Paul-André Linteau — René Durocher
Jean-Claude Robert — François Ricard

Quebec Since 1930

Translated by Robert Chodos and Ellen Garmaise

James Lorimer & Company, Publishers
Toronto, 1991

D1114099

This book has been published with the help of a grant from the Canadian Federation for the Humanities, using funds provided by the Social Sciences and Humanities Research Council of Canada.

Canadian Cataloguing in Publication Data

Quebec since 1930
    Translation of: Histoire de Quebec contemporain, v.2.
    Includes bibliographical references and index.
    ISBN 1-55028-298-0 (bound). -- ISBN 1-55028-296-4 (pbk.)

1. Quebec (Province) -- History -- 1936-1960. * 2. Quebec (Province) --
History -- 1960- I. Linteau, Paul-André, 1946-

FC2925.L5613 1991   971.4'04   C89-094964-6
F1053.2.L5613 1991

James Lorimer & Company, Publishers
Egerton Ryerson Memorial Building
35 Britain Street
Toronto, Ontario, M5A 1R7

Printed in Canada

CONTENTS

Maps

Figures

PREFACE

In this book, we follow much the same approach as we did in *Quebec: A History 1867-1929*, the first volume of our history of modern Quebec. Some of the principles that guided us in our work are worth mentioning here. The book proceeds from three major points of departure: history, Quebec, and the present.

Our goal is to understand and explain the significant phenomena and major changes that have characterized Quebec society. In this quest, we emphasize structures rather than circumstances, long-term developments rather than a chronological narration of events. We have tried to be open to contributions from all the social sciences and to take into account differences of interpretation among specialists.

For the purposes of our study, we define Quebec territorially rather than ethnically. We are interested in the phenomena that have occurred within the territory of Quebec and the men and women who have lived there. Thus, the term *Quebecers* has a very precise meaning throughout the book. It means all residents of Quebec: those whose ancestors came from the northwest thousands of years ago, from France at the time of Jean Talon, from Scotland in 1780, from an Ireland ravaged by the Famine, from eastern Europe to escape persecution and pogroms, from a Mezzogiorno offering only a bleak future, or from anywhere else. This is not a history of French Canadians, although of course they play a large role in it. Nor is it a history of Canada. Quebec history was constantly influenced by Canadian events, but we describe these events only briefly, emphasizing their effects on Quebec. For a fuller treatment of the Canadian context, readers can consult the many works on the history of Canada.

One of our goals is to cast light on the present by understanding how today's Quebec was fashioned. The roots of modern Quebec extend far back into the past. We do not believe that modern Quebec sprang suddenly from the Quiet Revolution or the Second World War: it is a product of long-term development. We don't see a strict division between a society called "old" or "traditional" and another labelled "new" or "modern." We see modernization as a process, consisting of both continuities and discontinuities. In each generation, it involves adapting to a new set of challenges, including the pressure of technological change and the arrival from other places of people, ideas and capital. It is not a linear process: it contains reexaminations, pitfalls and reverses, and is made up of some developments that occur rapidly and others that play themselves out at a very slow pace.

This is a synthesis, not an encyclopedic study. Seeking to encompass a period so rich in events of all kinds in a single volume and limited by the state of documentary evidence and the historical literature, we had to make choices. Many subjects are passed by or mentioned only briefly; thousands of people who at one time made headlines are relegated to historical obscurity. From this perspective, a synthesis such as this is only a starting point. A brief and highly selective bibliography providing guidelines for further study is given for each chapter.

The work is divided chronologically into three major periods. The first, from 1930 to 1945, was an unsettled period deeply marked by the Depression and the Second World War; this was followed by the postwar period, from 1945 to 1960, during which Quebec lived in the shadow of Maurice Duplessis; the last period began in 1960 and bears the stamp of the Quiet Revolution. In a departure from our practice in the first volume, we begin our discussion of each of these periods with an introduction in which we offer both a chronological outline and a synthesis of the major developments of the period.

Each chapter develops a specific theme. This approach renders possible a much more systematic and coherent examination of each dimension of the life of Quebec society, and makes the book easier to use for the reader who is particularly interested in specific questions. Many events are multifaceted and have to be mentioned in more than one chapter, but a detailed analysis of such events is given only once. Because of the scope of the material and the state of research in some fields, not all subjects could be treated explicitly for each of the three periods. This is why the most space is devoted to the most recent period. In cases where a theme is not treated for all three periods, a historical review is provided.

The same order is followed for all three periods. Developments relating to population (except for the first period) and the economy are treated first. Industry, natural resources, agriculture and the service sector are all discussed, as well as problems of dependency and government economic policies. Then comes a look at urban development, followed by chapters dealing with social groupings, work, living conditions, social policies, and selected social movements. Ethnic and language questions are also treated in this set of chapters. We discuss these questions primarily in relation to the last period, where two chapters are devoted to them. Next is an examination of two institutions that have a profound influence on society — church and school — followed by a look at ideologies. Then come the chapters dealing with politics: the state and its institutions, political parties, elections, governments and relations between governments. Our discussion of each period closes with an examination of the world of culture, encompassing both mass culture and arts and letters.

In attempting to measure phenomena quantitatively, we faced problems of consistency and continuity. In a number of cases, it proved impossible to compile a series of statistics that were completely comparable throughout. In the course of time, data-gathering agencies such as Statistics Canada have refined their methods of inquiry, changing the questions they ask, the definitions they use, the way they group their data or the scope of their coverage. In addition, the data we present here often come from specialized studies that cover only a limited period and have no equivalent for earlier or later years.

We consider the illustrations pieces of evidence that help us understand an era. They cast additional light on the text and are often complementary to it.

In closing, we would like to note that this book, like its predecessor, is the product of a genuine collective effort. François Ricard participated in this effort as a full partner along with the three original authors. We planned and developed the outline of the book together. Subjects were divided up for writing, with the preferences, specialization and availability of each author taken into account; as a result, the amount written varied from author to author. But we then reviewed, discussed and edited the entire manuscript as a group. Working together in this way was fruitful and stimulating for all of us.

Acknowledgements

We were helped by a number of researchers, who gathered some of the documentation and prepared working papers. We would especially like to thank Danielle Noiseux, as well as Wendy Johnston, Christine Lemaire and Lucia Ferretti. In the course of our work, we had the opportunity to participate in the production of two television series on Quebec history that appeared on Radio-Québec, *Le 30-60* and *Le 60-80*. The discussions and exchanges we had while working on these series — especially with the principal researcher, Lucien Régimbald — were very stimulating.

We would also like to thank the people who supported us in one way or another during the long process of bringing this work to fruition. We are especially grateful to the editor and publisher of the French edition, Antoine Del Busso, and his coworkers Louise Bourbonnais, Stéphane Dubois and Hélène Rudel-Tessier; to Ghyslaine Ethier, who typed most of the manuscript; to our colleagues Fernand Harvey, Gilles Marcotte, Normand Seguin, Esther Trépanier and François Vaillancourt, who read parts of the manuscript and gave us valuable feedback. Preparation of this book was helped by a Canadian Studies Writing Award from the Department of the Secretary of State of Canada. Finally, we wish to thank our dedicated translators, Robert Chodos and Ellen Garmaise, as well as the editor of the English version, Virginia Smith.

Paul-André Linteau
René Durocher
Jean-Claude Robert
François Ricard

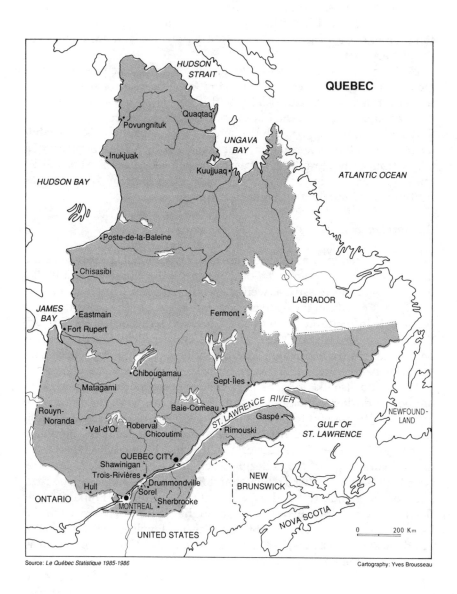

QUEBEC

HUDSON STRAIT

Quaqtaq

Povungnituk

UNGAVA BAY

Inukjuak

Kuujjuaq

HUDSON BAY

ATLANTIC OCEAN

Poste-de-la-Baleine

Chisasibi

LABRADOR

JAMES BAY

Eastmain

Fermont

Fort Rupert

Chibougamau

Sept-Îles

Matagami

Baie-Comeau

ST. LAWRENCE RIVER

Rouyn-Noranda

Val-d'Or

Roberval

Gaspé

NEWFOUND-LAND

Chicoutimi

Rimouski

GULF OF ST. LAWRENCE

QUEBEC CITY

Shawinigan

Trois-Rivières

Drummondville

NEW BRUNSWICK

Hull

Sorel

MONTREAL

Sherbrooke

ONTARIO

NOVA SCOTIA

UNITED STATES

0   200 Km

Source: Le Québec Statistique 1985-1986

Cartography: Yves Brousseau

Part 1:
The Depression and the War 1930–1945

Introduction

The years between 1930 and 1945 were an extremely troubled period in Quebec. The effects of two phenomena of international scope, the Depression and the Second World War, were strongly felt. The development of all aspects of society — the economy, work, politics, ideas, culture, daily life — was deeply affected by these phenomena, and all Quebecers felt their impact.

Quebec in 1929

On the eve of the Depression, Quebec showed the characteristics of an urban industrial society. It had reached this state as a result of changes that had begun in the previous century. The industrialization of Quebec really got off the ground in the mid-nineteenth century and proceeded by stages, affecting a growing number of sectors and regions. It provided a major impetus for urbanization and led to the formation of a working class and the emergence of the trade union movement, while at the same time strengthening the bourgeoisie. During the 1920s, new industrial investment broke all previous records.

However, 40 per cent of the population still lived in rural areas, which remained a very important part of Quebec society. Quebec agriculture began to become specialized in the nineteenth century, and it had increasingly been integrated into the market economy. Many people who had once worked in agriculture had left the countryside, becoming caught up in the exodus to the cities and especially emigration to the United States. Industry had replaced agriculture as Quebec's leading economic activity. However, rural Quebec still had considerable political clout and represented an element of stability in a rapidly changing society.

Politically, Quebec was a stronghold of the Liberal Party. The Liberals had been in power in Quebec City since 1897 and Louis-Alexandre Taschereau, premier since 1920, pursued the same policies as his predecessors: creating jobs through resource-based industrial development; adapting the education system to Quebec's new economic realities without upsetting the clergy, which dominated education; defending provincial autonomy within Confederation.

The Liberals' economic policies aroused opposition from nationalist intellectuals. These critics feared that Quebec was being industrialized too quickly and demanded increased efforts to develop agriculture and colonization. At the same time, they attacked the sale of resources to "foreigners" — English Canadians and Americans. In this way, their criticism raised the always delicate national question. Meanwhile, Quebec's Liberal leaders advocated accommodation in an effort to avoid arousing the animosity of English Canadians in the rest of the country and acknowledged Quebec's ethnic diversity, which had become more pronounced since the turn of the century. With the advent of the Depression, which appeared to provide clear evidence that the Liberal model of development had failed, this divergence of views took on a new dimension.

The Depression

The 1930s were marked by the Depression that engulfed the world. From the mid-nineteenth century onward, there had been recurring crises of overproduction in capitalist economies, each one coming at the end of a period of prosperity. These crises were felt as violent shocks, bringing with them falling prices, lower production and high unemployment. Each time, the economy adapted to these changes, but it was never an easy adjustment. The Depression of the 1930s surpassed previous crises in scope and seriousness, affecting the economy of the whole world and disrupting international trade. It was a number of years before the crisis was resolved. While the impact of the Depression was felt everywhere, how hard a country was hit depended on its economic structure. Among the countries that experienced the gravest problems and had the greatest difficulty coming out of the Depression was Canada.

The New York stock market crash of October 1929 has traditionally been regarded as the beginning of the Depression. However, the crisis was not simply a matter of stock prices or financial markets — it had much deeper roots, which went back to the prosperity of the 1920s. In many sectors of the economy, growth in demand led to major new investment, bringing about overproduction on a world scale. Agriculture is a good example. During and after the First World War, there was a substantial increase in agricultural production in countries outside Europe, which had easy access to postwar European markets. But during the 1920s, as Europe was rebuilt, most European countries sought to protect their agriculture in an effort to restore it to its prewar health. As a result, by the late 1920s, world investment in agriculture had reached a level where international markets could not absorb its output. The result was overproduction, and stockpiles of agricultural products accumulated. Prices began to fall in 1928, and the decline accelerated in the early 1930s.

The effects of these developments were strongly felt in countries such as Australia, Argentina and Canada that specialized in producing agricultural commodities for the world market. They still had to bear the high cost of investment in machinery but their return was much lower. A number of governments sought to protect their farmers by raising tariffs on imported foodstuffs and adopted a policy of self-sufficiency in an effort to resolve the crisis. The resulting disruption of international trade and the growth of protectionism quickly spread to other raw materials and manufactured goods.

What began as a commercial crisis degenerated into a financial and monetary one. With decreased revenues, many countries found it difficult to pay back the heavy foreign debt incurred during the preceding inflationary period. It became hard to obtain new capital. The whole system of international financial exchanges was compromised. Most countries gradually abandoned the gold standard, and a number of governments had to devalue their currencies.

As a world phenomenon, the Depression lasted until 1932. With all countries having taken protectionist measures, it was very difficult to revive international trade, and the economy recovered only gradually, beginning in 1932-33. By 1937, the world economy was almost back to its level of 1929, although the recovery did not extend in full measure to international trade.

In Canada, where the Depression was especially severe, the recovery was much slower than it was elsewhere. Between 1929 and 1933 the Canadian economy virtually collapsed, and it was only in 1940 that the Gross National Product exceeded the 1929 level. From 2.9 per cent in 1929, unemployment reached 25 per cent in 1933. With a quarter of its workforce idle, Canada faced economic and social problems on an unprecedented scale.

Canada was affected first of all as an exporter of wheat, which represented 32 per cent of its exports in the late 1920s. The prairie provinces were thrown into a severe slump. In Quebec the impact was felt in Montreal, where a portion of the economy was tied to western development, the export of prairie farm products to Europe, and the supply of manufactured goods to prairie farmers.

The other major industry tied to international trade was pulp and paper. Canada accounted for 65 per cent of world pulp and paper exports, and Quebec was the major producing province. Here too, excessive investment in the 1920s led to a crisis that began in 1927 and got steadily worse. This crisis touched a nerve in the Quebec economy, and whole regions specializing in natural resource exploitation suffered as a result.

The breakdown of export industries meant lower income for producers and hence a substantial reduction in their purchases of manufactured goods. As a result, industrial production was dragged into the crisis. Factories had to close, sometimes for long periods, and urban unemployment rose. The adoption of protective tariffs slowed down the collapse in some industries, but did not stop it.

Large-scale unemployment led to a reduction in disposable income and hence in consumption. Commerce and services were also drawn into the unemployment spiral. Construction came to a standstill, with unemployment levels nearing 100 per cent.

While consumption was declining, business investment also ground to a halt, as companies had to digest the substantial capital expenditures undertaken in the 1920s. Underlying the speculative fever of the late 1920s was an expansion of credit, and the stock market crash endangered financial institutions that now had to deal with large numbers of debtors who could not repay their debts. The result was a contraction of credit affecting not only stock market activity but all consumer markets.

Thus, the Depression in Canada was tied to a disorder in the international capitalist system, but its seriousness was accentuated by specific conditions, especially Canada's heavy reliance on exports and the substantial growth in investment — indeed, the excessive investment — that had taken place in the 1920s.

But not everyone was affected equally by the Depression. There were clear differences from region to region and from economic sector to economic sector; the western provinces and raw-material producers were the hardest hit. In Quebec, the impact was more severe in Montreal, whose economy was tied to international trade, than in agricultural areas, which were less specialized than the prairies.

Individuals and groups were also affected in varying degrees. In industrial centres, the unemployed bore the heaviest burden. Most Quebec workers were employed in low-wage industries and had had little opportunity to accumulate the kind of savings that would allow them to withstand the blow. There was no unemployment insurance or social assistance at the time, so that when their resources ran out the unemployed had to turn to charitable institutions. Governments slowly established financial assistance programs, but they remained fairly meagre.

Canadian governments were completely unequipped to deal with the scope of the Depression. Their first reaction was to treat it as comparable to the other depressions the country had experienced in the past and wait for the system to right itself on its own. However, they quickly realized that the Depression would last a long time and came around to the idea of intervening more actively. But their interventions were not part of any coherent overall policy. Instead, governments adopted temporary measures: palliatives that had only a limited effect and did not lead to genuine economic recovery.

At the same time, however, the situation forced governments to undertake an in-depth reassessment of their position and question some of their received ideas, and led to a redifinition of the role of government in the economy.

Thus, what was initially regarded as a depression that was a little more serious than previous ones but would resolve itself turned out to be a fundamental crisis of capitalism and rocked both the economic and the ideological foundations of the system. There was great human and economic cost, and the suffering and misery of the 1930s left an indelible imprint on the collective memory.

A Troubled Period

The impact of the Depression went beyond the economic sphere. The social and political instability it caused were evident throughout the decade.

It was a time of broken dreams: studies were interrupted, marriage plans were put off, people were unable to purchase essential goods. By the thousands, small property owners had their homes repossessed, while tenants were evicted from theirs. There was an all-pervasive climate of insecurity, which even extended to demographic behaviour. Between 1931 and 1941, Quebec's population increased by only 15.9 per cent, as compared with 21.8 per cent in the previous decade. The birth rate fell; immigrants no longer came; rural families, who over a period of decades had been leaving the countryside for the city, now stayed on the land which could at least feed them. Families made do with what they had, changing their diets and using their resources to the maximum. People resorted to expedients and learned to be ingenious. They had to learn to live from day to day, uncertain as to what tomorrow would bring.

Religion offered hope and escape from the misery of daily life. The 1930s were marked by a revival of religious fervour. It could be seen in the large crowds that gathered at St. Joseph's Oratory in Montreal, hoping for a miracle, or participated in novenas, processions and celebrations of the Sacred Heart.

If the 1930s were years of resignation, they were also years of searching for new solutions. It was a period of manifestos and ideological, social and political challenges. There were a wide variety of organizations, from far right to far left, and each proposed reforms that would radically change the capitalist system — or, in some cases, overthrow it. There were strong currents of anticommunism, xenophobia, and even antisemitism in Quebec.

The proliferation of ideologies was influenced by international phenomena such as the rise of fascism, the development of communism and the Spanish Civil War (1936-39). The expression of these ideologies was often tinged with violence. Incumbent governments were challenged, and their inability to solve the problems brought about by the Depression led to their defeat at the polls. In Ottawa, the Liberals under Mackenzie King were thrown out of power in 1930, but their Conservative successors didn't do any better and the government of R.B. Bennett was defeated in turn in 1935. In Quebec, Taschereau's Liberals held on despite significant Conservative strength in 1931, but subsequently crumbled under pressure coming from both the Conservatives and the breakaway Action Libérale Nationale. These two groups merged to form the Union Nationale and achieved power under Maurice Duplessis in 1936. However, Duplessis disappointed his supporters by failing to keep his promises of reform and was defeated in 1939 in an atmosphere marked by the outbreak of the Second World War.

The Second World War

In part, the war of 1939-45 had its roots in the Depression, which weakened the western democracies and made possible the rise of fascism. After Adolf Hitler took power in 1933, a process of militarization and territorial expansion began in Germany. The invasion of Poland led Britain and France to declare war on Germany on September 3, 1939. On September 10, Canada followed suit. Meanwhile, Japan followed its own parallel policy of expansionism in Asia during the 1930s.

The conflict took place on a planetwide scale, with two large blocs opposing each other. On one side were the Axis powers, led by Germany, Italy and Japan. On the other side were the Allies: initially France, Britain and the Commonwealth countries and then, from 1941 on, the Soviet Union and the United States as well.

In the first two years of the war, the Axis powers won victories on all fronts. After the Germans crushed British and French armies in 1940, France capitulated and the British were forced to evacuate their troops from Dunkirk. Germany invaded Denmark and Norway, then the Balkans, and finally, in 1941, the Soviet Union. In the Pacific, Japan launched offensives that gave it control of the area and then attacked the United States at Pearl Harbor.

Thus, in 1940, an isolated Britain faced a European continent under German domination. It counted on Canada to provide it with troops, foodstuffs and military matériel. The entry of the United States into the war in 1941 changed the balance of forces. The human and material resources the Americans injected into the struggle were a major factor. Starting in 1942, the Allies were in a position to take the offensive. They landed first in North Africa and then, in 1943, in Sicily, where they began the reconquest of Italy. With the Normandy landing in June 1944, the liberation of western Europe began, and Germany surrendered in May 1945. The Americans retook the territories conquered by the Japanese in the Pacific between 1942 and 1945, but Japan did not surrender until after nuclear bombs were dropped on Hiroshima and Nagasaki in August 1945.

The Second World War was the largest military conflict in history. The cost in human lives totalled more than fifty million dead, almost half of them civilians. Among these were the six million European Jews who were victims of the Holocaust. The war changed international power relationships and allowed the United States and the Soviet Union to expand their zones of influence considerably.

Quebec, like the rest of Canada, was spared the worst. Thousands of soldiers from Quebec did pay for the reconquest of Europe with their lives or came back from the battlefield permanently maimed. However, the country did not have to endure massive destruction or the massacre of civilians. For Quebecers, the war was even identified with the return of prosperity after the dark Depression years. Enlistment in the army and the needs of war industries meant that there were jobs for all able-bodied men and also brought a large number of women into the labour market. But there was also a price to be paid: society was militarized, government control was augmented, freedom was constrained, people did without a wide variety of goods.

Men were required to do military service for the defence of Canada. Some enlisted enthusiastically while others had to be conscripted. A large majority of Quebecers were opposed to conscription for overseas service and expressed their opinion forcefully in the 1942 plebiscite, but their vote failed to overcome a large majority in favour of conscription in English Canada.

To pursue the war effort to the maximum, the federal government assumed extraordinary powers. In addition to directing the workforce, allocating resources, fixing prices and rationing goods, the government also censored information and interned thousands of people. With the agreement of the provinces, it centralized state power and fiscal resources in Ottawa. Adélard Godbout, the Liberal leader who became premier of Quebec in 1939, cooperated fully with the war effort. A large number of voters disapproved of his conciliatory attitude, and the 1944 election returned Maurice Duplessis's Union Nationale to power.

Ottawa's centralism radically changed power relationships within Confederation. Most significantly, it created conditions in which the government could set in motion the mechanisms of the Keynesian state. By establishing major social programs — unemployment insurance and family allowances — Ottawa paved the way for a transition to a peace-time economy that would be better protected against violent fluctuations.

The war also provided the opportunity for a modernization of economic and social structures and of attitudes. With large-scale invest-ment in production, Quebec's industrial structure was substantially strengthened. Unionization took a giant step forward, bringing with it considerable improvement in working conditions. Women were called on to play a new role in a number of areas of activity. Another result of the international situation was a new openness to the world, with which Quebecers came in contact through radio, now in widespread use, and through the shift to Montreal of some of the cultural production of war-time France.

After the deprivation and regression of the 1930s, the war years saw a more active pursuit of modernity in Quebec. The intellectual climate and the social and economic reforms undertaken during the war were an early foretaste of the Quiet Revolution.

CHAPTER 1
INDUSTRY UNDER ATTACK

Quebec industry has always specialized in light manufacturing, mainly consumer goods. Industries based on the requirements of dress (clothing, textiles and shoes) and the food industry were particularly important. A second area of specialization was heavy industry (iron and steel products and transportation equipment), but it was much smaller than the light manufacturing sector. In the early twentieth century, a third area of specialization appeared consisting of industries — pulp and paper, chemicals and aluminum smelting — that relied on natural resources and hydroelectric power. By 1929, these new industries accounted for a quarter of total production.

Another aspect of the exploitation of natural resources is extraction: logging and mining. Overall, mining was still a small part of the economy, and did not lead to industrial development. The ore was often shipped out of Quebec in its raw state; at most, concentration or the initial stages of refining would be done in Quebec.

The industrial structure that had gradually fallen into place since the mid-nineteenth century was seriously shaken by the Depression and the war. The overall level of manufacturing output was affected, as was each of the main sectors individually.

Changes in Manufacturing Production

Industry remained the driving force of economic activly throughout the period. Manufacturing accounted for almost half the net value of production in Quebec in 1929, and three fifths in 1945. Hence ups and downs in manufacturing were inevitably reflected in the economy as a whole.

Industrial employment and output went through wide swings (table 1): first there was a substantial drop in the early Depression years, bottoming

Table 1
Manufacturing in Quebec, 1929-1946

Year	Number of establishments	Number of people employed	Gross value of production ($ million)
1929	6,948	206,580	1,109.0
1930	7,195	197,207	973.2
1931	7,287	173,605	801.6
1932	7,630	155,025	619.1
1933	7,856	157,481	604.5
1934	7,952	175,248	715.5
1935	7,727	182,987	769.1
1936	7,969	194,876	863.7
1937	8,518	219,033	1,046.0
1938	8,655	214,397	983.1
1939	8,373	220,321	1,046.0
1940	8,381	252,492	1,357.0
1941	8,711	327,591	1,841.0
1942	9,342	399,017	2,333.0
1943	9,372	437,247	2,851.0
1944	9,657	424,115	2,930.0
1945	10,038	384,031	2,532.0
1946	10,818	357,276	2,498.0

Source: François-Albert Angers and Roland Parenteau, *Statistiques manufactur-ières du Québec*, pp. 56, 76, 156.

out in 1932 and 1933, and then a dramatic rise during the war, reaching a peak in 1943 and 1944.

From 1930 to 1932, the value of manufacturing production declined steeply. The number of employees fell by 25 per cent between 1929 and 1933, and the total amount paid in wages fell by 40 per cent. Unemployment and underemployment were rampant in the manufacturing sector. When profits fall or inventories of unsold products accumulate, the first reaction of factory owners and managers is always to lay off workers and slow down production, or even shut their plants down entirely. Thus, it was the newly unemployed workers who bore the initial brunt of the Depression, while those who kept their jobs often had to accept pay cuts. In the darkest days of the Depression, there was no new investment to help create jobs and boost production. The economist A.E. Safarian has even found that there was disinvestment in Canada as a whole from 1932 to 1936. In many cases, companies decided not to replace or to delay replacing outdated equipment.

Employment and output began to rise in 1934, but recovery was slow and came to a halt again in 1938. The number of factories was increasing, reflecting the advent of small companies operating with fairly low production costs in sectors such as clothing and sawmills. Industrial production did not really revive, however, until the war. The initial effects were felt by 1940, when 1929 production levels were surpassed for the first time. In just four years, from 1939 to 1943, industrial employment doubled and the value of production and wages tripled. This indicates clearly that working conditions improved during the war.

The recovery did not affect all sectors equally, as we will see later. Its effects were most dramatic in arms-related industries. Factories that had operated at a fraction of capacity for ten years were now going full tilt. It also led to major additions to Quebec's industrial plant, as factories were built or expanded and new machinery was installed. New investment in fixed manufacturing capital had been low throughout the 1930s, but in 1940 it broke the record set in 1929, and it remained high throughout the war. Of course, some of the investment was linked to specific military needs. This extraordinary demand would fall at the end of the war, raising the question of reconverting military plants.

Canadian industry faced a labour shortage during the war. Large numbers of workers were enlisting in the armed forces, and women were increasingly called on to replace them. Authorities at the time saw this as a temporary expedient, but it did lead to the presence of more women in the workforce. Nonetheless, the total number of industrial workers fell after 1943. Some industries also had problems obtaining raw materials, which the government distributed according to military priorities. Paper companies were short of wood because there were not enough loggers. However, companies that received military contracts prospered.

Looking at Quebec's place in the Canadian economy as a whole, Quebec accounted for about 30 per cent of Canadian manufacturing. By contrast, Ontario accounted for half. When the Depression began, Quebec's share increased because its industrial structure, centred on consumer goods, was better able to withstand the drop in demand than Ontario's, characterized by heavy industry and capital goods. On the other hand, the recovery seemed to favour Ontario more, and its share of manufacturing grew slowly after 1934. During the war, the gap narrowed again, as Quebec had a greater number of industries engaged in military production. Quebec's share of Canadian manufacturing reached a peak of 32.7 per cent in 1943.

The Depression and Natural Resources

The exploitation of natural resources was hard hit by the Depression. World demand for raw materials tumbled and prices collapsed. In Quebec, forest and mineral resources were the most severely affected.

This process was especially conspicuous in pulp and paper. Between 1929 and 1933, the value of production fell from $129 million to $56 million, and the number of jobs fell from 15,890 to 9,850. Growth in the pulp and paper industry in the 1920s had been uncontrolled. A number of companies, attracted by the prospect of a large and quick return, invested heavily, leading to overproduction and a drop in prices. Starting in 1927, mills had to be closed and production reduced. The situation grew worse in the 1930s when the number of newspapers in the United States fell and their circulation dropped. Most Canadian pulp and paper companies were on the edge of bankruptcy and had to undergo financial reorganization. Only International Paper and its Canadian subsidiary, Canadian International Paper, were able to resist the trend because their operations were more diversified. Shutdowns of pulp and paper factories were responsible for considerable unemployment in the small towns and regions that were dependent on them.

Another forest industry, lumber, was also in serious difficulty. The number of jobs in the industry dropped from 9,676 to 2,937, and the value of production fell from $23.3 million to $6.6 million. With both residential and commercial construction at a standstill, the demand for lumber plummeted. The problems in the pulp and paper mills and sawmills had disastrous effects on logging. Thousands of farmers who habitually supplemented their meagre incomes by working as loggers in the winter found themselves unemployed or forced to accept pay cuts.

While the entire forest sector was affected, the situation in mining was more complicated. The value of mining production fell from $46 million in 1929 to $26 million in 1932. It rose again fairly quickly, however, and by 1936 surpassed its 1929 level. At the same time, the makeup of Quebec's mining output changed fundamentally with the opening of new mines in the Abitibi region.

During the 1920s, quarries supplying building materials accounted for at least half the value of mineral production in Quebec. This industry felt the repercussions of the standstill in construction, and its share of mining production fell to 13 per cent by 1936. The asbestos mines at Asbestos, Black Lake and Thetford Mines were also hard hit, although after bottoming out in 1932 they had begun to experience a strong recovery by the mid-1930s.

The situation was different in the metal mining sector. All but insignificant before 1927, this sector subsequently grew to the point where after 1933 it represented about 60 per cent of the value of mining production in Quebec. During the 1920s and 1930s, copper, gold, zinc and silver mines were discovered and put into operation around Rouyn, Malartic and Val d'Or-Bourlamaque in the Abitibi region. Gold was a special case. Contrary to other raw materials, demand for it is very high in times of economic depression when it is seen as the ideal safe investment. Thus, gold production increased substantially in Quebec and its value rose from under $2 million in 1929 to $34 million ten years later. Copper, found close to the gold, was mined mainly by the Noranda company, and production rose throughout the period. Output of other metals remained marginal.

The private companies that produced and distributed electricity were also affected by the Depression, and their revenues tumbled. It was not a time to build new power stations. Nonetheless, the projects begun in the euphoria of the 1920s had to be finished. One of these was the Rivière-des-Prairies station, built by Montreal Light, Heat and Power and opened in 1930. The largest project, however, was the first phase of the dam and power station at Beauharnois, on the St. Lawrence River. Construction began in 1929 and was completed in 1932. In the St. Maurice Valley, Shawinigan Water and Power completed work on Rapide Blanc, begun before the Depression, but had to delay the La Tuque power station, which came on stream only in 1940. It was not until after the war that construction of large hydroelectric projects began again in Quebec.

Other Industrial Sectors

Heavy industry and capital goods, directly affected by declining investment, suffer more severely than any other sector during times of recession. These industries represented a smaller proportion of Quebec's industrial structure than of Ontario's. The largest industry was railway rolling stock, located in Montreal, which was hurt when large-scale railway investment came to a halt. The crisis in international trade and the difficulties faced by western farmers in selling their wheat made the situation worse by reducing the demand for rail transportation. Production of rolling stock, valued at $70 million in 1929, fell to $11 million in 1933, and half the industry's 12,000 workers were laid off. Other industries in the sector were also affected — the value of machinery production fell from $17 million to $5 million, while steel production fell from $10 million to $2 million.

Light manufacturing is usually able to withstand economic downturns a little better, especially when its output consists of essential commodities. In the space of one year, 1929 to 1930, the value of cotton goods fell from $59 million to $34 million, hitting bottom at $27 million in 1932, but the industry began to recover in 1933. In women's clothing, the value of production fell from $27 million to $23 million between 1927 and 1933. However, this was probably due only to a drop in prices, because employment levels were maintained even in the early years of the Depression, except for 1932 when the number of workers was slightly lower than in 1929. The Canadian women's clothing industry became increasingly concentrated in Montreal during the 1930s, and the number of workers grew markedly after 1932. In men's clothing, there was a sharp drop in production, followed by a steady recovery beginning in 1933. The collapse of farm prices led to a fall in the value of food products, but few jobs were lost in the slaughterhouses, meat-packing plants, dairies, cheese factories and breweries.

Thus, the worst effects of the Depression were felt in the natural resource and capital goods industries rather than in industries producing everyday consumer goods.

The Impact of the War

As a result of Canada's entry into the war, industries that had served exclusively civilian needs were now redirected towards war production. Textile mills now manufactured khaki cloth, clothing factories produced uniforms, shoe factories made soldiers' boots, distilleries produced less whisky and more industrial alcohol to make synthetic rubber and explosives. But the most spectacular effect of the war on manufacturing was the phenomenal rise in the production of arms, including warships, planes, tanks, cannons, rifles, shells, explosives and other munitions. The war also gave impetus to the production of raw materials, mainly those of strategic importance, and to the construction of plants to process them.

In Quebec, the industries that underwent rapid growth were chemicals, nonferrous metal reduction and refining, aircraft construction and shipbuilding, iron and steel products, and electrical equipment. The chemical industry, which included explosives, led the way. The value of production was only $7.4 million in 1933 and $13.7 million in 1939, but it rose to $278 million in 1943. During the same period, the number of workers in the industry increased from 1,344 to 39,386. The industry includes both manufacturing basic chemicals and processing them into fertilizer, explosives and the like. In Quebec, basic manufacture had been centred in Shawinigan since the early part of the century. While the First World War had given a boost to the chemical industry there, the Second World War had a much greater effect. Shawinigan Chemicals, the largest producer, expanded its plant, which became one of the largest chemical factories in the British Commonwealth. Other producers, including Canadian Industries Limited (CIL), also opened plants in the city. Besides Shawinigan, the primary chemical industry was located in the Valleyfield-Beauharnois area southwest of Montreal, Arvida on the Saguenay where chemical production was related to aluminum, McMasterville in the Richelieu Valley, Buckingham in the Ottawa Valley, and Montreal.

The chemical processing industries included charcoal, paint, pharmaceuticals, perfume, soap, cleaning products, fertilizers, explosives and munitions. Obviously, munitions was the industry most affected by military demand, but its rapid expansion was also the most fragile, and many of the plants closed at the end of the war.

Reduction and refining of nonferrous metals also grew substantially. From 1933 to 1943, the value of production increased from $35 million to $260 million, and the number of workers rose from 964 to 12,739. One of the main components of the industry was aluminum. The war provided an opportunity for Alcan to carry out a major expansion of its Arvida plant with government aid. According to the historian Robert Rumilly, "the Arvida facilities produced more aluminum in 1942 than was produced in the whole world in 1939."

Because the automobile industry was concentrated there, Ontario became the main producer of tanks, jeeps and other motor vehicles. Quebec

Table 2
Percentage of Total Gross Value of Quebec
Manufacturing Production for Each Group of Industries,
1929-1945

Rank in 1945	Rank in 1929	Group	1929	1939	1943	1945
1	1	Food and beverages	18.3	19.3	11.4	15.5
4	2	Paper products	12.5	11.6	7.1	9.6
2	3	Clothing	9.7	11.5	8.5	10.7
6	4	Textile products	7.7	9.3	7.3	8.1
5	5	Transportation equipment	7.4	3.3	11.0	9.4
3	6	Iron and steel products	7.1	6.4	12.7	10.0
11	7	Tobacco and tobacco products	6.7	3.9	2.0	3.0
9	8	Wood products	5.4	3.8	3.4	4.9
7	9	Chemical products	4.1	4.9	13.2	7.6
10	10	Leather products	3.5	3.2	2.4	3.1
8	11	Nonferrous metal products	3.3	9.8	11.8	7.4
14	12	Printing, publishing, etc.	2.9	2.7	1.3	1.8
16	13	Miscellaneous manufacturing	2.6	1.1	0.8	1.1
13	14	Electrical appliances and equipment	2.5	1.9	2.6	2.5
15	15	Nonmetallic mineral products	2.3	1.8	1.5	1.6
12	16	Products of petroleum and coal	2.2	4.1	2.1	2.5
17	17	Rubber goods	1.8	1.4	1.0	1.1

Source: Marc Vallières, *Les industries manufacturières du Québec 1900-1959*, pp. 171, 173.

managed to obtain a larger share of the production of planes and ships. The Depression was a difficult period for Quebec's aircraft factories and shipyards. In 1939, neither industry produced more than $4 million worth of goods, and they employed only a few hundred workers. In 1943, the number of workers climbed to 27,093 in the aircraft industry and 23,225 in the shipyards. The value of aircraft produced was $95 million ($160 million in 1944) and the value of ships was $130 million. In the iron and steel industry, the value of production rose from $500,000 in 1933 to $166.7 million in 1943, while in the electrical equipment industry the increase was from $6.5 million to $73 million.

But the war also gave impetus to most other industries, even ones less directly related to war production. Despite rationing, prosperity and full

Construction of aeroplanes for Great Britain and the United States in Montreal, 1944. (National Archives of Canada C-32396)

employment stimulated consumption. Production rose significantly in industries such as pulp and paper, textiles and clothing, even though the rate of growth was slower than in the industries noted above.

Quebec's Industrial Structure

Thus, one of the effects of the war appears to have been to give heavy industry a more prominent place in Quebec's industrial structure. The breakdown of production by large industrial groups in 1943 (table 2) confirms this. Chemical products constituted the leading group, followed by iron and steel products and nonferrous metal products. But were these changes permanent ones? The new investment in heavy industry certainly left its mark, and the three groups that headed the list in 1943 still had a larger share of production in 1945 than they had had before the Depression. However, the industries that had led in 1929 remained among the top six — food and beverages, paper products, clothing and textile products. So even though heavy industry emerged from the war with a larger share, the industrial structure of Quebec had not fundamentally changed; in particular, light manufacturing still played a dominant role.

CHAPTER 2

AGRICULTURE: A REFUGE FROM THE DEPRESSION

Over the sixty years leading up to the beginning of the Depression in 1929, the position of agriculture in the economy was slowly whittled away to the benefit of other activities, mainly industry. At the same time, agriculture underwent profound changes. The base of production changed, as did agricultural methods. Grain production and self-sufficiency gave way to mixed farming dominated by dairy production.

The Depression had a direct but temporary effect. The slow, continuous development that had gone on since the late nineteenth century was interrupted. The exodus from rural areas stopped, production fell, and the number of farms increased; subsistence agriculture was given a reprieve from its steady decline. Then with the outbreak of hostilities in 1939, the exodus started again, with people leaving to work in factories or join the army. At the same time, demand and output increased very rapidly. Agriculture began to enjoy a period of intense prosperity, which affected all sectors.

Farmers

The percentage of the Quebec population living on farms fell steadily. It declined from 27 per cent in 1931 to 25.2 per cent in 1941 and then to 19.5 per cent in 1951. Similarly, the percentage of the labour force employed in agriculture, which stood at 22.5 per cent in 1931 and 20.8 per cent in 1941, was only 13.3 per cent in 1951. Even though its relative size fell, the agricultural labour force continued to grow in absolute terms until 1939, but it declined rapidly starting in 1940. Graph 1 clearly shows that the agricultural sector acted as a labour reserve, swelling in times of

Table 1 Area and Situation of Agricultural Lands, 1921-1951				
	1921	*1931*	*1941*	*1951*
Number of farms	137,619	135,957	154,669	134,336*
Total area under cultivation (acres)	5,964,154	6,140,299	6,137,521	5,790,359
Total area (acres)	17,257,012	17,304,164	18,062,562	16,786,405
Average farm size (acres)	125.4	127.3	116.8	124.9

*The definition of the farm used in the 1951 census was different from the one used in previous censuses; the real decrease in number of farms is estimated at 10,000.
Source: Censuses of Canada

economic crisis and emptying out at the first signs of recovery. It should be noted that the agricultural labour force was still essentially family-based — in 1931, only a little over a tenth of agricultural labourers were paid.

At the time, the agricultural sector seemed somewhat protected from urban misery. At least the essentials — food and shelter — were guaranteed. This is why one of Ringuet's characters says in *Thirty Acres*: "That's right, there's no depression back on the farm." However, the oversupply of farm labour exerted downward pressure on average agricultural wages.

In 1931, more than 42 per cent of the the agricultural population was concentrated in the St. Lawrence Lowlands. The Eastern Townships and Lower St. Lawrence-Gaspé regions each accounted for about 20 per cent, while the rest were scattered in the outlying areas. The opening up of new colonization regions had little effect on how the agricultural population was distributed.

Agricultural Output

Agriculture still accounted for about 20 per cent of Quebec production in 1929, but this figure had declined to barely 10 per cent by the latter years of the war. The three main sectors were field crops (primarily hay and oats used as animal feed); dairy; and cow, calf and hog raising. In addition to these major products, there were quite a few regional specialties whose production, while more limited, was significant in specific areas. In order of importance, these specialties were truck farming, which flourished around 1941; fruit growing, especially apples and strawberries; potatoes; and to a lesser degree, flax, peas and tobacco.

The work carried out by the geographer Raoul Blanchard between 1929 and 1948 has given us a picture of the range of regional production. Agriculture in the Lower St. Lawrence and the Gaspé suffered from inadequate markets. In the Lower St. Lawrence, the old parishes seemed to be in a better position, especially the ones closer to Quebec City, but in the Gaspé, as fishing gave way to the forest industry, farmers lost their markets and could produce only for subsistence. The situation was the same on the North Shore, where the main economic activities were forestry and tourism. In Saguenay-Lake St. John, the main activities were grain production, including oats; dairy farming; and blueberry picking. In Charlevoix, downstream from the Saguenay, three specialty products were developing out of the area's traditional agriculture: the potato, the turkey and the silver fox.

Heading up the St. Lawrence, Île d'Orléans was a veritable garden just outside Quebec City with potatoes, orchards, berries and flowers. Livestock was raised here as well. The parishes along the river between Quebec City and Trois-Rivières were a prosperous area engaged in dairy production and truck farming. Inland, the situation was different — in the Bois-Francs region southwest of Quebec City, for example, dairy and potato production were dominant in the old parishes, while in the newly settled areas there was only meagre subsistence farming.

Blanchard found the best agriculture in Quebec in the Montreal plain, which begins at Trois-Rivières and widens as you approach Montreal. The main products were hay, grain, dairy, flowers, tobacco and fruit. In the heart of the region, the Montreal archipelago, vegetable and dairy farming were the two main types of production. In the Eastern Townships, farming was divided between livestock raising and dairy production for the Montreal market.

On the north shore of the St. Lawrence between the Ottawa River and Trois-Rivières, the main products were potatoes, grain and dairy. Specialty products had been developed in some parishes, such as Saint-Félix near Joliette where farmers had been raising poultry since the 1920s. But the forest was never far away, and in many parishes in the Laurentians, a large proportion of the farmers worked in logging camps. The newest region, Abitibi-Témiscamingue, was virtually one huge dairy farm. Grain and hay were also grown, and raspberries and blueberries were picked for the Toronto and American markets.

Despite the vision of regional diversity that Blanchard conveys, only a few of the sectors were financially significant. Looking at the structure of farm income, livestock, eggs and dairy accounted for more than two thirds, while the sale of wood brought in about another tenth. But direct income from farm products was only one part of total farm income, to which foodstuffs consumed directly by farmers and their families and income derived from seasonal or occasional employment must be added.

Farmers' income was not stable during the period. Initially, falling prices and the general drop in production lowered incomes by about a third between 1926 and 1935. Then the war had the opposite effect. Not only did prices rise, but production increased rapidly, and income more than tripled between 1935 and 1945. Prevailing conditions were highly favourable, as markets were able to absorb all agricultural production. Some farmers, for the first time, were induced to increase production and sell their surplus.

Markets and Farming Methods

On the whole, agricultural markets — Quebec's urban areas and, for certain products, the United States and Britain — remained stable. But Quebec farmers did not take full advantage of the domestic urban market. In 1930, the Department of Agriculture reported that Montreal imported almost three quarters of its eggs and substantial quantities of vegetables, beef, pork and horses from outside Quebec. A new development was the growth of canning factories, stimulated by war needs and changes in eating habits.

Access to Quebec's traditional foreign markets, Britain and the United States, became more difficult during the Depression. The war increased demand in Britain for Quebec cheese, which had had a market there for many years. The most significant development, however, was the export of bacon to Britain, which had been deprived of its traditional sources of supply in Holland and Denmark by the Nazi invasion. At the same time, Quebec exported sheep, beef cattle and horses to the United States.

The trend towards concentration in agriculture — a reduction in the number of farms and an increase in average farm size — came to a halt during the Depression but picked up again in the 1940s (table 1). All observers, from Blanchard on down, agree that in well-established agricultural regions farmers tried to increase their holdings and did not hesitate to go into debt if necessary. The establishment of agricultural credit made the task easier.

Farm mechanization progressed slowly. In 1941, the census showed only 5,788 tractors, an average of one for every twenty-seven farms. This represented an increase, however, for ten years earlier there were fewer than one for every fifty-six farms. Obviously, the Depression slowed down mechanization considerably; lower incomes and easily available agricultural labour made the need to mechanize less pressing. Agronomists, aided by farm magazines and agricultural education, played a key role in making new techniques known. However, their efforts were hampered by farmers' mistrust, and agricultural education reached only some farmers' children.

Although there was real progress in some sectors and regions, agriculture in Quebec changed slowly between 1929 and 1945. It was based on the family farm, whose goals often did not go beyond subsistence. Paul-H. Vézina, writing in the early 1940s, observed that subsistence agriculture was prevalent in almost all the colonization regions as well as in areas where cash income came from forestry or fishing. On more commercial farms, there was the old problem of soil exhaustion; chemical fertilizers were being brought in, but too slowly to solve the problem. Nor was specialized dairy farming without its difficulties. On his tour of Quebec's regions, Raoul Blanchard noted that there were many undernourished cows producing only a fraction of the milk they were capable of giving. However, wartime needs made change come faster and had long-term effects.

Figure 1
Total Agricultural Labour Force, Quebec, 1935-1954

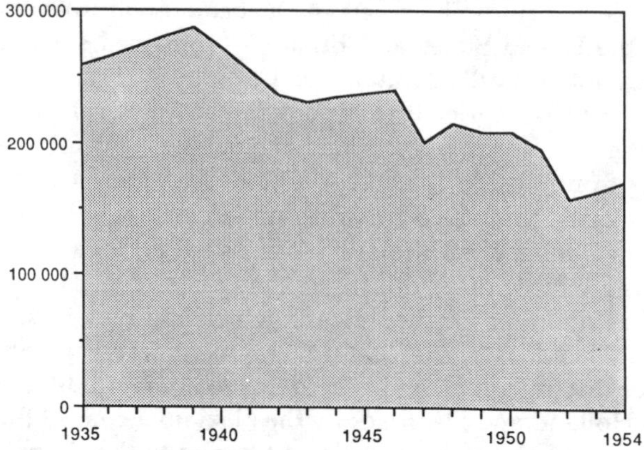

Source: Royal Commission on Canada's Economic Prospects, *Progress and Prospects of Canadian Agriculture.*

Government Intervention

From the nineteenth century on, Quebec government policy had been aimed at developing diversified agriculture based on dairy production. With the Depression, however, the methods used to achieve this goal changed. Apart from its aid to colonization, the government decided to confront two chronic problems: productivity, which it attempted to boost by instituting grants for draining land, and financing, which it dealt with by establishing a provincial farm credit program in 1936. Provincial farm credit was more accessible than the federal program set up in 1929. But both these measures had only a medium-term effect, and their impact was not really felt until after the war.

At the federal level, the period was characterized by growing, sustained government intervention. In 1934, Ottawa instituted aid for farmers in debt. After Canada entered the war, government intervention became broader in scope and more direct; thus, in 1942, Ottawa acted to delay drafting farm workers into the army. But the most significant government measure was control of agricultural prices, aimed both at avoiding inflation and at preventing particular sectors of production from becoming overdeveloped. Ottawa's most drastic action was the imposition of price ceilings in 1941. At the same time, by paying bonuses to producers, the government sought to stimulate the production of specific foodstuffs. For example, in 1942, bonuses were paid to farmers who produced tomatoes, corn, peas and beans for canning. In 1944, Ottawa legislated farm price support to prevent prices from falling below production costs.

The federal government established a number of agencies to administer all these measures, including the Wartime Prices and Trade Board, the Agricultural Supplies Board, the Bacon Board, the Dairy Products Board and the Special Products Board. The bacon, dairy and special products boards played a very active role in buying and exporting foodstuffs.

The Revival of Colonization

During the 1920s, the agricultural colonization movement had slowed considerably, but the Depression brought a complete about-face. Many people saw colonization as a cure-all for the unemployment and misery of the cities — on the land, at least subsistence was guaranteed. Pressed to do something, both levels of government set up programs specifically directed at colonization in the 1930s, thus reviving a movement that had seemed destined to disappear. The main result was the settlement of the Abitibi, but land was also occupied in the more remote areas of the Gaspé, Lower St. Lawrence and Lake St. John regions.

This wave of colonization was significantly different from previous ones. Largely controlled by the provincial and federal governments and colonization societies, the programs involved subsidies at various levels. The first program, the Gordon plan, organized by the federal government in 1932, offered unemployed city dwellers on relief $600 to go and settle on a piece of land. A few years later, in 1935, the Quebec government developed a more systematic program, the Vautrin plan. Rather than a one-time bonus, it provided a series of grants tied to all the aspects of land settlement — land clearance, house building, planting, and the like. In addition, the government funded the diocesan colonization societies, which acted as prime movers and assumed the costs of building roads and churches. Finally, a federal-provincial program known as Rogers-Auger was established in 1936. It was modelled on the Gordon plan and paid a $1,000 bonus. The Quebec government also had other ways of encouraging colonization: it gradually increased the bonuses for land clearance initiated in 1923, and in 1933 it set up a program to help farmers' sons become established on the land.

These programs had a pronounced impact on rural life and involved an estimated 42,000 to 54,000 people. Almost all of Quebec's dioceses sent colonists to the new parishes. However, observers are unanimous in noting that colonization was precarious — after a few years, the colonists decided they could do better by going back to the cities or working in the mines and forests. According to Raoul Blanchard, two thirds of the new colonists left the land.

The results of this last period of colonization are contradictory. On the one hand, settlement of Quebec's territory reached its furthest extent — even though many of the colonists did not stay, the 147 parishes they helped create between 1930 and 1941 are testimony to their presence. On the other hand, however, colonization was only a temporary solution. Its goal was to take the unemployed out of the cities, but it did not take into account difficulties of climate and distance, the fact that the colonists were insufficiently prepared, or the problem of making the new farms profitable.

CHAPTER 3

A NEW ECONOMIC ROLE FOR THE STATE

One of the most dramatic new developments during the period between 1930 and 1945 was unquestionably the part played by government in managing the economy. The Depression caused traditional policies based on the principles of laissez-faire to be called into question and led to a redefinition of government's role in regulating the economy. The war provided the first opportunity to put the new ideas into practice, and the resulting mechanisms remained in place after the war was over. The federal government was at the centre of these changes, while the Quebec government largely remained on the sidelines.

The Situation before 1930

Constitutionally, the federal government held the main levers of economic power — in particular, control of the banks, currency and foreign trade. At the heart of Ottawa's economic strategy was the National Policy, which was developed in the early years of Confederation and contained three elements. The first was a protective tariff, imposed in 1879 and designed to stimulate Canadian manufacturing and protect it from foreign competition. The second was aid for building the major railway lines, which were to link the provinces and make them interdependent by creating an integrated internal market. The third element was a policy of encouraging immigration to the prairies, where until 1930 Ottawa maintained ownership of public lands, distributing them to settlers and railway companies.

The Quebec government pursued its own economic policies, but their effects were more limited. Its main economic instrument was its ownership of huge tracts of public land. The way in which these lands were granted and managed affected the direction of economic development. The Liberal Party, in power from 1897 on, steadfastly upheld a policy of promoting natural resource development, mainly electricity and forests. In this way, the Liberals sought to encourage industrial development and job creation by large corporations, many of them American-owned. The government also pursued a policy of modernization, primarily in the areas of infrastructure and human resources. Thus, starting in the early years of the century, the government built roads in an effort to improve Quebec's internal communications network and adapt it to the automobile. At the same time, it developed occupational and technical training programs to meet the needs of the economy.

Economic liberalism was the guiding principle of government intervention, and private enterprise was seen as the driving force of economic development. The two levels of government were quick to provide financial support to private enterprise, but they did not seek to replace it. Some sectors required more direct intervention: governments took over canals, money-losing railways and some utilities. On the whole, however, governments were not major economic entities — in 1928, all governments together accounted for only 9.3 per cent of gross national expenditures; more than half that amount was spent by municipalities.

Ottawa and the Initial Impact of the Depression

When the Great Depression began, government economic policies were directed primarily towards encouraging long-term development. Unprepared to deal with cyclical crises, they generally resorted to traditional measures, believing that market forces would help the economy recover by itself.

As in a number of other countries, one of the Canadian government's first reactions was to raise customs duties sharply in 1930. However, this was far from a complete solution to the problem. It did provide better protection from imports for industries producing for the domestic market, notably textiles. But industries producing for export came up against the high tariff barriers established by other countries. The revival of protectionism accentuated the collapse of international trade, on which the Canadian economy was heavily dependent.

To get out of this impasse, Ottawa sought to reach reciprocal tariff reduction agreements with other countries, and after difficult negotiations arrived at agreements of this sort with Britain and its other major Commonwealth trading partners. At a conference in Ottawa in 1932, these countries agreed on list of goods on which reduced tariffs would be applicable. As a result, an increased share of Canadian exports went to Britain and other Commonwealth countries. A similar agreement was arrived at with the United States in 1935. In 1937 and 1938, further agreements between Canada and its two largest trading partners led to more reciprocal concessions and helped revive international trade.

But these customs agreements did not give consumers any more money to buy goods. The federal government had to provide financial support to entire sectors in difficulty, including railways, wheat production and coal mining. The largest recipients of aid were the provinces and municipalities, which were constitutionally responsible for helping the unemployed but did not have adequate financial resources to carry out this responsibility. Every year, Ottawa concluded temporary agreements with the provinces under which it provided grants to cover a share of relief for the jobless. Between 1930 and 1937, these grants represented 46 per cent of the costs incurred by the provinces. The share was higher in the western provinces, while in Quebec it was 29 per cent. To finance these temporary measures, Ottawa — like the provincial and municipal governments — had to run a budget deficit, borrow heavily and raise new taxes.

The Quebec Government and the Depression

In Quebec, apart from the new gold mines in the Abitibi region, the natural resources sector was among the hardest hit by the collapse of international trade. This made the Liberal government's policy of relying on natural resources impossible to implement. The government had no means of boosting the economy and had to try to deal with the most urgent problem, which was helping the tens of thousands of unemployed in the cities.

The government's first measure was to set up public works projects that gave work to some of the jobless. By 1932, it became clear that this was not going to be enough, and the government increasingly resorted to direct relief, making welfare payments to families in need without imposing any work requirements. But in 1937, the priority was shifted back to public works, although direct relief was maintained. The various levels of government together spent more than $24.8 million on such measures in Quebec throughout the 1930s. These measures and their social and ideological significance will be discussed in more detail further on.

While receiving federal aid, the Quebec government was passing on a large part of the bill to the municipalities. The Rowell-Sirois Commission found that Quebec was asking its municipal governments — and especially Montreal — to shoulder a much larger share of the burden than other provinces. Nonetheless, the provincial government still made the largest contribution to relief (table 1).

Quebec relied on aid to colonization more heavily than the other provinces. Some of the colonization programs were the result of federal-provincial agreements, while others were set up by the Quebec government, which spent $26 million between 1930 and 1937 helping colonists and subsidizing rural road construction.

The Quebec government and municipalities had to go heavily into debt to finance all their relief measures. According to the Rowell-Sirois Commission, "between 1930 and 1937 the per capita municipal-provincial deadweight debt rose from one of the lowest to one of the highest in the country."

Table 1
Funds Alloted to Aid to the Unemployed, Quebec,
1930-40 ($ million)

Level of government	Direct relief	Public works	Total
Federal	45.9	17.1	63.0
Provincial	59.6	56.4	116.0
Municipal	39.4	9.7	49.1
Total	145.0	83.2	248.1

Source: Michel Pelletier and Yves Vaillancourt, *Les politiques sociales et les travailleurs*, vol. 2, *Les années 30, pp. 198-99; Annuaire statistique du Québec, 1941-1943*, p. 442.

A New Direction

Increased public spending on temporary measures did not succeed in satisfactorily reviving the economy. By the middle of the decade, governments in Canada were calling into question some of the tenets of economic liberalism and considering permanent mechanisms for government intervention in the economy. This change was simply a rather belated adoption of new economic directions that had surfaced in other capitalist countries. In the United States, President Franklin Delano Roosevelt launched his New Deal, involving a whole series of social and economic programs, while in Britain, the economist J.M. Keynes put forward a new strategy for economic regulation based on increased government intervention through monetary and fiscal policy.

Following the recommendations of the 1933 report of the Macmillan Commission, the Bennett government acted to establish a central bank in 1934. Aimed at keeping tighter control over the monetary and financial system, the Bank of Canada came into existence in 1935. Its main role was to control the supply of money and credit in Canada and influence interest rates. It also served as the bank for the chartered banks, which had to deposit their reserves with it and for which it was the lender of last resort; acted as the banker or financial agent for the federal government, a role hitherto played by the Bank of Montreal; and issued currency, gradually replacing the chartered banks and the Department of Finance in this regard.

Also in 1934, the Stevens Royal Commission on Price Spreads revealed how monopolies used unfair practices to eliminate competition and showed that government had to regulate business. Prime Minister Bennett was sensitive to this pressure, and with an election coming up, he changed course in 1935 and proposed his own New Deal. Emphasizing the need to reform capitalism through government regulation and control, Bennett put a series of bills through Parliament. He created an unemployment insurance plan to replace direct relief, established a minimum wage, mandated a weekly day of rest and a maximum forty-eight-hour work week, tightened control over monopolies through an amendment to the Criminal Code and the establishment of a Dominion Trade and Industry Commission, improved programs for farm credit and the marketing of farm commodities, and set up an economic advisory council. But the Conservatives' New Deal legislation was later declared unconstitutional by the British Privy Council.

Thus, the Depression brought into play new views of economic policy and government's role in the economy. But in the 1930s there were many obstacles to the implementation of these views. While some prominent businesspeople saw the new economics as the only way of saving capitalism, they ran into opposition from sectors of the business community, from the Liberal Party, which was not yet convinced that government intervention was necessary, and from a number of provincial governments. With the outbreak of the Second World War, however, the Liberals changed their position, and Ottawa was given the chance to transform the rules of the game.

Winning the War

Constitutionally, the federal government enjoyed exceptional wartime powers, set out in the War Measures Act. This act was initially passed during the First World War and was put into force again in 1939. It gave the federal cabinet extremely broad powers which it could exercise through a simple order-in-council, without parliamentary approval.

Federal intervention during the war affected Quebecers in every aspect of their lives. In economic policy, the government's goal was to help win the war, and the entire economy was to to serve that goal. The National Resources Mobilization Act, passed in 1940, was designed to place all human and material resources at the service of the war effort.

The Department of Munitions and Supply was established to organize war production, and C.D. Howe, the King cabinet's strong man, was appointed minister. Private enterprise was given a major role: it received government aid to convert and expand factories for war production as well as many contracts for military supplies. The government itself entered into war production through the establishment of crown corporations. Canada became a huge arsenal, with two thirds of its output destined for the Allied armies.

But the war effort was not limited to military equipment. It affected all sectors of the economy, from farm production to paper manufacturing. The federal government stepped in by establishing a myriad of boards to control production and determine the allocation of resources. Civilian production was systematically subordinated to war needs and priority was given to industries that were deemed essential.

The system required tight control in order to function properly. Production or consumption of some products was forbidden or else

Cabinet minister C.D. Howe and a worker at the Cherrier plant, Montreal, 1944. (National Archives of Canada, PA-112908)

limited by quotas and rationing. The government imposed wage and price controls to avoid inflation and black marketeering, always a danger when there are shortages, and drew heavily on people's wages by raising income taxes and encouraging people to put their savings into victory bonds.

Thus, Ottawa implemented a highly centralized system of economic decision-making which the provincial governments accepted without protest. In exchange for partial compensation, they even agreed to yield the proceeds of all individual and corporate income taxes for the duration of the war. For a few years, Canada had a true command economy. Through this process, Ottawa gained valuable experience in managing the economy, which it could put to good use after the war. For a time, it also became the main buyer of goods and services, and its share of gross national expenditures reached a high of 37.7 per cent in 1944 (table 2).

Preparing for the Postwar Period

Long before the war ended, the federal government began to think about what its postwar economic policies would be. An advisory committee on economic policy was set up to coordinate its study of this question. The objective was twofold — to prepare a smooth transition to a peacetime economy and to avoid falling back into the prewar Depression.

Government propaganda during the war. (National Archives of Canada, C-91437)

A gradual loosening of government control was planned. As a product became available in sufficient quantities, its price and distribution would no longer be regulated by a government board. Arms factories would be liquidated and private companies could convert to civilian production with government aid. There would be a range of aid programs for the hundreds of thousands of demobilized soldiers — discharge bonuses, an opportunity to return to their former jobs, help to go back to school, and the like.

These were temporary measures, but the government was also considering permanent, long-term policies. The government had unequivocally converted to Keynesianism during the war, and henceforth there would be constant government intervention to regulate economic activity. At the heart of the new economic outlook were social security measures. Unemployment insurance came into being in 1940, and family allowances were established in 1945. The government looked at these measures largely in terms of their economic impact: they stimulated demand by redistributing substantial amounts of money to Canadians. The coherent social security program recommended by the Marsh Report in 1943 marked the birth of the welfare state in Canada. Another measure with similar aims was the National Housing Act of 1945, designed to revive the construction industry.

In taking the initiative to prepare for the postwar period, the federal government ensured that it would play a dominant role not only in the field of economic policy but in social policy as well. This was consistent with the recommendations of the Rowell-Sirois report and began a process of centralization that was to have considerable political consequences. We will return to this development further on.

Table 2
Governments' Share of Gross National Expenditures in Canada, 1929-46 (%)

Year	Federal	Provincial	Municipal	Total
1929	2.6	2.2	5.6	10.4
1930	3.0	2.8	6.8	12.6
1931	3.1	3.3	8.2	14.6
1932	3.1	3.3	8.8	15.2
1933	3.3	2.8	7.1	13.2
1934	3.2	3.2	6.2	12.6
1935	3.7	3.2	5.7	12.6
1936	3.3	3.0	5.4	11.7
1937	2.9	3.8	5.1	11.8
1938	3.3	4.1	5.2	12.6
1939	3.7	3.4	5.0	12.1
1940	10.1	2.3	4.2	16.6
1941	14.2	2.0	3.4	19.6
1942	31.3	1.5	2.8	35.6
1943	33.6	1.4	2.7	37.7
1944	37.7	1.5	2.8	42.0
1945	26.1	1.7	3.1	30.9
1946	9.1	2.4	3.7	15.2

Source: Dominion Bureau of Statistics, *National Accounts: Income and Expenditure, 1926-1956*, pp. 26-27.

Quebec Government Policies during the War

In Quebec, Adélard Godbout's Liberal government, elected in 1939, considered federal predominance justified by the exceptional circumstances of the war and accepted it fairly easily, agreeing to transfer income tax revenues. However, the government's conciliatory attitude towards Ottawa provoked hostility from Quebec nationalists. A turning point came in 1944 with the return to power of Maurice Duplessis's Union Nationale, which resisted centralist economic policies.

Nonetheless, the Godbout government did have some leeway to develop some internal economic policies for Quebec. In keeping with the new economic trends prevalent in Ottawa, it sought to modernize economic and social institutions. In 1943, it created an Economic Advisory Council whose purpose was to investigate the agricultural, forest, mineral and industrial resources of the province and to suggest the necessary measures to ensure that they were used as rationally and as completely as possible.

Its most spectacular initiative was, however, the establishment of Hydro-Quebec in 1944. Pressure for nationalization of the private electricity companies began to mount in the 1930s, and a Quebec City dentist, Dr. Philippe Hamel, launched a virtual crusade against the "electricity trust." In 1934, the Taschereau government set up a commission of inquiry (the Lapointe Commission), which found that the private companies had abused their power at the expense of consumers and recommended that the government establish some measure of public regulation. Thus, the Quebec Electricity Commission, later to become the Provincial Electricity Board, was set up to establish rates and regulate the production and distribution of electricity.

But the leaders of the Action Libérale Nationale wanted to go further and demanded nationalization. Maurice Duplessis disappointed many of his supporters by refusing to carry out this demand during his first term in office, and it was Adélard Godbout who finally proceeded with nationalization. Only Montreal Light, Heat and Power — the company that had exploited consumers most severely — and its affiliates were nationalized, but even partial nationalization was an extremely important economic measure. In the short term, it resulted in reduced residential, commercial and industrial electricity rates in the Montreal market. In the long term, it created openings for Francophone engineers, accountants and other senior executives and prepared the ground for the phenomenal expansion of electricity production in decades to come.

There were many other signs of change in Quebec as well: the government enacted a new labour code in 1944, and it undertook to review health and welfare policies. But this push for change stopped short with Godbout's defeat, as his successor had no intention of pursuing it.

CHAPTER 4

URBANIZATION ON HOLD

From the mid-nineteenth century on, Quebec had undergone a steady process of urbanization. Every census reported a significant increase in the percentage of Quebec's population living in cities. A number of cities in Quebec had experienced growth spurts, especially after 1900. The Depression seriously disrupted this trend, and cities became centres of unemployment and misery. There were even attempts to reverse the old trend by encouraging city dwellers to go back to the land. The war put a stop to urban stagnation by stimulating production, but special circumstances limited the physical growth of Quebec's cities.

Constraints on Urbanization

During the 1930s, urbanization seemed to have almost stopped in Quebec. The 1921 census showed that more than half the population of Quebec (51.8 per cent) already lived in urban areas, and further urbanization during the 1920s brought that figure to 59.5 per cent in the 1931 census. But ten years later, only 61.2 per cent of the population was urban. In absolute terms, the number of city dwellers in Quebec increased by almost half a million during the 1920s but by barely 300,000 in the 1930s. Thus, the urban population continued to grow, but at a much slower rate. The cities themselves appeared to have stopped growing, and residential construction fell to a very low level by the mid-1930s.

The main reasons why the trend towards urbanization was reversed are easily identifiable. Urban growth in the twentieth century was primarily the result of new people arriving in cities from other places. But with the Depression, both immigration and the rural exodus stopped almost completely. Although it is difficult to measure the scope of the phenomenon, it is clear that urban unemployment brought migration to the cities to a sudden halt. Surplus young people on the farms could no longer move to the cities if there were no jobs for them there. On the contrary, people who had just arrived in the cities tended to move back to the country — not to mention the people whom the government successfully convinced to move to colonization areas. What increase there was in urban population was natural rather than the result of in-migration. Government authorities did their part as well, limiting eligibility for relief payments to people who had lived in a municipality for at least a minimum required time (several months or even several years) so as to prevent the unemployed from streaming into the cities in search of public assistance.

The Depression placed municipal governments in a difficult position. On the one hand, their revenues were endangered by the collapse of land values and the inability of many ratepayers to pay their taxes, while on the other, they had to increase their expenditures to provide relief to the jobless. In applying the new social programs, the cities were on the front lines. They were responsible for local distribution of the sums granted by the federal and provincial governments for direct relief and for implementation of public works projects. In addition, they had to contribute financially to relief and public works in a proportion (usually between one quarter and one third) established by the higher levels of government. The cities emerged from the Depression deeply in debt and were unable to regain financial health until after the war. They were also

Tenants being evicted in Montreal. (National Archives of Canada, C-30811)

subject to stricter control from higher levels of government, which reduced their autonomy.

The demands of war production substantially strengthened the industrial structure of many Quebec cities and towns. New factories were built, many of them large ones, such as the Canadair aircraft plant in the Montreal suburb of Ville Saint-Laurent. Other factories underwent considerable expansion, such as the Alcan aluminum plant in Arvida.

These new conditions might have been expected to generate significant urban growth through an influx of new people, but this did not happen. On the whole, the growth of Quebec cities during the war was not as marked as the industrial statistics would suggest. A number of factors explain this situation. The cities lost many of their male residents to the armed forces, and the demand for civilian workers appeared to be satisfied more by increased participation of women in the labour force than by an influx of people from rural Quebec. Another factor in urban stagnation was the housing crisis. In allocating building materials, the government gave first priority to military needs, so that the demand for new housing could not be met. The population had to crowd into existing housing, and the vacancy rate was close to zero. As a partial solution to the problem, the government launched a campaign encouraging families to rent out rooms.

A certain amount of new housing was built, especially in smaller centres where there was not enough housing to meet the demand created by the new war plants. In 1941 the government established a crown corporation called Wartime Housing Limited, which in the six years that followed built more than 30,000 houses in Canada, including 4,172 in Quebec. They were intended initially for workers in war plants, and later for veterans. However, these houses only partially met the existing need, and there was a chronic housing shortage throughout the period. The housing problem was one of the major themes in the 1944 Quebec election campaign, and was the main focus of urban policy in the postwar period.

Urban Quebec

Even though the rate of growth of Quebec's cities had declined, most Quebecers still lived in urban areas. At the same time, some features of Quebec's urban areas that had developed over earlier decades were maintained.

Quebec continued to be one of the most urbanized provinces in Canada. Its rate of urbanization remained higher than the Canada-wide average, although it trailed Ontario and British Columbia. But the gap between Quebec and Ontario was widening — from 3.6 percentage points in 1931 to 6.3 points in 1941. Quebec and Ontario had very different urban structures. In Ontario, urbanization in the nineteenth century gave rise to a large number of middle-sized cities, each of which acted as a commercial and industrial centre for a rural area with which it had close links. These cities were not crushed by the rise of Toronto, which was not

Shack with no running water housing a war plant worker's family, 1942.
(National Archives of Canada, PA-108315)

as overwhelming in Ontario's urban system as Montreal was in Quebec's.
The urban system in Quebec had been highly centralized for many years,
with Montreal as the dominant centre and Quebec City as the secondary one.

By 1931, the greater Montreal area with its many suburbs contained
36 per cent of Quebec's total population and 61 per cent of its urban
population. These percentages fell slightly when urban growth slowed
during the Depression years, but the city's dominant position was not
shaken. Within a fifty-kilometre radius of the city, six small cities —
Saint-Jérôme, Joliette, Sorel, Saint-Hyacinthe, Saint-Jean and Valleyfield,
each with a population of 10,000 in 1931 — formed a satellite ring around
Montreal.

Other Quebec cities lagged far behind Montreal. The only other
metropolitan area of any importance was Quebec City. Three other cities
— Sherbrooke in the Eastern Townships, Trois-Rivières in the St. Maurice
Valley and Chicoutimi in the Saguenay region — played an important
role as regional centres, a role that had become increasingly significant
since the turn of the century because of rapid urbanization linked to
natural resource development. By 1930, Quebec's urban system had almost reached its full extent, and the only new development during the
decade was increased urbanization in the Abitibi region. All of southern
Quebec was highly urbanized except for its eastern portion, where both
banks of the St. Lawrence were still largely rural.

Urbanization is not just a matter of demographics and economics, but is also reflected in lifestyles and culture. Urban Quebec was the driving force of social change, even though the countryside still carried considerable weight politically. In the cities, and especially Montreal, a Francophone urban culture, American-influenced and disseminated through the popular press and radio, was developed and expressed.

Montreal

Between the census dates of 1931 and 1941, the population of the city of Montreal increased from 818,577 to 903,007, while that of the metropolitan area rose from 1,023,158 to 1,139,921. This increase was significantly lower than in the previous decade. Because of its strong industrial base and its role as a trading centre, Montreal was hard hit by the decline in manufacturing and suffered severe unemployment. The port of Montreal, always one of the cornerstones of its economy, reflected the difficulties the city was experiencing. The most noteworthy change was the decline in wheat exports — from 171 million bushels in 1928 to only 31 million bushels in 1935. The problems of western agriculture were not the only source of Montreal's difficulty. Montreal was also facing increased competition for Canadian grain exports from the ports of Vancouver, Quebec City, Sorel and Trois-Rivières, all of which had acquired grain handling facilities and were taking some wheat exports away from Montreal. Thus, in 1939 Quebec City, Sorel and Trois-Rivières handled almost half the wheat shipped from ports on the St. Lawrence. At the same time, imports — especially oil, coal and other raw materials used by Montreal industry — increased despite the Depression, causing further changes in Montreal's port traffic.

In addition to being a port city, Montreal was also Canada's largest industrial city and accounted for almost two thirds of the value of manufacturing output in Quebec. Its industrial structure had developed in the nineteenth century around two poles: light manufacturing (clothing, textiles, shoes, tobacco and food) and heavy industry (iron and steel and railway rolling stock). Diversification came in the twentieth centruy with the development of sectors such as electrical appliances, aircraft manufacturing and oil refineries. The Depression shook many companies and slowed production, but it did not affect the overall industrial structure, which in the 1930s and 1940s was dominated by light manufacturing. Clothing was extremely important, employing thousands of workers, both men and women, at very low wages. Montreal emerged as the leading centre for women's clothing, with 67 per cent of Canadian production in 1938. Tobacco processing was also concentrated in Montreal, which accounted for 73 per cent of Canadian output. Textiles and many food industries (slaughterhouses and meat-packing plants, breweries, biscuit factories and bakeries, and others) were well established in Montreal and employed a substantial part of the labour force.

During the war, heavy industrial production increased significantly. Iron and steel and transportation equipment benefited from war contracts. In 1942, this new industrial activity could be seen at the Canadian Vickers shipyards, at Canadian Pacific's Angus shops with their 9,700 employees, and at Canadair's brand new plant, which employed 7,500. Raoul Blanchard found that industries in the metal processing and transportation sectors employed 38.3 per cent of Montreal's manufacturing labour force. Thus, industry remained a basic component of Montreal's economy. It included a multitude of small concerns in industries such as clothing, each with only a few employees, as well as many large factories employing thousands of workers.

Montreal also remained the financial centre of Canada, although it increasingly had to share that role with Toronto. During the 1930s, the value of stock market transactions in the Toronto market surpassed Montreal's for the first time. As well, the value of cheques cleared in Toronto was almost always higher than in Montreal during the period. However, the head offices of the largest Canadian companies, including the Bank of Montreal, the Royal Bank, Sun Life, Canadian Pacific, Canadian National and the Bell Telephone Company of Canada were still in Montreal, and this had financial spinoff effects. Toronto's growth was much more dependent on Canadian subsidiaries of American companies.

As a trading, industrial and financial centre, Montreal was a city that looked outward, both to the Canadian hinterland and to the United States and Britain. Its openness could be seen in the character of its population. For more than a century, its growth had depended mainly on migration — immigration from other countries and the rural exodus of both English and French Canadians in Quebec. By putting a stop to population growth, the Depression reversed this long-term trend. The decline in immigration also affected the ethnic composition of the city. Since 1911, French Canadians had represented about 63 per cent of the population, but this figure rose to 66.3 per cent in 1941. Conversely, the percentage of Montrealers of British and other origins declined somewhat. These trends continued throughout the war as immigration remained low.

The city's physical growth was not as dramatic as in previous periods, as residential construction slowed down if not stopped. Nonetheless, some new neighbourhoods grew up during the war around the war plants, especially in the suburb of Ville Saint-Laurent, where the construction of an aircraft factory led to considerable population growth. On the whole, however, suburban growth before the end of the war was very slow.

The Montreal skyline continued to change with the addition of new public buildings. Modern skyscrapers, the largest of which was the Sun Life building, were built in downtown Montreal in the 1920s. The Aldred building on Place d'Armes was completed in the early 1930s. The most spectacular new structures of the period were on Mount Royal — the University of Montreal, with its imposing tower, and St. Joseph's Oratory. Another major achievement was the Jacques Cartier Bridge, opened in

1929. By providing another link to the south shore, it facilitated communications and stimulated the development of suburban Longueuil. Public projects undertaken as Depression make-work programs — improvements to Mount Royal park, the Botanical Gardens and railway overpasses to improve traffic — helped enhance Montreal's cityscape.

The financial burden of assistance to the unemployed was a strain on the city budget and made for a precarious situation. But the city's financial problems were mainly due to inadequate management and financial procedures inherited from previous decades. As a city that had undergone rapid growth, Montreal suffered from chronic revenue shortages. The level of taxation was much too low, as can be seen by comparing it with Toronto's, which was much higher. Large property owners — especially Anglophone ratepayers and executives of large companies — always opposed higher property taxes. The tax exemption for property owned by religious institutions also deprived the city of a significant source of revenue.

The city was also a victim of mismanagement. Corruption, patronage and managerial incompetence were continuing features of its public life, even though they were probably less serious than they had been early in the century. As well, the provincial government constantly threatened the city's autonomy. Montreal was underrepresented in Quebec City and the government was highly sensitive to financial interests that wanted municipalities run at the lowest possible cost. Camillien Houde, mayor from 1928 to 1932, 1934 to 1936 and 1938 to 1940, fiercely defended

The mayor of Montreal, Camillien Houde, with Premier Maurice Duplessis in the 1930s. (National Archives of Canada, C-27416)

ordinary Montrealers against the Board of Trade establishment and municipal autonomy against provincial government actions. His populist approach made him the target of attacks from the city's controlling interests.

Needing new sources of revenue to solve its problems, Montreal instituted a 2 per cent sales tax and borrowed heavily. It fell deeply into debt and was placed under trusteeship by the Quebec government in 1940. The Municipal Commission was given the task of instituting a stringent cleanup of the city's finances. A major reform of Montreal's political structures was also imposed. Under the new system, the mayor became largely a figurehead, while real power was invested in a city council made up of three groups of councillors, each with a third of the seats. "A" councillors were elected only by property owners, "B" councillors were elected by all voters, and "C" councillors were appointed by large institutions such as the Board of Trade, the chamber of commerce, the trade unions and the universities.

Quebec City

Quebec City lagged far behind Montreal in population. The population of the city proper grew from 130,000 in 1931 to 150,000 in 1941, while the census metropolitan area had 200,000 people in 1941, or 9.5 per cent of Quebec's urban population. However, Quebec City's importance was greater than its population would indicate. As the provincial capital, it was a major political decision-making centre, and it also served as the metropolis for eastern Quebec, the Beauce and the Saguenay-Lake St. John region.

As the seat of government, Quebec City was home to several thousand civil servants, who gave a distinctive character to the city's society and culture and constituted an important element in its economy. Quebec City was also a significant industrial centre. One of its main industries was shoes which, according to Raoul Blanchard, employed between 6,000 and 7,000 workers in 1933. However, the industry, which had a long history in Quebec City, began to encounter difficulties in the late 1920s. Other industries in the city included corset-making, tanneries, tobacco products, clothing, and pulp and paper.

Quebec City was also affected by the decline in port traffic during the Depression. But the Depression was not the only reason for the port's problems — as Blanchard emphasized, "Without a large and active hinterland, the port did not have enough merchandise to receive or export." The construction of grain elevators improved the situation without fundamentally changing it. However, commercial activities in Quebec City were not limited to water transport — there was considerable wholesale trade in wood, food products and hardware. These activities were the leading manifestation of Quebec City's function as a metropolis.

Quebec City's influence was also expressed through its university, colleges, archdiocese and religious institutions. Finally, it was a major tourist centre, attracting travellers from all over eastern North America.

Other Cities and Towns

Outside Montreal and Quebec City, the most populous urban agglomeration consisted of Trois-Rivières and Cap-de-la-Madeleine, which had a combined population of 54,000 in 1941. Trois-Rivières was the centre of a regional urban system on the St. Maurice River whose economy was based on natural resource development. The stagnation of the pulp and paper industry hit these small industrial towns hard, but the war revived the resource-related industries and started most of the towns growing again. Military needs brought new investment to the chemicals industry in Shawinigan, which along with Grand-Mère formed the second largest urban area in the St. Maurice Valley, with a population of 31,000 in 1941.

Towns on the Saguenay were also dependent on resource industries, and they too experienced the stagnation of the Depression and the rapid growth of the 1940s. The most spectacular growth took place in the aluminum town of Arvida, where expansion of the Alcan plant boosted the population from 4,600 in 1941 to 11,100 in 1951. The population of the large urban belt stretching from Chicoutimi to Jonquière jumped from only 26,000 in 1931 to 40,969 in 1941 and 69,668 in 1951.

In the Abitibi region, mining led to the formation of a regional urban belt because of the heavy demand for gold. Rouyn and Noranda had been founded in the late 1920s and had a population of 5,700 by 1931 (13,400 in 1941). Joining them were Duparquet (1933), Bourlamaque (1934), Val-d'Or (1935) and Malartic (1939). The St. Maurice, Saguenay and Abitibi regions were all dependent on natural resource exploitation, and the period from 1930 to 1945 was a good illustration of the wild swings, both upward and downward, that towns with a narrow economic base can be subject to.

The other region that was urbanized to a considerable degree was the Eastern Townships, with Sherbrooke at its centre. With an economy based on light manufacturing, forest industries and mining, the Eastern Townships had a more diversified economic structure than other regions. There were a dozen small towns with a variety of economic activities. The population of Drummondville and Granby, both at the edge of the Eastern Townships, grew considerably.

Thus, the Depression brought urban growth in Quebec to a temporary halt, while the war created conditions for a recovery that would hit its full stride after 1945.

CHAPTER 5

THE WORKING WORLD

Along with western farmers, the working class bore the brunt of the Depression. The working class was a heterogeneous group, divided by variations in skills, income and status as well as ethnic, linguistic, cultural and religious differences. It protected its interests through the trade union movement. Although only a minority of workers were unionized, unions succeeded in obtaining improvements in working and living conditions by bargaining with employers and pressuring governments to legislate against the worst abuses. According to the historian Bryan Palmer, workers in the manufacturing sector in 1928 could hope to support a family on their pay cheques alone. However, he adds, more than half of all workers had incomes of less than $1,000 a year. Whatever progress had been made was called into question after 1929 — employers were in a position of strength and they took advantage of it. The war changed the situation again, bringing increased unionization and substantial gains in wages and working conditions.

The Labour Force

From the turn of the century on, the labour force felt the effects of two developments. First, the growth of the service sector created new types of employment, notably office jobs. Second, more highly skilled labour was needed as a result of technological advances in manufacturing. The war redirected these trends, slowing the growth of the service sector, increasing the prominence of the manufacturing sector, and accentuating the need for skilled labour. Women made up about 20 per cent of employed people in 1931 and about 22 per cent during the war.

The Depression and the war had diametrically opposed effects on the workforce — the Depression brought massive unemployment while the war meant the beginning of a period of full employment. While estimates of the actual extent of unemployment vary, there is no question that the unemployment rate was higher than it had ever been. By 1930, it was above 10 per cent, and at the nadir of the Depression in 1933, more than a quarter of the Canadian labour force was unemployed. These are average figures — in some urban neighbourhoods and industrial towns the rate was even higher. After 1933 unemployment came down slightly, only to go up again after 1937. In addition, many other people were underemployed, working reduced numbers of hours or weeks. In Canada as a whole, people worked an average of only 44.3 weeks between June 1930 and June 1931. The Depression also caused wages to fall by an average of 40 per cent, although this was partly compensated for by falling prices.

The war brought many changes. For the first time, the labour force was registered and its movements controlled by the government. The government had three goals: to strengthen the armed forces, whose numbers rose from about 9,000 in 1939 to about 800,000 in 1944; to expand the industrial workforce to meet the needs of war production; and to maintain enough agricultural workers to meet Allied food requirements. In two years, a labour surplus turned into a shortage, and more women had to be called on. The National Resources Mobilization Act of 1940 and National Selective Service, instituted in 1942, placed a variety of controls on labour mobility. Among other provisions, young men were called up unless they had exemptions, farmers were not allowed to take industrial jobs, workers could not change jobs or be laid off without official permission, jobs could be offered only through official agencies, and all unemployed workers had to registered.

Another direct effect of the war was improved training. As the historian Desmond Morton has pointed out, many Canadian companies were not very efficient when the war began. High-quality products had to be turned out, and some required knowhow that did not yet exist. As a result, some workers had to be trained or retrained in short order.

Working conditions varied widely from sector to sector. Small clothing manufacturers and large industrial corporations represented two separate worlds. In the textile and shoe industries, both heavily represented in Quebec, conditions were still very difficult — shops were overheated, ventilation was poor and only minimal facilities were provided for employees. A long work day and a six-day week were still the norm. These conditions deteriorated further during the Depression, as studies of the period show, and wages also fell. In the construction industry in Montreal, carpenters' hourly wages fell from 83 cents in 1929 to 45 cents in 1933, and labourers who were paid 38 cents an hour in 1929 earned 25 cents an hour four years later — if they could find work. In the textile industry, wages were even lower. In 1934, in a factory in Louiseville, the average pay for a fifty-five-hour week was $13.43 for men and $9.73 for women.

However, the war brought a significant improvement in the situation. Wages rose substantially, and benefits such as pension funds and paid vacations began to be introduced. The work week came down to roughly forty-five hours at the end of the war, but people augmented their incomes significantly by working overtime. Looking again at the construction industry in Montreal, a carpenter's hourly wage was 70 cents in 1939 and 96 cents in 1945, while a labourer's increased from 40 cents to 61 cents over the same period. The average weekly wage rose from $21.26 in 1939 to $30.88 in 1945.

Women in the Workplace

Starting in the late nineteenth century, women had been entering the labour market in increasing numbers. A number of features of the female workforce are worth noting. Women were concentrated in a few sectors, especially manufacturing, office work, and services (mainly domestic work). A minority worked as teachers while a smaller number were nurses. On the whole, there was a wide wage gap between men and women. Women workers were mostly young and unmarried, and few of them remained in the workforce after marriage.

Women's participation in the labour force was not always looked on with approval; rather, it was tolerated and considered inevitable in some cases. In the Catholic Church and other traditional circles, it was seen as a threat to family values and the stability of society. During the Depression, other objections were raised that strengthened the traditional viewpoint — didn't women who worked take jobs from men who had to

Women workers inspecting parts for shells, Montreal, 1941. (National Archives of Canada, PA-112912)

support their families? This was a disturbing question for politicians, and even unions were sensitive to it.

During the war, however, all women were called on specifically to replace male workers who were needed for military service. The campaign to mobilize women was waged on several fronts. The three branches of the armed forces formed women's companies. Their members were considered auxiliaries at first and mainly did office work. In the civilian sector, women mostly did traditional work, but they also did jobs that had previously been performed only by men, working as mechanics and truck drivers. Women at home were also mobilized to participate in the war effort. They were asked to control what their families consumed, take care to avoid waste, and help solve the housing crisis by taking in lodgers.

But the underlying problems remained. Women were not paid the same as men, even in the army, and the careers available in the armed forces did not offer an escape from traditional jobs. Of course, women learned new skills in the war industries, but as soon as the war was over it was made clear that it was their duty to yield their jobs to the demobilized soldiers. According to historian Ruth Pierson, once the sense of urgency was gone, "traditional attitudes about women held sway once more." Nonetheless, women's place in the labour market expanded during the period and, contrary to expectations, it would continue to expand subsequently. Women workers filled a need that was not due only to the war, and women were now an integral part of the working world.

Labour Organizations

Unions had been in existence for quite a long time, since about the 1880s. But their progress was very slow and tended to occur mainly in sectors where workers were highly trained so that they were in something of a monopoly position. Thus, skilled workers who were difficult to replace became unionized well before unskilled labourers did. The unionization rate levelled off in 1921 at 17.4 per cent of the nonagricultural working population, fell to 9 per cent in 1931, and then rose again to almost 17 per cent in 1941. At the end of the war, about a quarter of all workers were unionized.

The 1930s were a difficult time for the labour movement, but during the war membership rose and unions gained greater recognition. The union movement's weakness, as reflected in its small number of members in 1931, was accentuated by its division into four separate factions, all vying for workers' allegiance. The main tendency was made up of the international unions affiliated to the Trades and Labour Congress of Canada (TLC), which encompassed almost two thirds of Quebec union members. It was followed by the Canadian and Catholic Confederation of Labour, the Canadian unions belonging to the All-Canadian Congress of Labour and, between 1929 and 1935, the Workers' Unity League, a small union federation linked to the Communist Party.

There were several factors causing these divisions. The first was the question of whether unions should be organized along craft or industrial lines. This debate dated back to the end of the nineteenth century, and became even more urgent with the advent of mass production techniques. Large companies employed not only skilled tradespeople but also large numbers of unskilled workers. Rather than dividing them up into many units, industrial unionism, which developed during this period, proposed to group them into a single union. In so doing it clashed head on with the interests of the traditional craft unions.

Another cause of division was the question of subservience to the so-called international unions, which were in reality American. The belief of some trade unionists that workers' interests were better served by independent Canadian organizations led to the formation of Canadian unions. The third divisive factor, and one peculiar to Quebec, was religion, which gave rise to a kind of unionism that was both French Canadian and Catholic. The Catholic unions tried as far as they could both to comply with the demands of the clergy and a section of the elite and to respond to the specific needs of French Canadian workers.

The Trades and Labour Congress of Canada was strongest in Montreal. Its craft unions, linked to the American Federation of Labor (AF of L), had a long history and considerable experience and were established in large industrial corporations. The TLC generally followed the directives of the AF of L. Like the AF of L, the TLC was shaken by the development of industrial unionism, which was a dominant force all over North America in the 1930s. The TLC's insensitivity to the new needs of workers at first led it to ignore industrial unionism, allowing the other union federations to reap the benefit. But beginning in 1935, following the AF of L's lead, it allowed industrial unions to develop. This led to an influx of experienced activists from the Workers' Unity League, which had been dissolved the same year. But industrial unionists and the TLC led an uneasy coexistence, and the TLC expelled some industrial unions in 1939, just as the AF of L had two years earlier. Despite the expulsions, the TLC's membership increased during the war. A number of industrial and semi-industrial unions remained affiliated to the TLC and contributed to its expansion. At about the same time, the Quebec unions affiliated to the TLC set up a new federation, the Quebec Provincial Federation of Labour, which acted mainly as a lobby and liaison group.

In 1938, before their expulsion, industrial unions had joined together in the Canadian committee of the U.S.-based Congress of Industrial Organizations (CIO). But in Quebec, these unions were badly organized and incurred the hostility of employers and the government, who were worried about this innovative, militant brand of trade unionism that they regarded as communist-dominated. In 1938, the Quebec provincial police invoked the Padlock Law and seized the files of the steelworkers' union, then just being formed. In 1940, the Canadian committee of the CIO merged with the Canadian unions in the All-Canadian Congress of Labour to form a new federation, the Canadian Congress of Labour. Industrial unionism also took advantage of the increase in unionization during the war, although only a small fraction of Quebec workers were members of industrial unions.

The Canadian and Catholic Confederation of Labour (CCCL) had been in existence since 1921. Most of its members were in Quebec, where it represented a little under a quarter of unionized workers. It was more firmly established outside of Montreal. According to the historian Jacques Rouillard, the CCCL's main problem was that it was torn between acting as a union and following the social doctrine of the church. Gradually, it began to behave more like other unions. But in the 1930s, it publicly espoused the goals of corporatism, which it did not give up until after the war. The active support of the church was important in certain sectors such as printing and especially construction, where contractors had to deal with CCCL unions on contracts for buildings serving religious purposes. The CCCL also organized the unorganized, so that its growth was not at the expense of the international unions, and its decentralized structure allowed room for industrial unionism. But its financial weakness, its lack of militancy and failures such as the 1937 textile strike led to some dissatisfaction, which the international unions took advantage of.

During the war, competition from the other union federations led the CCCL to change. It was poorly regarded by officials of the federal Department of Labour, who were often former members of rival unions, and was often distrusted because of its denominational nature and its reputation for collaborating with employers. To win full recognition, it had to be open to all the workers in a workplace, regardless of religion. In 1943, after a strike at the Price company in the Saguenay region, it changed its regulations to do that. By the end of the war, the CCCL behaved like the other union federations.

The short-lived Workers' Unity League, with its communist allegiance and obedience to Comintern directives, was clearly different from the other union federations. It was founded in 1929 when the Comintern launched its "class against class" orientation and ordered its members to fight organizations seen as class collaborationist, especially all groups with social democratic leanings. In 1935 it was dissolved on the order of the Soviet Communist Party, which ordered that popular fronts against fascism be built.

The Workers' Unity League was never very strong in Quebec, and at its peak had only a few hundred members. It never came close to its goal of mobilizing the French Canadian masses, and according to some historians, even during strikes its activities were dramatic but not especially effective. After 1935, communist trade unionists worked within existing unions, especially the industrial ones.

There were independent unions outside the federations, such as the railway unions and international unions that did not belong to the Canadian federations. As well, teachers' unions were created outside the existing federations during the 1930s, and they developed rapidly during the war. Teachers unions' first started among rural women teachers whose working and living conditions had deteriorated during the Depression and who earned only half as much as their male colleagues. In 1936, Laure Gaudreault founded the first union of rural women teachers in the Charlevoix area. The following year, the movement grew with the creation of the Fédération Catholique des Institutrices Rurales (Catholic federation of rural women teachers), which was soon followed by an organization of rural men teachers. Teachers in the cities followed suit in the early 1940s. A new labour relations act passed in 1944 gave these unions full accreditation.

Strikes and Labour Legislation

Strikes during the war were very different from those during the Depression. During the Depression, workers were in a relatively weak position, while during the war the balance of forces tipped to their side. The strikes during the Depression were manifestations of real misery, waged by workers who were pushed to the limit by poor working conditions, low wages and arrogant employers who knew they could replace recalcitrant employees. In 1934, Abitibi miners and women clothing workers in Montreal went out on strikes organized by activists from the Workers' Unity League. In neither case did the workers make any immediate gains, but they did obtain valuable experience in militancy, which the clothing workers used to make gains three years later. In 1937, unions affiliated to the CCCL waged two very tough strikes. The first, at the shipyards in Sorel, soon paralysed the whole town. The second took place in several Dominion Textiles plants where the work was especially hard and poorly paid. These strikes, however, did not go well for the unions. The government took a harder line towards all union activity after Maurice Duplessis came to power in 1936.

Canada's entry into the war was an important turning point. If high levels of production were to be achieved without interruption, social peace was required. Hence, the government tried to hold labour conflict to a minimum by encouraging unionization. But two problems remained: workers wanted to protect their wages from inflation, and employers were reluctant to accord union recognition. The number of strikes increased, reaching a peak in 1943. As a result, the government laid down clearer rules for unionization.

Thus, government intervention was a growing factor in labour relations. Regulations governing some aspects of work were already in place: hours of work for men and women, minimum working age, work accidents, conciliation in the case of labour disputes. Both levels of govern-

Strikers at Canadian Car Munitions in Montreal, 1943. (*The Gazette*, National Archives of Canada, PA-137223)

ment had jurisdiction in this area, although labour relations came mostly under provincial authority.

Before the war, the Quebec government introduced some major legislation. In 1934, as a result of pressure from the Canadian and Catholic Confederation of Labour, the Collective Agreements Extension Act was passed, based on similar French and Belgian laws. Under this law, conditions negotiated by an employer and a union could be extended to an entire sector. The other unions were not in favour of the new law, which they considered somewhat too corporatist and regarded as a threat to unionization, but it helped the CCCL make some gains. In 1937, the Duplessis government passed the Fair Wages Act, which would later become the Minimum Wage Act. However, this legislation was a double-edged sword, because it allowed employers to set wages arbitrarily when there was a labour conflict. The Padlock Law, authorizing the closure of any building used for communist propaganda, was passed the same year and was used against some union activists.

During the war, the federal government was predominant and its labour policy was quite clear — it wanted industrial peace. With labour problems persisting, it passed an order-in-council in 1944 that set clearer and more binding conditions on union recognition and forced the parties to negotiate in good faith. This measure was based largely on the Wagner Act, adopted in the United States in 1935 and considered the great charter of the American labour movement. The 1944 order-in-council played somewhat the same role in Canada. A few weeks before, Quebec had hastened to adopt its first labour code, based on the same principles. It also passed a law on disputes between utilities and their employees.

*   *   *   *   *   *

By the end of the war, the world of labour had changed. The workforce was larger, more diverse and better trained, and it had gained the experience of tight government management. The trade union movement had seen its numbers grow and had successfully fought for improved working conditions for its members. And finally, the question of union recognition, the source of numerous conflicts, was beginning to be regulated.

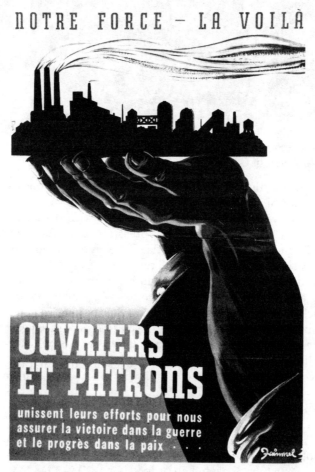

Government propaganda for worker-employer cooperation during the war. (National Archives of Canada, C-87501)

CHAPTER 6

DIRECT RELIEF

The Depression, with the suffering it brought in its wake, placed the impotence of traditional policies and institutions in sharp focus. With whatever means were at hand, society had to cope with widespread poverty. At the same time, it had to look at the unemployment problem in a new light and prevent the nightmarish situation from developing again. With the war came full employment and the emergence of a genuine system of social security.

Living Conditions during the Depression

Unemployment had always been a fact of life for workers. Its most common form was seasonal unemployment, with workers on the docks or in the construction industry being out of work for a few months each year. When unemployment dragged on longer than that, people's only choice was to look for work elsewhere. The United States had long acted as an outlet for Quebecers, easily absorbing the surplus labour force.

In the fall of 1929, it was still possible to believe that unemployment was merely seasonal. But once the spring of 1930 came, it was undeniable that unemployment was continuing and the traditional solutions were no longer working. Unemployment, which had always been thought of as temporary in duration and individual in scope, had now become a social problem. It remained at a high level throughout the 1930s — since there were no official unemployment statistics at the time, just how high can only be estimated. According to the historian John Thompson, the Canadian unemployment rate rose from 4.2 per cent in 1929 to 12.9 per cent in 1930, and jumped to almost 27 per cent in 1933. Subsequently, it declined very slowly, and then rose again in 1938; when war was declared, it was still 14.1 per cent. The Quebec rate is estimated to have been generally a little higher.

Some groups, particularly labourers and construction workers, were hit harder by unemployment than others. In the industrial sector, the slowdown was generalized, but it was worst in natural resource and capital goods industries.

Regional impact varied. Because of its strategic position in the Canadian economy, Montreal was hit hard; it had enjoyed the prosperity of the 1920s, but it suffered from the effects of the Depression more than any other large Canadian city. In 1933, Montreal had 60,000 unemployed; counting their dependents, an estimated 250,000 people, or 30 per cent of the population, were receiving relief from the city. This meant considerable loss in earnings for the local economy, and small businesses and professionals were also affected. It seemed that the spiral would never stop. The situation was made even worse by the influx of jobless from other regions of Quebec, Ontario, and even the United States, as Quebecers who had emigrated now returned. There were repercussions on public health — many schoolchildren had obvious symptoms of malnutrition, and the incidence of tuberculosis remained high.

Elsewhere in Quebec, the cities and towns most affected were those whose economies were dependent either on natural resources or on a single industry, such as Shawinigan in the St. Maurice Valley and Chandler in the Gaspé. Cities and towns that had more diversified industrial structures, such as Saint-Hyacinthe near Montreal, were in somewhat better shape.

Despite the high unemployment rate, most Quebecers had jobs during the Depression, although some who did suffered a decline in income, either through lower wages or through a reduction in hours worked. In Canada, the average annual manufacturing wage fell from $1,045 in 1929 to $785 in 1933. Falling prices made up for this to some extent: thus, a dozen eggs, which cost 47 cents in 1929, cost only 28 cents four years later, and the average rent in Montreal fell from $27.92 to $23.04 over the same period.

Some sectors of the population benefited from deflation and suffered no radical reduction in income, and thus actually saw their situation improve. Such was the case for civil servants, whose wages fell less than other employees', people with investment income, and part of the bourgeoisie. The prosperity of the few who had cars and servants and lived the high life stood in striking contrast to the misery of the unemployed.

The contrast was further emphasized by the improvement in living standards in the late 1920s, whose fruits had been dangled before Quebecers' eyes and remained accessible to people with means. Thus, the number of private cars rose by a third between 1927 and 1929, from 100,128 to 132,839. The Depression initially caused a small decline in the number of cars on the road, lasting until 1933; in 1934, however, the upward trend resumed. There had also been considerable growth in the number of telephones, reaching a total of about 300,000 stations in 1929; here the Depression caused a decline of about 12 per cent between 1929 and 1933.

Associations of the unemployed formed here and there in response to the hardships of the Depression. They organized street demonstrations, rallies at city halls, strikes at public works sites, and pilgrimages such as the one to St. Joseph's Oratory in 1933. These associations attracted many activists, from both the right and the left, but they encompassed only a minority of the unemployed. What is most striking is the absence of large-scale collective action on the part of the jobless.

The response to the Depression was mainly individual and was channelled through the basic support networks of family, neighbourhood and parish. The jobless used boundless ingenuity to try to turn things to their own advantage. People had to be resourceful, and in this respect women played a central role in the domestic economy, adjusting menus and altering clothes. In some circles, something approaching a parallel economy arose, with barter, payment in kind and exchange of services becoming increasingly common. When electricity was cut off in Montreal, some electricians "jumped" the meters in exchange for other services. When people couldn't pay the rent, they tried to get the landlord to agree to a postponement, and if this was not possible, they moved secretly during the night. It became essential for neighbours and relatives to help each other. In some cases, seizures of property were prevented or made difficult when neighbours intervened. At auctions, people agreed among themselves to buy the furniture at a ridiculously low price and give it back to its owner.

Housing conditions deteriorated significantly. In Montreal, this was caused by a lack of reasonably priced housing, as a large number of more expensive dwellings went unoccupied in 1933 and 1934. As a result, families crowded together. Many landlords rented at a loss, carrying out no maintenance or improvements. Shanty towns, the last resort of the homeless, appeared in Montreal, Valleyfield and Hull.

The cities did not have a monopoly on hardship. The rural areas had their share as well, although the situation was not as acute or desperate since food, housing and heating were usually guaranteed. But many farmers were encumbered with debt at a time when their incomes were collapsing, and some were even driven into bankruptcy. Their difficulties were made worse by the slowdown in logging, which traditionally provided extra income for farmers. Even lumberjacks who could still find work suffered from falling wages and deteriorating working conditions. Although colonization was promoted as a solution to urban hardship, a colonist's life was far from easy. It was hard to turn into a farmer overnight; for many, it was a life of hardship and deprivation.

Social Policy

When the Depression began, Quebec society was caught unawares. It had no system of social security, and the traditional view that individuals alone were responsible for their own wellbeing and the wellbeing of their dependents predominated. If individuals were unable to provide for

An impoverished family in Montreal, 1938. (*The Gazette*, National Archives of Canada, PA-129812)

themselves for one reason or another, the family had to take over. Charitable organizations mainly helped the "deserving" poor — the ones whose own behaviour was not considered to be the cause of their misfortunes. Naturally, this kind of charity was accompanied by moralizing, which varied in intensity from one religion to another. As a last resort, municipalities were responsible for indigents.

The increase in problems arising out of urbanization forced the government to step in, however hesitantly, to take care of those who had no families and were unable to work. The Public Assistance Act of 1921 provided for the maintenance of indigents placed in institutions, with the costs shared equally among the provincial government, the municipality and the institution. However, the conditions for receiving this assistance were very stringent — the recipient had to have no family support, be unable to work and be hospitalized. When this legislation was introduced it gave rise to a debate, with traditionalists fearing that government intrusion would spell the end of private charity and undermine the role of the family.

Less than ten years later, the Depression created another problem — what to do about people who were able to work but could not find jobs for reasons that were clearly beyond their control. There were two major ways to help them: handouts and work. Ideally, work was considered preferable, given the reluctance, in Quebec as elsewhere in North America, to give assistance to an able-bodied worker. So public works projects soon came to be seen as the best solution to the urgent problem of providing relief for the unemployed.

After an initial period of indecision, the first measures were taken in 1930. Some public works projects were undertaken on a shared-cost basis, with municipalities and higher levels of government all contributing to the cost. But it soon became obvious that this was not sufficient. First of all, the work was mainly excavation, which not all workers could do. In addition, there was not enough work for everyone. In accordance with the ideas of the time, priority was supposed be given to heads of families with the most children; unmarried workers, who were at the bottom of the list, were virtually excluded from these jobs. As well, these jobs were not meant for women. Finally, the projects drained the coffers of the municipalities, which had to shoulder a large portion of the costs.

Between 1932 and 1936, government programs were based on direct relief. For the first time, it became accepted that the government had to give assistance to able-bodied citizens without demanding work in exchange. Costs were divided in thirds among the federal government, the provincial government and the municipalities, making it possible for the higher levels of government to oversee what was handed out. The programs that were established provided for restrictions on allowable expenses, levels of benefits, categories of beneficiaries and methods of operation.

Initially, relief was supposed to be used only to pay for food and heating. Gradually, coverage was extended to include clothing, electricity, gas and part of the rent. The amounts provided were fairly paltry, since benefits were based on a typical menu providing a basic minimum. In Verdun in 1933, a family of two was allocated $3.16 a week, and a family of nine received $6.43. A little later in Montreal, a family of five received $5.05 weekly during the winter for food, $1.35 for heating, and 75 cents for clothing; in addition, it received monthly allowances of $10.50 for rent and 90 cents for electricity. In Montreal in 1935, single individuals not living with their parents received $1.80 per week for food, plus a housing allowance. Initially, the relief was distributed not in cash but in the form of vouchers that could be exchanged in the stores — sometimes only in certain stores. Later, because the system was so rigid and merchants were exerting pressure for change, the vouchers were replaced in some areas by coupons in fixed amounts or cheques. Recipients of relief could then buy what they wanted and avoid being identified as receiving direct assistance.

Throughout the period, public works and direct relief were both used, sometimes alternating and sometimes in conjunction with each other. However, there were three distinct phases: in the first, from 1930 to 1932, public works were predominant; in the second, from 1932 to 1936, relief was predominant; and in the third, from 1936 onwards, the emphasis shifted back to public works. Some municipalities, such as Saint-Hyacinthe, always required the unemployed to work if they received relief.

The various levels of government also adopted additional measures for particular categories of unemployed. Besides the colonization programs discussed in chapter 2, the federal government established a series of work camps in 1932, run by the army for young single men, who were highly mobile and a source of concern to the authorities. They were fed and paid a "wage" of 20 cents a day for working in the forests and building roads (they were nicknamed "vincennes" from the French *vingt cennes*). In Quebec, a camp was set up at Valcartier, where Jean-Louis Gagnon counted 1,700 rather dissatisfied inmates in the spring of 1935. The camps soon became highly unpopular with their occupants; the army and the government began to worry that they would become centres for propaganda and subversion and closed them down in 1936. Another form of assistance consisted of short-term shelters for the homeless in the cities. But there was massive pressure on the 700 beds in the Meurling shelter in Montreal every night, and people had to be turned away to seek the hospitality of the neighbouring police station or sleep in the open air in a park.

In addition to government measures, there were the more limited services provided by private charitable organizations, which financed a wide range of institutions aimed at helping the destitute. Each religious denomination performed a range of charitable works: the Jews had Family Welfare; the Catholics had l'Oeuvre de la Soupe, run by the Sisters

Meal for the jobless at the Old Brewery Mission in Montreal, 1937. (Conrad Poirier collection, National Archives of Quebec in Montreal)

of Providence, and the St. Vincent de Paul Society; and the Protestants had the Diet Dispensary. These organizations sponsored activities ranging from running playgrounds and summer camps through visiting the poor to operating hospices; in some cases, they even set up actual social service agencies. The assistance these organizations provided was essential, but their effectiveness was seriously hampered by the ethnic and religious divisions among them, the absence of coordination, and their narrowly defined religious and community outlook. Some were better funded than others, so that the level of assistance provided varied from organization to organization.

At the time, most municipalities did not have welfare departments, while private charitable organizations knew the community and had experience in helping the needy. As a result, the charitable organizations were initially given responsibility for managing the relief programs. In the Catholic community, this task was assigned to the St. Vincent de Paul Society, which had an efficient structure based on central diocesan councils and local conferences in every parish. Members of these conferences had experience in providing help in the home — something no municipal government had at the time. Similar organizations were called on for Protestants and Jews. But this solution soon had to be abandoned, because the organizations were overloaded with work and their management made government auditors shudder. Merchants complained that it took too long to receive payment for relief vouchers. In addition, the organizations retained their religious character and distributed relief as charity "according to their own regulations and methods," which left considerable latitude for arbitrary decisions. For example, a Montreal priest distributed vouchers directly at the church on Friday nights after the Benediction of the Blessed Sacrament; families who were not there had to wait until the following Friday.

So the municipalities decided to take responsibility for relief themselves and, beginning in 1933, set up departments towards that end. The situation did not always improve, however; there were cases of favouritism and, as a number of municipal relief officials came from the private organizations, the approach was often the same.

The relief programs had very serious ramifications. In simple financial terms, they caused municipalities to go into debt, and even pushed them to the edge of bankruptcy. In social terms, the government was forced for the first time to provide direct aid to individuals who were able to work. As well, labour force mobility was reduced: people were afraid to move to a new city because municipalities had minimum residency requirements for relief. In individual terms, the fact of accepting relief implied a degree of humiliation; many workers felt they had been stripped of their dignity as workers and heads of families, while young people on relief saw no future for themselves.

These considerations prompted a second look at relief. In 1930, the Quebec government mandated the Social Insurance Commission to examine the problem. The Commission's report made some concrete recommendations involving an increase in government intervention, which remained tentative and limited in a context where the role of the state still seen as secondary. As the decade went on, it became clear that the problems of the day were not temporary and that long-term solutions were needed, all of which involved recognition of government responsibility. In 1935, the federal government took a firm step onto that path when Prime Minister R.B. Bennett introduced his "New Deal," with unemployment insurance and health insurance as the centrepiece. These new measures were not well planned and did not take into account jurisdictional questions, and so ultimately had little concrete impact. But the first move had been made, and some of the recommendations of the Rowell-Sirois Commission, set up in 1937, were inspired by it.

The Quebec government enacted only limited measures — a good example of how political solutions had fallen behind social thought. Quebec accepted the federal old age pension program in 1936, and also established a mother's allowance and a pension for the blind. While these measures were new in some respects, they still followed the traditional approach of providing help only to the very needy.

Living Conditions during the War

When the war began, employment rose and much of the misery was relieved. But with the war also came unprecedented, open government intervention into all aspects of daily life. Whether it was urging people to buy victory bonds or to recover scrap metal, the government used massive advertising campaigns to try to influence their behaviour. Information was censored and people were warned to watch out for spies. Even clothing styles came under government scrutiny — outside pockets, large collars and decorative belts were eliminated to save material.

The government tried to mobilize women as much as possible. This was aimed not only at bringing them into the labour force in larger numbers but also at recruiting women at home for the war effort. Volunteers were needed to organize the metal recovery and victory bond campaigns, prepare packages for soldiers and keep an eye on prices. An effort was made to convince women that their individual commitment was essential to the war effort. Government propaganda gave them responsibility for upholding the morale of the men and of the whole country. So at least for a time, an image of women as dynamic and versatile, playing a role that went beyond the traditional confines of the home, came to the fore. After the war, however, the old ideal of womanhood was again promoted.

Day-to-day life was also affected by government control of consumption. Strategic commodities required for military purposes, such as rubber, gasoline and certain kinds of metal, became less easily available. As well, controlled allocation of raw materials to industry had an effect on consumption. For example, in 1942, car manufacturers stopped all production of civilian vehicles. The same held true in the construction industry: access to materials was restricted and there was little residential construction, which led to housing shortages in places where there was an influx of workers.

Consumers also had to submit to rationing. Housewives were given booklets of detachable coupons or tokens, which they presented to shopkeepers in exchange for items such as meat, butter and sugar. Drivers were also given coupons for gas. Although rationing was not as tight as it was in Europe, it did lead to reduced consumption. However, many shopkeepers bent the rules, and there was a black market that allowed people who could afford it to defy the restrictions, although this was not widespread.

Some young Quebecers had to get used to military life, either in the overseas force or in regiments stationed in Canada. Camp and garrison life was characterized by general boredom, which the soldiers tried to escape in any way they could. The Allied landing in Europe changed that aspect of army life, but it also brought a higher level of danger.

Towards the Welfare State

During the war, the state emerged more and more as the architect of social policy, even though a section of public opinion in Quebec was against this development. In 1940, the federal government passed the Unemployment Insurance Act, which established collective responsibility for unemployment. The burden was now shared among the individual, the employer and the government. Even though the scope of the legislation was limited by a host of conditions and barely 42 per cent of the labour force was eligible for benefits, it represented a recognition that workers had to be protected from unemployment without being considered indigents.

The Marsh Report, commissioned by the federal government and submitted in 1943, marked a turning point. Its philosophy permeated Ottawa's approach to social policy and, in a way, it signalled the birth of the welfare state. It was inspired by Britain's famous Beveridge Report of 1942, which set forth social policy goals for the postwar period. Beveridge considered that there were social risks and needs that should be covered by social insurance. Marsh based himself on these guiding principles, and his report urged the federal government to give Canada an integrated system of social security, where the notion of social insurance would replace social assistance. The report provided for a whole series of measures in addition to unemployment insurance, such as family allowances and health insurance. But the main proposals were not adopted immediately, although family allowances were enacted in 1945, as was the federal housing act, designed to improve housing conditions and access to home ownership.

Another concern of the government was the reintegration of veterans into civilian life. Various programs, including discharge allowances, access to unemployment insurance, occupational retraining and university education grants, helped veterans reestablish themselves. As well, a pension plan was introduced for disabled veterans.

The government of Quebec was responsive to these new developments in social policy. It widened the application of the old Public Assistance Act, which became less exclusively directed towards hospitalized indigents, and prepared to act in the health field. But this process was hampered by the return to power of Maurice Duplessis in 1944.

*   *   *   *   *   *

In the space of about fifteen years, there was a virtual revolution in social policy. After a situation of almost total laissez-faire, limited government intervention began during the Depression, followed during the war by the acceptance of the determining role of government in the economy and society.

CHAPTER 7
RELIGION AND EDUCATION

Two key institutions formed the organizational base of Quebec society: church and school. These institutions had a profound influence, which went beyond their immediate spiritual and intellectual objectives. Above all, they were places where collective religious, social, civic and cultural values were transmitted. In addition, some of the major goals towards which the energies of Quebec society were directed were developed in these institutions. A large part of the process of socialization of individuals also took place there. Because of the moral authority the two institutions enjoyed, they were powerful instruments of social control and even censorship. However, they were not monolithic. They had to adapt as best they could to the needs of society and they too felt the effects of the Depression and the war.

Religions and Churches

After the turn of the century, the percentage division of the population among different religious denominations remained essentially stable. Roman Catholics formed the overwhelming majority with 86 per cent of the population, with the other significant groups being Protestants (11 per cent) and Jews (2 per cent). These figures are based on the religious denominations people indicated on census forms, and do not necessarily reflect actual religious practice.

Minority Religions

Protestant Quebecers were mostly of English and Scottish origin. They were divided into a number of different denominations, three of which accounted for 90 per cent of their numbers. The Anglican Church, representing almost half of Protestant Quebecers, constituted the largest group, followed by the United and Presbyterian churches. During the period under study, the proportions represented by the Anglican and United churches increased slightly. The formation of the United Church in 1925, the most significant event of the previous period, had brought together the Methodists and some Presbyterians. The relative decline of the continuing Presyterians can probably be explained by further switches to the United Church.

In the 1920s, the social reform orientation represented by the social gospel movement declined among Canadian Protestants, but the Depression revived these concerns. Thus, in 1932, the General Council of the United Church expressed its desire to find a new way of raising social questions. But church adherents, apparently accepting the loss of the working class by the church, didn't want their ministers to flirt with ideas that were too radical. During the war, the Protestant churches were more critical than they had been in 1914, and they balked at regarding the war as strictly a crusade for the defence of Christian civilization.

While Jews did not represent a large group in relation to the population of Quebec as a whole, they were significant because of their concentration in specific neighbourhoods of Montreal, where they were in a position to develop their own institutions. There were tensions in the Jewish community brought on by recent immigration, as the new arrivals — those who had come since 1914 — tended to be more secular and politically more radical. Religious practice appeared to be confined more and more to the major holidays, and synagogues became as much places for social contact as houses of worship. These changes in Montreal Jewry were parallel to developments occurring among Jews in the United States. The acculturation they were experiencing was accentuated by the schools, where their children came in contact with the Anglo-Protestant system of values.

The Catholic Church

The Catholic Church was still a major force in Quebec. It was ubiquitous, and its activities went far beyond the religious sphere. Its power had its roots in the nineteenth century, and it had taken full advantage of the fact that Confederation allowed it much greater freedom of action in Quebec than elsewhere because of Quebec's Catholic majority. Its power and its social and cultural influence were based on three major factors. The first was faith, which was at the root of its prestige and imposed adherence and respect. The second was its position as a dispenser of services: through its network of schools, hospitals, and charitable and cultural organizations, it had made itself essential to Quebecers — all the more so in that the state did not play a large role in these areas. Finally, the church played a strong role in ideological orientation and definition.

However, its power was not without limits. In fact, industrialization and urbanization had been undermining the church for some time.

Against its will, the church had to recognize the increasing role of the state, and as early as the late nineteenth century it had not been able to indulge fully its desire to control Quebec's political parties. The Depression shook the church in a variety of ways. On the financial level, it had to learn to live with a significant reduction in income, and some of its institutions were on the verge of bankruptcy. In 1932, the *fabrique* (lay board of trustees) of a Montreal parish had to declare bankruptcy, a development that led to deep concern in financial circles. In subsequent years, the Legislative Assembly even had to bail out religious communities in difficulty. The result was that the development of the church's institutional network slowed down somewhat, and its charitable organizations were swamped. Even on the ideological level, the effervescence of the Depression years threatened the church's preeminence.

To carry out all its activities, the church needed a large number of people working for it. There were some 4,000 priests in Quebec in 1930, and more than 5,000 at the end of the war. In addition, there were more than 25,000 members of religious communities in 1931 and probably more than 35,000 in 1945. Exact figures cannot be obtained since some priests were also religious, but they do give an idea of the scale of the workforce on which the functioning of all the church's institutions depended. This workforce was made up primarily of women, who constituted more than 75 per cent of the membership of religious communities. However, women's role was limited to support and service. It is hard to tell whether communities recruited a larger number of people than usual because of the Depression. In any case, the church's workforce represented a considerable capacity for social control. In 1941, the proportion of religious, male and female, to the Catholic population as a whole reached a peak of one to eighty-seven.

The church's strategy of social control was implemented first and foremost through the parish. However, urbanization led to a change in organizational structures. In the city, some tasks had to be carried out in a wider context than the limited area of a parish, and diocesan institutions were strengthened as a result. Some of these institutions oversaw a group of parish organizations, while others fulfilled entirely new functions. Thus, the specialized Catholic Action movements established a structure that almost completely ignored the parish system and was organized instead around the workplace. As a result, the agencies around which Catholics' lives were organized proliferated and diversified. The strengthening of diocesan influence also led to tension and unease in the parishes where priests defended their autonomy. These developments did not affect rural Quebec to the same degree.

The church also had to fight a trend away from religion that began to be visible in the mid-1920s. An effort was made to adapt religious education to new circumstances. Thus, the church undertook the revision of the austere *Petit Catéchisme* and began to use radio: the program *L'heure catholique* was broadcast on the Montreal station CKAC.

Group weddings organized by the Jeunesse Ouvrière Catholique in 1939.
(*The Gazette*, National Archives of Canada, PA-137214)

On the ideological level, the church launched a virtual crusade against communist influence during the Depression. It was concerned about the communist sympathies that were apparent among recent immigrants to Montreal, and its efforts to limit the damage were carried out through the École Sociale Populaire, which was given the responsibility of mounting a counter-propaganda campaign on all fronts, especially in the city's workers' clubs.

Another way in which the church reacted to the Depression was by reviving an old project: colonization. With government support, the church urged unemployed city-dwellers to return to the land. Each diocese had its own colonization society and its own settlement, but the movement did not grow as large as the church had hoped. At the same time, the École Sociale Populaire developed the Programme de Restauration Sociale (program of social restoration), aimed at realizing its vision of a Catholic corporatist state. With the coming of the war, all these projects were more or less put on the shelf.

Within the church, forces challenging the established order began to be visible. For the moment, opposition was still expressed deferentially, but the day when the church would no longer be a monolithic body was in sight. On the spiritual level, Father Onésime Lacouture founded an ascetic movement advocating a return to evangelical purity and poverty.

Although his ideas would eventually be condemned, they had a great influence on both laity and clergy. The austerity and detachment he preached had considerable appeal in this insecure period.

Another challenge came from the Dominicans, who established institutions that would become focal points of renewal and change. With the founding of the Institut d'Études Médiévales came a new understanding of textual criticism and the rigour of scientific knowledge. Another institution whose influence would be felt was the École des Sciences Sociales, established by Father Georges-Henri Lévesque at Laval University in 1938.

Finally, within the Catholic Action movements, there was tension between "specialized" Catholic Action, which was oriented towards social issues, and the Association Catholique de la Jeunesse Canadienne-Française (ACJC), which was more concerned with the national question. Another innovation introduced by "specialized" Catholic Action was its new, more dynamic way of relating to its target population. By contrast, the activities of organizations such as the ACJC, the Ligues du Sacré-Coeur and the Ligue Catholique Féminine were of a traditional, classic sort, and were limited to campaigns for public morality.

At the level of the hierarchy, a challenge of sorts emerged to the prevailing conservatism and the leadership of Cardinal Rodrigue Villeneuve, archbishop of Quebec. The appointment of the first pro-labour bishop, Mgr Philippe Desranleau, who was named to head the Sherbrooke diocese in 1937, upset the tranquillity of the Quebec episcopate. It was followed by the appointment of Joseph Charbonneau as archbishop of Montreal in 1940. Charbonneau sought to adapt the church to the challenges of urban life and quickly came into conflict with his more traditional-minded colleagues.

From 1939 on, the Quebec hierarchy gave cautious support to the war effort. The bishops were divided. Cardinal Villeneuve favoured supporting the war effort vigorously, even agreeing to be photographed behind the wheel of a military vehicle. Others, such as Mgr Charbonneau, were more moderate, while some bishops greeted anything that smacked of war propaganda with outright hostility. Thus, Bishop Ross of Gaspé even forbade priests from reading announcements about victory bonds from the pulpit. Nevertheless, there was a basic consensus within the church on the principle of supporting the war effort. But clergy and laity alike would be jolted by conscription.

The years 1930-45 were a period of reflection and reorganization for the church, which had to learn to live with the new constraints of an urban industrial society. The church in 1945 had lost none of its power or presence, but currents of renewal had begun to flow within it.

Schools in Distress

During the 1920s, Quebec had made some progress in the field of education, but there were still serious weaknesses. Only a minority of young people could pursue their studies beyond the end of primary school. The Depression not only brought to a halt the momentum that had developed but also aggravated the chronic problems that beset the educational system. In a situation where it was hard for many Quebecers to meet their most basic needs, education was not a priority either for families or for society as a whole. And while progress began again during the war, it was very limited.

Educational Structures

The Quebec educational system in the early 1930s was distinguished by three major features. First, public education was denominational and was based on the coexistence of two autonomous subsystems, one Catholic and the other Protestant. Only a few specialized schools, responsible to a variety of government departments, were outside the denominational structure. Second, a plethora of private institutions operated parallel to the public schools or in competition with them. At some levels of education, these institutions — notably the classical colleges and the universities — had a monopoly. And finally, the system suffered from lack of coordination among its components and fragmentation of authority. The jumble of structures and programs that resulted from this situation led to serious social inequities.

At the primary level, Catholic schools offered a six-year program from 1923 on; this was increased to seven years in 1937. Primary school was followed by a two-year complementary primary course. Starting in 1937, students completing each of these levels took official examinations and received a diploma. By far the most significant innovation during this period was the superior primary course, introduced in Montreal in 1921 and officially established throughout Quebec in 1929. This three-year course for graduates of the complementary primary schools gave Catholics of modest means the long-awaited opportunity to get an education comparable to the one offered in the Protestant system's high schools. However, graduation from the superior primary course was not enough to allow admission to all university faculties.

There were also a number of other possibilities for primary-school graduates who wanted and could afford to further their education. Only a minority could go to the prestigious classical colleges, which offered an eight-year course and provided access to all university faculties. The colleges came under severe criticism from some quarters, and while they remained oriented principally towards the humanities, they were forced to allow greater scope for science and mathematics in their programs. In addition, there were art and trade schools, technical schools, normal schools and agricultural schools, which offered vocational programs of varying quality. While technical education stagnated during the Depression, a federal-provincial agreement in 1937 gave it a new impetus. Technical schools continued to grow during the war as a result of increased demand for skilled labour.

The options open to girls after primary school clearly bore the stamp of the ideology according to which a woman's place was in the home and her responsibility was taking care of her family. Thus, the complementary primary and superior primary courses tended to be less accessible to girls. At the same time, girls were encouraged to enrol in the regional domestic science schools, which enjoyed a new period of dynamism after 1937 under the leadership of Abbé Albert Tessier. The goal of these schools was to prepare *"femmes dépareillées"* (women without equal) to fulfil their calling as "mistresses of the house." A minority of girls did manage to go to private boarding schools, normal schools and classical colleges.

The Protestant system was less fragmented and better coordinated. It consisted of elementary schools, which went to grade seven, and high schools for both boys and girls. The final year of high school was grade eleven until 1935, when a twelfth grade was added; an intermediate certificate was available after grade nine. All university faculties were accessible to high school graduates. Thus, young Anglophones completed their undergraduate studies at about the same age as young Francophones obtained their classical college diplomas.

School Attendance

There was only a modest increase in the overall number of students enrolled in the Quebec school system (both Catholic and Protestant) during the period — from 653,351 in 1930 to 728,755 in 1945. The percentage of Quebecers of school age (five to nineteen years old) who were in school increased only slightly, from 67 per cent in 1930 to 69 per cent in 1945.

Just before the Depression, a large majority of Catholic students, especially in the rural areas, did not finish their primary course. Most of them left school around the age of twelve, at the time of their solemn communion. The situation improved during the 1930s, and the percentage of Catholic students who finished the primary course increased from 24 per cent in 1929 to 48 per cent in 1939. However, school attendance for Catholic students between seven and thirteen years of age was still very irregular and there was a substantial falling off in enrolment after grade four. During the Depression, many parents found it hard to pay school fees along with the cost of books, shoes, clothes and the adequate food and health care that would make regular school attendance possible. In 1940 the new superintendent of public instruction, Victor Doré, called the situation heartbreaking.

While the war brought economic recovery and improvement in Quebec families' material circumstances, it also had the effect of drawing some people into the labour market at a very young age. For a large majority of the population, school attendance came to a very early end. Just after the war, only 46 per cent of Catholic students reached grade seven, 25 per cent reached grade eight, 17 per cent reached grade nine and a mere 2 per cent reached grade twelve. In Protestant schools, by contrast, 80 per cent of the students reached grade eight, 34 per cent reached grade eleven and 7 per cent went as far as grade twelve.

The problem of premature school leaving was aggravated by the absence of any requirement for parents to send their children to school. This question had been a frequent subject of controversy from the late nineteenth century onward, as the clergy had always fiercely resisted any legislation that would make schooling compulsory. But the church had to revise its position when the pope himself imposed compulsory education in Vatican City in 1931. Nevertheless, it still took ten more years of debate, eye-opening inquiries by the Department of Public Instruction, (an administrative body, not a full government department), and the presence of a determined government led by Premier Adélard Godbout before compulsory education was legislated in Quebec. Adopted in 1942, the legislation went into effect in September 1943 and it required all children between six and fourteen years of age to attend school; parents who failed to send their children to school would be fined. It also abolished fees for public primary schools. In 1944 free education was extended to the complementary primary schools, and textbooks were also made free.

Educational Resources

The Depression had a disastrous effect on the financing of the educational system. Especially hard hit were the school commissions, which received about 80 per cent of their revenues from the property tax, divided according to the religion of taxpaying property owners. The inequities inherent in this system were accentuated when property assessments fell and difficulties in collecting taxes increased. Even though they reduced teachers' salaries, stopped building schools, raised school fees and took other measures to save money, more than 40 per cent of the 1,828 school commissions ran deficits. The Protestant school commissions, which received a disproportionate share of the fiscal pie because they served a wealthier population, did not suffer as much as the Catholic ones.

Government subsidies to school commissions covered only a small part of the costs of public education. During the war, the share of school commission expenditures covered by these subsidies rose from 20 to 27 per cent, but the subsidies were still insufficient to wipe out the debt inherited from the Depression and meet the commissions' needs.

The number of teachers rose from 22,318 in 1930 to 26,764 in 1945. There was little change in who these teachers were. Teaching remained primarily a women's profession, with women constituting 80 per cent of Quebec's teachers. The proportion of religious in the profession also remained fairly stable: about 45 per cent religious and 55 per cent lay teachers.

Overall, there were not enough teachers. The shortage was felt in the Catholic sector, where more teachers left each year — mostly women getting married — than were recruited into the profession. The situation got worse during the war when many teachers (primarily but not exclusively male ones) left teaching to enlist or to work in war industries offering more attractive wages. In 1945, the superintendent of public instruction reported that about a hundred schools were closed because of a lack of teachers.

Teacher training was often inadequate. Only a minority of teachers were normal school graduates. In 1930, almost 80 per cent of Catholic teachers had no teacher training and had only a diploma from the Central Board of Catholic Examiners, for which the only requirement was minimal knowledge of the subjects taught in primary school. With the abolition of the board in 1939, all teachers except religious had to go to a normal school. However, many people entering the profession still had only an elementary diploma, which boys could obtain with a year of study after grade eleven and girls with a year of study after grade nine.

The wages and working conditions that awaited them could hardly be considered inducements for prospective teachers to undertake long courses of study. Teachers' salaries were preposterously low even before the Depression and many school commissions, in an effort to reduce expenses, made further drastic cuts, especially after 1932. Working conditions were also very difficult: no job security, uncomfortable schools, overcrowded classes, and the like. In addition, there were wide gaps in pay between men and women, between lay and religious teachers, and between Protestants and Catholics (table 1). As the superintendent of public instruction noted in 1943, "much as we may want gifted people to enter and remain in the arduous profession of teaching, our efforts to attract them will be in vain so long as there is such a discrepancy between the remuneration offered and the task to be fulfilled." Women teachers in rural areas were in the most extreme situation. It was only by government regulation that they managed to obtain a minimum annual salary of $300 in 1938; it was raised to $600 in 1945. Teachers' unions first emerged among these underpaid teachers.

Table 1
Average Annual Salaries of Quebec Teachers ($)

	1930-31	1932-33	1934-35	1936-37	1938-39
Male religious	585	584	565	565	589
Female religious	386	379	359	360	389
Male Catholics	1,647	1,603	1,459	1,666	1,752
Male Protestants	2,596	2,543	2,034	2,008	2,169
Female Catholics	402	361	315	337	409
Female Protestants	1,127	1,125	980	980	1,060

Source, *Rapport du surintendant de l'Instruction publique*, 1931-32 and 1939-40.

The Universitsy of Montreal under construction, 1931. (Archives of the University of Montreal)

Universities and the Growth of Science

Universities and scientific activity in Quebec had begun to develop significantly during the 1920s. A number of events marked this turning point: the University of Montreal was split off from Laval University, many new faculties and schools were opened, successful public subscription campaigns brought greater financial resources, and the Association Canadienne-Française pour l'Avancement des Sciences (ACFAS) and the Institut Scientifique Franco-Canadien were established.

These initial efforts at modernization were brutally cut short by the Depression. The impact was especially severe in the two Francophone universities, as can be seen by a look at the University of Montreal. The university began construction of a lavish new building on the slopes of Mount Royal in 1928 to replace its overcrowded and antiquated facilities on Saint-Denis Street, but work was suspended and it was not completed until 1942. This "tower of hunger" symbolized the pathetic situation universities were in during the Depression. Professors' salaries were reduced and their pay was even suspended for a while amid talk of closing the university. The situation was almost as bleak at Laval. Even wealthy McGill University, with an endowment of $332 million in the late 1930s, had to take painful and controversial measures, such as the decision to close its School of Social Work in the midst of the Depression.

With the coming of the war, there was urgent demand for doctors, engineers, scientists and highly skilled workers in all areas. As a result, there was a new appreciation of the importance of universities, and governments increased the resources allotted to them. In return, they participated actively in the war effort. Thus, the training of doctors was speeded

University	Undergraduate	Master's level	Doctoral	Total
Laval	2,250	350	59	2,662
Montreal	3,079	816	83	3,978
McGill	4,137	440	275	4,852

Table 2
Number of Degrees Awarded by Laval University, the University of Montreal and McGill University, 1936-45

Source: Raymond Duchesne, *La science et le pouvoir au Québec*, p. 104.

up, students were required to undergo military training and those who failed their courses were expelled and became subject to conscription.

While there was a slight increase in the number of university students during the war, a university education was still a privilege reserved for an elite. Between 1936 and 1945, barely 10,000 students received undergraduate degrees, fewer than 1,700 completed master's-level studies and just over 400 received doctorates. There were significant differences between Francophones and Anglophones. A higher proportion of Anglophones received degrees, and Anglophones also had a greater tendency to study science and engineering, while medicine, law and the priesthood continued to attract large numbers of Francophones.

Despite these gaps and the economic difficulties of the 1930s, the growth of science in the Francophone community that had begun in the 1920s continued. This development was largely due to the determination and prestige of a few individuals who did pioneering work, such as Brother Marie-Victorin in botany, Adrien Pouliot in mathematics, Armand Frappier in microbiology and Abbé Alexandre Vachon in physics. Scientists played a major role within ACFAS, which held its first conference in 1933, and established such institutions as the Montreal Botanical Gardens and the Institut de Microbiologie de Montréal. There were significant new developments in the social sciences as well. Notable figures in this area included Édouard Montpetit and Esdras Minville at the University of Montreal, Father Georges-Henri Lévesque at Laval and Leonard Marsh at McGill.

*   *   *   *   *   *

The overall effect of the Depression was to interrupt the initial efforts to modernize Quebec education undertaken in the 1920s. As a result, Quebec lagged even further behind in educational resources, both human and material, as well as in access to education and proportion of the population attending school. The war set in motion a renewed process of development and modernization in the educational system, which would continue and intensify in succeeding decades.

CHAPTER 8
CHALLENGE TO LIBERALISM

In the area of ideology, the 1930s were a troubled period. We cannot give a detailed account of all the shadings of the various ideologies that were current at the time. Not all these ideologies had comparable significance or equivalent numbers of adherents. Further, within a single ideological current, there were often divergent views, even antagonisms, while apparently opposing ideologies intermingled or agreed on specific points. Faced with such a complex situation, it is necessary to concentrate on the essentials. We will look at the currents that were clearly important and more or less coherent: liberalism, left-wing ideologies, traditionalist nationalism and Catholic renewal. The situation changed during the war years, as a state of emergency was imposed and opinion became polarized on the issue of Canadian participation in the war.

The Effects of the Depression

As a result of the Depression, Quebec's ideological scene was livelier than it had been on all but a few occasions in the past. The seriousness of the situation and the unease it caused led intellectuals, politicians, journalists and clerics to try to explain the breakdown of the system and come up with solutions that would restore a sense of order.

The international tensions of the 1930s contributed to this ideological effervescence. The struggles of two major totalitarian, antiliberal ideologies in continental Europe — communism and fascism — were constantly in the news in Quebec. Communism, embodied in the Soviet Union after the Russian Revolution of October 1917 and propagated by organizations such as the Third Socialist International (Comintern), was supported by some left-wing trade unionists and intellectuals and made appreciable advances in a number of countries, notably Léon Blum's France and the Spain of the *Frente Popular*. Fascism manifested itself in the rise of authoritarian nationalism in Austria, Portugal and, a few years later, Franco's Spain. Its most significant expressions, however, were the Mussolini regime in Italy and, from 1933 on, Hitler's antisemitic Nazi regime in Germany. As the Second World War approached, the opposition between these two ideologies — played out in political and military events such as the Italian invasion of Ethiopia and, most notably, the Spanish Civil War — increasingly took on the characteristics of a major confrontation.

Quebec was also affected by phenomena closer to home. In English Canada, hitherto marginal ideologies such as communism, socialism (represented by the new Cooperative Commonwealth Federation) and social credit (which enjoyed spectacular success in Alberta) took on new importance. In the United States and Britain, the trade union movement became more radical while a significant reform current emerged within economic liberalism. And the Vatican, which had considerable international influence, worked out the details of its social doctrine in two major encyclicals, *Quadragesimo Anno* (1931) and *Divini Redemptoris* (1937).

In sum, the Depression brought with it a widespread intensification of ideological struggles. In Quebec, this development was affected by local circumstances as well: old debates continued, but they became more intense as a result of the difficulties and disorder of the times. The ideological effervescence of the 1930s can probably best be understood as a crisis of liberalism. The prestige of liberalism was put to a severe test. It was challenged both on specific points and as a system, and a variety of alternative ideologies were proposed in its stead. At the same time, however, it strengthened itself by changing from within under pressure from events and the criticism directed at it.

Liberalism in Trouble

In Quebec and the rest of Canada, as in the capitalist industrialized world as a whole, liberalism had held a dominant position in the ideological field since the late nineteenth century. The inspiration for the political institutions, laws and models of development established in Canada since Confederation came essentially from liberalism, and the prosperity of the late 1920s led to a further consolidation of liberal ideology. Its major proponents were politicians in the two major parties, businesspeople and the press. According to liberal ideology, economic and social progress was based on individual freedom and private property. Society was viewed as an arena of free competition, where everyone had the opportunity to achieve success without being hampered by social or governmental constraints. Social equilibrium and collective wealth were seen as the overall result of individuals' efforts and profits. Liberalism favoured industrialization, urbanization, changes in people's way of life, and the widest possible development of means of communication. In social policy, there were two currents within liberalism. One was a conservative current that emphasized individual responsibility. The other current, referred to as "reform" or "progressive," advocated government intervention to correct some of the inequities brought about by industrial society.

Liberalism may have been very influential, but it could hardly be described as a well-articulated doctrine in Quebec. As the ideology of powerful people and established institutions, it was diffuse and tended to be largely taken for granted. In addition, there was nothing really original in Quebec or Canadian liberalism, which took its inspiration essentially from Britain and the United States. Starting in the 1920s, British and American influence had been increasing in Quebec as a result both of investment and of the widespread dissemination of culture that followed British and American models through radio, movies and mass-circulation newspapers.

But the Depression was a severe blow to liberalism. It showed up the capitalist system's fragility and inability to bring about the necessary adjustments on its own. Attacks on liberal ideas and institutions, which were held responsible for the disaster, came from a variety of quarters. Formerly the heroes of "success stories," businessmen, captains of industry and speculators were now regarded as dangerous, greedy and insensitive to the suffering of ordinary people. As the historian Blair Neatby has written, they were "men who closed down factories and foreclosed mortgages, who worshiped profits with a callous disregard for the poverty and suffering they caused." The monopolies held by financial empires, large corporations and "trusts" were also bitterly denounced. In general, the liberal vision of society and model of development were called into serious question.

Antiliberalism spread rapidly starting in the early 1930s. One of the forms it took was a kind of populism. The populists of the era did not have a developed program of their own to offer, but they stood for ordinary people, the unemployed, low-wage earners and farmers against financiers, politicians and intellectuals. Traces of this attitude can be seen in almost all the opposition ideologies current at the time. However, it shows up most clearly in the rhetoric and the popularity of such political personalities as Camillien Houde, the early Maurice Duplessis and Ontario Premier Mitch Hepburn. It is also reflected in the wide public favour enjoyed by nonpolitical figures such as Brother André and La Bolduc.

But the real critics of liberalism were the proponents of "programmatic" ideologies — currents of thought that not only challenged liberalism but also offered alternative solutions. Antiliberalism of this sort can be divided into two major tendencies. One consisted of Marxism and socialism, which attacked the very foundations of liberalism and capitalism and wanted to replace them with a system based on collective ownership of the economy and massive government intervention. The second tendency, which attracted both progressives and traditionalists, proposed a variety of reforms and reorganizations that would correct or avoid the abuses of capitalism but would not abolish it or destroy its essential values. In Quebec, this second tendency was by far the stronger of the two.

The Left on the Margins

Social and economic conditions provided what in theory was fertile ground for the growth of left-wing ideologies. Nevertheless, these ideologies had little success in establishing a place for themselves in Depression-era Quebec, although their presence and influence were somewhat stronger than they had been in the previous period. This was an extension of developments in English Canada, where the left was making significant advances.

The most radical current was Marxism, represented by the Communist Party of Canada from 1921 on as well as a variety of affiliated organizations such as the Workers' Unity League and the National Unemployed Workers' Association, founded in 1930. Communists were very active despite the repression to which they were subjected. In their view, the Depression and its aftereffects were a highly graphic demonstration of the evils of the capitalist system. It was therefore necessary to overthrow the system and establish in its place a "Soviet Canada" based on the dictatorship of the proletariat and the nationalization of the entire economy. More immediately, they advocated better working and living conditions for workers, the right to unionize, and a variety of social measures such as unemployment insurance with no employee premiums and increased government spending for relief and public works. Canadian communists faithfully obeyed directives from the international movement. Thus, they initially followed a rigorous and fiercely anticapitalist policy of class struggle, but abandoned it after 1935 in favour of a "Popular Front" strategy that involved moderating their demands and trying to join with other, less radical antifascist groups.

Canadian socialists formed a new party, the Cooperative Commonwealth Federation (CCF), in 1932. They expressed their ideas in the party's Regina Manifesto (1933) as well as in the work of the League for Social Reconstruction, in which English-speaking Montreal intellectuals were especially active. This form of socialism was based on the ideology of labour, challenging capitalism in the name of "reconstruction" of a "new social order" based on the common good and meeting the needs of the majority rather than on profit. Its proponents advocated economic planning, nationalization of some sectors of production, and large-scale government intervention, especially in the area of social security. Unlike communists, from whom they tried to distinguish themselves, socialists believed it was possible to change society through peaceful means within the existing parliamentary system.

Both these movements tried to establish themselves in Quebec by supporting industrial trade unionism, participating in strikes, taking up the cause of the unemployed, organizing demonstrations and forming groups of activists. These efforts met with more success in some sectors of the population than in others. Left-wing ideas enjoyed a fairly warm reception among lower-class immigrants in Montreal, especially in the Jewish community, which brought with it from Europe a tradition in which the development and dissemination of socialism and Marxism had a place. In English Montreal, intellectuals, upper-class youth and some members of the middle class formed another group receptive to egalitarian ideologies. The best known members of this group were Frank R. Scott, a McGill University professor and active supporter of the CCF, and Dr. Norman Bethune, who became an active communist after a trip to the Soviet Union and joined left-wing forces fighting in Spain and later in China. Most Quebec recruits for the Mackenzie-Papineau Batallion, formed by Canadian communists in 1937 to come to the aid of the Spanish Republicans, came from this group.

However, neither communism nor socialism succeeded in making inroads among French Canadians. The Communist Party considered French Canadians "the most exploited masses in Canada" and assigned to the Workers' Unity League the task of recruiting 200,000 workers in Quebec industries, but it was in vain: the party never gained more than a few hundred members and sympathizers in Quebec, and none outside Montreal. The Marxist propaganda activities of the Université Ouvrière, founded by Albert Saint-Martin in 1925, were equally fruitless: it achieved only extremely limited influence in the Francophone community. Workers and the unemployed in Quebec were affected by left-wing organizations' campaigns, slogans and infiltration, but almost always without being aware of it and without supporting the overall ideologies these organizations represented.

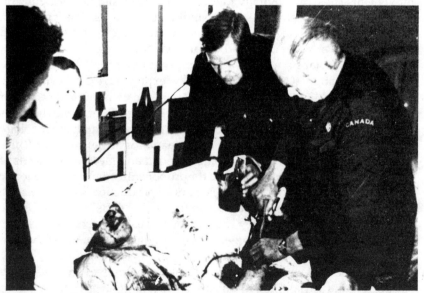

Dr. Norman Bethune performing a transfusion during the Spanish Civil War, 1936-38. (Geza Karphati, National Archives of Canada, C-64751)

Confiscation of communist publications, 1938. (Conrad Poirier collection, National Archives of Quebec in Montreal)

There were three major reasons for the left's marginal position among Francophone Quebecers. The first reason — and a decisive one — was the opposition of the church. With its concern for the maintenance of order and respect for constituted authority, the church rejected "Bolshevism" which, as one preacher told a crowd of 100,000 Catholics in Montreal in 1936, was fomenting "a night of anti-Christian debauchery and a great orgy of sacrilege." And even though the CCF was influenced by the social aspects of Christianity, it too was rejected because it offered "only a materialist conception of the social order."

A second factor was the attitude of governments, which not only joined the church's chorus of anticommunist propaganda but also carried out a vigorous policy of judicial, legislative and police repression. The federal government of R.B. Bennett began this campaign, and after 1936 it was picked up by the Quebec government under Maurice Duplessis, which virtually declared open season on communists and dissidents. Its chief weapon was the "Padlock Law," passed in 1937, under which any building where people were suspected of propagating communist ideas could be closed down. After the Nazi-Soviet Pact of 1939, the Communist Party was banned by the federal government.

And there were cultural and political factors as well. The Communist Party and the CCF not only failed to develop French Canadian leaders but also projected an overall image of movements alien to the Francophone community. They had difficulty understanding French Canadian nationalism and expressed a centralist view of federalism. In this way, they came in direct conflict with Francophone Quebecers' national feeling and traditional idea of provincial autonomy.

The Rapid Growth of Traditional Nationalism and Corporatism

While liberalism may have shaped Quebec's political institutions and economic system from the nineteenth century onward, another major ideological current developed parallel to it. This was nationalism, which placed a high value on the social and cultural aspects of collective existence, glorified French Canadians' particular characteristics, and emphasized maintaining the will to ensure that they would survive and develop. But nationalism can be understood in a variety of ways. There were many nationalist groups, sometimes with very different ideas of what the nation was and what were the most appropriate means, political or other, of promoting its interests. In varying degrees, all ideologies in Quebec after the mid-nineteenth century took account of nationalist concerns; thus, there was not one form of nationalism but several: liberal, reform, conservative, ultramontane and others.

Of all these tendencies, the most significant from the turn of the century onward was a current of thought that could be called "traditionalist." Even within that current, there were a number of formulations, which could differ substantially from group to group, generation to generation and school of thought to school of thought. But the essence of traditionalist nationalism was a view of French Canadians as a people (a "race," in the language of the time) whose specificity — and, for that matter, superiority — was primarily if not exclusively due to their attachment to traditions inherited from the past: their French peasant origins, their language, their religion. Also very important were the institutions through which they preserved this heritage: family, parish, rural life. Anything that could harm these values — urbanization, government intervention, or new cultural models imported from the United States — was viewed as a threat that had to be resisted.

The prestige and influence of traditionalist nationalism was due to the fact that its chief proponent was the Catholic Church, which for all practical purposes had made this ideology its official doctrine and used traditionalist nationalism to justify its own position of power and authority in Quebec society. This is why many writers have called this current of thought "clerical-nationalism." It was disseminated not only through preaching and pastoral works but also through all the mechanisms and institutions that the clergy controlled directly or indirectly: education, private social services, publishing, Catholic newspapers ("*bonne presse*"), Catholic trade unions, youth movements and the like. Another medium of transmission was orthodox literature and art, which incessantly repeated the lesson of *Maria Chapdelaine*: "In this land of Quebec naught shall die and naught shall suffer change." In addition, traditionalist nationalism had taken shape explicitly since 1900 in the writings of prestigious thinkers and activists such as Henri Bourassa, the editor of *Le*

Devoir, and Lionel Groulx, the editor of *L'Action Française*. As a result, it appeared clear, complete and well worked out and was supported by a rich historical literature.

A large part of the petty bourgeoisie, with close ties to the clergy, agreed with and advocated traditionalist nationalism. It is difficult, however, to determine how much support it had in other sectors of the population. In the 1920s in particular, the atmosphere of modernist euphoria and the explosion of American mass culture in the cities made traditionalist positions harder and harder to defend. The nationalists were reduced to the role of opposition to the political power embodied in the Taschereau Liberals. They came to be seen as reactionaries fixated on the past and fighting a rearguard action, and their ideas appeared to be systematically contradicted by reality.

But the Depression changed everything. The seriousness of the situation and the prevailing ideological confusion led the clergy and traditional elites to undertake a major campaign to revitalize traditionalist nationalism and bring it up to date. Most intellectuals, students, political thinkers and scholars in the humanities and social sciences who had any influence in Quebec quickly came to their support. Pamphlets, programs and declarations proliferated, especially after 1932. While there was an active group surrounding the newspaper *L'Action Catholique* in Quebec City, most of the ferment took place in Montreal, through such organizations as the Jesuit-run École Sociale Populaire, founded in 1911; *L'Action Nationale*, a magazine started in 1933 under the guidance of Lionel Groulx; the newspaper *Le Devoir*; the École des Hautes Études Commerciales, where Édouard Montpetit, Esdras Minville and Victor Barbeau were among the professors; the Saint-Jean-Baptiste Society; and the Jeune-Canada (Young Canada) movement, organized in 1932 around the *Manifeste de la jeune génération* (Manifesto of the Young Generation), written by André Laurendeau. The degree of conviction and activism was particularly high within these organizations, but the ideas and rhetoric developed there were heard in other circles as well: the regional press, trade unions affiliated to the Canadian and Catholic Confederation of Labour, the Union Catholique des Cultivateurs (Catholic farmers' union), cooperatives and caisses populaires — in other words, everywhere the clergy or the petty bourgeoisie had a preponderant influence.

While the basic values of French Canadian nationalism — the primacy of religion, language and agriculture, mistrust of the modern world, the importance of order and authority — may have remained the same since the turn of the century, some notable developments took place within this current in the 1930s under pressure from events.

One feature of 1930s nationalism was its critique of liberalism and capitalism. In the wake of *Quadragesimo Anno*, this critique was primarily moral in nature, as liberal society was taken to task for its lack of charity and justice, its materialism and the evils it gave rise to, especially in urban settings: moral corruption, disintegration of families, unemployment, misery. At the same time, the critique was consistent with nationalist motifs. The great industrial and financial monopolies were "foreign" (that is, not French Canadian), exploited Quebec's resources without regard for its national interest, showed contempt for its language and religion, and were largely responsible for the economic inferiority that French Canadians suffered from. But while the nationalists attacked capitalism's abuses and foreign aspect, they never questioned its foundations — private property and free enterprise.

Thus, the nationalists did not go nearly as far as the communists and socialists in criticizing liberalism. In fact, the nationalists regarded the communists and socialists as representing an even worse danger than unbridled capitalism. They saw communism as trying to take advantage of the Depression to overthrow the social order and inaugurate a reign of paganism, totalitarianism and hate. Condemned from on high by the pope, communism was the supreme enemy, and total war had to be waged against it. A noteworthy combatant in this struggle was the École Sociale Populaire, which published pamphlets, organized petitions and demonstrations, and called on governments and the police to stop the subversive schemings of the "godless communists." The nationalists were far from being alone in their anticommunism, which became one of the major ideological themes of the decade.

Just criticizing, however, was not enough. The urgency of the situation meant that the nationalists had to propose their own solutions for the Depression. Their most notable effort to do so was the drafting of the Programme de Restauration Sociale, published in 1933 under the auspices of the École Sociale Populaire. This document would be widely distributed and would remain a major reference point for the entire nationalist movement for a dozen years. The first goal of the program was to bring up to date the timeworn themes of traditionalism. Thus, the causes of the Depression were primarily moral. It had occurred because people had forgotten their traditions, Christian virtues and patriotic pride; only by recovering them could the chaos of the moment be ended. The words *"renaissance," "redressement"* (rectification), *"restauration"* (restoration) and *"ressaisie"* (recapture) all recur incessantly in the program, expressing the idea of a return to values and social structures that the modern world ignored or held in contempt.

At the same time, responding to the need to propose more concrete solutions, the program borrowed from a current of thought that had made its appearance within the nationalist intelligentsia over the preceding twenty years but had so far represented a minority position. The historian Yves Saint-Germain has called this minority the "ambivalent progressives," and they differed with the out-and-out traditionalists on three major points. First, instead of simply criticizing urbanization and industrialization, they acknowledged that these changes were irreversible and sought ways for French Canadians to adapt to them while preserving their traditional values. Second, they maintained that education and economic development were essential for collective survival. And finally, they recognized the importance of scientific progress. In this area, Brother Marie-Victorin and ACFAS (founded in 1923) played a leading role. This message fell on more receptive ears with the coming of the Depression and became one of the major inspirations for the Programme de Restauration Sociale.

Some of the measures the program advocated smacked of reform: the unemployed should be assisted; financial and utility monopolies should be nationalized or brought under local control. Other measures, however, were oriented more towards socioeconomic retreat: immigration should be restricted, women should return to the home, "rural restoration" should be brought about by giving priority to support for agriculture and colonization, craft industries and French Canadian small business should be encouraged, Quebecers should "buy Quebec," local cooperatives should be developed. And finally, the overarching idea that tied together all these specific proposals was the doctrine nationalist thinkers called corporatism, which would make possible the establishment of a "new order" and the complete reorganization of society and its institutions.

Corporatism was presented as a "third way" between liberalism and communism. It had the official support of the pope, who in *Quadragesimo Anno* had advocated the establishment of corporatism as a solution to the Depression. Supporters of corporatism liked to cite the models of their system that existed elsewhere in the world: Mussolini's Italy, Salazar's Portugal, some countries in Latin America. The Programme de Restauration Sociale made corporatism one of its major propositions, as did most nationalist ideologues and pressure groups throughout the 1930s.

Corporatist thought is not easy to summarize. Essentially, its vision was of all social groups, organized in "corporations" or "intermediate bodies" dedicated to the pursuit of the common good, working together in harmony to ensure order and social peace. In this way, class "collaboration" would replace class struggle: employers and workers in the same economic sector would belong to the same corporation and work together for the advancement both of their sector and of the nation as a whole. The nation would be, in a sense, the corporation of corporations and would be represented by a "social and economic council" whose members would be free of all partisanship and corruption in any form. Parliamentary democracy was a source of dissension, and corporatism would replace it with a unanimous society in which each person, imbued with the national mystique, would work towards — and at the same time benefit from — the general harmony and prosperity.

The traditionalist nationalists' adoption of corporatism reveals two basic characteristics of their thought. The first is its belief in the need for order, its desire to neutralize or prevent conflict in the name of national unity and its belief in authority as an organizing principle. In the ideal Quebec the nationalists dreamed of, everyone would be Catholic, French Canadian (by language and by blood) and respectful of religious and intellectual elites. For many nationalists, this vision was expressed in the cult of the *Chef* (leader): they waited for a French Canadian Mussolini or Dollfuss who would embody the essence of the nation and show the way to its future. The myth of Dollard des Ormeaux, enthusiastically propagated by Lionel Groulx and his disciples, was a symbolic response to this need.

The other significant characteristic was the nationalists' mistrust of the state as conceived in the emerging doctrine of reform liberalism and embodied in the newly activist government in Ottawa. They saw this increasingly interventionist state as dangerous on three counts: it was English-speaking and religiously neutral, it infringed on the traditional role of the church in society, and its "paternalism" threatened to take away the freedom and "natural" responsibilities of individuals and families. By contrast, social corporatism — which the nationalists were very careful to distinguish from state corporatism — would make possible organic social and economic planning by relying not on the state but on local "bodies," the most important being the church.

In sum, in advocating corporatism, the nationalists were proposing a social model that was highly structured, elitist, closed, completely dedicated to the defence of ethnic, linguistic and religious identity, and economically self-sufficient. As a number of writers have shown, this model was above all an expression of the interests of the traditional elites — the church and the petty bourgeoisie. They advanced it in an attempt to resist rising monopoly capitalism, social and cultural modernization, and increasing government intervention, all of which threatened their prestige and position in society.

Another way in which the traditionalist nationalism of the 1930s differed from previous forms was its political dimension. Although it has been described as "apolitical," it did succeed for a time in serving as the basis for a fairly coherent political party, the Action Libérale Nationale (ALN), whose reform-minded platform took its inspiration largely from social corporatism and nationalist themes. Even the early Union Nationale was regarded as embodying traditionalist nationalism. As a result, in the mid-1930s, the nationalists played a more significant role in electoral politics than they ever had before.

The political objectives of nationalism were also clarified somewhat. It had long wavered between Henri Bourassa's Canadian nationalism and the more Quebec-centred nationalism that the journal *L'Action Française* had begun to develop in the 1920s. In the 1930s, nationalism moved towards a resolution in favour of the Quebec-centred version. Some groups — the Jeunesses Patriotes, the Jeunes Laurentiens, the intellectuals surrounding the magazine *Vivre* (1934-35) and the newspaper *La Nation* (1936-38) — even suggested that Quebec should separate from Canada and form a right-wing independent state, which they liked to call "*Laurentie.*" Most nationalists didn't go that far, but they did gradually give priority to Quebec, which they saw as the national state of French

Canadians. They advocated a decentralized federal system and were ardent defenders of the principle of provincial autonomy. Lionel Groulx wrote that while French Canadians should remain loyal to their *"grande patrie"* (big homeland), Canada, they should devote themselves first and foremost to their *"petite patrie"* (little homeland), Quebec.

Finally, traditionalist nationalism was associated with other characteristic right-wing themes of the 1930s. One of these was admiration for fascism and its manifestations as well as for *"chefs"* such as Mussolini, Franco and Pétain. Another was antisemitism, which was fairly widespread. Many people saw Jewish merchants, financiers, trade unionists and intellectuals as a threat, and some even regarded them as agents of a vast international plot against the nation and the Catholic religion. No one symbolized foreignness better than the Jews. As a result they became scapegoats, and responsibility for all the evils of the time was attributed to them. At the same time, they were envied for their energy, determination and solidarity. But it was only among a few individuals and groups on the far right — such as Adrien Arcand and his group of Nazi followers, who published *Le Fasciste Canadien* between 1935 and 1938 — that suspicion of the Jews spilled over into open hatred or a call for such measures as expulsion or systematic discrimination.

The traditionalist nationalism of the 1930s has been called a "dominant" ideology. However, its effect on the political and economic life in Quebec was in reality a limited one, and it has been overrated while the

Antisemitic poster in Ste–Agathe, 1939. (*The Gazette*, National Archives of Canada, PA-107943)

effect of liberalism (disseminated in the mass-circulation press) and re-form liberalism (which was taking shape at that time) has been under-rated. However, it was probably the most conspicuous and explicit ideology: it was expressed in a variety of ways, took on many forms, and made its entry on the political stage through the ALN. Among intellec-tuals and some politicians, it was the ideology that exercised the greatest influence.

A New Way to Be Catholic?

Traditionalist nationalism was an extension and systematization of a current of thought that had a long history in Quebec. But there was also another movement that took shape in Catholic circles in the 1930s. Fairly small at the time, this movement would become much more significant after the war. Taking its inspiration primarily from the Catholic renewal in France and made up mostly of young classical college graduates, it neither broke with religion nor directly challenged clerical authority. On the contrary, it sought to breathe new life into religion by criticizing the prevailing religious conservatism and working towards forms of religious thought and action that would be better adapted to contemporary realities.

Two expressions of this current, both of which made their appearance in 1934, were of particular significance. One was the small intellectual magazine *La Relève*, whose founders had studied under the Jesuits, and the other was the "specialized" Catholic Action movements, especially the Jeunesse Étudiante Catholique (JEC). Both these groups refused to link nationalism closely with religion. In *La Relève*'s view, the key to ending the Depression was a spiritual revolution and the establishment of what the French philosopher Jacques Maritain called "integral humanism." Thus, the young Guy Frégault wrote in 1938 that "the new order must restore the dignity of the person....The new order will be personalist, that is, the exact opposite of any form of imperialism: impe-rialism of race, nation and state (fascism of the right), imperialism of class and productivist state (fascism of the left), imperialism of the digestive system and the bankers (typical example: British imperialism)."

While *La Relève*'s universalist arguments remained on an abstract level, the JEC tried to bring its own universalism into direct contact with real life. Towards this end it shunned both politics and the nationalism that had been the inspiration for Catholic Action in Quebec as practised by the Association Catholique de la Jeunesse Canadienne-Française, placing its emphasis instead on social reality and involvement in concrete issues. In the JEC's view religion should lead not to suspicion of the world but to willing acceptance of it, as a basis for knowing the world better, identifying its problems and transforming it through action suited to solving those problems.

This current of thought, which was supported by progressive elements within the clergy, represented a break with the traditional positions of Quebec Catholicism. It emphasized the responsibilities of laypeople within the church and the role of the individual rather than that of authority. The kind of religious practice it advocated would be more authentic, less triumphalist and more open to secular dimensions. And finally, it was optimistic about modernization in its various forms.

Towards New Forms of Liberalism

While liberalism was under attack from all sides during the 1930s, it was also undergoing a decisive transformation. Pure liberal principles were becoming harder and harder to justify, and liberals increasingly resorted to them only as a defensive manoeuvre against the threat of socialism, communism or fascism. At the same time, however, such currents as urban reform and the social gospel, which had been marginal tendencies within liberalism since their initial appearance early in the century, now made themselves more strongly felt. These currents maintained that liberalism should become "humanized," that is, more aware of such problems as socioeconomic inequality, unemployment and monopoly.

This reform movement within liberalism aimed to preserve basic liberal values while adapting them to the new evidence laid bare by the Depression. Most significantly, reform liberalism redefined the role of government, which it saw as being above particular groups and special interests. In its view, government would work through social and economic policies to prevent gross inequalities while still acting as the guardian of individual freedom.

The theories that underlay this redirection of liberalism were developed primarily in the great capitalist powers: Keynesianism emerged in Britain at this time, while President Franklin D. Roosevelt launched his New Deal in the United States in 1933. The conversion to reform liberalism took longer in Canada. Business people and politicians themselves — both Liberal and Conservative — regarded government intervention in the economy and social affairs as strictly temporary. They still believed in classical liberalism: they were social conservatives and continued to support "laissez-faire." Only an enlightened minority consisting primarily of academics, senior civil servants and reformist labour leaders in the Trades and Labour Congress of Canada were receptive to reform liberal ideas.

Reform liberalism had little impact on Francophone Quebec. Under both Taschereau and Duplessis, the Quebec government not only failed to adopt reform liberal ideas for itself but also resisted all of Ottawa's attempts at intervention, which it considered threats to free enterprise and family morality as well as interference in provincial affairs. In taking this stand, Quebec politicians had the support of the Anglophone bourgeoisie, the Montreal English newspapers, diehard liberal voices such as Jean-Charles Harvey's weekly *Le Jour* and Olivar Asselin's daily *L'Ordre*, and traditionalists in the church.

Wartime Interlude

While there was no clean break with the previous era, the ideological climate of the war years does present a strong contrast to that of the 1930s. First of all, economic circumstances changed rapidly: the Depression gave way to a new prosperity, which brought with it a steep fall in the unemployment rate and modernization of Quebecers' way of life. Thus, many of the debates occasioned by the problems of the Depression now became pointless. In addition, from 1939 on Canada was a country at war, living under a state of emergency, with a government that wielded its power much more forcefully than in ordinary circumstances. In the ideological arena, Ottawa was concerned with promoting the "war effort," and towards that end mounted a massive propaganda campaign and resorted to censorship. One result was a narrowing of the ideological spectrum. At the same time, the war directly influenced all ideological debates in Quebec. Its greatest effect was on the two major currents: it breathed new life into liberalism and speeded up its transformation, while nationalism became focused on the issue of participation in the war and provincial autonomy. There was not much change in the position of left-wing ideologies in Quebec.

War measures and Ottawa's mammoth intervention into all aspects of national life were, in principle, contrary to liberal ideology. Nevertheless liberalism, after suffering hard times during the Depression, regained all of its lost dynamism. Government propaganda was heavily based on liberal values: democracy, freedom, antifascism. At the same time, in the name of safeguarding these same values and in the interest of paving the way for the postwar era, reform liberal ideas gained increasing currency. Businesspeople and politicians overcame their previous reticence and accepted the Keynesian view of the state and a role for government in social security. In Quebec, reform liberalism of this sort was a large part of the inspiration for the policies of the Godbout government.

For nationalism, the war was a time of transition. For a variety of reasons, the traditionalist content of 1930s nationalism tended to fade. The renewed expansion of industry, the return of prosperity, the mobilization of young men and heads of family, the entry of women into the workforce, and people's increased awareness of the world as a result of the pervasive international situation had a dual effect. These developments helped move Quebecers' ways of living and thinking towards modernization and pluralism; at the same time, they weakened some of the bases for the influence of ideologies of retreat and preservation. In addition, the profascist sympathies the nationalists had shown during the 1930s — and the support they continued to express for the Vichy regime in France in the early part of the war — became increasingly suspect. Corporatism and anticommunism, for example, could now be seen as positions favourable to the enemy.

Henri Bourassa addressing a meeting of the Ligue pour la Défense du Canada in 1942. (*The Gazette*, National Archives of Canada, PA-108248)

While moving away from its traditionalist orientation, nationalism nevertheless flared up in the early years of the war. The prospect of again seeing Canada participate in a conflict in which it had no direct interest brought about a revival in Quebec of the anti-imperialist Canadian nationalism of the early part of the century. This position was still symbolized by Henri Bourassa, who regained his old prestige. This antiparticipationist stance was widely supported in all sectors of the Francophone population, and was forcefully expressed during the debate surrounding the conscription plebiscite of 1942. Quebec nationalism was rapidly politicized and moved towards a stronger pro-autonomy position. Although they stopped short of separatism, the traditional elites and a large proportion of the population now favoured a form of nationalism that was increasingly oriented towards Quebec and opposed to Ottawa's centralist version of federalism. In 1944, this pro-autonomy sentiment would bring down the Godbout government, which was too closely identified with the policies of the federal Liberals.

The content of nationalism remained somewhat vague. While the old themes — corporatism, anticommunism, protection of small business and cooperatives — still had some currency, they elicited much less enthusiasm than they had in the preceding decade. But new themes that could have replaced the old ones, such as promotion of the welfare state and modernization of Quebec's institutions, were identified with the opposing camp — the centralist ideology of the federal and Quebec Liberals. As a result, nationalism still did not bring its vision of society up to date;

in particular, it failed to develop a body of social thought suited to the new realities. For instance, the nationalists opposed a number of the social reforms of the era in the name of a traditional conception of the family. All in all, nationalism during the war years still appeared as a conservative body of thought, unable to move beyond its essentially defensive catchphrases and lacking an innovative plan for the future of Quebec.

The war provided an opportunity for left-wing movements to make some breakthroughs. Both the international situation and the rapid growth of trade unions in Canada helped create conditions favourable to wider dissemination of left-wing thought in the working class. In Quebec, the communists increased their influence slightly and even succeeded in twice electing a federal member of Parliament, Fred Rose, in a largely Jewish Montreal constituency. They also gained some support in Montreal intellectual and artistic circles where European influence and opposition to clerical traditionalism were strong.

While the communists' influence in the Francophone community remained very limited, it did grow somewhat, especially when they adopted an antiparticipationist position in the context of the Nazi-Soviet Pact of 1939. But with the entry of the Soviet Union into the war in 1941, their attitude changed completely. Banned in 1939, the Communist Party soon resurfaced under the name of the Labour Progressive Party and became for all practical purposes an ally of Mackenzie King's government. Setting aside its revolutionary goals, it advocated participation, denounced the anticonscriptionists as "profascists," and became, in Robert Comeau and Bernard Dionne's words, a "fervent propagandist for Canadian national unity as a necessary condition for a total war effort." In this way, failing to understand the full significance of the national question in the Francophone community, it once again alienated Quebec.

This same lack of understanding weakened the CCF. The CCF became a major political force in English Canada after 1940, and even took power in Saskatchewan in 1944. But in Quebec, while the church's negative attitude towards the CCF had faded somewhat, it was still seen as a party whose ideas were centralist and participationist, and as a result it appeared closed to Francophone aspirations.

* * * * * *

In succession, the Depression and the war each engendered a climate of ideological tension. While the tendencies and currents expressed between 1930 and 1945 were diverse and complex, their development can be grouped around two major themes. The first is the fortunes of liberalism, which initially went through a severe crisis of confidence. Subsequently, however, it succeeded in redefining itself in the form of reform liberalism and then, as a result of the Allied victory over the Axis powers, gained back its old prestige and effectiveness. The other theme is the path followed by traditionalist nationalism, which with the coming of the Depression entered one of the most vigorous periods of its history. The Depression made traditionalist nationalism more political and more aware — even if in a limited and awkward way — of social and economic concerns. During the war this form of nationalism was intensified by the conscription crisis, and while it shed some of its traditionalist content, it did not succeed in finding a new and more positive orientation.

CHAPTER 9
MANAGING THE DEPRESSION

The great ideological effervescence brought forth by the Depression had a direct impact on Quebec politics. A number of new parties, large and small, were founded; the old parties were rocked by dissension; and instability affected governments in both Ottawa and Quebec City. Despite this effervescence, however, the foundations of political life were not disturbed, as political institutions maintained their continuity and Quebec remained faithful to the liberal democratic tradition.

The New Parties

From the far right to the far left, new groups and parties were organized, and a few of them succeeded in establishing some kind of popular base. Notable among these was the Cooperative Commonwealth Federation (CCF), which became a significant force in the western provinces with the 1935 federal election. That same year another newly established party, Social Credit, came to power in Alberta under the leadership of William Aberhart and also won seventeen seats in the federal House of Commons.

In Quebec, however, these parties had only a few supporters. The CCF was clearly marginal among Francophone Quebecers, while the Ligue du Crédit Social de la Province de Québec, founded in 1936 by the journalist Louis Even, stayed outside the electoral arena. Its program tried to reconcile the economic doctrine of social credit, which aimed at increasing people's purchasing power through the distribution of a "social dividend," with the social doctrine of the church, and especially corporatism. Gilberte Côté soon joined the group, which gained approval from religious authorities and support from a few figures such as the mayor of Quebec City, Ernest Grégoire. However, it limited itself to political education and propaganda and did not run candidates in elections.

Another marginal group was the Parti National Social Chrétien, led by the fascist Adrien Arcand, which identified openly with Hitlerism — complete with blue shirts, swastikas, paramilitary demonstrations and virulent antisemitism. In 1938 Arcand's party joined with Canada's other Nazi groups and became the National Unity Party. Its activities came to an end with the outbreak of the war when Arcand and his associates were interned.

But another manifestation of the political effervescence of the Depression era was more significant in Quebec than any of these movements. The program formulated on the basis of the social doctrine of the church and the demands of nationalist intellectuals, defined in the Programme de Restauration Sociale and supported by a variety of pressure groups and youth movements, was taken up by a dissident political party, the Action Libérale Nationale. The ALN, in turn, paved the way for a new major party, Maurice Duplessis's Union Nationale.

From the Action Libérale Nationale to the Union Nationale

The Depression also shook the traditional big parties. The Liberals, in power since 1897, appeared increasingly old and sclerotic, incapable of adapting their policies to the problems of the times. Some of the party's younger activists began to advocate renewal and a change in orientation. In 1934 this group, whose central figure was Paul Gouin, formed itself into a public organization, the Action Libérale Nationale, which aimed to persuade the Liberal Party to take its inspiration from the ideas of the Programme de Restauration Sociale. Its main demands were greater emphasis on agriculture and colonization; a serious commitment to the fight against foreign trusts, especially the electricity trust; improved social policies; and replacement of the Legislative Council by a nonpartisan, corporatist-inspired institution called the Conseil d'Orientation Économique et Sociale. Made up of experts and representatives of various social bodies, this institution would be given the responsibility of recommending concrete solutions for the economic crisis. Finally, the ALN advocated that electoral and political practices be cleaned up.

Faced with the intransigence of Premier Louis-Alexandre Taschereau, the ALN broke with the Liberal Party just before the 1935 election. Knowing that it could not beat the Liberals on its own, it reluctantly negotiated an agreement with the Conservatives.

Mired in opposition since the turn of the century, the Conservatives had enjoyed a brief revival when the mayor of Montreal, Camillien Houde, became their leader in 1929. However, the 1931 election put a quick end to their hopes, and after internecine struggles the party chose a new leader, Maurice Duplessis, in 1933. But they had little success in shaking the Taschereau government and were hurt by the growing unpopularity of the federal Conservative government of R.B. Bennett. As the 1935 election approached the Conservatives were still going nowhere, and they had little choice but to join with the dissident Liberals of the ALN.

The Gouin-Duplessis alliance — initially a purely tactical one — did remarkably well in the 1935 election. After the election, Duplessis used the weakness of Gouin's leadership, his own parliamentary acumen and a variety of manoeuvres to emerge as the undisputed leader of a new party, the Union Nationale. He announced the formation of the Union Nationale in time for the 1936 election, and quickly succeeded in reducing the influence of the radical elements that had come into the party from the ALN and imposing an increasingly conservative orientation on the UN. Attempts to revive the ALN in subsequent years all failed.

The Liberal Party, meanwhile, was going through tough times; the 1934 split, the party's poor performance in the 1935 election, the scandals that developed around Taschereau, and the defeat of the Liberals in the 1936 election all took their toll. Nevertheless, the new Liberal leader, Adélard Godbout, took advantage of the party's spell in opposition to get rid of some elements of the old guard, establish closer ties with the federal Liberals (now back in power), and give the party a more innovative platform.

Political Life

After a period of realignment, a two-party system had thus been reestablished in Quebec politics by the late 1930s. For the first time, however, an exclusively Quebec party, the Union Nationale, had attained major-party status, while the other major party, the Liberals, remained closely linked to its federal counterpart.

The Depression affected political life in many other ways as well. Questioning the system and the desire for change were part of the general climate. Political debates, which had been more or less routine during the long reign of the provincial Liberals, were now redirected, became more intense, and took on a more pronounced ideological dimension. Politics became a central concern for a greater number of people and groups. Major changes in economic and social organization were advocated in the political arena: the fight against the trusts, the nationalization of electricity, farm credit, social security, labour legislation, colonization programs. This new intensity in political debates led to a questioning of solidly entrenched partisan loyalties, sometimes handed down from generation to generation. People who had always voted "rouge" supported the dissidents of the ALN and then went on to cast their lot with the "bleus" by voting for the Union Nationale. The founding of the UN went a long way towards breaking down the old Conservative-Liberal polarization that had dominated political life for decades.

While there was no radical change in the circles politicians came from, there was at least some diversification, with a few workers, rural Quebecers, small tradespeople and industrialists joining the ranks. There was also a tendency for politicians to be somewhat younger; the ALN played a significant role in this trend. In addition, politics was no longer regarded as the exclusive domain of politicians; other groups such as the

Table 1
Results of Quebec Elections, 1927-1939

Election	Party	% of popular vote	No. of seats
1927	Liberals	62.7	75
	Conservatives	36.6	9
	Other	0.7	1
1931	Liberals	55.6	79
	Conservatives	44.2	11
	Other	0.2	-
1935	Liberals	50.2	48
	Gouin-Duplessis alliance	48.7	42
	Other	1.1	-
1936	Union Nationale	57.5	76
	Liberals	41.8	14
	Other	0.7	-
1939	Liberals	54.2	70
	Union Nationale	39.2	15
	Other	6.6	1

Source: Jean Hamelin, Jean Letarte and Marcel Hamelin, "Les elections pro-vinciales dans le Quebec, 1867-1956."

clergy, trade unions, youth movements and feminist organizations took a more active part in political life.

The way in which politics was practised began to change as well. For the first time, Quebec political parties organized conventions to choose leaders or hammer out their platforms; the Conservatives held a convention in 1933, while the Liberals held one in 1938. While traditional media such as pamphlets, newspaper advertising and public meetings continued to be used for election propaganda, there was also a growing tendency to use radio. The Conservatives used radio extensively in their 1935 federal election campaign, and the ALN knew how to take full advantage of the new medium to persuade more voters by talking to them directly. Finally, corruption appeared all the more unfair in the context of the Depression, and it came under increasing criticism. It by no means disappeared, however, and could be seen in a deeply rooted system of favouritism and in election practices that made widespread use of fraud and violence.

Elections and Governments

The 1931 Quebec election, the first of the period, already reflected the effects of the Depression. Under the leadership of Camillien Houde, the Conservative Party criticized the Taschereau government for its inertia, promised to cooperate with Ottawa to fight unemployment and suffering, and attacked Liberal corruption. The Liberals reminded voters of their past achievements and argued that the Depression was a temporary phenomenon that had to be managed with prudence and thrift. Houde succeeded in substantially increasing the Conservative share of the popular vote, although he was defeated in his own constituency and there was little change in the distribution of seats (table 1). The Liberals, with deep roots in all parts of Quebec and with a powerful machine and patronage at their disposal, retained their overwhelming majority in the Legislative Assembly.

The Taschereau government tried to respond after a fashion to the province's persistent economic problems. It adopted the Vautrin Plan allocating $10 million to colonization, increased aid to municipalities for relief, took steps to revive the pulp and paper industry and established an Electricity Commission to regulate — hesitantly — the electricity trusts. However, the situation kept getting worse and dissatisfaction became more and more widespread.

In the 1935 election, the Liberals faced the Gouin-Duplessis alliance, which mounted a well-organized campaign highlighted by the publication of a *Catéchisme des électeurs* (catechism for voters), in which the bad management and corruption of the Taschereau regime were brought to light. Although they held onto power by a slender majority, the Liberals emerged from the election badly shaken. The real winners were the two parties in the opposition coalition and especially the ALN, which took twenty-six seats in its first try, as opposed to sixteen for the Conservatives.

This election would be followed by another only nine months later, in August 1936. In these intervening months, the Taschereau government, which went almost a year without convening the Assembly, fell apart,

Louis-Alexandre Taschereau, premier of Quebec (1920-36). Éditeur Officiel du Québec, 283-61H)

while the opposition, sensing that its accession to power was imminent, continued to campaign, harried the government, and reorganized around Duplessis. Duplessis managed to convene the Public Accounts Committee of the Assembly, which had not sat in ten years, and used it day after day to lay bare the government's corruption — illustrated by the fact that the premier's brother, who was entrusted with the Assembly's funds, was pocketing the interest on those funds. Taschereau had no choice but to resign, and he was succeeded by Adélard Godbout. But the Liberals were discredited and now faced a strongly united opposition. In the election that quickly followed, the Union Nationale won a convincing victory.

During the election campaign, Duplessis promised to fight corruption and put into effect measures advocated by the reformers to solve the problems of the Depression. But the achievements of the new government fell well short of its promises. Nothing changed with regard to patronage except its colour, and people continued to wait for reforms. In the economic sphere, Duplessis steered clear of ALN proposals such as the nationalization of electricity or the establishment of a social and economic council, and instead followed the same policies as the previous government, based on cooperation with foreign companies and private exploitation of natural resources. In the social sphere, apart from such cautious measures as the Fair Wages Act and assistance to needy mothers and the blind, all the government did was invest in public works to help the unemployed. The major distinguishing feature of the Union Nationale government was its increasingly pronounced conservatism, as shown especially in its virulent anticommunism, its vigorous campaigns against labour unions, and its efforts to join forces with religious leaders in defence of order, authority and traditional values. Duplessis also began to establish a reputation as the champion of provincial autonomy, thus addressing one of the major concerns of Quebec's nationalist groups. On the whole, the first Duplessis government gave the impression of being confused, disorganized and incapable of putting forward coherent policies or of fulfilling the expectations that had been held out for it. This image would not help the government in the 1939 election.

Federal Politics

The two federal elections held during the 1930s were also influenced by the Depression. Each of these elections resulted in a change of government (table 2).

When it faced the electorate in the 1930 campaign, Prime Minister Mackenzie King's Liberal government showed no awareness of how serious the situation was. Not long before, King had said that he would not give "a nickel" to Ontario, which was asking for federal aid to help the unemployed. His refusal confirmed the impression of a government that was insensitive to people's needs and ill prepared to deal with increasingly difficult circumstances. Meanwhile, R.B. Bennett, the new Conservative leader, viewed the Depression as a momentous develop-

Table 2
Federal Election Results in Quebec and Canada as a Whole, 1926-1940

Election	Party	Quebec % of popular vote	Quebec No. of seats	Other provinces % of popular vote	Other provinces No. of seats	Canada % of popular vote	Canada No. of seats
1926	Liberals	62.3	60	40.7	68	46.1	128
	Cons.	34.1	4	48.9	87	45.3	91
	Prog.	-	-	7.0	20	5.3	20
	Others	3.6	1	3.4	5	3.4	6
1930	Cons.	44.7	24	50.3	113	48.8	137
	Liberals	53.2	40	42.3	51	45.2	91
	Prog.	-	-	3.8	12	2.8	12
	Others	2.1	1	3.5	4	3.2	5
1935	Liberals	54.4	55	41.5	118	44.8	173
	Cons.	28.2	5	30.1	35	29.6	40
	CCF	0.6	-	11.6	7	8.8	7
	Soc. Cred.	-	-	5.5	17	4.1	17
	Recons.	8.7	-	8.7	1	8.7	1
	Other	8.1	5	2.5	2	3.9	7
1940	Liberals	63.3	61	47.5	120	51.5	181
	Cons.	19.8	1	34.3	39	30.7	40
	CCF	0.6	-	11.2	8	8.5	8
	Soc. Cred.	0.9	-	3.3	10	2.7	10
	Other	15.3	3	3.3	3	6.6	6

Cons. = Conservatives; Prog. = Progressives; CCF = Cooperative Commonwealth Federation; Soc. Cred. = Social Credit; Recons. = Reconstruction

Source: J.M. Beck, *Pendulum of Power: Canada's Federal Elections.*

ment and promised that if he was elected Ottawa would do everything possible to bring quick and effective relief to the unemployed and increase exports while protecting the home market.

This strategy led not only to a Canada-wide Conservative victory but also to a major Conservative breakthrough in Quebec. Quebec voters' concern with the effects of the Depression overrode their mistrust of the Conservatives, who had been identified with imperialism and the imposition of conscription in 1917.

But while the Depression helped Bennett come to power, it proved too much for his government to handle. The new prime minister failed either to bring about economic recovery or to alleviate misery, and the hopes that he had aroused turned to disappointment. People associated him with the difficulties of the time and he became increasingly unpopular. Just before the 1935 election, Bennett proposed a Roosevelt-style New

Deal, but the initiative was in vain, as widespread dissatisfaction led to a crushing defeat for the Conservatives. Disappointment with the old parties led many voters to switch their allegiance to new ones such as the CCF, Social Credit and former trade minister H.H. Stevens's Reconstruction Party, which campaigned on a platform of fighting the trusts. These third parties received considerable support but did not manage to win many seats. In the end, the main beneficiaries of dissatisfaction with the Bennett government were the King Liberals, especially in Quebec where the third parties did not do as well as elsewhere. Although they did not offer any concrete alternatives to Bennett's policies, the Liberals came out of the election with an impressive majority in the House of Commons.

The new government had to concentrate most of its energies in two areas. First, the ongoing Depression and its effects on the population required its continued attention. The King government maintained and strengthened programs introduced in the early 1930s and negotiated a trade agreement with the United States to stimulate exports. Second, with the international situation growing increasingly tense, the government had to devote considerable attention to foreign affairs. Its foreign policy was based primarily on avoiding confrontation. Thus, during the Spanish Civil War, it refused to take a position and made it illegal for Canadian citizens to serve with either of the two sides in the field. The government placed special emphasis on this cautious policy in Quebec, where Liberal representatives assured people that Canada had no intention of being drawn into external conflicts. Nevertheless, Ottawa felt it necessary to take such precautions as modestly increasing the defence budget and strengthening its alliances with the United States and Britain.

Richard Bedford Bennett, prime minister of Canada (1930-35). (National Archives of Canada, PA-37914)

Liberal Party of Canada election poster. (National Archives of Canada, C-85941)

Governments and the Depression

As already noted, one of the effects of the Depression was a wider role for governments. We will look at the impact of this development on the structures of government, the way it operated, and the means at its disposal. It would not be until the Second World War and the postwar period that decisive changes in these areas would take place.

For the time being, governments limited themselves to taking emergency precautions and did not call their traditional role and practices into question. The federal government's contribution to assistance programs was essentially financial in nature and did not involve a reorganization of the civil service. The number of civil servants remained steady at about 40,000 until 1939, and there was not much growth in spending either: $553 million in 1938 as compared with $442 million in 1930. However, there was some change in the distribution of the federal dollar: aid to the unemployed, on which the government spent nothing in 1928 and 1929, represented 8.5 per cent of total spending in 1931, 14.9 per cent in 1935 and 7.7 per cent in 1938.

For the Quebec government, a balanced budget had traditionally been the rule, but the Depression threatened to make it impossible. Despite misgivings, the government was forced to run a deficit in 1932, and more would follow in subsequent years. The reason was a dramatic increase in expenditures, from $49 million in 1929-30 to $108 million in 1939-40. In particular, spending on assistance to the unemployed represented 11.3 per cent of the budget in 1933 and 25.7 per cent in 1939. This increase made it necessary for Quebec to cut spending in other areas, such as transportation and communications, education and health. Overall, the provincial debt doubled between 1930 and 1936, then doubled again between 1936 and 1939; at the end of the decade it stood at almost $265 million.

Apart from the growing destabilizing effect on public finances, the Depression also slowly began to upset the balance among the different levels of government. The change in the division of expenditures and responsibilities between the provincial government and the municipalities was especially striking. The municipalities were traditionally responsible for social assistance, but they were swamped and had to depend on the Quebec government for an increasing share of the financing of relief and assistance to the unemployed. The federal government's share of expenditures, on the other hand, remained roughly constant until 1939, even if the idea that its role should be expanded through projects undertaken on a truly "national" — that is, Canada-wide — scale now had some currency. The Rowell-Sirois Commission debated these questions from the time of its appointment in 1937 into the early years of the war.

In summary, governments had to change in a number of significant ways because of the Depression: they had to intervene more, spend more, and hence tax more and go into debt more than they had before. But these changes were primarily quantitative, and traditional ideas and practices regarding the role and powers of government in the economy and society were not radically altered. At the federal level, however, there was a growing realization that a major restructuring would be necessary if similar depressions were to be avoided in the future.

CHAPTER 10

MANAGING THE WAR

On September 10, 1939, the Parliament of Canada, after a brief debate, declared war on Germany. Although ill prepared militarily, the country had to sustain a general mobilization of its human and material resources in a short time. The federal government, armed with its emergency powers under the constitution and the War Measures Act, took all the important decisions into its own hands and established its control over individuals, companies and even provincial governments.

The wartime political scene, dominated in both Ottawa and Quebec City by the Liberal Party, was of a special sort. The big issue that convulsed Quebec was conscription for overseas service, which Liberal leaders in 1939 promised not to impose. However, they resorted to a plebiscite to free themselves from that promise in 1942, and then imposed conscription in 1944. This issue also led to the defeat of Premier Adélard Godbout's reform-minded provincial government in 1944.

The Military

Canada was unlike European countries in that the army did not play a major role in Canadian society in peacetime. There was no compulsory military service, the regular army was small, and defence expenditures were low. The country maintained a volunteer militia that seemed more like a social club. In 1935, the chief of staff acknowledged that Canada's naval and air defence equipment was completely out of date and that "available stocks of ammunition for field artillery represented only 90 minutes' fire at normal rates." The great majority of the weapons used dated from the First World War. Canada was thus poorly prepared to deal with a large-scale armed conflict.

Very quickly, however, there was a radical change in the situation. Budgets and personnel increased dramatically and factories to build

Table 1 Canada's War Effort		
Year	Strength of armed forces (thousands of individuals)	Defence spending ($ million)
1931	5	18
1932	5	14
1933	5	13
1934	5	14
1935	5	17
1936	6	23
1937	6	33
1938	7	35
1939	9	126
1940	107	730
1941	296	1 268
1942	392	2 563
1943	716	4 242
1944	779	4 000
1945	736	2 942
1946	213	388

Source: *Historical Statistics of Canada*, series D-125 and H-19.

munitions and arms were created from scratch. All the country's resources would henceforth be poured into the war effort. The peak years were 1943 and 1944, when military spending was in the neighbourhood of $4 billion and military personnel reached almost 800,000 (table 1).

Canada participated in the world war in a wide variety of ways, of which three in particular are worth noting. The first is Canada's logistical support for the Allies, especially after the invasion of France and the evacuation of Dunkirk in 1940. Protected by its considerable distance from the major war theatres, Canada was in a position to produce large quantities of the foodstuffs and munitions that the allied forces needed. This role, in turn, provided a strong impetus to Canadian agriculture and industry. A related service was Canadian responsibility for training Commonwealth airmen, 50,000 of whom received their training in Canada.

A second aspect of Canada's involvement was its role as an intermediary between the United States, which was officially neutral until 1941, and Britain. This privileged relationship with the two great powers continued after 1941, as can be seen in the 1943 and 1944 Quebec conferences and in military-industrial cooperation in North America.

The third facet of Canadian involvement was active participation on the battlefield. Nearly 600,000 Canadians were sent overseas. There were almost 96,000 casualties, including 42,000 dead. The first major involvement of Canadian troops was the failed attempt to land at Dieppe in 1942.

William Lyon Mackenzie King, prime minister of Canada, flanked by
President Franklin Delano Roosevelt and Prime Minister Winston Churchilll at
the Quebec Conference, 1943. (National Archives of Canada, PA-115129)

Afterwards, Canadian troops took part in the Italian campaign, the Normandy invasion and the liberation of Europe, especially in northern
France, Belgium, the Netherlands and Germany.

Strengthening the State

As a result of the state of war, the government was given substantial
extraordinary powers so as to mobilize the human and material resources
of the country. The War Measures Act, originally passed during the First
World War, was again put into effect. One feature of government intervention was its authoritarianism: the federal government could govern
by decree without consulting Parliament, requisition any products or
services the army needed, intern people without trial, establish censorship, and place limits on the movement of people. A second feature was
the highly centralist character of government intervention: important
decisions were made by a small group of people in Ottawa, with the help
of specialized committees and a large bureaucracy. In addition, the
country's financial resources were strongly channelled towards the federal government which, at the height of the war, was responsible for more
than a third of gross national expenditures.

Strengthening the role of the government in this way inevitably involved a shakeup in its administrative structures. New departments were established to manage the war effort — notably Munitions and Supply, Air, and Naval Services — along with a large number of new sections and agencies. Within the cabinet, a War Committee was established whose members had control over most decisions relating to the conduct of the war. The government also set up some thirty publicly owned corporations — called crown corporations — each with its own specific goals and with greater freedom to manoeuvre than a government department. Overall, the number of federal civil servants increased from 46,000 in 1939 to 115,000 in 1945. As a result of this massive effort, the government incurred a large debt: from $5 billion in 1939, the federal debt grew to $18 billion in 1945.

The government apparatus was organized along more rational lines. An appeal went out to the most brilliant minds in the country, and experts in the pure and applied sciences were called on to invent new products and improve existing ones in areas such as munitions, drugs and foodstuffs. For the first time, the government also used the services of experts in economics, psychology, communications and other social sciences. They were brought in to help the government pursue the goals of the new welfare state and carry out other activities more effectively and "scientifically." Economic and social planning was the order of the day, and it was applied to financial management as well as to the management of human and material resources.

To gain acceptance for its goals and policies, the government systematically resorted to propaganda. The National Film Board and the government radio network were pressed into war service. The media were used as advertising tools, carrying campaigns for enlistment, volunteer work, conservation of resources, participation of women in the war effort, victory bond sales and the like. At the same time, all public expression of opposition to official policy had to be avoided. This was the task of censorship, which was imposed on all media. Thus, politicians in Quebec, as in other provinces, had to submit the texts of speeches they were to deliver on the radio to the censors. "Holding defeatist views" or "harming recruitment and the success of His Majesty's forces" was now punishable by a jail term. On these grounds, the mayor of Montreal, Camillien Houde, was interned in a detention camp for most of the war. Nor was he the only one. Thousands of Canadians of German, Italian and especially Japanese origin were imprisoned on the pretext that they came from enemy countries.

Conscription

The question of whether government coercion should extend to conscription for overseas military service, which had caused such acrimony during the First World War, again arose and became the subject of bitter debates. While there were opponents of conscription in all parts of Canada, the scope of the problem was greatest in Quebec.

Wartime propaganda poster. (National Archives of Canada, PA-137215)

During the 1939 provincial election campaign the leaders of the federal Liberal Party, in an effort to ensure the defeat of Duplessis, solemnly committed themselves to resisting conscription. Despite that promise, conscription would be imposed, but it happened in stages. In 1940 the National Resources Mobilization Act (NMRA) was passed, allowing for conscription for the defence of Canadian territory. All men and women between sixteen and sixty years of age were required to register. The government called men up group by group on the basis of these lists: first bachelors and the youngest age group, then married men. Those who were called up were initially mobilized for thirty days, then for four months. In 1941, compulsory military service became permanent for some age groups.

The government relied on volunteers for overseas service; great pressure was put on NMRA conscripts to volunteer. However, some groups in English Canada and the Conservative opposition in Parliament demanded that overseas service be made compulsory, arguing that French Canadians were not doing their fair share. The question was an emotional one and Ottawa decided to hold a plebiscite in 1942. It wanted to be released from its previous commitment so that could have a free hand in case the situation in Europe deteriorated. Prime Minister Mackenzie King would define his position in these terms: "Not necessarily conscription, but conscription if necessary."

The First World War had clearly demonstrated the opposition of French-speaking Quebecers to conscription. As soon as the plebiscite was announced, French Canadian nationalist leaders formed the Ligue pour la Défense du Canada, which opposed conscription for service outside Canada. The plebiscite campaign was marked by impassioned debates, and the results were unequivocal. In Quebec, 71.2 per cent of the population — and 85 per cent of the French-speaking population — refused to release the government from its promises, while in the rest of the country 80 per cent supported the government. The opposition between French and English Canadians was thus laid bare, and French Canadians had to submit to the will of the majority. However, the King government waited until 1944 before imposing conscription. That year, military leaders estimated that there would not be enough volunteers to replace killed and wounded soldiers in the field forces. King finally yielded to the numerous pressures and authorized the conscription of 16,000 men for overseas service. Although one cabinet minister resigned and a few Liberal MPs opposed their own party, French Canadians had to acquiesce.

Opposition to conscription was not the only aspect of Quebecers' attitude to the war. They had little awareness or information about the reasons for the war and the situation in Europe. However, many more French Canadians enlisted than in the First World War: they constituted 19 per cent of Canadian forces, as compared to 12 per cent in 1914-18. The desire to escape unemployment and a taste for adventure were no doubt factors that encouraged them to enlist, along with official propaganda and the songs of "Le Soldat Lebrun."

Nevertheless, the armed forces did little to welcome French Canadians. The top leadership was massively Anglophone. In the army, only three brigade commanders stationed in Europe and seven of the seventy-three high-ranking officers in Canada were French Canadian. The situation was even worse in the air force, which had two Francophone high-ranking officers, and the navy, which had only one. English was the only language of work in the air force and the navy and the use of French was often forbidden outright. Most Francophone candidates were thus excluded even from low-ranking positions. As a result, in 1944 the air force was only 8 per cent French Canadian. The situation was a little different in the army where there were French-speaking regiments such as the Royal 22e, the Régiment de Maisonneuve, the Fusiliers Mont-Royal and the Régiment de la Chaudière. There were not enough such regiments, however, to absorb all the Francophone recruits, many of whom were placed in English-language units. This was true especially of those who entered specialized units. The historian Jean-Yves Gravel has concluded:

> Before and during the Second World War, the armed forces did not grant equality of opportunity to French Canadians, and the equality of sacrifice that English Canada demanded so vigorously should not have been expected from them. The initiative to improve the lot of Francophones in the military came from politicians, who on more than one occasion had to order military authorities to carry out government decisions.

A demonstration against conscription in Montreal. (*The Gazette*, National Archives of Canada, PA-107910)

Federal Politics

Throughout the war, the federal political scene was indisputably dominated by the Liberal Party under the leadership of William Lyon Mackenzie King. After returning to power in 1935, King won a convincing
victory in the 1940 election that gave him a free hand for the duration of
the war.

King's handling of war policy was marked by a number of major
concerns. The prime minister wanted to ensure Canada's active participation, but he also wanted to protect the country's independence from
the implications of decisions taken by Britain and the United States. No
militarist, he took pains throughout the war to make sure that civilian
authority over the military was firmly maintained. To preserve the cohesion of his party and his government, King kept the power to make final
decisions in his own hands and did not hesitate to get rid of dissident
ministers where necessary. This did not prevent him, however, from
delegating a great deal of power to some ministers, especially C.D. Howe,
who was in charge of overall coordination of the war economy. And
finally, the prime minister was concerned with preserving Canadian
unity by taking French Canadians into account: he delayed the decision
to resort to conscription to the last possible moment and intervened
personally to improve the position of Francophones in the armed forces.

The Liberal government enjoyed solid support in Quebec, which provided it with a third of its seats in the 1940 election. This situation
explains why King wanted to avoid confrontations with French Canadians. But while the Quebec caucus was a large one, its size was not
reflected in the makeup of the cabinet, where there were few Francophone ministers. King relied on a "Quebec lieutenant" with considerable
influence in all matters concerning Quebec. This position was filled by
Ernest Lapointe until his death in 1941 and then by Louis Saint-Laurent.

The conscription issue, however, shook Liberal domination of Quebec.
After the 1942 plebiscite, dissident Liberals led by Maxime Raymond
established a new party, the Bloc Populaire Canadien. However, not all
the dissidents joined the Bloc: some MPs preferred to sit as independents.
The Bloc took only two seats in the 1945 election and went out of existence soon afterwards.

Meanwhile, the Conservatives, who formed the official opposition,
were disorganized. Between 1940 and 1945, the party had three leaders,
none of whom had a seat in Parliament. Its program never offered a real
alternative to the Liberals'; its only distinctive promises were conscription and an even more intense war effort. The collapse of the Conservatives in Quebec, where their share of the popular vote fell from 19.4 per
cent in 1940 to 8.4 per cent in 1945, was thus not surprising.

The Liberals were more worried by the rise of the CCF, which was
close behind them in the opinion polls and took power in Saskatchewan
in 1944. The Liberal government's reaction was an effective one: it stole

Table 2
Federal Election Results in Quebec and Canada
as a Whole, 1940-1945

Election	Party	Quebec % of popular vote	Quebec No. of seats	Other provinces % of popular vote	Other provinces No. of seats	Canada % of popular vote	Canada No. of seats
1940	Liberals	63.3	61	47.5	120	51.5	181
	Cons.	19.8	1	34.3	39	30.7	40
	CCF	0.6	-	11.2	8	8.5	8
	Soc. Cred.	0.9	-	3.3	10	2.7	10
	Other	15.3	3	3.3	3	6.6	6
1945	Liberals	50.8	53	37.3	72	40.9	125
	Cons.	8.4	2	34.3	65	27.4	67
	CCF	2.4	-	20.4	28	15.6	28
	Soc. Cred.	4.5	-	4.0	13	4.1	13
	Bloc Pop.	12.8	2	0.2	-	3.6	2
	Other	21.1	8	3.7	2	8.5	10

Cons. = Conservatives; CCF = Cooperative Commonwealth Federation; Soc. Cred. = Social Credit; Bloc Pop. = Bloc Populaire

Source: J.M. Beck, *Pendulum of Power: Canada's Federal Elections.*

their thunder by proposing a large-scale reconstruction program and socialist-inspired social policies. With little support in Quebec, the CCF did not manage to achieve major-party status alongside the Conservatives and the Liberals.

In the 1945 election, King won a narrower victory than in 1940. The Liberals' victory was due to their support in Quebec, despite the conscription crisis, which caused the defection of some Liberal voters to the Bloc Populaire and independent candidates. King's wartime attitude of conciliation and his innovative social policies helped his party survive the tensions of the war and put it in a good position to benefit from postwar prosperity.

Quebec Politics

The outbreak of the Second World War led to a confrontation between Maurice Duplessis's government in Quebec City and King's government in Ottawa. In an appeal to the voters, Duplessis attacked the federal Liberals who, he said, were taking advantage of the unusual wartime situation to place severe limits on Quebec's autonomy. The premier also raised the spectre of conscription. Quebec's federal ministers responded adroitly by claiming to be the "bulwarks" against conscription, adding that a vote for Duplessis would be a vote of nonconfidence in them. This would force them to resign and open the door to a proconscription Union government. They vowed that as long as they were in the government, there would be no conscription for overseas service.

The provincial Liberals, led by Adélard Godbout, were thus dragged along by the federal Liberals' strategy, and the conscription issue — which was not under the Quebec government's jurisdiction — played a determining role in the 1939 election. The Quebec Liberals also benefited from people's disillusionment with the Duplessis government. The Union Nationale had not lived up to the hopes raised in 1936, had disappointed many nationalists, and had had to deal with the latter years of the Depression by substantially increasing the provincial debt. As a result, the Liberals won an overwhelming victory in the 1939 election.

The Godbout government led Quebec firmly onto the path of reform. To avoid the stigma of patronage that had been associated with the Taschereau regime, it undertook a reform of the government apparatus aimed at establishing a career civil service. At the same time, it showed an increased awareness of the new responsibilities incumbent on the developing welfare state. Thus, Godbout immediately agreed to a constitutional amendment allowing the federal government to establish an unemployment insurance program. He subsequently tried to bring Quebec into the welfare state era by establishing a commission to study health insurance and an Economic Advisory Council.

The Godbout government's reformism also manifested itself in the stands it took on two questions that had deeply divided public opinion since the early part of the century. Despite resistance from the Catholic hierarchy and conservative circles, it gave women the right to vote in

Table 3
Results of Quebec Elections, 1939-1944

Election	Party	% of popular vote	No. of seats
1939	Liberals	54.2	70
	Union Nationale	39.2	15
	Other	6.6	1
1944	Union Nationale	38.2	48
	Liberals	40.0	37
	Bloc Populaire	15.2	4
	CCF	0.8	1
	Other	5.8	1

Source: Jean Hamelin, Jean Letarte and Marcel Hamelin, "Les elections provinciales dans le Quebec, 1867-1956."

Adélard Godbout, premier of Quebec (1936 and 1939-44). (Jacques La-coursière Collection)

1940 and made school attendance compulsory for children under four-teen in 1942. It also implemented a favourite nationalist idea by bringing electricity under partial public ownership and establishing Hydro-Que-bec. An agronomist by training, Godbout was very interested in agricul-ture, which he saw in economic rather than ideological terms. And finally, in the labour field, Godbout took his inspiration from the United States and the Canadian federal government, bringing in a labour code that recognized unions and sought to establish a framework for collective bargaining.

This reform program has led a number of historians to consider the Godbout government a precursor of the Quiet Revolution. However, the government proved unable to harmonize its reformism with a strong defence of Quebec's rights, which came under severe attack during the war. Godbout's zealous support of the war effort and his attitude during the plebiscite campaign made him appear to be a vassal of Ottawa and lost him the backing of a portion of the Francophone electorate.

The Bloc Populaire Canadien, established in 1942 by nationalists who had waged the plebiscite campaign under the banner of the Ligue pour la Défense du Canada, had a provincial wing led by André Laurendeau. While the Bloc placed primary emphasis on the fight against conscription, it also put forward a social reform program that stressed the need for family and housing policies.

Meanwhile, Maurice Duplessis rebuilt the Union Nationale, which had been in disarray since its 1939 defeat. Throughout the war, Duplessis skilfully followed a tortuous political path to avoid taking clear stands. While some nationalists were alienated by his deep-rooted conservatism and were more comfortable with the Bloc Populaire, Duplessis did stake out a position as a consistent and vigorous defender of provincial autonomy. The Union Nationale also had a solid organization and was well established in the country and small towns.

The 1944 election reflected these conflicting tendencies. The Liberals got the most votes, but they were concentrated in the cities and in English-speaking areas, which were underrepresented relative to rural areas by virtue of the electoral map. This bias favoured the Union Nationale, which won an absolute majority of seats with only 38.2 per cent of the popular vote. The Bloc Populaire got 15.2 per cent of the popular vote but won only four seats.

Thus, the Godbout government fell victim to special wartime circumstances, especially the conscription crisis. Meanwhile the intellectual nationalist movement, which had already failed once with the Action Libérale Nationale, tried again with the Bloc Populaire, but it did not succeed in taking full advantage of nationalist sentiment and carving out a large place for itself on the political scene. As a result, the way was clear for Maurice Duplessis's Union Nationale.

CHAPTER 11

A CHANGING FEDERAL SYSTEM

While the 1920s were a decade of relatively harmonious federal-provincial relations, the years 1930 to 1945 were a troubled period. The Depression, the war and the Keynesian revolution had decisive effects in this regard. While Ottawa proceeded in a hesitant, ad hoc fashion during the Depression years, wartime mobilization gave it the opportunity to impose its leadership and redirect the working of the Canadian system towards extreme centralization. Quebec tried to resist this wave. But events had moved too fast for Quebec's traditional defence of its autonomy: it was crushed by Ottawa, which had powerful instruments at its disposal as a result of wartime circumstances and its support among the country's English-speaking majority.

The Effects of the Depression

When the need for increased government intervention arises in a federal system, the question of which of the two levels of government will intervene and what procedures will be followed comes to the fore. The major issues of the period were whether the division of resources, powers and responsibilities between the federal government and the provinces that had prevailed in the past would continue and what degree of autonomy the provincial governments would be able to preserve.

In the early years of the Depression, federal-provincial relations were not unduly disturbed, except in the area of unemployment. Thus Ottawa, with the agreement of the other governments, transferred control over natural resources to the prairie provinces in 1930, and even compensated them financially for revenues they had missed out on in preceding years. The same year, it was no problem for the premiers of Quebec and Ontario to convince the federal prime minister that the British North America Act constituted an agreement among the provinces and that nothing in the

Statute of Westminster that London was about to adopt should violate
their rights.

With the Statute of Westminster of 1931, Canada became a formally
independent country. Although Canada maintained its official allegiance
to the British crown, the Statute stipulated that the Dominion was fully
empowered to pass laws in internal or external matters without requiring
Britain's consent; in addition, British legislation no longer had any force
in Canada. Canada thus attained formal sovereignty. However, because
the provinces and the federal government could not agree on an amending formula, its constitution — which was still the BNA Act — was not
repatriated and remained an act of the British Parliament. The Judicial
Committee of the Privy Council in London also continued to be Canada's
court of last resort.

While the distribution of powers between the two levels of government was not changed by the Statute of Westminster, it was called into
question by the Depression. The area of social assistance gained new
prominence and required urgent action on the part of governments.
Constitutionally, this area was under the jurisdiction of the provinces,
which exercised their responsibility with the help of the municipalities.
As a result of the magnitude of the Depression, however, the provinces
and municipalities were soon swamped and demanded financial aid
from Ottawa on the grounds that unemployment was "national" in
scope. Thus the federal government, with its greater financial resources,
was forced to intervene. It did so by establishing shared-cost programs
in the areas of public works, colonization assistance and direct relief to
the unemployed.

The Depression also highlighted the problem of regional disparities in
stark terms, as some provinces, with a less diversified economic structure
and a more limited tax base, were much more severely affected than
others. The western provinces were hit especially hard, and their governments were even threatened with bankruptcy. Here too, Ottawa had to
act, and it rescued them by taking responsibility for paying the interest
on their debts.

Dissatisfied with having to intervene in such an ad hoc manner and
swamped by the demands for assistance it was getting from all directions,
Ottawa became convinced of the need to rethink and rationalize its handling of the Depression and mount a direct attack on its causes. The New
Deal that Prime Minister Bennett proposed in 1935 was conceived in this
spirit. But the governments of Quebec and Ontario quickly attacked this
initiative as unconstitutional, maintaining that it infringed on their jurisdiction, especially in the areas of social assistance, civil law and control
of natural resources. Shortly afterwards, they won their case when the
Privy Council in London disallowed the Bennett proposals.

The federal government managed to extend the scope of its activity in
fields where its jurisdiction was recognized by the constitution, such as
money and banking (establishment of the Bank of Canada) and inter-

provincial transport (Trans-Canada Airlines). But the moment it tried to go beyond these limits — by regulating provincial expenditures and loans, for example, or by establishing a countrywide unemployment insurance program — it ran up against the principles of distribution of powers and provincial autonomy to which some provinces, especially Quebec and Ontario, were resolutely attached.

Federalism in Question

As a way out of the impasse, Ottawa decided to establish a Royal Commission on Dominion-Provincial Relations, known as the Rowell-Sirois Commission. Its mandate was to examine "the economic and financial basis of Confederation and the distribution of legislative powers in the light of the economic and social developments of the last seventy years."

The commission began its work in 1937. At the time, there was a new tendency among Canadians — especially English Canadians — to be increasingly critical of the concept of provincial autonomy, which was considered an obstacle to social justice. According to this view, there was a risk that provincial autonomy would destroy the country by preventing the federal government from acting, and the time had come to allow Ottawa to assume its "national" role in full measure. The compact theory of Confederation, according to which the constitution was an agreement among the provinces and could not be amended without their unanimous consent, came under intense scrutiny and was rejected by many people. It was argued that the BNA Act was a centralist document in both letter and spirit, and that Privy Council decisions had distorted its meaning in favour of the provinces.

This intellectual movement, which coincided with a resurgence of English Canadian nationalism, was supported by the poorest provinces, which were not interested in autonomy, and by the progressives in the new CCF party, who saw planning, nationalization and social justice as being largely incompatible with a decentralized form of federalism.

The conclusions of the Rowell-Sirois Commission, which submitted its report in 1940, were influenced by this state of mind. Among the commission's more noteworthy proposals were that the federal government establish and take responsibility for an unemployment insurance program and that it assume the full cost of old age pensions, which it had hitherto shared with the provinces. It also recommended that Ottawa have a monopoly of personal and corporate income taxes and succession duties. In exchange, it would assume the provincial debts and pay the provinces an unconditional annual grant determined by a "Canadian standard." In effect, the commissioners were saying that only the federal government was in a position to adapt fiscal policy to cyclical variations and regional diversity, and thus to provide the citizens of each province with decent social services while ensuring that the economy remained productive. In the commission's view, these recommendations were in conformity with the true spirit of 1867 and would even allow a greater degree of provincial autonomy in the real sense, since the provinces, in good years and bad, would have all the revenues they needed to run their affairs.

The Effects of the War

The debate on federalism during the 1930s and the work of the Rowell-Sirois Commission put new ideas into circulation and prepared people to think about an eventual readjustment of the federal system. But it was the war that both solved the economic crisis and gave Ottawa the opportunity and the means to put a thorough modification of the federal system into effect. The war made it possible for the federal government to concentrate all the instruments of power in its hands. The War Measures Act of 1914, which gave Ottawa unchallenged ascendancy over the provinces, was put back into force and became, so to speak, the constitution of the country.

Seeking to take advantage of the unusual situation, Ottawa called a federal-provincial conference in 1941 to study the Rowell-Sirois Report. Ontario, Alberta and British Columbia were vigorously opposed to the commission's recommendations, which they saw as too centralist, while Quebec, as represented by Premier Godbout, was ready to talk about them. Unable to reach a consensus, the conference came to an abrupt end, but this didn't prevent Prime Minister King from trying to put a number of the report's proposals into effect in stages. He had already, in 1940, secured the consent of all the provinces to a constitutional amendment that would allow unemployment insurance to be introduced. In 1942, he reached agreements with all the provinces giving the federal government the exclusive right to levy personal and corporate income taxes for the duration of the war, in exchange for which the provinces would get an annual subsidy from Ottawa.

The federal government's wartime experience and conversion to Keynesianism persuaded it that it would have to act to maintain control over the major direct tax fields and social legislation after the war ended. As a result, Ottawa created a federal department of health and welfare, established a family allowance program and passed the National Housing Act — all measures involving sectors that could be considered as being under provincial jurisdiction. Even if some provinces objected to one or another of these initiatives, there was no unanimity among them and they could not prevent the federal government from acting. Ottawa took advantage of the great popularity of these measures among broad sectors of the population. In its view, its policies implied that it had to maintain control over the major direct tax fields; this, however, it was not able to do.

Quebec

At the beginning of the Depression, it was Ottawa that appeared helpless; fifteen years later, at the end of the war, it was Quebec. And its impotence seemed total, for power relationships between the federal government and the provinces had been turned upside down in the interim. Quebec managed to maintain the traditional defence of its autonomy until 1939, but afterwards this position came under severe attack in Ottawa's centralizing offensive. Quebec's defence of its autonomy was based on the proposition that each level of government was sovereign in its own area of jurisdiction and that the BNA Act was a compact freely assented to by the provinces. This was, however, little more than a theoretical vision. In practice, Ottawa had the means to bend the apparently rigid rules of this form of federalism, as the technique of shared-cost programs showed.

Old age pensions constituted the most seductive of these programs. Ottawa instituted old age pensions in 1927, assuming 50 per cent — later 75 per cent — of the costs so long as the provinces agreed and paid their share. The Taschereau government saw this as an invasion of its jurisdiction in the social sphere and initially refused to join the program, even at the price of penalizing its own citizens. But under pressure from the opposition and public opinion, it finally yielded in 1936. Subsequently, Quebec successfully resisted the Bennett New Deal, but in radio and a number of other major areas it had to recognize federal jurisdiction after a fierce struggle.

As the Depression and the social problems it brought about deepened, Quebec had no other choice but to swallow its principles and join the other provinces in demanding financial aid from Ottawa. As it did so, however, it continued to proclaim its devotion to autonomy. The Ontario government shared its misgivings, fearing that centralization would limit its powers and force it to pay a large part of the bill for Ottawa's activities in other provinces. From 1936 on, Quebec and Ontario established an anti-Ottawa alliance that became known as the Duplessis-Hepburn alliance after the premiers of the two provinces. The two premiers' colourful personalities and populism and the deep animosity between both of them and King gave their struggle special prominence, even if all they were really doing was defending the traditional positions of their provinces.

While Quebec and Ontario wanted their share of federal aid to the unemployed, they were against the establishment of a federal unemployment insurance program, advocating instead a system that would be financed by Ottawa but administered by the provinces. Ottawa rejected this idea. Duplessis and Hepburn jointly resisted any attempt by Ottawa to regulate their governments' spending and borrowing. They also declared war on the Rowell-Sirois Commission, arguing that the federal government had no right to conduct an inquiry into provincial affairs and no power to amend the constitution without their consent. In opposition to the stance taken by the federal commissioners, they upheld the position that the provinces needed sufficient revenues to exercise their responsibilities and therefore should have priority in the field of direct taxation. Ontario and Quebec, they maintained, shouldn't have to pay for the extravagances of the western provinces. The two central provinces also had

L'INTRÉPIDE DÉFENSEUR DE NOS DROITS

COOPÉRATION OUI

ASSIMILATION JAMAIS

Union Nationale election poster. (National Archives of Canada, C-87690)

little sympathy for western complaints of being exploited by the east. It was up to each province to live within its means, and before developing Canada-wide social services, they said, it was important to develop the economy.

Thus, Quebec and Ontario advocated a decentralized form of federalism in the name of a conception of the constitution whose validity was challenged by many people at the time. In addition, the positions taken by the two "rich" provinces in response to the Rowell-Sirois Commission were inspired by an economic and social philosophy based on a form of liberalism that was handed down from the nineteenth century and unsuited to the needs of a Canada reeling from the Depression. Nevertheless, the federal government could not prevail over the simultaneous opposition of Quebec and Ontario, and Duplessis and Hepburn's strategy temporarily succeeded in holding the movement towards centralization in check. Here again the war, which completely changed the rules of the federal-provincial game, had a decisive effect.

Not only did the new premier, Adélard Godbout, owe his victory to the federal Liberals, but he was also deeply convinced that Canada and Quebec had to participate fully in the war effort, and on a cooperative basis (although he was committed to fighting conscription). With Godbout's accession, Ottawa-Quebec relations moved from the confrontation that had characterized the preceding years to a new era of harmony. Thus, by a simple letter of agreement, without consulting the Legislative Assembly, the Godbout cabinet assented in 1940 to complete federal jurisdiction over unemployment insurance. In the same spirit, it adopted a conciliatory attitude at the time of the 1941 federal-provincial conference and, despite opposition protests, yielded in 1942 to federal demands

Table 1
Percentage of Total Tax Revenues Accounted for by the Three Levels of Government in Quebec, 1933-1945

Government	1933	% 1939	1945
Federal	47.7	51.0	82.8
Provincial	10.0	16.5	7.3
Municipal	42.3	32.5	9.9

Source: Tremblay Report, vol. 4, table 10, pp. 34-35.

for an exclusive right to levy direct taxes for the duration of the war in exchange for an annual subsidy. Under this agreement, the federal government collected $2.26 billion in Quebec between 1941 and 1947 and paid Quebec only $103 million.

Despite this detente in relations between the two governments, vigorous pro-autonomy sentiment remained alive among Quebecers, especially in nationalist circles. Ottawa's aggressive centralism, the subordinate position of French Canadians in the civil service and the armed forces, and the conscription crisis that erupted in 1942 all exacerbated it significantly. This pro-autonomy sentiment, on which the opposition parties heavily based their appeal, eventually brought down the Godbout government in 1944.

*   *   *   *   *   *

In the years between 1930 and 1945, the old balance between federal and provincial powers was upset. Taking advantage of the Depression and especially of the war, Ottawa continually increased its influence relative to the Quebec government. Although Quebec put up a fight, it clearly lost ground during the period, as can be seen in the changes in the share of total tax revenues accounted for by each level of government (table 1).

The war showed that the federal government was capable of effectively planning and managing the Canadian economy. Strengthened by this experience and wanting to maintain the ground it had gained, Ottawa called another federal-provincial conference at the very end of the war, this time to discuss "reconstruction." At the conference it unveiled a vast program of action for bringing Canada into the welfare state era after the war. Some time before, however, Quebecers had returned Maurice Duplessis's Union Nationale to power, and this new government was fiercely determined to defend provincial autonomy.

CHAPTER 12

THE NEW CONSUMER CULTURE

The cultural development of a society such as modern Quebec is not easy to describe. First of all, the very concept of culture has recently been redefined in a way that makes it both richer and more complex and brings to light the deep interdependence between cultural activity and other dimensions of social life. It is important to specify at the start that what the sociologist Fernand Dumont calls "primary culture" (*culture première*) in the anthropological sense of the word — that is, modes of living, thinking and working — is not under examination here. All these areas are discussed directly or indirectly in other sections of this book. This section is devoted instead to activities and phenomena connected with "secondary culture" (*culture seconde*): entertainment, mass media, arts. These activities and phenomena, although tied to "primary culture" and other aspects of social, economic and ideological reality, nevertheless form a relatively autonomous area of study.

To make the discussion easier to follow, we will divide this vast area into two chapters for each period. In the first chapter, we will deal with mass culture — cultural activities either generated by or intended for the public at large. This heading includes such things as the press, mass media, popular theatre and popular music. In the second chapter, the more specialized area of artistic and literary creation will be discussed. This division is of course not an absolute one, and the two areas can overlap. And finally, it would be impossible to mention all the activities involved in culture in our discussion. In each period, we will concentrate on the phenomena that appear to be the most significant ones.

Another obstacle to writing the cultural history of Quebec is that knowledge is still fragmentary. Popular culture, the cultural life of Quebec's various ethnic groups and even the English community, and the material conditions in which writers, musicians and painters did their creative work are among the areas where no research has been done or where it has barely begun.

Despite these reservations, the period between 1930 and 1945 can be described in general terms as an important period of transition that saw the forms, ideas and methods that characterized the overall culture of western societies at the time become increasingly widespread in Quebec. This was the continuation of a process that had begun around the turn of the century and would be largely brought to completion during the war and the postwar years.

Through this process of modernization, the whole cultural landscape of Quebec was radically transformed. The most significant changes took place in the area of mass culture, where traditional activities were clearly in decline. The activities that replaced them were urban in nature and were increasingly integrated into the flow of commerce and consumption. Modernization was also visible in the arts and literature, in the form of an esthetic and ideological renewal marked by the abandonment of traditionalism and a more pronounced tendency towards conceptions and styles in which formal innovation and subjective expression were highly valued. In both areas, a virtual breakthrough occurred as a result of the Second World War, when culture was transformed and brought up to date at a noticeably faster pace.

A Traditional Culture Headed for Extinction

Traditional culture was based on oral transmission and a rural social structure. It consisted of songs, stories, legends, ceremonies and celebrations, and religion played an important role in it. This culture could survive only as long as the society that sustained it. Thus, in Quebec in the 1930s, it remained fairly vigorous in some regions that were still strongly rural, barely touched by radio, movies, newspapers and mass-market books, and not greatly influenced by urban life: Charlevoix, the upper St. Maurice Valley, Beauce-Dorchester, the Gaspé. It was in these regions that the last traces of this vanishing culture would be collected from increasingly elderly informants. The movement towards collection and scientific classification of Quebec folklore began in the late nineteenth century, was exemplified by the work of Marius Barbeau around the time of the First World War, and intensified with the establishment of the Archives de Folklore at Laval University by Luc Lacourcière in 1944. Once a living culture widely shared among Quebecers, traditional culture thus became frozen, and would soon be of interest only to ethnologists, folklorists and collectors.

One such scholar, Jean-Claude Dupont, met a storyteller named Isaïe Jolin in the course of his studies. About fifty years old in 1930, Isaïe had a repertoire of fifty stories, but his father had known about a hundred. On the other hand, his grandson, born around 1950, could barely remember Isaïe's two shortest stories. This example is a good illustration of how modernization severely weakens traditional culture and reduces its role. This process affects not only the content of traditional culture but also its place in a changing society, where a quick death is its inevitable fate.

By the late nineteenth century, most people in Quebec were already literate, even in the countryside. This meant that the cultural role of printed materials was increasing at the expense of oral transmission, and the mass-circulation press took advantage of this change and grew rapidly around the turn of the century. Subsequently, other phenomena presented an even more serious threat to the survival of traditional culture. The rural exodus, along with the development of transportation and communications of various kinds, shattered the relative isolation in which traditional culture had endured until then and subjected it to competition from cultural models and methods that came from the city. In all parts of Quebec, the mail brought newspapers and catalogues from large retailers. Travelling film projectionists, circuses and touring theatre troupes came to small towns and villages all over the province. Relatives and friends who had left the countryside for New England or the cities of Quebec came back for visits by train and car. Meanwhile, villagers and farmers made the reverse journey, going more and more frequently to a nearby town, or even to Montreal to see "St. Joseph's Oratory, the Wax Museum, Belmont Park and La Poune," in the description of "La Poune" herself, the popular comedienne Rose Ouellette. And finally, radio rapidly brought the voices and ideas of the modern world into the villages of Quebec.

The traditional elites and the clergy saw these changes as a direct threat to the whole system of values handed down from previous generations, including language and religion, and thus to the continuation of their own authority. There were a variety of attempts to protect the heritage of traditional culture and the values associated with it. Thus, festivals of folksongs and rural crafts were organized, and Quebec ecclesiastics, taking their cue from the papal encyclical *Divini Illius Magistri* (1929), denounced from the pulpit "impious and immoral books, often diabolically circulated at low prices;...cinema shows and broadcasts."

At the same time, however, attempts were made to use the new cultural instruments in the interests of tradition. Starting in 1937, Abbé Charles-Émile Gadbois's *La bonne chanson* songbooks were distributed in an effort to counter the influence of French and American popular songs by keeping folklore and old-time tunes alive in book form. As a weapon against sensationalistic books and newspapers, religious periodicals were published and the *"bonne presse"* (good press) — Catholic-inspired daily newspapers, often owned by a diocese or a religious community, such as *L'Action Catholique* of Quebec City, *Le Droit* of Ottawa and *Le Bien Public* of Trois-Rivières — was supported. In addition, uplifting biographies of

Gérard Raymond (1932), little Thérèse Gélinas (1936), and Marie-Rose Ferron, the "stigmatized girl of Woonsocket" (1941) were distributed through schools and parish libraries. All these books enjoyed exceptionally wide circulation for the period. Similarly radio, a powerful propaganda medium, was used to defend traditional values through religious discussions, the rebroadcasting of major ceremonies such as the Eucharistic Congress in Quebec City in 1938, and a weekly *Heure catholique* (Catholic hour) on Montreal radio station CKAC. And although film was denounced as a "school for corruption," it too was pressed into service. Thus, Abbé Albert Tessier made documentaries on nature, crafts and the education of women, notably *Femmes dépareillées* (1941 and 1948), Abbé Maurice Proulx produced didactic films on agriculture and colonization (*En pays neufs*, 1934-37; *Sainte-Anne-de-Roquemaure*, 1942), and Abbé Jean-Marie Poitevin made the missionary propaganda film *À la croisée des chemins* (1943).

The New Consumer Culture

This resistance no doubt helped slow down the process of cultural modernization. Under the conditions created by the Depression and the return to the land that accompanied it, conservatism rose sharply in public favour. Conservatives were thus able to defend traditional culture, at least in certain sectors of society, especially in rural areas. But this slowdown did not last long, and as soon as prosperity returned these sectors rejoined the overall trend towards what could be called the urbanization of culture. Starting in the 1920s, and especially after 1930, it was in the cities — and most notably in Montreal — that new cultural models were established. This was particularly true in the whole area of mass culture, which was rapidly taking on the features of a consumer culture in Quebec as in other industrial societies.

Even in an urban context, there were interesting examples of "recycling," or the adaptation of old practices to modern life, and traditional culture was continued in this way. From their rural past, French Canadians retained a set of ideas and habits that they adapted to their new environment with varying degrees of success. Traditional dances, participation songs, reels and jigs continued to enliven family evenings in the working-class neighbourhoods of Montreal and Quebec City. Corpus Christi and Rogation processions gathered at De Lorimier Stadium in Montreal or near the Basilica in Quebec City as they once had at the village crossroads. Radio programs and mass-circulation newspapers were haunted by werewolves and dancing devils, whose wondrous deeds were reported along with those of Lindbergh and the builders of the Empire State Building.

But even these surviving elements were destined to fade as new cultural products, coming mostly from the United States and laden with the prestige associated with modernity, became widespread. In opposition to traditional culture, where participation was of the essence, in this new context individuals were seen primarily as consumers of culture, and they were offered a variety of perishable goods to fill their leisure time, based on the tastes, wishes and means of the majority. In this way, a mass entertainment industry developed, dominated by a few large producers (almost all foreign) and dependent on such factors as disposable income and time, access to markets, and production and distribution capacity. All these factors were greatly encouraged by urbanization and the development of what would later be called mass media.

The daily press, with its serialized novels, columns and advertisements, was already well established. Circulation stagnated through the Depression years but began to grow again during the war. In Montreal, two large dailies, *La Presse* (founded in 1884) and the Montreal *Star* (1869), had circulations of more than 125,000 in 1940. At least four other papers also had substantial readerships; in order of circulation, they were the *Gazette* (1778), *La Patrie* (1879), *Le Devoir* (1910) and *Le Canada* (1903). In Quebec City, *Le Soleil* and *L'Action Catholique* had roughly equal circulations, with *L'Événement* (1867; called *L'Événement-Journal* after 1938) not far behind. There was also a newspaper in almost every region: *Le Nouvelliste* (1920) in Trois-Rivières, *La Tribune* (1910) in Sherbrooke, *Le Progrès du Saguenay* (1887) in Chicoutimi. Until the late 1930s, most of these newspapers were linked to the major political parties. However, with the change of government in Ottawa in 1935 and Quebec City in 1936 and the growth of paid advertising, they were able to break free of this domination and not only print a larger quantity of news but also present it in a more neutral manner and pitch it to the widest possible readership. Opinion journalism took refuge in the numerous partisan sheets that arose out of the ideological effervescence of the Depression. Very few of these survived the war.

Meanwhile, popular periodicals grew rapidly during the war. The *Revue Populaire* and the *Revue Moderne* had a combined circulation of about 150,000 in 1945. Three large Montreal weekly newspapers were distributed across the province — *Le Petit Journal* (1926), *La Patrie du Dimanche* (1935) and *Photo-Journal* (1937). With their populist-flavoured journalism, they quickly reached a combined circulation of almost half a million, and they continued to grow until the late 1960s.

But the most characteristic expressions of mass culture during the period were two new media: radio and talking pictures.

Radio

Radio was invented at the turn of the century, but it did not begin to become widespread until after the First World War, and even then it grew slowly. As late as 1931, according to the historian Elzéar Lavoie, there were only three radio stations in Quebec and only 27.8 per cent of households had radio sets — 37.5 per cent in the cities and a mere 8.4 per cent in rural areas, where most homes were still without electricity. Growth speeded up during the 1930s, although it was still much slower than in

Ontario or the United States. In 1941, there were sixteen stations in Quebec, fourteen of them French-language, and more than two thirds of households had sets. There was still a wide gap between the countryside, where only 41 per cent of households had radios, and the cities, where 85.1 per cent had them. Taking this gap (which would not be narrowed until the postwar period and the movement towards rural electrification) into account, Lavoie identifies 1936 as the approximate date when radio became, for Quebec as a whole, a major means of communication — a "mass medium."

From the early years of the century, Ottawa had endeavoured to assert its control over radio broadcasting in Canada, at least in principle. Before the Depression, however, it had left the field to the private sector, and the result was a rather anarchic situation that provided fertile ground for substantial penetration by American radio. In 1929, the Aird Commission reacted to this situation with proposals for Canadianization of the airwaves and vigorous intervention by the federal government. Three years later, despite strong opposition from the private sector and provincial governments, Ottawa established the Canadian Radio Broadcasting Commission (CRBC), which operated two stations in Quebec, in Chicoutimi and Montreal. But it was not until 1936, when the CRBC was transformed into a stronger organism under the name of the Canadian Broadcasting Corporation, that the federal government began to play a forceful role in radio broadcasting. The Aird Commission had recommended nationalizing the private stations, but Ottawa did not go quite that far. Nevertheless, it did place those stations under surveillance by the new CBC, which was given the task of regulating radio broadcasting across Canada. At the same time, the CBC was mandated to operate its own large national production and distribution system. In 1936, this network represented 75 per cent of the transmission power in Canada. The CBC's Quebec Regional Network, as of 1945, comprised owned and operated stations in Montreal, Quebec City and Chicoutimi and affiliated stations in a variety of regions. This network constituted the largest distributor of radio programming in Quebec, along with the private Montreal station CKAC, which had been founded by *La Presse* in 1922 and continued to occupy a leading position. In relation to community size, Anglophone Quebecers were better served than Francophones. In Montreal, for example, there were two stations — CBM (CBC) and CFCF (Marconi) — broadcasting entirely in English, while even on officially French-language CKAC, 34 per cent of the programs were in English in 1940. The reasons for this situation were that there was a higher proportion of radios in English-speaking neighbourhoods and that Anglophones represented a prime target group for advertisers.

Thus, radio was controlled either by the government or by newspaper corporations that wanted to preserve their advertising market. Programming was almost all live and was dominated by entertainment. On CKAC, for example, entertainment programming occupied about 75 per cent of air time and provided the context for the broadcast of a large number of commercials. On the CBC, a large part of entertainment programming consisted of classical music, with programs such as *L'heure symphonique* (1938) and the Metropolitan Opera broadcast from New York (1931), and drama, with series such as *Radio-théâtre* (1938) and *Le théâtre chez soi* (1939). But the highest ratings went to CKAC, which won listeners with its broadcasts of popular songs and comedies such as *Nazaire et Barnabé* (1939) and *Zézette* (1938). The advent of *Le curé de village* in 1935 marked the beginning of a form of programming that would be extremely popular until the 1950s: the radio serial. The popularity of this genre became firmly established between 1938 and 1940, when serials such as *La pension Velder* (1938), *Un homme et son péché (1939) and Jeunesse dorée* (1940) were introduced on the CBC's French-language CBF.

In the area of educational programming, the Quebec government sponsored a twice-weekly *Heure provinciale* (Provincial hour) on CKAC starting in 1929, while the CBC inaugurated its *Radio-Collège* in 1941. The *causerie* or radio talk was also much favoured, and provided a forum for many intellectuals and religious figures including Lionel Groulx, the thinkers of the Action Libérale Nationale, and Father Marcel-Marie Desmarais, who discussed the question "Is love a sin?" on the air. Information, meanwhile, accounted for only 10 per cent of programming during the 1930s. Radio stations were not very daring in their news programming, and most often simply repeated the contents of the newspapers that owned them. This situation changed when the CBC, in an effort to attract CKAC's listeners, used the royal visit of May 1939, the first by a reigning British monarch to Canada, and later the outbreak of hostilities in Europe to introduce a programming mix in which information played a large role. The commentator Louis Francoeur was an outstanding exemplar of this new emphasis. The CBC's French-language news service was established in 1941, and with information under federal control during the war, news and current affairs occupied an increasing proportion of the network's air time. Subject to censorship from 1939 on, CBC radio openly became an instrument of patriotic and government propaganda.

The impact of radio on cultural life cannot be overestimated. On the one hand, radio made it possible for new groups to have access to cultural activities — drama, literature, music — from which they had hitherto been practically cut off because of distance or lack of means. On the other, for professional artists — musicians, playwrights, actors, writers — radio represented a wider market and thus a significant source of income. This was especially true in Quebec, where American radio did not penetrate as strongly as in English Canada because of the language barrier. As a result, conditions were better for the production of a large number of local programs. The years from the mid-1930s to the mid-1950s can be described as the golden age of radio. Reaching almost all Quebec homes (88 per cent in 1947), it was the most powerful medium of communication and its influence was felt in all sectors of cultural activity.

Movies

Silent movies were very popular in Quebec in the 1920s. At the beginning of the Depression, a drop in attendance at movie theatres was noticed, but growth began again in 1934 and movies quickly became the most popular form of entertainment. The number of movie theatres in Quebec increased from 134 in 1933 to 190 in 1940 and 228 in 1945. The war marked the beginning of a virtual explosion that intensified after peace was restored.

The most important factor in this growth was the introduction in 1928 of talking pictures, which quickly became widespread in Quebec — as early as 1931, they were offered by half the movie theatres in the province. Another result of this new development was that an increased number of films from France were shown in Quebec. During the silent era, almost all the movies shown in Quebec came from the United States. These movies were shown with or without translation, as language was not a major problem. With the appearance of talking pictures, however, the

A CBC war correspondent in Italy, 1943. (CBC, National Archives of Canada, C-66238)

market changed, creating a favourable climate for films imported from France, which were now successfully offered by a number of French Canadian distribution companies, notably the Compagnie Cinémato-graphique Canadienne and France-Film, established in 1932, on which a large number of movie theatres across Quebec were dependent for their product. From 1930 on, the Saint-Denis Theatre in Monteal became the hub of French-language cinema in Quebec. In 1934, for example, it attracted more than 70,000 people to see Duvivier's Maria Chapdelaine. Of course, American distributors, led by Famous Players, continued to occupy a large share of the market, and Quebec theatres continued to show considerably more English-language than French-language films until after the war. Nevertheless, for the film-viewing public in Quebec, the discovery of the French sensibility — French directors, French movie stars, a French way of speaking — was a major development of the 1930s. Some people at the time, and especially the people in charge of France-Film, saw this development as a contribution to nationalism and patriotism.

The war and the occupation of France after 1940 represented a setback to this breakthrough by French film, as supply became a problem for the distributors. France-Film had to diversify into concerts and vaudeville. More than half the theatres that had shown French movies either closed their doors or turned to American movies instead. American film in-creased its market share significantly during this period, and more and more American movies were dubbed in French.

The lack of availability of French movies at a time when attendance at theatres was larger than ever also provided a modest spur to local pro-duction, which until then had been nonexistent or carried out on a very small scale. There was virtually no French-language component at the National Film Board, established by Ottawa in 1939, and until the end of the war almost all of the board's output consisted of short propaganda films. Outside the NFB, films produced in Quebec were few and far between; they generally contained a religious or patriotic message and rarely reached commercial theatres. During the war, however, the first Quebec feature films were produced: *Notre-Dame de la Mouïse* (1941), produced in France by the Montreal company France-Film; Jean-Marie Poitevin's *À la croisée des chemins* (1943); and especially *Le père Chopin* (1944). Produced by Renaissance Films and with a cast made up of actors from both France and Quebec, *Le père Chopin* was the first professional feature film shot in Quebec and was a notable popular success.

Popular Theatre

The growing popularity of movies brought about a thorough shakeup in the whole area of urban entertainment. Even in the First World War era, the popularity of silent movies brought to an end what John Hare has called the golden age of theatre in Montreal and seriously compromised the position of other forms of entertainment such as circuses and amusement parks. The situation became worse with the growing availability of talking pictures, and theatre in particular was thrown into a virtual crisis.

Some forms of popular theatre managed to survive, however, and even flourished to a degree after 1930. There was a wide audience for melodrama, vaudeville, light comedy, music hall and burlesque. These forms could also be combined with a movie in a single show, and this practice became widespread in the 1920s and remained common until the late 1930s.

The dominant form of popular theatre during the period was burlesque. Introduced before 1914 by touring American troupes, it remained an essentially English-language medium until 1920, when the troupe led by "Ti-Zoune" (Olivier Guimond, Sr.) began to present bilingual shows, and later ones that were entirely French. From then on, burlesque grew rapidly, especially after the Théâtre National in Montreal, founded in 1900 as a repertory theatre, switched over to the new form and became the mecca of burlesque and variety. It maintained this position until about 1950, notably because of the work of Rose Ouellette (La Poune), who ran the theatre from 1936 on. Scorned by the intellectual elite and suspected of immorality by the authorities, burlesque was a form that combined improvisation, humour, song, dance and colourful popular speech. Highly popular between 1930 and 1950, its success soon spread to all parts of Quebec, especially through the yearly tours of Jean Grimaldi and his troupe. Another popular form throughout the period was melodrama, as can be seen in the uninterrupted success of *Aurore la petite enfant martyre* from the time it was first produced in 1921. In quantitative terms at least, theatre in Quebec consisted essentially of burlesque, melodrama and similar forms during this period.

Music

Quebec had always had a particularly active musical life, consisting of traditional popular music, church music and, in the cities, even concerts and opera. Starting in the 1930s, as radio became increasingly available and the recording industry developed, the popularity of music grew steadily.

Thus, the promotion of the *"chanson canadienne"* helped traditional tunes remain popular in an urban context. Lionel Daunais, Paul-Émile Corbeil and the Quatuor Alouette sang old-time songs on the radio or in recitals such as the *"Veillées du bon vieux temps"* staged at the Monument National in Montreal from 1921 to 1941. Other artists, working within the spirit of the folk tradition, wrote new songs that evoked the vagaries and miseries of city life during the Great Depression for a wide audience. One such artist was Ovila Légaré, who wrote songs like "La Bastringue" and "Faut pas s'faire de bile" that gained considerable popular success.

But the most popular singer of the era was undoubtedly La Bolduc (née Mary Travers), who between 1928 and 1941 composed almost three hundred songs, many of which reached large audiences through records,

La Bolduc. (DOLQ)

and gave innumerable concerts throughout Quebec, Ontario and New England. Her songs were embellished with "turlutage," a technique comparable to mouth music or scat singing, and written in a language that was lively and close to popular speech. She came from the Gaspé to Montreal where she worked as a maid and a factory worker and became the mother of a large family. Many of her songs were inspired by these personal experiences, while others were taken from current events and daily life: unemployment ("Sans travail"), technological novelties ("Toujours l'R100"), politics ("Le nouveau gouvernement"), and miscellaneous occurrences ("Les cinq jumelles Dionne," "As-tu vu l'éclipse"). During the war, another popular singer, Roland Lebrun, known as "Le Soldat Lebrun," gained wide success with plaintive country tunes such as "Je suis loin de toi mignonne" and "L'adieu du soldat." He too became, in Gilles Potvin's description, "the bard of ordinary people up against the difficulties of daily life."

*   *   *   *   *   *

Despite the popularity of La Bolduc, La Poune and the Quebec radio stars of the era, two characteristics of the mass culture that spread through Quebec between 1930 and 1945 should not be forgotten. First, access to this culture and the new products that came with it was still very unequally distributed, and whole sectors of the population were largely or wholly left out of it for economic or geographic reasons. And second, this culture was largely conceived and distributed by foreign producers, and if Quebecers had a role in this entertainment industry, it was most often limited to presentation, translation or adaptation. But outside nationalist and clerical circles, few people were disturbed by this situation. For the public, it was much more important to participate in this new culture and enter fully into the modern world of which it was the most seductive manifestation.

CHAPTER 13

ORDER AND ADVENTURE

The audience for literature, visual arts, repertory theatre and classical music is characterized by a high level of education and membership in the economically favoured sectors of the population. While economic and commercial constraints have a significant influence on these forms of cultural expression just as they do on mass culture, it is not felt as directly or as definitively. As a result, ideological and esthetic issues are more immediately relevant and indigenous work has a more noticeable impact.

However, Quebec's cultural infrastructure was not highly developed between 1930 and 1945. Since government measures in the cultural sphere were sporadic and uncoordinated, the entire burden of support fell to private initiative. On the Anglophone side, a few wealthy Montreal families supported the major cultural institutions. In the Francophone community, cultural support was largely the responsibility of the church, notably through its classical colleges and seminaries, which outside Montreal were almost the only active cultural centres. Such institutions as the Collège de Joliette, the Collège de Rimouski and the Collège de Saint-Laurent played a key role in encouraging and disseminating literature, theatre, music and the visual arts. But despite these few oases, Quebec's cultural infrastructure as a whole was far from adequate.

Quebec's cultural community was essentially urban. It was small and could not grow much because of the Depression. Two groups were particularly influential: the clergy, which was in charge of education and the major cultural institutions within the Francophone community, and the Anglophone bourgeoisie. While there were disagreements within these groups, they both had distinct conservative tendencies in cultural matters. Some artists fell in with this conservatism, while others, insisting on greater autonomy and taking their inspiration from movements outside Quebec, sought to be freer in their artistic expression and to develop it along more modern lines. The title of this chapter, taken from a study of Quebec poetry between 1934 and 1944 by the critic Jacques Blais, is an attempt to evoke this duality.

On one side stood "order": a form of traditionalism tracing its roots to the second half of the nineteenth century that remained dominant in Quebec's cultural rhetoric and institutions until after the Depression. But because this traditionalism was so rigid and ill-suited to new realities, it came under increasing challenge. Thus another tendency, which also had earlier roots but had hitherto been able to express itself only occasionally or on the cultural margins, became a significant part of Quebec's cultural life during the 1930s, although it did not yet gain the upper hand. This was "adventure": the trend towards intellectual and artistic modernity. The new forms, new themes and new ideas that characterized twentieth-century culture increasingly insisted on making themselves heard.

A turning point in this development was the Second World War — a tragedy for Europe, but an opportunity for Quebec to become more open to international influences and to emerge for a few years as one of the most active artistic and intellectual centres in the French-speaking world. There was a proliferation of publishing houses, magazines and cultural productions. Many of the prestigious writers, musicians, philosophers, painters, theatre directors and actors who fled Europe landed in Montreal, either as a place of refuge or as a stop on the way to New York. They brought modern ideas with them, providing support for the forces of renewal already active within Quebec. From this starting point, the relative positions of the two tendencies would be reversed, and more and more of Quebec's literary and artistic output would contribute to the growing spirit of "adventure."

Artists

Little is known about the conditions under which painters, musicians, actors and writers worked at the time. There were many Anglophone artists, of British or Jewish origin, especially in music and the fine arts. Francophone artists were educated in the classical colleges and were generally members of the petty bourgeoisie: civil servants, clerics, lawyers, doctors, and especially journalists. Because there was hardly any government assistance and audiences generally preferred works from Paris, London or New York to local ones, very few artists could really make a living from their artistic output. In the case of painters, the Depression was a serious blow, as collectors and buyers were both less numerous and more cautious than they had been before. Writers almost all did their work in the context of intellectual movements, magazines, publishing houses or newspapers that owed their existence to church support; there were few independent writers. Radio rapidly became a significant source of income for actors and musicians, who supported themselves through whatever work they could get. Many artists — especially painters and musicians — chose to live in Europe, where the surroundings were more suited to the needs of their profession. But the war forced them to return home, and for a few years a new climate developed in Quebec encouraging innovation and change.

Literature

While books were a favourite means of expression for some groups, they had very little influence in the population as a whole. The reason for this was that distribution networks — libraries and bookstores — were completely ineffective. French-speaking Quebec was far behind English Canada in this regard. According to a 1937 study, 460 of Canada's 642 public libraries were in Ontario while only twenty-six were in Quebec. Furthermore, seventeen of the Quebec libraries were English-language ones. Anglophone Montrealers could borrow books from such large libraries as the Westmount Public Library, the Fraser Institute (closed during the Depression) and the Mechanics' Institute. Francophones, meanwhile, had to choose between the Saint-Sulpice Library (closed between 1931 and 1944) and the Montreal Municipal Library, housed in a lavish building on Sherbrooke Street but with a collection of only 70,000 books in 1933. Furthermore, use of the Municipal Library was limited by the fact that members were required to pay a deposit until 1943. Outside Montreal and Quebec City there were only parish libraries, with few resources and little activity. The result was that Francophone Quebecers had little opportunity to become interested in reading. Elsewhere in Canada, there was a large increase in library attendance and book borrowing because of the Depression, but this did not happen in Quebec. The low level of education already limited reading in Quebec, and the poor library system aggravated the situation. During the war, people began to become concerned about Quebec's backwardness in this regard and there were a few hesitant attempts to correct it, with the result that library attendance increased slightly from 1941 on. But it was not until the 1960s that any real policies were initiated in this area.

Quebec's bookstore network was not much better. At the end of the war there were only about forty bookstores in Quebec, including bookstores aimed at the school market. In Montreal, a few independent bookstores had a small clientèle made up of students, intellectuals and members of the liberal professions. These customers bought imported French books at Déom or Pony and second-hand books at Ducharme or the Librairie Françoyse, which Henri Tranquille opened in 1937. Other major bookstores were all associated with magazines, publishing houses or nationalist or other movements, and most of them were closely linked to the clergy.

The church's role in the literary world was a determining one, bordering on outright control. On one level, the clergy was itself a major publisher. Even more important was its position in the educational system — both private (classical colleges and universities) and public (the Catholic committee of the Council of Public Instruction), which made it the leading customer for bookstores and publishing houses. Beyond that, its moral authority was virtually unchallenged. In addition to the *Index* drawn up in Rome, which constituted a list of works forbidden throughout the Catholic world, each bishop could act within the limits of his diocese. Thus in 1934 the archbishop of Quebec, Cardinal Villeneuve, banned Jean-Charles Harvey's novel *Les demi-civilisés* "under pain of mortal sin." While in Montreal the book was a sensational bestseller, in Quebec City Harvey was quickly fired from his job as editor-in-chief of *Le Soleil*. And finally, the clergy was very active in the intellectual circles and nationalist movements that were the source of most of Quebec's literary output in the 1930s.

It was in this period that literary publishing in Quebec really got its start, as one of the activities of a revitalized nationalist movement that wanted to disseminate its views more widely among educated Quebecers. While publishing houses such as Beauchemin, Granger, Garneau, Fides (founded in 1937) and the Centre Pédagogique (1940) served the educational and religious market, new publishers directed at the general public were making their appearance under the sponsorship of bookstores and magazines. Among these were the Librairie d'Action Française, established in 1919 and acquired by Albert Lévesque in 1926; Éditions du Totem, founded in 1933 by Albert Pelletier, publisher of the magazine *Les Idées*; and Éditions du Zodiaque (1935).

While there were significant variations of emphasis from one publisher to the next, underlying all the works they published was a concern for developing and disseminating a distinctively "Canadian" literature, different in both form and substance from contemporary French literature, which some Quebecers considered decadent. This distinctive literature was seen as an expression of the national values of French Canada and consisted primarily of essays and novels, which were better vehicles than poetry for propagating ideology. In a time of crisis, essays could be used both to reaffirm the major conservative themes and to explore new avenues that did not represent a radical break with tradition. Lionel Groulx (*Directives*, 1937) and Camille Roy (*Pour conserver notre héritage français*, 1937) were still among the major nationalist thinkers, but they were joined by others who tried to adapt traditional nationalism to modern reality: social scientists such as Édouard Montpetit (*La conquête économique*, 1938) and Esdras Minville (*Notre milieu*, 1942), historians such as Gustave Lanctôt (*Le Canada d'hier et d'aujourd'hui*, 1934) and Jean Bruchési (*L'épopée canadienne*, 1934) and pamphleteers such as Victor Barbeau (*Pour nous grandir*, 1937) and Claude-Henri Grignon (*Les pamphlets de Valdombre*, 1936-43). The best novels of the period took their inspiration from older forms and themes: stories with pastoral (Claude-Henri Grignon's *Un homme et son péché*) [*The Woman and the Miser*], Ringuet's *Trente arpents* [*Thirty Acres*], Germaine Guèvremont's *Le Survenant* [*Outlander*] or forest (Félix-Antoine Savard's *Menaud maître-draveur* [*The Master of the River*], Léo-Paul Desrosiers's *Les engagés du Grand Portage* [*The*

Making of Nicholas Montour]) settings. Few works were at all innovative in their content or mode of expression.

But these novels' claim to carry forward traditional themes was undermined by their symbolic content, which showed that the worldview associated with conservative nationalism was a spent force — the madness of Séraphin Poudrier and Menaud, Euchariste Moisan's exile, the instability of the "Grand dieu des routes." While the nationalists still held centre–stage, and their doctrine remained the dominant one in literary institutions, another literary current was making its appearance in the wings. Its primary medium was poetry, its audience was very limited, and its exponents included the best writers of the period. The breath of universalism in Robert Choquette's *Metropolitan Museum* (1931), the love lyrics of Jovette Bernier (*Les masques déchirés*, 1932) and Medjé Vézina (*Chaque heure a son visage*, 1934) and the Depression-inspired social description of Jean Narrache (*J'parl' pour parler*, 1939) and Clément Marchand (*Les soirs rouges*, 1939) all marked a departure from the *terroir* school of the preceding decades. But the most significant break with the past came in 1934 when a group of writers and intellectuals founded *La Relève*, a magazine of ideas, criticism and creativity. These writers were more interested in a fully developed humanism than in national questions and saw art and literature as independent of ideology and politics. Rejecting the traditionalism of official circles, they embraced contemporary French literature in a quest for modes of expression that were personal and modern. Notable among these was the poet Saint-Denys Garneau, whose *Regards et jeux dans l'espace* was published in Montreal in 1937:

Je marche à côté d'une joie[1]
D'une joie qui n'est pas à moi
D'une joie à moi que je ne puis pas prendre....

In their disregard for classical conventions of versification, their quest for simple but novel imagery, and especially conception of poetry as a spiritual adventure in which the poet is intimately involved, such poems represented a major breakthrough which — as some readers and critics were able to see at the time — constituted the beginning of a renewal of Quebec literature. Other poets (such as Alain Grandbois, who published his first poems in Hankou, China, in 1934) were also paving the way for this renewal, as were a few critics and essayists who were more interested

1   I walk beside a joy
     A joy that is not mine
     A joy of mine that is not mine to enjoy....

in esthetic questions than in nationalist propaganda: Louis Dantin, who lived as an expatriate in the United States, René Garneau, François Hertel.

These new currents were marginal during the 1930s but came to sudden prominence when Quebec's literary world was shaken up by the war. With the French publishing industry paralysed by the Nazi occupation, Quebec publishers stepped into the breach; overnight, their vitality and variety reached new heights. There was a proliferation of new secular publishing houses: Valiquette (1939), L'Arbre (1940), Variétés (1941), Pascal (1943). A number of new magazines devoted to modern art and ideas were started: *Regards* (1940), *La Nouvelle Relève* (1941), *Amérique Française* (1941), *Gants du Ciel* (1943). Books that had previously been hard to get because of church control were now published freely in Montreal: the poetry of Arthur Rimbaud, the "dangerous" novels of André Gide and Georges Bernanos, Descartes's *Discourse on Method* and the writings of the French existentialists. There was a steep rise in editorial output, from eighty-two titles in 1940 to 417 in 1944. In all, nearly twenty-one million books were printed between 1940 and 1947. A large proportion of this output was exported to South America, the United States and even Australia, but the local market expanded as well. Newspapers devoted more space to books, which were no longer marginal as they had been in the past but had become a more available and abundant consumer item.

One effect of this explosion of publishing activity was to make it easier for readers to discover contemporary world literature. As a consequence, it also encouraged the emergence within Quebec of new works that were more open to modern influence. In poetry, this movement had begun during the 1930s, and it continued during the war with works such as Gilles Hénault's "L'invention de la roue" and Rina Lasnier's *Images et proses* in 1941, Anne Hébert's *Les songes en équilibre* in 1942, and Alain Grandbois's *Les îles de la nuit*, Carl Dubuc's *Jazz vers l'infini* and Edmond Labelle's *La quête de l'existence*, all published in 1944. Innovation soon spread from poetry, aimed at a small audience, to novels, which reached a much wider public. A number of works published between 1941 and 1945 paved the way for the new postwar Quebec novel. Robert Charbonneau's *Ils posséderont la terre* represented the beginning of the psychological novel in Quebec, while Roger Lemelin's *Au pied de la pente douce* and Gabrielle Roy's *Bonheur d'occasion* (*The Tin Flute*) made urban settings — which represented daily reality for a large majority of readers — part of the literary world. There was also Yves Thériault's *Contes pour un homme seul*, which provided an antidote to agrarian idealism in the form of a wilder, more pagan vision of nature.

At the same time, two works by Hugh MacLennan — *Barometer Rising* (1941) and *Two Solitudes* (1945) — inaugurated a comparable renewal in the English-language novel. Their realism and the immediacy of the problems they addressed represented a break with the past; until then, English Canadian fiction had been limited to regional idylls and historical novels, typified by the work of the prolific Alan Sullivan. But the dynamism of English Montreal writers was most clearly visible in poetry.

A notable development was the formation during the 1930s of the "Montreal group," made up of A.J.M. Smith, Frank R. Scott, Leo Kennedy and A.M. Klein, who published the joint collection *New Provinces* in 1936. Departing from the Victorian nationalist tradition, these poets wrote in spare, daring language and took up universal themes along with the social and political concerns that could not be ignored during the Depression. During the war, this activity not only continued but became more intense. Two magazines were started: *First Statement*, which published young poets such as Raymond Souster, Irving Layton and Louis Dudek, and *Preview*, where Patrick Anderson, P.K. Page and A.M. Klein expressed their social apprehensions. These magazines were initially rivals, but in 1945 they merged as the *Northern Review*, which continued publishing until 1956.

There was little contact between French-language and English-language literature. Their respective traditions, sources, foreign references (France on one side, Britain and the United States on the other), networks of writers and audiences all worked to keep them apart. In addition, while Montreal was still a significant centre of English Canadian literature, it was only one among several. The hub of English Canadian literary activity was Toronto, where the major publishers were located.

In conclusion, the war, with its short-lived publishing boom, represented a decisive turning point in Quebec literature and marked the transition from a conservative nationalism that defended the old "order" to a modernism that placed a higher value on novelty and "adventure."

Gabrielle Roy at the time of *The Tin Flute*. (Basil Zarov)

The Visual Arts

Painting in Quebec between 1930 and 1945 was also characterized by a clash between "order" and "adventure" and a gradual transition from one to the other. The Depression made art lovers and collectors, who were never much inclined to take a chance on novelty, even less so. They stuck to the tried and true, and above all to landscapes. Their taste included both the northern landscapes made popular in the 1920s by the Toronto-based Group of Seven and more intimate Quebec nature scenes in the manner of early-twentieth-century postimpressionist landscape painters such as Maurice Cullen, James Wilson Morrice, Marc-Aurèle de Foy Suzor-Côté and Clarence Gagnon. Suzor-Côté and Gagnon, both still active after 1930, also influenced some younger painters such as René Richard, the painter-trapper of Baie-Saint-Paul, and Rodolphe Duguay, who painted and engraved rural and traditional scenes in the Nicolet region.

Regionalist themes thus proved durable, and they took new strength from a revitalized traditionalist nationalism that tried to deal with the Depression by returning to the past. These themes were the occasion for a large number of conventional works, but a few artists treated them in a new way. While continuing to paint picturesque local scenes, these artists also pursued more formal objectives. Notable among them was Marc-Aurèle Fortin, whose rugged, passionate vision of the land was expressed in his treatment of the large elms in his native Sainte-Rose northwest of Montreal and of villages surrounded by mountains in Charlevoix and the Gaspé. His canvases, especially his "black enamel" works of the early 1930s, reflect a highly personal interpretation of nature, with strong lines and a vivid palette. Fortin's work was very popular among the Francophone upper classes until the war, then was out of fashion for several decades before coming back into favour after the artist's death in 1970. Goodridge Roberts, who settled in Montreal in 1936, was as prolific a painter as Fortin and continued to paint until the 1960s. The infinite variations in his oils and watercolours are inspired by the look of a number of regions of Quebec, especially the Eastern Townships. His work constitutes a long meditation on light, colour and the forms of nature as filtered through a specific view and temperament.

Although rural scenes dominated landscape painting during the period, perpetuating a rather traditional view of Quebec and its ways of life, some artists were interested in the city. Fortin himself painted a series of panoramas of Montreal harbour and the east-end Hochelaga neighbourhood, while Philip Surrey painted his first Montreal canvases in the late 1930s. But the leading urban painter of the period was Adrien Hébert, whose canvases consistently reflected the variety and richness of the Montreal cityscape and modern functionalist architecture. Urban settings were also a favourite theme of Montreal Jewish artists such as Louis Muhlstock, Jack Beder and Sam Borenstein.

Adrien Hébert, *Élévateur à grain no. 3.* (Musée du Québec)

Painting urban settings represented a break with the primitivism and ruralism of the conventional Canadian or Quebec landscape and reflected a desire to update the practice of art by bringing it closer to modern life. On the whole, however, there was a wide gap between these experiments and the avant-garde movements that had been transforming the European art scene since the turn of the century. The most significant of these movements was abstract or nonfigurative painting, which regarded the canvas as an autonomous object, subject to its own formal or expressive laws, rather than as a representation of external reality. Resistance to the "adventure" of modern art remained widespread in Quebec art circles, and it was not fully accepted until the late 1940s.

However, a movement in this direction began to take shape between 1930 and 1945. During this period, according to the art historian Esther Trépanier, there was a "crisis of the visual arts," characterized by a "struggle against the hegemony of national themes ... in the name of the universality of human experience, the absolute primacy of subjective expression, the right to experiment with form, and a greater openness to contemporary international movements." A number of critics, such as Henri Girard of the newspaper *Le Canada* and Robert Ayre of the Montreal *Standard*, supported this movement towards a "living art," as it was called at the time.

It was primarily in the Montreal Anglophone community that the movement in this direction began; John Lyman, who had lived in Europe for a long time and was in close touch with the theoretical and stylistic ferment taking place there, was a central figure. Through his own paintings, but even more through his work as an organizer and his articles in *The Montrealer*, he became the champion of new forms of painting both in artistic circles and among the general public, introducing Quebecers to such movements as expressionism, Fauvism, cubism and futurism. Other Anglophone artists, influenced by contemporary trends in the United States, were concerned both with formal investigation and with questions such as the social function and democratization of art and the social or even political involvement of the artist. Thus, the avant-garde painters Fritz Brandtner and Marian Scott were associates of Dr. Norman Bethune and became involved in a variety of progressive activities.

The Contemporary Art Society was founded by Lyman, Brandtner and others in 1939 and soon mounted an exhibition of contemporary European works entitled *Art of Our Day* at the Art Association in Montreal. A number of Francophones joined the Contemporary Art Society, which until its dissolution in 1948 organized an annual exhibition of paintings by its members and other activities aimed at promoting modern art.

But approval for what the regionalist painter Clarence Gagnon called "the huge joke of modern art" was far from being widespread. Here too, it was the war that made a real breakthrough possible. In 1940 Alfred Pellan, who had lived in France since 1926 and exhibited his works along with those of Fernand Léger, Max Ernst and Picasso, came back to Quebec. He mounted a major exhibition of 150 of his canvases, first in Quebec City and then in Montreal. Revealing the artist's superb command of line and colour, overflowing imagination and sensuality, and complete refusal to be bound by themes and forms received from the past, the exhibition constituted a "panorama of what can generally be referred to as modern art," in the words of the art historian Guy Robert. It was a revelation. Pellan quickly became the leader of the avant-garde. The École des Beaux-Arts in Montreal, which had refused to hire him in 1936, made him a professor in 1943. A number of young artists who sought to replace the prevailing conformity with innovation, spontaneity and art that was closer to contemporary sensibility gathered around Pellan. When Pellan's fervent opponent Charles Maillard was forced to resign as director of the École des Beaux-Arts in 1945, it represented an initial victory for these artists.

At the same time as Pellan, another painter, Paul-Émile Borduas, also exercised a decisive influence on the movement towards modernization. Borduas studied under Ozias Leduc in his youth, and was initially interested in church painting. In Europe he discovered the work of Maurice Denis, a French painter who sought to develop a form of religious art that incorporated the parameters of modern art. Back in Quebec, he continued his discovery of the whole spectrum of modern painting through reading, through his contact with John Lyman and other exponents of modernity, and through his experience as a teacher at the École du Meuble, founded in 1934. His ideas developed rapidly. In 1942 he began to exhibit non-figurative gouaches in which improvisation played a large role. He subsequently developed a technique of painting analogous to *écriture automatique*, the surrealist form of stream-of-consciousness writing, which he saw as a way of expressing the artists's drives and inner reality. He soon attracted a substantial following among young artists, and he served as the intellectual leader of the *automatiste* movement until the end of the decade.

Modern art became a major issue in Quebec art circles before and during the war. Group shows such as the exhibition of the *Indépendants* in Quebec City and Montreal in 1941 and that of the *Sagittaires* at the Dominion Gallery in 1943 became landmark events. Modern art became a cause for intellectuals: François Hertel published his "Plaidoyer en faveur de l'art abstrait" (plea for abstract art) in 1942 and the French Dominican Marie-Alain Couturier criticized "the divorce between artists and the public" in his lectures and writings. All the conditions had been created for modern painting to burst forth after the war as it never had before.

Paul-Émile Borduas, *Abstraction 14 ou Étude de torse*, gouache, 1942.
(Adrien Borduas Collection)

Repertory Theatre

After the First World War, "serious" theatre all but disappeared from the Quebec stage. This dark period persisted through the Depression, as can be seen in the difficulties faced by the Stella, which Fred Barry and Albert Duquesne established in 1930 to present plays from the French repertoire in Montreal. After two seasons, the rise of new forms of urban entertainment forced the Stella to deviate from its original purpose and present variety shows and melodramas before its stage was replaced by a movie screen in 1935. Establishment of the Stella was followed by a number of other initiatives, such as the 1935 performance of Yvette Mercier-Gouin's new three-act play *Cocktail*, but they were isolated endeavours and led nowhere.

Because repertory theatre could not operate profitably, its only possibility for renewal lay in amateur productions. In the late 1930s, as an extension of the Catholic Action movements active at the time, student troupes were formed with the aim of presenting what was then considered avant-garde theatre. Among these troupes were the Paraboliers du Roi, established by Father Gustave Lamarche in Joliette in 1939, and — most notably — the Compagnons de Saint-Laurent, founded by Father Émile Legault in Montreal in 1937. The Compagnons were influenced by new trends in French theatre and reacted against the realism that characterized the bourgeois and popular drama of the time. Their repertoire

Les Compagnons de Saint-Laurent.

— presented in Montreal and on tour in classical colleges — consisted of plays by major classical and contemporary French writers interpreted through a new esthetic based on poetry, faith and elegance in acting and speech. The Compagnons produced a whole generation of rigorously trained actors and directors. The fruit of their work began to be seen during the war when a former Compagnon, Pierre Dagenais, founded L'Équipe, which staged plays by Bernard Shaw and Jean Cocteau and even, in 1946, Jean-Paul Sartre's *No Exit.*

Music

Even though times were hard, classical music managed to improve its institutional framework and broaden its audience between 1930 and 1945. In Montreal, organizations such as the Ladies' Morning Musical Club, founded in 1892, and the Société Canadienne d'Opérette, which operated from 1925 to 1934 before being succeeded by the Variétés Lyriques (1936-55), continued their activities. A number of new organizations were also established, especially in the Francophone community, which until then had not been as well served musically as Anglophone Montreal. Thus, the new Société des Concerts Symphoniques, forerunner of the Montreal Symphony Orchestra, presented its first program at Plateau Hall in Montreal in January 1935, with Wilfrid Pelletier conducting. In 1940, under a new Belgian conductor, Désiré Defauw, a particularly intense period began for the orchestra, which became the city's only symphonic ensemble when the Montreal Orchestra (1930-41) disbanded. During the war, the Société des Concerts Symphoniques played host to conductors and soloists from all over the world. It also benefited from the wider audience that had begun to develop in the late 1930s as a result of such initiatives as the Matinées Symphoniques (1935), the Festivals de Montréal (1936) and the summer concerts at the chalet on Mount Royal (1938).

New organizations promoting classical music were also established elsewhere in Quebec. The Cercle Philharmonique, established in Quebec City in 1936, was aimed at the musical education of as wide a public as possible. In 1942, it merged with the Société Symphonique, which had been founded in 1903, to form the new Quebec Symphonic Orchestra. The orchestra's first conductor was Edwin Bélanger, who was succeeded after a short time by Wilfrid Pelletier. In smaller cities and towns, choirs and wind bands flourished between the wars, but most of these were destroyed by conscription.

In music education, the influence of the McGill Conservatorium of Music, founded in 1904 and headed by Douglas Clarke after 1929, was Canada-wide. The founding in 1932 of the École Vincent-d'Indy (which soon afterwards became affiliated with the University of Montreal) was an initial attempt to meet the need for a Francophone institution of higher education. New conservatories in Montreal (1943) and Quebec City (1944), established under the leadership of Wilfrid Pelletier and wholly financed by the Quebec government, were further efforts in this direction.

Pelletier played a large role and had considerable influence in Quebec's musical life during the period, as did Claude Champagne, a composer and, even more significantly, a leading music educator.

There were few composers, and they were interested primarily in religious music and in the creation of distinctively "Canadian" works based on folk music. There were some proponents of the new musical language developed in Europe during the 1910s, but taste both in musical circles and among the public ran primarily to nineteenth-century romanticism and the neoclassicism that had been flourishing since the First World War.

*   *   *   *   *   *

The Depression perpetuated conservative influences among French Canadian elites, in the cultural sphere as in education or politics. On the surface, clerical authority and traditionalist thinking appeared to be triumphant everywhere. But as the critic Gilles Marcotte has written, "the fox was among the chickens." Little by little, contradictions began to show up. Writers, painters and theatre directors began to ignore the old shibboleths, went ever deeper in their discovery of modern art and literature, and paved the way for a cultural renewal. The tumult of the war years provided an initial opportunity for these new trends to be expressed more openly, at least for a short time. Although the most decisive changes and real challenges would take place a little later, the esthetic and ideological foundations for them had already been laid.

Part 2:
The Duplessis Era
1945–1960

INTRODUCTION

The dominant features of the period between 1945 and 1960 were the figure of Premier Maurice Duplessis and his ascendancy over Quebec's government and political life. His unabashed conservatism, shared by portions of the clergy and the traditional elites, influenced the development of institutions in such areas as health, education and social services. At the same time, reactions to the prevailing conservatism in reform circles paved the way for what would become the Quiet Revolution.

In examining the Duplessis system, it is important to look first at the background of socioeconomic change against which the system was built. It was a period of population increase and economic growth that brought a new prosperity to Quebec, but this prosperity was not universal and substantial inequalities persisted.

Favourable Economic Circumstances

Throughout the postwar period Quebec, along with the rest of Canada and the United States, enjoyed rapid economic growth characterized by considerable increases in investment and production. This process was the result of a number of factors, most notably pent-up consumer demand. Because of Depression-era austerity and wartime rationing, consumers had had to postpone buying goods of all kinds, and especially durable goods such as cars and household appliances. With savings accumulated during the war and higher incomes after it, Quebecers were now in a position to acquire these goods, and the resulting demand propelled industrial output to unprecedented levels. The chronic housing shortage of the 1940s combined with population growth stimulated residential construction. The Quebec economy also benefited from demand in Europe, then in the midst of reconstruction, and — even more — from the growing American need for raw materials. There was substantial new investment in natural resources and related transportation infrastructure.

Quebec's production took off at a rapid rate immediately after the war. While the pace slowed somewhat towards the end of the decade, the Korean War (1950-53) pushed output to new heights. The war was followed by a brief slowdown in 1954, but it gave way to a new burst of growth that lasted until the recession of 1957, which ushered in a period of relative stagnation and significantly higher unemployment.

Until the recession, economic growth was strong enough to create as many new jobs as were needed. Quebec came closer to achieving virtual full employment in the immediate postwar years than at any other time in its history. The unemployment rate was only 2.7 per cent in 1947 and

Construction on the Quebec North Shore and Labrador Railway, 1951.
(National Archives of Canada, PA-133214)

1948, but it rose afterwards, reaching 6 per cent in 1957 and 9.1 per cent
in 1960.

Along with economic expansion, Quebec experienced rapid population growth. Quebec's population increased by 26.7 per cent between
1951 and 1961, from about four to five million. The birth rate, which had
declined significantly during the 1930s, took a leap forward in the forties
and fifties. As in the rest of North America, the baby boom changed
Quebec's demographic structure, making it a society in which children
were a major element. At the same time, internal and external migration,
which had come to a halt during the Depression and the war, showed
renewed vigour. The rural exodus speeded up and the Quebec countryside, where there was little growth in income, emptied out: the agricultural segment of the population declined proportionally from 20 to 11 per
cent between 1951 and 1961. There was also a new wave of immigration,
with more than 400,000 immigrants coming to Quebec between 1946 and 1960.

Quebecers enjoyed a standard of living completely different from what they had experienced in the 1930s. Per capita personal income increased much faster than inflation — from $655 in 1946 to $1,455 in 1961. At the same time, while prices rose rapidly in the immediate postwar years (the average annual increase in the consumer price index in Montreal between 1946 and 1951 was 8.7 per cent), they subsequently stabilized and inflation was very low throughout the 1950s (0.4 per cent between 1951 and 1956 and 1.8 per cent between 1956 and 1961).

The availability of steady employment, higher wages and government expenditures on new social programs (unemployment insurance, family allowances and more generous old age pensions) made the consumer society and modern comfort accessible to most Quebecers. Before the war, only a minority had hot water, a telephone, a radio or a car. All these things became common currency in the 1950s: household electrical appliances became widely available and television made a sudden and dramatic entrance onto the stage of daily life.

Gaps and Inequalities

While Quebec's postwar prosperity was undeniably real, it should not obscure the fact that not all Quebecers benefited from it in equal measure. Quebec society was still characterized by serious inequalities based on ethnic group, social class, sex and region.

French Canadians were still socioeconomic second-class citizens in their own land. In 1961, their average income was significantly lower than that of most other ethnic groups. They occupied the lower positions in corporations and had great difficulty getting middle-management or executive jobs. A French Canadian was paid less than an Anglophone with the same ability and experience. In the business world, most French Canadian companies were characterized by small size and low productivity. A large proportion of French Canadians were limited to the lowest-paying jobs by a low level of education and occupational training. Many of them worked in a milieu that was foreign to them, where the language was English and the values and culture followed British or American models. They were subtly discriminated against at all levels of the economy.

At the other end of the scale, Quebecers of British origin were in a dominant position in the economy and society, even though they were a minority. They had their own system of schools, hospitals, social services and cultural institutions, enabling them to live apart from the Francophone majority. Many of them spoke only English. Other ethnic groups — the largest of which were the Italians and the Jews — were in a variety of socioeconomic situations. Italians, like French Canadians, were largely confined to low-paying jobs. On the other hand the Jews, despite the open discrimination they had long been subjected to, rose rapidly in the postwar period as a result of their substantial presence in the business world and their insistence on giving their children a high level of education.

Averages aside, there were social differences within each group, although these were greater in some groups than in others. There were some rich French Canadians, while some English Quebecers lived below the poverty line.

A large proportion of the working class still lived in disadvantaged circumstances. Quebec's economic structure, built around consumer goods industries, resource extraction and transportation, was based on the availability of unskilled, low-wage labour. This situation also made it difficult to unionize large numbers of workers. The hostile attitude of the Duplessis government, which sided with the employers, was another obstacle to union militancy. However, those who were unionized, especially skilled workers and workers in the construction trades, were able to take advantage of the favourable economic circumstances to improve their situation. The gap between these workers and those who had to settle for the minimum wage (which was kept low) grew increasingly wide.

It was also a difficult period for farmers, who didn't benefit from the prevailing prosperity to the same extent as other Quebecers. Prices were stagnant and many farmers had a hard time making ends meet. However, their living conditions improved, notably as a result of rural electrification.

Another result of postwar prosperity was the development of a middle class whose aspirations reflected a clear desire for modernization and a higher social position. While Anglophone Quebecers were able to fulfil these aspirations through the growth of the service sector and large corporations with their expanding bureaucracies, Francophones champed at the bit. Francophones were disadvantaged in the Anglophone-controlled private sector, while services were dominated by the clergy. Stymied in this way, the Francophone middle class would provide the main seedbed for the Quiet Revolution.

Women were still clearly victims of discrimination. During the war, Quebec's elites had urged women to go beyond their traditional roles and fulfil a wide variety of tasks; now they wanted women to go back to the kitchen. But despite this regression, Quebec women did not passively accept the constrained existence that was being forced on them. Women's participation in the labour force increased steadily. At the same time, more and more girls received a more advanced education: although the domestic science schools were modernized, there was little interest in them, while women's classical colleges flourished. From a legal point of view, women — and especially married women — were still not considered equal to men.

There were regional inequalities as well. While the Montreal area experienced rapid growth and modernization, other regions were clearly disadvantaged, even underdeveloped. Thus the Gaspé and Abitibi regions, with economies that were heavily dependent on the primary sector, had inadequate, outdated infrastructure and incomes that were much lower than in the major centres. Even within the Montreal region there were substantial disparities. Slums were widespread in the east, centre and southwest of the city, where most poor families lived, while the north and west provided a home for the bourgeoisie and the new middle classes.

In addition to these internal disparities, there were wide gaps in some areas between Quebec and the rest of North America. Quebec's road system was clearly inadequate. Its social institutions — especially in education, health and social services — were in need of heavy investment and updating. But even though these institutions cried out for modernization, any such action was delayed by the very conservative policies of the Duplessis government.

The Duplessis System

Governments tend to be returned to office during times of economic growth, and it was not until the end of the period that there were any changes. The Liberals, in power federally since 1935, were reelected without great difficulty in 1945, 1949 and 1953 with the help of solid support in Quebec. Louis Saint-Laurent became prime minister in 1948 and held office until 1957, when his Liberals lost to John Diefenbaker's Conservatives. The Conservatives formed a minority government and then were reelected with an overwhelming majority in 1958.

In Quebec, after the Union Nationale won the hotly contested election of 1944, it was easily reelected in 1948, 1952 and 1956. Premier Duplessis remained in power until his death in 1959. He was succeeded by Paul Sauvé, who tried to initiate reforms, but Sauvé died after only a few months in office. The new premier, Antonio Barrette, had little time to make his mark as the Union Nationale's long reign came to an end with the election of June 1960.

In the economic, social and political spheres, the Duplessis government was deeply conservative. Duplessis supported private enterprise and trusted in big capitalists based in the United States and English Canada to spur economic growth in Quebec, with particular emphasis on natural resource development. He opposed the welfare state and increasing government intervention and defended the established order, resisting trade union militancy and labelling anyone who worked for social change a "communist." Relying on the traditional elites and the clergy to keep the population in line, he sang the praises of the old values and rural life in his speeches.

Politically, Duplessis exercised a highly personal form of power based on party loyalty and patronage. He took advantage of an outdated electoral map to minimize the strength and influence of the Liberal opposition in the legislature, but this situation contributed to the growth of an increasingly impatient extraparliamentary opposition during the 1950s. His methods of public administration and finance, which eschewed planning and expert advice, were patently obsolete.

Maurice Duplessis and Msgr. Joseph Charbonneau, Sainte-Thérèse, 1946. (*The Gazette*, National Archives of Canada, C-53641)

Duplessis skilfully played the nationalist card, vigorously defending provincial autonomy against the encroachments of a centralist federal government. But his nationalism, highly traditionalist in tone, was purely defensive, and he had little to offer as an alternative. The Tremblay Commission on constitutional problems (1952-56) presented him with a lot of new ideas, but apart from instituting a provincial income tax, he ignored them.

The Duplessis system cannot be explained in terms of one man's personality. Duplessis's ideas were widely shared by the traditional elites and the clergy, whose ascendancy over Quebec society was threatened by modernization. With its army of priests, nuns and brothers, the Catholic Church remained in control of education, health and social services. But the baby boom, urbanization and a higher standard of living increased the burden on these institutions to the point where the church could no longer cope. The growing number of laypeople whose help it had to enlist wanted a greater share of power. Elements within the church itself were beginning to demand that it adapt better to urban society and new values.

For a while, the alliance of elites managed to resist the pressures for change. But there was a widening gulf between institutions that were too inflexible and Quebec's rapidly changing socioeconomic reality.

The Rise of Reform Movements

The desire for change was very real and was expressed with increasing insistence as the period progressed. Urban Quebecers had a hunger for modernization that was initially channelled into consumption. But there were other desires as well that became stronger from year to year — for more and better schools, for a wider variety of government services, and simply for up-to-date roads. Television, which first appeared in 1952 and reached almost 90 per cent of Quebec homes by 1960, brought a greater openness to the world and conveyed new values.

The growing secularization of society was another source of ferment. The Catholic trade unions began to lose their clerical character at the end of the Second World War. There were more and more lay teachers, nurses and social workers and they regarded clerical control as a burden. The Catholic Action movements — which were increasingly influential, especially among young people — advocated a new relationship between Christians and society.

Openly challenging the Duplessis system, intellectuals, artists, trade unionists and politicians attacked the stifling ideological climate, which they called the *"grande noirceur"* (great darkness). They took their inspira-

Demonstration during the asbestos strike, 1949. (Montreal *Star*, National Archives of Canada, PA-130357)

tion from a variety of sources, ranging from Christian personalism through Keynesianism to the internationalism that flourished in the post-war era, and demanded that society and its values and institutions be modernized. They favoured greater social justice and a broadminded openness towards the world. For some, opposition to Duplessis meant a rejection of nationalism, while others sought a new synthesis between national and social concerns.

The Asbestos strike of 1949, harshly suppressed by the provincial police and condemned by Duplessis, became a symbol, as did other labour conflicts during the period, especially the strikes at Dupuis Frères (1952), Louiseville (1952), Murdochville (1957) and the CBC French network (1958-59). These strikes gave the trade union movement a new stature, and the support it won made it a major force in society.

By the late 1950s, Quebec society was ready to change course. Tension was inevitable between a population in the throes of rapid socioeconomic transformation and institutions that were too slow to adapt. The bubbling brew would boil over in 1960, leading to the headlong drive to modernize that became known as the Quiet Revolution.

CHAPTER 14

THE BABY BOOM

Population growth in Quebec between 1945 and 1960 had two major features: the marked increase in the birth rate known as the baby boom, and the resumption and intensification of immigration. Both these developments changed the face of Quebec society significantly, and they were all the more striking because they contrasted sharply with the population trends of the preceding fifteen years. The economic difficulties of the Depression slowed both the birth rate and immigration, and while the birth rate increased during the war, there was no increase in permanent immigration.

Overall Population Trends

Since the nineteenth century, Quebec's population had on the average doubled every twenty-five years. Between 1931 and 1961 (table 1), it didn't quite double: it grew by 83 per cent, with the rate varying from decade to decade. The Depression reduced the growth rate significantly, but it picked up again in the 1940s (especially after the war), returning to its level of the 1920s. During the 1950s, population growth shot up dramatically, largely making up for the time lost during the Depression.

Until the 1940s, Quebec's population growth far outstripped that of the majority Anglophone provinces and territories and therefore, to a lesser extent, that of Canada as a whole. This meant that Quebec represented a growing percentage of the country's population; it accounted for 26.9 per cent in 1921, 27.7 per cent in 1931, and 29 per cent in 1941. This trend also applied to the total number of French Canadians in Canada, and Quebec nationalists, basing themselves on rather flimsy projections, even thought that through the "revenge of the cradle," Catholic Francophones would one day be in the majority. However, they lost that illusion when the 1951 census showed that the population of English Canada was now growing as fast as Quebec's and that Quebec's share of the population had remained stable at 29 per cent. During the 1950s, Quebec's

			Table 1			
		Population of Quebec and Canada, 1931-1961				

	Quebec		Other provinces and territories		Canada	
Year	Population	Increase (%)*	Population	Increase (%)*	Population	Increase (%)*
1931	2,874,662	21.8	7,502,124	16.7	10,376,785	18.1
1941	3,331,882	15.9	8,174,773	9.0	11,506,655	10.9
1951	4,055,681	21.7	9,953,748	21.7	14,009,429	21.7
1961	5,259,211	29.7	12,979,036	30.4	18,238,247	30.2

*Since previous census
Source: Censuses of Canada

population growth rate even fell below the Canadian average, and in 1961, Quebec accounted for 28.8 per cent of the Canadian population.

Even more significant is the comparison between Quebec and Ontario, which were in many respects in competition with each other economically, financially and politically. From the turn of the century on, Ontario had had about half a million more inhabitants than Quebec. During the 1950s, however, although Quebec's growth rate was high, Ontario's was even higher (35.6 per cent), and in 1961 Ontario's population was one million greater than Quebec's.

The Birth Rate

Traditionally, natural increase, or the surplus of births over deaths, was the main factor in population growth in Quebec. This remained true until the late 1950s. The Depression brought a sharp fall in the birth rate (table 2); while traditionalist ideology still insisted on the duty to procreate, Quebec couples either delayed marriage or postponed having children because of the economic situation of the time. During the war, the growth rate began to rise again and this trend was accentuated in peacetime. The number of births each year reached record levels, which were maintained for more than a decade. This was the baby boom, a phenomenon Quebec shared with other societies, especially English Canada, the United States and Australia.

While the baby boom represented a dramatic increase in the number of births, it was not a radical reversal of long-term demographic trends, only a disturbance caused by the momentous events of the time. Thus, the birth rate (the number of live births per thousand population) had been falling steadily since the last third of the nineteenth century. With the Depression, the decline became much steeper, but the rise in the birth rate during and after the war made up for the sudden drop. So basic trends were maintained, even though they were slowed down tem-

Table 2
Birth and Fertility, Quebec, 1926-1961

Year	No. of births	Birth rate*	Total fertility rate**
1926	83,808	32.2	4.39
1931	85,278	29.7	4.08
1936	76,791	24.8	3.43
1941	90,993	27.3	3.45
1946	113,511	31.3	3.90
1951	123,196	30.4	3.84
1956	138,631	30.0	3.98
1961	139,857	26.6	3.77

*Number of births per thousand population
**Average number of children per woman between the ages of 15 and 49
Source: Bureau de la Statistique du Québec, *Démographie québécoise*, p. 93.

porarily. At the height of the baby boom, the birth rate was no higher than it had been in the early 1930s. The total fertility rate — the combined fertility rates of women in all age groups between fifteen and forty-nine — showed a similar trend.

So the baby boom was primarily a catch-up phenomenon, and not a return to the large families of earlier times. In the postwar period, more couples — not just young ones, but also ones who had had to wait because of the Depression and the war — married and had children. In other words, the birth rate jumped because more women had children, not because women had more children. The increased birth rate was a result of a general climate of optimism: prosperity had returned, and housing and consumer goods were more easily available. As well, a new feminine mystique was being propagated, idealizing young, dynamic, modern mothers.

This new influx of children had a profound influence on Quebec society, as changes in the age structure show (graph 1). In 1941, 21 per cent of Quebecers were under the age of ten; in 1951, this figure rose to 25 per cent. The increased number of young people put children at the centre of social and economic life in the 1950s. Departments of obstetrics and pediatrics had to be set up in hospitals and clinics. Elementary schools had to be built and teachers hired, and as the first wave of children grew older, the first few years of high school had to be made accessible. Recreational activities and playgrounds had to be better organized. Industries directed at children — food, clothing, toys and others — flourished. Tintin books and Walt Disney cartoons were widely popular, and on television, it was the era of *Lassie* and *Pépinot et Capucine*.

The Death Rate

There was another major factor behind the baby boom — the decline in the infant mortality rate, or the number of babies dying before their first birthday. It had been falling since the 1920s, continued its downward trend despite the Depression, and declined significantly in the 1940s and 1950s. The infant mortality rate fell from 120 to 32 per thousand births between 1931 and 1961. Improved public health, and especially more hygienic water and milk, played a determining role. Although the long-standing gap in this respect between country and city was closing, some groups were still clearly disadvantaged. Thus, in the 1950s, native people still had an infant mortality rate of more than 110 per thousand births.

Child mortality — the death rate for children from age one to fifteen — also dropped sharply, mainly because of greatly improved treatments for infectious diseases and the use of vaccines. In the early 1930s, child mortality was 5.4 per cent for girls and 5.8 per cent for boys; thirty years later, it was only 0.9 per cent for girls and 1.3 per cent for boys. For adults, the death rate for men aged sixteen and over barely changed at all, mainly because they were subject to accidents; but it did improve for young women as childbirth, formerly a major cause of death, became safer. In the adult population as a whole, some causes of death were disappearing while others — especially cancer and heart disease — were becoming more common. Cancer accounted for 17.5 per cent of deaths in 1961, compared to only 7 per cent in 1931, while heart disease accounted for 34 per cent of deaths in 1961, up from 10 per cent in 1931. Medical research became increasingly concerned with these two diseases, and general awareness of them grew.

The overall death rate in Quebec continued to fall, from 13.5 per thousand in 1931 to 7 per thousand in 1961. Life expectancy at birth improved significantly. A boy born in 1931 could expect to live 56.2 years, and a girl 57.8 years; by 1961, a boy could expect to live 67.3 years and a girl 72.8 years. So, as the demographers Desmond Dufour and Yves Péron have written, Quebecers coming into the world had a greater chance of "going through all the stages of a normal life cycle: childhood, youth, maturity and old age." But while children, adolescents and adults had a greater chance of reaching the age of sixty, life expectancy did not improve very much beyond that. In 1961, women aged sixty could expect to live a further 19 years and men 16.3 years. This was only a small improvement over 1931, when women could expect to live a further 16.4 years and men 15.8 years.

The Decrease in Immigration during the Depression and the War

Because of the relatively high overall birth rate and the sharp drop in the death rate, the natural increase of the Quebec population between 1930 and 1960 was substantial (table 3). A secondary factor in population

Figure 1
The Age Pyramid, Quebec, 1961

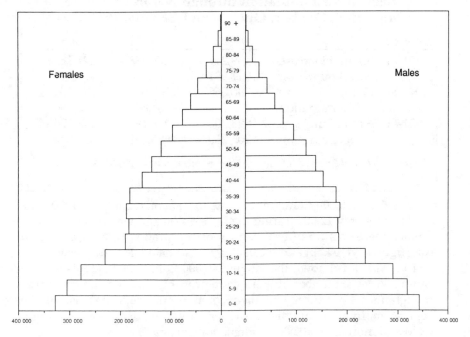

Source: Census of Canada, 1961.

growth was immigration, which went through two separate phases: stagnation during the Depression and the war, and a strong resumption in the postwar period, especially in the 1950s.

Canada as a whole and Quebec in particular received large numbers of foreign immigrants between the last quarter of the nineteenth century and the 1930s. But in Quebec's case, emigration to the United States was even higher, so Quebec's annual net international migration was always negative. The Depression brought migration — and especially emigration to the United States, which to all intents and purposes closed its borders to foreigners — to a quick end. Canada also tried to reduce immigration: government, business and unions all felt that with unemployment so high, the population had to be protected from competition from newcomers. The climate was ripe for xenophobia, and some people even wanted to send the foreign-born back home. Antisemitism, which was raging in Europe, was also spreading in Canada. The federal immigration department was extremely reluctant to accept Jews who were fleeing Nazi Germany, and there were antisemitic demonstrations in Quebec. During the war, mobilization in Europe and the problem of transportation across the Atlantic reduced immigration and emigration still further. Thus, immigration fell sharply between 1930 and 1945. While an annual average

Table 3
Changes in the Population through Natural Increase and Migration, Quebec, Ontario and Canada, 1931-1961

Decade		Quebec	Ontario	Canada
1931-41	Natural increase	459,211	278,488	1,221,787
	Net migration	-1,991	+77,484	-91,918
1941-51	Natural increase	736,058	505,034	1,972,394
	Net migration	-12,259	+304,853	+168,964
1951-61	Natural increase	998,300	953,493	3,148,198
	Net migration	+205,230	+685,057	+1,080,620

Source: *Historical Statistics of Canada*, 2nd edition, series A339-349.

of more than 110,000 immigrants came to Canada during the 1920s, the average was only 12,000 during the Depression and war years.

Since there was no official control or registration of emigration, no exact figures were kept and it can only be estimated. For the period from 1931 to 1941, it is known that about 240,000 Canadian residents left the country. A large number of them were probably recent or longstanding immigrants who returned to their countries of origin because of the Depression. In all, migratory movements over the decade resulted in a net loss of more than 90,000 residents for Canada.

Quebec had a slightly negative net migration between 1931 and 1941 (table 3), taking into account movements between Quebec and other provinces as well as movements to and from foreign countries. Here again, almost no figures are available, but it is believed that the negative balance was due to emigration to other countries and that contrary to what took place in the nineteenth century, interprovincial movements were in Quebec's favour. It may be assumed that the movement towards Quebec consisted largely of French Canadians who had gone to Ontario or the western provinces and came home to their families when they lost their jobs.

The decline in migration had repercussions on Quebec society, slowing down the process of ethnic and cultural diversification. In 1931, 8.7 per cent of Quebec's population consisted of people born outside Canada; ten years later, the figure was only 6.7 per cent. Similarly, the proportion of Quebecers of non-French and non-British origin rose from 4.9 per cent in 1921 to 6.1 per cent in 1931, but fell to 5.5 per cent in 1941. In 1941 Quebec's population was more homogeneous than it had been ten years earlier: French Canadians made up 80.9 per cent of the population, as compared to 78.9 per cent in 1931.

The Postwar Wave of Immigration

After the interruption of the Depression and the war, Canada opened its doors again to immigrants who wanted to escape postwar devastation and political turmoil and build new lives in North America. In 1948, more than 125,000 newcomers arrived in the country, and large numbers continued to come each year until 1960. In 1957 alone, 282,000 immigrants were admitted — more than came during the entire period from 1930 to 1945. In all, immigration to Canada totalled two million between 1946 and 1960. While the federal government, which was responsible for immigration policy, continued to make efforts to recruit and welcome new immigrants, it still considered entry into Canada a privilege granted more readily to some than to others. Europeans and Americans were welcome, while immigration from Asia, Africa and Latin America was severely limited.

Quebec received its share of this wave of immigration. From 1946 to 1960, 403,934 immigrants arrived in Quebec, settling mainly in Montreal. However, these immigrants represented only 21.6 per cent of total foreign immigration to Canada — less than Quebec's percentage of the total Canadian population. Ontario was the main beneficiary of immigration, attracting more than 50 per cent of the newcomers. As well, Quebec had more difficulty than Ontario in keeping its immigrants: about half left again after a few years, going to other provinces or the United States or returning to their home countries. This movement was undoubtedly due mainly to economic factors, although the challenge of integration into a bilingual culture should not be underestimated.

The new immigrants came from a much larger number of home countries than prewar immigrants had. Before the war, more than 40 per cent of all immigrants came from the British Isles, while after the war only 18 per cent came from there. The leading source of immigration was now southern Europe, which accounted for 32 per cent of foreigners settling in Quebec between 1946 and 1960. Italians alone made up half of this group. Quebec (especially Montreal) was greatly transformed by this wave of immigration, as we will see later on. For the moment, it is sufficient to note that the proportion of Quebecers born outside Canada rose from 5.6 per cent in 1951 to 7.4 per cent in 1961.

The Quebec government did not recognize the significance of immigration and saw no need to concern itself with integrating immigrants; as a result, there was no government agency responsible for receiving newcomers. Ethnic communities themselves took on the task of welcoming and assisting new immigrants. For instance, Montreal Jews had community organizations and voluntary associations that helped bring victims of Nazism into Canada and get them established here. In other groups, aid to immigrants often depended on family networks and village ties. Many Italian immigrants, for example, came to join family members or former inhabitants of their home villages already living in

Greek and Italian immigrants manufacturing television consoles in Montreal. (R. Beauchamp, *La Presse*, National Archives of Canada, PA-127037)

certain Montreal neighbourhoods. These people helped the newcomers find a job and a place to live and adjust to their new surroundings. New Quebecers themselves also had national parishes and organizations within their communities.

Although they often banded together and concentrated in neighbourhoods where they could keep their language and customs, new Quebecers generally tended to integrate into the Anglophone community. Before leaving for Canada, they were often unaware that the majority of Quebecers were Francophone, and their desire for success and social mobility made them opt for the language they felt had the most prestige — the language of most of the North American continent and of the economically dominant group in Quebec. At one time, most Italian Montrealers who sent their children to Catholic schools had chosen French-language education. In the postwar period, however, there was a clear change in attitude within the community and the great majority now chose English-language schools. Immigrants' attitudes were not the only factor in this situation: the French-language education system was not very open to immigrants and was hostile to non-Catholics, even French-speaking ones.

The massive integration of immigrants into the Anglophone community began to be a source of concern for some nationalist intellectuals, but the French Canadian community as a whole was largely indifferent to it.

They took scant notice of the new Quebecers and made little effort to attract them or develop contact.

There are still no precise data on numbers of people leaving Quebec for other countries during those years. Given the widespread prosperity and high employment, however, it may be assumed that many fewer left than came in. Canada as a whole had a positive net migration of more than a million people between 1951 and 1961. According to most estimates of movements between Quebec and the other provinces, by 1941 Quebec's net interprovincial migration was negative again, as it had always been before the Depression. However, foreign immigration put Quebec's overall net migration well into the plus column between 1951 and 1961 (table 3).

*   *   *   *   *   *

The baby boom and a large wave of foreign immigration made the post-war period a time of rapid population growth in Quebec. But Quebec's population growth remained much more heavily dependent on natural increase than immigration, while in Canada as a whole and Ontario in particular, immigration played a much larger role.

This dependence on natural increase had significant ramifications. Immigration makes a valuable contribution to the social and cultural fabric and provides large numbers of trained and educated adults who can play an immediate role in the economy as workers and consumers. Natural increase, on the other hand, involves major costs for the community, because children have to be cared for, trained and educated before they can join the workforce, although it does have the advantage of creating a younger population with great potential for the future. In 1961, more than 44 per cent of the Quebec population was under twenty, and this youthful population was a major factor in the Quiet Revolution.

CHAPTER 15

ECONOMIC DEPENDENCE

Throughout its history, Canada has been dependent on foreign powers. From the late nineteenth century on, it was dependent on both Britain and the United States, with a steadily increasing tendency towards the U.S. For a time, the Depression reduced foreign influence somewhat. But with the war, the trend resumed, with Canada leaning much more clearly towards the United States. Circumstances encouraged much closer cooperation between the Canadian and American governments and more extensive integration of their economies. This was the birth of continentalism, which was a coordinated strategy aimed at ensuring North American autonomy from German-dominated continental Europe.

The integration of the Canadian and American economies did not stop when the war ended. Relations between the two countries changed somewhat, but the direction was still towards further dependence in capital, technology, raw materials, finished products, and all other areas of economic activity. Nor was dependence restricted to the economic sphere — it increasingly extended to areas such as trade unions, communications and culture.

This phenomenon has to be looked at on a Canada-wide scale. Obviously, Quebec was part of the process of growing dependence on the United States, but most of the data available are for Canada as a whole, and it is not always possible to draw specific conclusions regarding Quebec.

Continentalism

Canada emerged from the war with a greatly strengthened economic structure. On the surface, it seemed to be in a good position to detach itself from foreign influence and affirm its autonomy. But the international situation exerted pressures in the opposite direction and led to increased dependence. The key factor was the increased strength of the American economy and the emergence of the United States as the leading world power. The United States was in a position to reorganize world trade to its own advantage and extend its political and economic influence over a large part of the globe. The fact that Europe, bled white by the war, was in disarray facilitated this process. Britain, Canada's traditional economic partner, emerged from the war in a considerably weakened position.

The Cold War between the United States and the Soviet Union heightened the importance of strategic alliances. Canada's geographic proximity to the United States and its longstanding unequal relations with its southern neighbour inevitably made it a satellite in the American orbit. American influence can be measured in terms of the volume of international trade and the level of foreign investment.

International Trade

In the early postwar years, Canada's international trade was substantially redirected, accentuating Canadian dependence on the United States. Before the war, Canada's trade was triangular, oriented to the United States on one side and Europe, mainly Britain, on the other. Canada usually ran a trade deficit with the United States, importing much more than it exported. But Canada's surplus in its trade with Britain and the other European powers outweighed this deficit.

After the war, the government wanted to maintain this triangular system and supported the development of multilateral trade relations on a world scale. But the disorganized state of the European economy prevented Canada from fully achieving its goals. The European countries were unable to pay for their foreign imports, so Canada had to lend them money to keep them as customers. Between 1945 and 1948, Canada advanced hundreds of millions of dollars in export credits. Britain in particular received large loans, mainly to buy wheat. There were outright grants in addition to the loans, and some debts were forgiven.

This system of credits had serious consequences for Canada's balance of payments. Less foreign currency was coming in to pay for exports, so Canada had to draw on its reserves to pay for its high level of imports from the United States. The situation very quickly reached a crisis point — Canadian reserves of American dollars ran out, and in 1947 the government had to impose import restrictions.

This however, was only a temporary solution, and something had to be done about the long-term imbalance in Canada's foreign trade. It was hoped that help would come from the Marshall Plan, the massive American program of economic aid to the European countries, whose effects began to be felt in 1948. The Canadian government's strategy was to have the U.S. administration allow some of the dollars advanced to European countries to be spent outside the United States. Under American law, such transfers were acceptable when European demand outstripped

American production capacity. So between 1948 and 1950, some of the Marshall Plan funds entered Canada, providing some respite and improving Canada's balance-of-payments position.

But the Marshall Plan was only temporary and its effects were slower and less dramatic than had been expected. Under the circumstances, Ottawa had to shelve its multilateral trade development policy, promote exports to the United States to alleviate Canada's chronic bilateral trade deficit and, as a consequence, increase Canadian dependence on the United States.

Canada became a major supplier of raw materials, and especially minerals, to the United States. Before the war the United States had been an exporter of metals; now rising demand made it an importer. Military requirements brought about by the Cold War played a large part in this development — Washington had to ensure an adequate supply of raw materials in case of armed conflict. The U.S. had begun strategic stockpiling of some commodities during the Second World War. When the Korean War broke out, Washington set up a major commission of inquiry into raw materials. The resulting Paley Report (*President's Report on Raw Materials*) found that American reserves of a number of basic materials were insufficient. The report recommended acceleration of the strategic stockpiling program and increased reliance on materials produced by allied countries. Towards this end, American capital was to be heavily invested in mining outside the U.S. and the minerals produced in this way brought into the country under low tariffs.

Thus, the Americans did not simply ask for Canadian minerals; they came to extract the minerals themselves. As the economist Hugh Aitken put it, American capital came to Canada mainly to speed up the development of industries that would meet the demand for raw materials in the American market. In this way, American investment helped create a Canadian economy that was complementary to that of the United States and in danger of becoming frozen in the role of supplier of unfinished and semifinished goods.

Quebec was central to this system of dependence. Because of its natural resources, it was one of the provinces that could best respond to American needs. Quebec was the main supplier of forest products which, despite the rapid growth in mineral production, still constituted the leading Canadian export to the United States. Quebec lumber was required for many purposes in the U.S., notably new housing, while newsprint production was also on the rise, mainly for the U.S. market.

The Americans were also interested in Quebec's mineral resources, and their decision to exploit the rich iron deposits of New Quebec was of strategic importance. The need to transport the ore to the large American steel mills in the Great Lakes region was a significant factor in speeding up the decision to undertake construction of the St. Lawrence Seaway. Completed in the late 1950s, the seaway contributed to Quebec's integration into the American economy.

Table 1 Percentage Distribution of Canada's Import and Export Trade, 1946-1960				
	% of total value			
	1946	*1950*	*1955*	*1960*
Exports				
United States	38.9	65.1	59.8	55.8
Britain	26.1	15.1	18.0	17.4
Other countries	35.0	19.8	22.2	26.8
Imports				
United States	75.3	66.9	72.9	67.2
Britain	7.5	12.8	8.6	10.8
Other countries	17.2	20.3	18.5	22.0

Source: *Canada Year Book 1967*, pp. 970-71.

Economic integration was not limited to natural resources alone. The Americans saw Canada as a natural market for their manufactured products, but they had to get around Canadian tariff barriers. To do so, they set up branch plants in Canada that mostly assembled products designed and developed in the United States. While such branch plants had existed for a long time, they became much more numerous after the war. Buying existing plants and building new ones, Americans obtained control over a large share of Canada's manufacturing industry. The trend that had emerged in the 1930s continued — most of the branch plants were located in southern Ontario, with Quebec trailing far behind.

Despite high tariffs, imports from the United States were on the rise. The United States clearly became Canada's largest customer and remained its main supplier (table 1). Canada-U.S. economic relations developed at the expense of Canada's longstanding privileged relationship with Britain, as Britain's share of Canada's export trade declined significantly.

Foreign Investment

Worldwide foreign investment increased spectacularly in the postwar period. From a total of $7.2 billion in 1946, it reached $22.2 billion in 1960. Throughout the period, the lion's share of foreign investment was held by the United States, which accounted for three quarters of the total. The enormous capital reserves held by large U.S. corporations that invested in all parts of the world helped maintain American dominance.

In 1946, close to 40 per cent of foreign capital in Canada took the form of direct investment; in 1960, it was 60 per cent. This represented a significant change in the degree of foreign control over the Canadian economy. The situation varied from sector to sector, with foreign control concentrated primarily in manufacturing and resources. In metal mining and refining, it rose from 43 to 61 per cent between 1948 and 1960; at the end of the period, it stood at 73 per cent in the oil and natural gas sector. In both cases, a heavy majority of the investment was American. In the utility sector, however, foreign control fell from 24 to 5 per cent during the period, most likely because of substantial Canadian investment by both private and government-owned companies in such areas as hydroelectric power.

In Quebec, although foreign control was less prevalent than in Ontario, it was still very much present. In the mining sector, foreign-controlled companies employed 40.4 per cent of the labour force in 1960 and produced 51.8 per cent of the value added. Foreign control in manufacturing in 1960 was concentrated in specific industries. Older industries that had existed since the nineteenth century, such as food and beverages and textiles, were still heavily controlled by Canadian capital, while foreign control was much stronger in newer industries that relied on more advanced technology. Looking at locus of control in relation to value added, the economist André Raynauld found that in Quebec in 1960, foreign-controlled companies were predominant in coal and oil, nonferrous metals, transportation equipment, chemicals, precision instruments, tobacco, machinery, iron and steel, and rubber.

Foreign control over the Canadian economy was not absolute. The financial sector (particularly the chartered banks), construction, real estate development and transportation were generally Canadian-owned. The growth of the public and parapublic sectors in the Canadian and Quebec economies also contributed to the development of fields that remained outside American control.

But concentrated as it was in key areas of the manufacturing and resource sectors, foreign investment was highly significant. In the short term, the influx of capital helped open new mineral deposits, build plants and create thousands of jobs, but these positive effects were offset by other, more negative ones. Having made its initial investment, the foreign parent company repatriated its profits to its country of origin, tended to promote flows of goods and services within the corporation itself, and concentrated research outside Canada. Thus, foreign-owned Canadian companies were subsidiaries in the full sense of the term, with only limited decision-making power over their own strategy and direction. Hence the ultimate consequence of foreign investment — and especially direct investment — was foreign control of decisions affecting the economic future of Canada and Quebec. Beginning in the 1950s, some intellectuals began to raise the issue, but their concerns seemed out of place at a time when billions of dollars in foreign investment were seen as bringing prosperity and progress to Canada.

St Lawrence Seaway, Lake St. Louis lock, 1959. (Chris Lund, NFB, National Archives of Canada, PA-151638)

Corporate Concentration

The presence of foreign capital accentuated the process of corporate concentration, which had begun early in the century and continued in the postwar period. Monopoly was at a more advanced stage in the United States than in Canada, and U.S. companies that set up Canadian subsidiaries transferred the effects of American concentration to Canada. In addition, the financial resources of large American corporations enabled them to buy Canadian companies, merge them, or extend the operations of their own subsidiaries, thus increasing concentration. Giant Canadian-owned corporations were also able to draw on large pools of capital and extend their operations.

Another trend among giant corporations was diversification. In most cases, this involved moving into areas connected to the company's main activity, but conglomerates began to appear that had operations in a variety of sectors not necessarily related to one another.

In a well-known study, the sociologist John Porter examined companies employing at least 500 workers in Canada between 1948 and 1950. He compiled a list of 183 leading companies that together accounted for 40 to 50 per cent of the gross value of manufacturing production, 60 per cent of the value of mineral production, 90 per cent of rail transportation, 88 per cent of gross revenues from cable and telegraph services, 88 per cent of revenues from air transportation, 83 per cent of telephone revenues and 60 to 70 per cent of the hydroelectric power produced by private companies.

However, concentration extended even further, as many of these large companies, while operating as separate entities, maintained very close ties with one another. Interlocking directorships, and especially the presence of senior officers of the Canadian chartered banks on the boards of many dominant corporations, represented one indication of these close relations.

Not including wholly owned subsidiaries of foreign companies, for which no figures were available, Porter found that eighteen large corporations had assets of more than $100 million in 1950. By 1960 the number of such corporations had increased to fifty-four. Many large corporations had become even larger, either through the natural expansion of their activities or through acquisitions. For dominant corporations, the 1950s were an intense period of takeovers and consolidation. The most significant mergers of the period, as noted by Porter, took place in iron and steel, transportation equipment, pulp and paper, breweries, flour mills, textiles and food. A number of paper companies operating in Quebec, such as Price Brothers, Howard Smith Paper and Brown Corporation, were affected.

A number of dominant corporations had their head offices in Quebec, especially in Montreal. But French Canadian business was all but shut out: only Marine Industries, owned by the Simard family, made Porter's list. The two French Canadian chartered banks, the Banque Canadienne Nationale and the Provincial Bank of Canada, were the smallest of the nine chartered banks, and none of the ten largest Canadian life insurance companies was French Canadian. But while French-Canadian-controlled companies were notable by their absence, this did not mean that there were no French Canadian investors. Some English Canadian corporations had Francophone directors, and French Canadians were shareholders — although very definitely minority shareholders — in many of these corporations.

Increasingly, therefore, the postwar Canadian economy — into which the Quebec economy was fully integrated — was controlled by a small number of large corporations and in a satellite position in the American economic orbit.

CHAPTER 16

A NEW INDUSTRIAL BOOM

The reconversion of industry to peacetime production took place without major problems. A number of factors contributed to the smooth transition, including the federal government's full employment policy, consumers' strong desire to catch up after the deprivation experienced during the Depression and the war, and the reconstruction of Europe. The postwar economic boom, which continued until the recession of 1957, created favourable conditions for industrial growth in Quebec. In the resource sector, heavy demand from the United States meant flush times both for unprocessed raw materials and for processed goods such as paper.

The Development of the Manufacturing Sector

Between 1946 and 1956, indices of manufacturing in Quebec — number of establishments, number of people employed and value of production — all increased steadily (table 1). Over these eleven years, employment increased by 25 per cent and the value of production by 165 per cent. During this period of growth, manufacturing represented about a third of Quebec's gross domestic product and a quarter of total employment. A slight decline began in 1957 as Canada entered a recession that lasted until 1960.

The manufacturing sector was in a phase of profound change. The value of production grew much more quickly than the size of the workforce, indicating that the productivity of each worker was increasing. Productivity gains that had occurred during the Second World War were now augmented as a result of mechanization and automation. The in-

Table 1
Statistics of Manufacturing Industries, Quebec, 1945-60

Year	Number of establishments	Number of people employed	Gross value of products ($ million)
1945	10,038	384,031	2,531.9
1946	10,818	357,276	2,498.0
1947	11,223	379,449	3,017.0
1948	11,107	383,835	3,598.9
1949	11,579	390,275	3,788.5
1950	11,670	390,163	4,142.5
1951	11,861	417,182	4,916.2
1952	12,024	429,678	5,176.2
1953	12,132	441,555	5,386.8
1954	12,191	424,095	5,395.8
1955	12,194	429,575	5,922.4
1956	12,112	446,137	6,622.5
1957	11,295	444,962	6,419.3
1958	10,896	425,260	6,512.9
1959	10,672	427,280	6,802.2
1960	11,093	429,442	7,075.5

Source: *Quebec Yearbook 1966-1967*, p. 671.

creasingly sophisticated machines offered by machinery manufacturers were constantly being modified, so that they quickly became obsolete and had to be replaced. But automation, although already present in some sectors, was still in its infancy; its full effects would not be felt until the 1960s and 1970s. There were also changes in the manufacturing workforce, although they were gradual and barely noticed at the time. During the 1950s, service-type jobs became more common in the manufacturing sector, and automation began to change the relationship between management and administrative staff (accounting, personnel, purchasing, and the like) and production workers.

Whether one looks at value of production or employment, the geographical distribution of manufacturing was very uneven. The Montreal region alone accounted for 70 per cent of manufacturing jobs, of which 55 per cent were on Montreal Island itself. Far behind were the Quebec City region with 9 per cent, Trois-Rivières with 8.5 per cent, Sherbrooke with 4.6 per cent and Saguenay-Lake St. John with 3.5 per cent. Farther afield, the Gaspé-Lower St. Lawrence, northwestern Quebec and North Shore regions each accounted for 1 per cent or less. The roots of this imbalance went back many years. Quebec's share of overall Canadian manufacturing remained stable at about 30 per cent of the value of production, as compared to slightly under 50 per cent for Ontario.

Table 2
Percentage of Total Gross Value of Quebec Manufacturing Production for Each Group of Industries, 1929-1945

Rank in 1959	Rank in 1945	Group	%			
			1945	1950	1955	1959
1	1	Food and beverages	15.5	18.5	16.0	17.8
4	2	Clothing	10.7	10.1	8.5	8.5
5	3	Iron and steel products	10.0	6.8	7.8	8.5
2	4	Paper products	9.6	12.4	11.6	10.8
9	5	Transportation equipment	9.4	3.8	4.8	4.9
6	6	Textile products	8.1	9.9	6.7	6.3
7	7	Chemical products	7.6	4.5	5.6	6.0
3	8	Nonferrous metal products	7.4	8.6	11.1	9.6
10	9	Wood products	4.9	5.1	4.8	4.6
16	10	Leather products	3.1	2.2	1.7	1.8
14	11	Tobacco and tobacco products	3.0	2.8	2.6	2.7
8	12	Products of petroleum and coal	2.5	5.0	6.5	5.5
11	13	Electrical appliances and equipment	2.5	3.4	4.2	4.2
12	14	Printing, publishing, etc.	1.8	2.7	2.9	3.3
13	15	Nonmetallic mineral products	1.6	2.0	2.6	2.8
15	16	Miscellaneous manufacturing	1.1	1.1	1.4	1.8
17	17	Rubber goods	1.1	1.0	1.0	0.9

Source: Marc Vallières, *Les industries manufacturières du Québec 1900-1959*, pp. 171, 173.

Quebec manufacturing seemed to have stabilized. It was growing at much the same rate as the gross domestic product, its geographical distribution changed very little, and its share of Canadian production was constant; on the whole, there was relatively little variation in the role of industry in Quebec's economy. But overall figures can be deceptive: they often mask significant differences from one industry to the next.

Quebec's Industrial Structure

The breakdown of value of production by large industrial groups (table 2) remained fairly stable. The leading groups were substantially the same in 1959 as in 1945: food and beverages, clothing, iron and steel products, paper products, textile products; nonferrous metal products was the only newcomer to the top six. But changes were clearly beginning, and they foreshadowed the difficulties some industries would encounter in the period that followed.

The decline of traditional industries had already begun. The clothing, textile, leather and tobacco industries were declining in relative although not in absolute terms — production in these industries was increasing, but not as quickly as in manufacturing as a whole. The leather industry had been in decline for a long time. For three decades in the late nineteenth century, shoe manufacturing had been the second largest industry in Quebec; in 1900, it still accounted for 13.7 per cent of the total value of production. By contrast, in 1959 the leather products group was in second to last place with less than 2 per cent. Even though the value of production was increasing slowly, many shoe factories closed and the number of jobs was falling.

The tobacco industry benefited from the popularity of smoking among a wider portion of the population, and the value of its production rose from $72 million to $182 million. However, the number of plants fell from fifty-one to fifteen and the workforce was reduced slightly. More sophisticated machines improved worker productivity significantly, and the industry became increasingly rationalized and concentrated.

The clothing industry fell from second place to fourth in value of production. Concentrated mainly in Montreal, the clothing industry relied heavily on low-paid labour and in part on work done at home. Most workers in the industry were poor immigrants. Expansion in the clothing

Dominion Textile plant in Montmorency, 1953. (George Hunter, NFB, Public Archives of Canada, PA–151651)

industry seemed to have reached a limit and growth in the value of production was well under the average for Quebec manufacturing. The number of shops declined only slightly, and its continuing high level reflected the relatively small degree of concentration in the industry. The textile products group was also losing ground, with production accounting for only 6.3 per cent of the Quebec total in 1959. The main textile industry was cotton which, after a period of expansion that lasted until 1951, began a sharp decline.

Not all the traditional industries were in decline. The highly heterogeneous food and beverages group maintained its first-place position, largely as a result of the rapid increase in population and the improvement in Quebecers' standard of living in the postwar period. The largest industries, in descending order, consisted of slaughterhouses and meat-packing plants; butter and cheese factories, based on Quebec agriculture's longtime specialization in dairy production; miscellaneous food producers; bakeries (bread and other baked goods); soft drink factories; breweries; and distilleries. The value of production in all these industries increased significantly, and in most cases the workforce increased as well.

Paper products, an important industry since the 1920s, regained the second-place position it had lost during the war. Pulp and paper employed more workers than any other industry in Quebec: 21,695 at the start of the period and 27,239 at its close, not including workers engaged in logging. The value of production jumped from $266 million to $585 million.

Refineries in East Montreal. (George Hunter, NFB, National Archives of Canada, PA-151652)

There was no single pattern of development for the industries that had grown up during the war. The most remarkable growth took place in nonferrous metals, especially aluminum, of which Alcan was the largest producer. There had been considerable investment in the aluminum industry during the war for military purposes. After a difficult postwar adjustment period, the industry took advantage of the growing civilian demand for aluminum in such areas as construction and aircraft manufacturing, among others. Iron and steel products, like nonferrous metals, suffered a decline in the immediate postwar period and then recovered gradually. It accounted for 8.5 per cent of the total value of production in 1959.

The end of the war had a much more dramatic impact on the transportation equipment group, which included industries with significant military components such as aircraft manufacturing and shipbuilding. From 9.4 per cent of production in 1945, this group declined to only 3.8 per cent in 1950, rising again to 4.9 per cent by 1959. The group included one of the oldest Quebec industries, railway rolling stock, located in Montreal. This industry suffered from the gradual move away from rail transportation, even though dieselization temporarily stimulated production in the 1950s. Employment reached a peak of 17,127 in 1952, dropping to 9,161 by 1959. The aeronautics industry, while clearly benefiting from the development of civil aviation, went through wild swings. Output plummeted after 1945, but the Korean War revived the industry, and the number of employees tripled between 1950 and 1953. Another slowdown followed, and then a recovery starting in 1956. Shipbuilding was a much smaller industry, employing only 6,036 people in 1959.

Two highly specialized industries are worthy of note: products of petroleum and coal and electrical appliances and equipment. The petroleum and coal products group had only 2.5 per cent of the value of production in 1945 and 5.5 per cent in 1959. Oil refineries were concentrated mainly in Montreal East, and since they were owned by the giant oil multinationals there were very few of them: only six to eight plants during the period. There were also very few employees — fewer than 3,000 — but wages were high. Between 1946 and 1959, the value of production increased sixfold, jumping from $63 million to $371 million. Electrical appliances and equipment also held a significant position in the industrial structure, but production was much more vulnerable to the economic cycle and the industry experienced a series of highs and lows over the fifteen-year period. Overall value increased markedly, however: from $59 million to $181 million.

Thus, while Quebec's industrial structure was maintained, it underwent some adjustments. Traditional industries declined in relative terms, while high-technology industries requiring a more skilled labour force were on the rise. This development presaged changes in Quebec's labour needs in coming years: there would be much greater demand for highly skilled technicians and much less demand for unskilled labour.

Natural Resources

Exploitation of natural resources expanded considerably in the postwar period. The needs of Canadian consumers and Canadian industry and strong American demand for raw materials contributed to this growth.

In the energy sector, hydroelectric power held the spotlight. The demand for electricity was rising quickly; in Montreal the rate of growth was 10 per cent a year. The main reason for this rapid growth was increased consumer use of electrical appliances — refrigerators, stoves, television sets, washers, dryers, and more. Greater urbanization and rising living standards contributed to this development. Industrial demand remained high, and the new mines needed electricity. Hydro-Quebec developed new hydroelectric sites: two new sections of the Beauharnois power station on the St. Lawrence, two power stations on the Bersimis River on the North Shore and two others on the Ottawa River (Rapide 2 and Carillon). Also during the period, studies and preliminary work were undertaken for the Manicouagan-Outardes complex, again on the North Shore, which would be built after 1960.

However, the most spectacular developments in the resource sector came in mining, where the value of production rose from $91.5 million in 1945 to $446.6 million in 1960. There was a significant addition during the period to the list of minerals produced in Quebec. This was iron ore, which had not been mined in Quebec since the deposits in the St. Maurice Valley were gradually abandoned in the nineteenth century. The postwar revival of iron ore mining took place in New Quebec. The existence of iron ore deposits there had long been known, and exploration carried out in the 1930s and 1940s had pinpointed their location straddling the Quebec-Labrador border. But this distant location made mining difficult. Conditions changed in the early 1950s, when the Cold War and the outbreak of the Korean War created strong demand for strategic raw materials. The Paley Report of 1950 aroused fears that American reserves would quickly run out. In this context the New Quebec deposits became very attractive, and the Iron Ore Company of Canada began work on developing them in 1951. It built a 574-kilometre rail link between the new town of Schefferville and the port of Sept-Îles. The first ore shipments took place in 1954. Another company, Quebec Cartier Mining, opened a new mine on Lac Jeannine, a new seaport at Port-Cartier and a 310-kilometre railway between 1958 and 1961. Iron ore production, non-existent before 1954, reached a value of $92 million in 1959.

At the same time, the growth of Quebec mining output extended to all minerals. Copper output tripled; asbestos output more than doubled and value of production increased fivefold. Gold, silver, zinc and molybdenum production increased significantly; only lead production fell. Quebec also became a titanium producer with the opening of the Lac Allard mine, near Havre-Saint-Pierre, in 1950. Massive amounts of Quebec ore continued to be exported without being processed locally. This was especially true of the iron ore from New Quebec, shipped directly from the North Shore to the United States by freighter. The opening of the St. Lawrence Seaway in 1959 facilitated delivery to the large American steel mills.

In the other major resource industry, forest products, economic recovery and the heightened demand for wood and paper products led to an increased cut, the value of which rose from $121 million in 1945 to $172 million in 1960. While developments in the forest industry were not as spectacular as those in electricity and mining, the industry did begin a thorough reorganization in the 1950s. Wood was cut and shipped in a much more mechanized fashion, which led to increased productivity. The nature of the work force also changed, as the farmer-logger gave way to the forest worker by trade. This spelled the end of the agro-forest economy, which had been in existence for more than a century.

CHAPTER 17

THE ROLE OF THE SERVICE SECTOR

The major role of the service sector in the economy has been a familiar phenomenon in recent decades not just in Quebec but in all industrialized countries. It is often forgotten, however, that this phenomenon has roots going back to the late nineteenth century and emerged along with the rise of urbanization, large-scale industry and the modern state. In Quebec, service activities were already a very large part of the economy by the end of the Second World War, and became even more so between 1946 and 1960.

An Expanding Service Sector

The service or tertiary sector, one of several facets of the economy and society, is itself made up of a number of components. It includes all activities not directly related either to agriculture and resource extraction (the primary sector) or to manufacturing or construction (the secondary sector). For statistical purposes, the service sector is divided into five main segments: finance, insurance and real estate; wholesale and retail trade; transportation and communication, including storage and distribution of electricity, gas and water; public administration and the armed forces; and personal and professional services.

The relative economic importance of the service sector grew significantly in the postwar period. It accounted for 51 per cent of Quebec's gross domestic product in 1946 and 55 per cent in 1960. The change in employment figures was even more noticeable. In the 1951 census, the five main segments of the service sector together provided employment for 623,448 people, or 42 per cent of the labour force aged fourteen and over; ten years later the figures were 921,527 and 52 per cent, for an average annual growth rate of 4 per cent. Most service sector activities

Switchboard operator at the Royal Victoria Hospital, 1953. (National Archives of Canada, PA-133210)

employ a large labour force whose productivity is lower than in manu-facturing industries.

In the 1950s, there was an appreciable growth in numbers in many occupations that were associated with white-collar work but required little skill and were low-paying: bank tellers, secretaries, office clerks, salespeople, telephone operators. More and more women were employed in so-called female job ghettos, generally working under male superiors.

A number of factors came together to spur the growth of the service sector. Service activities are much more common in urban than in rural areas, so the resumption of urbanization led to more service jobs. The higher standard of living led to increased demand for services. The emer-gence of the Keynesian state meant a larger civil service. The baby boom brought increased demand for education and health care. Even manufac-turing was affected, as management and sales personnel began to play a greater role.

The Financial Sector

The financial, insurance and real estate sector in Quebec had the greatest increase in value of production, with an average annual growth rate of 10.6 per cent between 1946 and 1960. Growth in employment was less impressive, with an average annual growth rate of 4.8 per cent between 1951 and 1961, but this was higher than in the four other segments of the service sector.

The financial sector was dominated by the chartered banks and the life insurance companies. Taken together in 1945, they owned 83 per cent of the assets held by financial intermediaries in the private sector in Canada. By 1960, this share had fallen to 63 per cent as a result of the rapid growth of other types of institutions such as credit unions and consumer loan companies. Despite this relative decline, the chartered banks remained the major force in this area, and their assets increased from $7 billion to $17 billion between 1946 and 1960. While they mainly provided financing for business, they were turning increasingly to consumers, devoting a growing share of their funds to personal loans and mortgages and counting more on individual savings accounts for their deposits.

After the wave of mergers at the turn of the century, the Canadian banking system stabilized in the 1920s. In 1946, there were nine chartered banks. The three largest institutions were the Royal Bank of Canada ($2 billion in assets), the Bank of Montreal ($1.8 billion) and the Canadian Bank of Commerce ($1.4 billion). The Bank of Nova Scotia ($667 million) was the largest of the medium-sized banks. It was followed by four banks with assets of between $300 million and $400 million each: the Bank of Toronto, the Dominion Bank, the Imperial Bank of Canada, and a Francophone bank, the Banque Canadienne Nationale. Far behind came the Provincial Bank of Canada ($137 million), also owned by Francophones, and Barclays Bank ($35 million), a subsidiary of a British bank.

This structure changed significantly in subsequent years. In 1955, the Bank of Toronto and the Dominion Bank merged; in 1956, the Imperial Bank absorbed Barclays; and in 1961, the Imperial Bank merged with the Bank of Commerce. Thus, Canada ended up with five large banks, which became known as the Big Five, and two minor banks, both French Canadian and with a total of between 6 and 7 per cent of Canadian banking assets. A newcomer, the Mercantile Bank of Canada, founded in 1953 by Dutch interests, was marginal.

In theory, Montreal was still the main financial centre of Canada because the two largest banks still had their head offices there, but Toronto was undermining its dominant position. The fact that large banks were based in Montreal did not necessarily mean that Quebec's interests were well served. For a long time, these banks neglected Francophone Quebec, concentrating their services in the cities and Anglophone neighbourhoods and leaving the rest to the French Canadian banks. During the 1950s, the large banks' attitude became a little more open, and they expanded their network of branches in Quebec. But it was still the Francophone banks that offered the widest coverage, with 60 per cent of all bank branches in Quebec in 1961.

So while the Banque Canadienne Nationale and the Provincial Bank were only small players on the Canadian scene, they carried considerable weight in Quebec where most of their operations were concentrated. But they were not alone in trying to attract Francophone customers. Two other types of institutions, savings banks and caisses populaires (credit unions), were competing for the same market.

Quebec's saving banks were set up in the nineteenth century, at a time when the chartered banks paid little attention to small savings account holders. The savings banks had much more limited powers than the chartered banks, and they invested most of their funds in government bonds. Offering secure savings above all, they were managed very prudently. There were two savings banks, each with branches: the Montreal City and District Savings Bank and the Banque d'Économie de Québec. In 1960, they had a total of $300 million in assets, of which 80 per cent belonged to the Montreal bank.

More significant were the caisses populaires, which grew quickly during and after the war. They numbered 549 in 1940 and 1,227 in 1960. Most were members of the Fédération de Québec and its ten regional unions, while some belonged to a dissident group, the Fédération de Montréal. The assets of the Fédération de Québec rose from $21 million to $687 million between 1940 and 1960. During this period the caisses, which had first taken root in rural areas, made a breakthrough in the cities — in twenty years, urban caisses saw their share of membership go from 31 to 56 per cent, while their share of assets went from 44 to 63 per cent. The caisses populaires played an active role in mortgage lending and contributed heavily to financing residential construction.

The postwar years also witnessed the very rapid rise of consumer loan companies, of which the best known was Household Finance (HFC). They granted loans more easily than the banks, but they charged much higher interest rates. These companies helped expand consumer credit and increased the indebtedness of working families.

The life insurance companies still played a very important role in the financial domain. They held between 20 and 25 per cent of the assets of private sector financial intermediaries in Canada and represented large pools of capital for long-term investment in stocks and bonds, government securities or mortgages. In the postwar period, there were a large number of life insurance companies, many of which had only regional penetration, but the market was dominated by a small number of English Canadian companies headed by Sun Life of Montreal. Foreign companies, mainly American and British, were also active and important. French Canadian companies were few and not very influential.

Most of these companies, even the Anglophone ones, serviced Quebec through very active insurance agents or brokers, of whom a large number were Francophone. Already in 1951, Quebec had more than 5,500 insurance brokers. At a time when life insurance was a preferred method of saving, brokerage gave some Francophones a way of rising socially and joining the ranks of local elites.

Throughout the financial world, French Canadians were still in a minority position after the war. Nonetheless, the companies they controlled were beginning to carry some weight and were growing as a result of the improved standard of living among Francophones. After 1960, these companies became the springboard for a new Quebec financial elite.

Commerce

Postwar prosperity was reflected not only in savings but also in consumption. Wholesale and retail trade grew quickly, at an annual average rate of 9.3 per cent. It represented 11 to 12 per cent of Quebec's gross domestic product and employed 173,070 people in 1951 and 248,038 in 1961, for an annual average increase of 3.7 per cent.

In retail trade, sales rose from $1.3 billion to $4.2 billion between 1946 and 1960. The most dramatic growth occurred in automobile sales, the value of which increased sevenfold, leading also to increased sales in garages and gas stations. For basic items such as food, clothing and shoes, sales in 1960 were three to four times higher than in 1946.

Retail trade was quite fragmented and there were a large number of outlets (about 45,000), the great majority of which belonged to small independent owners. Chain stores accounted for only 15 per cent of sales in 1946 and 18 per cent in 1960. Nonetheless, they represented the wave of the future because of their greater purchasing power and higher profitability. Chain stores were strongest in areas such as food, where Steinberg's and Dominion held sway. In response, independent merchants began to set up a different kind of chain that allowed members to take advantage of group purchasing while remaining in charge of their own businesses.

Transportation and Communications

In the transportation sector, the most important development was the rise of the automobile. Quebec lagged far behind in this regard at the end of the war. A car was a luxury few could afford. Even in 1953, only 36 per cent of households owned cars, while in Ontario the figure was 65 per cent. But Quebec was catching up quickly; there were 188,359 cars in 1946 and 843,731 in 1960, for an average annual growth rate of 11.3 per cent. In 1960, 56 per cent of Quebec households owned cars. Trucking was undergoing similar growth.

Cars, trucks and buses had clearly become the preferred means of transporting people and merchandise, but the extremely poor condition of Quebec's roads made it impossible to use them to the fullest. Progress was being made — roads were open in winter, a large number of roads were paved, the Metropolitan Boulevard in Montreal and the Laurentian Autoroute were built. But overall, the roads were unable to absorb the increase in the number of cars, and the problem was not solved until the 1960s.

Rail transportation was affected by competition from trucking, which was faster and more efficient. Although noncompetitive for short-distance hauling and for handling many manufactured products, rail remained very important for transporting raw materials in bulk, mainly ore, as well as commodities such as lumber and paper. The main additions to the railway system were lines serving the new mining centres.

Railways were often just a link in a transportation chain that also included shipping. For example, iron ore from New Quebec was sent by train to Sept-Îles and then loaded onto cargo ships bound for the United States. The St. Lawrence Seaway, officially opened in 1959, represented

St. Catherine Street, Montreal, 1952. (Gar Lunney, NFB, National Archives of Canada, PA-111582)

the largest investment made in shipping and had its greatest impact on the transportation of raw materials.

Air transport, whose expansion had been stimulated by the war, was a growing force in the transportation sector. During the war huge aircraft plants were constructed — including Canadair in the Montreal suburb of Ville Saint-Laurent, which produced tens of thousands of aircraft — and many airports were built, enlarged and modernized. Some of these facilities were then converted to civil aviation, which was also growing rapidly. Throughout the postwar period, air routes both within Canada and to other countries proliferated. The main airline was Trans-Canada Airlines/Air Canada, established in 1937 by the federal government with its head office in Montreal. The number of its paying passengers increased tenfold over the period. Canadian Pacific Airlines, founded in 1942, was smaller and initially operated mainly in western Canada and across the Pacific. In Quebec, it also operated some domestic routes, which it gave up in 1953. Quebecair, the result of a 1953 merger between Rimouski Airlines and Gulf Aviation, operated mainly in the Lower St. Lawrence, the Gaspé and the North Shore. The development of mining in this area encouraged its expansion and soon made it a regional carrier with routes to Montreal and Quebec City.

Aviation underwent more significant technological developments than any other transportation mode, including increased aircraft capacity, speed and range and the advent of jet engines. The DC-3 with twenty seats was replaced in 1948 by the North Star with forty. Then came the Super-Constellation in 1954, the Viscount in 1956, and in 1960 the DC-8, which with its 120 seats and new technology marked a real breakthrough and initiated the era of mass air travel.

In the world of communications, the most dramatic development was without a doubt the advent of television in 1952. Television had a considerable influence on culture and lifestyle. It turned the world of entertainment and communications upside down and forced other media to redefine themselves. In 1960, Quebec's nine television stations generated receipts of $4.4 million; the forty-two radio stations (up from twenty-five in 1948) generated $10.6 million. In that year, 97 per cent of Quebec households had at least one radio (one quarter had two or more) and 89 per cent had a television set. Radio and television became the main vehicles for advertising and speeded up the integration of Quebecers into the consumer society.

The telephone was a much older device, but it penetrated Quebec households more slowly, although the 84 per cent of households that had a telephone in 1960 represented a significant increase over the 33 per cent that had one at the beginning of the war. Telephone companies were major employers, with 13,485 employees in 1951 and 17,446 in 1961. Besides the powerful Bell Telephone Company of Canada, there were a number of small local or regional companies.

Public Administration and Services

The last two segments of the service sector were government and personal and professional services, which accounted for 16 to 17 per cent of gross domestic product. The percentage of the labour force employed in these areas rose from 19 to 25 per cent in ten years. They include such a wide range of activities that is is impossible to examine them all here. Some of the main ones — government, education and social services — are discussed in other chapters and will only be reviewed quickly in this section.

According to census figures, the three levels of government directly employed 61,723 people in Quebec in 1951 and 99,194 in 1961, not including what we would today call the parapublic sector. The federal government, mainly as a result of its defence personnel, was the largest employer, followed by municipal or local governments. Employment in education rose from 48,124 to 79,539, while employment in health and social affairs went up from 47,180 to 75,049. In all, jobs in government, education, health and social affairs accounted for less than 11 per cent of the workforce in 1951; this figure had increased to more than 14 per cent in 1961.

Business services — accounting, engineering, law and advertising — were smaller, with the number of jobs rising from 15,956 to 25,601. But their average annual growth rate, 4.8 per cent, was comparable to that of the public and parapublic sectors.

In personal and other services, the growth rate was lower but the absolute number of jobs was high: 93,568 in 1951 and 137,032 ten years later. Hotels and restaurants were the main employers, accounting for half the jobs. Typically urban services such as dry cleaners and beauty salons were growing. But the number of domestics was growing by only 1 per cent per year, an indication of the relative decline of this type of work from the nineteenth century on. In 1961, domestics made up only 1.7 per cent of the workforce, although census figures almost certainly underestimate the fairly widespread undeclared work performed by cleaning women paid by the day.

*   *   *   *   *   *

Not only was the service sector playing an increased role in the Quebec economy overall, but each of its segments was growing as well. The rise of the service sector after the war was a function of the growth of the primary and secondary sectors, to which it provided services, and of Quebecers' increased personal income, reflected in consumption and savings. Nonetheless, there were considerable differences among the various industries grouped rather arbitrarily into the service sector. There is a great distance between the concentration of the banking sector and the fragmentation of small retail trade and personal services, and this must be taken into account.

CHAPTER 18

THE MODERNIZATION OF AGRICULTURE

For agriculture, the postwar years were a period of transition. As in all other industrialized societies, agriculture in Quebec was evolving into agribusiness. Starting the period with a labour surplus and outdated techniques and management, it modernized by becoming generally more productive and better integrated with other sectors of the economy. In Quebec, where subsistence farming persisted and agriculture was accorded a special role in society, this development had some distinctive features.

Farmers

The most conspicuous phenomenon of the period was the rural exodus. This was nothing new — agriculture's place in the economy had been declining since the beginning of the century — but the sudden acceleration of the exodus in the 1950s was striking. Although the population of Quebec as a whole increased by more than 20 per cent between 1941 and 1951 and again between 1951 and 1961, the farm population fell by more than 5 per cent between 1941 and 1951 and then tumbled dramatically by 24 per cent in the second half of the 1950s. While the farm population represented one fifth of the total population in the 1951 census, it accounted for only 11 per cent ten years later.

An even stronger indicator of agriculture's decline was the drop in the agricultural sector's share of the labour force — from 20 per cent in 1946 to 7.5 per cent in 1960. The decline was sharpest among unpaid family labour, whose numbers were falling at an annual rate of 5.6 per cent, compared to 3.6 per cent for farm owners and 1.6 per cent for paid labourers. Thus, the very structure of the traditional family farm was threatened.

These rapid developments stood in direct contradiction to the myth of Quebec's agricultural destiny. One reason for the change was low agricultural income, which between 1946 and 1960 amounted to only about 40 per cent of nonfarm income. As well, improved communications and massive exposure to urban culture though radio and television made rural areas much more aware of disparities in standard of living between town and country. In outlying areas of Quebec, changes in working conditions in the forests lessened the need for labour, upsetting the traditional balance. Finally, in all marginal agricultural areas, colonists who had come during the Depression had tried to make the best of difficult conditions; facing an unpromising future, many now decided to go back to the cities.

Rural population distribution remained much the same despite the rural exodus. More than three fifths of the rural population was concentrated in the Montreal region, the Eastern Townships and the St. Lawrence Lowlands between Sorel and Quebec City. The Lower St. Lawrence, the Gaspé and the North Shore accounted for only 19.5 per cent and the Outaouais, Lake St. John and Abitibi-Temiscamingue regions for 16.5 per cent.

Agricultural Output

Although by 1961 agricultural production accounted for only 4 per cent of gross domestic product, this does not in itself mean that agriculture played a marginal role in the economy. Both upstream industries that provided farmers with fertilizer, machinery and other supplies and downstream industries that bought, transported, processed and distributed their products must be taken into account. Close ties of interdependence developed among these three components as agriculture became integrated into the capitalist economy. In 1961, the agribusiness sector employed about 15 per cent of Quebec's labour force and accounted for more than 14 per cent of its gross domestic product.

In agriculture as such, dairy products, poultry, pork, cattle and eggs were the five leading products. They accounted for more than 80 per cent of agricultural income in 1960, as compared to only 65 per cent in 1946. During the period, cattle production increased by 30 per cent, pork by 80 per cent and poultry by more than 700 per cent. There was little change in field crops, which remained dominated by crops grown for animal feed: 90 per cent of the growing area was devoted to hay and oats. Wood, which had always been an important part of agricultural income, was in steady decline. Regional specialties continued: vegetables in the Montreal area for market and for canning; tobacco in the Joliette area; orchards in Rouville and Deux-Montagnes counties; and sugar beets around Saint-Hyacinthe.

Productivity grew significantly during the period. With fewer workers, farmers made greater use of the other factors of production (machin-

Mechanization of dairy operations. (UPA)

ery, land, buildings) so that the agricultural productivity gap between Quebec and the rest of Canada began to shrink. Quebec's farm products were sold primarily within Quebec and then — especially in the case of dairy products — in the rest of Canada. Agricultural marketing was the focus of considerable attention in the postwar period, as producers wanted to have more control over the domestic market and better access to it. Overseas, the end of the war brought a resumption of international competition, especially in Britain, which during the war had absorbed a large part of Canadian agricultural output.

Government Intervention

When the war was over, the government gradually reduced its controls on prices and production, although it was still prepared to intervene to support agricultural prices in case they fell too quickly. It also continued to subsidize the shipping of western grain, which as a result became an important source of feed for Quebec livestock. When the Diefenbaker government took power in the late 1950s, it reviewed Ottawa's agricultural policies. In 1958, it set up the Agricultural Stabilization Board, and in 1959 it amended the Farm Credit Act to adapt it to the new conditions in Canadian agriculture. The same year, it passed the Crop Insurance Act, making it possible for Ottawa to help provinces offer this type of insurance.

The Quebec government retained its major instruments of intervention — farm credit and subsidies of various kinds. According to the political scientist André Blais, government efforts were directed mainly at the prosperous forms of agriculture and were organized around four main focal points: land drainage, farm improvement, schools and credit. In 1945, the government launched a rural electrification campaign and encouraged the formation of cooperatives to build distribution networks. This was a very important initiative, because the large electricity producers were not interested in providing service in areas where little profit was to be made.

One of the Quebec government's most noted measures was the establishment the Quebec Agricultural Marketing Board in 1956. This followed the recommendations of the Héon Commission of inquiry into the protection of farmers and consumers, set up in 1952. The board was to help market farm products through programs known as joint plans — agreements guaranteed by law that set the conditions of sale between producers and buyers and governed entire sectors of production. In 1961, the plans covered various dairy products, maple products, some vegetables, tobacco and wood products.

Farms and Farming Techniques

Farms and farming techniques were heavily affected by the postwar changes in agriculture. The number of farms fell from 154,669 in 1941 to 95,777 in 1961, while average farm area rose from 47.3 to 60.0 hectares. Marginal farms were eliminated, and productivity rose on the farms that remained. In this regard, the economist Jean-Pierre Wampach has shown that the increase in productivity after 1945 was largely due to farmers' willingness to invest more in machinery, fertilizer and related products — further evidence of the growing integration of agriculture into the capitalist economy.

Census figures began to distinguish between different categories of farms, making it possible to separate subsistence farms from commercial ones. In 1961, 65 per cent of farms fell into the commercial category, showing annual sales of more than $1,200. Meanwhile, 50 per cent of subsistence farms — those with sales between $50 and $1,200 — were run by part-time farmers, who also worked off the farm.

Clearly, however, the market economy had less and less room for farmers who also worked at other jobs. Logging, the main source of extra work, was changing, and it needed increasingly specialized labour. Thus, there were two very different kinds of farming in Quebec: one more prosperous than before, the other increasingly marginalized and low-level.

Increased productivity was based on improved farming techniques. In addition to the disappearance of less productive farms, improvements in land and buildings, greater use of fertilizers and progress in mechanization all helped increase productivity. Land drainage was subsidized on a large scale. The increase in mechanization, made necessary by the shrinking labour force, constituted a virtual revolution, of which the most striking manifestation was the growth in the number of tractors from 5,758 in 1941 to 60,481 in 1961. In 1961, 63 per cent of farms had tractors, up from only 23 per cent in 1951 and less than 4 per cent in 1941. The number of cars also grew. Rural electrification was another element in more rapid mechanization. Electric motors, refrigeration and lighting combined to change the conditions in which farm production took place. In 1961, almost all farms — 97.3 per cent — had electricity.

Knowledge of new techniques was spread by the two traditional means, farm newspapers and agronomists. Farm journalism adapted to the new media with programs such as *Réveil rural* on radio and *Les travaux et les jours* on television. In addition, both the federal and Quebec departments of agriculture provided publications on a wide range of farm topics, some of them highly specialized. Model farms also played a role; located right in the farm communities, they served as a reference point for agronomists and farmers.

Education was the other method of spreading information in rural communities. On the average, more than 1,600 students per year attended Quebec's seventeen agricultural colleges between 1945 and 1960, double the number for the period between 1934 and 1944. Thus, the influence of these institutions on farm practices was growing.

Farmers' Organizations

Farmers had two main types of organizations: farmers' cooperatives, which first appeared in the early years of the twentieth century, and a trade organization, the Union Catholique des Cultivateurs (UCC), founded in 1924. There were a number of sources of tension between the two. The main point of contention was whether the cooperative movement should be independent or act as the economic arm of the UCC. Over time, the gap between the two widened — the cooperatives operated more and more like big businesses, and the UCC became more like a farmers' union.

During the Depression, the cooperative movement was not very strong. Local cooperatives were often small, and only the central organization, the Coopérative Fédérée du Québec, was of significant size. The movement began to grow again during the war, and the number of cooperatives rose from 215 in 1938 to 645 in 1947. Sales grew even more quickly, increasing from $7.5 million in 1938 to $103 million in 1948. As the cooperative movement grew, it became more rationalized and concentrated: in 1960, there were only 482 cooperatives left, with total sales of $191 million. Some cooperatives, such as the Coopérative Agricole de Granby, became very powerful, controlling a large share of dairy production and processing. By the late 1950s, cooperatives were tending to become very large businesses, and the cooperative ideal of democratic operation took second place to the imperatives of efficient management.

The UCC was a small organization when the Depression began, with 10,251 members in 1930, and membership fell even further to 8,320 in 1933. But membership began to expand with the unionization of lumberjacks, which began in 1934, and growth continued during the war. By 1945 the UCC had 32,000 members, of whom only 1,000 were lumberjacks. Its activities consisted mainly of participation in the ideological debates going on at the time, in which the UCC defended family and rural values. Caught between its defence of traditional agriculture and agriculture's gradual integration into the market economy, the UCC went through a difficult time in the 1950s. Membership fell from 40,017 in 1952 to 28,156 in 1960. Hurt by the rural exodus and facing competition from independent organizations of specialized producers, it tried to redirect its efforts and act more like a union, defending farmers' interests. The UCC's new orientation emerged in the discussions surrounding the establishment of the Quebec Agricultural Marketing Board, when it protested the role given the cooperatives in managing the joint plans. The UCC felt it was better able to represent farmers, and it saw the cooperatives as removed from farmers' interests and comparable to privately owned businesses.

Farm women had their own organizations, the Cercles des Fermières. They were first established in 1915 and funded by the government, and they played an important role in communicating information and stimulating home crafts. In 1944 the UCC, worried about government influence, set up its own women's section, the Union Catholique des Fermières. Relations between the Union Catholique des Fermières and the Cercles des Fermières were tense throughout the period.

Colonization

The return of prosperity marked the end of colonization as a major phenomenon in Quebec. The government continued to offer some of its various bonuses, but there were no more colonization campaigns of the kind that had been launched during the Depression. While the recently opened colonization areas tried to survive as best they could, many people left the colonization regions and went — or came back — to the cities.

One of the main reasons for this development was the profound change that had occurred in the relation between agriculture and the forest industry. From its nineteenth century beginnings, colonization had depended on the complementary relationship between the two — the forest industry provided work for farmers during the winter, and the logging camps were a market for their meagre output. In their study of the development of forest work into a trade, "La professionalisation du travail en forêt," the sociologists Gérald Fortin and Émile Gosselin were among the first to describe the changes that undermined this relationship beginning in the 1950s. Entrepreneurs wanted to make woodcutting profitable, and so extended logging well beyond the winter and used increas-

Grain harvest in Abitibi. (Office du film du Québec, 1073-54)

ingly complex equipment. While farmers worked in the forest with familiar tools and traditional means of transport (essentially horses), loggers now had to use power saws, which were relatively expensive and required delicate handling. Sophisticated machines were now used in the various pruning and cartage operations.

Thus, logging became a trade in itself and went on almost year-round. At the same time, with logging operations restructured, the logging camps disappeared as a market, leaving the colonists deprived of their main outlet. From now on, the farms would have to survive on agriculture alone.

In some regions, tourism made up for the disappearance of the forest industry. The prosperity of many parishes in the Laurentians, north of Montreal, became tied to the growth of holiday resorts. Colonists and farmers turned into artisans, shopkeepers and small entrepreneurs serving the tourist trade, and gradually gave up farming.

The period from 1945 to 1960 was a crucial one. The gap between market-oriented agriculture and subsistence farming grew wider, and the links with the forest industry, which had helped subsistence farming survive, disappeared. This was not a new development, but it had been masked by the myth of Quebec's agricultural calling and the effects of the Depression. As a UCC brief put it, "agriculture in the province of Quebec is in the process of becoming a business instead of a way of life."

CHAPTER 19
ECONOMIC POLICIES

The postwar period marked a turning point in the history of peacetime economic policy in Quebec. The initiative came from Ottawa which, after the experience of the Depression and the war, applied Keynesian policies and tried to assume overall management of the Canadian economy. The Quebec government resisted this new direction and maintained its traditional policy of limited intervention and weak government supervision.

Federal Government Policy

At the end of the war, the federal governnment's greatest fear was a return to the large-scale unemployment of the 1930s. Mindful of the depression that had followed the First World War, it adopted Keynesian-based policies designed to ensure full employment, the main goal set forth in the White Paper on Work and Income issued in 1945.

Since the Canadian economy was heavily dependent on the export of raw materials, the federal government concentrated on getting international trade moving again. It hoped to carve out a market for Canada in Europe, whose infrastructure had been badly damaged by the war. But because European countries had been bled white, to do this it had to finance Canadian exports itself. As noted in chapter 15, the government granted a substantial loan to Britain, offered export credits to France, the Netherlands and Belgium, and made arrangements so that American dollars spent by the United States for reconstruction in Europe could be used to purchase Canadian products. In addition, Ottawa took an active part in negotiations to reduce trade barriers, which led to the General Agreement on Tariffs and Trade (GATT) in 1947.

But despite government efforts in Europe, the most dramatic increase was in exports of raw materials to the United States, whose economy was growing vigorously. Increased exports to the U.S. were mainly due to private sector initiatives, not federal government policies. However, Ottawa's 1951 decision to start work on the St. Lawrence Seaway strengthened the growing trend towards trade with the United States, although the seaway would also facilitate the shipping of western grain to Europe. Initially, the American government showed little interest in participating in the seaway project, but this changed when the Cold War and the Korean War made it see the strategic importance of Canadian resources for defence purposes. A Canadian-American agreement on joint construction of the seaway was signed in 1954.

Because of the scope of the investment required and the seaway's long-term implications, the project was one of the federal government's most important postwar economic decisions. The waterway made it easier to build hydroelectric power sites on the St. Lawrence. For Quebec, it meant the end of Montreal's position as a compulsory transshipment point for merchandise and pivot for water transport between the Great Lakes and the Atlantic, a role the city had played since the seventeenth century. On the positive side, the seaway contributed to the resource development and shipping boom on the North Shore.

Another goal of Canadian postwar economic policy was stimulating consumption. To let consumer demand reassert itself after being held in check for so long, the government lifted controls, eliminating production quotas and freeing prices. And it counted on transfer payments to act as long-term stimulants and prevent demand from burning itself out too quickly. Family allowances, approved in 1944 and put into effect a year later, were considered not just an equalization payment but also a means of stimulating consumption and redistributing large sums of money to families. Unemployment insurance, which had been in existence since 1940, was seen as a means of countering the effects of the business cycle — in times of full employment, large sums of money could be accumulated for redistribution when unemployment was high.

Other specific programs helped flesh out Ottawa's strategy. Thus, a number of measures were aimed at reintegrating demobilized soldiers into civilian life: veterans were to get their old jobs back, and there were grants for those who wanted to go back to school, financial aid for buying a house or a farm, pensions for the wounded and disabled, and other provisions.

But the most significant innovation in economic strategy after the war went beyond any of these specific measures. This was the use of government fiscal policy and the Bank of Canada's monetary policy as tools for managing the economy. Here again, Keynesian policies held sway, as budgets and monetary policy were periodically adjusted to the economic situation. In periods of vigorous growth, the government would curb spending and the Bank of Canada would try to tighten credit to control inflation; in periods of economic slowdown, the government would lower taxes and increase spending, incurring deficits if necessary, and the Bank would make credit easier.

In the decade following the war, Keynesianism worked fairly well because the economy was strong. Ottawa accumulated a sizable budget surplus. The slight economic slowdown that occurred in 1954 was swiftly countered: the Saint-Laurent government reduced taxes, stimulated investment and ran a deficit for the first time. The ensuing recovery restored the budget surplus the next year. But after 1957, Keynesianism experienced some failures when the most serious recession of the postwar period occurred and unemployment rose significantly.

The federal government could manage the economy only to a degree, because many economic elements were not under its control. The importance of international trade for the Canadian economy and increased Canadian dependence on the United States made Canada vulnerable to policies and decisions formulated elsewhere. As well, the federal government had no control over provincial and municipal spending, on which there was great demand, especially for infrastructure: schools, hospitals, roads, water and sewer systems, and other projects. Finally, it became clear that the most effective measures were not always the most popular ones, and economic policies had to be adjusted to electoral realities. So while in theory some types of government spending should have been drastically reduced when the economy was doing well, this proved difficult to do politically.

The Liberals, in power until 1957, favoured increased government intervention, as did their successors, the Conservatives, but both parties rejected the idea of the kind of planned economy the socialists in the CCF would have liked to see. Both Liberals and Conservatives believed that government should provide stimulants and incentives but economic development should remain in the hands of private enterprise. The Canadian government welcomed foreign — mainly American — investment with open arms, and American control over the economy grew substantially after 1945. At the same time, Ottawa withdrew from direct production, dismantling most of the crown corporations set up during the war or else handing them over to private enterprise. The federal government's share of gross national expenditure, which had risen to 37.7 per cent in 1944, reached a low of 4.5 per cent in 1948 and then varied between 9 and 10 per cent from 1952 on.

Ottawa's economic policy was a challenge to Canadian federalism and threatened to upset the balance that had gradually developed since 1867. The boosters of the new instruments of economic management in the House of Commons and the upper ranks of the civil service were convinced that for them to be effective, the federal government had to obtain more power over the provinces, which meant increased centralization of economic decision-making. Thus, they had the wartime agreements transferring income tax collection to the federal government renewed. We will return to this question in chapter 27.

Some provinces, mainly Quebec and Ontario, were against this kind of constitutional change, so federal strategists resorted to more indirect methods involving provincial participation. The government formulated so-called national objectives and proposed a set of concrete programs to realize them, with the costs shared by the two levels of government. In this way, the federal government entered into areas of provincial jurisdiction on the basis of rules it established itself. Examples of this procedure included construction of the Trans-Canada Highway, grants to universities and hospital insurance.

Ottawa would not have been able to meet its goals, or even formulate them coherently, without a new kind of civil service at the senior level. Since the latter years of the Depression, and particularly during the war, the federal government had recruited a bevy of brilliant young senior civil servants, including economists trained in Britain by the initiators of Keynesianism and the welfare state. Although they worked in the shadows, these new mandarins were key cogs in the wheel of the Canadian political system.

In these circles, dominated by Canadians of British origin, Quebecers could not keep up with Ontarians. Of course, Quebec benefited from the new federal policies, but it did not have a role in developing them. In the 1950s, many Francophone intellectuals felt torn between their support for the federal government's reform liberalism and their desire to protect Quebec's particularity.

Quebec Government Policies

Throughout the postwar period, the Duplessis government opposed Ottawa's reform liberalism and Keynesianism. Its economic and social outlook was profoundly conservative, and its credo was classic liberalism based on respect for private enterprise, through which it hoped to attract large corporations and capital investment to Quebec. It didn't matter if many of these companies were American, as long as they brought new investment.

This approach was most evident in the Duplessis government's attitude to business, especially in the resource sector. Companies enjoyed wide powers granted by provincial law, low prices for forest and mineral rights, and low taxes. The government took responsibility for such infrastructure items as roads, while companies had few obligations and were not heavily regulated.

The government also tried to create a favourable social climate for business. The minimum wage was kept low, there were few benefits, and standards for working conditions were minimal, worse than what unionized workers had. The Duplessis government used amendments to the labour code and the Provincial Police as weapons against union demands. The government's strategy helped keep Quebec as a large pool of unskilled, low-paid labour.

Specific economic measures were pursued within traditional areas of intervention favoured by Quebec governments for half a century: natural resources, roads and agriculture. In the resource sector, the Duplessis government departed from precedent by emphasizing mining. It promoted the opening of new mining regions in New Quebec, Chibougamau and the Gaspé. The Department of Mines contributed by building access roads, carrying out geological surveys and expanding its laboratories. The political scientist Gérard Boismenu has written: "The Union Nationale systematically granted exclusive mineral rights, shared in the start up costs of mining development, and asked only for a royalty in return. This policy of support for big capital contributed to the penetration of Quebec by large U.S. monopoly corporations, continental integration, and the export of unprocessed ore."

In the forest sector, Duplessis did not make any significant changes to the policy that had been developed several decades before, based on a system of forest concessions and payment of cutting rights. However, tax revenues from forestry were quite small compared to what they had been early in the century.

Duplessis inherited the partial nationalization of electricity carried out by his predecessor, Adélard Godbout. After opposing the nationalization as leader of the opposition, he had to accept it as premier. While he remained true to his conservative ideology in jacking up the compensation the Liberals had planned to pay the former sharehoders of Montreal Light, Heat and Power, he went against his own principles in assigning the Bersimis and Manicouagan hydroelectric projects on the North Shore to Hydro-Quebec, even though these two sites were far from the publicly owned utility's Montreal base. However, Hydro-Quebec was to sell some of the electricity from the two developments back to the private companies serving other regions of the province.

Since the era of Lomer Gouin, spending on roads had been one of the Quebec government's major areas of economic intervention. This was still the case in the postwar period. However, a study by Gérard Boismenu showed that Duplessis used this budgetary item in a special way — rather than make it an instrument of economic development or even a means of meeting a short-term need for jobs, he used roads basically for partisan electoral purposes. Spending on roads would reach record levels the year before an election and then fall back down again during the first three years of the next mandate. Duplessis repeated the trick in 1948, 1952 and 1956. "Roadwork," Boismenu concludes, "was a favourite channel for the distribution of patronage." It is not surprising that there was no coherent road building policy. The Union Nationale's strategy was essentially to improve rural roads and neglect major highways and roads serving cities. Roads around cities — especially Montreal — were constantly clogged with traffic. Construction of the Laurentian Autoroute and Montreal's Metropolitan Boulevard were exceptions to the rule.

In agricultural policy (see chapter 18), government intervention consisted mainly of building rural roads and providing grants for land drainage and equipment. Other measures included electrification and intervention to rationalize the marketing of farm products. On the whole, government assistance was directed mainly to the most prosperous forms of agriculture and helped consolidate them, even though there was a sprinkling of subsidies in marginal areas for electoral purposes.

Taken together, the Union Nationale's economic policies were limited, unrelated to any overall plan, and within the bounds of traditional Quebec government intervention. The main aim was to support private enterprise. Duplessis's refusal to involve the government in any active planning or coordinating role was also reflected in fiscal policy. Duplessis rejected Keynesianism and managed the government's finances like a family's: income had to exceed expenses. So balancing the budget became a priority, except at election time when increased patronage spending led to a deficit.

Duplessis had the same attitude to debt. He had been traumatized by the experience of his first term in office, when he had to borrow heavily because of the Depression and found himself at the mercy of the financial sector. When he got back into power, he tried to limit the Quebec government's debt, partly by using current revenues to cover capital spending and partly by paying back part of the existing debt. Thus, between 1945 and 1960, the government's consolidated debt fell from $341 million to $305 million. This meant placing severe limits on new capital spending and allowing Quebec's infrastructure to lag behind. By meeting only some of the need for roads, hospitals, schools and universities, the Union Nationale gave the impression of being a good financial manager, but it also created a wide social and economic gap, especially relative to Ontario.

The Union Nationale's economic policies encouraged resource-based development and foreign control of the economy, and thus contributed to Quebec's socioeconomic underdevelopment.

CHAPTER 20
URBAN GROWTH

Postwar economic growth was accompanied by increased urbanization. A large majority of the population lived in cities, and newcomers were attracted there in large numbers. Cities were changing physically, with a modernized infrastructure, tens of thousands of new houses, urban sprawl and growing suburbs. These changes were especially conspicuous in the Montreal metropolitan area, but they were also occurring elsewhere in Quebec. In addition, many new towns grew up in resource-extracting regions during the 1950s.

The Urbanization of the Population Resumes

The proportion of Quebecers living in urban areas rose quickly after the war, from 61.2 per cent in 1941 to 66.8 per cent in 1951 and 74.3 per cent in 1961. Quebec was still more urbanized than Canada as a whole, and while it was less urbanized than Ontario, the gap between the two was narrowing. In 1941 and 1951, Quebec was the third most urbanized province, after Ontario and British Columbia; in 1961 it was second.

There were a number of elements in the growth of the urban population. The birth rate, especially among urban French Canadians, remained high throughout the postwar period. The demographic catch-up process — the baby boom — was a contributing factor. Urban French Canadian families with five or six children were not uncommon, and progress in health care lowered the death rate significantly. Urban growth was also spurred by internal migration — the rural exodus, slowed down substantially by the Depression, resumed after the war and accelerated between 1956 and 1961. Finally, immigration resumed and was relatively high between 1951 and 1957, adding further to the urban population. Migrants were able to fill the urban economy's considerable demand for labour, both in the manufacturing sector and in the huge, and essentially urban, service sector, where large numbers of jobs were being created.

Bungalow in Saint-Léonard-de-Port-Maurice, built in the late 1950s. (INRS-Urbanisation)

Cities under Construction

The boom in residential and commercial construction and the major urban infrastructure projects being undertaken meant an expanding construction industry. There were more than 400,000 housing starts in Quebec between 1948 and 1960, of which 78 per cent were in urban centres with a population of at least 5,000. The 1961 census showed that 45 per cent of housing units then in existence had been built since the end of the war.

Government policy had a direct impact on the resumption of residential construction. The federal government set up the Central Mortgage and Housing Corporation in 1945 and then broadened its mandate with the National Housing Act of 1954. The CMHC's main purpose was to insure mortgage loans provided by certified lending institutions, but towards the end of the period it acted more and more as a direct lender. The CMHC's policies mainly encouraged the building of single-family dwellings for the middle class, which did not correspond to the needs of Quebec society at the time. Contrary to what happened in Ontario, only a minority of new housing units were financed with aid from the CMHC. Most new housing was built with loans from caisses populaires under Quebec legislation passed in 1948, which subsidized a 3 per cent portion of the mortgage interest under certain conditions. In this way, the government encouraged the construction of less costly housing for lower-income families.

While construction was booming in Quebec, wider access to home ownership came more slowly. Only a minority of urban Quebecers owned their own homes. In 1961, 67 per cent of people in the Montreal

Ruelle Leduc before work began under the Dozois Plan (Habitations Jeanne-Mance), Montreal, 1957. (Central Mortgage and Housing Corporation, National Archives of Canada, PA-123798)

area were tenants, as compared to only 33 per cent in Toronto. Although the North-American-style single family home was becoming more common towards the end of the period, the great majority of residences built were for two or more families.

People became increasingly concerned with urban renewal during the 1950s, and the CMHC devoted funds to it. In Montreal, where the large number of slums was widely criticized, there was fierce debate over the Dozois Plan, a scheme to demolish old dwellings in the downtown area and replace them with low-rent housing. The plan was finally carried out under the name Habitations Jeanne-Mance and was the only significant uran renewal initiative taken during the period.

General Features

Quebec's urban growth had its strongest impact in the Montreal area. From 1941 to 1961, the population of the metropolitan Montreal census area increased by almost a million; growth was fastest in the 1950s (table 1). In both 1941 and 1951, 34 per cent of the total population of Quebec lived in metropolitan Montreal, and in 1961, the figure rose to 40 per cent. Thus, the great concentration of population in Montreal, which had long

THE QUEBEC URBAN SYSTEM, 1961

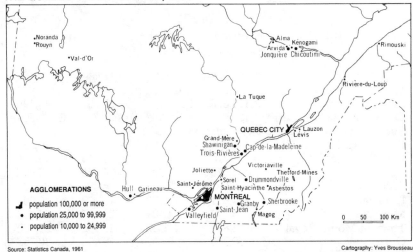

Source: Statistics Canada, 1961   Cartography: Yves Brousseau

been a major feature of urbanization in Quebec, was accentuated during the period.

This situation created further disparity among the components of the Quebec urban system. The second largest metropolitan area, Quebec City, contained only 6 to 7 per cent of the population. Other urban areas trailed far behind — there were only seven cities with a population of more than 30,000, two of which — Hull and Chicoutimi-Jonquière — had about 100,000 people each in 1961. In this sense, the Quebec urban system differed substantially from Ontario's. Ontario had many more middle-sized cities than Quebec, and these cities had larger populations.

In relatively old cities such as Quebec City, Trois-Rivières and Sherbrooke, population growth was much slower than than in Montreal, and the balance was thus further tipped towards the metropolis. Hull, however, was an exception. The urban system was also spreading outwards, with the rapidly increasing urbanization of the North Shore.

The slow growth of many cities was due in part to their fragile economic base. The initial development of many Quebec cities and towns was based on a small number of companies in a narrow range of industries, or even on a single dominant company. As a result, these cities and towns reached their full growth potential fairly quickly. Without industrial diversification, they could not count on continued expansion once the initial momentum was gone. Moreover, they were highly vulnerable to changes in the economic situation as it affected their main product. When the economy was slow, the whole town suffered. But in the post-war period, the rise of the service sector compensated for the economic weakness of these cities. In many cases, such a city came to serve as a regional metropolis or service centre, which gave new impetus to economic expansion. But with the rural hinterland in relative decline, growth possibilities for many cities remained fairly limited.

Table 1
Population of Major Cities and Towns in the Montreal Region, 1941-1961

	1941	1951	1956	1961
Montreal	903,007	1,021,520	1,109,439	1,191,062
Montreal Island	1,116,800	1,320,232	1,507,653	1,747,696
Census metropolitan area	1,139,921	1,395,400	1,620,758	2,109,509
Suburban municipalities on Montreal Island				
Beaconsfield	706	1,888	5,496	10,064
Côte-Saint-Luc	776	1,083	5,914	13,266
Dorval	2,048	5,293	14,055	18,592
Lachine	20,051	27,773	34,494	38,630
La Salle	4,651	11,633	18,973	30,904
Montreal North	6,152	14,081	25,407	48,433
Town of Mount Royal	4,888	11,352	16,990	21,182
Outremont	30,751	30,057	29,990	30,753
Pierrefonds	-	1,436	2,444	12,171
Pointe-aux-Trembles	4,314	8,241	11,981	21,926
Pointe-Claire	4,536	8,753	15,208	22,709
Rivière-des-Prairies	912	4,072	6,806	10,054
Ville Saint-Laurent	6,242	20,426	38,291	49,805
Verdun	67,349	77,391	78,262	78,317
Westmount	26,047	25,222	24,800	25,012
Other municipalities in the census metropolitan area in 1961				
Chomedey	-	7,732	16,649	30,455
Duvernay	-	1,529	3,095	10,939
Laval-des-Rapides	3,242	4,998	11,248	19,227
Pont-Viau	1,132	5,129	8,218	16,077
Saint-Vincent-de-Paul	4,275	4,372	6,784	11,214
Jacques-Cartier	-	22,450	33,132	40,807
Laflèche	-	6,494	9,958	10,984
Longueuil	7,087	11,103	14,332	24,131
Saint-Hubert	2,457	6,294	10,764	14,380
Saint-Lambert	6,417	8,615	12,224	14,531
Sainte-Thérèse	4,659	7,038	8,266	11,771
Muncipalities in the broader Montreal region				
Saint-Jérôme	11,329	17,685	20,645	24,546
Joliette	12,749	16,064	16,940	18,088
Sorel	12,251	14,961	16,476	17,147
Saint-Hyacinthe	17,798	20,236	20,439	22,354
Saint-Jean	13,646	19,305	24,367	26,988
Valleyfield	17,052	22,414	23,584	27,297

Source: *Quebec Yearbook*, 1958 and 1963.

Another feature of the period was the development of large agglomerations, each consisting of an urban population occupying a whole area with a central city at its core. The population of these agglomerations grew much more quickly than that of their central cities. Some agglomerations took the form of highly interdependent twin cities or conurbations constituting a single entity. This was the case with Shawinigan-Grand'Mère, Rouyn-Noranda and — perhaps the best example — Kénogami-Jonquière-Arvida-Chicoutimi. The main reason for the emergence of these large agglomerations was the growth of suburbs, as many small municipalities sprang up, all dependent on the central city. This was particularly true of Montreal and Quebec City, where population growth occurred mainly in the suburbs, but the same development could be seen around most of Quebec's middle-sized cities. The increase in the number of towns and cities, from 139 in 1945 to 227 in 1960, bears witness to this phenomenon.

The municipal system in Quebec after the war was managed in an archaic fashion. Municipal institutions that dated back to the 1870s and had not changed significantly since their founding were increasingly unable to cope with large-scale urbanization. The main problem was the division of administrative responsibility among a proliferation of small municipalities, often in competition with one another and with no coordinating structures. In the suburban areas of large agglomerations, regulation varied widely from one municipality to the next and uncontrolled development was a characteristic feature.

The proliferation of municipalities was matched by the fragmentation of the land development and residential construction industries. Since municipal governments took responsibility for servicing the land (building aqueducts, sewers and roads), Francophone entrepreneurs with little capital could play an active role in urban development. This situation also benefited a whole host of small builders and developers of Jewish and Italian origin in addition to French Canadians. In the same period, by contrast, big real estate development companies emerged in Ontario, acquiring large tracts of land around the cities and servicing these tracts themselves.

Municipal governments functioned on the basis of a kind of truncated democracy, in which many people affected by municipal decisions had little say in them. Heads of property-owning families carried the most weight in municipal politics. City and town councils were traditionally made up of local *notables* who ran the municipality in close cooperation with the developers and were conservative in social policy. There were no professional administrators. Political practice was based on patronage, and except in large cities municipal employees rarely had adequate training. The result was a laissez-faire system in which the interests of the few predominated over those of the community. There was no real plan for urban development: it was left in the hands of developers, who had no problem getting their projects approved by city and town councils that could not keep up with the scope and pace of the changes taking place.

Montreal

It took the Montreal metropolitan area until 1931 — almost three centuries — to reach a population of one million. Reaching its second million took only three decades. The rate of population growth during the 1950s was at a historic high: an annual average of 4.21 per cent for the decade as a whole and 5.41 per cent for the period between 1956 and 1961. This was basically a result of the phenomenal growth of the suburbs, as the population of the city proper grew fairly slowly, even though Montreal did have 300,000 more people in 1961 than in 1941.

Montreal grew because of its diversified economy and its role as a metropolis. Manufacturing was still a basic component of its economy and enjoyed another boom in the 1950s. Industry began to move out to the suburbs, a trend that would intensify in the 1960s. For example, Ville Saint-Laurent, where large-scale industrialization began with the opening of the Canadair aircraft plant during the war, attracted a number of aircraft, electronics and pharmaceuticals plants. By 1961 it had 18,546 industrial jobs, more than Quebec City.

Montreal was also a major commercial and financial centre, with more than a fifth of its labour force employed in these two sectors. Another 10 per cent was employed in transport and communications, but the city's role as the transportation hub of eastern Canada was changing. While the rise of air transportation could be seen at Dorval airport, Montreal's traditional strengths were eroding. Montreal had an underdeveloped road system at a time when trucking was overtaking rail transportation. Meanwhile the St. Lawrence Seaway, which opened in 1959, threatened to undermine Montreal's historic position as a port. For the first time in its history, Montreal was not a compulsory transshipment point for river navigation.

In addition to these activities, Montreal provided a wide variety of social, cultural, commercial and personal services, so that the service sector clearly dominated its occupational structure. Because Montreal's influence as a service centre extended far beyond its own territory, its function as a metropolis was a factor in its growth. However, it had to share its metropolitan role with its steadily rising rival, Toronto.

Montreal differed from other Quebec cities not only in its complex, diversified economic structure, but also in the makeup of its population. While many of its residents were native Montrealers, there was also a strong contingent of newcomers. In 1961, 16.8 per cent of its residents were born in foreign countries, 5 per cent were born in Canada outside Quebec, and there were also a large number of migrants from within Quebec. The resumption of immigration after the war made the city more cosmopolitan. The proportion of French Canadians in the population of Montreal Island remained steady at 62 per cent, but the proportion of residents who were of British origin fell from 24.5 per cent in 1941 to 18.1 per cent in 1961. The proportion belonging to other ethnic groups rose from 13 to 20 per cent, and Montrealers of Italian origin became more numerous than those of Jewish origin by the end of the period.

The city also changed physically during the period. Montreal's urbanized area extended much farther than it had previously, and new towns sprang up like mushrooms in all directions. In new neighbourhoods that grew up in the immediate postwar period, such as Ahuntsic, traditional Montreal features were retained: a preponderance of multifamily dwellings; long, narrow lots; flats laid out along a long corridor; and services concentrated on commercial streets. But during the 1950s, the new type of North American suburb became more common, with single-family homes (bungalow or split-level), smaller lots and shopping centres. Suburbs and neighbourhoods of this kind grew up on Montreal Island (Dorval, Ville Saint-Laurent, the new parts of Bordeaux and Rosemount), Île Jésus (Duvernay, Laval-des-Rapides, Chomedey) and the South Shore (Saint-Lambert).

These physical changes were brought about mainly by private interests, and the city government was unable to establish a coherent development policy. Its only major contribution was to build Dorchester Boulevard (now Boulevard René-Lévesque); this was a controversial project and when completed it created a breach in the fabric of the city. Montreal city council was paralysed by incessant fighting among competing cliques and factions. Corruption was rampant in local politics and the city administration. A huge anticorruption campaign in the early 1950s led to the retirement from politics of Mayor Camillien Houde, "Mr. Montreal," and a young lawyer, Jean Drapeau, was elected mayor in 1954 at the head of a reform group called the Civic Action League. In 1957, Drapeau was defeated by Sarto Fournier and his Ralliement du Grand Montréal. In neither election, however, did the winning party gain a clear majority. Furthermore, the elected councillors had to reckon with the appointed "C" councillors (see chapter 4), who held one third of the seats. The presence of these councillors was increasingly criticized as antidemocratic, and in a referendum in 1960, the voters opted to abolish the "C" category. In the 1950s, however, the incessant fighting in city council and Premier Duplessis' frequent interventions in Montreal's affairs paralysed the council and prevented it from playing an active role in guiding the city's development.

Suburban growth also posed the problem of coordination among municipalities. The Montreal Metropolitan Commission, formed in 1921 and replaced in 1959 by the Montreal Metropolitan Corporation, had only limited powers, and there was no agreement on what its role should be. Its only major accomplishment was the construction of the Metropolitan Boulevard, a project that had been under discussion since 1935. The other supramunicipal body was the Montreal Transportation Commission, es-

Table 2
Population of Major Quebec Cities and Towns outside the Montreal Region, 1941-1961

	1941	1951	1956	1961
Quebec City region				
Quebec City	150,757	164,016	170,703	171,979
Census metropolitan area	200,814	274,827	309,959	357,568
Beauport	725	5,390	6,735	9,192
Charlesbourg	2,789	5,734	8,202	14,308
Giffard	4,909	8,097	9,964	10,129
Sainte-Foy	2,682	5,236	14,615	29,716
Sillery	4,212	10,376	13,154	14,109
Lauzon	7,877	9,643	10,255	11,533
Lévis	11,991	13,162	13,644	15,112
Eastern Townships				
Sherbrooke	35,965	50,543	58,668	66,554
Magog	9,034	12,423	12,720	13,139
Thetford Mines	12,716	15,095	19,511	21,618
Victoriaville	8,516	13,124	16,031	18,720
Drummondville	10,555	14,341	26,284	27,709
Asbestos	5,711	8,190	8,969	11,083
Granby	14,197	21,989	27,095	31,463
St. Maurice Valley				
Trois-Rivières	42,007	46,074	50,483	53,477
Cap-de-la-Madeleine	11,961	18,667	22,943	26,925
Shawinigan	20,325	26,903	28,597	32,169
Shawinigan-Sud	2,282	6,637	10,947	12,683
Grand-Mère	8,608	11,089	14,023	15,806
La Tuque	7,919	9,538	11,096	13,023
Saguenay-Lake St. John				
Chicoutimi	16,040	23,111	24,878	31,657
Chicoutimi-Nord	-	3,966	6,446	11,229
Jonquière	13,769	21,618	25,550	28,588
Arvida	4,581	11,078	12,919	14,460
Kénogami	6,579	9,895	11,309	11,816
Alma	6,499	7,975	10,822	13,309
Eastern Quebec				
Rivière-du-Loup	8,713	9,425	9,964	10,835
Rimouski	7,009	11,565	14,630	17,739
Matane	4,633	6,435	8,069	9,190
Sept-Îles	1,305	1,866	5,592	14,196
Western Quebec				
Hull	32,947	43,483	49,243	56,929
Gatineau	2,822	5,771	8,423	13,022
Rouyn	8,808	14,633	17,076	18,716
Noranda	4,576	9,672	10,323	11,477
Val-d'Or	4,385	8,685	9,876	10,983

Source: *Quebec Yearbook.*

View of Quebec City at the mouth of the St. Charles, 1953. (George Hunter, NFB, National Archives of Canada, PA-151641)

tablished in 1951 to take over the management of public transit from private enterprise in the city and the near suburbs.

Quebec City

Changes in Quebec City were much less dramatic than in Montreal. The annual growth rate in the census metropolitan area was 2.67 per cent during the 1950s. The city itself reached a plateau, growing by fewer than 8,000 people over the decade. Even more than in Montreal, growth in Quebec City was concentrated in the suburbs.

Quebec City's relatively modest growth was due to its economic structure. In manufacturing, Quebec City continued to specialize in shoes, textiles, food, corsets, tobacco, shipbuilding and pulp and paper. Its markets were mainly local and regional. The traditional maufacturing industries did not expand in any significant way, and the shoe industry was actually in decline. The factories were all located near the port and the railways, although decentralization was beginning, with a few companies moving to the suburbs.

There was no fundamental change in commercial activity. The port was still an important part of the city's economy. Retail and wholesale trade, concentrated in the Lower Town, continued as before and remained unaffected by the upheavals taking place elsewhere in North America. The department stores in the Saint-Roch area dominated the retail sector, and were not yet challenged by shopping centres.

A new city: Sept-Iles, 1953. (George Hunter, NFB, National Archives of Canada, PA-151639)

Nor was the other major sector, the civil service, a dynamic factor in Quebec City's economy. Its numbers were growing, but the Duplessis government's highly conservative attitude to management and the role of government meant that the civil service did not give the economy the impetus that could be expected in a capital city. In postwar Quebec City, the civil service was synonymous with conservatism and inertia.

Thus, Quebec City was a city of low-paid workers and civil servants. Its population was 95 per cent Catholic and French Canadian, and it was controlled by a local elite that hung jealously onto power. The traditionalism that still held sway in the 1950s made the radical changes that would take place in the 1960s and 1970s all the more dramatic.

In physical terms, Quebec City was small, its housing stock was relatively old, and its road system was inadequate. Some of the old neighbourhoods were losing population, and only Limoilou was growing significantly. However, the urbanized area was expanding outside the city limits, to Sainte-Foy in the west, Charlesbourg in the north and Beauport in the east. Quebec's other significant cities, such as Sherbrooke and Trois-Rivières, were also outgrowing their older districts.

New Towns

One of the most noteworthy forms of urbanization in the postwar period was the proliferation of new towns and cities based on natural resource development. Some of these new communities were mining towns while others were port cities that shipped ore. Mining towns were nothing new in Quebec: the Eastern Townships had its asbestos region and the Abitibi had its copper-and gold-mining communities. But the towns built in the 1950s were in isolated regions, with no rural hinterland and far from the main communications networks. They were tightly controlled by the companies that founded them. The major new mining towns of the period were Chibougamau, northwest of Lake St. John, Schefferville in New Quebec and Murdochville in the Gaspé.

Mining development also stimulated the urbanization of the North Shore. Sept-Îles, a small fishing village with a population under 2,000 in 1951, became the port from which iron from Schefferville, Labrador City and Wabush was shipped. Sept-Îles grew quickly, and by 1961 its population had reached 14,000, equal to that of the North Shore's other significant urban area, the Baie-Comeau/Hauterive agglomeration.

But while the urbanization taking place in these outlying areas was remarkable, it did not profoundly change the Quebec urban system, which was still highly concentrated in the St. Lawrence Valley. Older cities and towns that had grown up around resource industries continued to develop, stimulated by American demand for Quebec's raw materials, and the population of some towns in the Saguenay, St. Maurice Valley and Abitibi grew significantly.

Thus, Quebec's urban system reached its full territorial extent in the postwar period. At the same time, however, it was increasingly dominated by Montreal.

CHAPTER 21
THE POWER STRUCTURE

There is a strong temptation to describe the social structure in terms of dichotomies: bourgeoisie/proletariat, rulers/ruled, elite/masses. Reality, however, is not so simple, and each of the major groups in society has its own divisions, power struggles and conflicting interests, compounded by ethnic cleavages. Not enough research has been done to allow these realities to be examined in all their complexity, but it is possible to describe some of the key groups.

Social scientists use various terms to describe the groups that hold power in society: bourgeoisie, dominant class, ruling class, elite, decision-makers. The composition and nature of these groups varies depending on whether their power is primarily economic, political, religious or cultural. For the postwar period, we will look at two main groupings: the bourgeoisie in the economic field and the traditional elites in the political and cultural fields.

The Capitalist Class

The bourgeoisie had a clearly distinct upper layer: a small group of very powerful individuals who dominated the large economic institutions. Many writers refer to this group as the economic elite; others prefer the term capitalist class (the term used here) or big bourgeoisie. In the early years of this century, members of the group had proudly referred to themselves as "capitalists" and made a show of their wealth. After the Depression they no longer used the term and were less open about flaunting their power, but in reality they were no less powerful than before. The capitalist class in Quebec was overwhelmingly Anglophone and was centred almost entirely in Montreal. The institutions it controlled were Canada-wide and sometimes international, and Quebec was only one among its many areas of activity.

In 1955, the sociologist John Porter conducted an analysis of the characteristics of the economic elite in Canada between 1948 and 1950. He identified 985 individuals who held directorships in one or more leading Canadian corporations. According to Porter, these men (there were no women) made up Canada's economic elite: a very small group with substantial economic power.

French Canadians accounted for only 6.7 per cent of this group, even though Francophones made up 30 per cent of the Canadian population. Only a few of the French Canadians, such as the Simard brothers, were major capitalists. Most of them were either directors of the two French Canadian banks or else corporate lawyers or politicians who sat on boards of directors because of their connections or technical expertise. This does not mean that there was no Francophone bourgeoisie, but very few Francophones were in the capitalist class. Jews, who made up only 1 per cent of the elite group, were in a similar position. Only the Bronfman family was a significant force in the leading corporations, and in 1950 there was still no Jewish director of any of the nine chartered banks. One reason for the marginal role of Jewish business people in the elite is that the industries in which they were strong were ones in which there was little concentration, such as the clothing industry or retail trade. Of course, discrimination was also a very real factor, for both Jews and French Canadians, although it is difficult to assess its impact, especially in a bygone era.

In addition to ethnic origin, Porter also identified some other ways in which recruitment of the elite was highly selective. Many members of the elite were university-educated and went to the most exclusive private colleges. He emphasized the importance of family connections; the sons of big capitalists quickly joined the boards of directors of the companies in which their families were major shareholders. The other path to membership in the elite was a career within a large company, for businesses set up by independent entrepreneurs hardly ever ended up among the leading corporations. So the elite was actually a small group of individuals with specific career profiles that tended to recruit new members from the same circles.

The Middle Bourgeoisie

Studies of the economic elite have provided only a partial view of reality. For while the elite gave overall direction to the economy, there was also a much larger group that ran the small and middle-sized companies, often family-owned, that were so important in Quebec, especially outside Montreal. This was the middle bourgeoisie, made up of thousands of business people of varying wealth, who were involved in a wide range of economic activities on a local or regional level and thus had a share of economic power. No equivalent study to Porter's has been done of the middle bourgeoisie, and much remains to learned about it. We will nonetheless attempt to point out some of its main features.

Much of the regional bourgeoisie was part of this middle stratum. In all the cities, there were entrepreneurs who were major employers of local labour and were involved in various fields of economic and noneconomic activity. Jules A. Brillant of Rimouski was a good example of this phenomenon. He owned the main local newspaper, an aviation company and the regional telephone company, and he was a presence in all fields of economic activity in eastern Quebec. There were similar entrepreneurs in all of Quebec's regions and, on a different scale, in big cities such as Montreal and Quebec City.

In the postwar period, the middle bourgeoisie benefited from Quebec's new prosperity and also took advantage of the greatly increased role of government in the economy. In the 1950s, many medium-sized general contractors were able to put their businesses on a solid footing through the construction of bridges, roads, schools, public buildings, classical colleges and private hospitals funded by the government. Manufacturers and transportation companies also benefited from government contracts, which amounted to indirect aid to small and middle-sized businesses. The government did not have an explicit "Buy Quebec" policy, but the Union Nationale's patronage system, later exposed by the Salvas Commission, amounted to the same thing. Entrepreneurs and small manufacturers made contributions to the party in power in exchange for government contracts. This made for very close ties between government and business and worked very well for middle-sized businesses.

Ethnically, the middle bourgeoisie was much more diverse than the capitalist class. French Canadian and Jewish business people, absent from the upper stratum, were largely concentrated in this group.

Although the bourgeoisie's power was mainly economic, it also exerted its influence outside the economic domain. Thus, as owners of the communications media, business people could promote particular economic and political positions. As philanthropists, they played a role in social welfare. But they had to share their power in these areas with other elites whom they tried to influence.

Business associations played an important role in this regard. The oldest were the local chambers of commerce, which were grouped in a Quebec-wide federation. The federation grew substantially between 1945 and 1960; the number of local chambers rose from 82 to 180 and membership doubled. Previously made up mainly of business people, especially merchants, the chambers of commerce now opened their doors to professionals, managers and academics. They became a forum where the middle bourgeoisie met with other elites and discussed not only economic issues but also any other problems facing the city or town where they were located. The chambers of commerce became one of the leading pressure groups in Quebec.

There were many employers' associations, typically organized along sectoral lines as in the case of the Quebec section of the Canadian Manufacturers' Association. Jean-Louis Roy has identified forty-seven such associations in existence in 1947, and others were created throughout the period. Their membership and functions varied. One of them, the Association Professionelle des Industriels, founded in 1943, was made up of Catholic employers, essentially Francophone, and took an active part in the social and political debates of the time. Initially very conservative and close to the Union Nationale, it fiercely defended private enterprise, opposed government intervention and denounced union militancy. Subsequently, it became more open to reform liberalism and trade unionism.

Montreal Anglophone business people expressed their views through the influential Montreal Board of Trade and in a number of employers' organizations. At the same time, the voice of Francophone business people was a much stronger one in the postwar period than it had been previously.

The Weaknesses of the Francophone Bourgeoisie

While there was undeniably a bourgeois Francophone business class, it did not play as large a role in the economy as the French Canadian proportion of the population would have warranted. The economist André Raynauld has calculated that in 1961, Francophone-controlled businesses and institutions accounted for only 47 per cent of all jobs in Quebec. French Canadians' minority position in the control of the Quebec economy was nothing new. In the postwar period, writings by sociologists, economists and historians helped reopen the debate on "French Canadians' economic inferiority."

Explanations for this situation have usually emphasized culture and attitudes. Maintaining that the cultural environment did not promote the development of French Canadian business people, social critics have criticized the church-run educational system and especially the kind of education given in the classical colleges. They said that clerical-nationalist ideology, with its insistence on Quebec's Catholicism and agricultural vocation, promoted a negative view of the business sector, and the prestige enjoyed by lawyers, doctors and priests turned young people away from careers in business. In this view, those who overcame all these obstacles and went into business anyway were too conservative, placed too much value on family-run businesses, direct employer control and personal relationships, and had a negative attitude towards modern methods of organization and management and publicly owned companies.

These views were widely held in the 1950s but have come under serious criticism since then. More recent observers have recognized that what was then interpreted as a cause of Quebec's economic inferiority could also be seen as the result. The values considered typical of French Canadian business people were actually the values of small entrepreneurs in general. Why then were French Canadian business people limited to small business and the less productive sectors, and why were they virtually absent from large corporations?

The work of the Montreal school of historians (Maurice Séguin, Guy Frégault and Michel Brunet) and their followers focused on the late development of the French Canadian bourgeoisie. After the British conquest in 1760, the Anglophone bourgeoisie, actively aided and supported by the new metropolis, quickly took control of the major sectors of the economy and accumulated large amounts of capital. From that point on, it became very difficult for French Canadian entrepreneurs to catch up. Later political developments, which placed French Canadians in a minority in the Anglophone-dominated Canadian state, helped perpetuate the situation.

More recent work has shown that despite these disadvantages, the French Canadian bourgeoisie continued to exist and even did quite well in the second half of the nineteenth century. But the trend towards economic concentration that began in the early twentieth century marginalized and sometimes even eliminated small and middle-sized companies in many sectors. French Canadians had to give way to the dominant forces in business and either join them on a minority basis or retreat to marginal sectors that were as yet untouched by concentration.

Whatever the full historical explanation, the French Canadian bourgeoisie in the postwar period faced a triple handicap: it lagged behind in accumulating capital, it was in a minority situation in Canada and it suffered from the effects of concentration and monopolization. French Canadian business people had two choices — to build their businesses and increase their market share or else find positions in large English Canadian or foreign-controlled companies.

Those who opted for the first alternative ran up against a shortage of available capital and lack of access to information. In Quebec as elsewhere, it is much harder for small and middle-sized businesses located far from large cities to find adequate financing than it is for big companies situated close to major financial institutions. As many analysts have pointed out, most French Canadian businesses faced this problem and were doomed to remain small. Entrepreneurs who tried to expand despite these difficulties often ran up against growth-related problems that they could only resolve by selling out to a larger company.

At the same time, Francophone entrepreneurs did not have access to the major sources of information that are so important to modern business. They were not privy to the kind of information about new technology and far-flung markets that could lead to growth. While the problem of access to capital and information would be a central concern of the Quebec government during the Quiet Revolution, the Francophone bourgeoisie before 1960 functioned in a relatively unfavourable environment in which its minority position in the economy was perpetuated.

Another means of access to economic power would be to join a large company as a manager or shareholder. In Quebec, big business was dominated by an Anglophone managerial elite that tended to recruit new members of the same culture and background. In the postwar period,

French Canadians who chose big business had to work in English in a culturally homogeneous milieu. They had to give up some of their cultural traits and regular use of their own language to integrate into the dominant group. Some did so, but it is no surprise that they were a minority. In addition, there were subtle forms of discrimination arising out of the recruitment practices of large corporations. Here again, it was not until the Quiet Revolution and the language laws of the 1970s that the situation changed significantly.

The Traditional Elites

Political and cultural power were the domain of the traditional elites, which writers have variously termed the petty bourgeoisie, the professional petty bourgeoisie, the elite, the French Canadian elites, and *notables*.

The groups that made up the traditional elites came from two main centres of power: the church and the state. For members of the traditional elites, government — which was practically run by members of the liberal professions — offered a real opportunity to wield power and influence with ramifications that extended beyond the political sphere. Thousands of jobs, both elective and nonelective, were open to them at all three levels of government, most notably the local level (municipalities and school boards). There were, after all, 1,600 municipalities, each with a mayor and six councillors — even more in the big cities. The growing role of government and the substantial increase in the funds available to it at all levels enhanced its attractiveness as a significant and desirable centre of power, promising both material and symbolic advantages to those who controlled it.

Obviously, the church was controlled by the clergy, but it also offered laypeople thousands of prestigious and influential positions as church trustees and leaders of religious or charitable parish associations. The church's influence also went beyond the strictly religious sphere and included many hospitals, social services and schools. The parish also provided a framework for the caisses populaires, a social and economic institution controlled by local *notables*.

Thus, the local scene — the town or village, parish and school board — was the main power base for the traditional elites, whose members dominated local life through the many positions they occupied. For some of them, it was a springboard to a higher level of power, either in federal or provincial politics or in the diocesan or provincial federations of religious and quasireligious organizations.

Lawyers, intermediaries par excellence with prestige and influence beyond the courtroom, were typical members of the traditional elites. Generally, postwar French Canadians saw the liberal professions (lawyers, notaries and doctors) as the fastest route into the elite. Priests enjoyed a similar status. They were numerous and had an effect on every sphere of life, although they were less influential in the political and economic arenas. Economic intermediaries — small shopkeepers, local entrepreneurs and insurance agents — also belonged to the traditional elites. So did some of the more substantial farmers in the rural areas and, at a higher level, intellectuals (college and university professors and journalists), engineers and accountants in the big cities.

There was still a substantial degree of social mobility at this level in the postwar period. There were a few dynasties, such as the Faribaults who had been notaries for generations, but many representatives of the traditional elites were of humble origin, as a study of the *notables* in the Saguenay region has shown.

At the same time, the traditional elites were very cohesive socially and ideologically, as a result of their common education and membership in the same organizations. The classical colleges, through which every future priest and member of the liberal professions passed, acted as melting pots and fostered a high degree of homogeneity. "Going to classical college," noted Maurice Tremblay in 1953, "is the first requirement for anyone who wants to be admitted to the upper class in society." For eight years, students were educated in the humanities, philosophy and religion, with little emphasis on the sciences or practical issues. As boarders, they spent most of their adolescence in the college, under the watchful eye of the priests. While the colleges changed in the postwar period — there were more of them, the number of students rose, there were more day students, and the course of study was modernized and diversified — these changes had little impact on the elites of the 1950s who had been educated before the war. They did, however, affect the elites of the 1960s and 1970s.

The other element providing cohesion for the elites was the network of organizations, which were very important at that time. There were parish organizations such as the St. Vincent de Paul Society, professional associations such as the Quebec Bar Association and economic groups such as the chambers of commerce. Parallel to these were service clubs (Kiwanis, Rotary, the Optimists) and more secret societies such as the Knights of Columbus and the Ordre de Jacques-Cartier, or "La Patente" as it was known.

Generally, the members of these elites were traditionalists, who resisted modernization and advocated a defensive kind of nationalism. They insisted that institutions remain Catholic and held an elitist view of society that left little room for democracy. But these views were not entirely homogeneous. Within the relative ideological unity of the elites was a range of sometimes shifting positions. There were numerous tensions, stemming from opposing partisan allegiances, personality and generational conflicts, and local and regional differences. Nor were political circles in perfect harmony with religious ones, for their goals were different and the growing secularization of society led to conflict. It is also important not to confuse village elites from rural areas with urban elites. Furthermore, Montreal was a special case: its size, degree of economic development and cosmopolitanism made it a complex environment and its elites were more diverse. They wielded power in a more diffuse way and had to arrive at compromises with the Anglophone and Francophone bourgeoisies and the trade union leadership.

The distinction between the traditional elites and the Francophone bourgeoisie was not always a clear one. The influence of business people extended beyond the economic field: they held a degree of political and cultural power, were active in local organizations and held elected positions. However, their prestige and influence was well below that of members of the liberal professions.

New Elites

In the postwar period, new groups developed outside the traditional elites and sometimes in opposition to them. An early manifestation of this was the emergence of new professions. Economic and social changes demanded increased specialization, professionalism and competence. In contrast to generalists such as lawyers and priests, a new kind of specialist was appearing in such fields as economics and psychology. This development was occurring in many sectors. In the corporations, new groups of career executives were slowly attaining influential positions in upper and middle management. They were more highly trained than their predecessors, usually in science, engineering or accounting. New professions such as social work and industrial relations were developing in the social field. The change was even more striking in the cultural and intellectual fields, where new lay thinkers were challenging the influence of the clergy. The new professions were especially conspicuous in the media, where reporters and radio and television hosts had the status of stars, and in the universities, which were growing and becoming more modern. The universities hired a whole new generation of young professors — historians, geographers, sociologists, economists, psychologists, educators, chemists, and others. In the discussions that were beginning to take place about new directions for Quebec society, these professors would be important participants and the approach they took — which bore the label of "scientific" — would command respect. In the trade union movement, new leaders emerged who kept their distance from political and religious powers.

Changes took place even within the groups that made up the traditional elites, although the ruling forces kept the reformers and protesters on the margins. Thus, Archbishop Joseph Charbonneau, Father Georges-Henri Lévesque and many other clerics wanted to see the church adapt to the social realities of the urban world. In the liberal professions, specialization was becoming more widespread and some people were attacking a power structure they said was cut off from the direction in which Quebec society was developing.

A number of factors contributed to the development of this kind of thinking among the new elites. In the colleges, the Jeunesse Étudiante

Catholique (Catholic student youth) sparked social awareness. In the universities, the new social sciences programs were stimulating change. Federal agencies — especially the CBC French network and the National Film Board — provided a platform and a place to learn over which the traditional elites had relatively little influence. Foreign influences, mainly French and American, were more visible and diverse and contributed to the development of new ideas and perceptions of society.

Many writers have grouped these new elites under the heading of the new middle class. This was an expanding class that profited from the rising standard of living and the growth of the service sector. Not all benefited equally, however. While the growth of management functions in business provided very attractive opportunities for Anglophones, Francophones ran up against a number of obstacles. In corporations, discrimination made promotions less available to Francophones. In education and social services, they came up against clerical control. There was hardly any room for them in public institutions under the Duplessis regime, and only federal agencies appeared open to them.

So the new Francophone elites were champing at the bit. They aspired to power and saw themselves as challengers to the traditional elites. As the period progressed, their attacks on the power structure for its traditionalism, incompetence and weak policies became sharper and sharper. After 1960, it would be the new elites who would spearhead the Quiet Revolution.

CHAPTER 22

FULL EMPLOYMENT AND THE RISE OF TRADE UNIONISM

For workers, the postwar period was a time of full employment and improved wages and working conditions. The kinds of jobs available and the composition of the labour force were changing. Having emerged strengthened from the war, the unions were now meeting increased resistance from employers and the Quebec government, who both wanted to regain control of the situation. But its frequent confrontations with the Duplessis government aside, the union movement was making progress in its quest for unity and was becoming a major social force.

The Labour Force

While the labour force grew in absolute numbers from 1,337,000 in 1946 to 1,768,000 in 1961, as a proportion of the population of working age (the participation rate) it remained stable at about 54 per cent. The composition of the labour force was changing. The number of women working was growing faster than the number of men: the percentage of women in the labour force rose from 22 to 23 per cent between 1941 and 1951 and then jumped to 27 per cent in 1961. At the same time, young people were staying in school longer and entering the job market later. This was one of the reasons why the labour force was aging: in both 1941 and 1951, 72 per cent of workers were over 25, while in 1961 the figure was 76 per cent. The educational level of workers was also rising.

The trend towards a service economy, stalled during the war, resumed: 55.7 per cent of the labour force had service jobs in 1961, as compared with 47.3 per cent in 1951. The number of manufacturing jobs increased in absolute terms but remained stable at about 28 per cent of the labour force. The number of resource extraction jobs declined not only as a percentage of the labour force — from 24.4 per cent in 1951 to 16.4 per cent in 1961 — but also in absolute terms. (This is not quite the same as the distribution of employment by economic sector, as reported in chapter 5 for the previous period, because there were service jobs in the manufacturing and resource sectors. Overall, however, it indicates the same trends.)

Wages more than doubled, with average weekly pay in Quebec rising from $31.37 in 1946 to $73.01 in 1961. In the cotton industry, for example, a spinner's daily salary rose from 46 cents to $1.36, and a set-up operator's from 71 cents to $1.63. In the construction industry in Montreal, a labourer's wages rose from 67 cents to $1.75, and a plumber's from $1.11 to $2.62. Wages increased faster than the cost of living, so that the standard of living was rising. Working conditions were improving as well: paid vacations, the forty-hour week and pension plans were becoming more common. However, not all workers benefited from these improvements to the same degree. There were differences between unionized and nonunionized workers, men and women, and office and factory workers.

The spectre of unemployment still loomed in the minds of many, even though the full employment level as defined by economists was attained for a few years. Unemployment remained at an extremely low average level of 3.3 per cent between 1946 and 1951. Subsequently, however, it rose, especially in the late 1950s when it approached 9 per cent. Unemployment was unequally distributed, with the Gaspé recording twice as high a rate as Montreal.

Automation was becoming a major concern. New machines could carry out many different operations without human intervention and were eliminating certain kinds of jobs. Trade unions were very much afraid of the effects these changes would have, and in collective bargaining demanded that new jobs be found for the affected workers.

White-collar workers were a fast-growing group. Automation and mechanization had not yet had a major impact on office work, and there was an increasing demand for personnel, fed by the growth of administrative functions in both government and private business. Office work was becoming increasingly hierarchical, with its executives, accounting staff, clerks and secretaries. Thus, white-collar workers, who had enjoyed a higher status than factory workers since the beginning of the century, were in fact a diverse group, within which there were distinctions similar to those between skilled and unskilled workers in industry and a continuing hierarchy of the sexes.

Women at Work

With the gradual closing of the war plants, women's participation in the labour force dropped markedly and returned to its 1941 level. Although no precise figures are available, it is known that many women returned

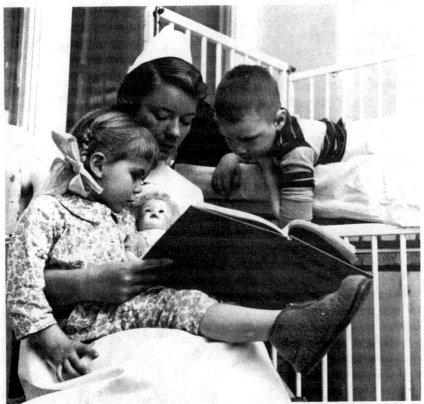

A nurse at the Royal Victoria Hospital, Montreal, 1953. (National Archives of Canada, PA-133209)

to the home. However, the trend towards women working outside the home soon resumed, and it intensified the 1950s.

The type of work women did gradually changed. While some women had access to a wider variety of jobs during the war, before 1961 women workers remained largely concentrated in job ghettos as clerks, teachers, secretaries, saleswomen and dressmakers. The average age of women workers increased, and while many young women still left their jobs when they got married, the pattern was changing — many chose to continue working until children were born, and sometimes even to go back afterwards. Inequality between men's and women's wages persisted. However, there were some indications of changing attitudes to women's work; for example, the Canadian and Catholic Confederation of Labour (CCCL) gave up its hostility to the idea in the early 1950s.

Government Intervention

The Quebec government began to play a determining role in labour relations with the adoption of the Labour Relations Act of 1944, which gave it responsibility for seeing that the mechanisms for union recognition and supervision of collective bargaining functioned properly. The federal government also intervened through its own labour code, although it applied only to a minority of workers in Quebec.

The Duplessis government was firmly antiunion and did not hide its pro-employer bias. To attract investment, it wanted to preserve Quebec's comparative advantages, and especially its docile and low-paid labour force. This meant that workers had to be "reasonable" in their demands. The government stated its goal of ensuring "employers a labour force that protects its rights but respects authority at the same time." In this regard, it was perfectly representative of the social conservatism of the traditional elites, who did not want to see workers escape their control and considered trade unionism a threat to social stability. In addition, there was a general rise in anticommunism in the postwar period. The international

Policemen during the asbestos strike, 1949. (Montreal *Star*, National Archives of Canada, PA-130356)

situation and the fallout from the Gouzenko Soviet spy affair helped create a climate of mistrust towards radicalism, which easily extended to the union movement and its leaders. Robert Rumilly was able to write in a 1956 political pamphlet that "class struggle does not exist in the province of Quebec."

The Godbout government's 1944 legislation provided a framework for union recognition, banned certain employer and employee practices and imposed an obligation to negotiate in good faith. In 1949, the Duplessis government sought to modify the framework of labour relations by introducing a bill designed to cut down on the concessions made to the unions and tighten government control. Based on the Taft-Hartley Act, passed in the United States in 1947, this bill met with unanimous union opposition and Duplessis had to back off. However, he managed to have parts of the bill passed later; thus, a clause preventing the certification of unions with organizers who were — or were presumed to be — communists went into force in 1954.

Besides introducing new legislation, the Duplessis government manipulated existing laws and regulations. It used all legally available procedures as stalling tactics to delay the start of legal strikes as long as possible. As well, the officials Duplessis appointed to implement labour legislation were biased towards the employers, especially in questions of certification. All this manipulation created such restrictive conditions that many strikes could be declared illegal and the solicitor general — none other than Duplessis himself — took legal action against the unions. The instrument for carrying out the solicitor general's decisions was the provincial police, who were sent to the scene of strikes where they escorted strikebreakers through the picket lines and engaged in pitched battles with strikers. Sometimes they acted as outright *agents provocateurs*, as in the Louiseville strike of 1952.

Trade Unions

At the end of the war, 25 per cent of the labour force was unionized; in 1960, the figure was 30 per cent. This was small progress, especially considering that teachers were included in the figures beginning in 1946. At the same time, however, trade unionism was changing. It was becoming both more militant, spurred by employer resistance and confrontations with the Duplessis government, and more strongly united, as unions established common fronts and tried to merge the different tendencies into which the movement was divided.

The social conservatism characteristic of the postwar era extended to the North American trade union movement, and it was accentuated by the gradual expulsion of communist union activists and the aging of the union rank-and-file. The anti-communist campaign sometimes degenerated into a witch hunt in which every possible means, including collusion with the government and sometimes with gangsters, was used to expel the communists.

The different tendencies in the trade union movement were converging. The craft unions gradually opened up to industrial unionism, and the Catholic unions too drew closer to the industrial unions as they became less denominational. The atmosphere of confrontation with the government made unity more important. It also turned unions towards the political arena, where they became a significant element in the anti-Duplessis opposition movement.

Major Strikes

Some of the strikes of the period have remained engraved in Quebec's memory for reasons that go beyond their immediate results. These strikes were waged over three central issues: union recognition, respect for the labour code and union financing. In the area of financing, there was growing demand for the application of the new Rand Formula, first developed to settle the 1945-46 Ford strike in Ontario. While refusing to enforce a closed shop, Mr. Justice Ivan Rand proposed that employers be obliged to deduct union dues from all employees, whether union members or not, on the grounds that the union was mandated to negotiate and administer the collective agreement. This formula meant that union finances were no longer dependent on employers' whims.

The most famous labour conflict of the period was the asbestos strike. It lasted from February to July 1949 and involved more than 5,000 miners whose demands concerned wages, the problem of asbestos dust, union dues, and some form of union participation in management. The workers decided not to wait for the legally imposed strike deadline to begin their walkout, so the government declared it illegal. The provincial police were sent to the town of Asbestos and brutally repressed the strike. A vast movement of solidarity with the strikers developed throughout Quebec, and even the church moved away from its legendary caution. On May 1, Archbishop Joseph Charbonneau of Montreal declared in his Sunday sermon: "The working class is a victim of a conspiracy which seeks to crush it, and when there is a conspiracy to crush the working class, the church has a duty to intervene." Collections for the strikers were organized in the various dioceses, and Archbishop Maurice Roy of Quebec mediated an end to the conflict. Even though the miners made few gains, the strike served as a revelation to Quebecers about the severity of workers' problems.

The strike that paralysed the Dupuis Frères department store in Montreal in 1952 also took on a symbolic character, in this case because it pitted a French Canadian Catholic union against a French Canadian Catholic employer. The union federation involved, the Canadian and Catholic Confederation of Labour, emerged from the strike with increased credibility.

However, the strikes at Louiseville (1952) and Murdochville (1957) showed how fragile union gains were. In each case, there was flagrant collusion between the company and the government and the provincial

Madeleine Parent, trade union activist, at the microphone. (National Archives of Canada, PA-130356)

police played an important role in protecting strikebreakers and repressing demonstrations by strikers. Finally, the CBC French network producers' strike (1958-59) raised the question of unionization of managerial staff.

The union consciousness of many Quebecers was shaped by these major strikes. The involvement of Catholic unions in a number of the strikes led to a changed image and new ways of operating for these unions. At the same time, the complexity of labour relations and the importance of the government's role in this area were clearly brought out.

Union Federations and the Move towards Unity

In 1935, the North American labour movement split over the question of industrial unionism. With time, however, tensions abated and the unions became more aware of the need to join forces. In the United States in 1955, the American Federation of Labour and the Congress of Industrial Organizations merged to form the AFL-CIO. The federations grouping the Canadian affiliates of the same unions followed suit the following year, as the Trades and Labour Congress of Canada (TLC) and the Canadian Congress of Labour (CCL) united to form the Canadian Labour Congress (CLC).

The movement towards unity went beyond mergers of union federations and was a characteristic of the entire period. After the war, the Catholic unions drew closer to Quebec's CCL unions, grouped from 1952 on in the Quebec Industrial Unions Federation (QIUF). But relations with the federation of TLC affiliates, the Quebec Provincial Federation of

Labour (QPFL), were more strained. The QPFL did take part in common fronts in 1949 in support of the asbestos strikers and against changes in the labour code. But QPFL affiliates tended to be the more conservative unions; the federation regarded the CCCL as revolutionary and during the 1950s it became friendlier to Duplessis. Nonetheless, the merger of the Canadian federations in 1956 forced the QIUF and the QPFL to overcome their differences and unite as the Quebec Federation of Labour (QFL) in 1957.

The leaders of the CCCL also favoured unity and advocated some form of association with the Canadian Labour Congress. But many CCCL members were reluctant to give up the special character of their federation and placed very strict conditions on any association. The CLC was not unanimous on this question either and set conditions of its own. In 1961, after several years of negotiations, the attempts to come to an agreement was abandoned.

Nonetheless, the union movement in the late 1950s was more united than it had ever been before. The old rivalry between craft unions and industrial unions had been overcome, and the traditional hostility and distrust of both groups towards the Catholic unions had disappeared. In numerical terms, the merger of the TLC and the CCL strengthened the international unions' dominant position in Quebec; in 1957, they represented about two thirds of all union members.

At the same time, the Catholic unions were rethinking their denominational character. During the war, they had had to open their ranks to non-Catholics without restrictions. With the advent of a new generation of more militant leaders and activists and a new conception of the role of laypeople in the church, the CCCL questioned clericalism and distanced itself from its religious base. But despite its new militancy, the CCCL's share of union membership fell from 24.2 per cent in 1946 to 22.6 per cent in 1960. To survive alongside the newly united international unions, it had to try to be more open to all workers. In this context, giving up all religious affiliation and the social doctrine of the church was a desirable option. Secularization was smooth and gradual. In 1960, the federation dropped the word "Catholic" from its name and became the Confederation of National Trade Unions (CNTU).

In addition to these unions, which represented the vast majority of the unionized labour force, there were other national and international trade unions, the largest being the railway unions.

Utility Employees and Teachers

The 1944 legislation created a separate group of unionized workers consisting of utility employees, municipal employees, firefighters, police, public transit employees and teachers. They had the right to unionize and negotiate with their employers, but they did not have the right to strike and they had to submit to compulsory arbitration when bargaining broke down.

Teachers were a special case. In 1945, the organizations of rural female teachers, rural male teachers and urban teachers merged and formed the Corporation Générale des Instituteurs et Institutrices Catholiques du Québec (Quebec guild of Catholic teachers). It started off with a membership of 10,000, which grew to 16,000 by 1959. Its status as a guild, while preventing it from being considered a true union and keeping it on the fringes of the union movement, did not save it from the Duplessis government's wrath. In 1946, the government deprived rural teachers of their only means of applying pressure by denying them recourse to arbitration. This was an especially severe blow to rural women teachers, who were both the largest group in the guild, constituting two thirds of its membership, and the most militant. It led to stagnation in their wages and working conditions, and in 1952-53, half of all rural women teachers earned less than $1,000 a year.

In the wake of a six-day strike by Montreal teachers in 1949, the government gave itself the right to change arbitration decisions for urban teachers. It also went after the Montreal Teachers Alliance, revoking its certification. After losing a court challenge, the government got rid of the union through retroactive legislation.

* * * * * *

Thus, conditions for workers continued to change in the postwar period. Trade unions played a more active role. The struggles of the period helped draw the different tendencies in the trade union movement closer together, and the union federations sought to widen their scope by taking positions on broad social issues. The union movement became a rallying point for opposition to the Duplessis government, and intellectuals, journalists and reform-minded lawyers became involved in its struggles. The trade union movement gradually became a major institution in society whose influence extended beyond its own membership and the labour relations sphere.

CHAPTER 23

PROSPERITY AND POVERTY

Postwar economic growth brought undeniable prosperity to Quebec. Even for the most impoverished, living conditions were significantly better than they had been during the 1930s. While the new prosperity touched all social classes to some degree, its benefits were not distributed equally. The middle class and skilled workers improved their financial standing and moved up the social ladder. But for other groups, improved material conditions and increased transfer payments were not enough to eliminate poverty and misery.

Improved Living Standards

Higher income is the first indication of an improved standard of living. Per capita income (including children) rose from $655 in 1946 to $1,455 in 1961. Regional inequalities persisted — the Lower St. Lawrence and the Gaspé, at the bottom of the ladder, had a per capita income less than half that of metropolitan Montreal — but incomes everywhere were rising. There was still significant seasonal unemployment in some industries, especially construction and water transport, but those who were temporarily out of work could now count on unemployment insurance. Unemployment insurance benefits paid in Quebec increased from $19 million in 1946 to $155 million in 1960.

Consumer prices underwent a period of rapid inflation towards the end of the 1940s but then rose very slowly throughout the 1950s. With incomes rising much faster than inflation, the purchasing power of most Quebecers increased. For most farmers, however, incomes rose much more slowly, with the predictable result that many of them decided to move to the cities.

The improvement in the standard of living was reflected in housing conditions. When the war ended, Quebec was in the midst of a housing crisis. Demand outstripped supply, leading to severe overcrowding. Prices also threatened to explode, despite the federal government's efforts to keep prices down by maintaining wartime rent controls until 1950. Fearing that deregulation would cause a rapid rise in housing costs for low-income families, the Quebec government set up a Rental Board in 1951 with authority over old housing only. The housing crisis was resolved through the large-scale construction of new single- and multiple-family homes with government-assisted financing.

The 400,000 new housing units built during the period provided all the modern comforts; as well, many old dwellings were modernized. Between 1951 and 1961, the proportion of dwellings with running water rose from 90 to 97 per cent; with hot water, from 50 to 90 per cent; with a flush toilet, from 82 to 91 per cent; and with a bath or shower, from 61 to 80 per cent. Houses were also heated more effectively. In 1961, more than half had central heating, as compared to less than a third in 1951, while the proportion of homes using stoves for heating fell from two thirds to one third. Meanwhile, heating oil came into general use and was found in 71 per cent of homes by 1961, replacing the two traditional fuel sources, wood (which declined from 41 to 19 per cent of homes) and coal (from 25 to 4 per cent).

Increased purchasing power was initially used to buy durable goods: cars, furniture and home appliances such as refrigerators (found in 47 per cent of homes in 1951 and 92 per cent in 1961) and television sets. Consumption also rose in general and was stimulated by increased advertising, which had new avenues opened to it by the expansion of radio and television. Advertising created needs that were beyond the capacity of regular household income to satisfy, leading many people into debt.

Access to credit became much easier. The growth of the mortgage market and the possibility of repayment over twenty-five years made home ownership much more accessible to middle-income families. Credit obtained from merchants and personal loans from finance companies, banks and credit unions made it much easier to acquire cars, furniture, home appliances and even nondurable goods.

Debt became an integral part of the increased standard of living, and in some cases was a heavy burden. In a 1959 survey of French Canadian wage-earning families in Quebec, the sociologists Marc-Adélard Tremblay and Gérald Fortin found that 74 per cent had borrowed money at least once and half were continually in debt at a level of about 12 per cent of their income.

The Change in Living Conditions

Barely 20 per cent of farmers had electricity in 1945, an indication of the wide gap between living conditions in urban and rural areas. Over the next ten years, the Duplessis government's Rural Electrification Bureau helped close the gap and brought rapid material and cultural changes. Electricity improved lighting, provided running water and gave access

Ford Motor Company advertising, 1954. (*La Terre de chez nous*)

to television, which introduced many rural Quebecers to the amenities of urban life and to forms of culture that had previously been inaccessible to them. Agricultural work was radically changed by electricity and by the process of mechanization as a whole, which reduced labour requirements drastically and improved productivity.

In the cities, improved facilities and public services and the rise of the automobile changed the way people lived. The effects were especially apparent in Montreal, which was Quebec's social testing ground as new developments surfaced there first. It was a mosaic of neighbourhoods, the successors to the former suburban municipalities that had been annexed at the turn of the century, and the city offered a variety of urban milieus characterized by social differences and ethnic diversity.

Montrealers enjoyed more and better-quality services than people living elsewhere in Quebec. Living conditions were much more hygienic than they had been early in the century, and the death rate had fallen in working-class districts. The city health department made its presence felt in the neighbourhoods and did preventive work. During the 1959 polio epidemic, for example, it took charge of the large-scale vaccination campaign. Montreal also had an active social welfare department and was in charge of recreation as well: it built playgrounds, skating rinks and swimming pools and opened branches of the municipal library. Throughout

Quebec, urban recreational facilities were designed with the baby boom generation in mind.

Along with the municipalities, the Catholic Church also provided recreational facilities, considering them part of the social works the clergy and Catholic Action groups should engage in. There had long been *patronages* — recreational and social organizations — in working-class neighbourhoods, and after the war, the more modern concept of recreation centre, of which the best known was the one in Montreal's Immaculée-Conception parish, caught hold. In boys' schools, the teaching brothers organized sports activities. The church also organized summer camps and gave religious guidance to the Boy Scouts and Girl Guides. The same kinds of organizations existed for Anglophones, but on a nondenominational basis. Since the 1930s, the clergy had also been very active in *l'oeuvre de terrains de jeux* (OTJ) — organizing playground activities. According to the sociologist Roger Levasseur, OTJ activities fulfilled two functions: "They brought together as many children as possible to protect them from being tempted to sin by the appeal of mass culture; and they provided a daily opportunity for national, civic and religious training." Thus, the church emphasized the community aspect of recreation. Although the number of practising Catholics was declining, urban parishes remained important centres for socializing and an organizational framework for part of the population.

The private sector also sought to tap the youth leisure market. Movie theatres and dance halls proliferated throughout Quebec, and private beaches and amusement parks attracted crowds. In working-class sections of Montreal, the "nowhere" was a great success. This was a bus that took young people out for an evening's entertainment, to a destination that was different every time and was unknown to the passengers until they arrived.

In Montreal, the flavour of neighbourhood life varied from ethnic group to ethnic group. In the Italian district, for example, people socialized in cafés, grocery stores and the Jean-Talon market and beautified the city with their gardens. Other neighbourhoods had large concentrations of Jews, who lived an active community life.

In the postwar period social clubs such as Kiwanis, the Optimists and the Richelieu Club became popular, and older organizations such as the Knights of Columbus and the chambers of commerce expanded their membership. They were mainly for men; women in the cities were excluded and were left with parish associations and family and neighbourhood relationships.

The most noteworthy change in urban life was the development of a new kind of suburb in the 1950s. These suburbs were located far from downtown and had poor transit service, making cars a necessity for their residents. The most common type of dwelling was the single-family detached house with a lawn. The house was most often a bungalow, but could also be a cottage or split-level. In the suburbs of Montreal, there were many multifamily homes as well.

Even more significant than the suburbs themselves was the idealized view people had of them. They represented the possibility of home ownership, symbolized by the single-family home, and offered a different kind of lifestyle from the city. In what were presented as rural surroundings, far from noise and pollution, the suburbs nevertheless had the latest in comfort and amenities. They were also family-centred: the mother stayed home and provided a healthier environment for her children than was possible in the old neighbourhoods. A new image of womanhood was an important part of the suburban mystique. Women were supposed to maintain all their traditional roles, but with home appliances alleviating much of the drudgery of housework, they were also supposed to have more time for child-rearing, giving each child individual attention. The image of femininity promoted by the ideology of the time did not always correspond to reality, but it was forcefully conveyed through developers' advertisements, newspapers, women's magazines and television. The new housing developments that sprang up on Île Jésus north of Montreal were typical of this new model of urban life.

The development of the suburbs was one expression of the increasingly central position of the car in Quebecers' lives. Tremblay and Fortin's study showed that in 1959, wage-earning Francophone families, both rural and urban, considered a car a necessity and devoted 7 to 8 per cent of their budget to their cars. Cars became both a means of daily transport, for getting to work and shopping, and a means of getting away, making it easier to go out, go away for the weekend or take a holiday.

The rise of summer resort areas after the war was closely linked to the car. Cottages sprang up on lakes and rivers close to the cities, and the Laurentian Mountains, north of Montreal, became a playground for city dwellers. It was no accident that the first modern limited-access highway built in Quebec was the Laurentian Autoroute, completed in 1957. The autoroute put an end to huge Sunday-night traffic jams with long lines of cars.

The growing prevalence of the forty-hour week and paid vacations helped make this new lifestyle possible. Paid vacations, rare before the war, became an established fact during the period. Employers were legally obliged to give employees with one year's service a week of paid vacation, and in unionized workplaces collective agreements provided for longer vacations after a few years of service. While most people spent their vacations in Quebec, many middle-class Quebecers headed to the beaches of New England, where they were exposed to new ideas for increased consumption and acquired a greater awareness of American culture. This section of the population was moving up socially, and the American way of life became a desirable symbol. Those who had no choice but to spend their vacations in the "balconvilles" of the city had somewhat different aspirations. By the late 1950s television had managed to standardize people's desires to some degree, but the gap between resources and needs was still greater for some people than for others.

Traffic in Montreal in the early 1950s. (Archives of the MUCTC, 3-953-017)

Poverty and Social Policy

A substantial part of the population lived in poverty and was unable to fulfil its basic needs. Obviously, this poverty was relative, as on a world scale Quebec society enjoyed great plenty and Quebecers' incomes were rather high. But in the North American context Quebec did not fare as well. Per capita income was chronically below the Canadian average. A number of writers have estimated that at the end of the period, at least a quarter of the nonagricultural population lived below the poverty line. And it was French Canadians who were most heavily affected.

Quebec's economic structure, based largely on low-wage industries, was a major factor in this situation. Although wages had risen, they were still inadequate, especially since French Canadian families tended to be larger. Structural unemployment, which set in permanently in the 1950s, also helped perpetuate poverty. In addition, there was poverty caused by misfortune — widows, women abandoned by their husbands, the handicapped, and workers who became sick all found themselves in a difficult position. Rural poverty was a problem as well. It was particularly serious in isolated regions and colonization areas; self-sufficiency in food alleviated its effects somewhat, but not enough to prevent genuine misery.

However, poor families had access to a number of social programs, most of which had been established fairly recently. Unemployment insurance was the cornerstone of the new system. Administered by a commission, it was designed to provide temporary help in difficult times. The scheme was funded by contributions from employees, employers and the federal government, and benefits were paid to unemployed individuals who had paid into it. At first, many jobs were excluded from the program and barely 40 per cent of the Canadian labour force was covered. Over the postwar period, coverage was gradually extended, so that it included 65 per cent of the labour force by the late 1950s. It was also broadened to take seasonal unemployment into account, and contributions and benefits were adjusted to keep abreast of higher wages.

Slums in Montreal, 1949. (McAllister, National Archives of Canada, P-151688)

Unemployment insurance was intended only for people able to work. Other programs targeted special population groups that were unable to work. The main program of this type was the old age pension. Before the war, very few private companies had pension plans, and while many such plans were established during the war, they were limited to large corporations. Many people who retired after the war had been unable to put money aside during their working years, having been deprived of income and savings during the Depression, and were in a particularly bad position. Since 1927, there had been a federal pension program, which Quebec did not join until 1936. Financed equally by the two levels of government, it was a welfare scheme for people over seventy who could pass a means test. In the early 1950s, only half of Quebec's elderly were eligible for benefits under this plan. In 1951, the federal government introduced sweeping changes to the plan, undertaking to provide old age pensions to everyone aged seventy and over regardless of needs or income. As well, a new program of old age assistance, whose costs were shared equally between the two levels of government, was set up for people in need between the ages of sixty-five and sixty-nine.

The main program developed and run by Quebec was public assistance, in existence since 1921. It provided support for indigents in institutions such as hospitals and hospices, and the costs were shared equally by the provincial government, municipalities and the institutions. It applied only to people who were unable to work, had absolutely no means of support, and met the strict criteria for indigents. Two changes were subsequently made to the program. Beginning in 1940, public assistance benefits were gradually extended to organizations working with indigents at home, such as social service agencies. The Quebec government also gradually took responsibility for the municipalities' contribution, eliminating it completely in 1960.

Other programs were designed for particular groups. Assistance for needy mothers, initiated by the Quebec government in 1937, was aimed at women who were heads of single-parent families and had little means of support. Unmarried mothers and divorced women, however, were excluded from the program. Pensions for the blind were enacted by the federal government in 1937 and financed jointly with the provinces on a 75/25 basis, and were restructured in 1951. In addition, in 1955 the federal government set up a 50/50 shared-cost disability benefits program.

These various assistance programs were significant in helping to relieve the poverty of society's most defenceless members. However, the benefits they provided remained quite low throughout the period, bringing the programs under increasing criticism. The programs were also inadequate because of their strict eligibility criteria, which excluded many people who were unable to work. People able to work who remained unemployed beyond the benefit period for unemployment insurance — often because their unemployment was structural rather than cyclical — also fell between the cracks. To respond to this need, the federal government launched an unemployment assistance program in 1956, with costs shared equally between the two levels of government. Quebec did not join until 1959, although the program was made retroactive to 1958. It was aimed at "unemployed persons who are in need" and was a forerunner of social welfare.

Thus, throughout the postwar period, new assistance programs kept being added to existing ones, with little coordination. As a result of strict eligibility criteria, many of these programs only partially met existing needs. Nonetheless, the system began to open up as new target groups gained access to one program or another, especially after unemployment assistance was established. The principle of universality, regardless of income, was initially introduced for family allowances and then extended to old age pensions for people seventy and over.

Enacted in 1944 and implemented in July 1945 when the first cheques went out, the federal family allowance program was not designed only to help the poor. It was also supposed to supplement workers' wages and farm incomes that were too low to provide children of large families with sufficient goods and services, as well as to help boost the postwar economy and stimulate consumption. With a birth rate higher than the Canadian average, Quebec's Francophone population derived particular benefit from family allowances, even though the amount fell after the fifth child (this discriminatory aspect was eliminated in 1949). Traditional groups in Quebec opposed family allowances, seeing them as an attack on provincial autonomy and the Christian concept of the family. They were particularly incensed by the fact that cheques were paid to the mother and not the father, who was considered the provider and the head of the family. While some traditionalists even suggested refusing the allowances, most people did not follow this recommendation.

These social programs had a substantial impact, and the funds paid out were a significant contribution to the economy. Tremblay and Fortin's study showed that in 1959, the money disbursed through social programs — most notably family allowances — represented 9.2 per cent of the income of wage-earning French Canadian families; the figure was even higher in rural areas.

Although they responded to obvious social needs, these programs also had an economic rationale, as noted in chapter 19. From a Keynesian point of view they could be regarded as transfer payments, transferring resources from some sectors of the population to others through taxation. They ensured that the poorest members of society would have a minimum level of purchasing power, and on the macroeconomic level they helped maintain consumption.

The proliferation of programs was testimony to the persistence of poverty amid plenty. While Quebec became more prosperous in the postwar period, it also became more aware of poverty, and the effects of that awareness would show up more clearly after 1960.

CHAPTER 24
TWO INSTITUTIONS IN CRISIS

At the end of the Second World War, the church and the educational system were still strongly traditional, but in the circumstances of postwar Quebec a serious reappraisal of these institutions became necessary. Needs that had long been held in check now burst forth, clearly indicating the urgency of renewal. The church and the educational system were unable to cope with the new situation and found it increasingly difficult to meet people's expectations.

Religions and Churches

The major features of Quebec's religious landscape remained unchanged. The Catholic Church continued to represent a large majority of the population — 87 per cent of Quebecers in the 1941 census and 88 per cent in 1961. As for the leading minority religions, the relative size of the Jewish community remained the same, at 2 per cent of the population, while Protestants declined slightly, from 10.6 to 8.8 per cent over two decades.

Minority Religions

The Anglican and United churches continued to account for three quarters of Quebec Protestants, while roughly another 15 per cent were Presbyterian. Of the remaining 10 per cent, some were members of smaller churches while a larger number belonged to a proliferation of sects, each with only a few hundred adherents.

Quebec Protestants were mostly Anglophone and were primarily concentrated in the Montreal metropolitan area and the Eastern Townships. Although Francophone Protestants were a small minority, they demanded recognition, especially within the Protestant school system.

The Protestant denominations flourished both materially and spiritually during the period. Protestant churches were built in the suburbs, religious observance was more consistent and church membership rose moderately. But the churches were affected by the prevailing conservative climate, and many of them abandoned the goals of social equality that had developed out of the social gospel.

For the Jewish community, two major developments marked the period after 1945. First, the scope of the Holocaust was just being discovered, and Quebec's Jews endeavoured to welcome its survivors. It was also a period of triumph for Zionism and the Zionist movement, which gained strength from the establishment of the state of Israel in 1948. The Jewish community benefited from the marked prosperity of the period and experienced a burst of upward social mobility. With a rising standard of living came a degree of falling away from religion. Jewish institutions became more secular and American, much to the dismay of cultural and religious traditionalists.

Like Jews elsewhere in North America, Quebec's Jewish community was of Ashkenazi background. Descended from a Jewish community that initially settled in the Rhineland in the Middle Ages ("Ashkenazi" means "German" in Hebrew) and spread throughout Europe and then to America, Ashkenazi Jews have their own distinctive cultural and religious

Demonstration in support of the state of Israel at the Montreal Forum, 1948. (*The Gazette*, National Archives of Canada, PA-116478)

characteristics. There are three major religious tendencies within the community: Orthodox, Conservative and Reform. In Quebec, Reform has been a minority denomination. Orthodoxy was strengthened by the arrival of Hasidic groups from eastern Europe at the end of the Second World War. Living in closely knit communities and unshakeable in their religious Orthodoxy, the Hasidim, although small in number, represented an adjustment problem for the Montreal Jewish community.

Sephardic Jews — members of the second major group in world Jewry after the Ashkenazim — began to arrive in Montreal in 1957. The Sephardim are descended from Jewish communities that originated in Spain and spread out around the Mediterranean perimeter, and their religious and cultural customs are different from those of the Ashkenazim. The fact that these "Arab Jews" — as they were sometimes referred to by the Ashkenazim — were French-speaking made their arrival in Quebec all the more disturbing to the equilibrium of the Jewish community. These tensions would become conspicuous during the 1960s.

On the whole, relations between minority religions and the Catholic Church were civil. Individual efforts to bring together adherents of different religions were undertaken during this period. It had also been clear to the churches for some time that it was best to live in peace and avoid any untoward efforts at conversion.

However, the militancy of a small sect, the Jehovah's Witnesses, led to a messy skirmish after the war. Quebec was apparently chosen as a major battleground by the American leadership of the sect. Starting in 1944, the Witnesses sent missionaries, committed funds, distributed pamphlets and set up open-air loudspeakers to denounce the Catholic Church and the clergy. Faced with this assault, priests appealed to the Catholic Action movements and municipal governments to fight the intruders. Premier Duplessis had the police keep a close watch on the Witnesses and launched a judicial guerrilla war against them. The climate in which these developments took place was one of intolerance on both sides. It was highlighted by the celebrated Roncarelli affair, involving a restaurant owner whose liquor licence was cancelled by the Liquor Commission on Duplessis's urging because he had posted bail for arrested Witnesses. In the 1950s, the Witnesses abandoned their strategy of confrontation and sought converts more discreetly, concentrating their efforts on individual contact through door-to-door proselytizing and selling newspapers and pamphlets.

The Catholic Church

It was a period of contrasts for the Catholic Church. Its wealth and power seemed more glittering than ever, but underneath this apparent triumphalism the very base of its power was being undermined. At the same time, there were a variety of tensions within the church, and they were becoming increasingly bitter.

The church's institutions and way of life reflected the prevailing prosperity. On the surface, the Catholic faith seemed in good health and church membership was still growing. Thus, the events of the 1947 Marian Congress in Montreal attracted huge crowds to the Botanical Gardens (50,000 people) and St. Joseph's Oratory (100,000). Numbers of priests and religious also reached new heights during the period. The total number of priests increased from 5,000 in 1940 to 8,400 twenty years later, while membership in religious communities grew from 33,398 in 1941 to 42,253 (of whom three quarters were women) in 1961. The result was a Catholic community closely supervised by priests and religious: around 1950, there was one priest for every 504 Catholics and one religious (father, brother or sister) for every eighty-nine Catholics.

But beneath these figures were two problems that became increasingly serious during the 1950s. One was a degree of falling off in recruitment of priests and religious: while numbers of priests and religious increased by more than 30 per cent for each decade between 1911 and 1941, this figure fell to 18.9 per cent between 1941 and 1951 and to 14 per cent between 1951 and 1961. Recruitment became one of the major concerns of Quebec's bishops during this period. The other problem was the inability of the clergy to cope with its many tasks, which were becoming more and more demanding. In 1945, it was estimated that barely 40 per cent of Quebec priests were involved in parish ministry, while 25 per cent were teachers, 10 per cent were chaplains and the rest were administrators, students or retired. Religious communities, faced with the rapid growth of schools, hospitals and social services, struggled with similar problems.

The organizational structures through which the church touched people's lives were changing too. The church tried to maintain the traditional form of pastoral organization in a context of rapid urbanization by establishing many new parishes in the cities. However, the shortage of priests had already reached the point where it was necessary to make parishes bigger, so that many of them exceeded the optimal size of 2,500 members. The various traditional movements, however, were still very active, and involved about one fifth of all Catholics in 1961. The specialized Catholic Action movements, which expected a higher degree of active participation from their members, had a much lower membership and continued to infiltrate particular target groups, such as students and specific occupations. At the diocesan level, efforts were made to mobilize Catholics through lange-scale programs such as the Family Rosary Crusade, begun in 1950, and Cardinal Paul-Émile Léger's Grande Mission in 1960.

The church also sought to broaden its field of activity by using the media. Through the Service de Presse et de Cinéma, established in 1946, the church was able to influence Catholic filmgoers by attaching a moral rating to every movie shown. At the same time, a film distributor loyal to the church, Rex Films (1951-56), was established to provide movies to the film clubs springing up in various places. On radio, the family rosary

The various elements of the organizational structure of a Catholic parish, Quebec City, 1945.

was a staple for many years, and while the hierarchy was suspicious of television, the church did not take long to realize that it had great potential. The appearance in 1954 of *Eaux vives*, with Father Émile Legault as host, marked the beginning of religious television programming.

Despite all these efforts, however, contemporary surveys revealed a growing lack of interest in religion, which made the hierarchy uneasy. Thus, in 1948, between 30 and 50 per cent of Montreal Catholics did not go to Sunday Mass, while surveys undertaken by the Jeunesse Étudiante Catholique showed that young people were indifferent to religion. Religion's hold on people seemed to be weakening everywhere. A striking instance of this phenomenon occurred in Montreal in 1951 when, at the archbishop's urging, activists in the church's morality campaign had the city adopt a regulation closing all stores for the Feast of the Immaculate Conception on December 8. But Catholics, ignoring their archbishop's wishes, went on with their Christmas shopping and flocked to stores in the western part of downtown Montreal, which stayed open despite the regulation.

Even among committed Catholics, there was a rising lay challenge to clerical power within the church. These laypeople were products of the Catholic Action movements who wanted an end to clerical control of all aspects of social and religious life. Their thinking was inspired by important trends within French Catholicism, then in the midst of a renaissance, and was expressed in a number of journals, of which *Cité Libre* was by far the best known. This same desire for autonomy was felt in the Catholic union movement, increasingly torn between its trade union goals and its religious affiliation. In addition, because the church no longer had enough priests and religious to staff them, its institutions had a growing number of lay employees, who were less and less inclined to accept the fact that leadership positions were systematically closed to them. The dominance of so many areas of social life by the church and its clerical personnel was gradually being called into question, and there was now a substantial group of laypeople who were ready to move into these positions.

Even within the clergy, there were new tensions between traditionalists and supporters of renewal. Cracks appeared within the hierarchy after the death of the archbishop of Quebec, Cardinal Rodrigue Villeneuve, in 1947. Three years later the archbishop of Montreal, Joseph Charbonneau, was forced to resign. Despite denials, his resignation seemed somehow related to the stands he had taken on social questions, and it marked a resurgence of conservative forces within the hierarchy. The nomination of Paul-Émile Léger to succeed Charbonneau confirmed this tendency. Nevertheless, there was a growing concern with social questions among some clerics, as manifested in the establishment of the Commission Sacerdotale d'Études Sociales (priests' social studies commission) in 1948, statements of support for the union during the Asbestos strike in 1949, and the bishops' statement on the labour problem in 1950. At the same time, other elements of the clergy fell into a bourgeois existence characterized by mediocrity, rote performance of their pastoral duties and lack of familiarity with the needs of their flock. The fact that many clerics were now paid employees of institutions instead of being involved in parish ministry intensified this trend.

The church was also weakened by changes in its relationship with the state. While the government did not challenge the church's prerogatives, the establishment of the Department of Youth and Social Welfare in 1946 and the growing commitment of public funds to hospital care and college education were indications that it was surrounding and besieging some of the church's strongholds. Increasingly, the church was unable to coordinate and maintain all the services Quebecers needed, and it was only natural for the government to pick up the slack.

A church triumphant: Cardinal Léger, Mayor Jean Drapeau and Maurice Duplessis surrounded by members of the clergy, Montreal, 1955. (*The Gazette*, National Archives of Canada, PA-119877)

The collusion between the Union Nationale and the church during the period ultimately constituted another factor leading to the weakening of the church. In a 1956 series of articles entitled "*L'immoralité politique dans la province de Québec*" (Political immorality in the province of Quebec), Abbé Gérard Dion and Abbé Louis O'Neill strongly criticized the amalgam of practices — with its elements of naïveté, wily opportunism, electoral corruption and abuse of confidence — to which this collusion led. In the final analysis, as a result of Duplessis's patronage system, not only did the government intrude more strongly into many areas occupied by religious institutions, but those institutions also became discredited in the eyes of the public.

Thus, while the Catholic Church in Quebec appeared to reach its zenith between 1945 and 1960, these were also the years when it first showed serious signs of weakness and inability to adapt to changes in society.

Education

There was considerable interest in educational questions in the postwar years. In part, this was due to rapid population growth and the return of prosperity, which encouraged individual and collective investment in education. But there were other factors as well: the development of science and technology, Quebec's new openness to the world, and its desire to modernize and catch up. Immediately after the war, the educational system was incapable of meeting people's needs and expectations. The result was an intense reappraisal and efforts to renew an institution that had become outdated.

Efforts to Adapt

From primary school to university, numbers of students grew in unprecedented fashion, increasing from a total of 728,755 in 1945 to about 1.3 million in 1960. How could the educational system cope with this rising tide?

The first problem was the serious inadequacy of the physical plant. As late as 1951, more than 70 per cent of Quebec's 8,780 schools were one-room schoolhouses, 60 per cent had no electricity and 40 per cent had no running water or indoor toilets. While the most serious deficiencies were corrected through rural electrification, the government also assisted school commissions in opening large numbers of new schools, so that in 1956 the Union Nationale could boast of having built more than 3,000 schools in ten years. However, most of these were range schools where children of all grades sat in one classroom with a single teacher. Public secondary schools were still inadequate and poorly equipped.

Nevertheless, there was a substantial increase in public spending on education. In the public sector, the school commissions assumed the largest share of educational spending at the primary and secondary levels: their expenditures rose from $69 million in 1951 to $213 million in 1959. At the same time, the government's contribution increased from 27 per cent of the total cost in 1945 to 35 per cent in 1959. The government also bore a share of the financing of other public and private educational institutions, so that its total spending on education rose from $46.7 million in 1950-51 to $181.5 million in 1960-61. Despite this increase in government spending, school commissions were underfinanced and some of them were heavily indebted. The Act to Ensure the Progress of Education, passed in 1946, authorized the government to turn substantial sums over to school commissions, but commissions resorting to this form of assistance had to submit to trusteeship by the Quebec Municipal Commission. Three years later, new legislation allowed some school commissions to levy a sales tax within their jurisdictions. The fact that more than half of Quebec's school commissions were still in trusteeship in 1954 indicates just how serious the problem was.

These financial changes represented scattered efforts to adjust the old system to new realities. Educational reforms undertaken during the period followed the same pattern. One of the most significant of these reforms involved secondary education. In 1956, the complementary primary and superior primary courses in the Catholic sector were combined into the public secondary course, with a new program of study lasting five years. The new course was divided into a number of tracks —

scientific, commercial and technical, among others — so that it could more appropriately meet the needs of the roughly 200,000 students registered at the secondary level.

The Duplessis government also took some initiatives in the area of technical and occupational education. In 1945 it set up apprenticeship centres, and the next year it established the Department of Youth and Social Welfare, which was given responsibility for trade schools and technical institutes. Forty schools of this type were opened between 1940 and 1961, but here too there was still a great deal of disorganization. The system operated parallel to the public secondary system, and it was poorly adapted to the needs of the labour market. There were also many private institutions in the technical and occupational sector, including 125 business colleges and about 150 other schools teaching languages, dressmaking, hairdressing and the like. Overall, only 23,000 boys were being trained in this sector in 1960-61, representing less than 8 per cent of the male population between fourteen and twenty years old.

The position of the private classical colleges in the educational system remained central. They grew rapidly during the period: 135 new colleges were founded between 1940 and 1965, while the number of students increased from 22,634 in 1940 to 38,000 in 1960. There were twice as many colleges for boys as for girls.

The colleges tried to tailor their programs to the times. They agreed to accommodate more day students, instituted a baccalaureate requiring Latin but not Greek, organized themselves into the Fédération des Collèges Classiques, and hired more lay teachers, although they resisted any challenge to their privileged place within Quebec education and refused to become part of a coherent public system. But the private colleges had neither the human nor the financial resources to cope with the growth in demand. As a result, classical sections were established within the school commissions starting in 1945, although it was only in 1954 that the Council of Public Instruction officially recognized this policy. In 1961 there were sixty-one such classical sections. Of these, only thirteen were for girls, who were disadvantaged in this area as they were in the rest of the educational system. Although these sections offered only the first four years of the classical course, they represented a crack in the classical colleges' monopoly.

Teachers

The number of Catholic teachers in the public system grew from about 27,000 in 1950 to 45,000 in 1960, but this increase was not enough to meet the demand created by the entry into the system of the baby boom generation. The normal schools did not produce enough graduates and many who entered teaching left after only a few years because working conditions were deplorable. Thus, in 1953, when office employees earned $1,600 a year on average, there were more than 5,500 teachers making less than $1,000 and about the same number making between $1,000 and

Typing class at William Dawson High School, Montreal, 1947. (*The Gazette* National Archives of Canada, PA-151687)

$1,500. It became necessary to increase the student-teacher ratio, and in the end to close schools and hire unqualified teachers. Even the secretary of the Council of Public Instruction estimated in the late 1950s that 48 per cent of Quebec's teachers did not meet the standards generally accepted in other provinces.

This situation was disturbing to the Corporation des Instituteurs et Institutrices, established in 1946 (see chapter 22), and the teachers' union federations. The solutions they proposed included professional recognition, higher wages, improved working conditions, upgrading courses, and mobilization of both teachers and public opinion. But the government and the school commissions resisted these urgent demands and the unions had to wage epic struggles to obtain decent conditions. It was not until 1959 that the minimum annual salary for teachers was raised from $600 to $1,500.

Women still constituted a large majority — 80 per cent — of teachers in the public system. In the Catholic schools, however, the proportion of religious teachers declined substantially, as religious communities were not able to recruit enough members to keep pace with increasing school enrolment. While priests, brothers and nuns were a majority of teachers in the system at the end of the war, they represented only 31 per cent in 1960.

Questioning the System

Neither increased spending nor changes in the program nor the building of new schools were enough to correct the deep-rooted inadequacies and inconsistencies in the school system. As a result, education was a central issue in the debates of the 1950s. What some people during the Duplessis

A nun and her pupils at church, Montreal, 1952. (Frank Royal, NFB, National Archives of Canada, PA-151654)

era liked to call "the best education system in the world" was in fact fragmented, underfinanced, underdeveloped, uncoordinated, undemocratic, elitist and sexist.

These characteristics of the system were acknowledged in a large number of inquiries, speeches and publications. Thus, of the 240 briefs presented to the Tremblay Royal Commission on constitutional problems between 1953 and 1955, more than 140 dealt with education. In 1958 some fifty organizations, representing almost all groups with an interest in education, got together to draw up a list of needs and seek solutions "to the prevailing anxiety."

The method of financing education was a basic problem. Relying on the property tax, distributed according to the religion of the taxpaying property-owners, it had remained essentially unchanged since the nineteenth century. The revenues this system produced were inadequate and inequitably distributed, and its perpetuation doomed education to underdevelopment. In particular, it offered little scope for financing secondary education, which needed to be regionalized and made accessible to all Quebecers. The question of financing was also directly related to difficulties in recruiting teachers. But the most serious problem was still the low educational level of Francophone Quebecers. As late as 1958, only 63 per cent of students who began primary school finished grade seven, 30 per cent went as far as grade nine and a mere 13 per cent completed grade eleven. By contrast, 36 per cent of students on the Protestant side reached grade eleven. Many people believed that only more government intervention, with better coordination, could correct the situation. The runaway success of *The Impertinences of Brother Anonymous* in 1960, with its denunciation of the weakness of the system and its recommendation that the Council of Public Instruction be closed down after giving all its officials the medal "for Solemn Mediocrity," indicated the extent to which Quebecers felt the need for reform.

Higher Education

The establishment of the University of Sherbrooke in 1954 brought the number of universities in Quebec to six. Three of these were French-language and three English-language, and all were private. While Anglophone students had little difficulty in reaching university, it was very different for Francophones. It is estimated that about 7,500 full-time students were registered in the regular programs of Quebec's French-language universities in 1953-54; of these only 15 per cent were women. In 1960, there were slightly fewer than 22,000 full-time students registered in all Quebec universities, representing 4.3 per cent of Quebecers between twenty and twenty-four years of age, but this overall figure conceals the substantial gap between the two language groups. While 11 per cent of Anglophones were in university, the figure for Francophones was only 2.9 per cent. The English-language universities produced more graduates than the French-language ones, and more than twice as many doctorates (table 1).

The Quebec government was not wholly insensitive to the needs of higher education and research. Between 1949 and 1959 it increased its grants from $2 million to $11 million and took such initiatives as establishing a school of veterinary medicine and a forestry school and allocating $6 million for the construction of new buildings needed by the École Polytechnique. But these measures fell far short of what was needed.

In academic and scientific circles, criticism of the Duplessis government focused principally on its lack of an overall strategy. It distributed

Table 1
Number of Degrees Awarded by Quebec Universities, by Level, 1946-55

University	Undergraduate	Master's level	Doctoral	Total
Laval	4,645	1,224	161	6,030
Montreal	5,597	1,394	226	7,217
McGill	9,860	1,217	823	12,000
Sir George Williams	1,448	-	-	1,448
Bishop's, Loyola & Marianopolis	802	40	-	842

Source: Raymond Duchesne, *La science et le pouvoir au Québec*, pp. 104-5.

its grants as it saw fit, and it didn't hesitate to intervene with university authorities to silence intellectuals who criticized its conservative policies.

The crisis in higher education affected all of Canada, and in 1951 the federal government implemented a recommendation of the Massey Royal Commission on National Development in the Arts, Letters and Sciences that federal grants be given to the country's universities in proportion to the population of each province. The Duplessis government's refusal to accept these grants touched off a heated controversy. Recognizing the seriousness of the situation, the Tremblay Commission also made two major recommendations regarding higher education: the creation of a Commission for Aid to Higher Education financed through the corporate income tax and the establishment of a Council of Universities, which would be made up of academics and would be responsible for distributing the government's grants to higher education without political interference.

The Duplessis government, however, refused to implement these recommendations. As a result the universities — which had support in the chambers of commerce, patriotic organizations and trade unions — increasingly became centres of opposition to the Union Nationale and joined other groups in demanding change.

In the education system as a whole, from the primary level to university, some progress was made as the number of students, the number of schools and educational spending all increased. However, many problems remained. An overhaul of the system, increasingly seen as indispensable in the 1950s, would have to wait until the next decade.

CHAPTER 25

THE ERA OF IMPATIENCE

The climate in postwar Quebec was conducive to the expression of new ideologies. Prosperity, the resumption of urbanization and industrialization, new lifestyles based on consumption and new means of communication, along with still-fresh memories of the Depression and the war, all contributed to this climate. Reform liberalism proposed its new models, and attempts were being made to recast nationalism and bring it up to date. But while these ideologies called for the modernization of Quebec, they had to face the rhetoric of a still influential traditionalist nationalism.

Traditionalist Nationalism and the Duplessis System

The position of traditionalist nationalism in postwar Quebec was paradoxical. On the one hand, its power and influence appeared greater than ever. On the other hand, it faced serious threats, and the reality of those threats would be confirmed by the speed with which it became marginalized only a few years later.

As we saw in chapter 8, the Depression had provided traditionalist nationalism with an opportunity to make its presence more strongly felt, restate its positions, and appear as a positive alternative to the difficulties of the time. But in the new conditions that prevailed after the war, Quebec society strayed further and further from the model put forward by the traditionalists, which was still based on the religious and agricultural vocation of the French Canadian people and the primacy of the old values: the patriarchal family, parish life, mistrust of the outside world, and worship of the past. To be sure, there were attempts to adapt the conservative message to contemporary reality without abandoning this vision or the principles underlying it. But these efforts were either too little or too late, so that proponents of this defensive form of nationalism tended to take refuge in a mainly negative attitude towards the modern world and its various manifestations and reject practically any possibility of change.

But despite the wide gulf separating traditionalist nationalism from the problems and needs of postwar Quebec, it still had considerable power. The reason for this was that it was supported by groups that continued to have a preponderant influence in Quebec through the positions they held in society and its institutions. These groups included a majority of the Catholic clergy and hierarchy and the traditional local elites. In addition, a number of pressure groups, such as the Saint-Jean-Baptiste societies and the secret Ordre de Jacques-Cartier, based their appeal on traditionalist nationalism. Clerical control of primary and secondary education resulted in large doses of traditionalist nationalism in the schools. This current also had its house intellectuals, such as the editors of the Quebec City newspaper *L'Action Catholique* and of the magazine *Relations*, published by the Jesuits in Montreal.

The most significant support, however, came from the Duplessis government. The government saw itself as both the incarnation and the official defender of traditionalist nationalism, from which Duplessis's Union Nationale drew the essential elements of its ideological program and the justification for its positions on constitutional and social issues. Thus, Duplessis appealed to French Canadian *survivance* in resisting Ottawa's centralist designs and fiercely defending provincial autonomy, and he gave Quebec an official flag in 1948 in the name of its French and Catholic identity. And when he suppressed militant trade unionism, denounced reform-minded intellectuals, or refused to encroach on the church's power in education and health services, this too was in the name of order and traditionalist values.

Another factor tended to strengthen the reactionary character of the ruling party's ideology even further: its partnership in the economic sphere with the old school of liberalism that remained committed to the principles of laissez-faire and opposed to any form of government intervention. This was a quite different position from the one taken by nationalists during the Depression, who had come to criticize at least some aspects of capitalism and advocate a form of regulation of the economy for the common good through corporatism and the fight against the trusts. By contrast, Duplessis and his allies argued that private enterprise, which was alone responsible for Quebec's prosperity, had to be allowed complete freedom of action. This was their justification for the generous welcome the government gave American capital, even to the point of contradicting the nationalist ideal it proclaimed on other occasions. At the same time, this ideal could be used to resist any attempt to revitalize the role of the state, which was seen as an instrument of centralist federalism and hence as a threat to the political and national integrity of Quebec.

Thus, the adoption of traditionalist nationalism by the Duplessis regime made it an ideology of decisive influence in Quebec's public life. But the very same development tended to drain traditionalist nationalism of its vitality and turn its message into an authoritarian one, closed to all discussion.

The Opposition to Duplessis

Throughout the period, the Duplessis version of traditionalist nationalism coloured the ideological landscape and formed a kind of permanent backdrop. However, opposition to this current arose in the late 1940s and continued throughout the 1950s. And even though it had only minority support, the opposition was undoubtedly the era's most significant ideological movement. Despite the apparent dominance of the traditionalist message, the period was characterized by intense questioning and crying out for renewal.

The opposition was both critical and constructive. On the critical side, it condemned not only the Duplessis system as such but also the values of traditionalist nationalism and the general state of Quebec's society and institutions, whose backwardness came under its scrutiny and attack. On the constructive side, it proposed new models and values to correct or replace the existing state of affairs and direct Quebec towards what it called *rattrapage* ("catching up") — in other words, towards renewal and modernization.

Opposition was expressed in a variety of circles. First, small communist, socialist and progressive groups were active in the Anglophone, Jewish and immigrant neighbourhoods of Montreal. In the Francophone community, a few artists and writers, such as the ones who issued the *Refus global* ("total rejection") in 1948, were among the first to express their impatience. The movement took on new dimensions after the Asbestos strike in 1949. The trade union movement — and especially the Canadian and Catholic Confederation of Labour and the Quebec Industrial Unions Federation — moved in the direction of protest. Some lay teachers, students involved in the Jeunesse Étudiante Catholique or campus journalism, and reform elements in the clergy and the hierarchy including Archbishop Joseph Charbonneau of Montreal also became part of the opposition.

But the group that took on the task of conceptualizing and explicitly formulating this program for change was made up of intellectuals, writers, journalists, university professors and social scientists, many of whom had been educated outside Quebec and were influenced by the new ideological currents circulating in postwar Europe and America. They belonged to the rising new elites that wanted to shape Quebec society according to their own values and interests. Their influence is difficult to measure in the period under study, although it would be decisive after 1960. But there is no doubt that even though their positions were worked out in small groups, their message gradually began to reach a large proportion of the population. A major factor in its dissemination was the CBC's French television network, which represented a platform of the highest importance for a number of opposition figures.

The thinking of these opposition groups was far from being perfectly homogeneous. Resistance to Duplessis and the call for modernization constituted common ground and made them allies in many debates. But within that context, they belonged to a fairly wide variety of tendencies, which often diverged or were even opposed to one another on important matters. Two of these tendencies stand out most clearly. One was the new reform liberalism, for which the magazine *Cité Libre* was one of the major platforms. The other was neonationalism, among whose proponents the journalist André Laurendeau commanded the widest attention.

Reform Liberalism and the New Federalism

As noted earlier, the Depression and the war created a favourable climate for the emergence of a new reform current within liberalism. While this current did not challenge the basic values of classical liberal thinking, it aimed at mitigating their negative effects by giving greater weight to ideas of social justice and economic balance. Only through a powerful, interventionist government could this dual objective be met.

During the war and the immediate postwar years, the federal government of Canada, led by the Liberal Party, adopted Keynesianism and brought in a number of measures inspired by this new form of liberalism. This redirection of socioeconomic thinking had significant political ramifications. The requirements of planning, it was argued, meant that the federal government had to have broad powers of intervention in all spheres, to the extent that the provinces, including Quebec, would be stripped of some of their fields of jurisdiction. Along with this "new federalism" went a new national policy that sought to promote the emergence of a common sense of identity and belonging among all citizens of Canada. This nationalist thrust was expressed on the diplomatic level by the assertion of Canada's presence internationally, notably in the activities of the United Nations (founded in 1945) and UNESCO (1946). Internally, it manifested itself in efforts to reduce the British character of some institutions and in initiatives to encourage the expression of Canadian culture, such as the establishment of the Massey Commission, the granting of a television monopoly to the CBC, and the founding of the Canada Council.

This growing linkage of reform liberalism with centralist federalism had a direct impact on the ideological scene in Quebec. The Union Nationale government, with the support of the traditional elites and a portion of the business community, adopted a rejectionist stance both towards Ottawa's new national policy and towards the new liberalism. Thus, it was outside of the ruling groups, in the opposition movements, that reform liberalism gained support. But their concerns went beyond economic theory and they were influenced by a variety of other currents of thought. Some of these influences came from outside Quebec: the new French Catholicism, expressed in the magazines *Esprit* and *Sept*; internationalism, embodied in the recently founded United Nations; and pacifism, which underlay the movements for nuclear disarmament.

Other influences came from currents that had sprung up in Quebec during the 1930s and 1940s. One of these was the intellectual modernist movement centred on *La Relève* (1934-41) and *La Nouvelle Relève* (1941-48). An even more direct influence was the Jeunesse Étudiante Catholique, which developed considerably during the 1940s and had firm roots in the classical colleges. Finally, many people have reported being inspired by the education they received in the years following 1938 at Laval University's Faculty of Social Sciences, headed by Father Georges-Henri Lévesque. It has often been said that the contribution of this "Quebec School" was the discovery of the "social" sphere as such. However, social affairs had been a concern of many, including some traditionalists, from the First World War on. The group surrounding the École Sociale Populaire had been a major force in this regard. What was new was the more modern and more scientific approach that sociologists, economists and political scientists of the Quebec School used to study social reality. Instead of using preconceived ideas borrowed from morals or religion as a starting point for looking at social reality, they regarded social affairs as an autonomous field that had its own laws of development and therefore required appropriate methods of inquiry and intervention.

Cité Libre

Starting in the early 1950s, a number of different organizations became vehicles for the development and expression of the new reform liberalism in Quebec. The Quebec Liberal Party, under the influence of leading figures such as Jean-Marie Nadeau and Georges-Émile Lapalme, who were as concerned with ideological formulation as with electoral activity, was an especially lively centre of reflection. The trade union movement and its numerous publications also played a significant role, as did the universities. However, historians still know little about this wider reform liberal movement, and they have tended to neglect it. Instead, they have focused their attention almost exclusively on *Cité Libre*, the magazine founded by Pierre Elliott Trudeau and Gérard Pelletier in 1950, and given the impression that it was practically the only forum in which the reform liberal current emerged. The historical reality behind this oversimplification — which historians are now beginning to criticize — is that *Cité Libre*, despite its small circulation, represented a major gathering place and channel of expression for reform liberals. Nevertheless, it is important to remember that the reform liberal movement extended far beyond *Cité Libre*.

It is as a journal of criticism that *Cité Libre* stands out. Its primary target was traditionalist nationalism, which it saw as harping on old themes, never seeing the socioeconomic reality in which French Canadians had

André Laurendeau, 1952. (Fondation Lionel-Groulx)

lived and continued to live. As Trudeau maintained in his introduction to *The Asbestos Strike* in 1956, the result of this ideological incongruity was that instead of adjusting effectively to this reality (industrialization, urbanization, proletarianization), instead of becoming masters of it and turning it to their advantage, French Canadians had become its passive victims, as could be seen in their current condition of exploitation, under-education, and social and political insignificance. In this way, political and religious elites had betrayed Quebec society by forcing it into outmoded institutions and ways of thinking, so that it was now seriously behind English Canada and other western societies. According to other contributors to *Cité Libre* such as Jean LeMoyne, Maurice Blain and Pierre Vadeboncoeur, the evils of the old nationalism could be seen in Quebec's cultural and intellectual life as well, in the form of Jansenism, fear of freedom, conformity and lack of creativity. In sum, Quebec in 1950 was a stifled and backward society, and the infusion of a new spirit and new values that could help it make up for lost time and bring it fully into the modern world was an urgent necessity.

The cornerstone of these new values was individual freedom, which was the basis for other changes that *Cité Libre* advocated: secularization, an attack on social inequality, strengthening the state, and antinationalism. Secularization meant not only that clericalism had to be removed from Quebec's institutions, intellectual life and the exercise of power in society but also that the role of laypeople within the church had to be revitalized. The editors of *Cité Libre* were not antireligious or even anticlerical. Instead, they stood for a Catholicism that would be progressive, open to dialogue and primarily a matter of individual conscience. By contrast, they saw the church's hegemony in secular spheres, its dogmatism, its intolerance towards even the slightest expression of nonconformity, and its collusion with political power as constituting a grave threat to freedom and one of the major causes of Quebec's backwardness. Therefore, they demanded that society be secularized. This was the only way to achieve pluralism, make Quebec truly democratic and modernize its institutions.

Social and economic inequality was another obstacle to freedom. *Cité Libre* argued that individuals had to have not only the right but also the means to develop their capacities fully and exercise their freedom. Exploitation prevented the majority of the population — specifically, the workers — from being able to act as free citizens. Only trade unions and the recognition of bargaining rights could correct this situation. Thus, *Cité Libre* supported the trade union movement in its struggles, especially when they were waged against the Duplessis regime and its allies. Only rarely, however, did the magazine's writers advocate the overthrow of the established order. More typically, they saw the capitalist system as being the best guarantee of individual rights, at least until a better one came along. Therefore, what had to be done was to correct its imbalances so that all citizens, whatever their social position, could benefit from the freedom the system provided. Towards the same end, *Cité Libre* demanded a thoroughgoing reform of the education system. This would involve modernizing its content and methods, secularizing its structures, and making education — another necessary condition for the exercise of freedom — accessible to everyone.

The chief instrument for attaining these goals could only be the state. The requirements for such a state were formulated in a theory called functionalism: it would be modern, interventionist, wholly dedicated to the protection of freedom, and strictly secular. It would also scrupulously respect the rules of democracy and not be subject to any consideration except carrying out its tasks effectively: redistributing wealth, establishing and administering services for citizens, economic planning.

Nor could such a state be based on nationalism. *Cité Libre* regarded all nationalist ideologies of whatever stripe as enemies to be fought. Recent European history showed that nationalism, by emphasizing collective interests at the cost of individual rights, would lead sooner or later to fascism. Thus, they saw the national ideal as being essentially antidemocratic. It could only be a right-wing ideal, using an appeal to national unanimity to disguise and justify the exploitation of underprivileged classes, the oppression of minorities, intellectual censorship and the denial of individual freedom. In contrast to nationalist self-absorption, the *Citélibristes* wanted to be "citizens of the world": they stood for openness to foreign influences and, within Quebec, for acceptance of cultural, ethnic, religious and political pluralism.

On constitutional issues, *Cité Libre* naturally gravitated towards the federalist camp. It regarded Duplessis's nationalist defence of autonomy as retrograde. However, *Cité Libre's* vision of federalism was not as unitary or centralist as the view then prevailing in Ottawa. Some of the magazine's writers and sympathizers, such as the economist Maurice Lamontagne and Father Lévesque, did come out in favour of centralization, accepting a reduction in Quebec's powers so that Canada's state machinery could function more smoothly. But the editors did not go that far, and when Quebec fought with Ottawa over taxes and university grants, they even took positions that were quite favourable to provincial autonomy. In their functionalist perspective, genuine efficiency required both a strong central government and the maintenance of provincial powers. They believed that while Quebec was not and should not become a national state, it should have the necessary authority and instruments to exercise the powers granted to it under the British North America Act.

Cité Libre's positions thus appear as directly opposed to the rhetoric of Duplessis. The Duplessis system saw itself as protecting Quebec against the changes brought about by modernization by encouraging it to be cosily wrapped up in preserving the past. By contrast, the *Citélibristes* called for Quebec to change, abandon its traditions, and democratize its institutions and behaviour. In short, they wanted Quebec to become part of the modern world, as defined by the new western liberalism of the time.

Neonationalism

The new liberalism and neonationalism should not be seen as opposed or even antagonistic to each other. On social, economic and political issues, they both drew from the same basic values, to the extent that they can be considered as two branches of the same central current, reform liberalism. However, they counted on different groups for support, had different attitudes to traditionalist nationalism and, most significantly, had different positions on the national question.

Neonationalism was a new reform version of nationalism. Among the circles in which it developed, the University of Montreal stands out: economists at the École des Hautes Études Commerciales and especially historians such as Guy Frégault, Maurice Séguin and Michel Brunet took a leading role in defining the new current. It also spread among students, prospective teachers, trade union staff, members of the cooperative movement, younger activists in some nationalist movements such as the Saint-Jean-Baptiste societies, and some business people, especially in the Montreal chamber of commerce.

A few of *Cité Libre*'s writers and editors, 1952: Pierre Vadeboncœur, Gérard Pelletier, Jean-Paul Geoffroy. (Private collection)

But the most influential neonationalist thinker and organizer was the journalist André Laurendeau. Laurendeau was born in Montreal in 1912 and in his youth was an activist in the Jeune-Canada movement, influenced by Lionel Groulx. In 1935 he left to spend two years in France, where he discovered social Catholicism and personalist philosophy. When he came back and assumed the editorship of the magazine *L'Action Nationale*, these influences led him to try to remodel French Canadian nationalism. During the war, he was drawn into the fight against conscription and became active in the Bloc Populaire, on whose ticket he was elected to the Quebec legislature in 1944. Soon after the war, however, he returned to the task of renewing nationalist thinking. His vehicles towards this end were *L'Action Nationale*, whose editorship he again held between 1948 and 1956, and especially the Montreal daily *Le Devoir*, of which he became assistant editor-in-chief in 1948. Laurendeau and his colleagues — Gérard Filion, Pierre Laporte, Jean-Marc Léger — made *Le Devoir* the leading platform for neonationalism throughout the 1950s. The Quebec Liberal Federation and the Quebec Liberal Party also embraced neonationalism and developed a program largely inspired by it.

As Laurendeau's career illustrates, neonationalism was the product of a tendency that had first appeared in the 1930s, notably in the form of the Action Libérale Nationale, and continued through the war with the Ligue pour la Défense du Canada and the Bloc Populaire. Hitherto somewhat confused and not well articulated, this tendency was characterized by a desire to rethink nationalism to adapt it to the realities and requirements of the urban industrial society that Quebec had become. Bringing nationalism up to date had two implications. One was that the heart of the old nationalism had to be preserved: the assertion of the national identity of the French Canadian people and their will to survive as a collectivity. The other was that the traditionalist, reactionary content that had so far been associated with that doctrine had to be renounced and replaced with a different content that would be more consistent with contemporary sociological and political reality and therefore more apt to lead to constructive action.

As already noted, the thinking of the neonationalists was very close to that of *Cité Libre*. Michel Brunet's 1957 essay "Trois dominantes de la pensée canadienne-française: l'agriculturisme, l'anti-étatisme et le messianisme" (Three dominant elements of French Canadian thought: agriculturalism, antistatism and messianism) is an example of how harsh they could be in their critique of traditionalist nationalism. It condemned the old nationalism for ignoring the transformation of French Canadian society and thus alienating a large part of the population — especially the urban working class — which no longer recognized itself in the old definitions and therefore tended to lose all national awareness. But unlike *Cité Libre*, whose response to this situation was to abandon nationalism, it proposed giving nationalism a new direction, especially in the area of social issues. "In many parts of our society," André Laurendeau wrote in 1948, "there is a kind of divorce between what are currently called the *social* and the *national*....Our task is to reconcile them, or more precisely to bring about a synthesis between them." Fulfilling this task involved a reform program directly inspired by the new liberalism, including opposition to the Duplessis system, secularization, support for the trade union movement, demands that the education system be modernized and democratized, and openness to immigrants and intercultural contact.

What ultimately separated the neonationalists from the leading writers for *Cité Libre* was the decisive importance, even primacy, that the neonationalists continued to give the idea of the nation. While they regarded individual rights as an essential value, they also believed that these rights would always be restricted or threatened in Quebec so long as the collective rights of the French Canadian nation in its entirety were not first assured. Inequality, they maintained, was not only social but also had an ethnic, linguistic and national dimension. From this view flowed their interpretation of French Canadian economic inferiority, which contemporary studies brought clearly to light. While *Cité Libre* saw this inferiority as mainly a question of "mentality," which could be blamed on the evils of the old nationalism and the ineptitude of the traditional elites, the neonationalists regarded it as being primarily due to the political and national domination of which Quebec had been and was still the victim within the Canadian federal system.

There was only one way to correct this situation and secure the future of the nation. It was necessary to establish a strong Quebec state dedicated to the interests of French Canadians. This state would be interventionist and geared towards planning, along the lines of the reform liberal model. The Quebec government would also take up the cause of protecting Francophones in the other provinces. It would thus act as a counterweight to the federal government and help improve the condition of French Canadians within Confederation. The neonationalists advocated a highly decentralized form of federalism in which Quebec would have all the powers that its position as the national state of French Canadians required. They criticized the Duplessis government for its purely negative conception of autonomy. In their view, by contrast, autonomy should be the means to create a modern, democratic Quebec that would be master of its own social and economic development. Their program for attaining this goal in the economic sphere was based on two major instruments: a strong public sector, which would serve as an outlet for Francophone managers, and the cooperative sector, another favourite theme of the neonationalists, who by now had left corporatism behind.

The neonationalists no longer defined the nation primarily in religious terms. Instead they proposed an economic, social and political definition of the nation, without losing sight of the historical dimension in which its existence was rooted. But the essence of their contribution was encouraging the transformation of the nationalist program, which for so long had been retrograde and conservative, into something more dynamic and consistent with the expectations of a growing number of Quebecers, especially those who made up the new urban elites. Instead of a nationalism of preservation and survival, Quebec now had a self-assertive, modernizing nationalism aimed at *rattrapage*. This current was thus one of the basic ideological sources of the Quiet Revolution.

Left-Wing Ideologies

The postwar era was a difficult one for the left in Quebec. Much of its rhetoric and many of its demands were taken up by reform liberalism and neonationalism. As a result, its only options were to become more radical or to form an alliance with reform groups, either of which amounted to a form of marginalization. In addition, the international situation was unfavourable to the left.

Most seriously affected was the Labour Progressive Party, which was faced with the new wave of anticommunism that the Cold War (1946-56) and the Korean War (1950-53) brought in their wake. In Canada the Gouzenko affair, which flared up in 1946, led to convictions of communists for espionage. In Quebec, the Duplessis government hunted down "Moscow agents" with increased ardour, with the clergy, nationalist groups and trade union federations joining in the hunt. At the same time, the positions of the federal LPP, which in its struggle against American imperialism fully supported the centralist version of federalism and

Canadian nationalism, continued to divide Quebec communists. The federal LPP finally recognized Quebec's national rights in 1952, but it was too late: the Quebec LPP had already lost its best elements when Henri Gagnon and his group were expelled for "nationalist deviationism" in 1947. Finally, the events of 1956 — Khrushchev's revelations about the horrors of Stalinism and the Soviet invasion of Hungary — completed the process of demoralizing Quebec communists and ushered in what amounted to a decade-long suspension of communist activity in Quebec.

Socialists fared a little better, but they too were unable to achieve a breakthrough. A number of writers for *Cité Libre* and a portion of the trade union movement were sympathetic to the social democratic, anti-communist CCF. But the CCF's centralist federalism and Anglophone image continued to stand in the way of a breakthrough among Francophone workers and the French Canadian population in general. To alleviate this difficulty, activists in the Quebec Industrial Unions Federation issued a *Manifeste au peuple du Québec* (Manifesto to the people of Quebec) in 1955. In it they advocated the establishment of a Quebec labour party "whose program would be closely related to that of the CCF but whose character would be distinctively Québécois." The proposed party never came about, but Quebec socialists did establish the Ligue d'Action Socialiste (Socialist action league). This group became the nexus for the development of a proposal for the independence of Quebec, which was expressed in small-circulation periodicals such as *Situations* (1959) and Raoul Roy's *Revue Socialiste du Québec*. Marginal in the 1950s, this current would become more significant in the 1960s.

* * * * * *

In the ideological sphere, traditionalist nationalism was criticized and discredited between 1945 and 1960, while new reform ideologies asserted themselves. The new currents were aimed at making Quebec a more modern society, aware of its problems and oriented towards the future — and also one in which the groups that formulated these ideologies, the new urban elites, would have greater influence and legitimacy. This ideological renewal took shape in two models, reform liberalism and neonationalism, which shared an impatience and a desire for change and were allies in the struggle against the stagnation of the Duplessis regime. Both these ideologies helped lay the foundations for the Quiet Revolution, but the differences between them and their separate visions of Quebec would begin to appear once that momentous change was underway.

CHAPTER 26
AN ERA OF STABLE GOVERNMENT

In contrast to the effervescent political scene of the Depression and war years, the regimes in power between 1945 and 1960 were very stable. Maurice Duplessis's Union Nationale governed uninterruptedly in Quebec City, while in Ottawa Louis Saint-Laurent's Liberals remained in power until 1957. Political life was still dominated by the traditional major parties, backed by powerful electoral organizations, largely financed by the business community, and offering little scope for internal democracy. Meanwhile, the federal bureaucracy, which had been given a major boost by the war, continued to develop rapidly after 1945. The Quebec bureaucracy, however, retained its traditional character.

Maurice Duplessis's Union Nationale

When the Union Nationale lost the 1939 election to Adélard Godbout's Liberals after three years in power, it was plunged into an internal crisis. Duplessis not only survived the crisis but emerged stronger than ever, and during the war the party took advantage of its stay in opposition to put its troops back in fighting shape. It manoeuvred adroitly between anticonscriptionist Quebecers and those who backed the war effort. Its main battle cry was provincial autonomy, which it saw as threatened by Ottawa's centralism and the acquiescence of the Godbout government. This strategy allowed the Union Nationale to win the 1944 election narrowly and slink back into power, where it would remain without a break until 1960.

Deeply conservative, Duplessis's party derived its main support from rural and small-town Quebec and had the backing of the traditional elites — the local *notables* and the clergy. Its pro-autonomy stance gradually brought nationalist groups to its side. At the same time, with its highly favourable attitude towards private enterprise, it also enjoyed the support of the business community, Anglophone as well as Francophone. Finally, its populism made even some working-class voters sympathetic to it.

The Union Nationale had no official membership and no internal mechanisms for consultation or decision-making. Its base consisted essentially of its MLAs and defeated candidates and their organizers, who between elections were responsible for distributing government favours and "patronage." At election time the party became a powerful machine, which used every possible method to ensure victory for its candidates. But real power in the Union Nationale was concentrated at the top. The treasurer looked after stocking the party's war-chest, the Caisse Électorale, which was accomplished primarily by collecting kickbacks from companies that had been awarded government contracts and by receiving "gifts" from friends of the regime. The publicity director determined the party's positions and propaganda. And supreme authority was in the hands of the "Chef," Maurice Duplessis himself, who knew and oversaw his party's operations in intimate detail.

Duplessis's domination of his party extended equally to the Legislative Assembly, where he had great influence on debates, and the Private Bills

Union Nationale election workers receiving their instructions, Saint-Georges-de-Beauce, 1945 byelection. (Louis Jacques, *Weekend Magazine*, National Archives of Canada, PA-115232)

Premier Duplessis voting, Trois-Rivières, 1952. (Montreal *Star*,
National Archives of Canada, PA-115820)

Committee, over which he presided with near-monarchical authority. In
cabinet, Duplessis not only served as both premier and attorney-general
but also exercised direct influence over all government departments. His
ministers held their portfolios almost in perpetuity, forming a cabinet that
made up in stability what it lacked in dynamism.

There was little change in the government's major policies during its
sixteen years in power. Their essential characteristic was conservatism.
Where possible, this took the form of perpetuating values and practices
that were consistent with tradition. When change had to be introduced,
the Union Nationale introduced it cautiously, making sure to avoid an
open break with the past.

Duplessis emphasized maintaining religious values and a conception of society based on respect for the established order. He used the courts, the police and, if necessary, legislation in his fight against groups and individuals he considered subversive: communists, Jehovah's Witnesses, trade union leaders and members, and journalists and intellectuals who favoured reform. The clergy generally supported Duplessis in these struggles, especially since the government maintained the church's traditional role and privileges, notably in the areas of education and social affairs.

Economically, three major policies reflected the regime's conservative thrust. First, it gave rhetorical support to agriculture and the struggle against the rural exodus in the name of the values of *survivance*. Second, it was very prudent in managing Quebec's finances, emphasizing debt reduction, a balanced budget and low taxes. And finally, it carried out a policy of industrialization based on welcoming foreign capital. These policies represented a return by the Union Nationale to the general direction Quebec governments had followed from the turn of the century until the Second World War.

Although the scope of the social problems brought about by the industrialization and urbanization of Quebec and the rapid growth of its population were beyond the Duplessis government's grasp, it nevertheless had to react to these problems. It devoted ever-increasing amounts of money to building and maintaining schools, hospitals and roads, but these initiatives were poorly planned, inadequate, belated or poorly adapted to needs.

Finally, the Union Nationale identified itself with traditionalist nationalism, centred on the French language, the Catholic faith and conservative values. Defending provincial autonomy became the instrument of choice for expressing traditionalist nationalism in the political arena, and this translated into systematic opposition to federal policies. Ottawa's centralism was seen as contrary to Quebec's constitutional rights while its reform liberalism was viewed as a threat to the values of French Canadian society.

One effect of the Duplessis system's rejection of government intervention and planning — a fundamental characteristic of its conception of politics — was that Quebec fell even further behind. Some of the Duplessis government's policies, such as farm credit, rural electrification and the development of the North Shore, may have contributed towards modernization in the longer term. In the short run, however, the way in which they were conceived and executed was usually true to their conservative inspiration, and the primary consideration was their electoral impact.

Duplessis died in Schefferville in September 1959, and Paul Sauvé succeeded him as leader of the Union Nationale and premier of Quebec. To many people, Sauvé's accession opened the possibility of political renewal, and the new premier promptly declared that *"désormais"* — from now on — a number of policies would change, especially in education

Paul Sauvé, premier of Quebec (1959-60). (National Assembly, publications director)

and social affairs, and the government would play a more active role. But only a few months later, before he could implement the promised changes, Sauvé died as well. After internal wrangling, Antonio Barrette became premier in January 1960, but his support within the party and his credibility with the public were both weak, and he was unable to pursue the reforms his predecessor had announced.

The Tribulations of the Quebec Liberal Party

After their defeat in 1944, the provincial Liberals were confined to opposition until 1960. However, they took advantage of this long period of purgatory, making it a time of renewal.

Until the mid-1950s, their main problem was their relationship with the federal Liberal Party, entrenched in power in Ottawa under Mackenzie King and then Saint-Laurent. The federal party had substantial means at its disposal to influence the provincial Liberals, who had a hard time staking out a clear position as a party dedicated first and foremost to the interests of Quebec. Adélard Godbout, who led the party until 1948, had no sense of the role the issue of autonomy played for Quebec voters. In the 1948 election, for example, he had no hesitation in asking the federal party — and especially Louis Saint-Laurent, soon to be prime minister — for support. Godbout was appointed to the Senate after he resigned as provincial leader; he was replaced on an interim basis by an Anglophone, George Marler, and then in 1950 by a federal backbencher, Georges-Émile Lapalme.

Lapalme undertook to emphasize social justice issues. Like Godbout he had little feel for the question of autonomy, and his federal allies often made his job more difficult for him. Thus, the federal Liberals openly supported the Duplessis government's policy of developing the Ungava Peninsula with foreign capital — a policy Lapalme criticized. Similarly, Lapalme attacked Duplessis's introduction of a provincial income tax, but Saint-Laurent, who had promised Lapalme he would never agree to such a measure, came around and acquiesced in 1954. All in all, while the Quebec Liberals did benefit from Liberal dominance in Ottawa in terms of patronage, they also appeared to be vassals of the federal "big brother," and Duplessis was quick to condemn them roundly on this score.

By the late 1950s, as a result of repeated election defeats, many Liberal activists sought to reorganize the party and rethink its orientation. They started a newspaper, *La Réforme*, under the editorship of Jean-Louis Gagnon. They also tried to strengthen the party's base by reinvigorating its riding associations and establishing new organizations for specific voter groups such as youth, women and students. And in 1955 they founded the Quebec Liberal Federation, which represented both the first specifically Quebec structure that the provincial Liberal Party had ever had and also a significant new feature in Quebec partisan politics: no other large party had ever gone this far in the direction of internal democracy.

This reorganization helped the Liberals continue to build support among the voters. While their traditional base — consisting mostly of a large majority of Anglophone voters and many urban Francophones — remained loyal to them, they also succeeded during the 1950s both in gaining additional urban support and in establishing a stronger presence in rural areas.

These changes did not result in immediate electoral victory, but the Liberals were increasingly striking a responsive chord. At the same time, they were able to give firmer foundations and greater precision to the positions they took. They were more cogent in their advocacy of social reform, while their constitutional position moved towards support for autonomy, but of a sort that was more dynamic and progressive than Duplessis's.

Lapalme was forced to resign because of his failure to lead the Liberals to power. He was replaced in 1958 by Jean Lesage, who came to the job with solid experience as a federal cabinet minister and whose skills as an orator and political pragmatism gave him considerable credibility. While Lapalme continued to lead the Liberal caucus in the Legislative Assembly and took charge of rewriting the party's platform, Lesage worked on building its support and resources, recruiting new personalities, and making the party the rallying point for anti-Duplessis forces by presenting it as the only alternative to the Union Nationale regime.

Thus, in the period preceding the 1960 election, the Liberal Party solidified its base substantially, becoming strongly identified both with the interests of Quebec and with the idea of change. In opposition to the traditional autonomist position, it came to incarnate a new and more modern political version of Quebec nationalism that was compatible with the reform liberal idea of the welfare state.

Other Parties

The existence of two parties is a logical consequence of the first-past-the-post electoral system. A third party can hope to displace one of the two major ones, but if it does not succeed it faces a very difficult struggle for existence.

The Bloc Populaire Canadien reached its zenith during the conscription crisis, but it enjoyed only limited success in the 1944 provincial and 1945 federal elections. The Bloc was unable to compete with the Union Nationale as a nationalist party or with the Liberals as a reform one. Furthermore, in 1948 it lost its leader, André Laurendeau, who resigned to become assistant editor-in-chief of *Le Devoir*. The Bloc did not run any candidates in that year's provincial election, and the party disappeared.

The Union des Électeurs, as Quebec's Social Credit Party was called, was founded in 1942. It too had little electoral success, although Réal Caouette won a federal byelection under its banner in 1946 and sat in the House of Commons for three years before being defeated in the 1949 general election. Social Credit ideas did have a degree of popularity in Quebec: the Social Credit newspaper, *Vers Demain*, had a circulation of 50,000, and the party won 9 per cent of the vote in the 1948 provincial election even if it did not win any seats. The Union des Électeurs subsequently abandoned electoral politics and with its trademark white berets became a pressure group rallying "pilgrims for a better world." In 1956 it supported George-Émile Lapalme's Liberals. Two years later, after a split in the movement, Réal Caouette formed a new party, the Ralliement des Créditistes, with federal ambitions that would be realized in the next decade.

Meanwhile, the left had little impact on the political scene. The communist Labour Progressive Party, discredited by the Soviet defector Igor Gouzenko's revelations about Soviet espionage and torn apart by internal struggles over the national question, became a completely marginal group. The socialist CCF was too closely identified with an English Canadian intellectual elite and the centralist version of federalism. Some Francophone socialists tried to reach the population by establishing the Parti Social-Démocrate under the leadership of Thérèse Casgrain in 1956, but their efforts were not notably more successful. In the same year, some progressive intellectuals who were part of the *Cité Libre* circle and distrusted the Liberal Party established an organization called the Rassemblement with the aim of unifying all the forces that favoured democracy and opposed the Duplessis regime, irrespective of partisan affiliation. But this intiative also failed, and in the end its supporters had no choice but to cast their lot with Jean Lesage's Liberal Party.

		Table 1		
	Results	**of Quebec Election**	**ns, 1944-1956**	
Election	*Party*	*% of popular vote*	*No. of seats*	
1944	Union Nationale	38.2	48	
	Liberals	40.0	37	
	Bloc Populaire	15.2	4	
	CCF	0.8	1	
	Other	5.8	1	
1948	Union Nationale	51.0	82	
	Liberals	38.3	8	
	Other	10.7	2	
1952	Union Nationale	51.5	68	
	Liberals	46.0	23	
	Other	2.5	1	
1956	Union Nationale	52.0	73	
	Liberals	44.5	19	
	Other	3.5	1	

Source: Jean Hamelin, Jean Letarte and Marcel Hamelin, "Les élections provinciales dans le Québec, 1867-1956."

Elections

The Union Nationale won all three elections during the period (table 1). In the first of these elections, in 1948, it consolidated its power in spectacular fashion. Its share of the popular vote increased to 51 per cent from 35.8 per cent in 1944, while the Liberal share remained below 40 per cent. The Union Nationale's nationalist appeal was symbolized by the fleur-de-lys, which the government had just adopted as the official flag of Quebec. At the same time, Duplessis's campaign was based more heavily than ever on opposition to Ottawa, which the premier criticized both for its centralism and for its policy of sending aid for the reconstruction of Europe. "Duplessis gives to his province," went the Union Nationale slogan, "while the Liberals give to foreigners." On election day, even Adélard Godbout lost his seat in the Union Nationale landslide.

The Union Nationale maintained its position in the 1952 and 1956 elections. While continuing to spare no effort in playing the autonomy card, Duplessis also used the theme of anticommunism to stigmatize his opponents and strongly emphasized his government's achievements: bridges, roads, hospitals, schools and the like. And even though the Liberals, revitalized by the presence of a new leader, improved their position, they were not a strong enough focal point for the forces of opposition to the regime.

Thus, the Union Nationale's repeated victories can be explained by three main factors: economic prosperity, which encouraged political stability; the skill with which Duplessis and his party were able to mobilize a majority of Quebecers around the question of provincial autonomy; and the highly effective Union Nationale machine.

But another factor that should not be ignored is the electoral system, aspects of which made it possible for the Union Nationale to win large majorities in the Legislative Assembly even though its share of the popular vote never went above 52 per cent. The nonproportional method of representation and the distorted electoral map both contributed to this skewed result. The imbalances in the electoral map were flagrant. While the member for the Eastern Townships riding of Brome represented only 7,648 voters, the member for the Montreal riding of Laval represented 135,733. Since these inequalities favoured rural areas at the expense of the cities, the Union Nationale, with its strong rural base, was the beneficiary. Analysing the 1956 election results, historians Jean Hamelin, Jean Letarte and Marcel Hamelin found that "the average number of voters in ridings won by the Liberal Party was 37,000, while in Union Nationale ridings it was only 23,000." A fairer electoral map would not have meant a Liberal government, but it would have made it possible for the Liberals to form a stronger opposition in the Assembly.

Finally, the lenient nature of existing election legislation and the widespread corruption in election practices also benefited the Union Nationale, which made great use of favouritism and a variety of fraudulent practices. After the 1956 election, Abbé Gérard Dion and Abbé Louis O'Neill brought out a pamphlet criticizing this situation, *Le chrétien et les élections* (Christians and the election), and it had considerable impact. The two priests especially attacked anticommunist demagoguery, misleading advertising, vote buying and the use of religion for electoral purposes.

Politicians

The liberal professions were still greatly overrepresented in the Legislative Assembly during the period, but there were some noteworthy changes. Notaries, doctors and lawyers all saw their numbers proportionately reduced, although lawyers still constituted a majority. There was an increase in the number of merchants and small business people, especially in the Union Nationale caucus. But the major new feature was what could be called the growing professionalization of politics. In the past, politics had often been a secondary activity for MLAs. Now, however, it took most of their time and energy, as a result of the increased length of Assembly sessions and the strategic role of the MLA as an intermediary in distributing public funds and patronage.

Union Nationale and Liberal MLAs were substantially the same kinds of people, but there were differences of degree. The Union Nationale caucus, with deeper roots in the community it represented, was more rural, less educated, and from a poorer background, while the Liberal caucus was a little younger and had a higher turnover.

Federal Politics

The Liberals had been in power in Ottawa since 1935, and under the leaderhip of Mackenzie King until 1948 and then of Louis Saint-Laurent, they remained there until 1957. In the postwar period, they were successful in managing the reconversion of Canada to a peace economy, in taking advantage of the prevailing prosperity to pursue policies whose inspiration came from the idea of the welfare state, and in reviving Canadian nationalism, especially by giving the country a position of prestige on the international stage. On the basis of this performance, they received strong support all across Canada in the 1949 and 1953 elections (table 2).

Quebec was in tune with the rest of Canada on this score. The presence of a French Canadian as party leader further enhanced Quebec's traditional confidence in the federal Liberals. It was a source of satisfaction to Quebecers to see one of their own as prime minister, following in the footsteps of Wilfrid Laurier, even if French Canadians occupied a relatively small place in the cabinet and the machinery of government as a whole. The Conservatives, meanwhile, were making some progress in Quebec. However, they still had an Anglophone and even anti-French-Canadian image, despite the efforts of their leader, George Drew, to identify the Conservatives with the cause of provincial autonomy in the hope of obtaining support from the Union Nationale. But while Duplessis left his organizers free to help the Conservatives in some ridings, he refused to give open support to the party and its leader. Third parties — the CCF and Social Credit — were successful in some parts of English Canada, but remained very weak in Quebec.

A break in Liberal dominance of the federal scene occurred in the 1957 election. By this time, the Liberals had lost some of their dynamism and even become a bit arrogant. While Quebec remained faithful to the Liberals, they lost the confidence of English Canada and the election resulted in a minority government for the Conservatives under their new leader, John Diefenbaker. The next year, Diefenbaker called another election. This time, Quebec followed English Canada's lead and for the first time in the twentieth century gave a majority of its seats to the Conservatives, who now had a solid grip on power. This reversal was not attributable to Diefenbaker's personality, as the Conservative leader had little affinity with French Canadians. A number of other factors were at work. First, Lester B. Pearson had succeeded Saint-Laurent as Liberal leader, thus removing one of the reasons for French Canadians' faithful support of the Liberals. In addition, the Union Nationale openly and actively supported Conservative candidates in this election, and this too played a determining role. And finally, Quebecers were affected by the Conservative tide that swept Canada as a whole. But in any case, the Conservatives had little success in taking advantage of this unique victory to bring about a real change in its image and sink lasting roots in Quebec.

Table 2
Federal Election Results in Quebec and Canada as a Whole, 1945-1958

Election	Party	Quebec % of popular vote	Quebec No. of seats	Other provinces % of popular vote	Other provinces No. of seats	Canada % of popular vote	Canada No. of seats
1945	Liberals	50.8	53	37.3	72	40.9	125
	Cons.	8.4	2	34.3	65	27.4	67
	CCF	2.4	-	20.4	28	15.6	28
	Soc. Cred.	4.5	-	4.0	13	4.1	13
	Bloc Pop.	12.8	2	0.2	-	3.6	2
	Other	21.1	8	3.7	2	8.5	10
1949	Liberals	60.4	68	45.5	125	49.5	193
	Cons.	24.6	2	31.6	39	29.7	41
	CCF	1.1	-	18.0	13	13.4	13
	Soc. Cred.	-	-	3.2	10	2.3	10
	Other	13.9	3	1.7	2	5.1	5
1953	Liberals	61.0	66	44.1	105	48.8	171
	Cons.	29.4	4	31.7	47	31.0	51
	CCF	1.5	-	15.0	23	11.3	23
	Soc. Cred.	-	-	7.5	15	5.4	15
	Other	8.1	5	1.8	-	3.5	5
1957	Cons.	31.1	9	41.9	103	38.9	112
	Liberals	57.6	62	34.7	43	40.9	105
	CCF	1.8	-	14.0	25	10.7	25
	Soc. Cred.	0.2	-	9.0	19	6.6	19
	Other	9.3	4	0.4	-	2.8	4
1958	Cons.	49.6	50	55.2	158	53.6	208
	Liberals	45.7	25	29.0	24	33.6	49
	CCF	2.3	-	12.3	8	9.5	8
	Soc. Cred.	0.6	-	3.3	-	2.6	-
	Other	1.9	-	0.2	-	0.7	-

Cons. = Conservatives; CCF = Cooperative Commonwealth Federation; Soc. Cred. = Social Credit; Bloc Pop. = Bloc Populaire

Source: J.M. Beck, *Pendulum of Power:* Canada's Federal Elections.

With the single exception of this upheaval on the federal scene in 1957-58, the dominant characteristic of governments during the period, in both Quebec City and Ottawa, was stability. The Quebec vote was also very stable, giving majorities to the Union Nationale provincially and the Liberals federally. This dual allegiance can appear to be a contradiction: Quebecers favoured a pro-autonomy conservative government at one level and a centralizing reform government at the other. Furthermore, these two governments were often vigorously antagonistic to each other.

In fact, many Quebecers voted *"bleu"* provincially and *"rouge"* federally because they were satisfied with both governments or because for ethnic reasons they preferred to see Saint-Laurent at the head of the Canadian government. In addition, until 1957, federal Liberal MPs and Union Nationale MLAs representing the same area often had a tacit agreement not to work against each other in their respective elections. The Quebec Liberal Party was never able to win the support of a large enough proportion of this bloc of voters and was thus condemned to remain in opposition.

Government Administration

Partisan struggles and electoral battles aside, the Quebec and federal governments differed significantly in the way they managed the state and its administrative machinery. While Ottawa had fully adopted the structures of the welfare state, the Quebec government was characterized by the persistence of old practices and the absence of administrative policies.

The war had forced the federal government to build up a large bureaucracy very quickly, and the civil service grew from 46,000 employees in 1939 to 120,000 in 1946. It had also given Ottawa the opportunity to become familiar with the instruments of planning and

John Diefenbaker, prime minister of Canada (1957-63), on a campaign visit to Montreal, 1958. (*The Gazette*, National Archives of Canada, PA-117494)

Civil servants at the Dominion Bureau of Statistics, 1952. (National Archives of Canada, PA-133212)

management that characterize the Keynesian state. Ottawa thus entered the postwar period with a modernized civil service led by a group of high officials with advanced university training. Trained in the British tradition and enjoying a large measure of power and prestige, these "mandarins" provided the machinery of government with a remarkable degree of cohesion. This select group had little place for French Canadians: in 1960, a number of key departments had no Francophone high officials, and a survey of eleven departments showed that of 163 civil servants earning at least $14,000 a year, only six were French Canadians.

The growth of the federal civil service continued between 1946 and 1960, although it was not as dramatic as it had been during the war. The number of civil servants reached 151,000 in 1960, to which must be added 120,000 military personnel, 150,000 employees of crown corporations, and 40,000 people working for the federal government in various other capacities. Ottawa thus directly or indirectly employed almost half a million people, distributed among 116 departments, corporations and commissions.

The machinery of the Quebec government operated on a much more modest scale, although it did grow substantially during the period. The number of Quebec government employees increased from 16,198 in 1944-45 to 36,766 in 1959-60. This growth reflected an increase in demand for the government's traditional services rather than a strategy of intervention on its part. In both 1944 and 1960, the administration of justice, roads and public works, Hydro-Quebec and the Quebec Liquor Commission accounted for more than half of all Quebec government employees.

The Quebec civil service was still characterized by traditional practices and outdated administrative methods. This can be explained by the Duplessis government's antistate attitude and the partisan, paternalistic way in which it administered public affairs. Hiring was often determined by patronage, so that many government employees were not highly skilled: in 1961, 31 per cent of Quebec government employees had no more than five years of schooling while only 16 per cent had been to school for thirteen or more years. Tasks were poorly defined, salaries were much lower than those paid in the federal civil service, and conditions did not make for attractive careers. There were far fewer specialists and experts than in Ottawa, and most of these were engineers, accountants, agronomists, doctors and lawyers. In 1959, there were not even as many as fifty social scientists (economists, urbanologists, social workers and the like) working for the Quebec government.

In sum, the Quebec civil service grew in size but its administrative and recruiting methods were not modernized. As a result, the effectiveness of government action was seriously reduced and the Quebec government was put in a position of inferiority relative to Ottawa. There was no overall plan or vision of public management at a time when the government was increasingly called on to pick up the slack left by local agencies that had become unable to meet the demand for services effectively, especially in the areas of education, health and social affairs. Because of the Duplessis government's lack of dynamism and coherence, Quebec fell even further behind, and the need to catch up after 1960 was rendered all the more urgent.

CHAPTER 27

THE NEW FEDERALISM AND PROVINCIAL AUTONOMY

More than ever, the initiative in federal-provincial relations lay with Ottawa. The exceptional circumstances of the Depression and — even more so — the war had led to a strong centralizing movement and a substantial strengthening of the federal government's powers. Ottawa wanted to use postwar conditions to maintain its position as the guiding force in the economic and social development of the entire country and to become a truly "national" government by transforming itself into a welfare state. In this spirit, it called together the provinces in 1945-46 for a federal-provincial conference on "reconstruction," during which it presented its plan of action for the coming years. This program was of such scope and implementing it would require such sustained effort that it can be referred to as a new "national policy," analogous to the Macdonald government's National Policy in the nineteenth century.

Most provinces were uneasy about Ottawa's initiative, seeing it as a fundamental change in the federal system and a threat to their own powers. However, with public opinion in English Canada supporting a dynamic federal government, they did not press the point for very long and yielded to Ottawa's position. Only Quebec remained fiercely opposed to the expansion of federal power throughout the period in the name of preserving its autonomy. In the end, Quebec's opposition forced Ottawa to compromise and revise its original plan.

Ottawa and the New National Policy

The lesson Ottawa had learned from the Depression and the war was that the slightly artificial country known as Canada had to be united politically, highly integrated economically, and brought under the unchallenged leadership of a central administration that Canadians would come to consider their "national" government. This was the new national policy that directly inspired the activities of the King and Saint-Laurent governments in the postwar period and marked them with a coherence and dynamism never seen before in Ottawa.

The federal government's policy was largely based on the new economic ideas of Keynesianism. According to Keynesian doctrine, the state had to be able to intervene in the economy on a massive scale, implementing a variety of countercyclical measures that would stabilize

Louis S. Saint-Laurent, prime minister of Canada (1948-57), at the time of his election as the leader of the Liberal Party, 1948. (National Archives of Canada, C-21524)

the economy and hence maintain a high level of consumption and employment. This would involve extensive activity in the social field, which proponents believed would not only serve humanitarian objectives and elicit goodwill from its many beneficiaries but also make it possible to avoid another depression, reduce regional disparities, and provide all citizens, from Atlantic to Pacific, with a decent standard of living and an opportunity to be productive.

Such a plan would require a large degree of centralization and a massive transfer of financial resources and legislative powers to the federal government, whose preponderance over the provinces would be unchallenged. Ottawa proposed to implement this major reform without resorting to constitutional amendments or court decisions. It was convinced that under the British North America Act, it had enough power to tax and spend to ensure the triumph of its new policy. Furthermore, its initiative had broad popular support. English Canada had become more aware of its unity and its identity during the war and appeared ready to back its determined "national" government, whose new prestige on the international scene was an additional major asset.

According to the Keynesian model, if the federal government wanted to act effectively it first had to have a near-monopoly of taxation. As a result, Ottawa sought to retain the fiscal powers that the provinces had ceded to it during the war in exchange for grants, following the recommendation of the Rowell-Sirois Report. After some hesitation, all the provinces except Quebec and Ontario signed an agreement to this effect in 1947, and Ontario signed five years later.

While this struggle over taxation was going on, Ottawa was making a vigorous effort to implement its economic and social development program. To do this, it made wide use of two familiar techniques: shared-cost programs and conditional grants. In this way, it established a variety of programs in fields that were in principle under provincial jurisdiction, such as natural resources, transportation, housing, agriculture and occupational training. It also intervened actively in the social sphere. In 1950-51, it obtained unanimous agreement from the provinces for a constitutional amendment that gave it authority over old age pensions, which now became universal and entirely paid for by Ottawa. It also established a shared-cost program to assist old people in need. A little later, it took responsibility for assisting people on welfare who were able to work. And finally, in the health field, it initially offered conditional grants for a number of programs and then in 1958 established a shared-cost hospital insurance program.

Conditional grants and shared-cost programs had clear advantages, making it possible to proceed with significant social legislation that benefited all Canadians and to carry out highly useful projects such as the Trans-Canada Highway. By acting in this way, however, the federal government in effect restricted provincial autonomy. Even more seriously, Ottawa's programs did not necessarily take provincial governments' priorities into account, and the provinces either had to conform to the "national" standards decreed by Ottawa or else forego federal funds. More often than not, these standards were established on the basis of the interests of Canada's Anglophone majority, and more specifically of the richest and most populous province, Ontario, which exercised a determining influence in the federal civil service, ministers' offices and institutions. For Quebec nationalists, a system of this sort was hard to accept, as it prevented Quebec from developing its own distinct policies that would meet the needs and objectives of its population.

In any case, conditional grants represented an ever-increasing share of the funds that Ottawa paid to provincial governments, thus tying the provinces more and more closely to the federal government. In 1960, 37 per cent of provincial revenues came from Ottawa, up from 29 per cent in 1947 and only 9 per cent in 1930. And while payments to provincial governments had been equivalent to only 4 per cent of federal revenues in 1930 and 6 per cent in 1947, that figure had risen to 17 per cent by 1960.

Another important dimension of the new national policy was the Canadianization of the country's symbols and institutions. Just after the war Ottawa brought in a Canadian Citizenship Act that put an end to the old practice of defining Canadians as British subjects. On its own authority, Ottawa also abolished appeals to the Privy Council in London, making the Supreme Court of Canada the court of last resort in civil, criminal and constitutional cases. Without provincial consent, it also obtained an amendment from London allowing it to amend on its own what could be called the federal constitution — the articles of the BNA Act that did not specifically deal with minority rights or exclusive provincial powers. In 1950, it made an unsuccessful attempt to obtain a consensus of the provinces for the repatriation of the whole constitution and the development of an amending formula. In 1952, the first Canadian governor general, Vincent Massey, was appointed, and the next year Elizabeth II was designated queen of Canada. The idea of introducing a distinctive Canadian flag was under discussion throughout the period, but Anglophones and Francophones could not come to an agreement on it and it had to be postponed. Also under discussion in the late 1950s was the need for a Canadian bill of rights; such a bill, applying only to federal institutions, was adopted in 1960.

Soon after the war, Ottawa entered the field of cultural policy in an effort to complement its economic and social policies. Its initial foray into the new field was the appointment in 1949 of the Royal Commission on National Development in the Arts, Letters and Sciences, chaired by Vincent Massey. The government had already carved out a place for itself in Canadian cultural life through such institutions as the Public Archives, the National Gallery, the CBC, the National Research Council and the National Film Board. By setting up the Massey Commission, the government sought to analyse the operation of these agencies and recommend "their most effective conduct in the national interest."

The commission set forth the dangers faced by cultural life in Canada — Americanization, materialism, lack of funds, and others — and concluded that it was the duty of a "national" government to assist individuals and groups in a variety of ways to overcome these obstacles. The government should help Canadian culture flower because the arts and letters "are also the foundations of national unity." It recommended that Ottawa increase the budgets of its existing cultural institutions and establish a new agency specially mandated to assist cultural creation. The government implemented this last recommendation by setting up the Canada Council in 1957. In addition, while the commissioners expressed their concern for maintaining provincial autonomy in education, they also emphasized the importance of universities and research, whose role, in their view, went beyond a purely provincial context. As a result, they recommended that the federal government come to the rescue of universities and researchers by giving them grants.

Quebec and Provincial Autonomy

The new national policy may have been appealing, coherent and imposing, but it also threatened to shake the Canadian federal system to its foundations. As a result, there was strong opposition to it in some quarters. Between 1896 and 1939, each level of government had been content to act more or less within the constitutional boundaries outlined for it by the original text of 1867 and the interpretations of the British Privy Council. During the war, Ottawa appropriated very broad powers, but many people expected that once peace was restored it would be possible to return to normal and revive what was referred to as "coordinate federalism."

While there was resistance in the other provinces as well, it was Quebec that mounted the most unyielding opposition to Ottawa's policy. It was said at the time that the new national policy threatened to take away from Quebec the minimum degree of autonomy it needed to develop as the national home of a minority people. Maurice Duplessis and the Union Nationale invested considerable energy in resisting Ottawa's centralist assault. Two factors contributed to the difficulty of Quebec's struggle. First, postwar circumstances appeared favourable to the success of the federal initiative. And second, the Quebec government too often lacked the imagination, daring and competence it needed. Thus, not understanding the nature or the consequences of the Keynesian revolution, Duplessis and his government refused to see the need for a more interventionist state.

Quebec's resistance to the new national policy took a variety of forms. On the symbolic level, Duplessis told Ottawa where he stood by proclaiming a distinctive Quebec flag, the fleur-de-lys. He also set up Radio-Québec and a provincial family allowance scheme, although neither program was put into effect. But in most cases, the choice for the Quebec government was essentially between accepting federal initiatives very cautiously and reluctantly and opposing them categorically.

Union Nationale election material during the 1956 campaign.

The first attitude is illustrated by the case of old age pensions, for which Ottawa sought to take exclusive responsibility through a constitutional agreement with the provinces. While Duplessis was opposed to the idea of yielding to Ottawa powers in the social field that in principle belonged to the Quebec government, he could not deprive Quebecers of the advantages of the federal program. He agreed to the constitutional amendment, but won his point of principle by having a clause included saying that it would not affect "the operation of any law present or future of a Provincial Legislature in relation to old age pensions."

The most striking example of the second attitude — outright rejection of a federal initiative — was the controversy over federal grants to universities. In 1951, Ottawa decided to implement the Massey Report's recommendation that it give financial aid to universities, even though universities were under provincial jurisdiction. Duplessis initially agreed to this intrusion but soon stiffened his attitude, and starting in 1953 he ordered Quebec universities to refuse the federal funds. Since the money was placed in trust and grew from year to year, and since the universities needed it urgently, the situation became increasingly tense and opinions were strongly held on both sides. To the end, Duplessis refused to yield.

But the development of the struggle for autonomy and the real issues at stake in it can best be seen in the federal-provincial struggle over taxes. Quebec categorically rejected Ottawa's attempt to obtain a monopoly of the major direct tax fields, arguing its case on both legal and political grounds. Duplessis appealed repeatedly to respect for the "Confedera-tion agreement of 1867" while also reiterating the point that there could not be autonomous provincial governments if they did not have the freedom to levy their own taxes.

Under Premier George Drew, Ontario adopted the same fiscal policy as Quebec, and the two provinces mounted a concerted resistance against Ottawa's proposals until 1952. In consequence, they did not receive com-pensatory grants; in Quebec's case, this financial penalty amounted to $136 million between 1947 and 1955, according to the Tremblay Commis-sion. In 1952, however, Ontario decided to agree to the federal proposals. Ottawa now appeared invincible, Quebec isolated and helpless.

The only way for the Quebec government to overcome its disarray was to go on the offensive, and this course was urged on it with increasing insistence by the neonationalists. In 1953, they succeeded in persuading the government to establish a Royal Commission on Constitutional Prob-lems, chaired by Judge Thomas Tremblay. Duplessis saw this commis-sion as having a straightforward, limited mandate and expected its report within a year. But the commissioners quickly became convinced of the need to do an in-depth study, and with the help of experts they worked for three years, travelled all across Quebec to hear testimony from hundreds of citizens and receive about 250 briefs, and finally submitted an extensive report accompanied by a number of specialized studies in 1956. The research done for the Tremblay Commission, the new aware-ness it evoked in many groups and the degree of identification with the Quebec government it uncovered all helped make its work one of the landmark events of the period.

In the short term, the commission made a decisive contribution to resolving the fiscal impasse. In late 1953, the commissioners persuaded Duplessis that the only effective way to fight for his *"butin"* (what belonged to him) was to exercise the rights granted to him under the constitution by levying his own personal income tax. Having begun to take the pulse of Quebec society, the commissioners knew that Quebecers were ready to back the autonomist point of view. Duplessis brought in a bill allowing the government to levy a personal income tax equivalent to 15 per cent of the federal tax. Ottawa objected, and a lively struggle ensued between the two governments. Finally, the pressure of public opinion forced Saint-Laurent to yield. A compromise was reached fixing the Quebec tax at 10 per cent of the federal tax, which would be corre-spondingly reduced for Quebec taxpayers.

Duplessis's apparently modest victory had wider significance. For the first time since the war, Ottawa had to draw back and temper its new national policy to take the demands of a province into account. The Quebec Liberal leader of the time, Georges-Émile Lapalme, would later say that Duplessis's "use of the tax issue changed the underlying assump-tions of Canadian politics over the long term."

Federalism in the Late 1950s

Ottawa's aggressive centralism and Quebec's equally tenacious defence of its autonomy were in dramatic conflict throughout the postwar period. By the late 1950s, this clash had brought about a new modus vivendi in federal-provincial relations, in which Ottawa imposed its leadership but agreed to a number of compromises in the face of claims from the provinces, especially Quebec.

Overall, the new national policy was a clear success. While federal preponderance was no longer as overwhelming in the late 1950s as it had been during the war, it remained beyond dispute. Ottawa accounted for the largest share of the country's public expenditures (58.5 per cent in 1959). It was also preeminent in taxation: not only did it have the right, according to the BNA Act, to raise money "by any Mode or System of Taxation," but the provinces had to bargain with it to obtain their share of the fiscal pie. It now also had a major role in the field of social policy. This role brought it closer to Canadians, to whom it distributed unemployment insurance, family allowances and old age pensions. These cheques represented direct, tangible contact with citizens, shoring up Ottawa's legitimacy and creating a stronger identification among Canadians with their "national" government. In addition, Ottawa's role in the cultural sector was essential and highly visible. And finally, by making extensive use of its spending power, Ottawa had managed to work its way into a number of fields under provincial jurisdiction, transforming the old division of powers into a new form of federalism with many grey areas.

But if Ottawa's initiative achieved results, so did Duplessis's struggle for autonomy. The concessions Duplessis extracted from Ottawa gave Quebec the instruments it would later be able to use to affirm its powers and its autonomy within Confederation. Three developments in particular are worth noting. First, with the adoption by Ottawa of the principle of equalization in 1957, some of the wealth of the richer provinces began to be redistributed to the poorer ones. Also in 1957, Ottawa granted to the provinces the freedom to levy their own taxes, which meant that Quebec could engage in taxation without being penalized. And finally, when the controversy over university grants was finally resolved in 1959-60, a formula was worked out allowing Quebec to opt out of a federal program with financial compensation.

As the period ended, Ottawa remained committed to a course of action leading to centralization and a strengthening of its role as a "national" government, while the Quebec government had the means to exercise its own powers. The elements were in place for the new federal-provincial dynamic that would characterize the succeeding decades.

CHAPTER 28

THE COMING OF TELEVISION

The new mass culture that made its appearance between the two world wars was a function of leisure time, a rising standard of living and increased urbanization. In the prosperous Quebec of the period between 1945 and 1960, this culture developed extremely rapidly. In some way or other it reached all sectors of society, including those that had previously been only marginally affected.

This process can be divided into two major stages. In the first stage, in the immediate postwar years, the effects of the media that had dominated the 1930s — especially movies and radio — were much more widely felt. Then in 1952, a new era began, centred on television, whose inception had a decisive impact on Quebec's cultural life as a whole. Quebec's traditional elites and religious authorities both resisted and tried to control these changes, which directly threatened their position in society, but there was little they could do in the face of the scope and power of the new developments.

The Golden Age of the Movies (1945-53)

The war had created conditions under which movies became by far the most popular form of entertainment in Quebec. This was all the more true in the climate of rapid urbanization and rising living standards that followed the war. The number of admissions increased from forty-four million in 1945 to fifty-four million in 1950 and reached a peak of fifty-nine million in 1952. This last figure represented an average of at least one trip to the movies a month for each Quebecer. Never in their whole history had movies been so popular.

It was primarily outside the big cities that this expansion of movie-going took place. Montreal and Quebec City had been well supplied with movie theatres since the late 1930s. In 1954, Montreal had seventy-three

A new movie theatre in Montreal during the 1940s. (*The Gazette*, National Archives of Canada, PA-137222)

movie theatres and Quebec City had twelve — not much different from the numbers of theatres they had had in 1939. It was in the rest of Quebec that movie theatres sprang up after the war: while there had been 146 theatres outside Montreal and Quebec City in 1945, there were 365 in 1954. Every small town had its own theatre, and it was not unusual to find a number of theatres in middle-sized communities. Rouyn, for example, had five, and Shawinigan had four.

What kinds of movies did these theatres show? The only figures available are for Canada as a whole, and they demonstrate that the largest source of new feature films shown in commercial theatres between 1946 and 1960 was still the United States. But while the American share of the market was overwhelming immediately after the war — 80 per cent in 1946 — it declined fairly rapidly in subsequent years, falling to 44 per cent by 1954. There was a corresponding rise in the proportion of movies from Europe, especially Britain, Italy and France. France had provided much of the fare shown in Quebec movie theatres in the 1930s, but French film production was almost completely paralysed during the war. After the war, however, Quebec moviegoers again had access to French films, which in 1954 represented 22.4 per cent of the new feature films shown in Canada. Clearly, the proportion in Quebec would have been higher. The figures suggest that Quebecers had fairly eclectic tastes in movies during the 1950s and divided their patronage more or less equally between American movies (dubbed or not) and French ones.

Locally produced films continued to occupy only a very limited share of the market, but the Quebec film industry did benefit from movies' huge popularity in the postwar era. Between roughly 1947 and 1953, some fifteen feature films were produced in Quebec, and these were generally well received by the public. Yvan Lamonde and P.-F. Hébert have called this development "the birth of a national film industry." Two production companies were especially active. The goal of Renaissance-Films, which was led by J.-A. De Sève and operated in association with elements in the European and Quebec clergy, was to make Montreal "a world centre of wholesome moviemaking." The city would produce Catholic-oriented films that would act as a counterweight to the "evil that bad films produce in the soul." In the event, only three fairly mediocre feature films were produced, although the last of these, *Les lumières de ma ville* (1950), gained considerable critical success. The other company, Québec-Productions, adapted works that were already very popular in other media for the screen; this success formula would be widely imitated. Under the leadership of Paul L'Anglais, Québec-Productions produced *Un homme et son péché* (1948), *Le curé de village* (1949) and *Séraphin* (1949), all based on highly popular radio serials of the time. Other producers followed a similar strategy, bringing out film versions of two popular stage plays, *La petite Aurore, l'enfant martyre* (1951) and *Tit-Coq* (1952). Both were huge successes: 300,000 people saw *Tit-Coq* in two months.

Thus, in these few years, Montreal became a very active film production centre. This activity had no equivalent anywhere else in Canada and was entirely concentrated in the private sector. However, the companies faced problems, rooted in the demands of the market, that the Quebec film industry would not be able to resolve for a long time. Should the Quebec film industry make movies of primarily domestic interest and hence shut itself out of the international market — the only market that could make its movies profitable? Or should it aim its movies at foreign markets, where it would have to compete from a position of weakness with much more powerful and better endowed American and European producers? A variety of solutions were tried: films brought out in two versions, French and American; coproductions; English-language films. None of these, however, dealt with the problem convincingly. Thus, from its inception, the "national film industry" was in a dubious and fragile position.

There were also government agencies, but they were more or less marginal. The Service de Ciné-photographie du Québec produced virtually nothing, although it had existed since 1941. Ottawa's National Film Board was more productive, but it continued to devote its energies almost exclusively to documentaries and animated films. In the latter field, this was the period when the illustrious Norman McLaren produced short subjects such as *La poulette grise* (1947) and *Neighbours* (1952). Until the late 1950s, the NFB had an essentially English face, and between 1946 and 1955 only 125 out of a total of 748 films, or a little more than 16 per cent, were original productions in French. The situation began to change only after the NFB moved from Ottawa to Montreal in 1956. A significant number of Francophone directors began to work at the Film Board, and they (sometimes vehemently) demanded that it establish an autonomous French-language section and gradually redirected the NFB towards the production of mass-market feature films.

By the time their efforts bore fruit, however, movies in Quebec operated in a completely different environment. The advent of television had changed everything.

Television

Television had begun to appear in some countries as early as the 1930s, but it took a while to develop in Canada. With its rapid growth in the United States during the 1940s, nearly 150,000 Canadian homes in areas near the border acquired television sets. But it was not until the fall of 1952 that domestic TV production and broadcasting began under the aegis of the CBC. The proportion of Quebec homes with TV sets grew at an astonishing rate: from 9.7 per cent in 1953, it reached 38.6 per cent in 1955, 79.4 per cent in 1958 and 88.8 per cent in 1960. Quebec was substantially ahead of the proportion for Canada as a whole, which was 80.6 per cent in 1960. In less than eight years, the people of Quebec had become a huge audience for television. Roofs were crowned with antennas, living-room furniture was rearranged to give a central place to the television set, and in city and country alike, people scheduled their evenings around this new wonder of the world.

Not only did everyone begin to watch television, but in the 1950s everyone watched the same programs. Following the recommendations of the Massey Report (1951), Ottawa decided that the CBC would have a television monopoly and that until this Canadian network was very widely established, the only private broadcasters who would get licences would be ones who agreed to act as CBC affiliates in areas where the CBC did not have its own transmitters. In Quebec, CBFT, channel 2 in Montreal, began broadcasting on September 6, 1952. Its programming was bilingual, and although there was dissatisfaction with this formula, it continued until 1954, when the English-language Montreal station CBMT, channel 6, began operation. At the beginning, the images transmitted from Mount Royal reached about half of Quebec's populated areas. But the CBC quickly extended its system of transmitters, so that by the end of the decade almost all Quebec homes could receive — without too much snow — the programs produced in the building on Dorchester Street West in Montreal where the CBC had centralized its radio and television operations in 1951.

Early television programming was more or less a continuation of what CBC radio was offering at the time. Entertainment occupied the largest share of air time. The radio serial format was recycled into TV serials such as *Les Plouffe* (along with its English version, *The Plouffe Family*) and *Le Survenant*; *La soirée du hockey* (the French version of *Hockey Night in Canada*) was now broadcast on television; there were game shows such as *La poule aux oeufs d'or* and *Le nez de Cléopâtre*; and much time was devoted to movies. For baby boom children there were adventure stories, educational programs and the puppet show *Pépinot et Capucine*. Programming also included a substantial cultural component, with such programs as *L'heure du concert* and the weekly *Téléthéâtre*, which was replaced in 1956 by *Théâtre populaire*. All these programs brought to a wider audience works that had hitherto been restricted to a minority.

The impact of television was also felt in the area of information and public affairs. Such programs as *Les idées en marche* (1954), *Carrefour* (1955) and *Point de mire* (1956) — generally regarded with displeasure by politicians in power and religious elites — made it possible for a new generation of leaders, whose influence had been limited almost entirely to cultured circles in Montreal, to spread their message all across Quebec. Program hosts such as René Lévesque, Gérard Pelletier, Judith Jasmin and Wilfrid Lemoine and commentators such as Pierre Elliott Trudeau and André Laurendeau became TV stars, and their call for change, critical thinking and modernization was heard everywhere.

In this sense, television clearly played a crucial role in the evolution of Quebec society in the 1950s. Not only did it provide a powerful means of disseminating information and new ideas but it also contributed to a more homogeneous way of life by transmitting the same values and the same ways of thinking and feeling to Quebec's different social groups and regions. Even more effectively than radio, it made rural life less isolated and made Quebec more open to the world. At the same time — contrary to what its founders in the federal government expected — the CBC French network, concentrated almost entirely in Quebec, came to be a force directly encouraging the emergence of a new solidarity among Quebecers. It helped make television viewers all across the province aware of being not only a single huge audience but also a distinct society, with its own particular characteristics and collective needs.

But whatever the sociopolitical repercussions of the advent of television, there was one area where its impact was revolutionary: entertainment and consumer culture. In this area, television did much more than add to what was already there. It upset old consumer habits, created new criteria of taste, and forced all other media to redefine themselves according to its standard.

The Decline of the Movies (1953-60)

The appearance and rapid spread of television was a serious blow for the movies, bringing an abrupt end to their golden age (1945-53) and ushering in a new phase of steep decline. Within a few years, the number of commercial movie theatres decreased by a hundred, while attendance fell

Wrestling was one of the most popular television shows. Two wrestling stars, Yvon Robert and Don Leo Jonathan, around 1955. (*La Presse*)

sharply. In 1960 there were barely twenty-five million admissions, four million fewer than there had been in 1937. Distributors and theatre owners tried to compete with television by presenting more feature films in colour, but it was in vain. Nothing could stop the trend away from moviegoing that by 1960 had made the commercial movie theatre business a very uncertain one.

The desertion of movie audiences also affected Quebec's film production, bringing to an end the activities of private producers, who were dependent on theatre showings. Except for low-budget independent films and NFB productions, no feature films were produced in Quebec between 1953 and 1963. So soon after its birth, Quebec's "national film industry" was dying. The only area of film production that survived, and even flourished, consisted of films intended for television: commercials, short subjects, documentaries and animated films produced both by the NFB and by small companies that proliferated in the late 1950s.

Radio

Another medium that had to adjust to the coming of television was radio. From the late 1930s on, radio steadily developed and extended its influence. During and after the war, it enjoyed a position in Quebec's cultural life similar to that of television a few years later. Everyone listened to radio, radio hosts and actors were stars, radio serials had a passionate following. Throughout Quebec, radio was the major channel of expression and dissemination not only of mass culture but also of ideas and information.

The CBC continued to expand its network and put more powerful transmitters into service after the war, so that in 1950 it was able to reach 90 per cent of Quebec's population. Its schedule was dominated by Canadian content and cultural and educational programming, notably concerts, drama, literature and the *Radio-Collège* series, which took up almost nine hours of air time a week in 1952.

However, most of the growth of radio took place in the private sector. In 1958, private stations had about 70 per cent of the transmitting power in Canada, as compared with only 25 per cent twenty years earlier. Private radio was essentially commercial and benefited directly from postwar prosperity. In Montreal, a number of new stations began operation during the period. On the French side CKVL, which began broadcasting from suburban Verdun in 1946, emerged as a strong competitor to CKAC by offering soap operas. CKAC countered in 1947 by going on air twenty-four hours a day. In 1953, Abbé Charles-Émile Gadbois, promoter of the *La bonne chanson* songbooks, started CJMS; the call letters stood for "*Canada, je me souviens*" ("Canada, I remember"). Meanwhile, CJAD and CFCF competed for English-language listeners. Outside Montreal, there were more than thirty stations in operation in 1957: four in Quebec City, two each in Chicoutimi and Trois-Rivières, and one in almost every town of any size.

The beginning of television caused only a momentary slowdown in the expansion of radio. Instead of being plunged into a crisis the way the movies were, radio redefined itself to take account of television and ended up being more popular than ever. Most radio stations quickly and successfully adjusted to television by concentrating their efforts on mornings and afternoons — times of day when television did not broadcast — and gearing their programming to their own specialized audiences, particularly women at home, young people and motorists. Radio stopped broadcasting serials, drama and other forms of spoken entertainment. Instead, it concentrated on regular, frequent newscasts and, above all, recorded popular music.

In the early 1940s, popular music in Quebec was dominated by American crooners and big bands, but the immediate postwar years saw the flowering of popular songs from France: Charles Trenet, Édith Piaf, Georges Guétary, les Compagnons de la Chanson. In the 1950s, however, American music was again dominant, with the birth of rock 'n' roll and the rise of such stars as Pat Boone, the Platters and Elvis Presley. The appearance of long-playing and 45-rpm records (in 1948 and 1949 respectively) contributed to this development. Thus, when CKVL went on air in 1946, it was initially the home of French songs, with Jacques Normand as disk jockey. Nine years later, an enraptured audience of teenagers infatuated with American rhythms, dances and fashions turned to CKVL for its daily hit parade, presented by Léon Lachance. Popular music produced in Quebec consisted essentially of adaptations of American hits and interpretations or imitations of popular French songs. Raymond Lévesque sang to small audiences and Félix Leclerc was a success in France in the early 1950s, but it was not until the 1960s that indigenous popular music really made its mark in Quebec.

Far from damaging radio, the coming of television provided it with an opportunity to find its niche. In the late 1950s, radio was growing rapidly in Quebec, new stations were coming on air, and with the increasing use of audience ratings, competition was becoming fierce.

Newspapers and Popular Literature

For the daily press, the postwar years were also a period of rapid growth and reorganization. Between 1945 and 1965, total circulation of English- and French-language daily newspapers in Quebec jumped by 62 per cent, from 680,000 to more than 1.1 million. A few well-established newspapers were the main beneficiaries of this expansion, while other papers failed to grow or even ceased publication. In Montreal, Le Canada closed down in 1954, followed by L'Autorité the next year, while La Patrie became a weekly in 1957. On the other hand, La Presse doubled its circulation to 286,000 between 1940 and 1962. On the English-speaking side, the Montreal Star continued to lead with a circulation of 180,000 in 1960. The Gazette, which had trailed far behind before the war, was an increasingly serious competitor, reaching a circulation of 129,000 by 1963. The reorganization was even more dramatic in Quebec City. With L'Action Catholique and L'Événement-Journal clearly in decline, Le Soleil became a regional daily for all of eastern Quebec, with a circulation of more than 120,000 in 1960.

The same phenomenon was occurring in other centres as well. Dailies such as Le Nouvelliste in Trois-Rivières and La Tribune in Sherbrooke had virtually no competition left and now served entire regions. All over Quebec, the daily press was becoming concentrated, with a few large newspapers accounting for most of the readers and advertising. Le Devoir was a special case. Although it remained small — its circulation grew from 20,000 to 40,000 between 1940 and 1962 — it was increasingly influential among Quebec's intellectual elites. It continued to be read by traditionalist nationalists, but under the leadership of Gérard Filion and

André Laurendeau it also became a rallying point for opposition to Duplessis and one of the leading forums for the emerging doctrine of neonationalism.

The rise of a variety of popular publications aimed at a mass audience
was a significant development of the postwar era. The prime example
was the daily tabloid *Montréal-Matin*. Begun in 1930 as *L'Illustration*, it
had little impact before the war. Then it changed its name and improved
its formula, concentrating on sensationalism, sports and pictures, and its
circulation began to climb, increasing from 11,000 in 1940 to more than
100,000 in 1960. The weekend press, aimed at essentially the same
audience, also grew rapidly, especially publications concentrating on
show business, radio and television. Existing newspapers — *Le Petit
Journal*, *Photo-Journal* and *Radio-Monde* (1939; known as *Téléradiomonde*
after 1950) — now reached a wider audience and were joined by new
ones such as *Dimanche-Matin* (1953), *Allô Police* (1953), *Nouvelles Illustrées*
(1954) and *Le Journal des Vedettes* (1954). There were also a large number
of scandalous or vaguely pornographic publications: the "yellow press."
In its zeal to purge Quebec of the yellow press, the church organized a
major campaign that ended up being aimed at all the weekend papers.
But the weekend press easily withstood this threat, and had a total circulation of more than a million in 1960. The postwar years were also a
period of significant growth for magazines. Aimed primarily at women,
the *Revue Populaire*, the *Revue Moderne* and *Le Samedi* were filled mostly
with escapist fiction and regular features. Together, they had a circulation
of more than 250,000 around 1955. But by far the largest-circulation
monthly was *Sélection du Reader's Digest*, which began publication in
French in 1947.

This period was also the heyday of the cheap popular novel. Even
before 1940, dime novels and comic books from the United States and
short sentimental novels from France were widely distributed through
Quebec newsstands and corner stores. A Montreal publisher, Édouard
Garand, successfully adapted the formula by bringing out his *"Roman
canadien"* series of brief, accessible and religiously orthodox stories. But
the growth of Quebec-produced popular novels really began in the mid-
1940s when the Lespérance brothers' print shop began publishing a new
weekly newspaper, *Police-Journal*, along with several series of novels in
instalments. These love and adventure stories appeared weekly in an
inexpensive thirty-page format with an attention-getting cover, and they
became enormously popular. The best known of the hundred or so series
published in this format was *Les aventures étranges de l'agent IXE-13, l'as
des espions canadiens* (The strange adventures of agent IXE-13, ace of the
Canadian spy team). Between 1947 and 1966, almost a thousand instalments of this series were published, with an average circulation of 20,000.

Nightclubs

With the growth of the new media, the various forms of popular theatre that had developed rapidly in the previous quarter-century — revues, vaudeville, melodrama, burlesque — now declined. Variety shows, however, still had a following in the postwar years, especially the risqué performances of Peaches and Lili Saint-Cyr at the Gayety Theatre in Montreal. This was also the golden age of Montreal night life, which flourished in such clubs as the Bellevue Casino, the El Morocco, the Faisan Doré and the Casa Loma. Quebec City had its night life as well, with the Chez Gérard café and the Porte Saint-Jean in full operation. Almost every night of the week, people came to these clubs to drink, dance, have a good time and be entertained by music and comedy, and they often stayed until the early morning hours. During the war, most of the featured performers were American, while after the war the clubs presented stars from France. Slowly, however, homegrown performers such as Fernand Robidoux, Alys Robi, Muriel Millard and Aglaé gained prominence. But this form of entertainment could not survive the combined effects of the bad reputation of many of the clubs and the coming of television, and its popularity declined rapidly after the 1950s.

* * * * * *

Quebec society in this period was heavily urban, substantially richer than it had been fifteen years earlier, and largely free from the control of traditional authorities. In these circumstances, it formed a huge and fairly unified cultural market that was hungry for novelty and could be reached effectively by a number of media: movies, newspapers, radio and especially television. These different media bolstered one another, employing the same people and increasingly making use of the same products. *Un homme et son péché* provides a striking example. It started as a novel, then became a radio serial, a play, a record, a movie and finally a television serial. Mass culture was now organized into a system of production and consumption, in which both the private sector and the government played major roles. This system grew steadily in power and extent in the postwar era, and it faced a future filled with both promise and pitfalls after 1960.

CHAPTER 29

THE TRIUMPH OF MODERNITY

In literature and the arts, the movement towards modernization that had begun in the 1930s and grown during the war gained strength and intensified after 1945, becoming dominant in almost all artistic sectors. This movement challenged and rejected the ideologies and forms associated with traditionalist conservatism and was open to the major international currents of the artistic and intellectual avant-garde. However, because of Quebec's backward education system, weak cultural infrastructure and distribution network, and absence of government policies and assistance before 1957, this change took place under precarious material conditions.

Artists

During the period, there were still hardly any artists who could make a living from their books, paintings or music. Nevertheless, the economic situation of the artistic community did improve somewhat in the early 1950s, notably as a result of the activities of two major federal cultural agencies, the CBC and the NFB, which commissioned works from artists or hired them as scriptwriters, directors, set designers, researchers and musicians. While few artists taught in colleges or universities, many taught in art, theatre and music schools, and journalism was still a source of livelihood for a significant number of writers.

The artistic and intellectual community grew and became more of a living, autonomous entity. The professional artist was slowly replacing the amateur, as writers, painters and musicians devoted most of their attention and energy to their art. Some magazines, galleries and publishing houses became forums for discussion and exchange and meeting places for members of this community.

The position of artists and intellectuals within Quebec society was also changing. Many artists and intellectuals were among the first to identify with the new ideologies of liberalization and *rattrapage*, which gained strength in Quebec between 1945 and 1960 as clerical influence waned. These people tended to define themselves not as defenders or propagators of traditional values but as members of the resistance and challengers to the system, whose role was to criticize traditional values and encourage Quebecers to reject them. Thus, many artists and intellectuals were involved in the opposition to the clergy, the Duplessis government and traditional institutions. This activity sometimes put them in a difficult position, but it also paved the way for the wide recognition that would be accorded them after 1960.

Literature

The situation of literature in Quebec was characterized by a striking contrast. A look at its economic circumstances shows that it was poorly organized, ineffective in reaching its audience, and based on a production and distribution system that was increasingly out of step with its needs. But from an ideological and esthetic point of view, literature underwent a radical change in these years, as a result of which the forces of renewal that had begun to appear in the late 1930s broadened their field of activity and made their presence very strongly felt.

There were multiple economic problems. Quebec had a mere twelve public libraries in 1949, only half of them French-language institutions. As a result, about 65 per cent of urban Quebecers and 95 per cent of rural Quebecers were without library service. The situation improved somewhat in the early 1950s: the Montreal Municipal Library extended its system of branches in the city's neighbourhoods, several young people's libraries were established, and about ten medium-sized towns set up small libraries, inadequately staffed with untrained personnel. Even though the work of the Tremblay Commission created a new awareness of the problem in some sections of Quebec's elites, the Duplessis government did nothing at all to resolve it. The situation was no better with regard to bookstores, most of which also sold stationery, school supplies and religious articles. The book trade was oriented towards educational institutions, which purchased directly from publishers, while individual consumers were poorly served. Around 1960 there were roughly a hundred bookstores in Quebec. Two thirds were in Montreal and Quebec City, and most of them were almost exclusively dependent on textbook sales. Only 30 per cent of sales were to individuals, and 85 per cent of the books they bought were imports from France and Belgium.

These difficulties had direct repercussions for the publishing industry, which was still dominated by religious houses and others specializing in the textbook market. The momentary wartime burst of activity in the literary publishing field came to an abrupt end after the war when French publishers began to recapture the domestic and international markets they had largely been forced to leave to their Quebec competitors. A number of the Quebec houses went bankrupt and there was a sudden reduction in literary publishing activity in Quebec: the total number of works published fell from 417 in 1944 to ninety-three in 1949. Although the situation improved somewhat thereafter, this "dark period" lasted until about 1957. Few new titles were published and those that were lost money. Among publishers that survived, some also sold to the educational market, such as Fides and Beauchemin; others distributed through book club sales, such as Cercle du Livre de France (1946); still others served a small audience, such as Les Écrits du Canada Français (1954); and the rest were small houses that published limited editions of works of poetry, often at the author's expense.

Novels, aimed at a wide audience and needing a reasonably effective marketing system to succeed, were most seriously affected by the publishing crisis. While the average number of novels published annually in Quebec had been twenty-seven during the war, between 1947 and 1959 it was only nineteen — roughly the same number as had been published each year during the 1930s. There were two major trends in the Quebec novel during the period, both of them rooted in contemporary reality and modern life, in contrast to the prewar novel's orientation towards rural life and the past. Gabrielle Roy's 1945 work *Bonheur d'occasion* (*The Tin Flute*) launched the first trend, the novel of urban life, with labourers and other working people as protagonists. Significant contributors to this current during the period were Roger Lemelin (*Les Plouffe*, 1948), Roy herself (*Alexandre Chenevert*, 1954), Jean-Jules Richard (*Le feu dans l'amiante*, 1956), Gérard Bessette (*La bagarre*, 1958) and Pierre Gélinas (*Les vivants, les morts et les autres*, 1959). The second major trend was the psychological novel, which like the novel of urban life was concerned with social criticism but pursued it in a more inward-looking way. This current is represented by the works of Robert Élie (*La fin des songes*, 1950), André Giroux (*Le gouffre a toujours soif*, 1953) and Anne Hébert (*Le torrent*, 1950; *Les chambres de bois*, 1958). The two currents come together in the work of the best known novelist of the period, André Langevin, the author of *Poussière sur la ville*, 1953), which both describes a small mining town and portrays a character haunted by modern existential anxieties. Somewhat outside these major currents was Yves Thériault, whose novel about the Inuit, *Agaguk* (1958), was an international success. In general, the Quebec novelists of the period were strongly influenced by their French contemporaries such as François Mauriac, Julien Green, Albert Camus and André Malraux, whose works began to become widely available in Quebec with the inception of the *"Livre de Poche"* series of pocket books in 1953.

In contrast to the difficulties faced by the novel, poetry flourished to the point that the critic Gilles Marcotte has called these years *"le temps des poètes"* — the time of the poets. There were at least as many works of poetry as novels published during the period, the quality was as high or higher, and the interest aroused among readers was at least as great. Poetry became the medium of expression for Quebec's most original writers. It asked the most urgent questions, and it blazed the trails that Quebec literature would follow until the late 1970s. This *"âge de la parole"* (age of the word), as the poet Roland Giguère has called it, was marked by three major developments. First, the established figures of the modernist movement in Quebec poetry published their major works during the period. Alain Grandbois brought new depth to his cosmic vision of love and death in *Rivages de l'homme* (1948) and *L'étoile pourpre* (1957). In *Le tombeau des rois* (1953), Anne Hébert's exploration of solitude and the night culminated in a vision of a "reflection of the dawn" heralding joy. Rina Lasnier continued her search for the invisible in *Présence de l'absence* (1956) and *Mémoire sans jours* (1960) with lush images of nature and tradition.

A significant movement developed among younger poets in the late 1940s, influenced by the Surrealist-inspired revolution in painting begun by Paul-Émile Borduas and Alfred Pellan. In their resolutely modern, esoteric and often provocative work, these poets sought not so much to evoke reality as to transform radically people's vision of what was real. Unsettling imagery, daring versification and passionate lyricism were tools to this end. The language used by poets such as Claude Gauvreau (*Les entrailles*, 1946), Gilles Hénault (*Théâtre en plein air*, 1946), Paul-Marie Lapointe (*Le vierge incendié*, 1948) and Roland Giguère (*Yeux fixes*, 1951) was in deliberate contrast to ordinary speech. They saw it as providing access to another reality, closer to the desires and real needs of the individual. Theirs was not only a philosophical, artistic and moral revolt: it also challenged the established sociopolitical order.

A new era began in 1953 with the founding of Éditions de l'Hexagone, which quickly developed into an extremely dynamic catalyst for poetry writing and related activities. The poets in this group — Gaston Miron (*Deux sangs*, 1953), Luc Perrier (*Des jours et des jours*, 1954), Jean-Guy Pilon (*Les cloîtres de l'été*, 1954), Fernand Ouellette (*Ces anges de sang*, 1955), Michel Van Schendel (*Poèmes de l'Amérique étrangère*, 1958) adopted the modern forms of their predecessors. At the same time, they sought to develop a language — a *"parole"* — that fully reflected their experience of existence, love, spirituality and even politics. Laden with both novelty and tradition, with inner anxiety and social concern, their poetry led to what would soon be called *"la poésie du pays"* (poetry of the homeland).

But while poetry may have blossomed between 1945 and 1960, it did so essentially outside the domain of commercial publishing, through a network of small presses (of which L'Hexagone was the most significant) that published in near-total obscurity and often vanished soon after they appeared. Most works of poetry produced in this period would not reach a wider audience until the 1960s and 1970s, when they were reissued and became part of school courses.

The most significant essays of the period were also published under marginal circumstances, were poorly distributed, and had little influence outside intellectual circles until after 1960. Unquestionably the landmark work in this area was *Refus global*, brought out by the painter Paul-Émile Borduas and his *automatiste* friends in 1948. This incendiary, violent manifesto denounced French Canadian society's conformism and attachment to the past, attacked the clergy and the educational system, and pleaded for the total liberation of the individual: "Make way for magic! Make way for objective mystery! Make way for love!" *Refus global* aroused the ire of the authorities and led to Borduas's being fired from the École du Meuble. During the 1950s, a number of essayists abandoned traditional doctrines and sought to express a more personal way of thinking that valued universal fellowship over the national cause, freedom over fidelity. This school of essayists included members of the *Cité Libre* circle such as Jean LeMoyne (*L'atmosphère religieuse au Canada français*, 1951), Ernest Gagnon (*L'Homme d'ici*, 1952), Pierre Vadeboncoeur (*La ligne du risque*, 1962) and Pierre Trottier (*Mon Babel*, 1963) who denounced the stagnation of a French Canadian culture trapped in conservatism and clericalism.

This movement also affected historians and social scientists, who suggested new interpretations of Quebec society, past and present. The establishment of historical institutes at Laval and the University of Montreal, the increasing number of Quebecers studying history outside the country and the founding of the *Revue d'Histoire de l'Amérique Française* all helped a more scientific and less rhetorical perspective emerge in Quebec historical literature. Notable figures in this movement were Guy

Some of the L'Hexagone poets, including Gaston Miron and Jean-Guy Pilon. (Private collection)

Frégault and Marcel Trudel, historians of New France, and Michel Brunet and Maurice Séguin, who developed a neonationalist interpretation of the history of Canada. At the same time, a new generation of sociologists, political scientists and economists appeared, many of them trained at the Faculty of Social Sciences at Laval University, established in 1938 by Father Georges-Henri Lévesque. Better acquainted with contemporary theories and making use of recent research, these scholars breathed new life into the analysis of the situation and social problems of modern Quebec in their studies and essays. Three collections of articles were especially eye-opening: the Paris journal *Esprit*'s special issue on French Canada in 1952, the sociologist Jean-Charles Falardeau's 1953 collection *Essais sur le Québec contemporain*, and the 1956 work *La grève de l'amiante* (*The Asbestos Strike*), whose contributors included Pierre Elliott Trudeau, Fernand Dumont, Gérard Pelletier and others.

Whatever difficulties it faced and however narrow its audience, Quebec literature underwent a major transformation during the period. It broke away from religion and conservative ideology, which in the past had been its means of support, its context and practically its master. With the greater degree of autonomy it now had, it could move closer to the major currents in modern literature and more seriously criticize and challenge Quebec's established order. It also became more independent of French influence. Instead of seeing itself as a "branch" of French literature, it became more aware of its specific character and more assertive as a national literature with its own tradition and laws of development. The writer Robert Charbonneau defended this view in a celebrated argument with some representatives of the Paris intellegentsia in 1946, and an increasing number of writers and critics expressed it during the 1950s. The critic Gilles Marcotte's description of Quebec literature as "a literature in the making" reflected a widespread belief.

Postwar English Canadian literature went through an analogous process. Quebec, however, tended to be a satellite of Toronto (the cultural centre for all of English Canada), New York and London in its English-language literary activity. Novelists such as Brian Moore and Mordecai Richler and poets such as Patrick Anderson and Leonard Cohen went to live in New York or London. Many writers continued to set their novels in Montreal — A.M. Klein (*The Second Scroll*, 1951), Morley Callaghan (*The Loved and the Lost*, 1951), Richler (*The Apprenticeship of Duddy Kravitz*, 1959), Cohen (*The Favourite Game*, 1963) — but all these works were published in Toronto or New York. On the other hand, Montreal (and especially McGill University) remained an intensely active centre of poetry writing until the mid-1950s. F.R. Scott, A.J.M. Smith and P.K. Page were still writing, and a new group — Louis Dudek, Irving Layton and the Toronto poet Raymond Souster — made its appearance with the publication of the joint collection *Cerebrus* in 1952. Their poetry was characterized by experimentation and social criticism. But the group disbanded soon afterwards and poetry writing also became concentrated in

Toronto and the cities of western Canada, especially Vancouver. From the 1950s onward, Montreal was a provincial centre in English Canadian literature, active but secondary.

Painting

Modernity asserted itself in painting perhaps more clearly than in any other field. The years between 1945 and 1960 were a period of effervescent change during which Montreal, and to a lesser extent Quebec City, became centres of modern painting in Canada. Leaving provincialism and local colour behind, the new Quebec painting moved resolutely along the path staked out by the rise of modernism after 1930. It had increasing affinity with the major contemporary currents in the French and American art worlds, and made its own contribution to those currents.

This effervescence was reflected in changes within the art community. Some artists who taught in the art schools — Paul-Émile Borduas at the École du Meuble, Albert Dumouchel at the Institut des Arts Graphiques, Alfred Pellan and Stanley Cosgrove at the École des Beaux-Arts in Montreal, and Jean-Paul Lemieux and Jean Dallaire at the École des Beaux-Arts in Quebec City — encouraged experimentation and discovery among their students. Exhibitions of modern art proliferated, notably at the Galerie Agnès Lefort in Montreal, which opened in 1950 and specialized in avant-garde painting. There was knowledgeable and sympathetic commentary on modern art in the newspapers, on the radio and in the journal *Vie des Arts*, which began publication in 1956. Elsewhere, however, there was still indifference, lack of understanding, even suspicion. Only a very few collectors were interested in the new forms of painting, while Quebec's two museums, the Montreal Museum of Fine Arts and the Musée de la Province in Quebec City, gave it only a very grudging place.

Because of their identification with international trends and the small audience for their art in Quebec, many younger artists — Jean-Paul Riopelle, Fernand Leduc, Marcelle Ferron, Marcelle Maltais and a number of others — went to live outside the country after serving their apprenticeship. The leaders of Quebec's art community were also outside the country. Pellan went back to France in 1952, while Borduas went to live in New York in 1953 and then in Paris from 1955 until his death in 1960. Riopelle and Pellan were notable among the painters who achieved success in their new places of residence. Most of the artists who left would return to Quebec after 1960.

The year 1948 marked a turning point in postwar Quebec painting. Two groups of artists who had already indicated their opposition to conformity in a number of exhibitions published manifestos in that year. First to appear, in February, was *Prisme d'yeux*, signed by fifteen artists grouped around Pellan. In their view, painting represented the exercise of absolute personal freedom, with no ideological or esthetic constraints of any kind. In August, Borduas and his group followed with *Refus global*, which argued that art should directly obey the dictates of the unconscious. Despite their differences, the two manifestos pointed in the same direction: towards spontaneity and experimentation and emphatically away from all forms of academic art and all attempts to subordinate art to anything outside its own internal requirements.

Both groups of artists disbanded soon afterwards, but the spark for the abundant and varied artistic output of the 1950s had been lit. There were two major trends in these years. The more significant was the triumph of nonfigurative painting — forms intended to add to the forms of the real world rather than represent them. Within this current there were two more or less distinct tendencies. The first consisted of works that can be grouped under the heading of Abstract Expressionism. Painters in this school were heirs to the *automatistes* and were influenced as well by American action painting and the *tachisme* of Paris. In their canvases, they sought to express the most spontaneous impulses of feeling, movement and imagination. This kind of painting, similar to French lyrical abstraction, is best illustrated by the work of Riopelle, along with Jean-Paul Mousseau, Marcelle Ferron, Marcel Barbeau and Pierre Gauvreau. Roland Giguère and Gérard Tremblay, whose work was based on dream images and inspired by Surrealism, can also be classified as part of this school.

The second tendency in nonfigurative painting, which made its appearance around 1955, was a reaction to the first and was influenced by analytic geometric abstraction. This was the *plasticien* movement, which

Jean-Paul Riopelle, *Composition*, 1947. (National Gallery of Canada)

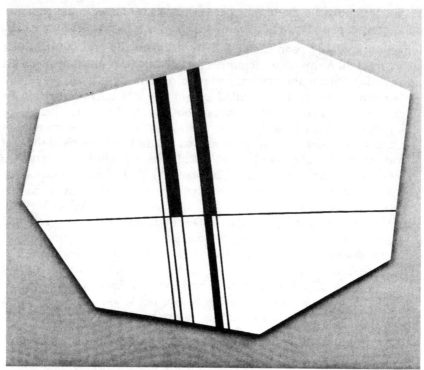

Fernand Toupin, *Aire des blanc différentiel*, 1956. (National Gallery of Canada)

included Jean-Paul Jérôme, Fernand Toupin, Louis Belzile and Rodolphe de Repentigny (who signed his paintings with the pseudonym Jauran). These artists rejected automatism as a subordination of art to expressive constraints and instead advocated a style of painting based only on purely formal and visual considerations. The *plasticiens* were enamoured of theory, and their canvases were in a sense scholarly studies of the properties of lines, surfaces and colours. Their influence in Montreal painting circles in the late 1950s was considerable.

The flowering of nonfigurative painting was unquestionably the dominant development of the period, but the figurative tradition did not by any means come to an abrupt end. Artists such as Léo Ayotte in the St. Maurice Valley, Albert Rousseau in the Quebec City region and René Richard in Baie-Saint-Paul continued the tradition of regionalist landscape painting, and their work was highly valued by collectors. At the same time, figurative painting was renewed in the 1950s by an effort to rejuvenate the treatment of figurative themes, and this movement constituted the second major trend of the decade. Artists in this current were stimulated by the rise of nonfigurative art and made use of the formal and stylistic contributions introduced by nonfigurative painters. Works in this category included Stanley Cosgrove's still life paintings, nudes and drawings, Paul V. Beaulieu's "roosters," and Jeanne Rhéaume's landscapes. The most vigorous expressions of this current took place in Quebec City, in Jean Dallaire's Surrealist-inspired portraits of women and fanciful scenes and especially in the work of Jean-Paul Lemieux. Lemieux had been active in promoting modern art since the 1930s. On the model of some Mexican and American artists of the 1920s and 1930s, his art had remained figurative while aiming to be both personal and open to social concerns, as can be seen in his 1944 painting *Fête-Dieu à Québec*. Subsequently, his painting became increasingly spare, heading towards a new style characterized by oblique horizons, motionless figures, muted colours, and an atmosphere of solitude and disorder. This style, which took shape in *Les Ursulines* (1951) and in the works he produced after 1955, would make him famous.

This classification of Quebec painting between 1945 and 1960 should not be taken as absolute. Categories are useful for study, but they were far from being airtight in practice. Thus, a number of nonfigurative painters borrowed from both major tendencies or moved from one to the other. Fernand Leduc, for example, was one of the signers of *Refus global* in 1948 but later turned to geometric painting. There was also frequent movement back and forth between figurative and nonfigurative painting, as with Jacques de Tonnancour or Pellan himself. All in all, there was great diversity, and each painter followed the logic of his or her own personal development, but the overall picture that emerged from these individual explorations was a fairly unified one, in which freedom, innovation and the emergence of some strongly individual styles were the dominant characteristics.

Theatre and Music

As we saw in chapter 28, almost all entertainment aimed at a popular audience tended to be replaced or coopted by television during the 1950s. Television's effect on forms of entertainment directed towards cultured audiences, however, appears to have been quite different. The development of repertory theatre and classical music, in particular, indicates that television played a galvanizing and supporting role, giving artists an opportunity to become more professional by providing them with work. And far from reducing the existing audience for these activities, it provided an entry point for a multitude of new enthusiasts.

In music, the television program *L'heure du concert* (1954-66) presented hundreds of operas, ballets, recitals and concerts of both well-established and contemporary music, often with Canadian artists. At the same time, a number of new ensembles began performing in concert halls: the McGill Chamber Orchestra (1945), the Ballets Chiraeff (1952; known as the Grands Ballets Canadiens after 1958), the Montreal String Quartet (1955), and the Baroque Trio of Montreal (1955).

For repertory theatre, the years between 1945 and 1960 were an especially propitious period. Even though there were few theatres and still fewer up-to-date ones, a number of new professional and semiprofessional companies began operation, mostly in Montreal. When the Compagnons de Saint-Laurent disbanded in 1952, the amateurs who had belonged to the troupe did not give up their theatre activities. In fact, many of them had already dispersed into a succession of more or less regularly performing companies: the Compagnie du Masque (1946); the Rideau-Vert (1948); and the Théâtre d'Essai (1947), which became the Théâtre du Nouveau-Monde (TNM) in 1951. More new companies sprang up after 1952: the Théâtre-Club (1954); the Théâtre de Quat'sous (1954); and the Théâtre International de la Poudrière (1958). These companies had to move frequently from one theatre to another and faced continual financial difficulties. Their repertoire consisted in more or less equal measure of classical works, light theatre and contemporary drama. The Théâtre de l'Estoc in Quebec City, founded in 1957, offered a similar mix. At the same time, small companies and *"théâtres de poche"* (pocket theatres) were started to present avant-garde theatre: the amateur Apprentis-sorciers (1954); the Théâtre de Dix Heures (1956); La Basoche (1958); and l'Egrégore (1959). And finally, the first summer stock companies began operation: the Chanteclerc in Sainte-Adèle; La Fenière in Ancienne-Lorette; and the Théâtre de la Marjolaine in Eastman.

Other factors also contributed to more intense musical and theatrical activity. The Jeunesses Musicales du Canada, founded in 1949, booked tours covering most of Quebec's cities and towns for performers from both Quebec and elsewhere. In 1951, the Jeunesses Musicales established a summer music camp at Mt. Orford to provide programs for students and present concerts. The same year, the city of Montreal started *"La Roulotte"* and *"Le Vagabond,"* which presented children's theatre and puppet shows in the city's parks. A number of other communities followed Montreal's example. Music and theatre education also improved. A Faculty of Music was founded at the University of Montreal in 1950, bringing together a number of existing institutions, while McGill reorganized its Conservatorium and Faculty of Music in 1955. This period marked the real beginning of theatre education in Quebec, with the establishment of dramatic art sections at the provincial conservatories in Montreal (1954) and Quebec City (1958) and the founding of the National Theatre School in Montreal (1960). The presence of better trained musicians, actors and directors, many of whom went on to finish their training in France or the United States, meant more frequent and higher-quality performances.

Visits by prestigious touring companies and artists from other countries also became more frequent and regular. The theatres welcomed major French companies such as the Compagnie Renaud-Barrault, the Compagnie Louis Jouvet, the Théâtre National Populaire and the Comédie Française. At the Montreal Forum, there was a proliferation of concerts: the Boston, Berlin and Vienna symphony orchestras, the Ballets Russes de Monte-Carlo, and a recital by Maria Callas. The Metropolitan Opera came to the Forum five times between 1952 and 1958. Montreal was now a stop on the international circuit. But while Montreal and to a lesser extent Quebec City were enjoying a relatively intense cultural life, this development largely passed the rest of the province by, and other communities had only very limited access to this kind of activity.

This richer cultural life benefited local creativity. In music, what Gilles Potvin has called "a genuine Montreal school" developed around the Society of Canadian Music, founded in 1953 to encourage the performance of locally written works. The Montreal school was made up of composers born around the time of the First World War, such as Violet Archer, Jean Papineau-Couture, Alexander Brott, Robert Turner, Jean Vallerand and Maurice Blackburn, whose works reflected the esthetic innovations of the first half of the twentieth century. In the 1950s, a younger generation of composers emerged, trained in France where a new wave of modernist activity was taking place, in which Olivier Messiaen and Pierre Boulez were the key figures. These composers — Serge Garant, Clermont Pépin, François Morel, Pierre Mercure, Gilles Tremblay — were open to such innovations as the twelve-tone scale, serialism and later electronic music. During the period they organized concerts of contemporary music and presented their first major works.

The postwar period is also regarded by some observers as the period when writing for the theatre had its real beginning in Quebec. Avant-garde presentations with a Surrealist and anarchic flavour, combining poetry, dance, music and the visual arts, were one manifestation of this development. But the most significant current was realist theatre. The groundwork for this form of theatre was laid in the large number of radio

Gratien Gélinas, author of Tit-Coq, in 1950. (Photo Jean Morantow, DOLQ)

plays produced from the 1930s onward, while television drama in the 1950s provided further support. Gratien Gélinas, who had already gained a huge following with his *Fridolinades* on radio and on tour, presented *Tit-Coq* at the Monument National in 1948. It was a revelation. "It creates the impression," one critic said, "that Canadian theatre is really making its presence felt for the first time." *Tit-Coq* played for five hundred performances and then went on tour, reaching New York. In subsequent years, Quebec playwrights had a number of outlets, notably the CBC, which was looking for locally written works, and the Théâtre du Nouveau-Monde, which organized a playwriting competition in 1956. As a result, Quebec-written plays in a variety of genres were produced: realist theatre such as Marcel Dubé's *Zone* (1953) and *Le temps des lilas* (1958); tragedy such as Paul Toupin's *Brutus* (1952); politically oriented theatre such as Jacques Ferron's *Les grands soleils* (1958); and avant-garde fantasy such as Jacques Languirand's *Les insolites* (1956). Another significant event for the performing arts was the opening of the Comédie Canadienne in Montreal in 1958. Under the direction of Gratien Gélinas, this modern facility would become a major centre of theatre and music in Quebec, and would later be home to the TNM.

In literature, painting, theatre and music, the years between 1945 and 1960 were far from being a *"grande noirceur"* (great darkness), as the period has commonly been described. High-quality and often daring works were created, artists and intellectuals redefined their role in society, and Quebec's efforts to "catch up" with modern ideas and forms gained speed. These developments — what Laurent Mailhot and Pierre Nepveu have described as Quebec's "great esthetic thaw" — were the product of a new generation of artists. But they also depended on the presence of a cultured audience that made up in openness and enthusiasm what it lacked in size. The scope of the renewal was limited by a number of continuing problems. Quebec's cultural infrastructure was outdated and rested on shaky foundations, artists still worked in difficult economic circumstances, and the authorities either tried to suppress this burst of creativity or else simply ignored it. Eventually this contradiction would reach the breaking point, and the resulting explosion would be a major factor in creating the climate of feverish liberation that would characterize the next decade.

Part 3:
The Quiet Revolution
and Its Aftermath 1960–

INTRODUCTION

Structurally, the socioeconomic development of Quebec in the 1960s and 1970s was characterized by unquestionable prosperity and a substantial rise in the standard of living. However, there were clouds on the horizon as well: problems such as the decline in Quebec's relative economic importance in Canada, the intensification of structural unemployment, and bureaucratization and rising deficits stemming from increasing government intervention proved difficult to resolve. Against this backdrop, two ideas — reform and nationalism — played a special role in Quebec society. These ideas were the driving force of the Quiet Revolution, remained deeply embedded in Quebec's social development for twenty years, and underlay its political theory and practice until the beginning of the 1980s. In the 1980s, however, a series of political, economic, social and ideological shock waves appeared to challenge what had come to be known as "the gains of the Quiet Revolution."

The Quiet Revolution

It was a journalist for the Toronto *Globe and Mail* who first used the expression *Quiet Revolution* to describe the changes undertaken in Quebec from 1960 onward. The expression was quickly taken up in French by Quebec's political leaders and intellectuals as *la Révolution tranquille* and had heavy symbolic connotations. The many writers who have examined the Quiet Revolution do not always agree on what the term means or on what period it applies to.

In the strict sense, the Quiet Revolution generally refers to the political, institutional and social reforms undertaken between 1960 and 1966 by the Liberal government of Premier Jean Lesage. Some writers trace the beginning of the Quiet Revolution to a slightly earlier date — the death of Maurice Duplessis and the accession to power of Paul Sauvé in 1959. Other writers identify 1964, when the pace of reform began to slow, as the end of the Quiet Revolution. The expression is also used in a wider sense to refer to the whole period between 1960 and 1980, as the ascendancy of reform liberalism and neonationalism marked this entire span and a remarkable continuity characterized the conduct of public affairs in Quebec City despite frequent changes of government.

The Quiet Revolution was also related to developments occurring outside Quebec. It took place while the West as a whole was going through a period of social and political reform, government intervention and economic prosperity and while the baby boom generation was reaching adolescence and then adulthood. The reappraisal of these orientations in the 1980s also had an international dimension: many countries were affected by the rise of conservatism and the wave of privatization.

Between 1960 and 1966, a series of reforms were rapidly put into effect, radically changing Quebec's institutions, image and self-concept. The key idea was *"rattrapage"* — catching up. This meant an acceleration of the process of modernizing Quebec society and bringing it up to date, which had begun after the Second World War but had been slowed down considerably by the conservatism of the Duplessis government. One implication of this process was that the state had to take responsibility for institutions that had hitherto been dominated by the private sector — notably the Catholic Church — so that they could be rationalized and access to them could be made more democratic. In three sectors in particular, structures and programs were reorganized from top to bottom: education, health and social affairs. From now on, Quebec would march proudly under the banner of the welfare state. This involved a major overhaul of the machinery of government: the civil service was reformed and government agencies — departments, boards and crown corporations — proliferated.

If the Quiet Revolution bore the stamp of reform liberalism, it also owed much to the new Quebec nationalism. The nationalization of Quebec's private electricity companies in 1962 became a symbol of this aspect of the Quiet Revolution. Self-confident and seeing itself as a modern movement, the new nationalism was expressed on three fronts at the same time. Within Quebec, nationalists challenged the ascendancy of the British minority and promoted the accession of members of the French majority to the leading positions in the economy and society. In Canada, they sought to end the process of federal centralization, which had been proceeding rapidly since the war, and obtain wider powers for Quebec within Confederation. Finally, they aimed to assert Quebec's presence internationally, notably by establishing a special relationship with France and other Francophone countries.

In endeavouring to implement its projected reforms, Lesage's *"équipe de tonnerre"* (thunder squad or "hell of a team"), as his government was called, had the advantage of a genuine consensus among the new elites in the trade unions, the corporations and intellectual and political circles. This consensus crumbled after 1966, and social and political strains intensified. Nevertheless, the governments that followed Lesage, under Daniel Johnson (1966-68), Jean-Jacques Bertrand (1968-70), Robert Bourassa (1970-76) and René Lévesque (1976-85), remained officially committed to "the spirit of the Quiet Revolution," and until the early 1980s they preserved and even extended its "gains." Thus, the Quiet Revolution became the main point of reference for the entire period.

The Glorious 1960s

When the Liberals came to power in 1960, Quebec was struggling with economic stagnation, which had begun with the recession of 1957 and

Exposition
Universelle et
Internationale,1967
Universal
and International
Exhibition,1967

Expo 67: one of the great events of the 1960s. (National Archives of Canada, C-56305)

brought about a rapid rise in the unemployment rate to 9.2 per cent of the labour force in 1960 and 9.3 per cent in 1961. In 1962, however, a period of strong expansion began; investment was up and unemployment was down, falling to 4.7 per cent in 1966. Then another period of contraction began in 1967 and lasted until 1971.

The economic growth of the 1960s was characterized by a new wave of investment in manufacturing and residential construction and by the rapid growth of public investment. To achieve its goal of *rattrapage*, the government allocated large sums of money to the construction of government buildings and schools and the modernization of Quebec's road system. It was an era of large projects that stimulated not only the economy but also the public imagination and national pride: the Montreal metro, which began operation in 1966; Expo 67, the 1967 world's fair in Montreal; and the Manicouagan 5 dam, opened in 1968.

Inflation was low in the early 1960s but increased in the second half of the decade. But incomes still rose faster than the consumer price index, so that the standard of living continued to rise, and the gap between Quebecers' incomes and their needs continued to narrow, as it had since the end of the Second World War.

The population was still growing, although at a slower rate than in the 1950s. Between 1961 and 1971, Quebec's population increased by less than a million — from 5,259,211 to 6,027,764. Population grew faster in the early 1960s, when the birth rate was still high and immigration was increasing, than in the second half of the decade; the birth rate fell rapidly after 1965 while immigration declined after 1967. At the same time, the urbanization rate continued its steady increase, from 74.3 per cent to 80.6 per cent; urban growth was most pronounced in the Montreal and Quebec City metropolitan areas.

The effect of the baby boom was strongly felt, and the 1960s were the decade of youth. Quebec pulled out all the stops to build new secondary schools and later cegeps (community colleges) and universities for its young people. As in other societies in different parts of the world, youth in Quebec boldly made their presence felt. Youth in the United States, shouting "peace and love!", resisted the war in Vietnam; youth in France brought the country to a halt in May 1968; youth in China launched the Cultural Revolution. Meanwhile, youth in Quebec organized their own student uprising in the fall of 1968. Quebec youth discovered marijuana, the counterculture and sexual liberation and made a new kind of music their own. Their large numbers also provided strong support for the new nationalism and especially for the Parti Québécois, founded in 1968. Older members of the baby boom generation benefited from the growth of the civil service and the parapublic sector, where they found interesting, well-paying jobs.

The new nationalism was a rising force, both politically and symbolically. Expressed in the songs of Quebec's artists and in the formulations of its intellectuals and technocrats and a new generation of politicians, it reached all sectors of the population with its message of building a strong Quebec. Its most radical wing, the independence movement, won the support of a substantial minority of Quebecers even if it did not succeed in assembling a majority.

Growing Pains

The wave of reforms and the ideological consensus that marked the Quiet Revolution could not be maintained indefinitely. The defeat of the Liberals in the 1966 election was an early sign that many Quebecers resisted or were tired of reform. Crises arose because the contradictory demands of different groups could not be satisfied simultaneously. The economic slowdown that began in 1967 exacerbated tensions.

The economy entered a new expansion phase in 1971, followed by a contraction in 1974-75. But the context for growth in the 1970s was very

The Manic 5 dam: one of the symbols of the new Quebec nationalism. (Hydro-Quebec)

different from what it had been in the 1960s. The world economy was severely shaken by the oil shock in 1973 and the resulting energy crisis. In Canada, the availability of oil made it possible for the federal government to moderate the rate at which energy prices rose, mitigating the effects of the crisis. This was not enough, however, to prevent accelerating inflation over the decade. In Montreal, the consumer price index, fixed at 100 in 1971, reached 138.1 in 1975 and 208.4 in 1980. In 1971 dollars, the purchasing power of a 1980 dollar was only 48 cents. Unlike previous bouts of inflation, this one did not come about at a time when the economy was overheated or human and material resources were used to overcapacity. The unemployment rate remained high. In Quebec, it rose from a level of about 7 per cent in the first half of the 1970s to 10 per cent in 1977, and remained in that neighbourhood for several years. *Stagflation*, or a simultaneous rise in inflation and unemployment, is an apt characterization of the economy of the 1970s, and it was a condition that appeared to leave governments helpless.

Business investment grew at a much slower rate than in the 1960s. Many businesses moved from Quebec to Ontario, complicating the situa-

Opening ceremonies at the 1976 Olympic Games. (*Le Journal de Montréal*)

tion. Economic growth in Quebec was increasingly dependent on investment by the government and its agencies. In this regard, a number of
large projects played a major role: the development of the area around
the National Assembly in Quebec City, the expansion of Quebec's ex-
pressway system, and especially the James Bay hydroelectric project and
the construction of the facilities for the 1976 Olympic Games in Montreal.
The scope of structural unemployment and the wage increases granted
to employees in the public and parapublic sectors placed an increasingly
heavy financial burden on the Quebec government, which ran large and
chronic deficits.

Population growth was also slower in the 1970s. Quebec's population
increased by less than half a million, from 6,027,764 in 1971 to 6,438,403
in 1981. A declining birth rate, a slowdown in immigration and the
departure of many Quebecers — especially Anglophones — for other
provinces were all contributing factors. The proportion of French Canadians in the population remained stable, but the proportion of people of
British origin fell below 10 per cent. Quebecers of other origins now
constituted a much more cosmopolitan group, and Quebec's cultural
diversity began to be more openly recognized. The 1970s also saw the
completion of the long process of urbanization. The proportion of the

The army in Montreal during the 1970 October Crisis. (National Archives of Canada, PA-129838)

population living in cities even began to decline, a phenomenon that reflected both the appearance of new ways of life and the economic difficulties of urban centres, especially Montreal.

The government of Robert Bourassa (1970-76) continued along the path laid out by its predecessors. It widened the scope of government intervention, increased the number of social programs and established new publicly owned corporations, making the government apparatus even more technocratic in character. The government was now Quebec's largest direct and indirect employer, and the unions representing its employees banded together in common fronts that challenged the government with forcefully expressed demands. In 1972 and 1976, the negotiation of collective agreements in the public and parapublic sectors degenerated into dramatic and highly political confrontations that became social crises. They resulted in a significant improvement in wages and working conditions for the government's employees, which had spinoff effects in other economic sectors, leading to an unprecedented standard of living for Quebecers.

The national question was another difficult area for the Bourassa government. Early in its term, in 1970, it had to deal with the October Crisis. Members of the Front de Libération du Québec kidnapped two people: first a British diplomat and then Quebec Labour Minister Pierre Laporte, who was later killed. The kidnappings elicited a firm response from the federal government of Prime Minister Pierre Elliott Trudeau, who refused to negotiate and proclaimed the War Measures Act to stop terrorism in its tracks. Another source of conflict through much of the

1970s was the language issue, which had first erupted when Jean-Jacques Bertrand was premier. Language battles pitted Francophones against Anglophones and supporters of a French Quebec against advocates of free choice.

The Parti Québécois became the vehicle for nationalist demands. Although it had only a few seats in the National Assembly in the early 1970s, the PQ gradually increased its support among voters until it finally took power in 1976. In this way, the Bourassa government fell victim to Quebec's economic, social and national growing pains.

The Great Debate

During the PQ's first term, all debates revolved around the national question and social struggles were relegated to the back burner. Language legislation, which had been worked out gradually by the two preceding governments, emerged in fully developed form in 1977 with Bill 101, the Charter of the French Language, which aimed at speeding up and intensifying the Francization of Quebec.

But above all, energies were mobilized around the PQ's promise to hold a referendum on Quebec's constitutional future. A battle of statistics broke out between Quebec and Ottawa and federal-provincial relations were turned into a form of trench warfare. Quebec was split in two over the national question, with little room left for nuances or compromises; the 1980 referendum, which resulted in a victory for the "no" side, revealed just how deeply it was divided. On the strength of its referendum victory, the federal government was in a position to begin the process of repatriating the constitution. When repatriation was achieved in 1982, it left Quebec isolated as the only province that refused to agree to the constitutional accord; the accord was imposed on it in any case.

In the social sphere, tensions eased somewhat. The PQ government declared that it had "a prejudice in favour of workers" and many union leaders actively supported it. It reformed Quebec's labour legislation and signed collective agreements that were advantageous to government employees.

Another major question that was the focus of increased attention in the late 1970s was the place of women in society. International Women's Year in 1975 helped bring this question to the fore. As a result of the growing participation of women in the work force and the arguments put forward by feminist groups, governments and sections of public opinion were forced to acknowledge that traditional ideas had to be reexamined. New agencies and programs were established, new laws were introduced and old ones were amended in an effort to allow women a larger role in society's institutions and move towards unequivocally recognizing the principle of equality of the sexes.

In its first term, the PQ was quite successful in navigating the rough seas of an inflation-ridden economy. Public investment remained a determining factor in economic growth. Anglophone private capital tended to stay away from Quebec, contributing to a more rapid flow of people and economic activity to Ontario, while government support helped enhance the stature of Francophone private capital.

Reappraisals

The PQ did not have the same degree of success during its second term (1981-85). In 1981-82, the most severe recession since the 1930s struck the western world. Quebec was hit was full force and it recovered more slowly than other places. Most companies incurred substantial losses, with many being driven into bankruptcy. Tens of thousands of workers suddenly lost their jobs and the unemployment rate approached 14 per cent in 1982 and 1983. Young people, with no prospects for the future and no place in the labour market, were the most seriously affected. The economy began to recover in 1983, but not as strongly as in the United States. The decline in the unemployment rate was slow.

The 1981-82 recession reduced the government's revenues and increased the financial burden of its social programs. Public finances were plunged into a crisis, leaving the government little room to implement countercyclical policies and forcing it to reduce spending. In 1982, it unilaterally decided to cut wages in the public and parapublic sectors, arousing vigorous social agitation, substantial bitterness, and disaffection with the Parti Québécois.

The crisis in public finance led to a reexamination of the welfare state inherited from the Quiet Revolution. Quebec was affected by the conservative tide that was sweeping Britain under Margaret Thatcher and the United States under Ronald Reagan, and ideas such as privatization and deregulation were very much in vogue. Policies of this sort were initiated under the PQ and were extended after the Liberals returned to power in 1985.

After the referendum and the repatriation of the constitution, the national question was put on the back burner. With its policy of sovereignty-association having been rejected by the voters, the PQ had to modify its platform. As a result, pro-independence elements left the party and a number of cabinet ministers and MNAs quit politics.

The first half of the 1980s can thus be seen as the end of an era dominated by the Quiet Revolution and its "gains": economic and political nationalism, social reform, government intervention and an affluent society. One by one, some of the leading figures of the era left the political scene. In 1984, Pierre Elliott Trudeau resigned and the Liberal Party, in power in Ottawa for two decades (except for a brief period in 1979-80), lost to the Conservatives. The following year, it was the turn of René Lévesque, who had led the Parti Québécois since its formation; soon after his resignation, the PQ was defeated by Robert Bourassa's Liberals. And finally, Jean Drapeau, who had been mayor of Montreal continuously since 1960 and had orchestrated some of the major projects of the era, decided not to seek reelection in 1986. This sense that an era was ending was accentuated by the death of René Lévesque in 1987 and the emotion it elicited among Quebecers.

Still, Quebec society had been radically transformed by the spirit of the Quiet Revolution. In all spheres and especially in the economy, Francophones now enjoyed a greatly enhanced position. Institutions were completely reorganized and people's standard of living improved considerably. But Quebec did not succeed in obtaining the reorganization of Confederation it had been fighting for, and its relative position within Canada was reduced over the period. At the same time, it did not succeed in solving the problems posed by the underemployment of a substantial portion of its human resources and the underdevelopment of some of its regions.

CHAPTER 30

THE IMPACT OF THE GENERATIONS

The high birth rate of the postwar period began to decline in the late 1950s and fell drastically after 1960, producing demographic upheavals that affected society as a whole. Quebec's population increased more slowly than it had in the past. The baby boom generation held centre stage throughout the period. The institution of marriage was questioned and birth control came into widespread use, transforming couple relationships and the family. The 1970s and 1980s saw an increase in the number of senior citizens and a general aging of the population.

The Decline in Population Growth

The Quebec population grew much more slowly than in previous periods (table 1), increasing by only 22.4 per cent between 1961 and 1981, as compared to an increase of 33.5 per cent in the population of Canada as a whole. As a result, Quebec represented a smaller proportion of the

Table 1
Population of Quebec and Canada, 1961-1981

	Quebec		Other provinces and territories		Canada	
Year	Population	Increase (%)*	Population	Increase (%)*	Population	Increase (%)*
1961	5,259,211	29.7	12,979,036	30.4	18,238,247	30.2
1971	6,027,764	14.6	15,540,547	19.7	21,568,311	18.3
1981	6,438,403	6.8	17,904,778	15.2	24,343,181	12.9

*Since previous census
Source: Censuses of Canada

	Table 2		
	Birth and Fertility, Quebec, 1961-81		
Year	*No. of births*	*Birth rate**	*Total fertility rate***
1961	139,857	26.6	3.77
1966	112,757	19.5	2.71
1971	93,743	15.6	1.98
1976	98,022	15.7	1.80
1981	95,247	14.8	1.62

*Number of births per thousand population
**Average number of children per woman between the ages of 15 and 49
Source: Bureau de la Statistique du Quebec, *Démographie québécoise*, p. 93.

Canadian population; from 28.8 per cent in 1961, its share fell to 27.9 per cent in 1971 and 26.4 per cent in 1981. Meanwhile, Ontario's population increased by 36.8 per cent. In 1981, it had over two million more inhabitants than Quebec and represented 35.1 per cent of the Canadian population, as compared to 34.2 per cent twenty years earlier. These developments had political implications, because the provinces are represented in the House of Commons in proportion to their population; the distribution of federal government services and resources was also at stake. At the same time, Quebec accounted for a smaller share of the Canadian economy.

Clearly the most dramatic and decisive factor in the decline in population growth was the fall in the birth rate (table 2). The annual number of live births fell drastically despite the increased population, so that the birth rate, which stood at 26.6 per thousand in 1961, was only 14.8 per thousand in 1981. Even more revealing was the total fertility rate. After 1970, it fell below the replacement rate of 2.1. While a decline was occurring in all western countries, it was particularly sharp in Quebec; thus, in 1983, Quebec's total fertility rate was 1.45, lower than in France (1.81), the United States (1.75) and Ontario (1.58). This situation represented a clear contrast with Quebec's traditionally high fertility rate and there would be serious misgivings about it among political leaders and in public opinion.

The immense progress of the preceding period in reducing the death rate continued. Infant mortality fell from 32 to 7.5 per thousand between 1961 and 1984, largely as a result of medical care for pregnant women, the development of pediatrics and improved living conditions. Child mortality also declined: in 1980, only 0.7 per cent of boys and 0.4 per cent of girls died between the ages of one and fifteen. Men of all ages had a higher death rate than women, but this was especially true for those between the ages of fifteen and thirty-five. For every 100 women in this age group who died in 1961, 213 men died; in 1981, this figure had risen to 271. Men ran a greater risk of violent death in the form of car and work accidents, suicide, and the like. For the population as a whole, the death

Table 3
Natural Increase and Net Migration by Five-Year
Period, Quebec, 1956-1981

Period	Natural increase	Net migration
1956-61	533,560	+97,275
1961-66	471,190	+50,455
1966-71	307,775	-60,855
1971-76	246,025	-39,345
1976-81	271,215	-67,255

Source: Bureau de la statistique du Québec, *Démographie québécoise*, table 1.7, p. 34.

rate remained steady at about 7 per thousand during the entire period, comparable to the rate in other industrialized countries. Cancer and diseases of the heart and circulatory system became increasingly frequent causes of death; they were responsible for 25 and 44 per cent respectively of all deaths in Quebec in 1983. Medical research was devoting considerable attention to these diseases; because they were related to lifestyle and behaviour, efforts were made to educate people and convince them to cut down on drinking and smoking, improve nutrition and exercise more.

Life expectancy continued to improve after 1960. Girls born in 1981 had an estimated life expectancy of 78.5 years as compared to 72.8 in 1961; for boys, life expectancy at birth was 70.7 years in 1981, compared to 67.3 in 1961. The gain was smaller than in the previous three decades, but it was significant nonetheless, particularly for women. The most important change was that many more people now reached the age of sixty. Beyond sixty, however, there was less progress in increasing life expectancy, especially for men.

Population growth in Quebec had always relied largely on natural increase. Because of the falling birth rate, however, natural increase declined sharply during the 1960s. The effects of this decline could have been at least partially offset by migration. But while immigration exceeded emigration until 1967, the trend subsequently reversed itself and net migration became negative, cancelling out a large part of what little growth occurred through natural increase (table 3).

Although it fell off somewhat in the early 1960s, the wave of immigration to Canada that had begun after the war continued (table 4). As in the period from 1946 to 1960, Quebec continued until about 1965 to attract about a fifth of the newcomers, which was less than its proportion of the Canadian population as a whole. After that, the rate of attraction of new immigrants fell, and it was difficult to get immigrants to stay in Quebec permanently. Nevertheless, because not many people from Quebec left Canada, international net migration remained positive throughout the period. However, interprovincial migration continued to be to Quebec's disadvantage (graph 1), as had generally been true in the past except

Figure 1
Interprovincial Migration, Quebec, 1961-1982

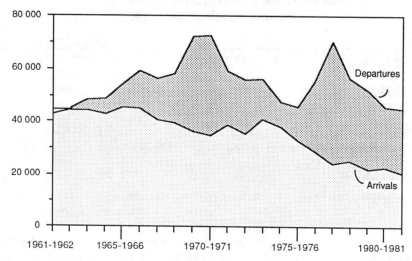

Source: *Démographie québécoise*, p.356.

Figure 2
The Age Pyramid, Quebec, 1985

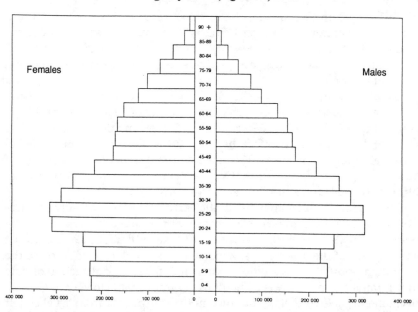

Source: Statistics Canada, *Postcensal Annual Estimates of Population by Marital Status, Age, Sex and Components of Growth for Canada, Provinces and Territories, June 1, 1985.*

Table 4
Immigration from Foreign Countries by Five-Year Period,
Canada and Quebec, 1956-1980

Period	Canada	Quebec	Quebec's attraction rate (%)
1956-60	782,911	163,502	20.9
1961-65	498,790	115,635	23.2
1966-70	910,837	172,126	18.9
1971-75	834,452	126,175	15.1
1976-80	605,869	104,489	17.2

Source: Bureau de la statistique du Québec, *Démographie québécoise*, table 9.2, p. 322.

during the Depression. The number of arrivals from other provinces varied through the period according to Quebec's economic, social and political situation. In total, arrivals numbered 722,851 between 1961 and 1981, while departures numbered 1,009,852. The total deficit of 376,701 was higher than the gains from international migration and explains why overall net migration was negative from the mid-1960s on (table 3).

Thus, the two main reasons for the decline in population growth in Quebec were the falling birth rate and the deficit in interprovincial migration. This had significant implications not only for the linguistic and ethnic makeup of the population, which will be discussed in later chapters, but also for distribution according to age.

There are three noteworthy features to the age pyramid for 1985, as shown in graph 2. The first is the low proportion of children and adolescents under the age of nineteen; while these age groups represented 44.2 per cent of the total population in 1961, they represented only 28.3 per cent in 1985. This drop reflects the decline in the fertility rate after 1965. The second feature is the high proportion of twenty- to thirty-five-year-olds — the baby boom generation. Finally, the pyramid shows a high proportion of individuals aged sixty and over — especially among women, an indication of the higher death rate for men.

The Effects of the Baby Boom

The generation born between the end of the 1940s and the beginning of the 1960s was so much larger than the ones that preceded and succeeded it that as it grew older, it set the pace and imposed its values and needs on society as a whole. The 1950s belonged to children, the 1960s to adolescents and the 1970s to young adults.

Between 1960 and 1970, 1.2 million Quebecers reached the age of fourteen. The decade was deeply marked by what was called the youth phenomenon and by the atmosphere of euphoria and excitement associated with it. Having taken care of baby boomers when they were children, society continued to give them everything they needed as adolescents. Most notably, it provided a better education system after elementary school, so that the baby boom generation was better educated than its elders. It questioned traditional values of family, religion, morality and lifestyle, no matter how firmly established, and advocated its own values of freedom and change, often in a sensational way. There has always been youthful protest and rebellion, but in the 1960s it had more impact because young people were so numerous and conscious of their strength. In addition, the prosperity and technological progress that characterized the sixties instilled an optimism in young people that heightened their expectations and made them believe they could change society politically, socioeconomically and culturally. It was a time of student unions, the rise of the independence movement, hippies and rock music. Their numbers, high level of consumption, and mass identification with the latest youth styles made all these adolescents a particularly alluring market for business. A whole range of products were targeted at this market: records, clothes, soft drinks, sporting goods, beauty products. Sales of all these items rose dramatically.

The excitement continued until about the mid-1970s, when it began to die down and make way for new concerns as the baby boom generation became more mature. Having reached adulthood, the young people of the 1960s calmed down, settled in, showed an increased need for stability,

Young people frequently took to the streets to demonstrate. (*Le Journal de Montréal*)

and became somewhat more conservative. Some of the protesters of the 1960s were now teachers, executives and civil servants. They were married, parents, owners of houses and cars, and concerned about succeeding in their careers and protecting their job security and incomes. Just as society had been created in the image of the children and adolescents they had been, in the 1980s it geared itself to meet the needs of the adults they had now become.

These developments were especially advantageous to the first wave of baby boomers. For younger ones, born between about 1955 and 1965, the situation was more difficult. Even more numerous than their immediate predecessors, they benefited from the improved secondary and post-secondary education system but found that the job market was not as open to them as it had been to older baby boomers, who had found jobs easily and kept them. As the last cohort of the baby boom generation arrived on the job market, openings were rarer — increasingly so as time went on. Unemployment among young people soon reached alarming levels. In 1983, 21 per cent of workers aged twenty to twenty-four were unemployed, as compared to only 11 per cent in 1971 and as little as 5 per cent in 1966. The problem was even more serious for fifteen- to nineteen-year-olds, for whom unemployment stood at 27 per cent in 1983. Many young people who were employed worked in highly unstable part-time, piecework and temporary jobs. The rest stayed in school because there were no jobs for them, or else relied on government assistance. In 1984, there were more than 150,000 single people and heads of families under thirty on social assistance. Many considered the youth of the 1980s a lost generation.

Challenges to the Family

Another significant development since 1960 has consisted of changes in behaviour and attitudes relating to marriage and the family. Practices began to change after the war because of large-scale urbanization and changes in lifestyle. The family unit, which had once included a broad range of relatives, now tended to consist of a single nucleus of parents and children. More married women worked outside the home. Values and role models, however, changed very little. Marriage, celebrated with the obligatory religious ceremony, marked the passage to adulthood and was supposed to last forever. Married life was centred on the children, and husband and wife each had clearly defined roles: the father was the provider and authority figure, while the mother was the housekeeper and brought up the children. But the 1960s and 1970s brought a new way of looking at all these matters, and radical changes occurred very suddenly.

First of all, for many young adults, marriage stopped being the only desirable lifestyle. The number of marriages continued to increase until 1972, reaching a peak of 54,000, and then declined steadily. In 1983, there were 36,000, of which 23 per cent were civil marriages (legal from 1968 on). However, since the number of individuals of marriageable age in-

creased as the baby boomers reached adulthood, demographers estimated that the likelihood of marriage for a single individual between the
ages of fifteen and forty-nine dropped from 90 per cent in 1972 to about
50 per cent in 1984 — one of the lowest rates in the western world. While
partially attributable to economic factors, especially the high youth unemployment rate, the low rate was mainly due to the change in attitude
towards couple relationships, the family and lifestyles. Instead of marry-
ing, an increasing number of couples chose to live together. More than
242,000 Quebecers were in such relationships in 1981.

Both married and unmarried couples questioned traditional marital
roles. Although the division of labour was not perfect, household tasks
tended to be shared more equally; the attitude towards women working
outside the home changed radically; each partner had greater financial
independence; and, most important of all, more emphasis was placed on
the development of the relationship itself, with children no longer seen
as the main reason for the couple being together.

Between 1961 and 1981, the number of families rose from 1.1 million
to 1.6 million, but the families themselves became much smaller. The
relatively large family of the pre-1960 era was being replaced by a new
kind of family, with one or two children and a lifestyle that did not follow
the traditional model. The baby boom adolescents of the 1960s had begun
to challenge that model by questioning parental authority and demanding more independence. When they became parents themselves, they
tended to have a more open — even permissive — attitude towards their
own children. These children were brought up in a different environment
from postwar children: they had fewer brothers and sisters and less
contact with children their own age, their relationships with adults were
different, and since both parents were likely to work, they often went to
daycare centres or were looked after in other people's homes as young
children and then began school earlier, entering kindergarten at the age
of five.

The major change in couple relationships and family life was the
widespread availability and use of birth control. The birth control pill,
which became available in the early 1960s, quickly replaced the so-called
natural methods in use to that point. Although subject to legal restrictions
and banned by the church, use of the pill rapidly became widespread in
the 1970s, not only among married women but also among teenagers and
single women. Subsequently, because of the inconvenience and risk associated with the pill, other methods came into use, including condoms,
IUDs and voluntary sterilization — tubal ligations for women and vasec-
tomies for men. The number of these operations performed rose from
12,000 in 1971 to more than 41,000 in 1979, and a significant number of
those who had them were under thirty. Contraceptive use changed
sexual behaviour enormously, especially for women. More than before,
having a child or not became a matter of choice. This was a major factor
in the so-called sexual revolution of the 1960s and 1970s; however, the

new sexual freedom created health risks that became a major concern in the 1980s. It should also be pointed out that the burden of contraception lay largely with women, who had to bear the responsibility and the risks.

While abortion was not a method of contraception as such, it became a means of birth control. Abortion was treated as a criminal act — although it was carried out secretly, often in dangerous and traumatic conditions — until 1969, when it was legalized under specified circumstances. With the new legislation in effect, abortion became much more common in the 1970s and 1980s: the number of declared abortions (which excludes illegal ones) rose from 1,275 in 1971 to 6,004 in 1984, or 18.3 per cent of the number of live births. This was lower than the U.S. rate of more than 40 per cent and the Ontario rate of about 23 per cent. From the late 1970s on, there has been an intense debate between believers in free access to abortion and people who want to see it severely restricted.

Another significant change in the 1960s and 1970s was a weakening of the link between procreation and marriage. The proportion of babies born out of wedlock rose from only 3.7 per cent in 1961 to 10 per cent in 1976 and 22 per cent in 1984. The number of single-parent families also rose markedly over the same period, from 95,818 to 208,430. In addition, while most single-parent families had once been headed by widows or widowers, such families were now headed mainly by single, divorced or separated women.

Less universal and less centred on procreation, marriage was also less stable than it had been before. Before the 1960s, divorce, although legal, was expensive, complicated, looked down on in the community, and therefore rare. Virtually the only choice for Quebec couples was legal separation, which authorized them to live apart but did not put an end to the marriage and therefore did not permit remarriage. New legislation enacted in 1968 and 1985 made divorce much cheaper and easier. The number of divorces rose from 2,930 in 1969 to 16,485 in 1984, while the likelihood of divorce rose from 8.7 per cent in 1969 to 38.1 per cent in 1984.

Thus, beginning with the Quiet Revolution, family life and couple relationships changed enormously, largely because of the baby boom generation, which challenged traditional values and practices. Of course, for the majority of the population, including young people, the married couple with children remained an ideal. In pursuit of this ideal, however, people behaved in unprecedented ways, so that there was greater scope for individual choice and diversity. The government tried as best it could to adapt its policies and legislation to the new reality.

Senior Citizens

As a combined effect of longer life expectancy and the falling birth rate, the proportion of children and adolescents in the population declined while the proportion of elderly people correspondingly increased. In 1985, as the age pyramid shows (graph 2), 9.6 per cent of Quebecers were over sixty-five, which represented a significant increase over 1961 (5.8 per cent) and 1971 (6.9 per cent). During the 1970s, senior citizens became more visible and forced the government and society as a whole to become aware of their particular needs and problems.

As well, the elderly themselves organized and made their voices heard on issues that concerned them. They set up golden age clubs and combined these clubs into federations. Seniors also became more active in political parties, social and cultural groups, and other organizations. In addition to old age pensions and other pension plans, pressure from seniors led to the adoption of a number of new measures aimed at improving their situation. Thus, retirement at age sixty-five was no longer mandatory, a tax deduction was granted to the elderly, an income supplement was provided for the neediest, prescription drugs became free and reduced rates were established for various services.

But despite these improvements, living conditions for the elderly were often precarious, especially for women, who made up the majority of seniors. Many suffered from poverty, health problems, poor treatment and loneliness.

The increase in the number of senior citizens, the falling birth rate and the baby boomers' arrival at maturity were all factors contributing to a basic characteristic of the period — the aging of the population. This had short-term advantages, because there were more productive individuals in the population and fewer dependent young and old people. In the longer term, however, the aging population would become an enormous challenge as the older population grew and succeeding generations became smaller. Many observers also feared that an aging population could mean a loss of dynamism and fear of change in society as a whole.

CHAPTER 31

CORPORATE CONCENTRATION AND CONTROL

In 1986, the Quebec economy was quite different from what it had been in 1960. Apart from changes that occurred sector by sector, which we will examine in subsequent chapters, the structures of the capitalist system in Quebec, and in Canada as a whole, were developing and changing.

Three main issues were widely and sometimes hotly debated over the period: corporate control, including the problem of foreign investment, Canadian investment in foreign countries and the role of Francophones in corporate ownership; the growth of monopolies and the position of small and middle-sized business; and the role of government in the economy.

Foreign Control: Expansion and Decline

Foreign control of the Canadian economy went through two stages. The first stage, the 1960s and early 1970s, was a continuation of the preceding period and saw a considerable increase in foreign control. In the mid-1970s, however, the trend began to be reversed, as Canadian corporations and governments regained control over many foreign-owned companies, so that foreign control was on the decline by the early 1980s.

During the 1960s, foreign direct and indirect investment in Canada grew rapidly, as it had since the end of the war, rising from a total of $22 billion in 1960 to $29 billion in 1965 and $44 billion in 1970. The lion's share of foreign investment — 70 to 80 per cent — continued to be American. Foreign control reached a peak of 38 per cent of the assets of nonfinancial companies in Canada in 1968. Natural resources and manufacturing were the most heavily affected sectors: in 1970, for example,

69 per cent of mining assets and 58 per cent of manufacturing assets were under foreign control. The impact was not as great in Quebec as in Ontario and the prairie provinces, where foreign investment and the jobs resulting from it were primarily concentrated. Nonetheless, Quebec did feel the negative effects of foreign control.

Foreign control took various forms. Most commonly, American branch plants expanded their activities; thus, General Motors established an assembly plant in a Montreal suburb. In other cases, existing Canadian companies were bought out. A good example is the snowmobile industry, where the major Quebec manufacturers, with the exception of Bombardier, were taken over by large American corporations. European investors also made efforts to gain a foothold in Quebec and elsewhere in Canada. Powerful Belgian interests acquired the Miron building materials concern, while the French-owned Ciments Lafarge opened a Quebec subsidiary and bought Canada Cement. As well, large British, German, Swiss, Italian and South African corporations invested in Quebec resources, manufacturing and real estate development.

For years, some intellectuals and politicians had pointed out the dangers in allowing such extensive foreign ownership of the Canadian economy. Their warnings remained unheeded for a long time, but in the late 1960s, awareness of the problem began to grow, especially in English Canada. Studies by economists such as Mel Watkins and Kari Levitt shook the public out of its apathy. The Waffle — the left wing of the New Democratic Party — put forward a program of Canadian economic nationalism in response to what it considered American imperialism. Government had always extended a warm welcome to foreign investment, but with this partial shift in public opinion, it had to reconsider its position. Studies were undertaken: Ottawa's Gray Report on foreign ownership, the Tetley Report in Quebec, and many other studies carried out by government agencies.

The Gray Report, published in 1971, provided a good overview of the situation and described the wide-ranging harmful consequences of foreign investment: reduced Canadian control of Canadian companies, dependence on foreign technology, and the negative impact on decision-making in Canada, export potential, procurement and import practices, competition, balance of payments, and even culture, society and politics. The report recommended a number of corrective measures, including the establishment of a screening agency for new foreign investment to slow down the trend.

This new awareness was an important factor in the turnabout that occurred in the first half of the 1970s, when private firms and governments began to regain control of the Canadian economy. A number of elements converged to make this possible. First of all, in 1973, the federal government, under pressure from the New Democratic Party, stopped dithering and set up the Foreign Investment Review Agency (FIRA), which was to review all projected foreign investment in Canada and block it if necessary. As well, Ottawa established the Canada Development Corporation, controlled by the federal government but with some private capital. Its purpose was to buy back foreign-controlled Canadian companies and to develop high-technology industries, in which foreign investment tends to be concentrated. Later, Ottawa set up a federally owned petroleum corporation, Petro-Canada, which made a series of purchases of foreign oil companies, buying four between 1976 and 1980. It also announced its National Energy Program, designed to increase Canadian control of the energy sector. Provincial governments moved in similar directions, setting up crown corporations to increase Canadian control over natural resources.

Quebec government policy followed a different path from that of other governments. Except in the asbestos industry, government-owned corporations were set up not to counter foreign investment but rather to increase Francophone economic influence in the face of English Canadian capital. As the Tetley Report (1973-74) noted, Quebec had always been open to foreign investment, which was seen as a source of job creation. In the government's view, Quebec needed new investment and any measures to block it would only benefit Ontario and lead to a net loss for Quebec if they were adopted before the Quebec economy could be restructured so that it could fulfil the role played by foreign investment. The Tetley Report challenged the notion of the existence of a single, undifferentiated Canadian economy that underlay federal policy, and insisted on the particular structural character of regional economies. Instead, the report suggested a policy aimed at better integrating foreign companies into the Quebec economy and making industrial structures more dynamic by strengthening innovation in Quebec. However, it acknowledged the need to protect some sectors it considered vital — culture, natural resources, financial institutions and utilities.

Parallel to these new government initiatives, the private sector appeared more willing and able to participate in increasing Canadian control. Large Canadian corporations had grown stronger because of the expansion of the 1960s and the increase in corporate concentration. In addition, the rapid growth of the Canadian banks gave the private sector the means of buying back giant foreign-owned corporations. Thus, in 1981, Canadian Pacific bought Canadian International Paper, which had its head office in Montreal and had been solidly established in Quebec since the 1920s, from its American parent, International Paper. The large American corporations that had acquired the Moto-ski snowmobile factory and Montreal Locomotive Works sold these concerns to Bombardier. This trend was not limited to very large corporations. During this period, many small and middle-sized Quebec firms that had been sold to foreign interests were bought back and reinvigorated by Quebec business people.

Within a few years, the efforts at Canadianization showed results. Between 1970 and 1982, foreign control declined from 69 to 43 per cent of assets in the mining sector and from 58 to 49 per cent in manufacturing. In the petroleum industry, foreign control fell to 45 per cent in 1982, and even in sectors such as retail trade and services, where foreign interests had not been dominant, Canadian control increased. Overall, in all non-financial industries, foreign control fell from 36 per cent of assets to 26 per cent. Of course, Canada was far from being completely free of foreign control, which remained strong in the petroleum, mining and manufacturing sectors. Total long-term foreign investment was $205 billion in 1984, of which $83 billion was direct investment. Nonetheless, a qualitative change had occurred in the space of a few years.

But this progress was precarious, and the Conservative election victory of 1984 cast federal policies in this area into doubt. The Mulroney government replaced FIRA with the more pliable Investment Canada and abolished the National Energy Program, indicating clearly that foreign investment was welcome in Canada once again. The most significant development, however, was the adoption of a free trade agreement with the United States in 1988. In Quebec, openness to foreign investment was maintained under the Lévesque government, as the establishment of plants by Pechiney and Hyundai indicates. When he returned to power in 1985, Robert Bourassa set out to encourage foreign investment still further.

The Growth of Canadian Investment in Foreign Countries

Canada, while a major importer of capital, has also for a long time been an exporter, although in smaller quantities. But during the 1960s and 1970s, Canadian direct investment in foreign countries increased dramatically, from $2.5 billion in 1960 to $41.4 billion in 1984. Including indirect investment and other kinds of assets, long-term Canadian foreign investment totalled $79 billion in 1984.

Banks accounted for a large portion of the Canadian presence in foreign countries. In the 1970s, they became true financial multinationals. Their international operations accounted for a growing share of their revenues and proved much more profitable than their activities within Canada. In the early 1980s, they suffered heavy losses when many developing countries, suffering from excessive debt burdens, were unable to repay their creditors. In the wake of these losses, the banks redirected their international investments to the United States and the rapidly growing countries of Asia.

Canadian multinationals were active in other sectors as well, and their international expansion gained speed between 1960 and 1980. Companies that had operated exclusively in Canada until that time became multinationals. Dominion Textile is a good example of this process. From the time it was founded in 1905, its production had been concentrated in Canada — mainly in Quebec, where it formed an integral part of the history of the cotton industry. In 1975, it launched an international expansion program. Similarly, Bombardier, originally established in Valcourt in the Eastern Townships, became a multinational. In the early 1980s, it manufactured transportation equipment and recreational products in a number of Quebec plants, motors and streetcars in Austria, buses in Ireland and rolling stock in Vermont. Attracted by the proximity of the United States and the size of the American market, many Quebec companies, even relatively small ones, acquired subsidiaries south of the border.

Canadian expansion in the United States did not go unnoticed, especially when Canadian companies sought to take over very large American firms. Beginning in 1980, there was a nationalist reaction in American financial circles against large Canadian corporations such as Canadian Pacific and Seagram that were involved in takeover bids for large American corporations. Within Canada, there was criticism of the negative effects of the massive export of capital on the value of the Canadian dollar. However, this situation reflected the extent to which Canadian capital had gained strength over the two decades.

Corporate Ownership in Quebec

As can be seen from some of the examples given earlier, such as Bombardier and the asbestos industry, increased Canadian control of the economy sometimes amounted to increased Quebec control. But aside from buying back foreign companies, other questions can be asked about corporate ownership and control. Specifically, there is the question of the position of French Canadians compared to English Canadians and foreigners. It was clearly marginal in the rest of Canada, but what was the situation in Quebec?? The fact that Francophones were in a minority position in terms of control of the Quebec economy is well established, widely known and much discussed, but it is also well known that the situation changed after 1960. What was the scope and significance of the changes that occurred during this period?

Two studies on corporate ownership in Quebec give an indication of these changes: one by André Raynauld for 1961 and a second, by Raynauld and François Vaillancourt, for 1978. The main yardstick used was the number of jobs in both privately and publicly owned establishments, categorized by the linguistic and national origins of the people who controlled them (table 1). For the Quebec economy as a whole, the French Canadian share increased from 47 per cent to nearly 55 per cent, while the English Canadian share declined from 39 to 31 per cent and the foreign-controlled share remained stable at 14 per cent.

Francophone progress was not due simply to higher growth in sectors where Francophones were already firmly established. Progress was general and involved all sectors, although to varying degrees. The most dramatic increases in Francophone control were in construction and financial institutions. In both 1961 and 1978, Francophone control was weak in mining and manufacturing, and Francophones were clearly underrepresented in transportation, communication and utilities, financial

Table 1
Percentage of Jobs Accounted for by Francophone-controlled, Anglophone-controlled and Foreign-controlled Estabishments by Sector, Quebec, 1961 and 1978

Sector	Year	Francophone-controlled establishments	Anglophone-controlled establishments	Foreign-controlled establishments
Agriculture	1961	91.3	8.7	0
	1978	91.8	8.2	0
Mining	1961	6.5	53.1	40.4
	1978	9.2	17.9	73.0
Manufacturing	1961	21.7	47.0	31.3
	1978	27.8	38.6	33.5
Construction	1961	50.7	35.2	14.1
	1978	74.4	18.5	7.1
Transportation, communication and utilities	1961	36.4	55.3	8.3
	1978	42.2	53.4	4.4
Commerce	1961	50.4	39.5	11.5
	1978	51.0	32.0	17.0
Financial institutions	1961	25.8	53.1	21.1
	1978	44.8	43.1	12.1
Services	1961	71.4	28.6	0
	1978	75.0	21.2	3.8
Public administration	1961	51.8	47.7	0.5
	1978	67.2	32.8	0
Total	1961	47.1	39.3	13.6
	1978	54.8	31.2	13.9

Source: André Raynauld and François Vaillancourt, *L'appartenance des entreprises: le cas du Québec en 1978*, p. 81.

institutions and commerce. Their strong points were agriculture, services, construction and public administration.

Conversely, the relative decline in Anglophone control appeared in all sectors. Sometimes it was to the benefit of foreigners, as in mining and commerce, but on the whole it was to the benefit of Francophones. While the percentage of control by foreign interests remained stable, there were wide variations from one sector to another.

Even though Francophones were far from dominant in the Quebec economy and their share in it was disproportionately low compared to their percentage of the population, there was undeniable progress over the seventeen-year period, and this progress appears to have continued after 1978. The fact that English Canadians moved their businesses to other provinces was not the only reason for this. A number of factors were involved, including the emergence of new Francophone elites, improvements in French Canadians' standard of living and the role of the government.

But the degree of control is far from being the only significant variable in measuring the development of the capitalist system in Quebec. The kinds of activities and businesses Francophones were involved in must also be taken into account.

Increased Corporate Concentration

The process of monopolization and concentration that had begun in the late nineteenth century gained new impetus after 1960. Large companies became even larger through the acquisition of other firms and through rapid growth that strengthened their monopoly position. The restructuring of the economy also affected many of the thousands of smaller firms whose scope was regional or local.

As noted in chapter 15, for the period 1948-50, the sociologist John Porter identified 183 dominant corporations — companies that owned the majority of assets in a number of major sectors of the Canadian economy. Another sociologist, Wallace Clement, undertook a similar study for 1971-72. Taking as his sample all corporations with assets of more than $250 million and sales of more than $50 million, Clement ended up with a list even smaller than Porter's: 113 dominant corporations representing 97 per cent of the assets in the communications sector, 90 per cent in transportation and petroleum, 66 per cent in machinery and food and beverages, and similar percentages in a number of other sectors. In the financial sector, these large corporations controlled 90 per cent of the assets of chartered banks, 86 per cent of the assets of life insurance companies and 80 per cent of the assets of trust companies. Some sectors, such as nonmetallic minerals, electrical equipment, miscellaneous manufacturing and wholesale and retail trade, had lower levels of concentration.

Alongside these large corporations, there were thousands of other firms of varying size. Every year many such companies disappeared while many new ones were formed, but the general trend was towards increased corporate concentration and centralization of economic power.

One of the features of concentration was the sharp rise in the number of conglomerates, as witnessed by the creation of holding companies controlling firms in a wide variety of industries. The classic example is Power Corporation, controlled by the corporate acquisitor Paul Desmarais. In 1980, Power controlled a number of large companies and their subsidiaries in four main sectors: financial services (Great West Life, Investors Group, Montreal Trust), transportation (Canada Steamship Lines), pulp and paper (Consolidated-Bathurst) and communications (*La Presse* and Trans-Canada newspapers). It also had minority interests in the petroleum industry. In the early 1980s, Power Corporation reorganized. It divested itself of Canada Steamship Lines, made an unsuccessful bid to take control of Canadian Pacific, restructured its financial services subsidiaries, and entered the international scene by investing in a number of financial companies in partnership with European interests. In 1984,

Power Corporation had assets of $1 billion, but the companies under its control had total assets of $21 billion (and almost double that if the assets administered in trust by Montreal Trust are included).

Other conglomerates were formed when firms long identified with a single industry diversified their interests. Examples of this process are the Molson Companies and Imperial Tobacco, which became Imasco in 1970 and invested in the retail sector and financial services.

Corporate concentration raised some concerns that prompted the federal government to set up a royal commission, the Bryce Commission, to look into the question. In its 1978 report, the commission concluded that it was to Canada's advantage to have large corporations that could compete with leading foreign companies and did not make any recommendations to restrict concentration significantly. The trend towards concentration continued throughout the 1970s and intensified in the 1980s, when a number of major Canadian companies changed hands through takeovers where billions of dollars were at play and that in some cases involved struggles among corporate giants. Huge new conglomerates — CEMP Investments, belonging to the Bronfman family of Montreal, Edper Equities, owned by the Toronto branch of the Bronfmans, and Olympia & York, the central corporate instrument for the Reichmann brothers' interests — appeared on the scene, joining the older giants Canadian Pacific, Power Corporation, Argus Corporation and Weston. The financial situation in the 1970s partially explains the trend towards takeovers — with high construction costs and astronomical interest rates, it was more economical for a large company to buy an existing firm than to try to set one up from scratch.

In a finding similar to Porter's, Clement's study showed that in 1971-72 very few companies controlled by French Canadians from Quebec were among Canada's dominant corporations. Power Corporation, whose rise was a striking new development, provided the only exception. Apart from financial institutions, the only other large private company controlled by Quebec Francophones was Bombardier, which Clement classified as middle-sized rather than dominant. However, the situation changed in the 1970s with the emergence of new Francophone business groups and the rise of Quebec government-owned corporations.

During the 1970s, French Canadian companies, like their English Canadian counterparts, launched a campaign of acquisition and concentration, extending to sectors in which there had hitherto been a degree of fragmentation. The impact was felt most heavily in financial services and commerce, but some manufacturing industries such as food (dairy products, bakeries and biscuit manufacturing), sawmills and printing were affected as well. Concentration also took place in transportation and other services.

Thus, French Canadian industrial and financial groups have been forming and developing. They play a much larger role in Quebec than they did previously, and they have been making efforts to expand their operations throughout Canada and internationally as well. Notable among these groups are the National Bank of Canada, the Laurentian Group, Provigo, Bombardier, Gaz Métro, Québecor, UniMédia, Lavalin and SNC, as well as the large number of cooperatives and companies making up the Desjardins group. Also under Francophone control are the many Quebec government corporations, most of them set up since 1960; the most significant of these are Hydro-Quebec, the Société Générale de Financement and the Caisse de Dépôt. Thus, the prevailing trend observed elsewhere in Canada and in other industrialized countries — a large role for big business, strengthened by corporate concentration — has affected Quebec as well. Two decades after the beginning of the Quiet Revolution, Quebec capitalism had been profoundly transformed by this process.

Small Business

However, even if there was a breakthrough by big business, most Francophone business activity took place through small and medium-sized business. In both Quebec and the rest of Canada, small and middle-sized businesses represented more than 90 per cent of all companies. Because they accounted for only a small part of the value of production and profits, however, their actual importance in the economy was much smaller. In Quebec, small business played a greater role than in Ontario — not because Quebec small business was particularly dynamic, but because big business, particularly heavy industry, was primarily established in Ontario.

The expression "small business" or the French expression *"PME"* (small and middle-sized business) encompasses a wide variety of business endeavours, but the greatest attention has been devoted to the manufacturing sector. Raynauld and Vaillancourt showed that in 1978, just as in 1961, Francophone control and size of company were inversely related (table 2). But in studying the average size of businesses, they found that

Table 2
Percentage of Value Added by Size of Establishment and Ownership, Manufacturing Sector, Quebec, 1978

Size of establishment (shipments in $)	Francophone-controlled establishments	Anglophone-controlled establishments	Foreign-controlled establishments
0 - 999,999	53.8	38.9	7.3
1,000,000 - 2,499,999	47.0	42.1	10.9
2,500,000 - 4,999,999	39.2	42.8	18.0
5,000,000 - 9,999,999	28.6	42.5	28.9
10,000,000 or more	15.8	35.0	49.2

Source: André Raynauld and François Vaillancourt, *L'appartenance des entreprises: le cas du Québec en 1978*, p. 94.

the gap that separated Francophones from Anglophones and foreigners had shrunk significantly. Supporting the overall conclusions of other researchers, they noted that in the manufacturing sector, Francophone firms were "those with the smallest plants, the lowest productivity and the lowest wages but with the highest labour costs. They mainly serve the local market."

The government, aware of the weaknesses and shortcomings of Quebec small business and its impact on job creation, developed policies to improve its management, financing and productivity. This was viewed as a question of survival, because lack of efficiency made many Quebec firms unprepared to face competition.

Thus, although Francophones made an undeniable breakthrough into economic leadership during the period, their accomplishments were fragile in many sectors.

The Role of Government

The role of government was another element that changed the face of capitalism in both Quebec and the rest of Canada. As a share of Quebec's gross domestic product, government spending on goods and services rose from 17 per cent in 1961 to 26 per cent in 1983.

As we will see in subsequent chapters, government intervention was multifaceted and affected all areas of Quebec life from the economy to culture. In the economic field, government intervened in five major ways that had a major impact on private enterprise: through legislation, regulation and inspection; through subsidies and other forms of assistance; through purchases of goods and services; as a direct and indirect employer; and as an entrepreneur, mainly through government-owned corporations. The government changed from being a passive partner to being an active player in business.

In the next chapter to come, we will examine these forms of government intervention more closely. Suffice it to say that federal and provincial government intervention played a significant part in the developments discussed above, especially the trend towards Canadianization and the rise of Francophone entrepreneurs.

CHAPTER 32
THE GOVERNMENT AND THE ECONOMY

The attitude of Quebec political leaders to government intervention and economic policy changed radically after 1960. The new elites favoured government intervention as strongly as Duplessis and his supporters had opposed it. The redefinition of the role of government had many facets — political and administrative, social, ideological, and even cultural — that will be examined in other chapters. Here we will look at government's role in the economy. The Quebec government clearly offered new leadership, but its effectiveness was limited in a capitalist economy and a country where the central government was the real architect of economic policy.

A New Strategy

The election of Jean Lesage marked a reversal of the kind of economic strategy applied since 1897 by the Liberals and then by the Union Nationale. There were elements of continuity — natural resources and roads were still important concerns, although they were no longer central to government policy but rather part of a much wider overall strategy. This strategy, developed during the Quiet Revolution, was maintained through the changes in government of the 1960s and 1970s.

The new direction was inspired both by reform liberalism and by nationalism, and was part of the general goal of modernizing Quebec society. In the economic domain, there were three specific objectives. The first was to increase the role of government. Quebec political leaders, like their federal counterparts, embraced the principles of Keynesianism and the welfare state. They wanted to make the Quebec government a major player in the economy and a partner with private enterprise. As well, they sought to regulate business activity much more closely.

The second objective was to modernize the Quebec economy, as expressed in what was called the ideology of *"rattrapage"* (catching up). The main concern here was to transform Quebec's industrial structure by promoting the modernization of traditional manufacturing facilities and the establishment of new companies involved in the production of capital goods and high-technology industry. There was also an effort to compensate for the lag in infrastructure investment, particularly roads and hydroelectricity.

A third objective, this one inspired by nationalism, was to change the role played by French Canadians in the economy. There was an attempt to improve the socioeconomic status of Francophones and raise their standard of living through more advanced, better-quality education, better working conditions and more highly developed social policies. Particular emphasis was placed on greater participation by Francophone managers and business people in economic leadership. From this perspective, the Quebec government was seen as an instrument at the service of French Canadians. Finally, Quebec government intervention was to be used to counter the negative effects of federal policies on Francophones.

These three objectives were part of an ongoing concern with stimulating economic growth, attracting investment and creating jobs. Carrying out such an ambitious program required a broad range of approaches. The break with Duplessis's strategy was especially apparent in the use of fiscal and budgetary policy. A balanced budget stopped being the golden rule for ministers of finance, and government spending grew significantly. Duplessis's traditional, cautious policies left the Quebec government with considerable borrowing capacity, which the Lesage government and its successors did not hesitate to use. In addition to its own investments in infrastructure, the government tried to stimulate private investment through tax breaks and subsidies.

The government paid increasing attention to the impact of public spending. The gradual development of a clearly protectionist purchasing policy was an example of this. Beginning in 1962, Hydro-Quebec agreed to pay up to 10 per cent more for products manufactured in Quebec. The list of drugs recognized by the Department of Social Affairs favoured those produced in Quebec laboratories. The manufacture of city buses and educational computers was encouraged by bulk purchasing and subsidies.

From the 1960s on, the government saw publicly owned corporations as both an important instrument of economic intervention and a way of strengthening the Francophone presence in a variety of sectors. New government-owned corporations were set up (table 1), in addition to the existing Liquor Board and Hydro-Quebec. As well, the government made liberal use of its power to monitor and regulate business. For example, it established and improved standards for work and fringe benefits, and imposed rules regarding the use of French to help Francophones.

Table 1
Major Quebec Government-owned Corporations, 1978

Name	Year of establishment
Société des Alcools	1921
Hydro-Quebec	1944
Société Générale de Financement (SGF)	1962
Sidérurgie du Québec (SIDBEC)	1964
Société Québécoise d'Exploration Minière (SOQUEM)	1965
Caisse de Dépôt et Placement du Québec	1965
Société d'Habitation du Québec (SHQ)	1967
Société d'Exploitation des Loteries et Courses (Loto-Québec)	1969
Société de Récupération, d'Exploitation et de Développement Forestiers (REXFOR)	1969
Société Québécoise d'Initiatives Pétrolières (SOQUIP)	1969
James Bay Energy Corporation (JBEC)	1971
James Bay Development Corporation (JBDC)	1971
Société de Développement Industriel (SDI)	1971
Société Québécoise d'Initiatives Agro-alimentaires (SOQUIA)	1975
Société Nationale de l'Amiante (SNA)	1978

Although the government had powerful and varied means at its disposal to implement its economic strategy, its capacity to intervene was subject to serious limitations. It had to reckon with Ottawa, which held the major levers of economic power under the constitution, intervened heavily in economic development, provided assistance to business, and had considerable fiscal resources. As well, the Quebec government was operating in an environment dominated by private enterprise, to which technocrats and politicians had to adapt. Private capital was relatively mobile and could move when it was not happy with the constraints placed on it. In addition, Quebec faced competition from the other Canadian provinces and gradually lost ground to Ontario, Alberta and British Columbia. Finally, the government had to adjust to cyclical conditions — for example, in the 1970s, the high level of unemployment often meant that it had to put its long-term strategy on hold and attend to the urgent question of creating jobs through short-term measures.

Despite these limitations, the Quebec government managed to carve out a role for itself and even, in some cases, to have some influence on long-term tendencies. We will now examine some of the forms Quebec government intervention took and the results it obtained.

Tighter Control over Natural Resources

Since the Quebec government was the owner of public land and could use it for economic development, natural resources always had a central role in government strategy. However, the government had always preferred to allow the private sector to actually develop those resources. After 1960, there was a move to exercise tighter control over natural resource industries and even to participate in them through government-owned corporations.

In the energy sector, the government's most dramatic and far-reaching move was its nationalization of private electricity production and distribution companies outside Montreal, which were integrated into Hydro-Quebec in 1963. Companies affected included Shawinigan Water and Power and a number of smaller utilities. Industrial firms that generated electricity for their own needs — some twenty companies including Alcan — and a few municipally owned concerns and local cooperatives were the only electrical utilities that remained outside Hydro-Quebec.

The nationalization of hydroelectric power had both political and economic significance. As a result of nationalization, rates could be made uniform throughout Quebec and better service could be provided in distant regions such as Abitibi and the Gaspé. The growing needs of industry and urban consumers could be met more adequately. The burden of the substantial investments required to satisfy the demand for electricity was shifted to the government, and hence to society as a whole. The former owners of the electricity companies, such as Power Corporation, acquired large amounts of cash to be channelled into more profitable sectors. Finally, a huge corporation was created where thousands of Francophones, many of them professionals, could work and excel in French.

Hydro-Quebec quickly became a symbol of the new Quebec nationalism and the government's new economic strategy. The scope of its investments gave it some influence on the manufacturing sector, and the volume of its purchases attracted some new businesses and helped others grow. Because Quebec produced cheaper electricity than other regions of North America, it was able to attract energy-intensive industries, although it was not until the 1980s that it offered them reduced rates. The accumulation of surplus energy that began in the mid-1970s forced it to take this step as well as to become an exporter of electricity.

Propelled into the position of Quebec's largest corporation, Hydro-Quebec had considerable influence over the economy and began to look like a "state within a state." Premier Robert Bourassa even tried to limit its power in 1971 when he tried to set up the James Bay Energy Corporation outside of Hydro-Quebec's control, but he was subsequently pressured into making the JBEC a mere subsidiary of Hydro-Quebec.

The energy crisis of the 1970s forced the government to try to develop an energy policy that would reduce Quebec's dependence on imported

Hydro-Quebec's head office on Dorchester Street (Now Boulevard René–Lévesque) in Montreal, 1962. (Hydro-Quebec)

oil and increase the proportion of electricity, and especially Canadian natural gas, in Quebec's energy consumption. Another government-owned corporation, SOQUIP, founded in 1969 to carry out petroleum exploration in Quebec, played an important role in this regard. The government several times toyed with the idea of having SOQUIP participate in oil refining and retail sales, but it had to back down under pressure from business circles. After 1976, SOQUIP extended its

The hydroelectric complex at La Grande, James Bay. (Hydro-Québec)

explorations outside Quebec, particularly in western Canada where it was involved in natural gas discoveries. During the 1980s, its operations expanded: at the distribution end it took control of Gaz Métropolitain, while at the exploration end it took over Sundance Oil. While the government also tried to maintain and stimulate the petrochemical industry by participating in the establishment of Petromont, results were disappointing, as Quebec increasingly operated at a disadvantage in relation to Alberta and Ontario.

In the forest sector, a far-reaching reform abolished the system of concessions that had existed for more than a century. Under Bill 27, in preparation for a number of years before its adoption in 1974, the government took over the management of public forests. The Department of Lands and Forests began to ensure better distribution of forest resources by drawing up plans for allocating wood to each region's processing plants. Along with grants for plant modernization, this measure gave producers a better guarantee of supplies and promoted a thorough reorganization of Quebec's sawmills. Meanwhile, under a federal-provincial plant modernization program for pulp and paper, several hundred million dollars in new investment were injected into that industry.

The Quebec government also intervened directly in production through the Société de Récupération, d'Exploitation et de Développement Forestiers (REXFOR) and the Société Générale de Financement

(SGF). Initially, many of these agencies' acquisitions involved saving sawmills owned by French Canadians from bankruptcy. During the 1970s, however, their activities became more specialized. While REXFOR became sole or part owner of a number of wood-processing plants, the SGF concentrated on the paper industry, becoming a partner with Donohue in a newly established plant in Saint-Félicien on Lake St. John and then taking over Domtar in conjunction with the Caisse de Dépôt.

The mining sector posed problems, dominated as it was by giant English Canadian and American corporations, many of them multi-nationals. Unlike the situation in the forest industry, little processing was done in Quebec. Furthermore, Quebec's comparative advantages were eroded when large ore deposits were opened up in Third World countries, and Quebec was powerless to stop this process.

Clearly the most significant action undertaken by the Quebec government in this sector was its support for mineral exploration, particularly along the Cadillac fault in the Abitibi region. As in other resource industries, it set up its own corporations. The Société Québécoise d'Exploration Minière (SOQUEM), established in 1965, had some notable successes. It discovered a number of deposits and operated several mines, often in partnership with private interests. Nonetheless, it was small compared to the large corporations. Much less sucessful was SIDBEC, which through its subsidiary SIDBEC-Normines operated an iron mine that was unable to make a profit because of the fall in the world price of iron ore and was later abandoned.

Asbestos was a special case because of its symbolic character. Quebec was the leading world producer, but production was carried out by large foreign corporations that exported the asbestos in its unprocessed state. Throughout the period, there was considerable discussion of the need to process asbestos in Quebec, but no action was taken. The Parti Québécois put forward a proposal for partial nationalization of the industry, and in 1978 it established the Société Nationale de l'Amiante, which acquired Bell Asbestos and the Asbestos Corporation. However, these acquisitions took place at a time when sales of asbestos were suffering because of widespread publicity given reports of its harmful effects on health. In this context, far from producing the results the government had hoped for, nationalization proved to be a costly mistake.

Thus, in the resource sector, government intervention led to increased control by Quebecers, and by Francophones, in the energy and forest sectors, but only a marginal degree of control in the mining industry.

The Financial Sector

The Quebec government also intervened substantially in the financial sector. Under the constitution, it had jurisdiction over part of this sector, including caisses populaires, insurance companies, provincially incorporated trust companies, stock brokerage and real estate. These institutions grew rapidly in the 1960s and 1970s, forcing the Quebec government, along with the federal and other provincial governments, to modernize its mechanisms for supervising and monitoring them. Thus, in 1968, the Department of Financial Institutions, Corporations and Cooperatives and the Régie de l'Assurance-Dépôts, designed to protect small depositors, were established.

But the government measure that had the greatest effect was the creation in 1965 of the Caisse de Dépôt et Placement, which administered the huge sums of money collected by the Quebec Pension Plan. Gradually, responsibility for managing the funds of several other government agencies was also transferred to the Caisse. Its task was not just to make profitable investments with the large amounts of capital at its disposal but also to contribute to Quebec's development by helping to finance public agencies and private companies. In its first ten years, the Caisse moved cautiously and invested mainly in government bonds. But in the late 1970s, the Parti Québécois pushed it to intervene much more actively in the private sector, buying large blocks of stock in Quebec companies. In a short time, it acquired the largest stock portfolio in Canada and became a significant presence on financial markets. The English Canadian establishment did not welcome this development, and in the early 1980s, fearing a takeover of Canadian Pacific, it persuaded the federal government to table legislation limiting the participation of provincially owned corporations in the ownership of transportation companies. The general outcry this bill aroused in Quebec forced the Trudeau government to withdraw it, but the affair brought the overall reaction to the rise of Francophone businesses, especially when the Quebec government was involved, into the open.

Successive Quebec governments were concerned with strengthening private financial institutions that belonged to Francophones. The Parti Québécois, once in power, placed particular emphasis on this question, and besides giving new direction to the Caisse de Dépôt, it allowed the Desjardins movement to engage in new financial activities, opposed the sale of the Crédit Foncier to non-Quebec interests, launched the Quebec Stock Savings Plan and promoted the deregulation — and consequently the increased concentration — of financial institutions, as we will see in chapter 35.

The existence of the Caisse de Dépôt also helped resolve the old problem of financial syndicates. For a long time, Quebec government loans had been underwritten primarily by Anglophone brokerage houses, grouped into financial syndicates that were able to impose conditions on the loans and exert pressure on the government. Through the resources of the Caisse de Dépôt and the growth of Francophone institutions such as the caisses populaires, the government was able to free itself from the hold of the syndicates in the 1970s and diversify its borrowing.

Aid to Business

Beginning in the 1960s, the Quebec government increased and diversified its assistance to private enterprise, especially in the manufacturing sector. Municipalities had long played an important role in this area and continued to do so, setting up industrial commissions and industrial parks. However, the Quebec government was a much more active player in this area during the period, developing new programs and making more funds available. It sought to supplement federal government programs, of which there were many, rather than compete with them.

Most government intervention was aimed at promoting investment that created new jobs. Beginning in 1971, Quebec left it up to the federal government to provide direct subsidies and concentrated on supporting investment through such measures as no-interest loans, loan guarantees, and equity participation; like Ottawa, it also offered tax breaks. Government aid involved areas other than investment as well. The Department of Industry and Commerce made agents and advisers available to firms, export initiatives were supported by Quebec delegations in foreign countries as well as by the federal Export Development Corporation, and the Centre de Recherche Industrielle du Québec (CRIQ — Quebec industrial research centre) helped manufacturers develop new products. The government report *Bâtir le Québec* took note of the more than 160 programs or forms of assistance Quebec companies, especially manufacturing companies, had access to in 1978. These programs were administered by more than eighty granting bodies, including a variety of government agencies, and gave these bodies considerable scope for intervention.

Governments of the period also differed from their predecessors in seeking to modernize Quebec business and change the industrial structure. The initial spearhead of this new strategy was the Société Générale de Financement (SGF), established in 1962. Owned jointly by the government and private interests, it brought the government into partnership with financial institutions as well as the general public. Its purpose was to set failing Quebec companies back on their feet and develop new industries, and during the 1960s it intervened in many areas, from automobile assembly to food production. But its efforts were too scattered and it had management problems, which led to disappointing results and prompted a major reorganization in 1971. The SGF then came under exclusive government control with the goal of developing and restructuring firms in specific sectors; it also undertook joint ventures with large private companies. Turned into a virtual conglomerate, the SGF discovered the path to profitability and became one of the largest Quebec industrial corporations in the 1970s. Aid to Quebec business, and especially Francophone business, now became the responsibility of the Société de Développement Industriel (SDI), which acted as an investment bank and management consultant. It was also responsible for promoting changes in the industrial structure by supporting the development of the heavy industrial and capital goods sectors.

As the 1980s began, the Quebec government was looking for ways to broaden the scope of its intervention. It set up programs to aid investment in tourism infrastructure and paid greater attention to small business and its management, innovation and marketing problems.

Managing the Labour Force

Government economic policy also includes the economic impact of social measures, especially those affecting the labour force. The most significant such measure in Quebec during the period was the educational reform of the 1960s, which had clear economic goals. These included raising the overall level of skills in the labour force, developing vocational education to meet the demand for technically skilled workers, and encouraging the training of Francophone managers through higher education. In addition, adult education served to help the generations that had suffered from the slow development of earlier periods catch up.

The government also grappled with high unemployment through much of the period. Throughout the 1970s and 1980s, job creation programs proliferated, but many of the jobs were seasonal or temporary and the programs were only partially successful.

Federal Policies and the Economy

While the Quebec government was intervening in a much broader range of areas than before, the federal government also made its presence felt in a variety of ways. The Canadian government carries considerable weight in the Quebec economy. Tens of thousands of federal public servants live and work in Quebec. Some crown corporations, including Air Canada and Canadian National, have their head offices in Montreal. The federal government invests in Quebec, purchases goods and services, and makes large transfer payments. But it is mainly through policy that it influences the economy's direction. In fact, all federal policies have a direct or indirect effect on Quebec. A complete analysis of federal economic policy is beyond the scope of this book, and we will only highlight a few aspects of it.

The Canadian government had a clearly defined goal: economic integration. It wanted to develop a healthy, harmonious domestic market in which all the regions of the country would participate, each with its own areas of specialization, complementing those of other regions. The reality was quite different. Some provinces — principally Ontario — were dominant, while the others were dependent. For federal politicians in the 1960s, the challenge was to deal with these inequalities, or regional disparities as they were called. Starting in 1957, Ottawa made equalization payments in an effort to redistribute federal funds to the poorer provinces, including Quebec. In 1969, it established the Department of Regional Economic Expansion, which provided subsidies for investment in designated regions, partially replacing a variety of tax incentives instituted earlier. These measures were designed to ensure that all Canadians received the same level of government services and to stimulate development in depressed areas. The results were not encouraging. Redistribution was not able to offset the concentration of economic activity in Ontario, which was promoted by so-called national policies whose goals and standards primarily met Ontario's needs.

Canadian economic integration soon became synonymous with federal centralization, especially after the election of Pierre Elliott Trudeau in 1968. The federal government now intervened on all fronts, frequently cooperating with the provinces but engaging in many confrontations with them as well. In the energy sector, for example, Ottawa carried on a dispute with the Atlantic provinces over the control of offshore oil resources and imposed its National Energy Program on the west.

Ottawa was also active in trying to define Canada's external economic relations. One of the major questions was the growth of foreign control in the private sector. Indifference and passivity on this question in the 1960s gave way to a new awareness of the problem, which led to the creation of the Foreign Investment Review Agency (FIRA) in 1973.

Another question with major implications for Quebec was the effect of foreign competition on traditional manufacturing industries such as textiles, clothing and shoes, which became known as soft sectors. To slow down the decline of these industries, the government decided to restrict imports by imposing quotas on the major exporting countries. At the end of the period, however, the Canada-U.S. free trade agreement along with new GATT agreements aimed at liberalizing international trade and reducing tariff barriers limited the government's room for manoeuvre in this area.

The presence of Trudeau as prime minister and many Francophone ministers in the cabinet was in some ways a boon to Quebec. "French Power" had economic dimensions and resulted in lucrative contracts going to Francophone Quebec companies. However, this did not mean that Ontario was no longer the most favoured province, as it had been for so long. Even short-term policy was adjusted to Ontario's needs rather than Quebec's. For example, Ottawa's emphasis on fighting inflation starting in the mid-1970s led to much higher interet rates and increased unemployment. Quebec was hit doubly hard, because its unemployment rate was significantly higher than Ontario's and the financial base of Quebec companies was weaker.

Many analysts have noted that federal policies were among the factors contributing to the deterioration of Quebec's position in the Canadian economy. Huge transfer payments could not make up for the negative effects of overall policies and served only to make the Quebec economy more dependent.

Too Much Government in the Economy?

Throughout the 1960s and 1970s, growing government intervention in the economy enjoyed wide public support. It even came to be viewed as government's role to solve the problem when a company or region found itself in difficulty. Protests against excessive government intervention were heard in business organizations, but few people outside these circles paid much attention.

The 1980s, however, brought a challenge to the certitudes of the preceding decades. Keynesian policies seemed more difficult to apply when governments were forced into severe budget restraint, had very little room to manoeuvre and ran large deficits. In addition, Keynesianism was designed to deal with short-term fluctuations and offered no solutions to long-term problems such as chronic high unemployment or the aging of the industrial structure. The serious recession of 1981-82 highlighted these weaknesses.

Inspired by the resurgence of conservatism in the United States after the election of Ronald Reagan, Canadian and Quebec business circles and a growing number of politicians called for reduced government intervention. They wanted entire sectors to be deregulated and publicly owned corporations to be privatized. Even the Parti Québécois, long the standardbearer of interventionism, took a new approach and developed policies that were more supportive of private enterprise. This new direction was strengthened by the Liberal election victory of 1985. The new Bourassa government even had a minister specifically responsible for privatization and deregulation, and he sold off some government-owned corporations. Similar developments took place on the federal level after the election of Brian Mulroney's Conservatives in 1984.

The recession of 1981-82 was thus a turning point, marking the end of an era and the beginning of an overhaul of the strategies developed during the Quiet Revolution. The new Francophone bourgeoisie, made strong by two decades of government support, felt ready to stand on its own two feet.

CHAPTER 33

INDUSTRIAL DECLINE

In the postwar period, manufacturing, construction and natural resources were extremely important components in Quebec's economic growth. They remained major elements after 1960, but their share of overall economic activity tended to fall, while Quebec's position in relation to the rest of Canada deteriorated. A phenomenon that became known as deindustrialization was showing up throughout the industrialized world. The rise of the service sector was one reason for the relative decline of the industrial and resource sectors, but developments within those sectors were also involved: a redistribution of production on a world scale and relocation of industry.

The Relative Decline of Manufacturing

Quebec manufacturing underwent a growth spurt in the first half of the 1960s (table 1). It accounted for 450,000 jobs at the start of the decade, and this figure rose quickly to 500,000 in 1965. A period of relative stability followed this rapid increase, and for the next fifteen years, employment fluctuated between 500,000 and 540,000. In twenty years, the value of production jumped from $7 billion to $50 billion (the figures for the 1970s were obviously swollen by inflation). The recession of the early 1980s hit hard, as Quebec lost tens of thousands of manufacturing jobs, many companies went bankrupt and others had to cut production drastically. Quebec was slow to recover from the impact of the recession.

Throughout the 1950s, about 29 per cent of Quebec's jobs were in the manufacturing sector, and this level was maintained through the industrial growth of the early 1960s. Decline began in 1966, and manufacturing's share of employment fell to 26.3 per cent in 1971 and 23 per cent by 1980. The same trend could be seen in output figures: the manufacturing sector contributed 30 per cent of Quebec's gross domestic product in 1961, but only 26 per cent in 1970 and 23 per cent in 1976.

Table 1
Manufacturing in Quebec, 1961-82

Year	Number of establishments	Number of employees production	total	Shipments ($ million)	Value added ($ million)
1961	11,217	319,231	452,543	7,022	3,332
1962	11,102	326,257	459,926	7,589	3,583
1963	10,980	328,495	462,014	8,073	3,724
1964	11,097	342,907	479,518	8,774	4,125
1965	10,952	356,780	499,177	9,492	4,517
1966	10,877	368,450	516,154	10,465	4,949
1967	10,772	372,408	524,688	10,966	5,088
1968	10,513	370,537	521,250	11,743	5,445
1969	10,466	379,869	529,027	12,810	5,968
1970	10,176	369,896	514,150	13,084	6,092
1971	10,135	366,198	508,591	13,833	6,406
1972	10,025	377,802	517,878	15,092	7,021
1973	9,947	391,518	533,759	17,464	8,026
1974	9,974	398,857	541,500	22,397	10,045
1975	9,375	394,333	532,932	23,967	10,459
1976	9,020	386,985	524,632	25,803	11,223
1977	8,476	367,207	500,098	28,010	12,395
1978	9,701	386,664	523,452	33,146	14,431
1979	10,381	395,810	535,742	39,117	17,096
1980	10,740	389,901	527,925	44,603	19,177
1981	10,915	386,698	525,839	50,139	21,201
1982	10,753	348,333	482,337	49,179	19,520

Source: Statistics Canada, cat. no. 31-205.

While not peculiar to Quebec, the relative decline of manufacturing was somewhat sharper there, and Quebec's share of Canadian manufacturing output decreased over the period.

Industry in Transformation

The process of rapid modernization of Quebec industry that had begun in the 1950s intensified after 1960. It took several forms: increasingly sophisticated and automated machines, computerization of administrative functions and even a completely new kind of industrial architecture.

These upheavals were felt first in the labour force. Increased automation often resulted in fewer jobs, and a skilled technician could now supervise a machine that performed operations formerly carried out by dozens of employees.

Modernization also meant plant relocation. Old factories located in old industrial districts were no longer suitable. Access to major highways, rather than to railways and waterways, became an important factor in factory location. In some cases, old plants could accommodate new machinery; often, however, companies preferred to move, so that there was mass relocation of manufacturing industry. This was especially conspicuous in the Montreal area, where the old manufacturing districts along the Lachine Canal in the west end and along the St. Lawrence River in Hochelaga and Maisonneuve in the east end were gradually left behind for new sites in the suburbs. New plants were built in industrial parks in suburban municipalities such as Dorval, Saint-Laurent, Anjou and Montreal North, located close to major highways. Even the long-established clothing industry, which for decades had been crowded into the downtown area, migrated to modern buildings in new districts. A similar decentralization occurred in Quebec City, where the old industrial districts on the banks of the St. Charles River were abandoned for new sites along Charest and Hamel boulevards, and in other urban centres.

Table 2
Percentage of Total Gross Value of Quebec Manufacturing Production for Each Group of Industries, 1929-1945

Rank in 1982	Rank in 1960	Category	1960	1970	1978	1982
1	1	Food and beverages	17.8	18.2	17.4	17.9
4	2	Primary metals	11.7	8.2	8.4	6.9
3	3	Paper and allied industries	10.7	10.5	10.2	10.2
8	4	Clothing	6.9	7.0	6.1	5.0
10	5	Textiles	6.2	6.3	4.9	4.2
6	6	Chemicals and chemical products	5.7	5.6	5.8	6.5
2	7	Petroleum and coal products	5.3	3.9	8.8	11.3
7	8	Metal fabricating	5.1	6.0	5.6	6.3
5	9	Transportation equipment	5.0	6.8	6.5	6.9
9	10	Electrical appliances and equipment	4.7	5.7	4.3	4.5
11	11	Printing, publishing, etc.	3.5	3.4	3.6	3.9
12	12	Wood	2.8	2.7	4.1	3.1
18	13	Tobacco	2.6	1.8	1.3	1.4
15	14	Nonmetallic mineral products	2.5	2.4	2.5	1.9
16	15	Miscellaneous	2.1	1.9	2.0	1.7
20	16	Leather	1.8	1.6	1.0	0.9
17	17	Furniture and fixtures	1.7	2.1	1.8	1.5
13	18	Machinery	1.5	2.0	2.4	2.8
19	19	Knitting mills	1.5	2.1	1.3	1.2
14	20	Rubber	0.9	2.1	2.0	2.0

Source: Statistics Canada, cat. nos. 31-203 and 31-205.

Industrial modernization sometimes had negative consequences. Faced with the need to relocate, a company's management often wondered whether it was necessary to stay in Quebec. The westward shift of economic activity and Ontario's vigorous growth prompted many companies to move closer to their main markets by closing their out-moded factories in Quebec and replacing them with new ones in Ontario. Quebec lost a large number of plants and industrial jobs, especially in the 1970s, and this was a major reason for the relative decline of Quebec industry. The large degree of American control over Canadian manufacturing also contributed to the migration of industry out of Quebec.

The need to modernize also speeded up concentration in industries where there were still a large number of middle-sized firms in 1960, as the cost of modernization and the increase in productivity that resulted from it led inexorably in that direction. The result was that a number of traditional plants closed and much larger ones were built in such industries as sawmills, dairy processing and baked goods.

Small factories did not disappear from the industrial scene, however. Many of them remained in the clothing, furniture, wood products, printing and food processing industries. In other industries such as mechanical engineering and toolmaking, small plants survived on a different basis: as highly specialized operations with a very specific niche, doing most of their business through subcontracts from large companies. In 1978, 80 per cent of industrial establishments still had fewer than fifty employees, but these companies accounted for only a little over 20 per cent of manufacturing jobs and 15 per cent of the value of production.

Industrial Structure

To what extent did the changes in the manufacturing sector transform Quebec's industrial structure?? The distribution of production according to industrial group (table 2) shows elements of continuity. Overall, non-durable consumer goods and light industry still occupied a larger place than durable goods and heavy industry. Food and beverages remained in first rank with 17 to 18 per cent of the value of production, followed by paper and allied products with 10 per cent. But despite this apparent stability, there were significant changes, of which the most notable and noted was the decline of traditional light industries or "soft sectors." There was a sharp decrease in the share of production accounted for by leather, textiles, clothing and tobacco — old industries that began to face a variety of problems in the 1960s, and even earlier in some cases.

Firms in these industries faced increasingly tough foreign competition. The shoe, clothing, and textile industries had prospered in Quebec for many years by relying on cheap labour and tariff protection. But with industrialization in many Third World countries, where wages were much lower than in Quebec, products that were very inexpensive even with the tariff barriers could be brought onto the Canadian market. Quebec firms tried to fight this competition by having Ottawa impose quotas on imports from the countries involved, but this was only a temporary solution.

Inefficient management was another problem. The traditional family business, still common in these industries, did not always succeed in adjusting to changes in the industrial environment. Other difficulties had to do with aging plants and lack of access to the capital required to modernize them. While the most financially solid companies, such as Dominion Textile, were able to undertake a systematic modernization program, such a program involved shutting down the most outdated and least profitable plants. In some cases, the low end of the market, consisting of mass-produced items, had to be left to foreign companies, while Quebec firms concentrated on more specialized segments of the market or developed new products. In the end, even though some industrial groups and firms were able to make the changes the situation required, factory closings were a common feature of the 1970s and 1980s.

A government study found that between 1961 and 1976, "the most significant structural change...was without question the growing share accounted for by metal-processing industries, including industries producing intermediate products (primary metal processing, metal products) and those producing finished products (machinery, transportation equipment, electrical appliances." Government policies designed to strengthen these industries undoubtedly contributed to this development. The availability of cheap electricity was also a significant factor, especially for the aluminum industry, which increased its production capacity during the period.

New industries were also emerging. Automobile assembly, which had never been part of the Quebec scene, appeared with the opening of a General Motors assembly plant in Sainte-Thérèse near Montreal and the creation of the short-lived Société de Montage Automobile (SOMA), which assembled Renaults. Plants making snowmobiles opened in response to their growing popularity in the 1960s. While many of these plants subsequently closed, the Bombardier company continued to grow, and became one of the first Francophone-controlled Quebec industrial giants. The rise of the new electronics industry encouraged new companies to spring up and old plants to redirect their production. Aeronautics, concentrated in the Montreal area, experienced a surge, although the industry was heavily cyclical.

However, heavy industry in Quebec became stronger only in relative terms. Quebec trailed far behind Ontario in this sector. Analysts all emphasized that Quebec did not attract enough highly productive companies in the most innovative industries, and traditional sectors remained a major element of Quebec's industrial structure.

Construction

Construction was an important area of economic activity. Between 1961 and 1976, investment in new construction represented 15 per cent of Quebec's gross domestic product.

Public investment, of greater importance in Quebec than in Ontario, was largely responsible for the prominence of the construction sector. During the 1960s, the government financed the construction of many polyvalent high schools, cegeps and university buildings and the expansion of a number of hospitals. It invested in the construction of many government buildings, creating a whole new complex in the area around the National Assembly in Quebec City and building new buildings in Montreal and regional administrative centres as well. The federal government was also active in this area, building the new CBC building and the Guy Favreau complex in Montreal along with post offices and administrative centres. Large investments were made in transportation infrastructure, including the Montreal subway system, repair and modernization of the road system, and construction of the Trans-Canada Highway, the Eastern Townships Autoroute, the North Shore Autoroute, the Décarie and Ville-Marie expressways in Montreal, the highways surrounding Montreal and Quebec City, the Louis-Hippolyte Lafontaine Tunnel and the Pierre Laporte Bridge. The federal government built Mirabel Airport and upgraded other airports and harbours. Hydro-Quebec also made large investments, notably at its huge sites on the Manicouagan and Outardes rivers on the North Shore and later James Bay. Expo 67 and the 1976 Olympic Games brought substantial public investment to Montreal.

Private construction for commercial and industrial purposes was another important facet of the construction sector, and here too there was heavy investment throughout the 1960s and 1970s, although not as much in Quebec as in Ontario. Montreal's new downtown, with its many skyscrapers, was built during these two decades. The modernization and relocation of industrial enterprises stimulated the construction of new buildings, as did the growth of the shopping centres that began to dot the suburbs.

In twenty years, the built environment in Quebec was completely transformed. Nonresidential construction represented about 70 per cent of new investment. The rest went into housing, which also grew rapidly, although here too the upsurge was smaller than Ontario's. According to a study by the Office de Planification et de Développement du Québec, a major reason for the investment gap between the two provinces has been the weaker performance of the housing sector in Quebec.

Construction generally employs local labour and uses locally produced raw materials. As a result it has a large economic impact, so that in times of economic slowdown governments seek to revive the economy by stimulating construction. Thus, the first Bourassa government

A skyscraper under construction in downtown Montreal, 1961. (G. Lunney, Montreal *Star*, National Achives of Canada, PA-129265)

launched road-building projects after it took power in 1970, and the Lévesque government followed the same strategy with its "Corvée-habitation" program.

However, construction continued to be subject to major cyclical fluctuations. The years 1964-66 and 1973-76 were times of intense activity, the first associated with Expo 67 and the second with James Bay and the Olympics, but they were followed by periods of marked slowdown. There was also considerable instability in the construction sector. While a few large companies worked on the major construction projects, there were also a multitude of small contractors, many of them financially shaky. The situation was also highly unstable for construction workers, especially labourers and unskilled workers. Between 1961 and 1981, the proportion of the Quebec labour force working in construction fell from 7 to 5 per cent.

Natural Resources

The resource sector continued to make strides during the 1960s and 1970s, as it had during the postwar period. At the end of the period, however, it encountered major difficulties that called into question the direction the sector had taken since 1945.

Electricity is a good example of this process. From the end of the war on, demand rose quickly. Hydro-Quebec was entirely responsible for meeting that demand, and the utility raced to produce enough hydroelectric power to keep up with it by building ever larger power stations at increasingly distant sites. There were three large projects in the 1960s and 1970s: the Manicouagan-Outardes project; Churchill Falls, which although located in Labrador sold its hydro power almost exclusively to Hydro-Quebec; and James Bay.

Since these large power stations were able to meet Quebec's peak demand, which occurred in winter, Quebec had a surplus in summer, and the excess electricity was sold to the United States. Quebec sold increasing amounts of electricity to New York State and New England throughout the 1970s. These were sales of surplus power only: the government always refused to enter into contracts for firm power sales, which would mean exporting jobs. However, the concern with energy conservation spawned by the energy crisis, along with the recession, had the unexpected effect of slowing the growth of demand in Quebec. Production capacity soon outstripped electricity requirements, and during the 1980s Quebec broke with its long-established policy and began selling firm power to the Americans. The same factors led to postponement of plans to build new power stations.

Mining is not a major element of the economy as a whole, accounting for only 3 per cent of Quebec's gross domestic product, but it is quite important in some regions, especially the North Shore (iron ore), Abitibi (copper, zinc and gold), and to a lesser extent the Eastern Townships (asbestos) and the Gaspé (copper). Overall, it experienced an upsurge in the 1960s and 1970s, despite major cyclical variations and different rates of growth from one industry to another.

Iron ore was unquestionably Quebec's most important mineral resource. Iron mining had begun in Schefferville in the preceding period, and new mines were opened after 1960, notably at Lac Jeannine in 1961 and Mount Wright and Fire Lake in the 1970s. New mining towns such as Gagnon and Fermont sprang up, while other communities, such as Port-Cartier and Pointe-Noire, took shape where the ore was concentrated and shipped. For a time, the North Shore appeared to be a virtual El Dorado, and this made the collapse of the early 1980s all the more brutal. The worldwide surplus of iron ore production, worsened by the recession, led to the closing of Iron Ore's operations in Schefferville and the failure of SIDBEC-Normines. This setback did not mean the end of iron ore production in Quebec, but it signalled the end of the growth that had characterized the preceding three decades.

The production of copper and zinc, two metals that are often mined together, was on the rise in the 1960s. New mines opened in Abitibi and the towns of Matagami and Joutel grew up around them. During the 1970s and 1980s, production fell substantially. As in the case of iron ore, the opening of new mines in Third World countries created increased competition.

Gold mining followed a different pattern. Production declined steadily throughout the 1960s and 1970s, and many Abibiti mines closed. But the explosion in the price of gold in the early 1980s along with the recession gave gold mining a new lease on life. Prospecting resumed, stronger than ever, new mines came on stream, and old ones were reopened.

Output of asbestos, Quebec's other leading mineral product, remained high throughout the 1960s and 1970s, but afterwards it fell into a deep slump. Asbestos was hit not only by the effects of the recession of the 1980s but also by disfavour in the industrialized countries caused by reports that it was carcinogenic. In addition, new deposits were found in other countries, and Quebec lost its position as the world's leading producer.

In short, after three decades of expansion, Quebec's mining sector experienced some failures in the 1980s and had to make its way in an environment of worldwide overproduction of raw materials.

The forest sector is similar to mining in being strongly export-oriented but differs in that much more processing of forest products is done in Quebec. The primary forest industry — logging — has represented barely 1 per cent of gross domestic product. Mechanization, which began in the 1950s, continued on an even larger scale in the 1960s. The labour force was cut by almost 50 per cent, while productivity rose. The rules for distributing resources within the forest industry were completely reworked under a new policy adopted by the Quebec government. However, at the end of the period, the industry was threatened by severe overcutting and insufficient reforestation.

More significant for Quebec's economy are industrial activities deriving from forest resources. Pulp and paper and wood products make a substantial contribution to manufacturing production (table 2). Firms in these industries were subject to cyclical variations and experienced periods of both expansion and stagnation. They faced much stronger competition in the American market.

Thus, both manufacturing and the resource sector showed signs of weakness. Quebec's position in Canada and North America was deteriorating in a context of growing world competition.

CHAPTER 34
THE ADVENT OF AGRIBUSINESS

Agriculture completed the transition that began after the war, becoming ever more closely integrated into the market. The development of the agribusiness economy continued, so that the face of Quebec agriculture in the early 1980s was profoundly different from what it had been in the immediate postwar period. A number of features characterized this development, which occurred in other industrialized countries as well: a rural exodus; declining importance of agriculture in the economy; increased average farm size; higher total output; more specialized farms; and persistent problems of stability and income distribution.

Agribusiness

Integration into the economy had profound and lasting consequences. On the one hand, farmers were increasingly dependent on outside suppliers for their factors of production, including tractors, feed grain and fertilizer; on the other, they relied on large companies to sell their output. With the mechanisms linking them to the economy becoming more integrated and complex, farmers were no longer independent producers who could intervene directly and freely in the market.

Nonetheless, different farmers were in different situations, ranging from a degree of autonomy to almost total dependence. Marketing programs administered by the cooperatives and the Union des Producteurs Agricoles (UPA) allowed many producers to maintain some manoeuvring room in their relations with downstream concerns. However, other industries such as pork and broiling chickens were so vertically integrated that farmers sometimes supplied only the buildings — even the land had become useless. The animals and their feed were supplied by a company that often took care of the marketing as well.

Auction at a farm in Saint-Michel-de-Bellechasse, 1975. (Linda Walker, National Archives of Canada, PA-128926)

The most severe constraint was the cost-price squeeze. Farmers were caught between the prices they had to pay for the materials they needed for production and the prices they were paid for their products. Industrial prices tended to rise while farm prices were constantly being pushed down. The result was a constant gap, and when it was combined with a rise in interest rates, as occurred in the early 1980s, a very serious financial crisis could ensue. Purchases of machinery and land led to an ever increasing farm debt load, and farmers were constantly seeking some form of support for agricultural prices.

Farmers

The trend towards fewer farmers, already very strong in the 1950s, continued. The farm population was fading away: it dropped by more than 50 per cent in fifteen years and totalled only 200,000 in 1976. The agricultural labour force also declined sharply and numbered only 78,115, or 2.6 per cent of the total labour force, in 1981. But there was not enough agricultural work for even this drastically reduced labour force, so that employment off the farm remained important for about a third of all farm owners surveyed in the 1981 census (this proportion is overstated, as it includes those who had a regular job elsewhere and only ran a farm on the side).

Farmers did not form a homogeneous group. In 1970, a study divided Canadian farmers into three groups: one third were prosperous, one third "moderately well-off" and one third poor. The direction in which the

Farmers' demonstration. *(Le Journal de Montréal)*

economy was developing meant that farmers who were too small could not long survive. During these years, the government tried to redirect the surplus farm population into other kinds of work, but these programs had only mixed success and many former farmers ended up unemployed in the cities.

Farmers became even more heavily concentrated in the St. Lawrence Lowlands, and 74 per cent of the farm population lived in the Montreal-Quebec City-Sherbrooke triangle in 1976. Some regions had virtually no farmers; the Gaspé, for example, had only 1.3 per cent of the total.

Even if there were fewer farmers, farm unions became stronger. From the turn of the century on, farmers promoted their interests through two kinds of organizations: the cooperatives and the farmers' association, the Union des Cultivateurs Catholiques (UCC). But beginning in the 1950s, while cooperatives grew to resemble capitalist enterprises and confined their activity to the marketplace, the association became more active as a union.

The early 1960s saw a sharp rise in farm militancy. Membership in the UCC increased from 28,216 in 1960 to 43,448 in 1963, and then stabilized at that level. The UCC had every intention of gaining recognition for its new strength and set out to create more stable structures for itself. In 1963, it obtained an amendment to farm marketing legislation allowing unions to administer joint marketing programs and thus compete with the cooperatives. In 1972, it attained another of its goals when the government adopted the Farm Producers Act governing farm organizations. The same year, the farmers accepted the principle of compulsory dues by a 70 per cent majority. The UCC changed its name to the Union des Producteurs Agricoles (UPA); representing all Quebec farmers, it had become one of the strongest farm organizations in North America.

The rise in farm militancy also led to greater capacity to mobilize farmers, and starting in the 1960s there were farmers' demonstrations in Quebec City and Ottawa. Protests also took other forms, such as blocking roads and, in 1974, public slaughter of animals. Farmers were determined to be closely involved in developing policies that affected them.

Output

Agriculture accounted for less than 2 per cent of Quebec's gross domestic product. However, this did not reflect its real importance, because it was linked to a whole series of industrial activities both upstream and downstream, such as the manufacture of farm supplies and the processing of farm products into food. Taken together, these agriculture--related industries constituted a significant element in the economy.

There was not much change in the overall shape of Quebec's commercial farm output. The leading product, in both 1960 and 1980, was milk, accounting for one third of income, followed by pork, accounting for almost 20 per cent of income between 1976 and 1980, and eggs and poultry, with 13 per cent. Then came cattle with 10 per cent, and miscellaneous crops, which include potatoes, fruits, vegetables and tobacco. All in all, these commodities accounted for almost 90 per cent of income. Field crops, primarily hay and to a lesser extent oats, were also grown in Quebec; these products were used as livestock feed, and only a small proportion of output was marketed. The index of overall production, fixed at 100 in 1961, had risen to 115 by 1975. Thus, even with fewer and fewer farmers, output continued to increase.

But despite this relative stability in overall terms, there were problems in specific sectors during these years. The importance of dairy production lay in the fact that since the late nineteenth century it had been the surest way for farmers to guarantee financial return. This made them very sensitive to anything that could affect the industry. Chronic overproduction led the federal government to establish the Canadian Dairy Commission in 1966. Since then, dairy production has been regulated through a supply management system assigning a quota to each producer.

Income from hog production rose. No longer associated with dairy production as it had been traditionally, the pork industry became a specialized branch of agriculture in its own right and grew quickly: the average herd increased from nineteen to 430 head between 1961 and 1981. It was also highly concentrated — farmers who owned herds of more than 1,100 head, a little less than 11 per cent of all producers, controlled 56 per cent of the total hog population. This was a long way from the few hogs that used to be found on every farm.

There was overproduction of eggs and broiling chickens. Ontario's resistance to allowing Quebec eggs and poultry onto the market led to the establishment of Canadian marketing boards. Structures of production also changed radically — small farmers lost ground to industrial poultry producers, and as in the case of pork, integration was accompanied by concentration.

Quebec cattle producers also sought to make changes. Most of Quebec's cattle were dairy cattle, and the beef industry, like the pork industry, was traditionally associated with dairy production. Attempts were made to stimulate the production of slaughter cattle, which meant higher--quality livestock and increased average weight. But there were obstacles to this development: competition from western Canada and the increasing cost of feeding the cattle.

Apart from animal feed, crops grown in Quebec included some specialized commodities that were marketed directly. While accounting for about 10 per cent of income overall, they were concentrated in certain regions and so became very important to the economies of those areas. This was the case with blueberries in the Lake St. John area and vegetables around Sherrington southeast of Montreal. Urbanization led to the decline of some kinds of farming, such as market gardening in Île Jésus and orchards in the Richelieu Valley. Others were endangered by changes in the market; for example, the trend away from cigarette smoking brought about a fall in tobacco production in the Joliette region, while chronically depressed world sugar prices led to the gradual disappearance of sugar beet farming around Saint-Hilaire east of Montreal.

As agriculture became integrated into the capitalist economy, the question of markets took on primary importance. Instead of trying to produce everything they needed for their own consumption, farmers had to rely on marketing one commodity. If the market turned sour, disaster could ensue: the farm would no longer cover its expenses and support the family. Farmers also faced other pressures related to overproduction in North American agriculture as a whole.

Farm products were sold first in Quebec, then in the rest of Canada and then in other countries. Growth required a constant search for new markets. During the 1960s and 1970s, in a context of overproduction in the dairy industry and intense competition in other branches of agriculture, the Quebec market seemed the most promising. Starting in the 1960s, Quebec sought greater agricultural self-sufficiency; other provinces followed a similar strategy. The resulting competition led the federal government to intervene to prevent trade wars among the provinces and regulate output.

Farms themselves were changing, becoming larger and more mechanized. So-called subsistence farms were disappearing while the remaining farms were becoming consolidated. In 1961, Quebec had 95,777 farms, with an average area of 60 hectares, while in 1981 there were 48,144 farms with an average area of 78 hectares.

Farms were generally better equipped than before. One indication of this development was the more than tenfold increase in average capitalization in twenty years, from $16,965 in 1961 to $196,665 in 1981 — well above inflation for the two decades. The number of tractors also increased markedly, from 0.7 to 1.9 per farm in twenty years. However, even though productivity rose considerably, Quebec was still behind other parts of North America in this regard.

The growth in productivity was partly due to progress in farmers' educational level. Increased access to education reduced the gap that separated farmers from other social groups. Dissemination of knowledge of new techniques was also facilitated by the opening of regional branches of the Department of Agriculture, the activities of cooperatives and other farm associations, and the heightened demands of buyers.

However, these changes masked the serious problem of unequal farm incomes. Integration into the market, the fight for outlets and the race for productivity all took place in a context of very harsh rivalries both in agriculture and in the economy in general, and only the most efficient farms could withstand the pressure on farm prices.

Farmers began to use increasingly complex equipment. (UPA)

Agriculture and the Government

Agriculture continued to be marked by substantial government intervention. It had three main facets: supporting farm prices, encouraging the production of particular commodities, and influencing farmers' practices. While the Quebec and federal governments agreed on the main goals, their priorities and the directions they sought to give to agricultural development were sometimes different.

In the early 1960s, the Quebec government's policies were still the traditional ones based on farm credit and subsidies. The government also began to be involved in marketing. But it found that more coherent policies were required, and in 1965 it set up a royal commission on agriculture in Quebec, the April Commission. The commission's report, published between 1967 and 1969, highlighted the main problems in the agricultural sector. It recommended measures to help make agriculture competitive, with the government taking the lead in bringing about the required changes. Potential outlets were to be identified and incomes stabilized through marketing programs.

Even before 1960, Quebec policy had sought to strengthen the profitable segments of agriculture, and this goal was pursued more strongly in the 1970s. The various small-scale subsidy programs were abandoned and efforts were concentrated on prosperous agricultural regions. A consistent policy of trying to improve marketing was maintained despite successive changes of government. The government's concern with having Quebec farm products occupy a larger share of the domestic market led to a number of initiatives: the 1963 reorganization of the Office des Marchés Agricoles, which had been set up in the late 1950s; establishment of the Société Québécoise d'Initiative Agro-alimenataire (SOQUIA) in 1975; and meetings on the agriculture and food sector in the late 1970s. While in the 1960s the main concern was with marketing existing output, in the 1970s there was a push to diversify production to meet more varied needs and stimulate food-processing industries. Agricultural zoning legislation adopted in 1978 was aimed at protecting the most fertile land from speculation and keeping it in production in areas around cities, especially Montreal.

The federal government was not as clear about the direction it wanted Canadian agriculture to take. It was caught between pressure from eastern and western farmers, and had to intervene to support farm prices and organize the marketing of dairy products, eggs and poultry. It tried as best it could to arbitrate conflicts among different provinces, all of which wanted to be self-sufficient in agriculture and market their products outside their borders. The government was also active in the area of farm credit. In 1967, it set up the Federal Task Force on Agriculture, which issued a report recommending a gradual decrease in farm subsidies. In the inflationary environment of the 1970s, however, its recommendations were not followed.

In the 1960s, major cost-sharing programs were set up with the provinces, including the Agricultural and Rural Development Act, adopted by Ottawa in 1961, and a crop-insurance program, which began in 1959.

By the end of the 1970s, agriculture had emerged as a relatively dynamic sector of the economy. Its role as a reserve of labour power declined as the excess agricultural population left the farms to live elsewhere. Market forces were dominant, forcing farmers to adapt and making government adjust to the new realities of agribusiness.

CHAPTER 35
A SERVICE ECONOMY

The service sector has played an increasing role in the economies of all industrialized countries, and this process is a characteristic feature of what is termed postindustrial society. In Quebec, the process occurred extremely rapidly after 1960, to the point where the service sector occupies a larger share of the economy than in Canada as a whole or most other countries. Many writers regard the excessive growth of the service sector as a serious problem, because it indicates that the other two sectors of the economy, resources and especially manufacturing, are increasingly weak.

The growth of Quebec's service sector was already very evident in the postwar period and continued after 1960. The activities that make up the service sector accounted for 57 per cent of Quebec's gross domestic product in 1961, 66 per cent in 1981 and close to 71 per cent in 1983. The proportion of the labour force involved in service activities also increased, from 52 per cent in 1961 to close to 63 per cent in 1981 (table 1).

The service sector is highly disparate. A distinction is often made between dynamic services and traditional and nonmarket services. Dynamic services are activities with close ties to other sectors of production. These include financial activities, transportation and communication. Traditional and nonmarket services have fewer spinoff effects and include commerce, public administration and sociocultural, commercial and personal services. Over the period, traditional and nonmarket grew much faster than dynamic services. Thus, the growth of the service sector was a sign not so much of the maturity of Quebec's economic structure as of serious deficiencies.

Low productivity had long been characteristic of the service sector and technological progress had had little impact on it, but major changes took place after 1960. A wide variation in kinds of employment is also characteristic of the sector. Thus, while the service sector includes highly skilled, well-paid professionals such as doctors, university professors, lawyers and engineers, it contains much larger numbers of low-skill,

Table 1
Quebecers Aged 15 and Over Working in
Service Activities, 1961-81

	1961		1971		1981	
	No. of workers	*% labour force*	*No. of workers*	*% labour force*	*No. of workers*	*% labour force*
Transportation, communication & other utilities	161,268	9.1	171,785	7.7	234,495	7.6
Commerce	248,038	14.3	294,595	13.1	472,135	15.2
Finance, insurance & real estate	62,163	3.5	90,570	4.0	146,320	4.7
Sociocultural, commercial & personal services	350,864	19.8	521,500	23.3	876,310	28.3
Public administration and defence	99,194	5.6	140,010	6.2	217,275	7.0
Service sector total	921,527	52.0	1,218,460	54.3	1,946,535	62.8
Total labour force	**1,768,119**	**100.0**	**2,242,840**	**100.0**	**3,100,425**	**100.0**

Source: Censuses of Canada

low-paid workers: office employees, housecleaners, restaurant servers and others. These are also the occupations where women workers tend to be concentrated. During the period, work in the service sector was heavily affected by the technological revolution. The advent of computers and rapid communications systems changed many job descriptions and reduced personnel requirements considerably, especially in administrative work.

The public and parapublic sectors account for a significant share of service activity, but there is also a large private sector, made up mostly of small and middle-sized businesses. Many service sector activities require little investment, which makes entry easy for a large number of small entrepreneurs. However, concentration appeared here as well, and it increased significantly in the 1970s and 1980s.

The service sector is so vast and complex that it is not possible to deal with it in a single chapter. Some of its components, such as government activity, education, culture and social services, are examined in more detail elsewhere. The following pages provide an overview of the role of services in the economic structure.

The Financial World

Finance, insurance and real estate activities are key elements of Quebec's economic structure. Throughout the 1960s and 1970s, their share of GDP remained between 11 and 12.5 per cent. Their share of total employment was smaller, but it was growing, from 3.5 per cent in 1961 to 4.7 per cent in 1981. These figures do not convey the full significance of financial institutions (real estate is not examined here). They channel a large proportion of savings, act as intermediaries among individuals, companies and the government, and often play a determining role in production.

The expansion of the financial sector was due to a number of factors, notably the growth and transformation of Quebec's economy between 1960 and 1981 and the improved standard of living and increase in personal income, which meant that more Quebecers had personal savings. Beginning in the 1970s, with higher levels of education and economic information, Quebecers became more aware of the variety of financial products available and the money that could be earned through them. High inflation contributed to this awareness as well. In addition, tax shelters established over the years by governments, such as the Registered Retirement Savings Plan (RRSP) and the Registered Home Ownership Savings Plan (RHOSP), created reservoirs of capital managed by financial institutions. Contributions to the Quebec Pension Plan administered by the Caisse de Dépôt et Placement constituted a similar pool of capital. Governments intervened substantially in financial markets, primarily by borrowing heavily. The availability of capital also led to an expansion of credit to individuals and firms.

Long dominated by the chartered banks and insurance companies, the financial sector had become more diversified since the war. This trend continued throughout the 1960s. Near-banks, such as savings banks, credit unions and trust companies, accounted for a steadily growing share of the assets of financial institutions, as did investment houses. There was also a significant trend towards vertical and horizontal corporate concentration in the 1960s and 1970s.

Despite the expansion of its financial sector, Montreal was losing its position as Canada's main financial centre to Toronto. Montreal's decline had been underway for a long time, but it became much more pronounced after 1960, as head offices moved away and financial activity grew in Toronto. Montreal was reduced to the role of financial metropolis of Quebec and intermediary for the large Toronto institutions.

Banks. There were two major reforms of the Canadian banking system during the period. In 1967, Parliament allowed the chartered banks to enter new fields of activity, making them better able to resist competition from the near-banks and even increase their market share. In 1980, the very tight controls that had made the banking sector almost completely closed to foreign institutions were loosened, so that foreign banks were authorized, within limits, to set up Canadian branches.

The Big Five English Canadian banks still dominated the scene, but other banks came and went. The two French Canadian banks merged, the Industrial Acceptance Corp. became the Continental Bank (later Lloyds Bank Canada), and six new Canadian banks were set up in the west (two of them failed in 1985). As well, fifty-seven foreign banks came into Canada in the first half of the 1980s. In 1960, the banks' total assets

Automatic banking machines provide banking services twenty-four hours a day. (*Le Journal de Montréal*)

were \$17 billion; twenty-five years later, they were \$421 billion, of which 84 per cent was controlled by the five largest institutions.

The Big Five were not as clearly dominant in the Quebec market, where the operations of the Francophone banks were concentrated. These banks grew substantially, especially the smaller of the two, the Provincial Bank, which successively absorbed the Banque Populaire (formerly the Banque d'Économie de Québec) in 1970, then the Unity Bank of Toronto in 1976, and finally, in 1979, Laurentide Financial Corp. of Vancouver. It also reached a merger agreement with the Banque Canadienne Nationale, which resulted in the formation of the National Bank of Canada in 1980. The integration of these two institutions operating in the same markets initially created serious problems, but in 1983 the new Francophone bank became profitable, and with $21 billion in assets in 1985 it was even able to acquire the Mercantile Bank, which was then in difficulty.

The share of Canadian banking assets held by Francophone banks varied between 6 and 7 per cent throughout the 1960s and 1970s, and then declined in the 1980s. Their presence in the Quebec market was much more substantial, but they had difficulty making a breakthrough in English Canada. In 1978, for example, they had only 10 per cent of the bank branches in Canada but 43 per cent in Quebec.

In Montreal, they were also in competition with the Montreal City and District Savings Bank, a unique financial institution that came to resemble a chartered bank more and more over the period. Its assets, which were only $258 million in 1960, totaled $5.6 billion in 1984. It played an important role in the mortgage market. In 1987, it became the Laurentian Bank of Canada.

The caisses populaires and the Desjardins movement. However, the most serious competition for the Francophone banks came from the caisses populaires. There were almost as many local caisses as there were bank branches in Quebec. By 1960, Quebec was dotted with 1,227 caisses grouped into ten regional unions. In 1984, while the number of caisses had gone up only slightly to 1,408, their membership had tripled (from 1,211,000 to 3,975,000) and their assets had skyrocketed from from $688 million to $20 billion.

Almost every Francophone Quebecer, man, woman and child, had an account in a caisse populaire. The strength of the Desjardins movement came from its deep roots in the population, based on institutions that were cooperatively structured and attentive to the needs of the community. However, it had to resolve the problems inherent in coordinating such a decentralized network. During the 1970s, the federations (as the regional unions had become) and the confederation (the new name for the central body) were shored up, a system linking the caisses was established, and customer service was standardized. In strengthening the central bodies and the their full-time, specialized staff, these measures reduced the autonomy of the members and local caisses.

The movement expanded not only through internal growth and rationalization but also by integrating other credit cooperatives that until then had remained independent. Beginning in 1978, the Confédération des Caisses d'Économie, which had operated in workplaces, some mutual aid cooperatives that were in difficulty, and the Fédération de Montréal des Caisses Desjardins, a dissident group founded in 1946, joined the Desjardins movement.

The Desjardins movement also embarked on a diversification program. As the movement's assets grew, the federations and the confederation, which kept some of the reserves of the local caisses, accumulated increasingly large sums of money and invested these funds in purely capitalist firms with a view to offering caisse members a range of financial services. The movement's two existing insurance companies were joined by two others, La Sauvegarde in 1962 and La Sécurité in 1963. Then followed a move into trust companies in 1963 with the Fiducie du Québec. During the 1970s, the leadership of the Desjardins movement took an additional step, deciding to intervene in sectors other than financial services and thus become more involved in influencing the direction of Quebec's economic development. This led to the creation of the Société d'Investissement Desjardins, which acquired interests in industrial corporations, in 1974, and the Crédit Industriel Desjardins, which offered loans to business, in 1975. Finally, the Caisse Centrale Desjardins was set up in 1981 to intervene in the money market.

By 1984, the Desjardins movement was much more than a grouping of local caisses — it had become a holding company with assets of more than $22 billion. While it still drew its strength from its more than 1,000 affiliated caisses and its millions of members, it also owned financial and industrial concerns.

Insurance. The insurance sector, traditionally one of the pillars of the financial system, underwent profound change. Life insurance was particularly affected. Consumers had long been attracted by the security it offered, but they discovered that it had disadvantages during periods of rapid inflation such as the 1970s and turned to other methods of saving. Life insurance companies lost some of their share of the market. The nature of their business changed; group insurance grew more quickly than individual, and term policies more quickly than whole life insurance. Life insurance companies also played more of a role in managing retirement and pension funds. Because of the large sums of capital they administered, these companies remained extremely important in the area of long-term investment, including government bonds, corporate financing and mortgages.

General insurance companies also operated in a highly competitive market, and one that had long been dominated by British and American firms. The establishment of the Régie de l'Assurance Automobile (automobile insurance board) forced them to reorient their operations somewhat. Protection for property damage resulting from automobile accidents and property insurance remained their main sectors of activity.

The main feature of the period was unquestionably the rise of Francophone insurance companies in Quebec, such as Assurance-Vie Desjardins, L'Industrielle and La Laurentienne in life insurance and the Commerce and Desjardins groups in general insurance. Like the Francophone banks and caisses, they operated essentially in the Quebec market where, according to a government survey, they collected 28.6 per cent of premiums in 1972 and 34 per cent in 1978 — considerably larger than their share of the market in Canada as a whole.

Trust companies. Trust companies grew dramatically after 1960 and gained a larger share of the financial market. Until then, they had mainly acted as trustees, managing private portfolios, administering estates, and keeping lists of corporate shareholders. But now they began to act as financial intermediaries, accepting deposits from individuals, even offering chequing accounts in some cases, and opening more and more branches to reach the public at large. Total assets of trust companies in Canada rose from $1.3 billion in 1960 to $58.5 billion in 1984.

In Quebec, the trust field was dominated by large Canadian companies such as Royal Trust and Montreal Trust. Francophone companies, while smaller, managed to make a breakthrough. Older ones — Trust Général du Canada (1902) and the Société Nationale de Fiducie (1918) — were joined by new companies like Fiducie Prêt et Revenu (1961) and the Fiducie du Québec (1963). As well, Francophones took control of Anglophone companies such as Montreal Trust and Guardian Trust.

The stock market. In 1960, there were two stock exchanges in Montreal, the Montreal Stock Exchange and the Canadian Stock Exchange. Shares of large companies were traded on the Montreal exchange, established in 1874, while the Canadian exchange, founded in 1926, specialized in new companies and middle-sized businesses. However, the Canadian Stock Exchange did not have a very good reputation, and in an effort to make financial markets healthier it merged with the Montreal exchange in 1974.

The stock market had ups and downs, but over the period as a whole it grew in terms of both volume and value of transactions. However, the Montreal-based exchanges declined in importance compared to the Toronto Stock Exchange. In 1963, 33 per cent of the value of share transactions in Canada was processed in Montreal, as compared to 62 per cent for Toronto and 5 per cent for Calgary and Winnipeg. By 1980, the Montreal Stock Exchange's share had tumbled to 11 per cent, while Toronto had 84 per cent. There was a reversal after 1980, and in 1984, the Montreal Stock Exchange had a 19 per cent share, while Toronto's share had declined to 76 per cent.

A number of factors converged to bring about Montreal's decline: the emergence of Toronto as the financial centre of the country; the fact that many American companies chose to list their shares only in Toronto; the departure from Montreal of many Anglophone individual and institutional investors; and the lack of Francophone interest in the stock market. The recovery of the Montreal Stock Exchange after 1980 was due partly to more innovative leadership but also to the changing attitudes of Francophones, more of whom were purchasing stocks. A determining factor in this regard was the establishment by the Quebec government of the Quebec Stock Savings Plan. This program made it easier for Francophones to become stockholders and also encouraged many middle-sized companies to be listed on the stock exchange, at least until the October 1987 crash dampened enthusiasm for the stock market. The Caisse de Dépôt also played a crucial role, carrying out some large transactions on the Montreal exchange.

The growth of the stock market helped securities brokers, who in addition to dealing in stocks and bonds played a key role in underwriting bond issues for private companies, governments, municipalities, and school and hospital boards. The concentration of the financial market in Toronto clearly worked to the advantage of large Canadian and even American brokerage houses. In 1984, only one of the fifteen largest brokerage companies, Lévesque Beaubien, was Francophone. However, the growth of the market in Quebec helped the Francophone brokerage houses. While remaining small by Canadian standards, these houses took a larger share of the Quebec market where their operations were concentrated.

Other institutions. The period 1960-85 saw the decline of the finance companies, institutions specializing in small loans at high interest rates, as consumer credit from other sources became widely available and a large majority of Quebecers had access to it. Two developments were significant here: banks became increasingly active in the area of consumer loans following the 1967 banking reform, and the use of credit cards — Chargex (later Visa) and MasterCard — became widespread in subsequent years.

There was also improvement in the possibilities for corporate financing. At the beginning of the period, difficulty in obtaining capital was often an obstacle to a company's growth. Small and middle-sized companies were generally at a disadvantage, especially if they were just starting out, had to carry out a major expansion, were owned by Francophones, or were located far from the big cities. Therefore, financial institutions were set up to help small and middle-sized Francophone companies and support regional development. One such group of institutions was the Sociétés d'Entraide Économique. Born in the Saguenay, they spread to other regions and grew spectacularly in the 1970s. However, they were shaken by a deep crisis in 1981 and had to completely reorganize, liquidating a large part of their assets. The government-backed Sociétés de Développement de l'Entreprise Québécoise (SODEQ), which were were supposed to provide venture capital to small business and obtained funds by granting tax deductions to investors, failed miserably. On the other hand, other companies seeking to provide venture capital and support new companies were set up on a firmer foundation. Most large financial institutions established subsidiaries for this purpose, among them Novacap, the Société d'Investissement Desjardins and Crédit Industriel Desjardins. The Quebec government also intervened in this area through the Société de Développement Industriel. At the end of the period, a commission of inquiry concluded that the problem for small business was no longer access to financing but rather chronic undercapitalization and, as a result, excessive debt.

Other types of financial institutions included mutual funds, whose popularity was growing.

Financial groups. There was a trend towards concentration that began to break down the barriers separating the subsectors making up the financial sector. Throughout much of the period, the Canadian and Quebec financial world was dominated by the theory of "four pillars," according to which the four basic financial operations — banking, insurance, trust and brokerage — were to be carried out separately by separate companies. However, in the early 1980s, there was a trend towards deregulation in both Canada and the United States, leading to one-stop financial shopping where the consumer could carry out banking transactions, buy insurance and sell shares all at the same time.

More significant than decompartmentalization has been the formation of financial groups with companies operating in separate but complementary sectors. The Desjardins movement is a good example of this process, and a number of Quebec Francophone groups have been established in this way. The largest one was built by the corporate acquisitor Paul Desmarais, who through Power Corporation came to control one of the large Canadian insurance companies, Great West Life, a trust company, Montreal Trust, and an investment and mutual fund company, Investors Group. Similiarly, the Laurentian Group of Quebec City acquired control of a number of insurance companies as well as the Montreal City and District Savings Bank and shares in various financial companies. Other groups — Prêt et Revenu, Sodarcan and Les Coopérants — are examples of the same phenomenon, although on a more modest scale.

French Canadian finance. In the period between 1960 and 1985, Francophones made a real breakthrough in the financial world. Many factors contributed to this development, including a significant rise in income for French-speaking Quebecers, higher levels of education, the rise of a new generation of managers, the impact of nationalism and the substantial support of the Quebec government and its agencies, especially the Caisse de Dépôt. The breakthrough did not develop out of thin air but was based on financial institutions such as the banks and caisses populaires that had been solidly established for decades and had a broad presence in the Quebec market. Francophone institutions modernized their structures and operations and were able to attract the much more substantial savings French Canadians now had at their disposal. However, their activities were still highly concentrated in Quebec, and despite several attempts they had difficulty making a breakthrough in English Canada.

By contrast, Anglophone financial institutions had long shown little interest in the Quebec market, and their reaction to the rise of Quebec nationalism was hesitancy and even confusion. In the early 1970s, however, there was a turnaround. Large Anglophone companies decided to adapt rather than resist, and they set out to win back the Quebec market through more far-reaching Francization of their operations and personnel in Quebec. By the end of the period, both through businesses they controlled themselves and as managers of Canadian companies, Francophones occupied a much more substantial position on the financial scene than they had in 1960.

Christmas shopping in a Montreal department store, 1961. (G. Lunney, National Archives of Canada, PA-151640)

Commerce

As it had in the postwar period, commercial activity represented 11 to 12 per cent of Quebec's GDP and employed 13 to 15 per cent of its labour force. The number of people employed in commerce almost doubled in twenty years, and the average annual growth rate was 3.3 per cent, only slightly lower than the postwar rate of 3.7 per cent.

In retail trade, sales rose from $4.2 billion to $14.3 billion between 1960 and 1976. Food stores accounted for the lion's share with one third of sales, followed by car dealers. At 9.8 per cent, car dealers showed the highest annual growth rate, as they had in the postwar period.

Rising personal incomes were only one factor in the growth in the commercial sector. Others included the replacement of domestic production by products bought outside the home, especially food and clothing; the spread of credit, first through instalment buying and then through credit cards; the development of advertising; more sophisticated marketing strategies; the speed with which some goods became obsolescent; and the proliferation of disposable products. All these factors converged to stimulate consumption, even overconsumption.

The overhaul of retail trade that had begun in the postwar period intensified after 1960. One of the most significant developments was the emergence of shopping centres, linked to suburban growth and increased use of cars. Quebec had fifty-five shopping centres in 1961; by 1975, the number had grown to 223. They are found both on the outskirts of large cities and in every middle-sized city: Saint-Hyacinthe, Drummondville, Sept-Îles and many others. They were a threat to the old downtown commercial streets, which had to redefine their purpose. In Montreal, the density of population in older neighbourhoods kept the commercial streets busy, and in the early 1980s, the city government brought in revitalization programs to give them new impetus.

The appearance of shopping centres changed as well. In the early 1960s, a shopping centre was simply a row of stores, each with an outside door, and it was generally small and designed to serve the surrounding neighbourhood. But beginning in the 1970s, a new style of shopping centre, a covered mall where all the activity was inside, became prevalent. Many shopping centres of the 1970s were also much larger and were intended to serve entire regions, with hundreds of stores, boutiques and restaurants and a cultural component. Yet another type of shopping centre also emerged, with stores in downtown office buildings; the prototype was Place Ville-Marie in Montreal.

In the 1960s, retailers continued to direct their marketing strategies to a homogeneous market, so that stores selling everything under the same roof were on the rise. Drug stores became discount centres, hardware

The Fairview shopping centre in Pointe-Claire. (*Le Journal de Montréal*)

stores sold home renovation supplies, giant supermarkets sprang up and department stores opened branches in the suburbs. In the 1970s, however, a new trend towards specialization and market segmentation took hold. Stores not only carried a specialized product line but also sought to attract a specific clientele, based on socioeconomic level (high end of the market, low end of the market), sex and age. Small stores began to attract a larger proportion of consumers at the expense of department stores.

During this period, chain stores also made headway, accounting for 18 per cent of retail sales in 1960 and 35 per cent in 1976. To resist competiton from the chains, independent retailers grouped together, either under the aegis of a wholesaler — Provigo, for example — or by forming purchasing and distribution cooperatives, such as Métro-Richelieu and Ro-Na. During the 1970s and 1980s, franchising also developed, not just in retailing but also in the restaurant business and other service activities.

Some Quebec chains reached a respectable size, through either internal growth or acquisitions. The first to do so in food retailing was Steinberg's, which gradually extended its operations from Montreal to other parts of Quebec and Ontario, and then to the United States. Steinberg's became involved in department stores, real estate and, for a time, manufacturing. Then came Provigo, the product of the 1969 merger of three regional wholesalers. Through a series of acquisitions, Provigo pulled itself up into first place in the retail food sector, at the same time buying chains of stores in other fields, including drug stores, sporting goods and catalogue retailing. Quebec companies also carved out a place for themselves in other retail sectors, but none of them reached the size of the food retailing giants and they faced competition from Ontario and U.S. companies. The

The Montreal metro. (*Le Journal de Montréal*)

composite nature of the retail trade accounts for this wide variation from sector to sector.

Transportation and Communication

Like other components of the service sector, transportation, communication and utilities (electricity, gas and water) represent a diverse group of activities. We will look mainly at transportation and communication. As a whole, this component accounted for 13.2 per cent of Quebec's GDP and employed 9.1 per cent of its labour force in 1961, while it accounted for 11.5 per cent of GDP and employed 7.6 per cent of the labour force in 1981.

Transportation. Cars had become common after the war, and their primacy grew after 1960. The proportion of households owning at least one car rose from 56 per cent in 1960 to 75 per cent in 1976, while the proportion of households with two or more cars, very small at the beginning of the period, had reached 15 per cent by 1976. Between 1960 and 1970, the number of vehicles on the road rose from 1.1 million to 3.2 million, including 2.6 million private cars. This development created a society that was virtually based on the automobile and organized its habitat and daily life around it. It also had specific effects on transportation as such.

During the Duplesis era, Quebec fell behind in developing and modernizing its road system. From 1960 until the mid-1970s, the government had to make enormous investments to catch up and respond to growing needs. Gravel roads were paved, most existing roads were widened and repaired, and a network of superhighways was built.

People's preference for cars has led them to have a negative view of public transportation. In the cities, mass transit riders are mainly the young and the elderly, except during rush hours when commuters ride to and from work. The deficits incurred by mass transit systems led to government intervention beginning in the early 1970s. The government provided subsidies, reorganized the sector, and set up regional transportation commissions.

The flexibility of road transportation also explains the success of trucking. With 373,768 vehicles in 1979, trucking is a complex sector that ranges from store delivery personnel to long-distance haulers, from thousands of owner-operators with one truck each to large companaies with hundreds of vehicles. As in other sectors, concentration was increasing.

Containers were a new development that revolutionized the transportation of goods in the 1960s. They offered increased flexibility, especially for overseas shipping, since the containers could be loaded onto boats or trains for long-distance hauling and then onto a truck for delivery to the final destination. In the 1970s, containers were a key factor in the revival of the port of Quebec City and later the port of Montreal.

Air transportation also played a larger role. The development of air freight was one factor in its growth, but the real revolution in this sector was the advent of mass air travel, made possible as aircraft of increased

Container shipping in the port of Montreal (Le Journal de Montréal)

size and range came on the market. The long-haul aircraft of the early 1960s, the DC-8 and Boeing 707, were replaced by the wide-bodied Boeing 747, DC-10 and L-1011. The new shorter-haul aircraft, the DC-9 and Boeing 727 and 737, were also markedly different from their predecessors. The number of scheduled flights and passengers rose quickly after 1960. The growing popularity of charter flights to holiday destinations made air travel more accessible than before. But the rise in oil prices in the late 1970s and the 1982 recession put a halt to the rapid growth of air travel and left the sector unsettled for a few years.

In Quebec, air transport was still dominated by Air Canada, but regional carriers also established a place for themselves. Québécair linked Montreal and Quebec City with the Abitibi, Saguenay, Lower St. Lawrence, Gaspé and North Shore regions. Québécair changed ownership several times and encountered serious problems in the early 1980s. It was taken in hand by the Quebec government, which sold it to a private company in 1986. Nordair, which served the Canadian north and some Ontario and Quebec towns and cities from its base in Montreal, showed strong growth and became the centre of a battle between Quebec, which wanted to merge it with Québécair, and the federal government. The result was that Ottawa integrated Nordair into Air Canada and then privatized it. Nordair and Québécair both wound up as part of CP Air, which itself became the main component of the new Canadian Airlines International.

Communication. Communication constitutes an important sector, and at almost 3 per cent its proportion of GDP is greater than that of agriculture or mining. The number of employees rose from 41,370 in 1971 to

66,250 in 1981. The largest employers were the telephone companies, followed by the post office and radio and television.

The world of communications was acutely affected by the technological revolution. With the introduction of computers, transistors, satellites and fibre optics, new equipment was used and information was transmitted in new ways. Both telephone switching and letter sorting became increasingly automated. Television alone underwent a large number of technological changes after 1960, including the introduction of colour, the use of tape instead of film, the downsizing of cameras, cable TV and the cable converter.

Broadcasting also became big business. Between 1960 and 1979, the number of television stations rose from nine to sixteen, and their operating revenues shot up from $4.4 million to $120 million. In the same period, the number of radio stations rose from forty-two to eighty-six and their revenues increased from $10.6 million to $77 million. Cable television companies, which were quite small in 1960, generated revenues of $61 million in 1979. The most profitable television company was Télé-Métropole, which until 1986 was the only private Francophone station operating in the rich Montreal market. In addition to the public networks, the CBC and Radio-Québec, there were private networks: Télémédia and Radio-mutuel in radio and TVA, Quatre Saisons and Toronto-based CTV in television. Other private groups controlling several stations and sometimes other media as well were formed. Thus, Télémédia, in addition to being involved in radio, also published mass-circulation magazines and invested in cellular telephones. Henri-Paul Audet, the owner of stations in Trois-Rivières and Sherbrooke, formed the Cogéco group; in Montreal, Jean Pouliot acquired CFCF and then founded Quatre Saisons. Vidéotron, founded in 1964 by André Chagnon, became the largest company in the cable television field by acquiring Quebec City's Télécable in 1978 and then Cablevision Nationale in 1980.

Newspapers are part of the media, even though statistics place them under industry (publishing) rather than communications. They too showed an increasing trend towards concentration. In 1968, Paul Desmarais acquired *La Presse*, which had long been owned by the Berthiaume-Du Tremblay family. In 1973 he added *Montréal-Matin*; however, he had to close it a few years later. His group also owns regional dailies. But the rising star was Pierre Péladeau, who began by owning neighbourhood weeklies, started *Le Journal de Montréal* in 1964 and then founded Québecor, a large printing and publishing group. A third group, Uni-Média, publishes weekly newspapers and purchased Quebec City's *Le Soleil*. It was owned by Jacques Francoeur before becoming part of the empire of Toronto financier Conrad Black. The concentration of English-language newspapers had repercussions in Montreal, where the Montreal *Star* closed down, leaving the Southam-owned *Gazette* as the only English-language daily.

Concentration was also evident in the telephone industry. In 1979, Bell Canada, its subsidiary Télébec, and the American-owned Québec-Téléphone, which served eastern Quebec, accounted for 99 per cent of telephones in Quebec. These companies enjoy a monopoly in the areas they serve and have benefited from the considerable increase in demand for telephone services. To meet it, they have invested in more automated equipment rather than create thousands of jobs for telephone operators.

In both the telephone industry and the media, technological changes increased the speed and volume of communications and ultimately changed their very nature, especially their cultural content. This fundamental change will be discussed later.

Sociocultural, Commercial and Personal Services

Clearly the largest component of the service sector is sociocultural, commercial and personal services, which accounted for 14 per cent of GDP in 1961, 21 per cent in 1971 and 24 per cent in 1981. The proportion of the labour force employed in these activities has been significant and rising — from 20 to 28 per cent over the same period (table 1).

Sociocultural services. Education, health and social services were the largest part of this subsector, together employing 8.7 per cent of the labour force in 1961 and 14.2 per cent twenty years later. The chapters on education and social policy will examine these services in more detail.

The number of people employed in entertainment and leisure activities was small but increasing. It rose from 9,944 in 1961 to 17,125 ten years later and 34,660 in 1981, reflecting the growth of these activities. Employment by religious organizations took a different direction as a result of the questioning of the role of the church in the 1960s, falling from 23,699 to 17,065. In the 1970s, there was a slight recovery to 21,735 in 1981.

Corporate services. Although representing a much smaller proportion of the labour force than sociocultural services, corporate services grew much more quickly. The number of people employed in this field doubled each decade, increasing from 25,601 in 1961 to 105,930 in 1981.

The number of people employed in accounting and engineering firms grew at an average annual rate of about 6 per cent, while lawyers' and notaries' offices grew at a 4.6 per cent rate. New kinds of services were emerging, such as management consulting and computer services, while security and investigative agencies grew considerably.

The growth in services of this sort was a reflection of the development of corporate culture, as companies increasingly called on experts to solve specific problems, and of profound changes in the professions. In 1981, Quebec had 27,850 architects and engineers, 37,620 accountants, auditors and other financial agents, and 8,665 lawyers and notaries. No longer did these professionals work independently in their own offices. While many were still in private practice, a much larger number were either on salary in government or large corporations or partners or employees in large firms.

In this area as well, there was a trend towards concentration and large companies, especially in accounting and engineering. The consulting engineering firms Lavalin and SNC, each with thousands of employees, emerged as leaders in their field, and many other firms reached a respectable size. The rise of Francophone consulting engineering firms and their international presence owed much to the support they received from the Quebec government and to French Power in Ottawa. The construction of roads and large dams gave them expertise that they were able to export to Third World countries through projects financed by the Canadian International Development Agency (CIDA).

In accounting, activity was more limited to Quebec or, at most, Canada. Large Francophone companies were formed through mergers of firms that were well established in their home cities. In the corporate services field as a whole, Francophones carved out a much larger role for themselves than in other fields, although in certain areas, such as advertising, Anglophone companies maintained an important presence.

Other services. Among other services, the hotel and restaurant sector, which employed 161,510 people in 1981, occupied a significant place, reflecting both the major role of tourism in the Quebec economy and the increasing number of meals eaten outside the home. It was a low-wage sector, some of it part-time or seasonal, and it was dominated by small, family-run businesses. Chains were becoming more common, but in many cases the establishments were run as franchises by individual owners. While some Quebec chains developed (including the Auberge des Gouverneurs hotels and the Marie-Antoinette and St-Hubert restaurants), American chains (notably Holiday Inn and McDonald's) also had a strong presence. In Montreal, the restaurant sector was the preferred form of entrepreneurship for Quebecers of Greek origin, who came to own most of the city's restaurants.

Government and Defence

The percentage of the labour force employed directly by the three levels of government rose from 5.6 per cent in 1961 to 7 per cent in 1981 (table 1). These figures do not include the huge parapublic sector (teachers, hospital employees and employees of publicly owned corporations), who are included under other headings. Even though defence personnel declined slightly, from 24,417 to 22,020, the federal government continued to employ more people than the Quebec government. But its lead was diminishing: it led by 43,962 to 20,971 in 1961 and by 81,230 to 75,510 in 1981. Municipal governments, which with 33,747 had more employees than the Quebec government in 1961, came in third with 60,125 in 1981.

The direct share of government and defence in Quebec's GDP rose from 5.1 per cent in 1961 to 8.2 per cent in 1981. However, government's share in the economy was much greater than that, because of its strong presence in other sectors such as transportation, communication, utilities and sociocultural services. Government activity is examined in more detail in other chapters.

* * * * * *

The service sector includes a wide variety of economic activities. Each component of the sector has its own characteristics, but beginning in 1960, there were basic features common to them all — the impact of new technology, corporate concentration and the rise of Francophone companies.

CHAPTER 36
REGIONAL INEQUALITY AND ECONOMIC DEVELOPMENT

In any industrialized country, different regions feel the effects of economic development in different ways. Because each region has its own particular combination of resources, the country as a whole can be seen as a mosaic of zones at different stages of development and prosperity.

Distribution of population is usually the easiest index of economic development to identify. People tend to move towards places that offer the best possibilities for work and therefore for income, and Quebec is no exception to the rule. From the starting point of primitive agricultural settlement, regions developed with different growth rates that set them apart from one another. Industrialization, which promoted concentration in the cities, heightened the imbalance.

Political authorities became interested in these problems as the rural exodus came to an end during the 1960s. Public opinion also became more sensitive to regional disparities. In addition, it came to be widely believed that regional inequalities could be corrected through consultation and systematic government action.

The Extent of Regional Disparity

Quebec can be divided into regions in several ways: according to physical characteristics, history or the perceptions of people who live in a particular place. In 1965, the Quebec Department of Industry and Commerce

QUEBEC'S ADMINISTRATIVE REGIONS

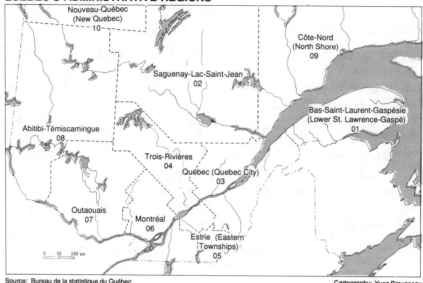

Source: Bureau de la statistique du Québec   Cartography: Yves Brousseau

proposed a division into ten administrative regions; despite criticism, this division has been widely used and accepted ever since (map 1).

From a population standpoint, the most striking feature has been the disproportionate size of the Montreal region, which contains more than half of all Quebecers. This means that all the other regions except the Quebec City region have had relatively low populations. While this situation is not new — the dominance of the Montreal region dates back to the nineteenth century — regional imbalance has continued to grow: in 1931, three regions outside of Montreal each accounted for more than 9 per cent of the population, while fifty years later, only one such region remained. Between 1961 and 1981, all regions saw their share of the population decline except for the Montreal region, the Outaouais and the North Shore-New Quebec.

Data on disposable per capita income (table 2) also reveal wide gaps. For example, in 1961, income in the Lower St. Lawrence-Gaspé, the poorest region, was barely over half the Quebec average, while the sub-region of Montreal Centre (Montreal Island and Île Jésus) showed disposable income well above the average. The trend between 1971 and 1981 was clearly towards reducing the income gap. This trend was undoubtedly in part the result of government action, but it was also attributable to the slowdown in the Montreal region, the resource boom on the North Shore and urban development in the Outaouais. Nonetheless, large disparities remained.

The unemployment rate is another indicator of regional disparity. Although unemployment rose everywhere between 1961 and 1981, the

Table 1
Regional Distribution of Population, Quebec, 1931-81 (%)

Region		1931	1961	1981
01	Lower St. Lawrence-Gaspé	9.4	4.7	3.6
02	Saguenay-Lake St. John	3.7	5.2	4.7
03	Quebec City Region	13.9	16.3	16.0
04	Trois-Rivières Region	6.7	7.9	6.9
05	Eastern Townships	9.8	4.0	3.7
06	Montreal Region	50.2	53.5	56.4
07	Outaouais	4.0	3.9	4.2
08	Abitibi-Temiscamingue	1.5	2.9	2.4
09	North Shore	0.7	1.5	1.8
10	New Quebec	0.1	0.1	0.3

Source: *Annuaires du Québec*; censuses.

Table 2
Per Capita Disposable Income, by Region, 1961-81

Region	1961 $	1961 Index	1971 $	1971 Index	1981 $	1981 Index
Lower St. Lawrence-Gaspé	739	55.0	1,616	65.0	4,981	62.1
Saguenay-Lake St. John	972	72.0	1,914	78.0	7,379	92.0
Quebec City Region	1,088	81.0	2,374	96.0	7,580	94.6
Trois-Rivières Region	1,037	77.0	2,122	86.0	6,535	81.5
Eastern Townships	1,032	77.0	2,253	91.0	6,834	85.2
Montreal Region	1,642	122.0	2,718	110.0	8,752	109.1
(Montreal South)	1,218	90.0	2,307	93.0	8,443	105.3
(Montreal Centre)	1,864	138.0	2,969	120.0	9,218	115.0
(Montreal North)	1,154	86.0	2,195	89.0	7,547	94.1
Outaouais	1,119	83.0	2,217	90.0	7,713	96.1
Abitibi-Temiscamingue	917	68.0	2,020	82.0	7,086	88.3
North Shore-New Quebec	1,235	92.0	2,377	96.0	9,013	112.4
Quebec average	1,347	100.0	2,470	100.0	8,018	100.0

Source: *Annuaire du Québec 1979-1980*; *The Financial Post, Canadian Markets, 1982*, p. 119.

Table 3
Unemployment Rate by Region, 1961-81

Region	1961	1971	1981
Lower St. Lawrence-Gaspé	8.25	15.99	17.9
Saguenay-Lake St. John	8.63	15.37	12.9
Quebec City Region	3.68	8.69	10.7
Trois-Rivières Region	4.83	12.24	11.3
Eastern Townships	3.75	9.25	11.1
Montreal Region	3.64	9.36	9.3
Outaouais	5.02	9.25	11.6
Abitibi-Temiscamingue	8.66	12.77	14.9
Quebec average	4.4	10.05	10.4

Source: A.-G. Gagnon, *Développement régional, État et groupes populaires*, p. 68.

rate in the central regions of Quebec, such as Montreal and Quebec City, remained well below what it was in the other regions (table 3).

A New Awareness

Thus, regional equality was an inescapable reality. Before 1960, however, it was taken for granted and no efforts were made to reduce it. Rural areas had acted as buffers against the Depression; in the rush of postwar prosperity, it was not surprising that people should leave these poor regions and go to the more developed centres.

This acceptance of things as they were was rooted in the history of regional development. From the time most of the regions were opened up for agricultural settlement, the initiative for economic development had always come from the outside. Any decision to develop a region's natural resources or to undertake colonization during the Depression was made in Montreal and Quebec City, if not Toronto or New York. Moreover, the decisions were generally made by the private sector. Federal and provincial government intervention in regional affairs was limited in scope, disorganized in implementation and partisan in motive. The way roads were built is the classic example.

The will to change the situation emerged only slowly. The Depression caused an initial awareness of the problem, which took concrete form in research on the regions and a series of regional inventories directed by Esdras Minville in the 1930s. During the 1940s and 1950s, there was the short-lived Economic Advisory Council set up by the Godbout government in 1943, and local associations such as the chambers of commerce began to call for dialogue to find ways of stimulating economic development. In 1946, the Saguenay set up an economic development council, and the Lower St. Lawrence followed its example in 1956.

However, it was not before a number of other events had occurred that even the idea of regional development would gain acceptance by government and then by the population at large. An inquiry conducted by the Canadian Senate in the late 1950s aroused concern about severe rural poverty. Shortly afterwards, in 1961, Ottawa adopted the Agricultural and Rural Development Act (ARDA), giving it the means to intervene in regional development in conjunction with participating provinces. Also in 1961, the new Quebec government of Premier Jean Lesage established the Economic Advisory Council. It had a dual mandate: to prepare an overall development plan and to advise the government on economic matters. This was Quebec's first planning structure at a time when post-war European experiments were making the notion of economic planning increasingly popular.

Eastern Quebec: A Pilot Area

However, in terms of regional planning, the most significant initiative came from the Lower St. Lawrence economic development council, which in 1963 proposed that the government make it a pilot planning region. The Quebec government quickly accepted the proposal, and after agreeing to take part in ARDA, it set up the Bureau d'Aménagement de l'Est du Québec (BAEQ), one of the most advanced experiments in regional planning Quebec, or Canada, had ever known.

BAEQ's structure was relatively flexible and allowed room for a certain amount of regional representation. In establishing BAEQ in 1963, the government gave it a very large mandate: to prepare a planning blueprint for 1966. From the very beginning, BAEQ's strategy was to involve the target population. A team was sent into the field to help people organize. At the same time, a series of studies was undertaken on the various facets of life in the region, drawing on social science methods and techniques. BAEQ has been called a virtual social science laboratory: at the height of its activities in 1965, sixty-five researchers and twenty community organizers, most of them young university graduates, were involved in the project. BAEQ's preparatory work represented a wealth of documentary information.

In 1966, BAEQ tabled its plan in ten volumes. The goal was to help the region catch up to the Quebec average, especially in employment, productivity and income. Four objectives were laid out: geographical and occupational mobility for the labour force; the establishment of an institutional framework for planning and participation; the creation of regional awareness; and the rational structuring of regional land.

For many long months, there was no follow-up to the plan. In the region, a liaison committee was organized, and then in 1967 a regional development council was set up to exert pressure on government. Finally, in the spring of 1968, Ottawa and Quebec City signed an agreement to spend $258 million over five years to develop the region. The second phase of the operation was ready to begin.

After the initial period of euphoria in the region, people's enthusiasm declined very quickly. They realized that very popular projects, such as reorganizing the road system and industrializing the area, had not been accepted as part of the plan. When it was learned that the largest projects had to do with relocating the population and would lead to the closing down of a dozen villages, there was widespread disappointment. Then, when it appeared that more villages would be closed and — as in the case of Cabano near Rivière-du-Loup — the region's forest products would be processed elsewhere, there was an explosion of anger. With the resistance to these aspects of the plan, and the fact that getting other aspects off the ground was a slow and complex process, the goal of closing the gap between eastern Quebec and other regions appeared to be compromised. At the end of the period, there were still large disparities between the region and the rest of Quebec. Only the income gap had been reduced, and this had been accomplished through transfer payments rather than a real economic turnaround.

Regional Development and Decentralization

As the Lower St. Lawrence-Gaspé experiment was going on, both levels of government found it necessary to establish new agencies to structure their activities. In 1968, Quebec replaced the Economic Advisory Council with a new agency, the Office de Planification et de Développement du Québec (OPDQ), whose role included overall planning and management of regional projects. The OPDQ interacted with a series of regional bodies, the Conseils Régionaux de Développement (CRDs), made up of community representatives and established in almost all of Quebec's regions during the 1960s.

The federal government adopted a different strategy. After creating the ARDA program, it took a number of other initiatives: for example, it set up the Area Development Agency in 1963 and the Fund for Rural Economic Development in 1966. In 1969, it established the Department of Regional Economic Expansion (DREE) in an effort to control the direction of government action in this important area where the provinces were very active. DREE administered existing programs, provided subsidies, established employment programs and initiated studies and research.

In addition to structures directly linked to regional development, governments had a fairly systematic policy of decentralizing their operations. The Quebec government set up offices in all the administrative regions while the federal government opened regional offices in smaller cities, relocated administrative offices within the Ottawa-Hull area and moved some government services outside the capital region. These policies benefited smaller cities by stimulating employment in the service sector. Hull and its immediate area were transformed by the construction of office buildings and new residential areas.

Parallel to this process, the Quebec government implemented a policy of decentralizing its health, education, social security and cultural services. Cities and towns where hospitals, CLSCs, polyvalent high schools, cegeps and University of Quebec campuses were established or expanded reaped significant direct and indirect economic benefits. In cities and towns in poor regions, the presence of public and parapublic sector employees both ensured a solid economic base and helped enliven local cultural, social and political life.

Despite these efforts, major policy problems remained. After a period of indecision, the Quebec government opted in the 1960s for an overall strategy of decentralizing economic growth. Simply put, it tried to reverse the trend towards the development of a sole industrial centre, Montreal, and stimulate growth in other regions. But in the 1970s, in the aftermath of the Higgins-Raynauld-Martin report, which guided the policies of the federal Department of Regional Economic Expansion, there was a return to the idea of protecting and strengthening existing centres of development, especially Montreal. But these divergent points of view did not prevent the two governments from coordinating their activities and reaching agreements to cooperate on specific development projects. When the Parti Québécois took power in 1976 there was an upsurge in federal-provincial tension, but in the economic climate of the late 1970s the time for large-scale projects was past in any case.

In the regions concerned, all this activity in the 1960s and 1970s brought a renewal that was manifested in several ways. The example of eastern Quebec is revealing. When the people of the region disagreed profoundly with development projects they considered unsuitable, they made alternative proposals. The resistance was initially organized parish by parish with the launching of the first Opération Dignité in 1970. It was followed by several others, which met with varying degrees of success. In addition to spontaneous protest movements, some parishes grouped together to plan their development and survival themselves; thus, Saint-Juste, Auclair and Lejeune formed the JAL in 1973. While many of these experiments were barely viable financially, their social and cultural effects were often pivotal.

Between 1960 and 1980, the poorest regions of Quebec experienced a degree of development they never dreamed of before. While their economic base, too often dependent on a single resource, was fragile, the experience of regional development had a positive side — even though planning did not change the outlying regions into centres of development, it did contribute to the development of vibrant regional communities.

A new regional dynamism arose during the period. In terms of economic development, desire for coordination and regional promotion was much more intense in the outlying areas than in the Quebec City and Montreal metropolitan areas, as could be seen in the CRDs and older bodies such as the chambers of commerce. Some regions — the Beauce is often cited in this regard — served as a base for more dynamic and growth-oriented entrepreneurship. Some regional small businesses reached a respectable size in just a few years. In most cases, however, entrepreneurs ran up against initial financing difficulties, which prompted them to set up venture capital companies, such as the Sociétés d'Entraide Économique and the SODEQs. Despite the weaknesses of these institutions, they helped pave the way for radical improvements in the financing of regional companies by government and large lending institutions.

Coordination also took on a political dimension, as some local structures were reorganized on a regional basis. Regional school boards were set up, municipalities were urged to amalgamate, and county councils changed into regional municipalities. As well, the Quebec government established coordinating bodies in the social affairs and cultural sectors, and the new colleges and universities became centres of expression of a community-based cultural dynamism.

CHAPTER 37
THE INESCAPABLE CITY

By 1960, the influence of the cities and urban culture spread throughout most of Quebec, including rural Quebec. But Quebec's urban areas still changed markedly during the period: urbanized space, city administration and, more generally, the relationship between the city and society were all completely transformed.

An Urban Society

The longstanding trend towards an increasingly urban population continued in the 1960s, but it levelled off in the early 1970s. The proportion of Quebecers living in urban centres increased especially rapidly between 1961 and 1966, rising from 74.3 to 78.3 per cent. It grew more slowly in the second half of the decade, reaching 80.6 per cent in 1971, and then it declined: in 1981 it was 77.6 per cent. The decline was probably due to the growing number of people who worked in the cities but lived outside them, forming part of the nonagricultural rural population. The proportion of people in Quebec who lived in urban centres remained above the Canadian average, which rose from 69.7 per cent in 1961 to 75.6 per cent in 1981. In Quebec, there were obviously significant regional variations — between two thirds and three quarters of the people in most regions lived in urban centres in 1971, but the figure was 91 per cent in the Montreal region and only 47 per cent in eastern Quebec.

Urban growth in the 1960s was the product of rising employment in the service sector. In addition, the first wave of baby boomers reached adulthood, leading to the formation of a greater number of new households. The 1960s were also a time of increased government investment, which influenced the direction of urban growth. For example, major elements of Quebec's transportation infrastructure were built at that time, as were schools and hospitals. As well, the needs of new households and

Figure 1
**Housing Starts in Agglomerations with 10,000
or More People, Quebec, 1960-1980**

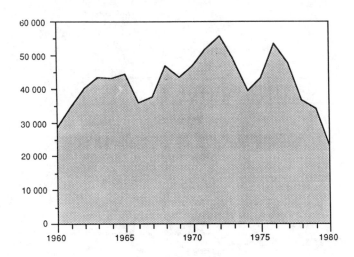

Source: *Quebec Yearbooks.*

easier access to home ownership led to a significant expansion in residential construction (graph 1) and urban space. The cost of materials and labour was still relatively low, and mortgage financing was not expensive.

Population statistics were the first to show the levelling off that took place in the 1970s. The falling birth rate hit the urban areas with full force at the same time as immigration declined. People leaving rural Quebec had already filled up Quebec's towns and cities. Thus, all the factors that had until then contributed to rapid growth were no longer in play.

Nonetheless, demand for housing among young people setting up new households led to continued expansion of urban space. In the first half of the 1970s, housing starts were at high levels while housing remained affordable. However, the kind of rapid, disorganized development towns and cities had undergone since the war was called into question by the 1973 energy crisis and the economic uncertainty characteristic of the 1970s. Towards the end of the decade, rising construction costs and interest rates caused a marked slowdown in residential construction and large public works.

Municipalities were finding it more expensive to run their own administrations. The model of development based on a proliferation of suburban towns and the construction of single-family dwellings was becoming more and more burdensome. Increasingly expensive services — water, sewers, roads and others — had to be provided to a low-density population. Municipal governments could no longer finance large-scale projects

THE MONTREAL METROPOLITAN AREA, 1981

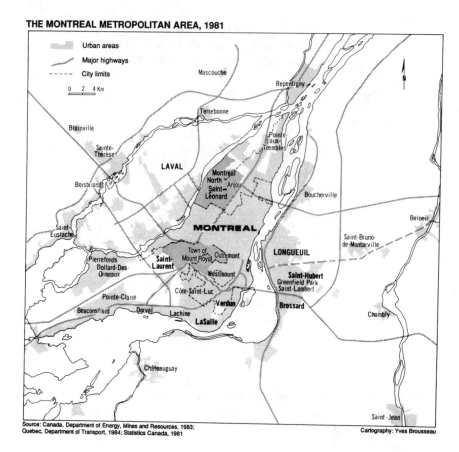

Source: Canada, Department of Energy, Mines and Resources, 1983;
Quebec, Department of Transport, 1984; Statistics Canada, 1981

Cartography: Yves Brousseau

on the assumption of future population growth. On the basis of costs and travelling time, some people began to find it more advantageous to renovate aging houses in older neignbourhoods than to move to increasingly distant suburbs. This situation was partly responsible for the trend towards repopulating downtown areas that appeared in the early 1980s.

Thus, all sectors of the Quebec's population — including Quebecers who live in the country — generally have an urban lifestyle. The rural-urban contrast no longer holds the same significance as it did in the past. In most cases, divergences in culture and outlook are due to differences internal to the urban system itself. Montreal's urban culture is different from Quebec City's, while within the same agglomeration life in the suburbs is different in many respects from life downtown. But despite these differences, there is profound convergence, widely expressed in the mass media.

THE QUEBEC CITY METROPOLITAN AREA, 1981

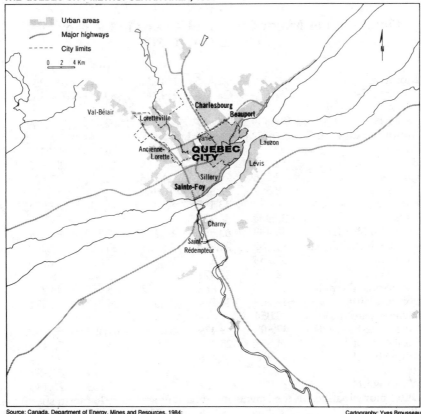

Source: Canada, Department of Energy, Mines and Resources, 1984; Quebec, Department of Transport, 1984; Statistics Canada, 1981

Cartography: Yves Brousseau

The Growth of Metropolitan Regions

Another significant feature of the period was the growth of metropolitan areas, each encompassing a large city and suburban municipalities closely linked to it.

Montreal and Quebec City had always been the leading components of the Quebec urban system. Their importance continued to grow, and a majority of Quebec's total population now lived in these two metropolitan areas: from 1961 to 1976, the Montreal census metropolitan area's share of the population jumped from 40 per cent to 45 per cent, while the Quebec City metropolitan area's climbed from 6.8 per cent to 8.7 per cent. The population of metropolitan Montreal grew from 2,100,000 to 2,800,000, while metropolitan Quebec City had a population of more than 500,000 at the end of the period. Taking account as well of the metropolitan areas of Hull and Chicoutimi-Jonquière and the agglomerations of Trois-Rivières-Cap-de-la-Madeleine, Sherbrooke and Shawinigan-Grand-Mère, it is clear that most Quebecers live in large agglomerations.

Table 1
Population of Major Cities and Towns in the Montreal Region, 1941-1961

	1961	1966	1971	1976	1981
Montreal	1,191,062	1,222,235	1,214,352	1,080,546	980,354
Montreal Island	1,747,696	1,923,178	1,959,143	1,869,641	1,760,122
Census metropolitan area	2,109,509	2,436,817	2,743,208	2,802,485	2,828,349
Suburban municipalities on Montreal Island					
Anjou	9,511	22,477	33,886	36,596	37,346
Beaconsfield	10,064	15,702	19,389	20,417	19,613
Côte-Saint-Luc	13,266	20,546	24,375	25,721	27,531
Dorval	18,592	20,905	20,469	19,131	17,722
Lachine	38,630	43,155	44,423	41,503	37,521
La Salle	30,904	48,322	72,912	76,713	76,299
Montreal North	48,433	67,806	89,139	97,250	94,914
Town of Mount Royal	21,182	21,845	21,561	20,514	19,247
Outremont	30,753	30,881	28,552	27,089	24,338
Pierrefonds	12,171	27,924	33,010	35,402	38,390
Pointe-aux-Trembles	21,926	29,888	35,567	35,618	36,270
Pointe-Claire	22,709	26,784	27,303	25,917	24,571
Rivière-des-Prairies	10,054	-	-	-	-
Ville Saint-Laurent	49,805	59,479	62,955	64,404	65,900
Saint-Léonard	4,893	25,328	52,040	78,452	79,429
Saint-Michel	55,978	71,446	-	-	-
Verdun	78,317	76,832	74,718	68,013	61,287
Westmount	25,012	24,107	23,606	22,153	20,480
Other municipalities in the census metropolitan area in 1976 (north shore)					
Blainville	4,459	6,258	9,630	12,517	14,682
Boisbriand	2,502	3,498	7,278	10,132	13,471
Laval	124,741	196,088	228,010	246,243	268,335
Mascouche	3,977	5,953	8,812	14,266	20,345
Repentigny	9,139	14,976	19,520	26,698	34,419
Sainte-Thérèse	11,771	15,628	17,175	17,479	18,750
Sainte-Eustache	5,463	7,319	9,479	21,248	29,716
Terrebonne	6,207	7,480	9,212	11,204	11,769

The agglomerations also underwent internal reorganization. The most notable development was the rise of the suburbs, which was conspicuous in the case of both Quebec City and Montreal. While the population of the core city fell and that of older suburban towns stabilized or even declined, newer suburban municipalities grew very quickly (tables 1 and 2).

While suburban municipalities were proliferating, there were also consolidations and mergers, as some suburban towns combined to form municipalities of respectable size. The best-known example is Laval, produced by the fusion of fourteen Île-Jésus municipalities in 1965. There was also the merger of Jacques-Cartier and Longueuil on Montreal's south shore, as well as the fusions that led to the formation of Charlesbourg and Beauport in the Quebec City area. There were also annexations

Table 1 (continued)				
1961	**1966**	**1971**	**1976**	**1981**
Other municipalities in the census metropolitan area in 1976 (south shore)				
Beloeil	6,283	10,152	12,724	15,913	17,540
Boucherville	7,403	15,338	19,997	25,530	29,704
Brossard	3,778	11,884	23,452	37,641	52,232
Chambly	3,737	10,798	11,469	11,815	12,190
Châteauguay	7,570	12,460	15,797	36,329	36,928
Greenfield Park	7,807	12,288	15,348	18,430	18,527
Longueuil	24,131	25,593	97,590	122,429	124,320
Jacques-Cartier	40,807	52,527			
Saint-Bruno-de Montarville	6,760	10,712	15,780	21,272	22,880
Saint-Hubert	14,380	17,215	21,741	49,706	60,573
Laflèche	10,984	13,433	15,113		
Saint-Lambert	14,531	16,003	18,616	20,318	20,557
Muncipalities in the broader Montreal region				
Joliette	18,088	19,188	20,127	18,118	16,987
Lachute	7,560	10,215	11,813	11,928	11,729
Mirabel	-	-	-	13,486	14,080
Saint-Hyacinthe	22,354	23,781	24,562	37,500	38,246
Saint-Jean	26,988	27,784	32,863	34,363	35,640
Saint-Jérôme	24,546	26,511	26,524	25,175	25,123
Salaberry-de-Valleyfield	27,297	29,111	30,173	29,716	29,574
Sorel	17,147	19,021	19,347	19,666	20,347
Tracy	8,171	10,918	11,842	12,284	12,843

Source: *Annuaire du Québec*, 1973 and 1977-1978; Census of Canada, 1981.

to the core city in Montreal, Quebec City and smaller centres such as Drummondville and Saint-Hyacinthe.

The formation of these larger municipalities was only one aspect of a challenge to the entire municipal structure. Administrative fragmentation and the proliferation of decision-making centres led to problems of coordination that the Quebec government had to deal with. Its initial move, in 1970, was to set up the first urban communities, in Montreal, Quebec City and the Outaouais. In each case, coordinating structures were established that respected municipal autonomy while pooling some services such as police and municipal assessment. In the late 1970s, these early efforts led to a much broader reform of municipal coordinating structures with the creation of regional county municipalities.

The Physical Reorganization of Large Urban Areas

One of most spectacular aspects of urban development during the period was the reorganization of space and transformation of architecture in

Table 2
Population of Major Quebec Cities and Towns
outside the Montreal Region, 1961-1981

	1961	1966	1971	1976	1981
Quebec City region					
Quebec City	171,979	166,984	186,088	177,082	166,474
Census metropolitan area	357,568	413,397	480,502	542,158	576,075
Ancienne-Lorette	3,361	5,691	8,304	11,694	12,935
Beauport	9,192	11,742	14,681	55,339	60,447
Charlesbourg	14,308	24,926	33,443	63,147	68,326
Giffard	10,129	12,585	13,135	-	-
Loretteville	6,522	9,465	11,644	14,767	15,060
Sainte-Foy	29,716	48,298	68,385	71,237	68,883
Sillery	14,109	14,737	13,932	13,580	12,825
Val-Bélair	2,629	3,408	4,505	10,716	12,695
Vanier	8,733	9,362	9,717	10,683	10,725
Lauzon	11,533	12,877	12,809	12,663	13,362
Lévis	15,112	15,627	16,597	17,819	17,895
Eastern Townships and Bois-Francs					
Sherbrooke	66,554	75,690	80,711	76,804	74,075
Magog	13,139	13,797	13,281	13,290	13,604
Cowansville	7,050	10,692	11,920	11,902	12,240
Drummondville	27,709	29,216	31,813	29,286	27,347
Granby	31,463	34,349	34,385	37,132	38,069
Thetford Mines	21,618	21,614	22,003	20,784	19,965
Victoriaville	18,720	21,320	21,813	21,825	21,838
St. Maurice Valley					
Trois-Rivières	53,477	57,540	55,869	52,518	50,466
Cap-de-la-Madeleine	26,925	29,433	31,463	32,126	32,626
Trois-Rivières-Ouest	4,094	6,345	8,037	10,564	13,107
Shawinigan	32,169	30,777	27,792	24,921	23,011
Shawinigan-Sud	12,683	12,250	11,470	11,155	11,325
Grand-Mère	15,806	16,407	17,137	15,999	15,442
La Tuque	13,023	13,554	13,099	12,067	11,556

Quebec's main towns and cities. This change, the first significant modification in years in the way urban space was structured, was based on a new kind of urban planning, which largely followed the example of the United States. This new wave began to appear in the early 1950s, but it was in the next two decades that its full effects were felt.

The automobile was at the heart of these changes. Autoroutes (as multilane divided highways are known in Quebec) provided a means of rapid travel between large cities, while urban expressways were built to connect downtown cores with suburban areas. Montreal and Quebec City in particular were surrounded by limited-access highways that made mass travel easier and had a significant impact on suburban growth. At the same time, in a move that went somewhat against the flow in a society

Table 2 (continued)					
	1961	1966	1971	1976	1981
Saguenay-Lake St. John					
Chicoutimi-Jonquière					
census metropolitan area	-	132,954	133,703	128,643	135,172
Chicoutimi	31,657	32,526	33,893	57,737	60,064
Chicoutimi-Nord	11,229	12,814	14,086	-	-
Jonquière	28,588	29,663	28,430	60,691	60,354
Arvida	14,460	15,342	18,448	-	-
Kénogami	11,816	11,534	10,970	-	-
Alma	13,309	22,195	22,622	25,638	26,322
Chibougamau	4,765	8,902	9,701	10,536	10,732
La Baie	-	-	-	20,116	20,935
Lower St. Lawrence-Gaspé					
Gaspé	2,603	2,938	17,211	16,842	17,261
Matane	9,190	11,109	11,841	12,726	13,612
Rimouski	17,739	20,330	26,887	27,897	29,120
Rivière-du-Loup	10,835	11,637	12,760	13,103	13,459
North Shore					
Baie-Comeau	7,956	12,236	12,109	11,911	12,866
Hauterive	5,980	11,366	13,181	14,724	13,995
Sept-Îles	14,196	18,957	24,320	30,617	29,262
Outaouais					
Hull	56,929	60,176	63,580	61,039	56,225
Aylmer	6,286	7,231	7,198	25,714	26,695
Buckingham	7,421	7,227	7,304	14,328	7,992
Gatineau	13,022	17,727	22,321	73,479	74,988
Abitibi-Temiscamingue					
Rouyn	18,716	18,581	17,821	17,678	17,224
Noranda	11,477	11,521	10,741	9,809	8,767
Val-d'Or	10,983	12,147	17,421	19,915	21,371

Source: *Annuaire du Québec*, 1977-1978; Census of Canada, 1981.

where the car was king, Montreal built a subway, greatly facilitating travel within the city.

Downtown areas were also changing. The growth of government and the service sector led to a marked increase in the need for office space, which resulted in the construction of many highrise buildings. The old residential districts were reduced through demolition. In Montreal, a new central business district emerged to the northwest of the older one. In Quebec City, the development of the area around the National Assembly completely transformed the cityscape. Even a small or middle-sized city could not be without its own "skyscraper." The new buildings were architecturally modern, with stripped-down lines and glass and aluminum surfaces, and multifunctional, containing shops, restaurants and movie theatres. In this way, they contributed to the decline of the old commercial streets, which had already suffered considerably from competition from the new suburban shopping centres.

Housing was also affected in a variety of ways. Bungalows — one-storey single-family dwellings — became the rule, especially in the suburbs. While multifamily dwellings did not disappear, they took different forms. In some areas, there were still many two-storey houses containing two or three flats, but most new multifamily buildings contained larger numbers of dwellings. Some of these were three- or four-storey walkups; far more common, however, were highrise apartment buildings.

These changes occurred in an environment dominated by private developers, who had little difficulty in gaining municipal approval for their plans. The municipalities recognized urban planning as a concern, but it usually only went as far as passing zoning regulations and making improvements to public spaces. In the euphoria of the 1960s, developers' plans were seen as symbols of progress, but in the 1970s reactions against them began to appear. Community groups concerned with environmental protection and historical preservation opposed large-scale demolition. As we will see later, pressure from these groups gradually forced government to show concern for the quality of urban life and make an effort to preserve historic areas.

Cities and Their Residents

Urban environmental protection groups were only one facet of a broader phenomenon: a proliferation of community groups in the larger cities and towns, especially Montreal. Citizens' organizations had existed in urban areas since the late nineteenth century, but most represented business or middle-class interests, and they were often associated with chambers of commerce. Beginning in 1963, a new kind of community group emerged. Rooted in working-class areas, these groups demanded improved living conditions and better services for specific neighbourhoods or blocks. They criticized the way city governments operated and called for the establishment of consultation mechanisms and neighbourhood democracy. Their existence was testimony to the considerable distance that had developed between city dwellers and their local governments, as more powers had become concentrated in the hands of executive committees at the expense of elected councillors.

According to political scientist Louise Quesnel, a new conception of the role of municipal government developed within the Quebec government in the mid-1960s: "The municipalities must serve the whole population, and not property owners as they did in the past." With this goal in mind, attempts were made to make municipal politics more democratic — in 1968, all residents aged eighteen and over were given the right to vote and eligibility for office was extended. However, the acquired rights of corporate bodies (such as companies) were maintained, and they did not lose their right to vote until 1978. The 1968 voting law also established criteria for the remuneration of elected officials according to the size of the municipality, and the 1978 law recognized municipal political parties and provided for the reimbursement of a share of election expenses. However, the provincial and municipal governments refused to set up neighbourhood councils, as demanded by the community groups.

The Cost of Urban Growth

There was growing concern about the economic and social costs of urban growth. Municipal governments were the first to feel the pinch. There were increasing numbers of municipal civil servants, with rapidly rising salaries. Beginning in the late 1970s, municipal governments reduced services and cut personnel to slow the increase in the wage burden. At the same time, rising construction costs made infrastructure expenditures extremely burdensome, while declining population growth added further to the growing pressure on municipal finances.

The situations of different municipalities varied, and they competed to attract new residents and industrial investment. This only made the problems worse. Costly public and private industrial parks sprang up, most of them only partially occupied. Within a single agglomeration, municipalities differed in age, economic structure and the wealth of their residents. The core cities sheltered the poorest part of the population and faced high costs for social services and police. A debate began in the late 1960s over the fairest way to share the costs of certain services, such as police, that benefited the whole agglomeration. The establishment of urban communities was aimed especially at resolving this problem.

Another solution to the financial problems faced by towns and cities was municipal tax reform, which was carried out in the 1970s. The main source of revenue for towns and cities had always been property taxes, which they had to share with school boards. The goal of the reform was to gradually reduce the proportion of taxes handed over to the school boards and leave virtually all property tax revenue to the municipalities. As well, the provincial government, having taken away the municipalities' share of the sales tax in 1980, increased its subsidies in areas such as mass transit, water treatment and historical preservation.

The costs of urban growth went beyond municipal finances. Observers pointed to the waste of space and resources caused by uncontrolled urban development. In the 1970s, there was much discussion of the harmful effects on agriculture of this kind of development, which was using up some of the best land in Quebec for nonagricultural purposes, especially in the Montreal plain. The Lévesque government passed an agricultural zoning law in 1978 to remedy the problem.

Montreal

The giant city of Montreal continued to grow in the 1960s as it had in the previous decade, but it appeared to reach the limits of its expansion in the 1970s. For the whole census metropolitan area, the average annual rate of population growth was still 2.66 per cent between 1961 and 1971, but it fell to 0.30 per cent in the next decade. The city itself lost population to the suburbs; from a peak of 1,222,255 in 1966, its population fell below the million mark in 1981. Nonetheless, the agglomeration had a population of a little over 2.8 million at the end of the period.

Montreal's growth reached a ceiling because its traditional activities were in decline or had moved elsewhere. The city suffered from the consequences of the inexorable westward shift of Canada's economic centre of gravity. While it could be said that Montreal and Toronto shared the role of Canada's metropolis in the 1960s, this was no longer the case in the 1980s — Toronto had become the main centre of economic decision-making. Departures of head offices from Montreal, which accelerated in the 1970s, were eloquent testimony to this. It is important to note, however, that Montreal's difficulties have deep historic roots and have been due more to economic and demographic factors than to political ones. From the turn of the century on, American companies chose to set up their branch plants in Ontario; as early as 1936, 66 per cent of American branch plants were located there as opposed to 16 per cent in Quebec. Thus, the subsequent expansion of American control contributed to Toronto's steady rise. Moroever, the rapid, resource-driven growth of western Canada not only strengthened regional metropolitan centres such as Vancouver and Calgary but also favoured Toronto over Montreal. The Francization process in Montreal may have been a factor in a company's decision to move, and may even have served as a convenient pretext. Taken on its own, however, it is not sufficient to explain the rise of Toronto at the expense of Montreal.

Montreal's industrial structure also put it at something of a disadvantage. Plants in many industries were old and inefficient and had to be replaced by more modern facilities; this often gave companies the opportunity to move closer to Canada's main consumer market, Ontario. In addition, Montreal had many light manufacturing industries whose decline was speeded up by foreign competition. Finally, the energy crisis put an abrupt halt to the growth of the petroleum products and petrochemicals industries, which until then had benefited from the low price of imported oil. In the 1980s, several of the Montreal oil refineries closed.

Nonetheless, manufacturing continued to play in important role in the Montreal agglomeration. Factories left the central districts and moved to the new industrial parks in the north end of the city and the suburbs. But most jobs in Montreal were in the quickly expanding service sector.

Transportation remained a central element in Montreal's economy. With the construction of a network of multilane highways and several new bridges, Montreal was now at the heart of a road system connecting it to large Canadian and American cities. The dazzling growth of air traffic in the 1960s prompted the federal government to begin construction of a new international airport at Mirabel, but because of the energy crisis and the rise of Toronto as the gateway to Canada at the expense of Montreal, the planners' optimistic forecasts were not realized. The port

Jean Drapeau, mayor of Montreal (1954-57 and 1960-86)

of Montreal was adversely affected by the opening of the St. Lawrence Seaway in 1959, as ships carrying raw materials passed by the city without stopping. After some slow years, the port was revived by the development of container shipping.

Montreal's role as the economic and cultural metropolis of Quebec was strengthened. Most large Francophone companies set up their head offices in Montreal, and television production, publishing and the major French-language sociocultural activities became concentrated there. Starting in the 1960s, negative reactions to the influence wielded by Montreal on Quebec life developed, and there were calls for decentralization. They subsided, however, when it appeared that Montreal's growth had reached its peak.

Montreal even worked to develop an international vocation. Expo 67 and the 1976 Olympic Games were held in Montreal at the instigation of Mayor Jean Drapeau, whose strong personality marked the entire period. Drapeau enjoyed considerable personal popularity, and he stayed in power at the head of a Civic Party administration from 1960 to 1986. This stability gave the Montreal city government remarkable continuity and unity of views. Favouring development based on large projects, Drapeau neglected problems related to the decline of Montreal, its aging industrial base and the deterioration of living conditions in the older neighbour-hoods. It was not until the 1980s that there was any change of policy in this regard. Opposition to the mayor organized around neighbourhood citizens' committees and Anglophone and Francophone middle-class re-form groups. These groups formed the Front d'Action Politique (FRAP) to contest the municipal election of 1970, but FRAP did poorly when the election took place against the troubled backdrop of the October Crisis. But the opposition resumed its campaign in the 1974 election with the Montreal Citizens' Movement (MCM). The MCM succeeded in gaining a foothold in city council, where it served as a strong opposition until 1986, when it gained power under the leadership of Jean Doré.

The Montreal cityscape changed considerably. A new central business district emerged, with a covering of tall buildings and a maze of under-ground shopping areas. Older downtown residential neighbourhoods were gutted by large-scale demolition and an invasion of cafés, restau-rants and shops. In the early 1980s, the process of gentrification under-way in other North American cities reached Montreal, as old working class neighbourhoods were taken over by people from better-off social strata.

Clearly the most important development, however, was the territorial explosion of the suburbs, which now spread for dozens of kilometres, from the banks of the Richelieu to the far side of the Rivière des Mille-Îles. On Montreal Island itself, almost all areas were now urbanized: Anglo-phones became concentrated in the West Island, while the rapid growth of Anjou, Saint-Léonard and Montreal North made the development of the east even more dramatic. On the South Shore, still largely rural in 1961, towns such as Brossard, Boucherville and Saint-Bruno mush-roomed; the area had a population of close to half a million by the end of the period. North of the city, the population of Île Jésus — now the city of Laval — grew from 124,741 in 1961 to 260,033 twenty years later. And suburbs spread out even farther, from Saint-Eustache to Repentigny.

Quebec City

After a century of slow growth, if not stagnation, Quebec City ex-perienced a surge of expansion. Between 1961 and 1971, the population of the Quebec City metropolitan region grew at an annual rate of 3 per cent, and the rate remained at 1.8 per cent over the following decade. Here again, the increase came from the suburbs, because the central core, like Montrreal, experienced a population decline during the 1970s. In 1981, the agglomeration as a whole had a population of 576,075.

Clearly the main factor in Quebec City's growth was the major expan-sion of the civil service that began during the Quiet Revolution and continued until the mid-1970s. The number of government employees, both federal and provincial, in the agglomeration rose from 15,000 to 45,000 in twenty years. But people directly employed by government represented only part of this phenomenon, and civil servants' higher wages had effects on the local economy as a whole. Increased government activity has also affected the city physically. With its heavy requirements for office buildings, government was directly and indirectly responsible for the construction of the many large buildings that transformed the urban landscape. The most significant project associated with government was the development of the area around the National Assembly, which led to the elimination of many older houses. The government also gave the agglomeration an impressive multilane highway system, which was completed in the 1970s.

The presence of the government has also had a substantial impact on the growth of the hotel industry, which also relies on tourism, another important element in the city's economy. Visitors are attracted by the European flavour of Quebec City's older districts. However, the redevelopment of the Place Royale ended up being a partial failure.

Quebec City has continued to serve as a regional commercial centre. Shopping centres — including one that for a time was one of the largest in North America — proliferated to an extent unmatched elswhere in Quebec and led to the decline of the old commercial sector in the Saint-Roch district.

This was only one aspect of the transformation of Quebec City's urban culture, now subject to outside as well as local influences. The growth of the civil service attracted many people from other areas of the province. A new middle class made up of government officials and academics joined the old elite of *notables* and merchants.

Suburban growth has been encouraged by the autoroute system, which now extends in all directions. The main suburban areas are Sainte-Foy, Charlesbourg and Beauport. The Pierre Laporte Bridge, opened in 1970, facilitated the development of a number of small municipalities on the south shore.

Other Towns and Cities

While Quebec City is an extreme example of urbanization based on the growth of the public and parapublic sector, this development could also be observed in many other towns and cities. For the growth of government did not affect the capital alone. Middle-sized cities where the Quebec or federal government opened regional offices became administrative centres. This role was often strengthened by the establishment or expansion of regional institutions such as hospitals, cegeps and even universities, and such a city became a kind of regional metropolitan centre.

The new service jobs often took over from declining traditional industries. Too far from major markets, middle-sized cities have found it difficult to attract new companies. Towns and cities that relied on processing natural resources have been especially threatened. During the period, most of them reached the limits to growth imposed by an overly narrow economic base. Thus, in Abitibi, the St. Maurice Valley, the

Saguenay and the North Shore, many localities have lived at the mercy of a factory shutdown or a significant reduction in personnel. Shawinigan and Port-Cartier have been particularly affected, but there are also many other centres where the population has stagnated, declined, or in some cases almost disappeared.

CHAPTER 38

DOMINANT GROUPS AND THE RISE OF NEW ELITES

Quebec's social structure underwent profound changes after 1960, especially at the level of the groups in power. The changes that had begun to appear in the postwar period were now in full swing. In the political, cultural and social fields, the traditional elites gave way to a new ruling class, while a new Francophone bourgeoisie rose to the forefront in the economic field.

The New Ruling Class

The power of the traditional elites, made up mainly of local *notables* and the clergy, eroded quickly during the Quiet Revolution. They did not completely disappear, but they lost their old status and their near-monopoly over institutions and the government as a new elite came to the fore in these arenas. Many sociologists, political scientists, essayists and journalists have pondered and commented on this development. For example, a number of Marxist writers use the term "new petty bourgeoisie" to distinguish the new group from the traditional petty bourgeoisie, but they define it in a narrow way. The sociologist Jean-Jacques Simard talks about "the long march of the technocrats," while the essayist Jacques Grand'Maison condemns the "new class" that has seized power by imposing its own agenda on the government and society.

Particular groups within this ruling class — mainly provincial politicians and civil servants, but also some professions and the heads of specific institutions — have also been studied. However, no in-depth studies have been done of the new elites as a whole, so our discussion here can only provide a broad outline.

While a lawyer in a locally based private practice could be taken as a prototype of the traditional elites, the symbol of the new ruling class was a highly placed government technocrat with a specialized university education who could influence the major trends in society. The technocrats in some ways personified the new class, but they were not its only members, for it was made up of several distinct groups.

The numbers and influence of the new managers of public and parapublic institutions increased rapidly as government services and crown corporations proliferated. These managers also benefited from the secularization of education, health and social services and their takeover by the government. Most were career civil servants, starting out as professionals and then climbing the bureaucratic ladder. During the early years of the Quiet Revolution when demand was high, these managers rose quickly and some found themselves in positions of power while still quite young. Later on, the situation was not as fluid and upward mobility became a slower process.

Another important group was made up of managers and executives in the private sector. In the early 1960s, most were Anglophone and therefore had little interest in identifying with the new Francophone class, which was not only Francophone but, worse yet, nationalist; they had much closer ties with federal technocrats. But during the 1970s, the situation changed gradually as more Francophone companies came into existence and large English Canadian and foreign companies sought more French-speaking executives. Meanwhile, the growth of government institutions tailed off, so that the influence of the private sector group was on the rise within the ruling class.

Intellectuals, in the broad sense of the term, formed a third and extremely important group within the new Quebec elite. They comprised two subgroups. The first consisted of professionals such as lawyers, engineers and accountants, working in universities or large firms, who put their talent and expertise at the service of the technocrats and politicians, supplying them with studies and policy proposals. The second consisted of communicators — journalists, teachers, radio and television personalities, advertising people — who promoted the idea of change and thus helped to gain acceptance for the new approaches. However, the intellectuals were a complex group, and some of them challenged or opposed the power structure.

Trade union elites enjoyed much greater influence than they had in earlier periods. These too were new elites, and they were led by career trade union officials, many of them university-educated, and included few genuine workers.

As we will see in chapter 49, more and more politicians — especially cabinet ministers but backbenchers as well — came from these groups, whose goals and aspirations they shared. While the premiers of the 1960s still came from the traditional elites, the premiers of the 1970s — Robert

Bourassa, an economist, and René Lévesque, a journalist and television personality — were perfectly representative of the new ruling class.

The traditional elites had based their position on a defensive kind of nationalism with religious, cultural and legal components. The groups that made up the new class, on the other hand, professed an aggressive nationalism whose field of endeavour extended to all aspects of Quebec life and even the international stage. They presented themselves as the embodiment of the nation, which they sought to revitalize and bring up to date. They made no secret of their intention to Francize Quebec by making it a strong state, which for some included independence.

The focus of power for the new ruling class was the political field. From there, power could spread to the economic, social and cultural domains. In the development strategies implemented by this class, the government had the role of initiating change. The government was to act as a source of support and guidance for Francophones in a society that until then had treated them as a minority, and all classes of society should be able to benefit from its role as promoter of the collective welfare.

The erosion of the power of the church contributed to the concentration of resources and influence in the government. Although power became more centralized through this process, there were still a variety of areas where it could be exercised, in fact a greater variety than there had been before. Local institutions remained active, although some of them, especially school boards, hospitals and social services, had their autonomy eroded by Quebec government regulation. Regionalization and the establishment of new institutions in a number of sectors increased the availability of prestigious and influential positions.

One respect in which members of the new elites were quite different from their predecessors was education. Generalists trained for the priesthood or the bar were replaced by experts with more specialized university training and often more than one degree. The rapid and dramatic growth of the Francophone university system contributed to this. As well, an influential minority received part of its education outside Canada, in French, American and British universities. A degree from Harvard or the London School of Economics conferred considerable symbolic advantage on its owner.

During the Quiet Revolution, the people at the forefront were recent social science graduates, particularly in economics and sociology. In the civil service, economists were held in high regard and almost magical creative powers were attributed to them, until the economic difficulties of the 1970s and 1980s somewhat tarnished their image. During the 1970s, the social sciences gradually lost their attraction and were replaced by business administration, epitomized by the MBA degree. This switch was also reflected in goals and priorities — the concern with competence and scientific rationality that prevailed during the Quiet Revolution gave way at the end of the period to a preoccupation with efficiency and productivity.

Despite these new trends, careers in the traditional fields of law, medicine, engineering and accounting were still much sought after and the number of graduates in these disciplines increased rapidly. But there were profound changes in the way they were practised. There were still family doctors and neighbourhood lawyers who practised alone or with a colleague, but it was far more common for professionals to form large firms or teams with complementary specialties. Increased specialization, acquired either at university or on the job, was becoming a hallmark of career development. The very definition of a professional was changing as many became salaried employees.

Thus, a completely new ruling class rapidly occupied positions of power after 1960, and its members reaped clear benefits from their new situation — affluence, prestige, authority, influence and respect. The new ruling class had a solid foothold in the political sphere, but it had to come to terms with another elite that was emerging in the economic sphere.

The New Francophone Bourgeoisie

Quebec's social structure was characterized after 1960 by the emergence of a new Francophone bourgeoisie that developed out of the economic prosperity of the postwar period and established itself more firmly in the 1960s and 1970s. Early in the period, Jean-Louis Lévesque and the Simard and Brillant families were the biggest names in French Canadian financial circles, but later on the circle widened. One manifestation of this process was the extraordinary and dazzling rise of Paul Desmarais, who took control of Power Corporation and became the head of an industrial and financial empire. At a different level, there were many other well-known names — Pierre Péladeau, Jacques Francoeur, J.-A. DeSève, Jean A. Pouliot and Philippe de Gaspé-Beaubien in the media, the Perron brothers and Guylaine Saucier in the forest industry, Alfred Hamel in transportation, the Bombardier family, the Lemaire brothers and Marcel Dutil in manufacturing, the Parizeau, Saint-Germain and Tardif families in insurance, and Antoine Turmel in food distribution. Researchers have taken an interest in this new phenomenon and carried out a number of studies.

While the Francophone bourgeoisie includes many newcomers, it also has historical roots. By the end of the war, some French Canadian companies — especially the Francophone banks, the caisses populaires and some insurance and trust companies — already had a long history, although they were small compared to the large Canadian institutions. As well, French Canadian fortunes were built over the years, often in the form of investment portfolios. Thus, there were existing institutions and accumulated capital that could play a role in the expansion and consolidation of the new bourgeoisie. During the period, some of these institutions were acquired by new Quebec companies, which thus gained a reserve of savings that had been accumulated earlier.

Paul Desmarais, chair and chief executive officer of Power Corporation. (*Le Journal de Montréal*)

However, historic roots are not enough to explain the rise of a Francophone bourgeoisie. The changes that had occurred in the Quebec market since the war — increased population, greater urbanization, and a pronounced rise in educational level and standard of living — constituted another factor in its development. Thus broadened, the Quebec market was more integrated into the system of consumption, and the Francophone bourgeoisie was able to take advantage of this quantitative and qualitative growth.

Changes in ideology and attitudes are also worth noting. With the Quiet Revolution, a wave of modernization spread over Quebec, along with a form of nationalism that sought to expand Francophone influence, especially by taking charge of the economy. Some writers have maintained that because of clerical control over education and the influence of religion, until 1960, French Canadians were given little encouragement to become interested in business. The effect of this factor has certainly been exaggerated. But whatever its impact, it no longer operated after 1960, when the quick collapse of religious beliefs and the clergy's loss of influence removed any obstacle there had been. From that time on, reform liberal ideology became all-pervasive, challenged only by the Marxist-inspired left in the late 1960s and then by the move back to classical liberalism in the 1980s.

The effects of modernization were most conspicuous in the education system, which now gave more Quebecers an opportunity to prepare for careers in business. Engineering, commerce and business administration programs underwent phenomenal growth, and more of their graduates went into business. Through the normal process of promotion, a growing number of French Canadians reached the upper echelons of large corporations. However, education was not a panacea. Business has always been, and continues to be, an area where "self-made men," more interested in doing than in studying, can make it on their own account. Many business people did their learning and acquired skills within the corporation.

The term "businessmen" increasingly gave way to "business people" to reflect another new development during the period: the entry of women into management positions. Although still in the minority, there were many more of them than before, and during the 1980s, the media recognized this new development and devoted more attention to women in business. Businesswomen such as Claire Léger, Guylaine Saucier and Jeannine Guillevin-Wood became well known. These women did not have an easy time of it, since corporate culture had always been highly sexist, but the success achieved by women in business helped bring about a gradual change in attitudes.

Another set of factors contributing to the rise of the new Francophone bourgeoisie had to do with the nature of the areas of activity in which Quebec entrepreneurs operated. They concentrated mainly on sectors such as commerce, finance, personal services, real estate and publishing, where technological barriers to entry were not difficult to overcome and growth was strong from the postwar years on. As well, as noted in chapter 31, the trend towards concentration in the 1970s and 1980s gave rise to Francophone corporations with an enhanced financial position, greater economic influence, and a capacity to support one another.

Quebec government intervention was also a determining factor in the consolidation and expansion of the Francophone bourgeoisie. Through its purchasing policy and financial assistance programs, the government helped strengthen companies belonging to French Canadians. Crown corporations also played a role in this regard, notably the Caisse de Dépôt et Placement, which helped maintain or increase Francophone control in some companies.

Thus, a whole series of factors contributed to the establishment of a new Francophone bourgeoisie. But clearly, the Quebec bourgeoisie was not limited to the Francophone bourgeoisie: it also had large contingents of Jewish and British Quebecers, among others. The question of ethnic origin has given rise to a debate. Should the Francophone bourgeoisie be seen as a relatively integrated whole, as the sociologist Jorge Niosi has argued? Or is the political scientist Pierre Fournier right to make a distinction within the Francophone bourgeoisie between a Quebec bourgeoisie, whose base of accumulation is mainly or exclusively Quebec, and a Canadian bourgeoisie, which operates Canada-wide and even internationally? The ethnic aspect is only one facet of the question, and the economic power each component of the bourgeoisie holds and seeks must also be taken into account.

A comparison with the situation elsewhere in Canada may be useful. Beginning in the nineteenth century, a distinction was established between the capitalist class with pan-Canadian and international ambitions and the middle bourgeoisie with a more geographically limited scope. Regional bourgeoisies have existed not only in Quebec but in other provinces as well; as Niosi points out, some of them have risen rapidly in recent decades, especially in British Columbia and the prairie provinces in addition to Quebec. These bourgeoisies have sometimes asserted themselves by resisting the big Canadian monopolies, which were increasingly Toronto-based. However, they have also sought to expand and operate on a Canada-wide basis. Their starting point was regional, but their operations have extended further. Thus, it must be concluded that there is no clearcut opposition between the Canadian and Quebec bourgeoisies; rather, new groups have formed among Francophones, and these groups, sometimes in competition with one another, have aspired to extend their operations outside Quebec. In doing so, they have come into conflict with other groups that have different ethnic origins and come from other regions of Canada.

The Canadian capitalist class, also known as the economic elite, had been solidly established in Quebec since its formation and had been closely associated with Montreal's role as metropolis. When the economic centre of gravity shifted westward, many members of the economic elite left Montreal for Toronto. St. James Street and Westmount faded as major symbols of Canadian high finance, and this trend accelerated in the 1970s.

The results of the study of the economic elite conducted by John Porter in the 1950s and Wallace Clement's similar survey for 1972 were discussed in chapters 21 and 31. Examining the characteristics of the directors of the 113 dominant corporations in Canada, Clement confirmed Porter's findings and found that the phenomena he identified had intensified. After the war, the Canadian economic elite was a small group of a few hundred carefully chosen individuals, whose social and family background played a central role in their inclusion. Clement found that the elite was even more closed in 1972: three fifths of its members were born into the upper class, and a growing number of them owed their accession to the boards of directors of dominant corporations to their family ties. Fewer individuals were able to make it on their own account.

The economic elite in 1972 was still overwhelmingly Anglophone. While the proportion accounted for by French Canadians increased slightly, from 6.7 per cent in the early 1950s to 8.4 per cent in 1972, they were still clearly underrepresented, as were other ethnic groups, whose share rose from 1 per cent to 5.4 per cent. Private schools continued to be the breeding ground for future members of the economic elite, and a large majority of them received a college or university education. Membership in private clubs, trade associations and charitable organizations was another distinguishing feature of this class. Clement also brought to light the close relations between the economic elite and other elites in Canada, especially the political and mass media elites.

Although no similar study has been carried out for a more recent period, it is generally considered that the 1970s brought about major changes within the Canadian capitalist class. As the 1980s began, there were still families of British origin at the top of the social pyramid — the Westons, the Thomsons, the Blacks — but there were also important Jewish families (the Reichmanns and the two branches of the Bronfman family) and Paul Desmarais. In 1984, the Toronto *Globe and Mail* estimated that the nine richest families in Canada controlled about half the value of the shares of companies (not counting the banks) that made up the Toronto Stock Exchange index.

The 1970s saw the rise of the "acquisitors," as the journalist Peter C. Newman termed the many newcomers to the ranks of the superrich during the decade. Many of them had a regional base, especially in western Canada, and built empires based on oil, real estate development and finance. While the 1982 recession shook some of these instant fortunes, the changes that had taken place continued to mark the Canadian bourgeoisie.

The new Francophone bourgeoisie developed in a similar way. It was based in Quebec, but sought to extend its influence outside the province. On the whole, it was federalist and did not seek to challenge the Canadian political system. But while it became more Canadian and international in its activities, it did not stop being Francophone and Quebec-oriented.

The Quebec bourgeoisie continued to rely on its own organizations, which acted as representatives of business in its dealings with the government and the public. In addition to the chambers of commerce and the large number of sectoral associations, many of which were long established, a new and unique organization emerged, the Centre des Dirigeants d'Entreprises. This body represented the most reform-minded element in the business community in the 1960s and 1970s, and its main concern was developing better cooperation among government, unions and employers.

In 1969, all these organizations except for the chambers of commerce decided to join together by setting up the Conseil du Patronat to express the point of view of firms and employers to the public and the government. Within a few years, the Conseil became the main mouthpiece of the business community and regularly pressured the government into taking employers' interests into account when developing policy. The Conseil du Patronat did not replace the various business associations, which continued to be active on their own, but it gave the corporate sector greater influence and a more unified voice.

Convergence and Divergence

Between the new Francophone bourgeoisie and the new ruling class, there were many points of convergence. The dual objective of modernizing Quebec and strengthening Francophone economic control could only bring these two groups together, and they supported each other in many ways. The pursuit of power necessarily brought about a convergence of the elites and the different groups they contained. Comings and goings of individuals between the corporate world and government, although not as common as in the United States, were nonetheless significant. The benefits these groups drew from the new political and economic order strengthened their cohesion into what appeared to be a true alliance of privileged people.

However, each of the groups that made up the elite had its own interests, which sometimes placed it in opposition to other groups. An initial source of tension was the dynamic relationship between the public and private sectors. While they supported each other in many ways, the private sector reacted strongly against the ambitions of the technocrats and the unwieldy bureaucracy these ambitions created. For its part, government tried to use social programs as a counterweight to the concentration of wealth and the inequality of private property.

Other tensions also showed up regularly in union-employer relations. The new trade union elites maintained clear links of solidarity with other elements in the ruling class. They supported the growth of the bureaucracy, whose employees made up a growing portion of union membership. They were supported publicly by many intellectuals and communicators. Even in their opposition to business, they received support from the political and technocratic elites, who designed new labour laws that were more favourable to the union movement. However, the trade union elites came into violent opposition with the political and technocratic elites in negotiations with the government as employer. The radicalization of trade union leaders and many intellectuals in the early 1970s heightened the existing tensions and made the trade union leaders and intellectuals a kind of opposition within the ruling class.

A third source of tension came from the dynamics of the relationship between Ottawa and Quebec. While they generally shared a basic nationalism, the members of the new elites were divided on the best way to strengthen Quebec and Francophones. These tensions were played out on the political scene in election battles and conflicts over the national question.

But despite their differences, all these groups shared a fundamental goal: holding power.

CHAPTER 39
WORKERS

The working world was in a state of flux during the 1960s. The labour force continued to adjust to economic and technological change. At the same time, it grew younger with the arrival of the baby boom generation on the job market, diversified, became more educated, and included more women. The trade union movement, while representing only part of the labour force, increased its membership considerably, and its influence extended throughout society. And the government pursued a policy of cooperation instead of the confrontation of the preceding period.

The Working World

The labour force grew from 1.8 million people in 1960 to 2.3 million in 1983. This increase reflected not only population growth but also an increase in the rate of participation in the labour force, from 54 per cent in 1960 to 61 per cent in 1984. This meant that a larger portion of the population aged fifteen and over was in the labour market. In particular, women's participation rate almost doubled, rising from 26.5 per cent in 1960 to almost 48 per cent in 1983, while men's participation fell from 81.5 per cent to less than 75 per cent.

The longstanding trend towards the growth of the service sector continued: in 1981, almost 70 per cent of employment was in service jobs, while primary jobs accounted for 5.6 per cent and secondary jobs for 24.6 per cent. This brought about a number of changes. As office workers grew in number, their prestige diminished and their tasks were increasingly fragmented and mechanized. At the same time, companies hired more executives and professionals, who enjoyed high salaries and a large measure of autonomy. The emergence of government as a major employer strengthened these tendencies.

Another set of transformations arose out of technological change. Some of these changes led to a deterioration in working conditions, status and wages, while others led to an improvement. In mining and manufacturing, increases in productivity always resulted in a reduction in the

Getting off work at a factory in Sorel. (National Archives of Canada, PA-133213)

labour force and a wage increase for the workers who remained, usually accompanied by a faster pace of work. Wherever this process operated, the jobs involved were profoundly transformed, after a transition period that was often long and difficult.

As the 1980s began, a new trend emerged. Part-time work became more common, accounting for 13 per cent of jobs in 1983 as compared with 7.4 per cent in 1976. Young people and women were most heavily affected by the increase in part-time employment, which was caused by the recession of the early 1980s and employers' desire to reduce their permanent labour force, as well as by changing attitudes to work.

One of the goals of the Quiet Revolution was to improve the educational level of the population, and the effects of this change were felt quickly in the labour force. While barely 44.5 per cent of the active population had more than a primary school education in 1960, the figure was 67 per cent in 1977 and 82 per cent in 1984. The standard of living improved greatly after 1960, with wages rising faster than prices. The average weekly wage rose from $73.01 in 1960 to $199.22 in 1975, and then to $427.49 in 1984.

Of all these major changes, the greater participation of women in the labour force was the most significant. Female labour, which had previously consisted mainly of young women who left their jobs when they got married, became more of a permanent fixture as the participation of married women increased markedly. Women had fewer children, which meant that they usually stopped working temporarily rather than permanently. However, broadening of the kinds of jobs women workers did lagged behind their increase in numbers. While the improved average educational level led to some diversification, 60 per cent of the female labour force was concentrated in seven occupations in 1981: stenographer-typist, office clerk, nurse, teacher, waitress (in restaurants and hotels), salesperson, and textile or clothing worker.

A more acute awareness of the wage gap between male and female workers led to the demand for "equal pay for equal work," around which trade unions and feminist groups mobilized. The government began to respect this prinicple and prohibited all wage discrimination on the basis of sex. Nonetheless, large discrepancies persisted, especially in private sector service occupations. Even in areas were wages were nominally the same, wage inequalities persisted because of factors such as seniority, job security, and part-time work. There was also a growing awareness that many women — an estimated 150,000 in 1966 — worked alongside their husbands in small businesses, usually on an unpaid basis.

The labour market was afflicted by endemic unemployment, which affected all regions of Quebec although it was unevenly distributed. The unemployment rate went up and down with the economic cycle, but unemployment was now not only a cyclical phenomenon but also contained a permanent or "structural" component, caused by deficiencies in economic development, the aging industrial structure and the swelling labour force. Newcomers to the labour market — young people between the ages of fifteen and twenty-four and women — were most severely affected by unemployment.

A variety of groups remained on the fringes of the working world. One such group was made up of all the women who stayed at home and whose economic contribution, although essential, was unpaid and did not appear in official statistics. Then there were the unemployed who had given up all attempts at finding a job and joined the ranks of welfare recipients. Some of these were people who were discouraged by what seemed an impossible quest, while others rejected a working world they considered alientating and settled for a life of near-poverty on the fringes of society. In 1984, the welfare rolls included 250,000 people who were able to work.

The working world has become so diverse that it is no longer accurate to include all the individuals in it under the umbrella of one social class, the working class. Because of the wide variation in status, income and educational levels, it is becoming more common to refer to them simply as workers.

Trade Unions

The trade union movement felt the impact of changes in the labour market. Membership climbed sharply, rising from a little under 400,000 in 1961 to 850,000 in 1984. While the rate of unionization is subject to disagreement, the most reliable estimates indicate that it rose steadily until the mid-1970s, increasing from 30 to 40 per cent, and then declined to 34 per cent by 1984. In 1960, the union movement was still dominated by international unions, which represented two thirds of union members, and by the Confederation of National Trade Unions, which represented about a quarter. Other unions included the Corporation des Instituteurs et Institutrices Catholiques and a variety of independent unions.

Trade unions took on greater importance in Quebec life between 1960 and 1983. At the same time, three major changes took place: Canadianization of the international unions; the rise of the Confederation of National Trade Union (CNTU), followed by a split that weakened it; and the rise of independent unions.

The role of the Quebec Federation of Labour (QFL) has been substantially transformed and enhanced over the period. In 1960, only 40 per cent of the members of international unions affiliated with the Canadian Labour Congress belonged to the QFL, but the proportion grew with time and in 1983 exceeded 80 per cent. Its leaders became recognized and respected representatives of the labour movement.

While the QFL did not have all the powers of a true union federation, it did acquire greater autonomy from the CLC and played a greater role on the Quebec trade union scene. As the trend towards Canadianization grew within the CLC, the QFL began to identify more closely with Quebec and took more nationalist positions. It benefited from the growing trend towards unionization in the public and parapublic sector, although less so than the CNTU. However, it has a more solid base in the private sector, where most of its membership is concentrated. It has taken a less radical approach than the CNTU and has openly supported the Parti Québécois and the New Democratic Party. It remains the largest trade union organization in Quebec, representing 33 per cent of trade union members.

The second largest organization, the Confederation of National Trade Unions (CNTU), grew substantially in the 1960s. It very quickly shed what remained of its Catholic trade union heritage and became more radical and militant as the years went by. It retained the strong base it had developed in the social services sector, especially hospitals, and was the main beneficiary of the huge wave of unionization in the public and parapublic sector, doubling its membership between 1960 and 1966. The composition of its membership was profoundly changed by this development — in 1966 less than half of its members were in the private sector, as compared to three quarters in 1960. The CNTU increasingly established itself as the union federation representing government employees.

Confrontation during the *La Presse* strike, 1971. (*La Presse*)

In 1972, a major split divided the CNTU and it lost several thousand members, who founded the Confederation of Democratic Unions (CDU). The CDU unions, which mainly represented private sector workers, rejected the militant trade unionism and class struggle ideology embraced by the CNTU. The departure of the CDU unions strengthened the influence of the public sector unions within the CNTU, although large unions such as the provincial civil servants and the Alliance des Infirmières also left the federation. By 1983, the CNTU represented only 22 per cent of Quebec trade union members and appeared to be drifting somewhat, in contrast to its previous dynamism.

With a membership made up entirely of teachers, the Corporation des Instituteurs et des Institutrices Catholiques (CIC) was relatively isolated from the two other union federations at the beginning. It dropped the word "Catholic" from its name in 1967 and increasingly modelled itself along union lines, adopting the new name of Centrale de l'Enseignement du Québec (CEQ). Its membership grew very quickly during the time of the great educational reforms, rising from 30,000 in 1960 to 68,000 in 1968. Membership levelled off at between 70,000 and 80,000 during the 1970s. Although the CEQ has tried to diversify its membership to include non-teaching personnel and CEGEP and university teachers, the vast majority of its members are still primary and secondary school teachers.

In the early 1960s, the union federations, and especially the CNTU, shared the main objectives of the Quiet Revolution. They took part in the heated debates taking place in Quebec and cooperated with the government, which needed their support to carry out reforms. But the atmosphere in the second half of the decade was different. The government

Common front demonstration in 1972, led by the presidents of the three union federations, Louis Laberge (QFL), Yvon Charbonneau (CEQ) and Marcel Pépin (CNTU). (John Daggett, Montreal *Star*, National Archives of Canada, PA-1116453)

took on the role of employer, while the union federations, influenced by the ideological and political radicalism characteristic of the period, adopted new methods and views. Going beyond traditional union activity, they suggested that a "second front" be opened, consisting of a radical critique of the economic system and open participation in politics. From that time on, the union movement became mistrustful of political parties and governments; cooperation and working together appeared to them to be a trap. This was also the period when Marxist ideas flourished within the trade union federations. Although they were more prevalent in the CNTU and the CEQ than in the QFL, they coloured all the debates taking place within the unions on the nature of society. Each union published a provocative manifesto: *L'État, rouage de notre exploitation* (The state, instrument of our exploitation: QFL, 1971); *Ne comptons que sur nos propres moyens* (Let us rely only on our own means: CNTU, 1971); and *L'École au service de la classe dominante* (Schools at the service of the ruling class: CEQ, 1972).

The radicalization of the union federations also affected labour relations, and some negotiations degenerated into conflict and even violence. This was the case with the strikes at Seven-Up (1967-68), *La Presse* (1971), the Firestone plant in Joliette (1973-74) and United Aircraft (1974-75). Also during the 1970s, negotiations in the public and parapublic sectors took on great significance. The establishment of interunion united fronts to negotiate with the government was a North American first; never had a government sought to negotiate with all its employees at once. These negotiations turned very quickly into confrontation, with strikes involving tens of thousands of employees and retaliation in the form of injunctions and back-to-work legislation. In 1972, the presidents of the three union federations were found guilty of defying a court order and sent to jail. While subsequent common fronts (1975-76 and 1979-80) did not go that far, they occupied the attention of the unions and the government for months at a time and mobilized public opinion. Repeated utility strikes irritated users and tarnished the unions' public image.

Other signs that the unions were losing their vitality appeared in the mid-1970s. The rate of unionization declined somewhat and the recession of the early 1980s pushed it down still further. Independent unions also grew considerably. Trade unionism appeared to have reached a plateau; most of the growth in membership came from the civil service, which was no longer expanding. In 1983, the public and parapublic sector accounted for 44 per cent of trade union members and had a unionization rate of 63 per cent, much higher than the 24 per cent in the private sector. This imbalance was a source of tension within the union movement.

As the number of women workers grew, unions made timid efforts to make a place for women in their structures. They set up women's committees, but progress has been slow, as shown by the small number of women in leadership positions in the unions. Even in the CEQ, where women constitute two thirds of the membership, they are far from being represented in the leadership in proportion to their numbers.

Government Action

The Quebec government's first initiative in the labour field in the early 1960s was to revamp the labour code. Dating back to the 1940s, the code was no longer adequate, and Duplessis's use of the code to fight the labour movement had discredited it. The government therefore sought to develop an entirely new labour code that would meet the needs of an industrial society. The new code was adopted in 1964 after intense negotiations between the government and the unions. The new code shortened the mandatory time periods for negotiating collective agreements. It also recognized the right to strike in public services, except for firefighters, police, civil servants and teachers. Civil servants and teachers were granted the right to strike the following year.

The Lesage government also raised the minimum wage, a measure that had considerable impact because it affected a large number of wage-earners who had no union protection. In addition, the establishment of the Quebec Pension Plan in 1964 ensured that workers with no retirement pension would have a minimum income.

In 1967, when the Johnson government was in power, the legislature passed special legislation ordering striking teachers back to work. This was the first time the Quebec government resorted to back-to-work legislation, which would become a common practice in public service strikes in the decades to come.

Under the Bourassa government of the 1970s, public and parapublic sector negotiations were at the forefront of labour relations. The government also legislated with regard to the construction industry, mass lay-offs and the minimum wage. The election of the Parti Québécois government, with its "prejudice in favour of workers," marked a change in attitude. The new government sought to promote cooperation among the major partners in society by organizing a series of summits beginning in 1977, where unions, employers and government met to discuss Quebec's future development. At the same time, it undertook to review and systematize all labour-related legislation. It made changes to the labour code from 1977 on; the most noteworthy ones forbade the use of strike-breakers and made it compulsory for union dues to be withheld at source (the Rand formula). In 1979, it modernized all regulations affecting non-unionized workers through work standards legislation, which governed such matters as the minimum wage, working conditions, paid vacations and maternity leave. Finally, an occupational health and safety act replaced the old work accidents legislation and provided better protection, mainly by allowing any worker to refuse to perform any work dangerous to his or her health. As well, it made employers financially responsible for the work accident insurance plan.

The federal government has its own immigration, training and labour force management programs, as well as the Unemployment Insurance Commission. But it has influenced the labour force mainly through its economic policies. In the mid-1970s, when the fight against inflation was in full swing, Ottawa introduced wage and price controls, which had direct effects on labour contracts and provoked strong reaction in trade union circles. As well, even though federal labour regulation covers only about 10 per cent of Quebec workers, it has had substantial ripple effects.

* * * * * *

Thus, in the space of a quarter of a century, the working world, like the society of which it is a part, experienced far-reaching changes. Trade unions improved their structures, and until the early 1980s they were able on the whole to win better wages and working conditions for their members. During the same period, they became very important social partners, taking an active part in developing the policies that guided Quebec's development. Subsequently, however, the recession of 1981-82 created new power relationships that were much less favourable to the trade unions, both in Quebec and elsewhere in North America, and the unions entered into a period of difficulty and even crisis.

CHAPTER 40
ETHNIC DIVERSITY

Quebec's ethnic and cultural diversity occupied a substantial degree of public attention from the late 1960s on. It was not a new phenomenon, having been part of Quebec life since the early twentieth century, but it took on new significance as a growing variety of ethnic groups were represented in Quebec and it became necessary for Quebecers of old Francophone and Anglophone stock to redefine their positions and attitudes towards these groups.

Immigration is the initial cause of Quebec's ethnic diversity. As time goes on, however, newcomers become citizens and have children in Quebec, so that it is no longer a question of immigrants but rather one of Quebecers of diverse ethnic origins.

Immigration

The impact of migratory movements on population has already been examined (see chapter 30). We will now explore the newcomers' social and ethnic characteristics and the development of government policy towards them.

After a period when its borders were all but closed because of the particular circumstances of the Depression and the war, Canada again became a receiving country for immigrants in the postwar period. Between 1946 and 1982, 5,896,873 immigrants came to Canada; Quebec was the first destination for 965,075 of them, or 16.4 per cent of the total. Quebec's rate of attraction was highest between 1951 and 1967, when it generally fluctuated between 20 and 25 per cent; subsequently, it held steady between 15 and 17 per cent. The proportion of Quebecers born outside Canada rose from 5.6 per cent in 1951 to 8.3 per cent in 1981.

When Ottawa opened the doors again after the war, it implemented a policy similar to the one in force in the early twentieth century. This consisted of attracting a large number of immigrants, even unskilled ones, to meet the country's labour requirements and stimulate economic growth. Recruitment was concentrated in Europe, and immigration from other parts of the world was restricted. Some attention was paid to war refugees, but newcomers were admitted mainly through sponsorship by relatives and friends already settled in Canada. Between 1946 and 1961, Italian and British immigrants to Quebec were the largest contingents (a little over 75,000 each), followed by the German and Austrian, French, and Jewish groups. There was also the beginning of a wave of Greek immigrants (about 20,000) and a strong Hungarian contingent after the failed revolution of 1956.

During the 1960s, federal immigration policy gradually changed. Restrictions on non-European immigration were lifted, but at the same time numbers coming in were controlled in an effort to adjust the influx to the needs of the labour market. This was accomplished through a selection system designed to take into account prospective immigrants' skills and training and the demand for labour in their area of specialization, which was put into place in 1967. At the same time, illegal immigration of individuals who did not meet the new criteria was on the rise.

Between 1962 and 1970, the main countries of origin for immigrants to Quebec were Italy, France and Britain, followed by Greece and the United States. The 1960s represented an exceptional period for immigration from France, with almost 40,000 newcomers. The southern European countries — Italy, Greece and a new source country, Portugal — supplied more than a quarter of the new arrivals. The range of immigrants broadened with the arrival of fairly large numbers from the Caribbean, Egypt and other parts of the Third World.

Immigrants arrived from an ever-growing variety of countries as federal restrictions were lifted in the decade that followed. Unsettled conditions in many countries brought more political refugees from areas such as southeast Asia, Lebanon, Chile and Central America. Haiti was one of the main sources of immigration, followed by the United States, France, Vietnam and Britain. Immigration from southern Europe declined; Italy, the main source of immigration since the end of the war, was now in eighth place with fewer than 10,000 immigrants.

Even though constitutional responsibility for immigration was shared between the federal and provincial governments, it had been a long time since the Quebec government had played any active role in it. But from the early twentieth century on, Quebec nationalists had attacked federal policy in this area because they felt it might upset the traditional balance between the country's two main ethnic groups. Starting in the postwar period, intellectuals had been demanding that the Quebec government intervene in the area of immigration, but without success — immigrants headed for Quebec were chosen by federal civil servants, who did not take into account the French character of the immigrants' new home. On arrival, private associations, set up by ethnic groups themselves or by churches, took charge of the newcomers.

It was not until 1965 that the Quebec government established an immigration section, coming initially under the Department of Cultural

Affairs and then under the provincial secretary's department. During this period, the question of what language immigrants would be educated in, which soon sparked a full-blown language crisis, brought immigration into the political arena. The government realized it had to intervene to ensure the harmonious integration of immigrants into the Francophone community, and the Quebec Department of Immigration was created for that purpose in 1968. The same year, immigrant guidance and training centres, known as Centres d'Orientation et de Formation des Immigrants or COFIs, were set up.

The Quebec government's first measures in the area of immigration had to do with receiving and integrating immigrants, but the initial selection of immigrants was still done by federal authorities. As a second stage, Quebec demanded the right to have input into the selection process, to give potential immigrants better information on the Francophone nature of Quebec society and especially to attract more individuals who would be likely to fit in easily. Ottawa agreed in stages, from 1971 to 1978, to make room for Quebec's representatives, who were given a role in the selection process beginning in 1978.

Post-1960 immigrants were diverse not only ethnically but socially as well. The immigrant experience took very different forms depending on what kind of milieu the immigrants came from, their age, their educational background and even the colour of their skin. Managers, engineers and highly skilled technicians, mostly from Britain, Germany and the United States, were in demand in industry. To meet the needs of the educational system, which was growing quickly in the 1960s, French, Belgian and Egyptian teachers were recruited for Francophone schools, as were British and American teachers for Anglophone schools. Jews from Morocco and the Middle East brought capital and business experience with them. Moreover, the government was on the lookout for immigrant investors who could create jobs.

However, the situation was not as rosy for the majority of immigrants. Peasants from southern Europe and Third World countries moved into the most arduous and lowest-paying jobs in construction, manufacturing and services. Many Haitians, for example, became taxi drivers. Immigrant women were even more heavily exploited by clothing manufacturers and office cleaning contractors. Each immigrant group that managed to improve its lot after years of hard work was replaced by another wave of newcomers who took over the least desirable jobs.

But even if it subjected them to exploitation, immigration offered many people a real opportunity for social and economic mobility that did not exist in their countries of origin. Many immigrant groups — and especially the largest group, the Italians — developed an economic strategy based on family solidarity and pooled resources, with home ownership as the material and symbolic goal. Immigrants who arrived after the war benefited from postwar prosperity, but more recent arrivals, particularly Third World immigrants belonging to what became known as visible

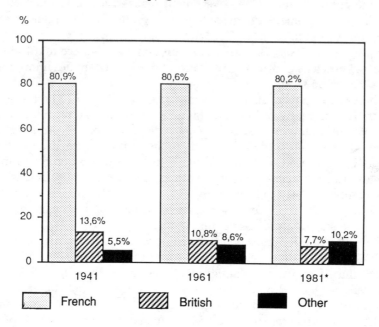

Figure 1
Population Distribution by Ethnic
Group, Quebec, 1941-1981

*The 1981 data are not entirely comparable with those of previous years. They are based on a sample of 20 per cent of the population; 2 per cent of respondents indicated more than one ethnic origin.

Source: Hubert Charbonneau and Robert Maheu, *Les aspects démographiques de la question linguistique*; Censuses of Canada, 1971 and 1981.

minorities, ran up against more open discrimination and had to deal with the more difficult economic situation prevailing at the end of the period. Their precarious existence gave them little hope of rapid mobility, and they often had to resort to social assistance.

Quebec's Ethnic Composition

Quebec's ethnic makeup was inevitably influenced by immigration, and in particular by the new structure of immigration that developed during the period. Other influences included the return of some immigrants to their country of origin, interprovincial migration, and the different rates

A class at James Bay. (Hydro-Québec)

of natural increase for different ethnic groups. In the Canadian census, ethnic origin has been defined by the first male ancestor who arrived in North America, except in the 1981 census where the question was left open to interpretation by respondents. In recent years, with the proliferation of interethnic marriages, information on ethnic origin has posed problems for researchers, and other variables such as mother tongue and language of use are now also considered. We will discuss the language aspect more specifically in the next chapter.

Graph 1 and table 1 show the numbers of the main ethnic groups in Quebec and their proportion of the Quebec population as a whole. Three main trends emerge: the French Canadian population has remained fairly stable at around 80 per cent, the proportion of Quebecers who are of British origin has been in steady decline, and their place has been taken by a rising proportion of Quebecers of other ethnic origins. Researchers in the 1970s and 1980s took great interest in studying the history of each group, tracing the story of how it arrived in Quebec and examining its socioeconomic and cultural characteristics. However, such a detailed ex-

Table 1
Population of Major Ethnic Groups in Quebec, 1961-81

Ethnic origin	1961	1971	1981*
French	4,241,354	4,759,360	5,105,670
British	567,057	640,045	487,380
Italian	108,552	169,655	163,735
Jewish	74,677	115,990	90,355
Greek	19,390	42,870	49,420
Aboriginal	21,343	36,590	46,855
German	39,457	53,870	33,770
Portuguese	n.a.	16,555	27,375
Polish	30,790	23,970	19,755
Chinese	4,749	11,905	19,255
Spanish	n.a.	10,825	15,460
Indochinese	n.a.	n.a.	15,125
Haitian	n.a.	n.a.	14,915
Ukrainian	16,588	20,325	14,640
Indo-Pakistani	n.a.	5,000	14,150
Armenian	n.a.	n.a.	10,380
Hungarian	15,561	12,570	9,750
Syrian/Lebanese	5,302	8,235	8,635
Netherlander	10,442	12,590	8,055
Belgian	12,092	8,220	6,465
Yugoslav	5,577	6,810	6,460
African	4,287	5,225	6,215
West Indian	n.a.	5,050	5,890
Egyptian	n.a.	n.a.	4,990
Filipino	n.a.	n.a.	4,460
Scandinavian	11,295	8,510	4,225
Russian	13,694	4,060	2,945
Romanian	7,101	2,320	2,785
Lithuanian	5,883	3,990	2,745
Austrian	7,423	2,500	2,275
British and French			62,270
British and other			20,645
French and other			21,790
Other mixed origins			23,250

n.a.: not available

*The 1981 data are not entirely comparable with those of previous years. They are based on a sample of 20 per cent of the population; 2 per cent of respondents indicated more than one ethnic origin.
Source: Censuses of Canada, 1961, 1971 and 1981.

amination is beyond the scope of this study, and here we will draw an overall picture only.

Native people. While Amerindians and Inuit are not very significant on the basis of numbers (they constitute less than 1 per cent of Quebec's population), they represent a unique group because they were the country's first inhabitants, because of where they live, and because of their special status. The native people of southern Quebec — such as the Mohawks of Kahnawake and the Hurons of Ancienne-Lorette — who live on reserves and whose way of life has been profoundly influenced by white society, can be distinguished from the native people of the Far and Middle North, who have maintained their traditional customs and way of life longer. For northern native people, the situation changed quickly as a result of the impact of government policies aimed at settling them in villages and offering them better educational, health and social services. On the whole, native people have continued to lead a precarious existence and have been marginalized under the guardianship of higher levels of government. However, there has been a revival of native pride during the period in both Canada and the United States, and native people have demanded greater political, economic and social autonomy. In Quebec, this new mood began to be evident in the negotiations over the James Bay Agreement, signed in 1975. The agreement recognized the right of the Cree and Inuit to occupy and use part of the land in question and provided for substantial financial compensation which the native people later used to set up their own businesses. The assertion of native rights has sometimes led to conflict with the Quebec government, notably at Oka and Kahnawake in the summer of 1990. The Quebec government had previously left native affairs to the federal government, but in the 1960s it began to play a greater role, exercising its jurisdiction in areas that came under its constitutional purview.

French Canadians. Since the nineteenth century, French Canadians had managed to consolidate their position in Quebec by compensating for the effects of migration through a high birth rate. But this traditional balance was upset in the mid-1960s. The falling birth rate became a cause for great concern and brought to light the extent to which Quebecers of other ethnic origins had become Anglicized. The upsurge of nationalism in these years led to a burst of ethnic consciousness centred on Quebec and what it meant to be a Quebecer, and the term "Québécois" tended to replace "French Canadian."

Despite their numbers, Quebecers of French origin were, in socio-economic terms, a dominated majority in 1960: they were second-class citizens in their own territory. Their average income was well below that of most other ethnic groups. During the Quiet Revolution and the years that followed, the situation changed radically. Quebecers of French origin gained greater control of the economy and their standard of living improved.

Quebecers of British origin. The new nationalism was directed primarily against the dominant minority: Quebecers of British origin, whom one Anglophone observer called "Westmount Rhodesians." Of course, in the early 1960s many of the 567,057 English Quebecers lived modestly, but a large proportion of them were at the top of the social scale. Their influence over society and especially the economy was disproportionate to their numbers. They were mainly concentrated in Montreal, living mostly in a relatively autonomous Anglophone community, with no ongoing contact with the Francophone majority and no need to speak French.

The English Quebec community continued to grow during the 1960s, but beginning in the 1970s their numbers fell dramatically, and in 1981 there were fewer Quebecers of British origin than there had been in 1961 (table 1). The English Montreal community was severely shaken by the shift of the centre of Canadian economic activity to Toronto and by the shock of growing Francization, which prompted many to leave the city. Those who remained went through a painful period of adjustment and learned to live as a minority. They became more open to the French fact while at the same time they fiercely defended their rights. Even as their numbers fell, Quebecers of British origin were nonetheless strengthened by the growing number of individuals of other ethnic origins who chose English as their language of use and thus integrated into the Anglophone bloc.

Jewish Quebecers. While Jews come from different countries of origin and identify themselves primarily in relation to a common religion, Canadian census takers have considered them an ethnic group. Their presence in Quebec is a longstanding one, although the largest numbers of Jews arrived around the turn of the century. Until 1960, they were the largest group of non-French and non-British origin. Through their business people, trade unionists, scientists and intellectuals, the Jews have played and continue to play an important role in the history of Quebec. Because they have been concentrated in Montreal, they have been able to maintain a presence in the federal, provincial and municipal political arenas.

Their upward social mobility has been more rapid than that of any other group. By 1961, the descendants of poor turn-of-the-century immigrants had the highest average income of all ethnic groups in Quebec, even including the British. The majority were members of the Ashkenazi community, one of the two main groupings in world Jewry. They or their parents came mainly from Poland and Russia and shared a common language, Yiddish, and an eastern European culure. Even though their culture changed in the North American environment and the use of Yiddish declined, Montreal Jews maintained tight social and geographical cohesion based on a solidly established religious and institutional system. Beginning in 1957, Jewish homogeneity was broken up by the arrival of Sephardic Jews, mainly from Morocco, who spoke French and whose culture was shaped by centuries of living in the Arab world. The differences between the two groups were a source of tension within the community, and the newcomers, who were in the minority, had to carve out a place for themselves in a society where they spoke the language of the majority but their coreligionists had chosen English.

Quebec Jews became part of the migration of some Quebec Anglophones to Toronto. Along with significant aging within the group, this movement was responsible for their declining numbers after 1971 (see table 1).

Italian Quebecers. Since 1961, Quebecers of Italian origin have constituted the largest non-British minority, and because of their numbers they occupy a special place in the ethnic mosaic. As with the Jews, an organized community had come into existence by the turn of the century, and reinforcements arrived with the heavy wave of immigration of the 1950s. Although the immigrants came from all parts of Italy, the largest contingents were from the south — Molise, Campania and Calabria.

The first immigrants often had to work as labourers in construction and lived under very difficult conditions. However, their successors were able to take advantage of the prosperous postwar economic environment. While their socioeconomic rise was not as marked and rapid as that of the Jews, they did achieve upward mobility in the 1960s and 1970s. A new class of construction and industrial entrepreneurs, small merchants and professionals took over the leadership of the community from the priests and notables who had exercised it to that point. The younger generation had more education and achieved positions in society that their parents could never attain.

Because it was long-established in Quebec, the Italian community had a network of institutions: Italian parishes, organizations of *paesani* from the same village or province, cafés and grocery stores, and Italian-language print and electronic media. The language debates of the 1960s and 1970s led to the establishment of new, more political organizations. Among these was the Quebec section of the Congresso Nazionale degli Italo-Canadesi, founded in 1974, which became the community's main representative; it lobbied the government and tried to influence public opinion on behalf of the interests of Italian Quebecers. A new search for Italian identity on the part of poets, playwrights and filmmakers emerged around 1980.

The Italian community is by no means homogeneous. Because it is so large, there are many divisions within it — socioeconomic, ideological, cultural and even linguistic, since some Italian Quebecers have associated with Francophones while most opted to integrate into the Anglophone community. The experience of the Italian community reveals the contradictions all ethnic minorities have faced in attempting to integrate into and participate in Quebec and Canadian society.

Other groups. Aside from the main communities, Quebec has been home to a wide variety of ethnic groups (table 1), and this diversity increased with the migratory movements of the 1970s. The 1981 census probably underestimated the numbers of many groups, but it nonetheless showed an increase in the size of the Greek, Portuguese and Spanish communities, as well as a significant presence of visible minorities, particularly Chinese, Indochinese, Haitians and South Asians. These groups were generally concentrated in the Montreal region, heightening that area's ethnic diversity.

Cosmopolitan Montreal. Montreal had been the main entry point for immigrants for a long time. While the rest of Quebec was overwhelmingly French, the cosmopolitan character of the Montreal metropolitan area stood out. Francophones, with between 64 and 65 per cent of the population, represented only a relatively fragile majority there. The British, who had been solidly established for a long time in certain rural areas such as the Eastern Townships, the Gaspé and the Outaouais region, had been gradually retreating to Montreal since the nineteenth century; after 1960, three quarters of them lived in the Montreal area. However, in twenty years their share of the Montreal population fell from 18 to 11 per cent, and other ethnic groups — accounting for almost one fifth of the total population in 1981 — overtook them in numbers.

Ethnic makeup has also had a geographical dimension. Each group has tended to concentrate in certain neighbourhoods or suburbs. The British hold sway in the West Island. The Jews have a strong presence in the Snowdon and Côte-des-Neiges neighbourhoods and in Côte-St-Luc, one of the few municipalities with a Jewish majority outside of Israel. Large numbers of Italians live in Saint-Michel and Saint-Léonard, while many Greeks live in Park Extension. Churches, commmunity centres and even grocery stores and restaurants bear witness to Montreal's cultural diversity, symbolized by St. Lawrence Boulevard, virtually a multiethnic marketplace.

Managing Interethnic Relations

Growing ethnic diversity created new challenges for Quebec society. For a long time, attempts were made to reduce friction by isolating the groups from each other. Beginning in the nineteenth century, both the Francophone and Anglophone elites chose to have ethnically exclusive institutions. In practice, this resulted in a triple school system: French Catholic for the French Canadians, English Catholic for the Irish and English Protestant for the Scottish and English. Similarly, each ethnic group had its own ethnic society (St. Jean Baptiste, St. Patrick, St. George and St. Andrew) and charitable and religious organizations. This situation continued when new ethnic groups began to arrive early in the century. Thus, the Catholic Church established national parishes for Italians, Ukrainians and other groups. However, the school system was not further fragmented, and immigrant children had to integrate into already existing schools. This process caused some tension, as can be seen in the experiences of the Jews in the first half of the century.

Education was not the only issue; the whole question of integrating minorities into Quebec society arose after the war. The Francophone elites were slow to react to the new situation and chose to ignore the presence in Quebec of immigrants, whom they saw as outsiders. But the language issue forced them to put the problem of integrating minorities at the top of their list of priorities.

The federal government was the first to recognize Canada's growing ethnic diversity when it developed its multiculturalism policy in the 1960s. But multiculturalism had political connotations — its purpose was to depolarize the English-French debate and pave the way towards acceptance of the new policy of bilingualism it was also developing. While only two official languages were recognized, the richness of cultural diversity was praised as an expression of the Canadian mosaic.

The Quebec government's awareness of the issue came much later. Its policies were based on promoting French Canadians and Francization and left little room for minorities, who were to be simply forced to integrate into the Francophone majority. However, in the early 1980s the situation changed. Political recognition of ethnic contribution to Quebec society came in 1981, when the Department for Immigration became the Department of Cultural Communities and Immigration and the government initiated aid programs for various ethnic groups.

An awareness of the richness of Quebec's cultural diversity grew gradually throughout the period. By contrast, the language issue, which we will now examine, sparked an explosion.

CHAPTER 41

THE LANGUAGE ISSUE

The language issue was in the forefront of the debates taking place in Quebec society in the 1960s and 1970s. It was not a new problem. Several times since the conquest in 1760, French Canadian political leaders had had to defend the constitutional rights of the French language in the British country that was Canada. The 1867 constitution officially designated certain federal and Quebec government institutions as bilingual. In the twentieth century, Quebec nationalist intellectuals denounced the numerous infringements on these language rights, especially their failure to be observed outside Quebec, and at the same time attacked the Anglicization of Quebec society.

However, the debates of the 1960s and 1970s were very different in nature and scope. They took place in both the federal and provincial arenas, and two distinct and competing objectives were set out: on the one hand a bilingual Canada, and on the other a French Quebec. Studies were done, public opinion heated up and the legislation and regulations that governments adopted represented a complete break with their inaction of earlier periods.

The Languages Spoken in Quebec

At the heart of the debate were individual language choices. Census figures showed that French Canadians outside Quebec, even those living in areas of high geographic concentration such as Franco-Ontarians in eastern Ontario and Acadians in New Brunswick, were being gradually assimilated. Quebec was the only province where French was maintaining its position, although even there the language seemed threatened by the fairly widespread adoption of English by recent immigrants.

In an effort to distinguish language groups from ethnic groups, a new set of terms, based on mother tongue, began to be used (in both French and English): Francophone for French speakers, Anglophone for English speakers, and allophone for individuals whose mother tongue is neither French nor English.

Data on mother tongue (table 1) — the first language learned and still understood by the individual — show some parallels with the trends noted in chapter 40 with respect to othnic groups. Francophones maintained their position, Anglophones declined, and the proportion of allophones was on the rise after 1951. However, the congruence between language group and ethnic group is greater in some cases than in others. The percentage of Francophones is barely higher than the percentage of Quebecers of French origin (see graph 1 in chapter 40), indicating the weak attraction of French for other ethnic groups. The gap between Anglophones and Quebecers of British origin became proportionally wider beginning in 1951. This means that many descendants of immigrants learned English first rather than the language of their ethnic group. The same phenomenon is reflected in the percentage of allophones, which is lower than that of ethnic groups of origins other than French or British. The Anglicization of allophones appears even more strikingly in data on language of use — the language usually used at home (table 2) — which was not available until the 1971 census. The percentage of Quebecers who

Table 1
Distribution of Quebec's Population by Mother Tongue, 1931-81 (%)

Year	French	English	Other
1931	79.8	15.0	5.3
1941	81.6	14.1	4.4
1951	82.5	13.8	3.7
1961	81.2	13.3	5.6
1971	80.7	13.1	6.2
1981*	82.4	10.9	6.7

*1981 data are based only on a sample of 20 per cent of the population.

Sources: Hubert Charbonneau and Robert Maheu, *Les aspects démographiques de la question linguistique*; censuses of Canada, 1971 and 1981.

Table 2
Distribution of Quebec's Population by Language of Use, 1971-81 (%)

Year	French	English	Other
1971	80.8	14.7	4.5
1981*	82.5	12.7	4.8

*1981 data are based only on a sample of 20 per cent of the population.

Source: Censuses of Canada, 1971 and 1981.

The English face of Montreal, 1961. (Gar Lunney, NFB, National Archives
of Canada, PA-133218)l

have French as their language of use corresponds to the percentage with
French as their mother tongue. However, some of those who normally
use English at home have a different mother tongue.

Thus, language shift, which was usually permanent, worked mainly
to the advantage of English. While the Anglophone bloc lost members
with the departure of many Quebecers of British origin, it managed to
maintain itself by drawing in individuals of other ethnic origins. Assimilation to English, while varying in degree from ethnic group to ethnic
group, represented a huge trend that was especially significant in Montreal.

The strong attraction of English was due both to the mobility it offered
within Anglophone North America and to its undeniable status as the
language of business and therefore of economic success. The choice immigrants made was logical: they had left their countries of origin precisely to improve their economic situation, and so they learned the
language that offered them the best chance of success. The rise of the new
Francophone bourgeoisie and the increased Francization of the Quebec
economy occurred too late to alter these choices, which had often been
made before 1960. However, they did prompt a growing number of
Anglophones of all ethnic origins to learn French as a second language.

The degree of bilingualism rose during the period. The percentage of
Quebecers who could speak Canada's two official languages rose from
25.4 per cent in 1961 to 32.4 per cent in 1981. The gap between the sexes
tended to grow wider, since the percentage for men climbed from 29.7
per cent to 36.3 per cent, while it rose only from 25.4 per cent to 28.6 per

Executives from Shawinigan Water and Power taking French lessons after the nationalization of electricity. (Hydro-Québec)

cent for women. The demographers Hubert Charbonneau and Robert Maheu have shown that the gap between the sexes is primarily due to the difference in their degree of participation in economic life. Since women's participation increased significantly, a greater increase in bilingualism might have been expected; that it did not occur may perhaps be explained by the circumstance that women often work in jobs that do not require a knowledge of English.

The increase in bilingualism was also due to demographic factors, such as the decline in the number of children under the age of five, who are less bilingual than adults. There were certainly political factors as well. There was a considerable increase (from 28.7 per cent to 53.4 per cent) in bilingualism among Quebecers whose mother tongue was English, while the increase was much smaller (from 24.4 per cent to 28.7 per cent) among those whose mother tongue was French.

In the 1981 census, 60.1 per cent of the population (as compared to 61.9 per cent in 1961) still consisted of unilingual French speakers. Thus, counting bilinguals, 92.5 per cent of Quebecers could speak French (as compared to 87.3 per cent in 1961), so that even though many allophones were assimilated into the Anglophone bloc, the Francization of Quebec appeared to be an undeniable fact. English nevertheless maintained considerable strength.

Francophone elites had long been concerned about the quality and local authenticity of the French language in Quebec. The Société du Parler Français, founded in 1902, was the main forum for these concerns. Beginning in 1960, the issue was broadened and refocused as the poor and deteriorating French spoken by working-class Quebecers, particularly in urban areas, became a widespread source of anxiety. This type of French was given the derogatory nickname *"joual,"* and according to the intellectuals of the *Parti Pris* group, the situation could be corrected only if the sociopolitical and cultural alienation suffered by French Canadian society, and especially its underprivileged classes, was brought to an end. For others, the solution lay in democratizing education and establishing standards for "proper usage." This was the task undertaken by the Quebec government's Office de la Langue Française, established in 1961. At the same time, considerable work was done in the area of terminology, as French lexicons were distributed and, where necessary, prepared for various sectors where English was widely dominant: technology, computers, law, accounting, and others. Other influences, such as the growth of television and other communications media and the increasing number of exchanges with the international Francophone world (France, Belgium and French-speaking African countries), also affected the language situation.

It is difficult to measure the effects of these changes. Although claims are sometimes made for the existence of a Quebec language distinct from French, most observers agree that the French spoken by the elites and the middle class tended to move closer over the period to what is termed international French. This is not to say that the special features of Quebec French disappeared or that the very strong pressure exerted by English let up: in fact it intensified. It should also be noted that Quebec was not exempt from a North America-wide trend towards a deterioration in written language that began in the 1970s.

Francization and bilingualism were the two main aspects of the development of language in Quebec. But the changes that took place were not smooth ones. Battles were waged for recognition of the right to use French, both in Canada as a whole and in Quebec.

Ottawa and Bilingualism

The federal government was the first to make a move in the language field. As a result of the rise of the new Quebec nationalism beginning in the early 1960s, the government's legitimacy was called into question among Francophones, who saw it as representing English Canadians. Of course, under the constitution, federal institutions were officially bilingual and their major publications appeared in both languages. But this bilingualism was usually just for show, or else was based on one-way translation — reports, policies and laws were generally designed, developed and written in English and then translated into French. In theory, public services were available in French, but the situation varied from department to department and region to region. Almost all Francophone civil servants had to work part of the time in English, and the burden of bilingualism was theirs alone. In addition, they were heavily underrepresented among the senior civil servants and managers who made the real decisions.

Quebec nationalist intellectuals had denounced the situation regularly since the turn of the century, but without much effect. However, when Lester B. Pearson became prime minister in 1963, changes began to occur. The government set up the Royal Commission on Bilingualism and Biculturalism, cochaired by André Laurendeau and Davidson Dunton, and the B&B Commission, as it was familiarly known, carried out an in-depth study of the question. After issuing a preliminary report in 1965, it did not present its final report until 1969. Among other things, it recommended more bilingualism in the federal government and the establishment of Francophone work units. It also suggested that bilingual districts be set up in every region of Canada where there was a significant minority speaking one of the two official languages; under this proposal, Quebec would become a huge bilingual district.

After Pierre Elliott Trudeau succeeded Pearson in 1968, pressure grew for increased bilingualism in federal institutions. The new policy was set forth in the Official Languages Act, passed in 1969. A commissioner of official languages was appointed to oversee the implementation of bilingualism in the government. French courses for Anglophone civil servants were stepped up, and for a few years bilingualism bonuses were instituted for positions officially designated as bilingual. Federal bilingualism policy was also aimed at the provinces: they were given generous grants for education in the minority official language and pressure was placed on provincial governments to offer Francophone minorities services in French, as Quebec already did for Anglophones.

The new federal policy received much support from English Canadian intellectuals, but it also provoked negative reactions from the Anglophone provinces and from representatives of non-British and non-French ethnic groups. To assuage the fears of these ethnic groups, multiculturalism programs were developed simultaneously. In Quebec, the Anglophone minority and many French Canadian leaders supported the federal government, but it was denounced by Quebec nationalists who saw official bilingualism as an obstacle to their goal of increased Francization in Quebec.

Federal language policy resulted in a significant increase in French-language services. However, it failed to bring significant changes to the civil service, where Francophones remained notoriously underrepresented in the upper echelons. Resistance to bilingualism took many forms; one notable manifestation of it was the controversy that broke out over the use of French in air traffic control in 1976. Quebec pilots and air traffic controllers, who formed a group called the Association des Gens de l'Air, demanded the right to use French in communications with airport control towers in Quebec. Their Anglophone colleagues objected vehemently, invoking safety arguments. The Trudeau government had to back down and set up a commission of inquiry, which concluded that French communications presented no danger and thus paved the way for the use of French at some Quebec airports.

Federal language policy lost steam in the 1970s, not only because of resistance of this sort from English Canada but also because Quebec policy took a diametrically opposed direction.

The Language Battle

During the Quiet Revolution, the Quebec government was not particularly conscious of the language issue. The main concern was the ethnic dimension of power relationships rather than their language aspect, and the goal was to place more French Canadians in leading positions in the government and the economy. The fact that it was often necessary to work in English in the private sector was not called into question. For most Quebec leaders, learning English remained an economic necessity, although some pro-independence groups began to denounce this situation, calling openly for French unilingualism.

The first real awareness of the language issue developed in the field of education, where the government was forced to react to growing pressure from public opinion. During the second half of the 1960s, many

Confrontation between Italian Quebecers and French Canadians in Saint-Léonard, 1969. (Edwards, Montreal *Star*, National Archives of Canada, PA-137177)

observers pointed out that recent immigrants were chosing assimilation into the Anglophone community by sending their children to English schools. This was occurring at a time when the decline in the birth rate was preventing French Canadians from compensating for this language shift. The most alarmist observers predicted that in the long term, Francophones ran the risk of becoming a minority in their own territory unless corrective action were taken. The language choices made by allophones were seen as a threat to the very survival of the Francophone community. The language battleground would clearly be Montreal, and the first reactions to government inaction on the issue came from there.

The crisis broke out in the Montreal suburb of Saint-Léonard, where Italian minority parents sent their children to so-called bilingual classes, of which three quarters were given in English. In 1967, the school board trustees decided that bilingual education would be replaced with unilingual Francophone education. The Italian Quebecers resisted and established the Saint Leonard English Catholic Association of Parents. In reaction, Francophones set up the Mouvement pour l'Intégration Scolaire (MIS). The battle was waged on several fronts at once — with the government, before the courts, in the media and even in the streets. One demonstration organized in Saint-Léonard by the MIS in 1969 turned into a riot. Each group obtained outside support and the conflict took on Quebec-wide proportions.

With the developments in Saint-Léonard, the stakes became clear. On the one hand, supporters of freedom of choice wanted to leave all parents in Quebec free to choose their children's language of education. On the other hand, defenders of French unilingualism wanted to impose French-language education on everyone, although some of them were prepared to recognize the acquired rights of the minority of British origin. Thus, a position supporting the primacy of individual rights squared off against one supporting the primacy of collective rights. The Italian Quebecers were both players and prizes in the conflict. They upheld their own position by choosing English for their children and opposing what they considered a discriminatory attitude that insisted on treating them differently from people of British origin. At the same time, they found themselves involved in a conflict that was not primarily their own but rather a power struggle between English and French Canadians. The English used the Italian Quebecers as shock troops to defend their own interests, while the French wanted to draw them into the Francophone orbit or at least prevent them from swelling Anglophone ranks.

After an initial attempt to bring in language legislation in 1968, Jean-Jacques Bertrand's Union Nationale government introduced Bill 63 in 1969, establishing the principle of freedom of choice while offering incentives to promote the use of French in Quebec. This policy was greeted with sharp protest in Francophone nationalist circles. A Front du Québec Français was organized, and it waged a vigorous campaign to win over public opinion. Four members conducted the battle against Bill 63 in the

National Assembly while a series of demonstrations took place in the streets. This agitation contributed to the defeat of the Bertrand government in 1970.

Before taking action in this area, the new premier, Robert Bourassa, decided to wait for the report of the Commission of Inquiry on the Position of the French Language and on Language Rights in Quebec, set up by the Bertrand government in 1968 and presided over by the linguist Jean-Denis Gendron. When the commission finally presented its report in late 1972, it made many recommendations on a variety of aspects of the language question. The first recommendation set the tone for the rest. "We recommend that the Quebec government set itself the general goal of making French the common language of Quebecers, that is, a language known by everyone which can thus serve as an instrument of communication in contact situations between French-speaking people and Quebecers of other language groups." The commission was particularly interested in establishing French as the language of work. It maintained that the government had the necessary power to legislate in the area of language of education, but did not propose any policy in this regard.

On the basis of the Gendron Report's recommendations, the Bourassa government passed Bill 22 in 1974. This legislation established French as Quebec's official language and sought to ensure its preeminence in the workplace and in other sectors of activity. Freedom to choose the language of education was now limited: only children who could show through tests that they knew English were allowed to attend English schools. The passage of Bill 22 revived the language battle. Nationalist and pro-independence groups criticized it for granting too many privileges to English and not asserting French-language rights strongly enough, while many Anglophones attacked it for the opposite reasons. In the eyes of Anglophones and allophones, the language tests soon became the symbol of Francophone authoritarianism and the unequal treatment they felt subjected to. In 1976, the language issue again contributed to the defeat of a government.

When René Lévesque and the Parti Québécois came to power, they put forward their own solution to the problem. Bill 101 went much further than Bill 22 in asserting the preeminence of French in the workplace and public places, further limited access to English schools, and overall was much more restrictive than Bill 22. It was passed after a long and stormy debate in the National Assembly and enjoyed solid support in Francophone public opinion. But it was fought vigorously by Anglophone and allophone leaders, organized in a group called Alliance Quebec. They decided to challenge the law before the courts and succeeded in having a number of sections of it struck down. While debates on the language question continue, the material base of the problem had changed by the late 1970s, with Francophones more solidly in command of the economy and society in general than they had been a decade earlier.

Language Policy

Thus, over the course of a decade, successive Quebec governments, under pressure from Francophone public opinion and with tensions running high, developed a true language policy. Three major bills and a host of regulations for implementing them marked the development of this policy: Bill 63, the Act to Promote the French Language in Quebec, passed in 1969; Bill 22, the Official Language Act, passed in 1974; and Bill 101, the Charter of the French Language, passed in 1977. Despite their differences, there was a remarkable continuity among these language laws, and they reflected gradually widening concerns. Denise Daoust has summed up this progression as follows: "a) from one law to the next, the question of enhancing the social and economic value of the French language became more important; b) the emphasis gradually changed from language of education to language of work; c) there was a similar change in the guiding principles behind the laws, which started out by asserting collective identity and then gradually asserted territorial identity; d) the laws started out promoting bilingualism and ended up proclaiming French unilingualism; e) from one law to the next, mechanisms for implementation were refined and supplemented; and f) the laws at first offered incentives but later became coercive."

One of the main goals of Quebec government language policy was to ensure a preeminent position for French in Quebec society. Bill 63 sought to attain this objective slowly, through incentives, while Bill 22 made French the official language, although it recognized both French and English as national languages. Bill 101 did away with this perspective, retaining only French as the official language.

The bone of contention that set Anglophones and Francophones against each other was the school question. Quebec's language policy recognized the acquired rights of the British minority but restricted enrolment in English schools for French and allophone children. Bill 22 limited enrolment to those who already spoke English, while Bill 101 went even further, allowing access to English schools only to children with at least one parent who went to an English-language school in Quebec (the "Quebec clause"), or to children who were already attending English schools. The 1982 constitution modified this provision, replacing the "Quebec clause" with the "Canada clause," allowing access to English schools only to children with at least one parent who went to an English-language school in Canada. However, the effects of these restrictions were limited because they came fairly late — the main language shifts had occurred in previous decades and immigration was declining. In addition, education in French did not guarantee integration into Francophone society. Nothing prevented children from speaking English at home and in the street. Nonetheless, the language laws did mean that these children could work in a Francophone setting when they grew up.

Francization of the workplace was an important element in language policy. Bill 63 contained no specific provisions on this question but entrusted the Office de la Langue Française with the task of proposing measures to the government and developing French-language programs. One of the goals of Bill 22 was to make French the language of business, and it introduced the idea of a Francization certificate for businesses. This was meant as an incentive, but the certificates were nonetheless compulsory for companies doing business with the government. Bill 101 made the certificate compulsory for all businesses. Bill 22 made ability to use French compulsory for employment in the civil service and for obtaining a professional licence. These requirements were maintained in Bill 101, which also strengthened measures aimed at making French the language of internal and external communication in government and business.

One of the most visible effects of language policy was its impact on signs. Under Bill 22, signs had to be in French, although another language could be used as well. Under Bill 101, signs had to be in French only. Within a few years, the face of Montreal, where English had had a strong presence, was radically transformed. In 1988, however, the Supreme Court of Canada declared this part of Bill 101 unconstitutional. In response, the Bourassa government adopted Bill 178, under which bilingual signs are allowed inside small establishments but all outside signs must be in French.

Under Quebec language policy, special bodies were established to administer the laws. The Office de la Langue Française was set up in 1961 to improve the quality of French in Quebec. Bill 63 widened its mandate, giving it the power to investigate language complaints and make recommendations. Bill 22 replaced it with a Régie de la Langue Française, which had much more wide-ranging powers and was given the responsibility of seeing that the law was implemented and respected. Bill 101 set up three bodies: an Office de la Langue Française, in charge of Francization programs and work on terminology; a Conseil de la Langue Française to assess the language situation; and a Commission de Surveillance, a virtual "language police force" to deal with contraventions of the law.

By the end of the period, Francization was much more clearly established in Quebec. It is not clear whether this was due to the Quebec government's language policy or to a more general process of Francophone self-assertion. There is no simple and easily verifiable answer to this question. The Francization of Quebec seems to have been the result of a complex dynamic in which both individual and collective action played a role. At the same time, Francization remained a fragile accomplishment in a society subject to political, cultural and socioeconomic pressures from North America as a whole and more immediately from Canada and Anglophone Quebec. It also came up against the provisions of the Canadian constitution, especially with regard to official bilingualism and the primacy of individual rights.

CHAPTER 42

THE WOMEN'S MOVEMENT

Beginning in the mid-1960s and increasingly in the 1970s, women's issues were front and centre in Quebec's social, political and ideological life. Feminism, dormant since the war, resurfaced, and its reform and radical tendencies both gained widespread support. At the same time, women played more prominent and more varied roles in society, as changes in attitude and lifestyle challenged old models of femininity. Reforms promoting the equality of the sexes and greater freedom for women were a concrete political expression of these changes, but life in Quebec still failed to reflect the principle of equality in a consistent way. In this chapter, rather than discussing all the aspects of women's role in society touched on elsewhere, we examine the struggles waged by the major organized women's movements.

The Changes behind the Continuity

Between the war and the mid-1960s, there was virtually no discussion of women's role and position in society, and the women's emancipation movement seemed to be marking time.

In 1940, feminists finally won their struggle for the right to vote in Quebec provincial elections, which was very much a live issue as late as the 1930s and in which they faced strong opposition from the church, conservative nationalist circles and even major women's organizations such as the Cercles de Fermières. The suffrage question, feminist activism's main raison d'être for fifty years, was now gone. A brief controversy flared up in 1945, when Thérèse Casgrain succeeded in having the federal government pay the newly established family allowances to mothers, rather than to their husbands as Quebec's religious and political authorities had wanted. After that, however, feminism disappeared from the public arena.

While there were still a variety of women's organizations with a substantial number of members, they were not openly concerned with emancipation or equality. The Voice of Women was an organization devoted to pacifism and the struggle for disarmament. Unions of women workers and teachers worked mainly towards socioeconomic goals and, in any case, were primarily controlled by male executives. There were also large, Quebec-wide associations such as the Cercles des Fermières (founded in 1915), which were concerned mainly with crafts, and the two women's organizations set up after the war by the church: the Union Catholique des Femmes Rurales and, in the cities, the Cercles d'Économie Domestique. These denominational associations saw themselves as bulwarks against the damaging effects of emancipation; their essentially conservative orientation and the positions they took were very close to the traditional vision upheld by the church and the authorities. According to this vision, women were by nature inferior to men, or at least fundamentally different from them. Thus, in order not to betray her femininity, a woman had to stay out of the strictly male domains of gainful employment, the professions and politics and fulfil herself in her own sphere as a loving, faithful wife, devoted mother and industrious housekeeper.

Even outside traditional circles, this vision of women as dependent and submissive was widely propagated by the media, in a slightly altered version that became known as the new feminine mystique. Large numbers of women had participated in the war effort by working in factories and at home, doing volunteer work, and limiting domestic consumption. But once the war was over, women were urged to return to the home and resume their "natural" role, made more attractive by the new mystique. The emphasis was not on sacrifice but on the joy of being a wife and "modern" mother. The ideal woman was capable and active, keeping herself beautiful, decorating her house, providing support for her husband, and keeping abreast of the latest developments in medicine and psychology to care for and educate her children.

Thus, conceptions about the status and condition of women were unchanging, and the period from 1950 to 1964, as the historians of the Clio collective put it, the years between 1950 and 1964 were a "period when women's activism and feminist militancy could be described as silent."

But underneath the surface and away from view, changes were taking place. Even though the vast majority of women continued to marry and have children, contraception became common in the 1950s and use of the pill became widespread starting in the early 1960s. As a result, smaller families became common and the work involved in having children became less onerous. Meanwhile, in the context of the postwar industrial boom, the growth of the service sector, and the increasing secularization of the health care and education systems, more and more women entered the labour market. Some of them were married women who, defying prejudice, continued working or returned to their jobs while raising their families. In addition, even though the educational system still systemati- cally put girls at a disadvantage, more women succeeded in obtaining a higher education and embarking on careers that had previously been reserved for men. In the public arena, women made their presence felt in journalism, literature, the arts, Catholic Action movements, women's groups and trade unions.

While there were not yet feminist groups making demands, the changes taking place gradually modified women's image and self-image. The new needs that were created and the expectations aroused laid the groundwork for the awareness to come.

These changes in attitude were responsible for the passage in 1964 of Bill 16, aimed at bringing women's legal status into line with the way reality had evolved. The Civil Code continued to deny married women many of the rights enjoyed by men. Some minor changes were introduced in the early 1930s as a result of the work of the Dorion Commission on women's civil rights, and the articles dealing with adultery were amended in 1954. But to all intents and purposes, the Code treated women as minors, with no responsibility, completely subject to their husbands' authority. Bill 16 put an end to this state of affairs by recog- nizing the legal equality of the two spouses and women's right to civil and financial responsibilities that had previously been denied them.

Reform Feminism

Modern Quebec feminism originated in 1965-66 with the founding of two major organizations devoted to upholding women's legal and economic rights and fighting for equality.

The first was the Fédération des Femmes du Québec, which came into existence in 1965 at a conference on the condition of women organized to mark the twenty-fifth anniversary of female suffrage in Quebec. Non- denominational and ethnically mixed, the FFQ brought together about twenty women's groups and a few hundred individual members, mostly lawyers, trade unionists and social workers. It was influenced by the atmosphere of reform, and saw itself as a tool for promoting women's interests and a pressure group lobbying for reforms and legislation that might improve the condition of women and abolish all the forms of discrimination they were subject to. The FFQ quickly became one of the major feminist organizations in Quebec.

The other organization was the Association Féminine pour l'Éducation et l'Action Sociale, born in 1966 from the merger of the Union Catholique des Femmes Rurales and the Cercles d'Économie Domestique. Avowedly denominational and apolitical, the AFEAS was based mainly in the countryside and small towns. While less visible than the FFQ, it was closer to women from ordinary backgrounds. It was concerned with women's economic status and the work they did in the family and society, and had a special interest in women who worked alongside their husbands in family businesses.

These two movements marked the inception of the "first wave" of feminism — what some writers have termed reform feminism. Setting out to modify the social system rather than totally transform it, this type of liberal-inspired feminism aimed to make it possible for women to enjoy all the rights and advantages granted to men instead of suffering inequality and discrimination. It is to be distinguished from the much more radical leftist feminism that emerged in the early 1970s.

Radical Feminism

The relationship between reform and radical feminism should not be viewed simply as a progression. One branch did not replace or eliminate the other. In fact, throughout the 1970s, the reform movement remained extremely strong, and may have been larger than the radical groups. In 1980, for example, the FFQ grouped together thirty-five associations representing more than 100,000 women. It took up new issues such as the decriminalization of abortion, the elimination of sexist stereotypes, the fight for daycare and maternity leave. But it was the radical groups, many of which clashed with the reform ones, that gave 1970s feminism its particular impact.

According to the historian Martine Lanctôt, radical feminism did not limit itself to fighting for the "emancipation" of women in order to win equal rights with men. Instead, the women's movement was seen as engaged in a struggle for "liberation," implying the complete overthrow of the structures of society and a fundamental modification of the relationship between men and women, which was viewed as a relationship of domination and oppression. This goal was to be achieved by making demands, speaking out publicly, and taking part in demonstrations and other forms of direct action — even, when necessary, defying laws regarded as unjust and standing in the way of women's freedom and development.

The two tendencies also had different ways of operating. While the reform movement worked through large associations with well-established, hierarchical structures, radical feminists organized small groups that operated independently and spurned all forms of hierarchical leadership as characteristic of male power structures. Men were also excluded from participating.

The radical feminist tendency originated in the United States, emerging out of the movement against the Vietnam War and the fight for black civil rights. Two phases in the development of radical feminism in Quebec can be identified.

The first phase lasted from 1969 to about 1975, when the movement was developing in and around the socialist left wing of the nationalist movement. During this phase, a small number of activists were organized in various groups such as the Front de Libération des Femmes du Québec,

Demonstration in defence of Dr. Henry Morgentaler and in favour of liberalizing access to abortion. (*Le Journal de Montréal*)

the Montreal Women's Liberation Movement and the Centre des
Femmes. They broke off from the main body of the left, which rejected
their demand for autonomy, from the trade unions, which did not seem
sufficiently receptive to their cause, and from the nationalists, whom they
considered a reactionary movement that was trying to coopt them. As a
result, they became isolated and their influence was reduced.

The year 1975, proclaimed as International Women's Year by the
United Nations, was the beginning of a new phase of expansion and
decentralization for radical feminism. In the years that followed, many
groups were set up in Montreal and other Quebec towns and cities.
Ideologically, Marxist-inspired feminism ceased to be the main reference
point of the movement, giving way to a broad pluralism that included a
number of tendencies: nonsocialist radical feminism, what Diane
Lamoureux has called "identity" feminism, lesbian feminism, and the
many women's collectives that were less interested in ideological issues
than in concrete work towards specific goals. At the same time, Francophones and Anglophones increasingly acted together, rather than against

each other as they had before. Radical groups were in agreement on insisting that their struggle was an autonomous one and in refusing to subordinate it to any other political or social cause.

Martine Lanctôt divides the work these groups did into three main areas. Some groups worked mainly on aspects of the oppression of women relating to their bodies — rape, battered women, excessive medical control of childbirth, "macho" psychiatry and the like. Others were more interested in women in the labour force and in education, dealing with such issues as discrimination, sexual harassment, unionization, wages for housework, and access to daycare. Finally, some groups organized around magazines (such as *Les Têtes de Pioche*, 1976-79, and *La Vie en Rose*, 1980-87), publishing houses, theatre troupes, and other cultural expressions.

These groups served as a base for an increasing number of artists and intellectuals to promote writing, reflection and other activities giving expression to women's voices in a way that accommodated the new expectations and consciousness created by feminism. Women's studies courses and research at universities were another sign of the new awareness of feminist issues, as was the struggle for the right to abortion, in which radical feminists were joined by many other groups.

A woman's voice: Denise Boucher's play *Les fées ont soif*, 1976. (*Le Journal de Montréal*)

In the early 1980s, the feminist movement, both reform and radical, entered into a period of retreat and reexamination. While it had succeeded in making many of its main points, the movement itself, and especially its most militant segments, appeared to have lost most of its power to mobilize women, especially younger ones.

The women's movement went beyond feminism as such. In addition to the feminist organizations, there were many groups that existed simply to provide communication and solidarity. Among these were business and professional women's groups and the organizations that mounted the annual Salon de la Femme and published the *Bottin des Femmes*. Even though these groups were not militant and did not put forward any demands, they nevertheless contributed to the visibility and diversity of women's participation in public life.

From Theoretical to Real Equality

The 1970s began with the publication of the report of the Bird Royal Commission on the Status of Women in Canada. Set up in 1967 in response to pressure from women's organizations in Quebec and English Canada, the commission created great excitement within all women's groups, and its report had enormous impact. The Bird Report showed clearly that even though women theoretically had the same rights as men, they nonetheless suffered flagrant injustices that affected the actual social conditions under which they lived. The commission recommended that men and women be completely equal, in law and in fact, with respect to jobs, wages, promotions, education and family responsiblities. It also emphasized the importance of family planning clinics and even affirmed the right to abortion, although the commissioners were divided on this issue.

Spurred on by the Bird Report, women's groups intensified the struggle for equality, mainly by exerting pressure on governments, where only a handful of women had positions as cabinet ministers and back-benchers. The Canadian and Quebec governments soon promised to set up official structures where women's concerns could be heard. In 1973, Ottawa established the Advisory Council on the Status of Women. Quebec set up the Conseil du Statut de la Femme the same year, and three years later the Lévesque government mandated it to develop an overall policy on the status of women. Its report, entitled *Pour les Québécoises: égalité et indépendance*, was published in 1978. The following year, a standing cabinet committee on the status of women was given the responsibility of implementing this policy, mainly through affirmative action. Results, however, were slow in coming. This foot-dragging aroused the ire of reform feminists, despite their belief in government action, as well as radical feminists, who saw the councils' work as a way for governments to turn women's demands to their own advantage without actually satisfying those demands.

In any case, amendments to legislation permanently enshrined the principle of equality between the sexes and officially recognized the changes that had occurred in attitudes and lifestyles. In the area of family law, the most important measure was Bill 89, passed in 1980, which abolished the last vestiges of inequality between spouses. Under this legislation, both spouses have the same rights and obligations in marriage. Each keeps his or her own name, and the mother's name can be given to their children. Moreover, both spouses are responsible for the family's moral and material wellbeing, and both exercise parental authority and carry out the tasks involved in it.

Other measures banned discrimination on the job. Legislation to that effect had been on the books since 1964, but it was vague. The passage of the Quebec Charter of Rights and Freedoms in 1975 made all forms of discrimination on the basis of sex illegal and also established the principle of equal pay for work of equal value.

Birth control legislation was also further liberalized. Provisions prohibiting the advertising and sale of contraceptive products or providing information on contraception were withdrawn from the Criminal Code in 1969, and therapeutic abortion was permitted under specified conditions. In 1988, however, the Supreme Court of Canada overturned the abortion provision of the Criminal Code, and the issue remains the centre of intense controversy.

Other new measures served to protect pregnant women. Demands made by women's organizations and some unions gradually created an awareness that maternity is not just a private matter but has a social dimension as well. In 1978, a Quebec government order in council made it illegal to fire women for being pregnant, made it possible for a pregnant woman to be given different job duties with no change in working conditions to protect her or the fetus from hazardous work, and instituted an eighteen-week maternity leave.

In general, governments recognized their responsibility to women to a much greater extent than in the past, primarily because of increased awareness of the problem of sexual equality and sensitivity to women's demands in many segments of society, including feminist and nonfeminist women's organizations, trade unions, political parties and pressure groups. The changes that occurred were ultimately also due to changes in customs and attitudes and to the many new developments that benefited women — the democratization of education, contraception, liberalized divorce laws, and the increased importance placed on individual rights and freedoms.

The Continuity behind the Changes

These changes, however, by no means resulted in perfect equality between the sexes. Despite the new legislation, changed attitudes, and disappearance or alleviation of the most flagrant forms of discrimination, inequality persists in many forms.

Thus, even though about 48 per cent of women were in the labour force in 1981 as compared to 28 per cent twenty years earlier, many problems remain. Housework is still generally the woman's responsibility, so that women who work face a double work day. For most working women, having to cope with work, motherhood and housework remains a major problem. Moreover, as a general rule, women are promoted less often than men, lose their jobs more easily and are more likely to work part-time. Women fill most of Quebec's low-paying jobs, even though they have made breakthroughs in some occupations that used to be closed to them or were very difficult for them to enter.

In addition to wage-earning women workers, there are women who work alongside their husbands in family businesses and others who work at home. In 1980, as a result of pressure from the AFEAS, the government recognized women working in family businesses as employees who could receive some benefits. But women at home are still far from gaining social recognition, even though they still accounted for more than half of adult Quebec women in 1981. According to a 1984 study by the AFEAS, the reason women most often gave for staying at home was that they had to care for their children. Almost half the respondents said they were prepared to return to the labour market once their family was raised.

While liberalized divorce laws have benefited many women, they still suffer most of the financial and social consequences of divorce, as indicated by the fact that 85 per cent of single-parent families in 1981 were headed by women. Women also bear almost the entire burden of contraception, voluntary sterilization and abortion, sometimes at the risk of their lives and health, while both men and women enjoy the increased sexual freedom these measures allow. Women continue to face problems in the area of education as well, as we will see in chapter 46.

*   *   *   *   *   *

Between 1960 and the mid-1980s, Quebec society abandoned the old restrictive values to which women were subject in favour of much greater freedom and equality. In practice, however, there was still a long way to go before women were completely free and equal.

CHAPTER 43
THE CONSUMER SOCIETY

Postwar Quebec became part of the consumer society in a headlong, almost frenzied manner. The trend intensified even further after 1960 as a result of higher incomes and a changing marketplace where more and more products were hyped through advertising and sold on credit. Some people became concerned about this development and pressed for more consumer protection, while others worried about the environmental damage caused by consumerism and by what appeared to be unbridled production.

At the same time, the leisure society became part of daily life and gave new meaning to free time, vacations and the outdoors. As in previous periods, however, some groups in society did not benefit as much as others from the general prosperity and the new freedom it provided.

Standard of Living and Consumption

Purchasing power continued to increase throughout the 1960s and 1970s, as it had in the postwar years. According to data compiled by the journalist Alain Dubuc, the wage index in Canada rose by close to 500 per cent between 1960 and 1985, while the price index increased by a little over 300 per cent. As a result, the index of real wages rose by 47 per cent. The increase in purchasing power began to become more pronounced in the mid-1960s and was especially steep in the early 1970s, when despite growing inflation, workers obtained wage hikes that were well above increases in prices. The situation changed after 1977, first because of the wage and price controls imposed by the federal government in 1975 and subsequently by the Quebec government, and then because of the recession of 1981-82. Real wages fell slightly, but the drop was small compared to the spectacular gains achieved in the three preceding decades.

Statistics show that personal income rose from $7.8 billion in 1961 to $87.8 billion in 1984. Governments extracted part of this increase through taxes: the portion of personal income paid by individuals in direct taxes rose from 9 per cent to 21 per cent. Nonetheless, the disposable income individuals retained was considerable, and it increased by 866 per cent over the period. As a result, Quebecers were able to save more: personal savings represented 4 per cent of personal income in 1961 and 10 per cent in 1984, with a peak of 14 per cent reached in 1982, at the height of the recession. They were also able to consume more, and even though personal spending on consumer goods and services fell as a share of personal income, its value rose by 777 per cent.

A real explosion in consumption occurred during the 1960s and 1970s. Men and women, young people and adults — all took part in their own way. An increasingly wide range of products was offered. Progress in transportation and storage and distribution methods meant improved accessibility and availability. Quebec consumption patterns closely followed those of the United States and were subject to the fashions that brought retail commodities into the limelight and then destroyed them. Disposable products, ready-to-wear clothes, prepared foods and fast food became more common, along with different sizes and varieties of products (regular, light, enriched, natural and the like).

The food industry was a good example of the changes that took place. The food basket of 1980 was very different from the one of 1960. The basic traditional vegetables — potatoes, carrots, green beans and peas — were supplemented by broccoli, different kinds of lettuce, squash and others. Most of these vegetables became available throughout the year. Exotic fruits such as kiwis and clementines made their appearance on grocery shelves. The consumption of wine shot up. Freezing improved preservation and made even more foods available.

In the car market, the range of choice broadened with the arrival of imported cars onto the market, while the oil crisis of the 1970s sounded the death knell for big multicylinder engines. New technology gave birth to the portable radio, the personal computer and the videocassette recorder.

The race to consume was intensified by the pervasiveness of advertising, which came in so many forms that no one could escape it. Television became the main advertising medium and TV ad slogans often remained engraved in people's memories for decades. While advertising in the 1960s was undifferentiated and without subtelty, in the 1970s it became more complex, identifying specific target groups and adjusting to a fragmented market.

The consumption boom was given strong support by the growth of credit. Banks and caisses populaires, with their huge reservoirs of savings, became increasingly involved in consumer credit, and the launching of major credit cards that could be used almost everywhere gave them an even firmer hold on this field of activity. Interest paid on consumer debts, which totalled $37 million in 1961, was more than $1 billion twenty years later.

Credit cards became ubiquitous. (Gilles Savoie)

Consumer Protection

A market where people were avid consumers and did not think twice about going into debt to buy things put producers and sellers at a considerable advantage and allowed them to set the ground rules. The fact that they were often large companies enjoying monopoly or oligopoly control increased their power. Isolated individuals had little capacity to avoid the traps of the marketplace.

Public resistance to this situation first began to develop in the United States, where Ralph Nader and some other prophets of consumer protection founded a genuine social movement in the 1960s. Consumer protection organizations emerged in Quebec in the early 1970s, establishing a public presence and attracting media attention.

The new movement wanted to transform complacent buyers into informed consumers, and it demanded government intervention to regulate the market and protect the individual consumer. It addressed two kinds of problems. The first was product quality and safety — from cars to drugs to food and suntan lotion, thousands of items were examined, brands and models were compared, and their faults and dangers were publicly exposed. Second, business practices were subjected to scrutiny, from contract language to terms of financing, and campaigns were waged against misleading advertising, high-pressure sales and hidden costs.

Some victories won in the United States, such as the many automobile safety measures that were adopted, had repercussions in Quebec. Pressure was also put on the Quebec government to regulate certain sectors of activity. The 1971 consumer protection act was an important step. It stipulated the form sales contracts had to take, especially the ones used by travelling sales people, gave consumers the right to cancel their purchases within five days, regulated terms of credit, and established the Consumer Protection Bureau. Seven years later a new act, even more favourable to consumers, strengthened the provisions on contracts, warranties and sales methods.

Numerous other consumer protection measures supplemented this general legislation. In 1967, a deposit insurance bill was passed after a similar measure was adopted by the federal government. The following year, the position of Public Protector was created, on the Scandinavian model of the ombudsman. The government revamped securities legislation and legislation dealing with food inspection, and it established supervision of travel agents to protect their clients' deposits. It also took action to improve access to the legal system: it set up a small claims court in 1971 where costs were reduced to a minimum, established a system of legal aid for low-income Quebecers the following year, and later allowed class-action suits. It specified the terms for housing rental and granted additional powers to the Rental Board.

The 1970s belonged to consumers. In addition to obtaining regulation of the marketplace, consumer groups forced companies to become aware of questions such as sexism in advertising and the dangers posed by chemicals in food.

Environmental Protection

The expansion of consumption and production created great stresses on the environment, and ultimately on the people living in it. Here again, awareness of the problem led to the birth of a social movement. The movement to protect the environment from the consumer society became widespread throughout the western world, and in several European countries it took the form of political action. In Quebec, groups such as the Société pour Vaincre la Pollution and the Quebec Wildlife Federation worked to raise public consciousness.

Environmental or ecological groups had two targets. They criticized the waste and destruction of resources brought about by industrial production, agriculture and urbanization and demanded measures to protect and conserve our heritage, both natural and built. As well, they denounced the harmful effects of pollution on the environment and public health.

The government also intervened in this field. In 1972, an environmental quality act was passed and a minister responsible for the area was appointed. Six years later new legislation, stronger than the original, was adopted. The municipalities' responsibility for many public facilities gave them an important role as well.

The first problem to be dealt with was air pollution, which reached alarming levels in urban areas in the late 1960s. Municipalities passed antipollution bylaws that helped bring about a significant reduction in the average concentration of particles suspended in the air. The shift from oil to electricity as the main source of heat, the installation of antipollution devices on cars and the use of unleaded gasoline also contributed to lowering the level of air pollution.

Water pollution was another important problem. Efforts were concentrated on the major industrial polluters, the pulp and paper producers — 94 per cent of the $611 million invested in waste treatment between 1978 and 1984 went into dealing with this source of pollution. But in the area of sewage treatment in big cities, Quebec was far behind the rest of the continent and became aware of the problem quite late. In 1984, sewage treatment plants served only 6.2 per cent of the population, as compared to 84 per cent in Ontario. Attempts were also made, with mixed success, to control pollution caused by farmers, especially pork producers.

During the 1980s, the ravages of acid rain in lakes and forests became a major concern. Quebec could only try to exert political pressure, adding its voice to that of the other Canadian provinces and the northeastern American states, because the pollution came largely from outside its boundaries.

The concern for environmental protection also extended to urbanization. The agricultural zoning act of 1978 was designed to stop urban areas from spreading onto Quebec's best agricultural land. Pressure groups were formed, mainly in Montreal, to preserve historic buildings, which were under constant threat of demolition. Development-oriented city governments needed considerable persuasion before they could recognize the importance and benefit of conservation and the value of preserving buildings that were reminders of the past and contributed to the quality of life. Anglophone Montrealers were in the forefront of this movement. They initially became alarmed when buildings recalling the past grandeur of their group — Windsor Station and the beautiful bourgeois mansions of the Square Mile — were threatened with destruction. They were also concerned with the preservation of green spaces in the city. To a certain extent, they were able to reverse the trend and interest many Francophones in the problem.

By the end of the period, the words heritage, environment and ecology were part of the political vocabulary, reflecting a new balance that was being struck between consumption and conservation.

The Leisure Society

Improved living standards, reduced work time and longer vacations all contributed to the increased importance of spare time in day-to-day life. Leisure time became integrated into the market as a consumer item. During the 1960s, many people believed that in the future, increases in productivity would be such that work time would be radically shortened and free time proportionally expanded. Attempts were made to determine what the "leisure society" of the future would be like. Reality tempered the dream somewhat: while flexible hours, the four-day week and part-time work made their appearance in some sectors, the vast majority of Quebec workers still worked a five-day week in the 1980s. Nonetheless, free time began to be viewed differently and became qualitatively more important.

The community approach to leisure that prevailed in the 1950s was replaced by a more individualist attitude emphasizing personal fulfilment. The rise of hedonism in society contributed to this development, and the quest for pleasure and the desire to satisfy individual needs and to fulfil oneself as a person became central to the values shared by most Quebecers. Decisions about how to use free time are now basically individual ones. The leisure field has become ever more diverse and specialized, changing as fashions changed.

But it also became a public, political issue. As in many other areas, the church was forced to give way to the government as the chief organizing force by the early 1960s. The government tried to ensure greater access for various segments of the population by establishing recreational facilities in all communities and by contributing to the cost of recreational activities. It also tried to rationalize leisure activities further by establishing policies which, after 1976, became integrated into its strategy for cultural development. In this way, the government became the guardian of organized leisure activities.

The municipalities remained directly responsible for community facilities, and their role in this area continued to grow as cultural and sports centres, libraries, parks and playgrounds proliferated. They also took a more direct role in organizing the activities in these facilities. However, the quantity and quality of services offered varied widely from one municipality to the next, depending on the municipality's resources and the socioeconomic and demographic characteristics of its population. The Quebec government, for its part, set up political and administrative structures for dealing with leisure. In 1965, it established the Bureau des Sports et Loisirs, which became the Haut Commissariat à la Jeunesse, aux Loisirs et aux Sports in 1968, and finally, in 1979, the Department of Recreation. It also developed its own facilities (in particular provincial parks), while at the same time contributing to municipal facilities. It became the main sponsor of sports and recreation associations and exerted tight control over them.

Leisure activities became better structured and were supervised by professionals, such as physical education instructors, recreation directors and community cultural workers. However, volunteer work remained significant, and in 1976 an estimated 15,000 volunteers were active in the area of sports and recreation. Participation in clubs and associations is also an important feature of the organization of leisure activities.

The leisure field is extremely heterogeneous, with groups that want to encourage mass participation rubbing shoulders with others that target the elite. Participants are divided according to age, social milieu and degree of skill. Four main sectors have emerged: sports, outdoor activities, sociocultural activities and tourism.

Sports, some of which enjoy a long tradition, constitute the most highly structured sector, with hockey and baseball leagues, ski clubs, and armies of coaches, trainers and referees. New sporting facilities were built during the period, including sports centres, indoor skating rinks and playgrounds. The development of physical education in schools also contributed to the development of the sports sector. Sporting competitions of all kinds (races, marathons, championships) proliferated and the creation of the Quebec Games gave them increased prestige.

The boom in outdoor activities, many of which have a sporting dimension, has been a feature of the period. It is a mass phenomenon: for example, in 1982, 2,339,000 Quebec households owned skis (as compared to 541,000 in 1976), and about a million had bicycles for adults or camping equipment. The growing concern with physical fitness and the increased access to recreational areas contributed to the boom, while improved living standards allowed people to buy equipment that was often expensive.

It was also a time of change and growth for the huge field of sociocultural activities, which include such varied interests as yoga, handicrafts, parlour games and scientific pursuits. Many of these activities were organized by senior citizens' clubs, an important new feature of the period; other activities were aimed especially at young people.

The growth of tourism was linked to the increase in vacation time. Workers now had the right to at least two weeks of paid vacation, as compared to only one in the postwar period, and many had even longer vacations of up to five weeks. This was reflected in the development of cottage communities, which had already begun in the preceding period. But the travel industry was the main beneficiary of the situation. The modernization of the road system in the 1960s was the main factor in the growth of tourism, along with heavy investment in hotel facilities and the popularity of camping. Plane travel, a rarity in 1960, had become common twenty years later. Wintertime "getaways to the sun" enjoyed unprecedented popularity and the number of Quebecers travelling to Europe, mainly France and Spain, shot up.

On the Fringes of the Consumer Society

The consumer society had its outcasts who lived on the fringes of the economic system. But even people who had to rely on government assistance, under the table work arrangements and marginal part-time jobs to survive were drawn towards the consumer society.

This sector of the population was highly heterogeneous and included people in diverse circumstances, varying according to age, sex, family size and place of residence (rural or urban). One notable group consisted of the elderly, many of whom lived solely on their old age pensions and income supplements. Another was made up of people who had been displaced from rural areas in the 1960s and sent to small towns and villages, where they had to go on welfare. A major component of the population living outside the consumer society were women who headed single-parent families. Many of them lived below the poverty line, and their numbers grew significantly during the period. Another substantial group consisted of unemployed people who had used up their unemployment insurance benefits and had no recourse other than going on welfare. People who were not actually unemployed but worked in conditions that maintained them in poverty were also among society's second-class citizens. This group included a number of categories of workers earning the minimum wage, along with recent immigrants, particularly women.

Of course, these people were better off than they would have been in the postwar period. The social programs of the 1960s and 1970s were better coordinated and provided them with more decent living conditions. Access to medical care was probably the area where the most progress was made. These social programs will be examined in more detail in the next chapter.

However, the development of the welfare state had the effect of keeping the beneficiaries of social programs in a state of dependence, often for life. While groups were formed to protect their interests, senior citizens, welfare recipients and the unemployed remained divided and isolated, and were rarely able to wage effective campaigns for their demands.

In the late 1970s, conditions for these marginal sectors of society began to change dramatically as their numbers became inflated by mass unemployment. This was a result of two factors. The first was the rapid growth of the labour force as the number of working women increased and the youngest members of the baby boom generation reached working age. The second was the reduced availability of work as increased automation and productivity led companies to employ a smaller work force and more and more employers used part-time labour. The situation was made even worse by the 1981-82 recession, with its series of massive layoffs and factory closings, as well as by job cuts and reduced hiring in the public sector.

Unemployment statistics reveal only part of the real situation, because they only count the unemployed who are looking for work. However, many people became discouraged and either stopped looking for work or took marginal part-time jobs because there was nothing better. According to the economist Rodrigue Tremblay, the real unemployment rate was much higher than the official rate: for example, he estimates that in 1983, when the official rate was 13.9 per cent, the real rate was 18.9 per cent. Governments had to step in to help, and they paid out astronomical sums of money — between 1975 and 1983, the total amount of unemployment insurance benefits paid in Quebec rose from $1 billion to $3 billion and welfare payments rose from $504 million to $1.8 billion.

The immediate victims were young people who were unable to find steady work. Those who had to go on welfare were at an even further disadvantage, because the benefits they received were well below those that older people were entitled to. But young people were not the only ones affected. Unemployment was so widespread that it had an impact on all age groups to varying degrees. Entire regions, such as the North Shore and the east end of Montreal, were hit by plant closings. For the tens of thousands of unemployed who wanted to work, social programs provided poor compensation for the anguish of living every day without work and facing a future with no opportunities.

Thus, a sharp contrast remains between the advantages of the consumer society and the affluence enjoyed by most Quebecers on the one hand, and the life of poverty and social assistance to which a minority is condemned on the other.

CHAPTER 44
THE WELFARE STATE

The welfare state is the product of a long process that began during the war. It reached maturity in the 1960s and 1970s, when the panoply of social programs that constitute its most visible aspect were put in place. All areas of social life and all Quebecers were affected by its intervention, which took three forms: regulation, redistribution and insurance. Governments' concerns now appeared to know no bounds. They expanded, reformed and integrated their social programs and moved to occupy the whole area of health care. This was the era when governments fought the "war on poverty" and promised a "just society," winning popular support with these slogans. Quebec made substantial progress, building a well developed and integrated arsenal of social security measures. However, the major objectives of redressing social inequalities were not achieved, and administering the system became an increasingly heavy and costly burden.

Development of the Welfare State

During and after the war, it was the federal government that played the leading role in orienting social policy and establishing the welfare state. Following the example of Britain and the guidelines suggested by the social scientist Leonard Marsh in his 1943 *Report on Social Security for Canada*, Ottawa began to build a social security strategy on the foundation of unemployment insurance, family allowances and its reform of old age pensions. Before 1960, the Quebec government was more hesitant, rejecting both the principle of the welfare state and the intrusion of the federal government in social affairs. However, the pressure of social need and public opinion forced it to intervene in an ad hoc fashion and even to participate in shared-cost programs such as unemployment insurance.

In the 1960s, a fundamental change occurred. The Quebec government came under the influence of Keynesianism and became an exponent of increased government intervention. Implementing this new direction was a huge task, as the government moved to take responsibility for social affairs and bring its policies up to date, which involved taking innovative measures and playing a more dynamic role in developing and carrying out new programs. Meanwhile, Ottawa continued to build on the structure it had started, taking on the problem of hospitalization in the 1950s and health in the 1960s. In 1966 it established the Canada Assistance Plan, under which it assumed half the cost of social assistance programs administered by the provinces. Social affairs became a particularly sensitive area of friction in Quebec-Ottawa relations, with conflicts frequently erupting over the orientation and financing of programs. Beyond federal-provincial rivalry, however, neither level of government developed its social policies in isolation: each government produced reports whose influence extended beyond the jurisdiction in which they originated.

The broadening of social policy was a significant new element. Existing programs were made more accessible, while some new measures, such as hospital and health insurance, were aimed at the entire population. Social policy was broadened in another sense as well, as health care, formerly considered an individual or family matter, now became a public responsibility, on the same footing as income security and social assistance.

People's attitudes as well as governments' approaches changed considerably. A variety of studies exposed the extent of poverty and misery in the midst of urban affluence as well as the reality of rural misery and all the problems associated with unequal regional development. Old notions of indigence and public charity gave way to new ideas of citizens' rights and social justice. Poverty and the unequal distribution of income were multifaceted problems that had to be attacked on all fronts. As a result, the idea took hold that if social programs were to be effective, they had to be integrated into a coherent whole. Short-term measures such as social assistance were necessary, but corrective policies and programs that would work over the longer term also had to be put in place.

The Quebec government's activity in this area was based on two important reports that served as a foundation for integrating social policies: the report of the Study Committee on Public Assistance, appointed in 1961 (the Boucher Report), and the report of the Castonguay-Nepveu Royal Commission on Health and Social Welfare, appointed in 1966. During the 1970s, the welfare state became a daily reality for Quebecers.

As attitudes towards social policy became more open, organization of the social affairs sector also improved. Citizens' groups were formed, especially in disadvantaged urban neighbourhoods, and offered residents such services as medical and legal clinics, day care centres and food cooperatives. Initially, the movement was supported by diocesan organizations such as the Conseils des Oeuvres; in the late 1960s it was provided with paid organizers by the Company of Young Canadians, a federal agency established to involve young people in community development. Emphasizing grassroots participation, these citizens' groups developed rapidly. A number of these groups became more politicized and radical, leading to the formation of the Front d'Action Politique (FRAP), which ran candidates in the Montreal municipal election of October 1970. People in authority were upset by the direction taken by the community groups. This reaction (accentuated by the atmosphere of the October Crisis), along with increasingly intense ideological struggles among community activists, led to disaffection with the groups. Still more people drifted away as the government subsequently took over responsibility for some community services, such as the medical and legal clinics. The community groups that remained lacked the old spark, but they did bear witness to the maintenance of a tradition of grassroots organization.

Income Security

Early on, the idea of income security became the keystone around which governments sought to structure their social policies. This meant that if individuals or households ran into difficulty, a minimum capacity for consumption could be maintained. A range of programs were set up towards this end, and the number, field of application and eligibility criteria of these programs were all steadily extended.

The centrepiece of the system was unemployment insurance, which underwent a major reform in 1971. The program became nearly universal, covering 96 per cent of wage earners, as compared with 61 per cent in 1960. Benefits were increased so that workers with dependents could obtain up to 75 per cent of their pay. The minimum number of weeks during which a worker had to pay premiums to qualify for benefits was reduced from twenty to eight. And finally, the program was made to serve specific social goals as workers who had to leave their jobs because of illness and women on maternity leave were made eligible for benefits.

In the late 1970s, with the cost of the program increasing as a result of rising unemployment, the government reduced maximum benefits to 60 per cent of wages and lengthened the qualifying period again. At the same time, the program was fine-tuned to take regional variations in unemployment into account: in areas of higher unemployment, benefits were now more generous, more accessible and longer lasting. The steep rise in unemployment in the early 1980s led to another increase in the cost of the program, and as unemployment persisted, the number of people who had to fall back on social assistance because their benefits ran out grew.

There were also radical changes in the other major program, social assistance. In 1960, Quebec's social assistance program was still essentially based on the old Public Charities Act of 1921 and subsequent legislation aimed at specific groups, such as needy mothers and the blind. There was also the unemployment assistance program, whose cost was shared equally by the two levels of government; under this program, social assistance benefits could be extended to people who were able to work. Change came in two stages. The first stage, corresponding to the adoption of the Canada Assistance Plan in 1966, enshrined the principle that social assistance should be accessible to all citizens who needed it, including the working poor, and provided for costs to be shared equally by Ottawa and the provinces. The second, embodied in Quebec's Social Aid Act of 1969, reorganized all existing social assistance measures and recognized the right of all citizens to government assistance.

This new act greatly simplified the way social assistance worked. The government paid a monthly sum to cover shelter, food and clothing to all individuals and households that could not earn income. The scale of benefits was adjusted for inflation and took age and family size into account. For people under thirty who were able to work, there was a provision designed to compel them to find a job. The overall number of people dependent on social assistance increased from just under 500,000 in 1970 to more than 700,000 in 1983. Initially, it was primarily people unable to work who received benefits, but by the 1980s the proportion represented by people who were able to work and people under thirty was increasing.

Many people suffer a drop in their standard of living when they retire. For a long time, the old age pensions paid by the federal government had been the main income support measure for retired people. This universal program was also broadened during the 1960s. Between 1966 and 1970, the age of eligibility was gradually reduced from seventy to sixty-five. The pension was increased several times and then indexed to the cost of living. In addition, a guaranteed income supplement program was established for the neediest old people.

Another response to income uncertainty in old age was the establishment of a contributory pension plan in 1965. This had the character of an insurance plan, with premiums paid by workers and their employers. In Quebec, the plan was administered by the Quebec government, but it was completely compatible with the federal Canada Pension Plan that covered workers in other provinces. In time, provision was also made for benefits to be paid to a surviving spouse. This was an especially valuable benefit for women who had never entered the labour market and whose incomes were drastically reduced when their husbands died.

Like old age pensions, family allowances were a universal federal program. Since 1944, benefits had been fixed at $6 for a child up to age nine and $8 for a child between ten and sixteen. In 1961, Quebec decided to pay allowances for youths aged seventeen and eighteen who were still in school. This measure was taken over by the federal government three years later. In a 1973 reform of family allowance legislation, allowances were tripled, indexed to the cost of living, and made taxable. As part of a budget-cutting campaign in 1979, family allowances were deindexed and scaled back to 1974 levels, but a child tax credit was introduced in compensation. The program also allowed provinces to decide how the overall amount allotted should be distributed, and Quebec used this clause to favour large families. Meanwhile, the Quebec government decided to pay its own family allowances in 1968.

Table 1
Major Components of the Income Security System, 1984

Basic Minimum Income
Social assistance
Provisions for social assistance recipients with special needs
Guaranteed income supplement
Allowances for spouses between 60 and 64 years old
Low-rent accommodation for low income earners and senior citizens
Housing allowances for senior citizens (Logirente)
Reimbursement of property taxes
Veterans' allowances
Allowances for Cree hunters and trappers

Income Replacement
Unemployment Insurance
Old Age Security
Quebec Pension Plan
Age tax exemption
Pension income tax deduction
Maternity allowances
Unemployment insurance for maternity leave
Workers' compensation
Compensation for automobile accident victims
Allowances for the death of a spouse (Régime des Rentes du Québec)
Disability pensions
Compensation for victims of criminal acts
Disability tax deduction
Veterans' pensions

Compensation for Dependent Children or Spouse
Family allowances
Child tax credit
Tax exemption for dependent children
Married tax exemption
Availability allowances
Allowances for parents of handicapped children

Aid to Participation in the Labour Force
Work income supplement
Child care allowances
Child care expense tax deduction
Supplement to income allowed under unemployment insurance
Supplement to income allowed under social assistance
Occupational training allowances

Source: *Le Québec statistique*, 1985-86

Governments also sought to use the tax system as a means of redressing specific inequalities. Thus, tax rates were lowered for the poorest groups while some categories of people benefited from particular exemptions. Finally, there were private instruments that made it possible for individuals to protect their income and benefit from tax deductions. These instruments were aimed primarily at high-income groups and affected only a minority of the working population. The best known are pension plans financed jointly by employers and employees, which covered 39 per cent of the working population in 1982, and individual retirement savings plans.

Thus, the major programs became increasingly accessible and were targeted to more needs. Table 1 shows the major components of the income security system, both federal and provincial, as of the mid-1980s. Given the proliferation of these programs and especially their high administrative costs, specialists in the field repeatedly suggested that they be replaced by a single program — a guaranteed annual income. However, because such a scheme would have an exorbitant cost and be difficult to apply, governments held back from introducing it.

Health Care

Illness represented another significant risk for individuals and families, as medical and hospital costs could run into large sums of money. As a result, health care quickly became an essential dimension of social policy. Before 1960, only the poor received a form of government assistance. For other people, there were private insurance programs, but they covered only 43 per cent of Quebecers in 1960. The government initially moved to deal with the rising cost of hospitalization. The public hospital insurance program, which took effect in Quebec in 1961, made hospital care free and hence genuinely accessible to everyone. This program made it necessary for the government to oversee and coordinate the hospital system and put services on a regional basis. This was a major challenge: the hospitals were private institutions and there was a great deal of diversity within the system, in terms of both services offered and quality of care and equipment. Even allowing for the fact that it took some time for the government to organize its administration of the system efficiently, there was a surprisingly steep rise in costs, from $139 million in 1961 to $343 million in 1966. The reason for this rise was that care became institutionalized: doctors preferred to take care of their patients in hospitals rather than in their offices or at home. Partly in response to this problem, consideration began to be given to establishing a health insurance program, which would allow everyone access to a doctor without having to be hospitalized.

Developed by the federal government, this proposal was accepted by Quebec and came into effect in 1970, making all health care free for the user. In an effort to improve cost control and rationalize services, Quebec tried to introduce changes in medical practice, but the doctors resisted

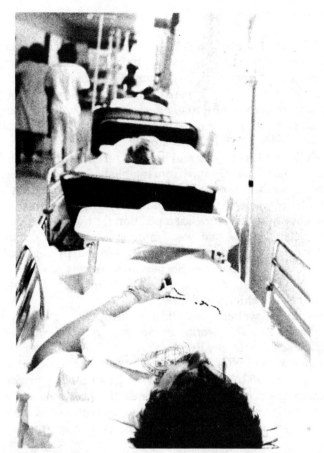

A crowded emergency room, 1986. (*Le Journal de Montréal*)

any intrusion, fearing the socialization of their profession. The fee-for-service method of payment eventually put into effect led to a rapid rise in costs. The government dealt with this problem by adopting policies that increasingly emphasized prevention. However, the institutions that were made responsible for implementing these policies, the Centres Locaux de Services Communautaires (CLSCs), found it hard to carry out this task, partly because of resistance from doctors. The government also established specialized programs, such as free dental care for children and adolescents and reimbursement of the cost of drugs for senior citizens and people on social assistance.

Even though problems remained, there was significant progress in making hospital and medical care more accessible and democratic. This represented a marked contrast to the situation before 1960.

Other Social Services

The establishment of the CLSCs was aimed at decentralizing counselling and health services and encouraging increased participation by users. They replaced private social agencies that had developed from the nineteenth century on. They were geared towards prevention and took on a significant community role, offering a wide varity of services. The CLSCs had their origin in a recommendation of the Castonguay-Nepveu Commission, which saw them as a point of entry and switching station for the whole system of social and medical services. In practice, however, they had to deal with resistance from established institutions and doctors as well as constraints imposed by the government. As a result, they never fully played the role that was initially assigned to them and had to struggle tenaciously to carve out a position for themselves.

Some social services that were more specialized in nature, such as protection of youth and adoption, were offered by regional agencies known as Centres de Services Sociaux. All regions of Quebec also had homes that provided shelter for specific target populations: orphans, convalescents, the elderly and others.

The rise of the welfare state did not mean the end of philanthropic, volunteer and charitable work. On the contrary: they continued to play a significant role, especially in urban settings. They now served an auxiliary function with regard to the state, reversing the situation that had prevailed before 1960. Among the services performed by private charities were financing a portion of medical research, meeting social needs neglected by institutions, and helping people who could not adjust to bureaucratic requirements and whom the system therefore left by the wayside.

In other fields, the government sought to make services more accessible to the poorest Quebecers. An example is the justice system, where small claims court was introduced in 1971 and legal aid was introduced in 1972. Meanwhile, the Rental Board offered protection against excessive rent increases. Another significant development was the general policy of making public places more accessible to handicapped people.

The Reassessment

The achievements of the welfare state were impressive. Social services were integrated and modernized, health services were made more accessible, and Quebecers were better protected against loss of income. The free services from which Quebecers in general, and disadvantaged groups in particular, could benefit were many and varied.

However, the system came under criticism on a number of grounds. The first was cost. In Canada, combined expenditures on social security, including health services, grew from $3 billion in 1961 to almost $25 billion in 1976 — an increase of more than 700 per cent. The Quebec government allocated a growing proportion of its expenditures to this sector, reaching 39 per cent in 1983-84. The quality of the care and services offered also came under attack. Thus, in the hospital sector, bureaucratized and depersonalized services and an incompletely regionalized system often led to difficult conditions for both patients and staff. Long waiting lists were a symptom of inefficient services, inadequate resources and overuse. In addition, dependence of individuals on the government — in some cases permanent dependence — was criticized by both the left and the right. Finally, the welfare state was seen in some quarters as an instrument of social control that operated primarily for the benefit of the ruling classes.

During the 1980s, there was a reassessment of the welfare state. Many people wondered whether it was really possible for society to provide all these services — and do it efficiently. The principle of universality was also challenged: why provide everyone with services and programs that only some people really need? On the other hand, the population as a whole regarded the services offered by the welfare state as gains that had been made, so that attempts to reduce these services were vigorously resisted.

*   *   *   *   *   *

Issues relating to the welfare state are major ones because of the scope of the services it offers and the importance it has taken on. The problems that face the welfare state are real, but its role in Quebec's collective life remains an essential one.

CHAPTER 45

SECULARIZATION

In the period following 1960, religious life in Quebec was shaken to its foundations. Two major factors influenced the direction taken by changes in religious life. First, in Quebec as elsewhere in North America, society was becoming increasingly secularized; religious practice declined sharply and churches, temples and synagogues stood empty. Second, the prestige, influence and power that had marked the position of the Catholic Church in the social life of Catholic Quebecers also declined rapidly. At the same time, new trends began to appear. Some groups, notably women, began to demand change, and the pressures for reform had an impact on existing institutions. In addition, people could now express their spirituality through a wider variety of experiences, and the organized churches were no longer the only outlets for religious feeling.

None of these changes were reflected in census data. Thus, in 1981, 88 per cent of Quebecers continued to list themselves as Catholic, the same percentage as in 1961. But religious affiliation did not have the same depth or meaning now that it was not supported by regular practice.

Minority Religions

Religions other than Catholicism accounted for less than 10 per cent of Quebecers. Protestants, with 6.1 per cent of the population, and Jews, with 1.6 per cent, were still the two major groups, but the number of adherents of other religions was increasing, mostly as a result of new immigration. Thus, Eastern Orthodox groups constituted 1.2 per cent of the population in 1981, while religions outside the Judaeo-Christian tradition represented 0.5 per cent.

The Anglican, United and Presbyterian churches were still the three major Protestant denominations, but they now accounted for only three quarters of all Protestants. The Anglican and United churches each represented about a third of the Protestant population, while 9 per cent of Protestants were Presbyterians. This relative decline of the three major groups is attributable to the rise of other denominations and sects, especially the rapid expansion of the Pentecostals and Jehovah's Witnesses.

Two major developments of the period for Protestants were acknowledgement of their minority status and recognition of their ethnic diversity. Protestant churches were affected by the secularization of Quebec society, as Protestants lost powers they had traditionally held, particularly in education and social services. Although Quebec Protestantism was historically linked to white Anglo-Saxons, an increasing number of Protestants came from other groups. According to Nathan H. Mair's estimate, 40 per cent of Quebec Protestants in the late 1970s were not white Anglo-Saxons, and half of these were Francophones. The prevailing indifference to religion and the departure of some Anglophone Quebecers also affected the Protestant community: Protestants were an aging group and their churches had difficulty finding clergy.

There was a slight decline in the number of Jews in Quebec between 1961 and 1981. Here too, an overall aging of the population was involved, accentuated by the departure of younger Jews. Characteristics observed in earlier periods persisted. There were still three major religious tendencies within the Jewish community, and religious practice continued to decline. The sociologist Morton Weinfeld has pointed out that 20 per cent of Montreal Jews never go to synagogue and 30 per cent go only for the major holidays. However, he also notes the persistence of other religious customs: home observance of holidays and practices such as the fast on Yom Kippur and the marking of major life-cycle events such as birth, Bar or Bat Mitzvah, marriage and death.

Until the late 1950s, the Jews of Quebec had been a very homogeneous community, with their geographic origins, their common Ashkenazi background, their use of English and their identification with the Anglophone group all holding them together. The development of a significant Sephardic and Francophone minority represented a problem for the community. The newcomers had different traditions, came from different places and spoke a different language. They tended to become part of the Francophone community and wanted to maintain their identity. In 1965, they established the Association Sépharade Francophone (since 1975, the Communauté Sépharade du Québec) to protect their interests and advance their position within the Jewish community. However, the established community was somewhat resistant, as can be seen in the story of the first French-language Jewish school in Montreal, the Maimonedes School. Founded in 1969, the school encountered problems in trying to obtain recognition from the Association of Jewish Day Schools, which was necessary to gain access to large grants. Relations improved over time, but there were still tensions. Around 1980, a fifth of the Jews in Quebec were Sephardim.

The Catholic Church

The 1960s saw a radical transformation of the Catholic Church's relationship with its own adherents and with Quebec society as a whole. From the preeminence to which it had become accustomed, the church's role was reduced to specifically pastoral activities. The changes that took place in a span of ten years were fundamental: the Catholic hierarchy lost its decision-making power in education; priests and religious dwindled in numbers and gradually disappeared from Quebec's schools, colleges and hospitals; those who did not leave religious life dressed more discreetly, as priests stopped wearing the cassock and nuns gave up the habit and veil. The collapse of religious practice resulted in severe financial difficulties, the demolition of churches and the conversion of some religious buildings to other purposes. These changes were caused by complex factors that had been operating over a long period of time. It was in the 1960s, however, that the contradictions became insurmountable and the situation reached a critical point.

In the social sphere, the church was faced with the increasing pluralism of Quebec society and, in consequence, a clearer separation between civil and religious life — an idea that took hold even among Catholics. The church could no longer serve as a guide and common denominator for all of Quebec society, and a broad consensus developed in favour of its going back to its primary vocation. Sector after sector slipped out of the church's sphere of influence into lay hands. The school system, however, was an area of resistance, and it remained denominational, despite pressure from groups such as the Mouvement Laïc de Langue Française (lay French-language movement), founded in 1961, and the journal *Parti Pris*.

Another problem for the church was declericalization — the gradual replacement of religious institutions and their members by the state and its civil servants in the areas of education, health and social security. Since 1945, needs in these areas had grown beyond the point where the church had the resources or even the potential to meet them, so that the way it carried out these responsibilities no longer corresponded to people's expectations. With the rise of the welfare state, education and social services were seen as entitlements that should be available to all citizens, without any distinctions and especially without reference to religious values. These factors led the church to give way to the state during the 1960s as a provider of these services.

The church also faced serious problems in the religious sphere. Pastoral services and parish organization were still very traditional and out of tune with modern sensibilities. The church's rigid structures, which maintained both clerics and laypeople under a yoke of blind obedience, were increasingly indefensible. These structures were roundly criticized in the 1960 bestseller *Les insolences du frère Untel* (published in English as *The Impertinences of Brother Anonymous*). This book's runaway commercial success — twenty-eight printings and 130,000 copies sold, including

The sensational *Impertinences of Brother Anonymous*, 1960.

17,000 in the first ten days after its publication — was evidence of the scope of the problem. Confronted with difficulties that seemed to be springing up everywhere, the Catholic Church in the 1960s was a church in disarray, a church that no longer knew how to respond, a church in the throes of a deep crisis that affected both clergy and laity.

One symptom of this crisis was the decline in the number of priests and religious. In the early 1960s, recruitment of both priests and religious seemed to be slowly drying up. In the middle of the decade, a rapid exodus from the priesthood and male religious communities began, which later spread to communities of women. The figures speak eloquently. There were 8,400 priests in Quebec around 1960, while in 1981 there were only 4,285. Meanwhile, membership in religious communities fell from 45,253 in 1961 to 29,173 in 1978. This trend was especially devastating to communities of men, whose membership declined by 75 per cent.

The collapse of religious practice was a second symptom. Between 1961 and 1971, the proportion of Catholics in the archdiocese of Montreal who practised their religion fell from 61 to 30 per cent, while in the south shore diocese of Saint-Jean the decline was even more precipitous: from 65 to 27 per cent. In the late 1970s, survey results for all Quebec Catholics showed a proportion of practising Catholics varying between 37 and 45 per cent. Separating out urban and rural areas reveals marked differences. According to the sociologist Raymond Lemieux, in the cities the proportion of practising Catholics can be anywhere from 7 to 70 per cent, depending on the neighbourhood, while in the countryside, where attachment to religion is traditionally stronger, the proportion varies between 60 and 75 per cent.

At the same time as these transformations were taking place, the church was also going through a period of renewal. The example came from Rome, where the election of Pope John XXIII in 1958 represented a break with elements of the church's tradition. While his predecessor, Pius XII, had represented the austere grandeur of the Catholic magisterium, John XXIII — although initially seen as a caretaker pope — left an indelible mark on the church by instigating a movement to return to its sources. With his simplicity and his emphasis on the pastoral aspects of his job, he also set a new tone for all Catholic clergy. In 1959 Pope John summoned the Second Vatican Council, which met in Rome between 1962 and 1965. The council established the thrust of the church's reforms and was a focus of intense interest among Catholics.

The Quebec church, which always paid close attention to developments in Rome, joined the reform movement, but the pace of change was faster in some dioceses than in others. Montreal, Quebec's largest diocese, was a leader. According to the historian Jean Hamelin, this was partly a result of changes in the thinking of its archbishop, Cardinal Paul-Émile Léger. After his appointment in 1950, Léger was initially associated with traditionalist elements, but in the late 1950s he became more open to new values. From that time on, he took on a decisive leadership role within the Quebec episcopate. Thus, Léger tempered the zeal of those who wanted to discipline Frère Untel (Jean-Paul Desbiens) and showed a new openness to other religions.

The rise of ecumenism was another area of renewal within the church. In 1952 a Jesuit, Father Irénée Beaubien, organized the Catholic Inquiry Forum, which sponsored interdenominational meetings in Montreal with the aim of improving Protestants' understanding of Catholicism. This initial intention was gradually modified, so that by the late 1950s the missionary goal had given way to ecumenism. When the Forum celebrated its tenth anniversary in 1962, Cardinal Léger went even further, acknowledging that the Catholic Church had not had a monopoly on the truth of the Gospel in the past. The same year, he authorized the formation of a diocesan commission on ecumenism and published a pastoral letter, *Chrétiens désunis* (disunited Christians), in which he recognized the responsibility of all Christians to seek unity. This attitude represented a radical departure from all previous positions taken by the Quebec episcopate.

A final area of renewal was a larger role for the laity. The specialized Catholic Action movements had already taken initial steps towards this change. Gradually, the laity was allowed a new and more dynamic role within the church; from being passive spectators, laypeople became participants, not only in worship but also in some pastoral activities.

The combination of all these factors plunged the church into a decade of reexamination and crisis. Initially, until the mid-1960s, a spirit of change prevailed: declericalization and the new separation between the civil and religious spheres had a liberating effect on the church, while a new vision of Catholicism was being worked out in the wake of Vatican II. Traditional methods of maintaining control of the faithful were questioned. Starting in the late 1950s, experiments with common pastoral services were undertaken in an effort to compensate for the weakening of parish organization in the urban context; the idea was to strengthen the sense of belonging to a larger Christian community by working at the diocesan level.

A new start was also made in the area of liturgy and religious art. The discordance between the liturgy and atmosphere of worship on the one hand and the tastes of ordinary Catholics on the other had long been regarded as a problem. Here too, a series of changes began in the late 1950s. Starting in 1954, the ceremonial use of French in combination with Latin was allowed. A new form of religious architecture that used simpler lines and modern forms and created more intimate places of worship made its appearance. Vatican II, with its thrust towards simplifying cere.nonies and encouraging lay participation, had a determining influence in this area. At Sunday Mass on March 7, 1965, the full scope of the changes was brought home to Quebec Catholics. Undoubtedly the most striking innovation was that the proceedings took place entirely in French, English or Italian, depending on the language of the parishioners.

For a time, in an effort to retain the interest of parishioners or attract new ones, sometimes unorthodox experiments were undertaken in the wave of enthusiasm that Vatican II's directives set in motion. Thus, one parish would stage a Mass "à gogo" in an effort to attract a younger clientele, while another would present a program of "à la carte" Masses, each designed for a different audience. However, these experiments set more traditionally minded Catholics to trembling with indignation and incomprehension without stopping the growing drift away from the church.

The church's attitude towards questions of marriage and birth control was a source of further disaffection. The strong positions the church took against divorce in 1967 and against abortion and contraception in 1968 established a gulf between it and many Catholics, especially women. The 1968 encyclical *Humanae Vitae* officially condemned the use of the birth control pill, which had recently become widespread. The consternation with which the encyclical was greeted soon gave way to indifference.

By the early 1970s, signs of disaffection were everywhere: recruitment was at a standstill, priests and religious were leaving, and religious practice was falling off. But religious practice did not disappear entirely, and new forms made their appearance to complement the traditional parish structure. The charismatic movement grew rapidly, developing outside the hierarchical structure and involving more than 50,000 Quebecers. By

Followers of Krishna Consciousness (*Le Journal de Montréal*)

the late 1970s, it had been coopted into the institutional church. There were also experiments that took place in small group settings. Notable among these were the Base Communities — groups of people who lived their faith collectively in a particular milieu — but there were also Christian political activists and even Christian cafés. None of these movements brought the disaffected back to the church en masse. However, the church did learn to live with smaller numbers and its financial situation gradually stabilized.

Despite everything, the church continues to exercise considerable influence in society, disproportionate to the number of practising Catholics. This has been especially true in the area of education, where the government has had to negotiate any reform with the Catholic hierarchy. This influence could be seen in the success of the Association des Parents Catholiques, which with the support of the clergy controlled the Montreal Catholic School Commission from 1973 on.

New Forms of Spirituality

Some people have sought to express their religious feeling and spirituality in a different fashion, outside the established churches. In Quebec, as in other western societies, sects of all sorts grew rapidly, the most conspicuous being the Krishna Consciousness Movement.

In this proliferation of sects, three major tendencies could be identified: sects linked to Christianity, such as the Jesus Freaks and the charismatics; sects linked to eastern religions or spiritual traditions, such as Krishna Consciousness or the followers of the Guru Maharaj Ji, the "living God"; and political-religious movements such as Rev. Sun Myung Moon's Unification Church.

While these sects gained a degree of popularity, especially in the 1970s, they were still a minority phenomenon. Along with the success of television evangelists, whose sermons were broadcast every Sunday, they represented a new way, less closely tied to traditional institutions, for people to express their belief and the mystical side of their nature.

In less than twenty years, the religious picture in Quebec changed radically. The new situation was marked by a diversity of religions and religious experiments and by the waning of the influence of the Catholic Church.

CHAPTER 46

ACCESS TO EDUCATION

In the 1950s, the weakness of the education system became a favourite target for opponents of the Duplessis regime. Reform of the system was begun under Paul Sauvé in 1959 but it became fully operative under the succeeding Liberal government, which made it one of the major elements of its political program. The central goal was to make education accessible to all Quebecers, and pursuit of this goal set in motion a process of change that affected all aspects of the system: the roles of the church, the government, school boards and citizens were redefined; attempts were made to coordinate the various levels of education, from primary to university; teaching methods, teacher training and school financing were all submitted to reexamination. People were forced to make difficult choices, tensions were created, obstructions were thrown up, and substantial resources were mobilized before the wave of reform finally began to subside.

Reforming the System

Educational reform was a longstanding wish that became a major theme of the 1960s. It raised the hopes of many Quebecers and enthusiasm for it went far beyond the educational community as such. Seen as a tool of social change and national development, education became a major concern of the government.

The process began to get moving during the premiership of Paul Sauvé. Using his famous slogan *"désormais"* — henceforth — Sauvé announced that government grants to educational institutions not only would be increased but also would no longer be distributed at the government's discretion. In addition, Sauvé began negotiations with the federal government to recover the money that Ottawa set aside for higher education. Under his successor, Antonio Barrette, the government intro-

Table 1 Major Education Bills Introduced in 1961
Royal Commission on Education (Parent Commission) established
School boards required to ensure that secondary education be offered through grade eleven, either directly or through other institutions (requirement previously extended only to grade seven)
Free education and textbooks through grade eleven
Compulsory education to age fifteen
Statutory grants to school boards increased
Grants for establishment of kindergartens
Statutory grants to private educational institutions
Five-year plan for university financing
All parents of children under eighteen given the right to vote in school board elections
Education allowances of $10 per month for students aged sixteen and seventeen
System of loans and bursaries for college and university students established
Bursaries established for university training of teachers
Source: L.-P. Audet, *Histoire de l'enseignement* 2, pp. 401-3

duced a number of bills to increase grants to universities, classical colleges and school boards and improve the situation of Quebec's teachers.

After coming to power in 1960, the new Liberal government increased the pace and scale of the reform movement. For the first time, responsibility for all policies and budgets related to education, which had been split among a number of ministerial departments and the Department of Public Instruction, was given to a single minister, Paul Gérin-Lajoie. Starting with its first legislative session, the government introduced an impressive series of measures that became known as the *"grande charte de l'éducation"* — the great charter of education (table 1).

In addition to these legislative initiatives, the government also made a number of administrative and pedagogical decisions that strengthened Gérin-Lajoie's Department of Youth at the expense of the Department of Public Instruction. The government set up a large number of commissions of inquiry and study committees to examine every area of education thoroughly. This activity culminated in the establishment of a Royal Commission on Education headed by Alphonse-Marie Parent. The commission's mandate was a broad one, extending to the organization and financing of education at all levels. In the course of its work, which lasted from 1961 to 1966, the commission heard 300 briefs and visited many educational institutions in Canada, the United States and Europe.

Liberal Party election material, 1960.

The commission submitted its first recommendations in 1963. They included the abolition of the Department of Public Instruction and the establishment of a Department of Education along with an advisory body, the Superior Council of Education. But when the government introduced a bill to implement these recommendations, there was a strong reaction from a number of groups, especially the Catholic bishops, and the government had to retreat temporarily. While Youth Minister Gérin-Lajoie toured Quebec to mobilize public opinion, difficult negotiations were undertaken with the bishops, which led to a compromise in 1964. The Department of Education was established, but the denominational character of the public school system was ensured through a variety of measures, such as the appointment of Catholic and Protestant associate deputy ministers and the setting up of Catholic and Protestant committees with supervisory powers within the Superior Council of Education. The council had the power to inquire into any matter relating to education and make its recommendations public; it was believed that it could serve as a counterweight to the department.

One of the new department's priorities was to make sure that all young people had access to secondary education. The roughly 1,500 local school boards were in no position to ensure that secondary education would be available everywhere. Therefore, the government initiated a process of consolidation that led to the rapid establishment of fifty-five regional Catholic and Protestant school boards, covering all of Quebec. This "Operation 55" involved people at the local level and as a result was successfully carried out.

So strong was the dynamic of change in education that when the Union Nationale returned to power in 1966, it had to ratify the measures that had already been put in place and continue to implement the reforms recommended in the Parent Report. The Union Nationale government set up a system of community colleges (cegeps), established the University of Quebec and provided for teacher training in the universities. As a result of these reforms, along with the effect of the baby boom, the number of students grew substantially (table 2).

This rapid increase in the number of students in the public system below the college level led to rising educational expenditures. In 1960-61, the Quebec government spent about $181 million, or 24.4 per cent of its total expenditures, on education. By contrast, in 1970-71, educational expenditures were more than $1 billion (29 per cent), while in 1982-83 they were more than $6 billion (27.4 per cent).

In the 1970s, the effect of Quebec's reduced birth rate was strongly felt in the school system, as the number of students at the primary and secondary levels declined significantly (table 2). Efforts were also made to control the system's growing cost. Thus, the euphoric, effervescent atmosphere of the 1960s did not continue in the 1970s. It was a period of

Table 2
Students Enrolled in Public Schools, Quebec, 1960-84

Year	Kindergarten*	Primary	Secondary	Total
1960-61	11,769	870,046	204,772	1,086,587
1970-71	108,127	865,620	591,734	1,565,481
1979-80	83,430	554,367	524,547	1,162,344
1983-84	89,134	529,868	429,711	1,048,713

*Does not include preschool classes for children under five.

Source: *Annuaire du Québec*, 1961 to 1985-86.

consolidation, with few major institutional changes. In the 1980s, the quality of education became the leading concern.

The linguistic and religious dimensions of education also became major issues. The language laws — 63, 22 and 101 — had direct repercussions on the school system and people affected by them responded vigorously. The debate centred on restructuring Quebec's school boards, whose basis for existence was denominational. The problem was especially intense in Montreal, where rigid denominational structures were poorly adapted to the needs of a population characterized by ethnic and linguistic as well as religious diversity. Two solutions were proposed: either unified school boards or division along language lines. Either way, the same school board would administer Catholic, Protestant and neutral schools.

Repeated attempts by successive governments to resolve the problem ran into determined opposition from the existing school boards and from pressure groups, especially English Protestants and conservative Catholics. With the constraints imposed by article 93 of the British North America Act on their side, the opponents of change succeeded in blocking any significant reform. The government succeeded only in reducing the number of school boards and in establishing the School Council of the Island of Montreal in 1972; this body's mandate was limited to specific responsibilities for coordination.

Another aspect of educational reform had to do with financing, where the government played an increased role. School boards now depended on the government for a much larger share of their budgets. The property tax, a much smaller proportion of which went to the school boards, was of declining importance. In addition, the cegeps were entirely government-financed and the universities primarily so. At the same time, the government took a much more active role in monitoring the management and spending of educational institutions, which now had to meet exacting standards administered by a heavy-handed bureaucracy. The effect of this change was to limit the autonomy of local and private authorities. However, the system also contributed towards reducing inequality of opportunity and resources.

Programs and Teaching

In addition to structural reform, educational programs and teaching were modified as well. The sequence of education was unified and coordinated. Everywhere in Quebec, education now takes place in four distinct stages, each with a standard duration. The primary couse, reduced to six years, is followed by a five-year secondary course, then by a college program lasting two or three years depending on which stream the student enters, and finally by a university program, itself divided into three levels.

Other innovations were also aimed at establishing uniformity. Thus, the government mandated a standard age for starting school and instituted new programs. The new teaching methods introduced in Quebec had their origins in the United States. Education was to be less teacher-directed and book-oriented. Rather, it would be better adapted to the child's personality and take account of the different rates at which children in a large heterogeneous population learn. Rigid discipline, it was hoped, would be replaced by freedom, creativity and spontaneity.

In the 1950s, kindergarten was not integrated into the public system. Few school boards offered it, and it was left to private agencies. In 1960-61, for the first time, the government provided for grants to school boards for kindergarten programs, and the number of kindergartens grew rapidly (table 2). At the primary level, change affected the content of education more than structures. Beyond teaching the three Rs, primary education was now directed towards developing the whole child.

Regionalization at the secondary level made it possible to establish polyvalent schools in which general and vocational education took place in the same building. Breaking down the traditional barriers between mutually exclusive sectors made secondary education a more open program, with compulsory general courses and a series of options. With the integration of technical training into the polyvalent schools, a number of specialized institutions — such as trade schools and family institutes (successors to the domestic science schools) — disappeared. Between 1,000 and 4,000 girls and boys from twelve to eighteen years of age and from all sectors of the population came together in the new secondary school, often travelling a substantial distance from their homes to get there. Among parents and students, the organization of the polyvalent school and the education that took place there were the cause of considerable concern and protest. Some demanded a return to more traditional, authoritarian, rigidly organized education, while others sent their children to private schools.

The wave of reform also buffeted the private school system, which is a significant part of the Quebec educational scene. However, grants to some private schools under the terms of the Private Education Act, passed in 1968, made it possible for these schools to survive and grow. These grants are equivalent to 60 or 80 per cent of the average cost of education in the public system and represent the most generous subsidies to private education in Canada. The growth of the private sector was all the more significant in that it came at a time of declining primary and secondary school enrolment. In 1970-71, 62,683 students, or 3.7 per cent of the total, attended private schools, from kindergarten to the college level. By 1983-84, the total was 108,212 (8.3 per cent); one child in thirteen was enrolled in a private primary or secondary school in 1982.

Colleges and Universities

With the implementation of the Parent Commission's recommendation that a new system of colleges be established, an institution that had been part of Quebec's educational system for more than a hundred years, the classical college, disappeared. This reform also represented a major change on the Anglophone side, for it marked the end of the direct transition from high school to university that still prevails in the rest of North America. The first *collèges d'enseignement général et professionel* (cegeps) were set up in 1967. The network of cegeps soon covered all of Quebec, providing free, accessible college-level programs for all students. The cegeps offered both general education, which for most students was preparatory to university studies, and vocational training, which usually led directly to the job market. The number of students enrolled in cegeps increased rapidly, from 71,858 in the late 1960s to 156,658 in 1983-84. Initially, most students (65 per cent) chose the general program, but in 1983-84 almost half of all students enrolled in Quebec's private and public cegeps opted for the vocational course.

More accessible college-level education also led to a larger number of students attending university. The many changes that occurred in structures and programs make comparisons difficult, but the most significant statistic is undoubtedly the number of degrees granted by Quebec universities. Table 3 shows that in the five-year period between 1966 and 1970, there were more university graduates than in the ten preceding years, and at the end of the period (1983), there were substantially more graduates per year than there had been before.

While there was considerable growth in the whole system from the late 1960s on, Anglophone universities continued to produce a disproportionately high number of graduates, especially at the doctoral level.

Table 3
Number of Degrees Awarded by Quebec Universities, by Level, 1956-70 and 1983

	Francophone	Anglophone	Total
A - 1956-65			
Undergraduate	19,832	14,831	34,663
Master's level	5,403	913	6,316
Doctoral	446	1,174	1,620
B - 1966-70			
Undergraduate	21,145	16,135	37,460
Master's level	5,604	2,811	8,415
Doctoral	470	1,006	1,476
C - 1983			
Undergraduate	15,451	6,708	22,159
Master's level	2,392	1,202	3,594
Doctoral	249	169	418

Sources: Raymond Duchesne, *La science et le pouvoir au Québec*, pp. 104-5; *Le Québec statistique, Édition 1985-1986*, pp. 444-45.

The gap narrowed by the end of the period, but in 1983 Anglophone universities still granted 30 per cent of the bachelors' degrees, 33 per cent of the masters' degrees and 40 per cent of the doctorates.

Moreover, despite the progress that was achieved, Quebec still has a long way to go before graduation from university is as common as it is in Ontario. In 1982, according to the Science and Technology Council of Quebec, there were 346.8 bachelors' degrees awarded in Quebec per hundred thousand population as compared with 466.9 in Ontario. At the master's level, the figures were 53.1 in Quebec and 71 in Ontario, while at the doctoral level they were 6.1 in Quebec and 9.5 in Ontario. At the same time, there was an increasing tendency for Francophone students to study the natural sciences, engineering and management. Another change was the increasing number of women students: in 1960, only about 14 per cent of university students were women, while in 1983 women represented 50.2 per cent of the graduates.

Among the changes that produced these results were an increase in the number of universities and decentralization of the university system. The various campuses of the University of Quebec began to be put into operation in 1968. As a result, a second French-language university was opened in Montreal and university education was now available in previously poorly served cities such as Trois-Rivières, Chicoutimi, Rimouski, Hull and Rouyn-Noranda. At the same time, the University of Montreal, the University of Sherbrooke and Laval University underwent considerable expansion. On the Anglophone side, Sir George Williams University

The University of Quebec at Montreal, which opened in 1968. (Gilles Lavoie)

and Loyola College merged to form Concordia University. In 1968, to coordinate the system's growth, the government established the Council of Universities and assigned it the task of formulating and regularly updating a development and financing plan.

The place of scientific research in Quebec universities has been a growing one. Efforts have been made to develop applied research and provide for the transfer of knowledge between the universities and business, but basic research and the training of researchers remain the most significant activities in this field.

Teachers

Although Quebec had 114 normal schools in 1958, its teachers, according to the historian L.-P. Audet, were the most poorly trained in Canada. As a result, from the beginning of the Quiet Revolution, the government made it a priority to raise the educational level of Quebec's teachers by making it easier for them to obtain university training. The Parent Commission recommended that the universities take over teacher training from the normal schools, and this recommendation was implemented. The opening of the new University of Quebec campuses made it possible to meet the demand for university spaces that this change created. The reform succeeded in raising teachers' educational level and professional status.

In the late 1950s, teaching was still considered a "calling." Working conditions were poor, wages were low, job security was nonexistent and education and experience were barely recognized. There were wide gaps between men and women, between urban and rural areas and between the English Protestant and French Catholic systems.

By 1960, however, the huge demand on the educational system imposed by the advent of the baby boom generation created a climate favourable to change and to the upgrading of teachers' status. Starting in 1959, membership in the teachers' guild, the CIC, was compulsory for lay teachers in French Catholic elementary and secondary schools. The CIC's membership jumped from 16,000 to 28,000, and its capacity to organize its members and work in their interests was greatly enhanced. The CIC gradually developed into a real union, the Centrale de l'Enseignement du Québec (CEQ). Quebec-wide negotiations led to substantial wage hikes and made it possible for female teachers, who had always been grossly underpaid, to obtain parity with male ones. But the union's struggles often ended up being very difficult ones, leading to strikes and back-to-work legislation. The collective agreements that came out of these battles were heavy-handed, minutely detailed documents that specified everything. Teachers progressively lost their autonomy in a squeeze among the local school administration, the government and the union. Almost all college and university professors were also organized into unions during the period.

A student demonstration. (John Daggett, Montreal *Star*, National Archives of Canada, PA-139981)

In the early 1980s, some fundamental changes occurred. With the substantial decline in the number of primary and secondary students, the number of teachers dropped from 73,408 in 1979 to 63,609 in 1984. As a group, teachers were aging, and teachers with ten years' seniority were no longer assured of keeping their jobs. The situation led to a deep-seated malaise. Women still represented a substantial majority of Quebec's teachers, but they were concentrated at the primary and secondary levels. In 1982-83, 63.5 per cent of primary and secondary teachers employed by Quebec school boards were women. At the same time, women accounted for only 33.4 per cent of college teachers and less than 20 per cent of university professors.

The Student Movement

During the 1960s, students at the university and later the college level made efforts to organize and to become an influential pressure group. Adopting trade union structures, they established the Union Générale des Étudiants du Québec (UGEQ) in 1964. UGEQ was the flagship organization for a group of well-organized local student unions, which along with the student press served as organs for participation in the major social debates of the time. In 1968, students went on strike and occupied buildings in the cegeps and some university faculties. They were critical of the quality of education and insisted on greater participation in decisions that affected them. They demanded free education through university and more financial support from the government. After this feverish period, however, the student structures broke down. One by one, the major associations fell apart under the weight of internal contradictions, financial problems and the alienation of their members. The succeeding period was marked by drift and by conflicts among small groups. Then in the late 1970s, the student movement surfaced again. More pragmatic this time, student associations encouraged student participation, offered services and sought to improve the quality of education. The new Quebec-wide organizations — Rassemblement des Étudiants Universitaires and Association Nationale des Étudiants du Québec — found it difficult to mobilize their troops except on issues of fees, loans and bursaries and the financing of postsecondary education.

Under Bill 32, passed in 1983, educational institutions were required to grant official recognition to student associations and provide for their financing at source when they represented a majority of students. In some cases, the legislation has led to fairly intense internecine struggles that have weakened the student movement. Where there is no internal division, however, student associations have enough resources at their disposal to play a significant role.

*   *   *   *   *   *

Never in its history has Quebec devoted as much energy and resources to the progress of education as during this period. Undoubtedly the most significant achievement of educational reform has been to make schooling widely accessible and to improve the educational level of the popu-

Table 4
Educational Level of Quebec's Population, by Age Group, 1971 and 1981

	% completed grade nine	% with secondary school diploma	% with at least some university
1971			
Total population	57.7	n.a.	9.8
15-24	83.6	n.a.	10.2
25-34	66.2	n.a.	15.1
35 and over	40.5	n.a.	7.5
1981			
Total population	73.6	53.9	13.5
15-24	94.2	59.2	9.5
25-34	89.8	73.2	21.1
35 and over	56.6	42.8	12.2

n.a.: not available

Source: *Le Québec statistique, Édition 1985-1986*, p. 447.

lation substantially. Almost all children between the ages of five and fifteen now attend school. While in 1971 only 57.7 per cent of the population fifteen and over had completed grade nine, in 1981 the figure was 73.6 per cent. Also in 1981, 53.9 per cent of the population had a secondary or trade school diploma. Looking at the educational level of the population by age group indicates the scope of the changes that have occurred (table 4). However, opportunity and accessibility are still not equally distributed according to social class, sex and ethnic group. Moreover, there are still hundreds of thousands of illiterates in Quebec. In other words, educational reform is still incomplete.

CHAPTER 47

PLURALISM AND THE DESIRE FOR CHANGE

In the period between the Quiet Revolution and our own time, Quebec's ideological landscape has been unusually varied and complex. This is no doubt in part an optical illusion: we are looking at this period from very close range. But it is also in part a result of some characteristics of the period itself: the development of means of communication that have speeded up and intensified the circulation of ideas both within Quebec and between Quebec and other societies; the availability of secondary and postsecondary education to new sectors of the population; the maturing of the baby boom generation; the increased number of places in which ideologies are developed and disseminated. All these factors have contributed to increased pluralism and a greater diversity of currents of thought and opinion.

Another feature of the period has been the leading role played by ideologies favourable to change. The profusion of ideological currents promoting innovation and a break with the past rapidly relegated traditionalism, which strongly marked the years between 1930 and 1945 and — even while coming under criticism — still exercised a determining influence between 1945 and 1960, to a defensive minority position.

We do not treat this ideological ferment exhaustively here. In the first part of the chapter, we sketch the general development of the ideological scene during the period. Then we look more closely, one by one, at the major currents — those that appear to us to be most representative, most influential and most fully worked out. In doing so, we have had to ignore other tendencies that, while significant, are too marginal to allow a full discussion.

From Consensus to Polarization

The years between the beginning of the Quiet Revolution in 1960 and the 1980 referendum on sovereignty-association can be divided into three unequal periods, each of them shaped both by Quebec's internal political, social and economic situation and by the international context. The first period (1960-65) was marked by a fairly broad consensus on the major goals of the Quiet Revolution. This consensus then broke apart, to be followed by a period of dissension on a range of issues (1965-76), in which choices became more varied and debates became more intense. Then in the final period (1976-80), Quebec was highly polarized on the national question.

With the death of Maurice Duplessis in 1959 and the election of Jean Lesage's Liberals the next year, the new elites that had formed since the war began to rally round a few major ideas. While these groups were very diverse and included Anglophones as well as Francophones, they agreed on enough ideas to make it appropriate to talk about a genuine ideological consensus.

The ideas on which the consensus developed were products of the reform liberal current. The first of these ideas was rejection of the old conservative values and an attack on Quebec's backwardness in all its forms. There had been a rumble of discontent and impatience for a decade, and it burst into the open with the huge success of *Les insolences du Frère Untel* (*The Impertinences of Brother Anonymous*) in 1960 and political slogans such as Paul Sauvé's *"Désormais"* (Henceforth) and the Liberals' *"C'est le temps que ça change"* (It's time for a change).

The positive side of the same coin — the idea of modernization and catching up — was another area of consensus. No longer was Quebec seen as a marginal society, essentially rural and traditional. The new ideological consensus instead emphasized Quebec's urban, industrial character and the need to adapt its political and institutional structures to this reality through wholesale reforms. Quebec would thus be in step with the rest of the world, modelling itself after modern, dynamic societies such as John F. Kennedy's America and Gaullist France.

It was also agreed that the primary instrument for such a program of modernization had to be a strong Quebec state, run by a large, competent civil service under the leadership of an elite made up of experts in management. Along with this positive view of the state went a new, affirmative Quebec nationalism, as clearly symbolized in the gradual replacement of the terms "Province of Quebec" and "French Canadian" by "State of Quebec" and "Québécois."

The final area of consensus appeared to contradict this large degree of confidence in the technocratic state. This was participation — a desire to democratize Quebec's institutions and involve different groups of citizens in the process of making decisions that affected them. Among the expressions of this desire were better relations between the government and trade unions, the establishment of a large number of consultative and parity committees, and broad consultation campaigns. These concepts represented a clear contrast with the authoritarianism of the Duplessis era.

On the one hand, this ideological consensus — which could be seen in full flower during the campaign to nationalize Quebec's private electricity companies in 1962 — was one of the factors that made the Quiet Revolution such an exceptional period. On the other hand, it also helps explain why the period was so brief. For while the directions taken during the Quiet Revolution had the near-unanimous support of the most conspicuous leaders and groups, they were also a source of dissatisfaction.

Some Quebecers agreed with the idea of modernization but rejected specific aspects of it. For example, business people and employers favoured limiting social programs and government intervention. Others, such as the editors of *Cité Libre*, applauded the reforms but did not agree with the openly nationalist orientation that went along with them. Resistance also came from traditionalist groups that rejected modernization in key sectors. Examples are the Créditistes and the Catholic integrist groups that resisted the establishment of the Department of Education. At the same time, other groups saw the reforms as inadequate or too slow. The Mouvement Laïc de Langue Française, for example, wanted Quebec to be more radically secularized and declericalized. The independence movement wanted Quebec's self-assertion to go all the way to the rejection of federalism and the proclamation of Quebec independence. And the left wanted to carry participation and democratization to the point of overthrowing the socioeconomic system through revolution. The most notable expression of this radical current was the journal *Parti Pris* (1963-68), which conducted its struggle on three fronts: secularism, independence, socialism.

These dissatisfactions began germinating in the early 1960s and soon found expression in better organized ideological currents, which made the years between 1965 and 1976 a much more fragmented and troubled period than the previous one. The ideological climate was increasingly one of criticism, systematic challenge to existing structures and experimentation with new values. In particular, the left became more visible and active, while nationalism became more radical. New currents also began to make their presence felt: the counterculture, the ecology movement, and later radical feminism. Most social and labour conflicts showed signs of this ferment, which led to increasingly intense struggles within intellectual and artistic circles and on the political scene. This intensification of debates was largely the result of changes internal to Quebec, such as the youth phenomenon, the growth of the universities and the new stature of the state. But ideological currents that originated outside Quebec also had an influence, especially the rise of radicalism and the challenge to the system in France in May 1968 and in the United States under Richard Nixon. In fact, the Quebec situation can be seen as one instance of a general crisis of values that occurred throughout the West at the time.

The St. Jean Baptiste Day celebrations in 1968 turned into a riot. (Canada Wide)

This ideological climate was further upset by the Parti Québécois's victory in the 1976 election and its promise of a referendum on the question of sovereignty-association. The national question had been an issue for a long time, and an increasingly crucial one since the Quiet Revolution. Now, for four years, it was at the centre of every debate. All other concerns, notably social questions, were subordinated or relegated to the back burner. Public opinion divided into two diametrically opposed blocs on the question of Quebec's constitutional position and its relationship with the rest of Canada. While each side may have brought together highly diverse groups and tendencies, political circumstances and the referendum legislation under which "umbrella" Yes and No committees were established forced both sides to keep their differences under wraps and present a united front.

On the No side, Canadian nationalists such as representatives of Ottawa's "French Power" and well-known Quebec nationalists such as Quebec Liberal Party leader Claude Ryan worked side by side. So did social democrats and elements of the left along with conservative groups such as the Conseil du Patronat (Employers' council), the Créditistes and the leaders of the "Yvette" movement of women opposed to independence. The Yes side was also characterized by diversity, although to a lesser extent. Radical independentists worked together with supporters of decentralized federalism, and traditionalists like the leaders of the

Saint Jean–Baptiste Society made common cause with trade unionists and socialists.

The fight to the finish between Quebec Premier René Lévesque and Canadian Prime Minister Pierre Elliott Trudeau was the most dramatic expression of the polarization on the national question. While tension had surrounded the new Quebec nationalism for two decades, this polarization reflected a further hardening of positions. At the same time, it marked a narrowing of the Quebec ideological spectrum, which had been a very broad one after 1965.

The Major Currents

Even though the period has been characterized by ideological diversity, a few major currents of thought can be identified. Each of these ideologies has a substantial degree of coherence and represents what the political scientists Kenneth McRoberts and Dale Posgate have called "beliefs about the purpose and character of society and polity." While the major ideologies have been widely disseminated, they have been formulated by small groups belonging to Quebec's social, political and intellectual elites. These groups aim to direct Quebec's social organization and collective life along a path consistent with their interests and values. We will examine three of these currents: reform Quebec nationalism, Canadian nationalism and left-wing egalitarianism. The last section will look at some more limited currents of thought: feminism, the ecology movement, the counterculture and Catholic integrism.

It is important to note two caveats. First, none of these currents is completely homogeneous. Each contains tendencies that can differ significantly from one another, and internal conflicts can arise within each current over the best means of attaining goals on which everyone agrees. Second, even though in general terms these ideologies are opposed to one another, they are not always separated by unbridgeable gulfs. They often agree on certain points while disagreeing on others.

A large part of the reason for these complexities is that in the social and political context of the period, supporters of each ideology have had to take a position on both national and social questions. Thus, there has been room for different positions on some of these questions, and for different sets of priorities, within each current; at the same time, on some issues there has been no clear distinction between one ideology and another.

Reform Quebec Nationalism

One of these ideologies can be seen as the backdrop to the whole period: reform Quebec nationalism. It originated in the neonationalism of the 1945-60 period, and although it has been formulated in different and sometimes conflicting ways, it is based on two fundamental themes. The first is a new definition of the nation, stripped of its religious and backward-looking dimensions and with new content given to its other distinctive features. Language rights and an enhanced place for French in all areas of political and economic life are a priority. Culture is no longer identified simply with maintaining traditions; instead it has to be open to innovation and involved in social and political struggles. Most important, the nation is now identified with the people of a specific territory, Quebec, who despite a degree of regional diversity are unified by the circumstance of living under the same government. Within that territory, French Canadians — increasingly referred to as Québécois — constitute a majority, forming a distinct society.

The second characteristic theme of this new nationalism is its association with a vision of social reform. It sees modernization in all forms as the best guarantee of Quebec's future as a collectivity. If Quebec is to flourish, it has to catch up and be in the vanguard of reform in all areas. The defensive attitudes of the past gave way to an assertive, challenging, change-oriented nationalism that has given a strongly distinctive character to the political life and cultural output of the period.

In the social and economic spheres, this reform spirit was expressed through reform liberal ideas in the 1960s, while in the 1970s it developed into support, at least on the rhetorical level, for social democratic values. Through this transition, reform Quebec nationalists remained consistent in their broad confidence in the forces of change — especially the state, whose role was to embody the nation and organize its development.

Reform nationalism based on the state was the central ideology of the Quiet Revolution and was forcefully expressed in its slogan "*Maîtres chez nous*" (Masters in our own house). But it was far from being the exclusive property of Jean Lesage's Liberals. Other governments and political parties of the period drew from it as well: Daniel Johnson's Union Nationale, with its slogan "*Égalité ou indépendance*" (Equality or independence); Robert Bourassa's Liberals, with their concept of "cultural sovereignty"; and René Lévesque's Parti Québécois, whose platform was based on the twin pillars of nationalist affirmation and social and political reform. Outside the political arena, a variety of other groups were motivated by the same ideology — student movements, trade unions, intellectuals, teachers, journalists, Francophone business people, even some bishops and other clergy influenced by the Second Vatican Council.

Because reform Quebec nationalism has been the dominant ideology and because it is very diffuse, its unity and cohesion are sometimes ignored and the differences among those who identify with it are emphasized instead. However, these differences are not so much about fundamental issues or major goals as about the means of reaching these goals. The most significant and conspicuous of these differences, appearing first in the early 1960s and powerfully in evidence during the 1970s, has to do with Quebec's constitutional position and its relationship with the rest of Canada. Two major tendencies confronted each other on this question. One, which might be called the federalist nationalist tendency,

proposed that Quebec's powers be expanded within a substantially decentralized Canadian federation. Some federalist nationalists went as far
as demanding special status for Quebec within Confederation, and many
of them found themselves in frequent and fairly vigorous opposition to
Ottawa. But all of them agreed that the political link with the rest of
Canada was essential and a separate Quebec — as advocated by the
supporters of the second tendency, the independence movement — was
risky if not impossible.

While individuals had put forward the idea of independence at
various times in the past, it was only around 1960 that a real pro-independence current began to develop. Decolonization movements in
Africa, both black and Arab, were a significant influence on this current,
which considered the federal link an obstacle to Quebec's development
and saw Quebec as a victim of domination that made it an "alienated"
and "dispossessed" society. The independence movement saw itself as
socially and economically progressive, and its goals were Quebec
sovereignty, French unilingualism and more or less radical reforms. In
the 1960s it gained a significant number of adherents, especially among
youth, but it was a long way from attracting broad support in the population as a whole. After 1967, under René Lévesque's influence, the idea
of independence was redefined in the more moderate form of
sovereignty-association. Diluted in this way, the idea of independence
made rapid progress during the 1970s, only to be ultimately rejected in
the 1980 referendum. However, even if federalist nationalism represented
the dominant current of the period, pro-independence nationalism was
a major ideological factor.

Canadian Nationalism

Quebec nationalists, federalist and pro-independence alike, agreed on the
need to identify with Quebec first and therefore to make the Quebec
government's powers as broad as possible. In this belief, they were opposed to another major current of the period, Canadian nationalism,
which placed primary emphasis on membership in the Canadian nation
and saw Quebec as first and foremost a component of a larger bilingual
and bicultural federal unit.

This current had its origins in the new federalism of the 1950s. On the
Francophone side, the *Cité Libre* group, a major component of the reform
liberal intelligentsia of that period, became its most significant representatives. This group initially allied itself with the New Democratic
Party, but from 1965 on it switched its allegiance, following three of its
leaders, Pierre Elliott Trudeau, Gérard Pelletier and Jean Marchand, to
the federal Liberal Party. Once in office, Trudeau, Pelletier and Marchand
— nicknamed "the three wise men" — were the architects of what became known as "French Power" (the English term was used in French as
well).

The Canadian nationalists' vision of Canada and Quebec's place in it is not a new one. In the first quarter of the twentieth century, it had taken shape in the ideas of Henri Bourassa. Bourassa, however, had linked it to a conservative, clericalist position that was not much different from similar ideas within traditionalist nationalism. By contrast, the Canadian nationalism of the 1960s and 1970s, like the new Quebec nationalism, took its inspiration from reform liberalism. Like Quebec nationalists, its supporters argued for the modernization, democratization and secularization of society and saw the state as a choice instrument of economic and social organization. As a result, they initially supported the reforms of the Quiet Revolution. However, Canadian nationalists saw the Quebec nationalist orientation of the Quiet Revolution, and later the rise of the independence movement, as a dangerous deviation, even — in Trudeau's description — a "new treason of the intellectuals." In other words, they regarded it as simply a resurgence of the old conservative, provincialist, authoritarian nationalism.

In opposition to this nationalism, which in their judgement was "tribal" and closed in on itself, they put forward a form of universalist humanism. This position translates into identification with Canada, which they conceive of as a bilingual, multicultural state that guarantees basic freedoms and democracy. On the basis of this conception of Canada, they have fought to strengthen the position of Francophones within federal institutions. At the same time, they support a centralist form of federalism opposed to Quebec nationalism in all its manifestations.

Canadian nationalism acknowledges that French Canadians form a specific group within Canada, but their specificity is seen in terms of language and culture alone. It is not enough to make them a distinct society. Still less does Quebec constitute a territory with the right to govern itself. The Canadian nation is a mosaic of various cultures, with French Canadians as one of its essential components, but politically it is a single unified entity. The federal government's role is to preserve both this diversity and this unity.

Roughly from the late 1960s on, a large majority of Anglophone Quebecers supported this vision. Their support was reflected in the English-language press and in business circles as well as among intellectuals and politicians. The Anglophones saw themselves primarily as Canadians and could not identify with the new Quebec nationalism, which many of them saw as a threat directed expressly against them. Initially, their conception of Canada was a rather traditional one, in which they along with Anglophones of other provinces formed the majority and Quebec was a bilingual region whose powers had to remain limited. However, under the influence of Quebec nationalist self-assertion and the Francization movement, they increasingly saw themselves as a minority group, and as a result supported the vision of a bilingual Canada implied in the French Power movement. At the same time, often in alliance with Francophone minorities elsewhere in Canada, they fought to defend their language and community rights in Quebec. These new positions were expressed primarily through Alliance Quebec, an organization founded in the late 1970s. Finally, around 1980, an increasing number of English-speaking Quebecers — especially in what the journalists Dominique Clift and Sheila McLeod Arnopolous called "the new Anglophone leadership" — began to identify with Quebec to a greater extent, acknowledging its predominantly French character and even accepting its political demands in its struggle with Ottawa. It should also be noted that even if the Anglophone community has taken a relatively homogeneous position on the national question, its positions on other issues, like those of the Francophone community, have been characterized by broad ideological pluralism.

Left-Wing Ideologies and the Social Question

While Quebec nationalists and Canadian nationalists were in conflict over political and constitutional issues, their positions on social and economic questions were often very similar. The values that underlay their attitudes on these questions were the same — in essence, those of reform liberalism. As noted in chapter 25, reform liberalism was an ideology whose major tenets had been developed in the aftermath of the Depression. Recognizing the need to reduce flagrant inequalities, it assigned to the state the responsibility of guaranteeing an adequate education and decent living conditions to all citizens and making social security as extensive as possible. At the same time, it did not challenge the foundations of liberalism: private property, free enterprise and the profit motive. Even though some groups, such as business, have wanted government's role to be limited primarily to assisting private enterprise, reform liberalism has been the dominant ideology of the period in the social sphere.

The left differs from reform liberalism in that it places primary emphasis on social questions and seeks to transform the economic and political system so that all groups of citizens will be as equal as possible. Achieving this kind of equality means putting an end to the exploitation that victimizes workers, the unemployed, people on welfare and all other disadvantaged groups.

Relatively marginal before 1960, left-wing ideologies made a breakthrough during the period and became a significant factor in social debates. The growth of the left was a feature of most western societies. In Quebec, it took the form of increased penetration by left-wing ideas in the Francophone community, which until then had been largely closed to these ideas. As clerical and conservative influence waned and institutions and attitudes were liberalized, Francophones' traditional hostility to the left softened. At the same time, the political, ideological and even judicial censorship to which left-wing groups had been subject in the past was relaxed (although not completely eliminated), while the growth of the trade union movement, the youth phenomenon and the development of the education system gave the left a wider potential audience.

While all groups on the left share a common ideal — the replacement of capitalism by an egalitarian society — there have been a number of different tendencies, which can be grouped into two major currents. The first, characterized by its radicalism, is Marxist communism, which advocates the abolition of private property; the nationalization of the economy; the overthrow of the state, which it sees as an instrument of the ruling class; and the installation of a proletarian government entirely devoted to the interests of the working class. It seeks to realize these goals by intensifying social conflict and radicalizing labour struggles, especially those directly involving the state. Marxism had little impact in the early 1960s. But it subsequently became stronger and more widespread in the universities and cegeps under the influence of a new generation of professors trained in France, where a renewal of Marxist thought was taking place. People started Marxist study groups, magazines and newspapers. There were an increasing number of "models" and tendencies: Maoism, Trotskyism, Leninism and others. At the same time, groups of militant partisans gained a foothold in a variety of associations: trade unions, citizens' committees, community organizations, pressure groups. Marxism reached its high point in Quebec in the early 1970s, when large organizations such as the CEQ and the CNTU adopted increasingly radical positions. Revolutionary rhetoric was a major feature of the trade union common fronts of 1972 and 1976. But after that, the movement quickly lost its strength. Marxism was divided into squabbling factions and cells seeking to destroy one another, shunned by growing numbers of trade unionists, and discredited by the statements of Soviet dissidents who defected to the West. It was increasingly seen as a rigid, dogmatic system of thought that did not have much of a hold on the reality it claimed to want to change.

The second major left-wing ideology was socialism, which also advocated collective ownership of the economy and more power for workers. More moderate than Marxism, it believes that its goals can be achieved through parliamentary democracy and does not propose to intensify class struggle or establish the dictatorship of the proletariat. The early 1960s were an auspicious period for socialism. The Parti Socialiste du Québec and the Quebec NDP were founded, attracting many of the intellectuals and trade unionists in the *Cité Libre* circle. Socialism was also one of the fundamental goals of the journal *Parti Pris*. The movement subsequently lost some of its force, as Marxism became the leading channel for the expression of egalitarian thought. But by 1980, with Marxism on the wane, there was a revival of socialism. In its new manifestation, it is an ideology of participation as it was in the 1960s, but it has largely given up its emphasis on government intervention in favour of such themes as worker management, community life and grassroots mutual support.

Although left-wing ideologies unquestionably made progress in Quebec after 1960, their position and influence should not be overestimated. There were a large number of speeches, publications and demonstrations expressing left-wing ideologies, and much work was done in the area of analysis and theoretical development, most of it based on foreign and especially French models. However, left-wing thought still had little impact on the concrete organization of society. Outside of intellectual groups and trade union offices, it reached only a small number of supporters. This limited influence could be seen in the failure of all the political organizations started by communists and socialists during the period.

Part of the reason for the difficulties faced by the Quebec left was its ambiguous relationship with nationalism. In an effort to avoid the trap into which their predecessors had fallen, socialists and Marxists initially tried to integrate the national question into their programs, arguing that Quebec should assert itself or become independent as a preliminary step leading towards social revolution. As the nationalist movement developed, however, some of them modified their position. These groups saw nationalism as a bourgeois issue: Quebec workers had to turn away from the nationalist illusion and give first priority to their solidarity with the Canadian working class as a whole. At the same time, other groups did not share these views and continued to support nationalism. The result was that nationalism became an area of further dissension, weakening and disorienting the movement and undermining its credibility.

Other Ideologies

While the currents discussed above have been the major features of the ideological landscape, they are far from being the only ones. In the pluralist atmosphere of the period — and especially the 1970s — a number of other currents have made their presence felt. These ideologies, characterized by their emphasis on issues other than the national and social questions, have often had considerable influence, directly or indirectly, on large sectors of the population.

The first of these currents is feminism (see chapter 42). The feminism of the 1960s was an ideology of reform, emphasizing legal equality. In the 1970s, under the influence of developments in the United States, a new, more radical form of feminism that challenged all of society's practices and values related to sex role division grew up alongside reform feminism. Radical feminism had relatively few supporters and declined after 1980. However, the feminist message has had an increasing influence not only on women but on society as a whole, prodding political structures, trade unions, corporations, the media and other institutions into beginning to take its ideas and proposals into account.

The ecology movement, which seeks to protect the natural and built environment, has achieved a somewhat similar position. This current has expressed itself most characteristically through very specific controversies involving such issues as public transportation, green spaces, neighbourhood development, the construction of a factory or dam, and non-smokers' rights. The movement's supporters have included many Montreal Anglophones. The ecology movement has not achieved the same political stature in Quebec as in some European countries, but it has succeeded in making some of its concerns felt well beyond its own groups of supporters. Towards the end of the period, peace issues and opposition to the use of nuclear power also became prominent concerns.

Another current had considerable influence, especially among young people, around 1970: the counterculture. This was an umbrella for a wide variety of tendencies, covering such phenomena as the use of psychedelic drugs, fascination with eastern cultures and religions, the occult, vegetarianism and transcendental meditation. All these tendencies came from California, and they placed a common emphasis on the moral, sexual, psychological and spiritual liberation of the individual and the community. Their social and political ideas were not worked out in detail, being generally limited to a radical opposition to conformity and a disdain for established norms and values.

Finally, another part of the ideological landscape consisted of a number of ultraconservative movements. One such was *naturisme social*, which promoted order and discipline. More significant, however, were the various forms of Catholic integrism, which ranged from the Créditiste *Bérets Blancs* through groups campaigning against the liberalization of abortion laws to the Association de Parents Catholiques, which fought to maintain denominational schools.

Narcissism and the Resurgence of Liberalism

The early 1980s marked a break with the past in the ideological sphere. The large questions that had aroused passions among so many activists and groups and sparked such vigorous debates over the previous two decades now seemed to have lost their potency. Quebec nationalism found it difficult to recover from the despondency into which it was cast by the No victory in the referendum. The faith that reform liberalism and social democracy placed in the state turned to doubt. Feminism was in crisis and had a hard time mobilizing young people. There was a climate of disillusionment among onetime activists, and some people even spoke of "the end of ideology." This development, which took place in most western societies, was due to several factors, notably the 1981-82 recession and the aging of the baby boom generation.

Whatever the reason for the new disaffection with ideologies that challenge the established order and emphasize the role of collective movements, it made possible the emergence — or resurgence — of two other currents that appear to have been the characteristic ideological expressions of the 1980s. The first consists of "ideologies of the self," — hedonistic ideologies that place primary emphasis on private life and the physical or psychological wellbeing of the individual rather than questioning the organization of society. Therapies and doctrines leading to "personal growth," various methods of achieving "wellness," and the worship of physical form and emotional equilibrium have flourished. The commercial and advertising sectors have made considerable use of these developments.

The other significant current is neoconservatism, which represents a critique of Keynesian reform liberalism and a return to the values of classical liberalism: smaller government, deregulation, privatization of the economy, cutbacks in social programs and belief in free enterprise. The influence of this new conservatism, which came to Quebec in the wake of the triumph of Reaganism in the United States, has been felt in all areas of social and political life. It promotes individualism, discipline, strict economic rationality and, in general, stability rather than change.

CHAPTER 48

REFORM OF THE STATE

The Quiet Revolution signalled the beginning of a thorough reform of Quebec's government institutions. At the same time, it marked an acceleration of the long-term trend towards increased government intervention in a variety of spheres of activity. In 1867, the Quebec government did not amount to much. Over the years, however, circumstances had required it to broaden its initial role, so that it had steadily acquired greater resources and an enhanced capacity for action. This development had become more pronounced after the Second World War, and the Quebec civil service had grown substantially in size. In addition, before 1960, local governments (municipalities and school boards) had taken on a significant portion of the burden of public administration and investment. And the federal government had preceded the Quebec government in developing and modernizing its administrative institutions to adjust to the new requirements of the welfare state.

The Broadening of Government Intervention

Early on in the 1960s, the Quebec government centralized some of the powers and responsibilities belonging to school boards and municipalities, thus taking charge of areas of activity that had hitherto been handled primarily at the local level. In addition, it brought areas that had been monopolized by the private sector, and especially the church, under public control: hospitals, social services, parts of the education system. These initiatives set in motion a process of centralization of decision-making, management and resources that the political scientist James Iain Gow describes as one of the basic characteristics of modern public administration.

Successive governments in Quebec City did not limit themselves to taking charge of existing institutions. New government intervention covered many areas. Governments entered fields of activity such as the economy and culture much more systematically than before and increased their hold over citizens' lives. Government intervention in specific sectors and the policies underlying it are discussed in the chapters dealing with those sectors.

To make these new roles possible, the government needed a considerably more complex administrative machine than it had before. As a result, a number of new departments were established: Cultural Affairs (1961), Revenue (1961), Federal-Provincial Affairs (1961), Education (1964), Immigration (1968), the Public Service (1969), Communications (1969), Recreation (1979), the Environment (1979), Science and Technology (1983). Some of these departments consolidated and expanded functions previously assumed by other government agencies, while others represented an extension of government concerns. Most existing departments were reorganized, merged or split, in some cases more than once. Thus, Agriculture and Colonization were combined into a single department, and Fisheries and Food were later added to it. Similarly, the departments of Health and Welfare were combined into the Department of Social Affairs. To ensure that government activity as a whole would be better coordinated, new cabinet committees with permanent structures were established, as was a treasury board whose influence increased steadily.

The period has also been marked by an explosion of public corporations, which function as the economic arm of the state (see chapter 32). The government also established or reorganized and gave new powers to a large number of boards. Some were responsible for overseeing private activity in areas ranging from liquor sales through lotteries and horse racing to rent control. Others were established to manage specific government programs, such as pensions, health insurance and automobile insurance.

A look at the distribution of government expenditures by department provides an indication of the scope of these changes, even if the many administrative upheavals often make exact comparisons impossible. Comparing the fiscal year 1983-84 with 1960-61, it can be seen that some of the government's traditional activities declined in relative terms. The share of expenditures accounted for by Agriculture and Colonization fell from 8.3 to 1.7 per cent; by Roads, from 10.7 to 6.5 per cent; and by Public Works, from 3.4 to 1.2 per cent. Others, such as Finance and Manpower and Income Security, accounted for a much larger share. Throughout the period, however, more than half of all government expenditures went to two areas: education and social affairs. In 1960-61, education represented 24.4 per cent of government expenditures while the departments of Health and Welfare accounted for 30.7 per cent. In 1983-84, 26.9 per cent of government expenditures went to the Department of Education and 27.7 per cent went to Social Affairs and the Quebec Health Insurance Board. These figures show that the Quebec government's educational and social function developed before the Quiet Revolution. What changed was not the relative importance of education and social affairs but the way they were managed and organized. These two government services, more than any others, serve as evidence of the development of bureaucratic centralization.

Bureaucratization

The success or failure of government intervention depends in large part on the people who are responsible for implementing it. How many civil servants the government employs and how qualified they are represent basic parameters of its effectiveness. The leaders of the Quiet Revolution clearly recognized the importance of civil service reform. They saw it as an urgent priority and it constituted one of the most significant measures taken by the Lesage government's *"équipe du tonnerre."* Civil service reform became an ongoing process, and all subsequent governments contributed to it. The result was a transformation of the Quebec civil service in both quantitative and qualitative terms.

Because of substantial differences in job definition and status, figures on the size of the Quebec civil service vary from source to source and it is not easy to obtain an exact measure. Overall, the civil service in the narrow sense — employees of government departments and agencies — nearly doubled in size during the 1960s, from about 29,000 to 53,000 people. The most rapid increase took place between 1966 and 1968, when the government hired almost 10,000 new civil servants. In subsequent years, the rate of increase slowed down, and the number of employees in 1983-84 was about 65,000. Measures taken by the government around that time in an effort to control the growth of its payroll contributed to the slowdown.

In addition to the civil service in the narrow sense, public employees include people who work for publicly owned corporations. There was a sharp increase in the number of these employees in Quebec during the 1960s as a result of the proliferation of publicly owned corporations and especially the rapid growth of Hydro-Quebec. At the same time, the government took responsiblity for paying the employees of the education and social affairs systems, which became known as the parapublic sector. According to figures compiled by Gow, the Quebec civil service represented 3.4 per cent of Quebec's overall work force in 1968, while the public and parapublic sectors together represented 11.4 per cent. All public employees — including those working for municipal governments and federal government employees working in Quebec — represented the respectable total of 16.6 per cent.

Developments on the qualitative side were no less striking than these quantitative changes. All aspects of the way Quebec civil servants were recruited, paid and managed were transformed. Under Duplessis, as the political scientist Jocelyn Jacques has noted, "political favouritism and patronage constituted the two main access routes to the civil service." The system was decentralized and discretionary, tasks were ill defined, pay was very poor and job security was nonexistent. There was a substantial pay increase during Paul Sauvé's brief premiership, but it was the Lesage government that undertook a thorough reform of the civil service. It was spurred on by the civil servants themselves, who didn't hesitate to speak up and now had a union through which to channel their demands.

The civil service was unionized in 1964. This was a major development representing a vast change in labour relations between the government and its employees. A large majority of civil servants voted to join the Quebec Government Employees' Union, affiliated to the CNTU. There were also other bargaining units representing specific groups of employees, such as professionals. Initial negotiations between the unions and the government led to legislation, passed in 1965, that reformed the civil service and its management methods. Civil servants gained union recognition, collective bargaining rights and the right to strike.

Under the 1965 legislation, permanent employees won job security, and further negotiations resulted in an improvement in the conditions under which civil servants became permanent employees. Job classification was revised from top to bottom, making possible a genuine career path with the potential for promotion and advancement. In addition, the pension plan was improved and gradually extended to other categories of government employees, including people working for publicly owned corporations. As a result of these changes, working for the government as a career became a much more real prospect.

Management of working conditions — including movement of personnel, classification and salaries — also became highly centralized under the new legislation. Three agencies shared responsibility for this area: a remodelled Civil Service Commission; the Treasury Board and the Executive Council. Their respective responsibilities were subsequently changed several times, notably when the Department of the Public Service was established in 1969 and at the time of the administrative reform of 1978.

While the Liberals sought to reorganize the civil service systematically, they were especially concerned with its leaders. Top civil servants acquired new importance and visibility. Following the example set by Ottawa two decades earlier, the Lesage government went outside the civil service to recruit a team of new deputy ministers, trained in the social sciences and still relatively young. These newcomers, whom the media quickly identified as "mandarins," played a central role in the reform of the state and provided the government's actions with a degree of cohesion. Union Nationale leader Daniel Johnson attacked them during the 1966 election campaign, but after he won the election and became premier, he realized how important they were and kept them in their jobs. Reform of the higher reaches of the civil service went beyond the deputy minister level. Many upper- and middle-level managers, much younger than their predecessors and generally with experience outside the Quebec government, were hired during the 1960s.

Like the managers, the government's substantial corps of professionals was rejuvenated and renewed. The government's concern with developing a more qualified and competent civil service and with increasing the number of specialists was a factor in this development. In 1959, the government employed only one professional for every fifteen office workers and technicians; by 1968 the ratio was one to six and by 1978 it was one to three. There was also a radical change in the kinds of professionals employed, with specialists in the social sciences and management occupying a much more prominent place. The sociologist Jean-Jacques Simard has noted that the ratio of experts in the biological and physical sciences to experts in the social sciences and management was two to one in 1964. By 1971, the situation was reversed: the social science and management experts were now on the top end of a two-to-one ratio. According to Simard's figures, the number of professionals in "human and socioeconomic engineering" increased by 420.5 per cent between 1964 and 1971 and the number in "legal and administrative support" by 246.7 per cent, while the number in the biological and physical sciences increased by only 20.5 per cent.

Thus, the Quebec government apparatus not only became more bureaucratic after 1960 but also more technocratic, as the presence of these new specialists shows. Both individually and collectively, the technocrats had an interest in the growth of government intervention, which gave significance to their work, extended their power and made their career opportunities more attractive and varied.

New Management Methods

As the government apparatus became more technocratic, it sought to make its actions more "scientific" and systematic. The instruments for achieving this goal were research and planning. From now on, every major initiative would be preceded by a thorough inquiry into the problems that had to be tackled, the needs of the population and the various solutions that could be envisioned. Social science research methods were widely used.

Governments began to make much more frequent use of a time-honoured instrument, the commission of inquiry, and modernized its composition and operation. While commissions had previously consisted essentially of judges and lawyers, the new professions were now increasingly represented on them. Commissions have had substantial research budgets and have used the services of legions of experts and specialists. Some of them have studied questions of great scope and complexity and have had considerable influence as a result. Among the most significant have been the Parent Commission on education, the Bélanger Commission on taxation, the April Commission on agriculture, the Castonguay-Nepveu Commission on health and welfare, the Gendron Commission on the French language and the Prévost Commission on the administration of justice. The political scientist Lionel Ouellet has calculated that between 1960 and 1978 a total of 176 commissions and committees of inquiry were established by the Quebec government. In addition, thousands of research projects and inquiries have been carried out on a regular basis by civil servants on subjects ranging from the classification of a building as a historic site to the industrial inventory of a region. The preliminary study has become part of the government decision-making process.

Planning initiatives are a natural consequence of the technocratic perspective. At the beginning of the Quiet Revolution, officials dreamed of following the French example and working out an economic development plan for Quebec. This task was given to the Economic Advisory Council in 1961, but by 1965 it was forced to accept the evidence that such a plan was unrealistic and could not be implemented. In an economic environment where private enterprise is dominant and government responsibilities are divided between Quebec City and Ottawa, the Quebec government did not have the resources or the means to bring an economic development plan to fruition. This conclusion was confirmed a few years later by the failure of the attempt at regional planning in eastern Quebec carried out by the Bureau d'Aménagement de l'Est du Québec.

The government had to be satisfied with sectoral planning in fields where it exercised more direct control. Thus, planning offices were established in a number of departments and policy statements aimed at making government action more coherent became commonplace. This effort at coherence was hampered by the fragmentation of authority among many departments and decision-making centres, which often failed to coordinate their actions and policies. But despite these difficulties, the government succeeded in developing more rigorous and cohesive sectoral strategies, even if it did not manage to integrate all government intervention into a genuine overall plan. In addition, no matter how well conceived a policy was, many difficulties could still arise in its implementation.

One of the risks of establishing a modern, technocratic, centralized administration was a widening of the gap between the government and citizens. Governments tried to solve this problem by setting up mechanisms of information, consultation and participation and by decentralizing services.

The most notable progress was made in the area of information. The number of government publications and the rate at which they were issued exploded after 1960. Each department and agency had information officers who published bulletins and journals. Many government reports were made available by the Quebec Official Publisher through its bookstores. Towards the end of the period, the access to information legislation reduced government secrecy. The most striking development, however, was the proliferation of information aimed directly at citizens through the Department of Communications, which became a dispenser of government advertising and propaganda. Hesitantly in the 1960s and then massively from the 1970s on, the government used the print and electronic media to let citizens know about the programs and services at their disposal — and, of course, at least implicitly about the merits of the party in power.

However, government information has been a one-way street, and efforts to establish a flow of information from individuals to the government have been less successful. Governments have had two favoured methods of consultation. The first consists of establishing consultative councils or committees made up of representatives of interest groups. The Superior Council of Education is the most significant of these bodies, of which several dozen were set up during the 1960s with widely varying roles and mandates. Most analysts agree that they have not been very representative and have tended to become instruments serving the government. In general, the groups involved have preferred to make their views known directly to cabinet ministers and senior civil servants rather than go through consultative committees.

The other method has been direct consultation through public hearings held by commissions of inquiry, boards, parliamentary committees and some permanent bodies such as the Commission de Réforme de la Carte Électorale and the Bureau des Audiences sur la Protection de l'Environnement. Here too, it is primarily organized groups that make their voices heard. And in any case, their views are mediated through and interpreted by the body holding the hearing. Opposition groups are poorly represented in consultative bodies and have little hope of getting their ideas accepted. As a result, they have tended to impress their points of view directly on public opinion and the government through dramatic action: demonstrations, sit-ins and occupations, all of which became commonplace starting in the late 1960s.

Efforts at decentralization have taken the form of local and regional offices of some departments and have covered a variety of activities, from social assistance to the Quebec archives. But decentralization has been implemented only in part. It is essentially the delivery of services, an activity closer to citizens, that has been decentralized, while decision-making and policy development have remained centralized in Quebec City. In some cases, along with the decentralization of activities, participation mechanisms have been instituted: user committees have been established, parent committees have been recognized, and user representatives have been elected to the boards of directors of local agencies such as CLSCs, hospitals and cegeps. However, these positions have quickly become monopolized by professionals and ordinary consumers have had little opportunity to be represented.

Table 1
Revenues and Expenditures of the Quebec Government, 1960-84 ($ million)

Year	Gross Revenues	Gross Expenditures
1960-61	744.5	860.2
1961-62	947.3	1,059.4
1962-63	1,092.5	1,222.8
1963-64	1,204.0	1,386.3
1964-65	1,556.2	1,778.4
1965-66	1,779.4	2,049.4
1966-67	2,117.2	2,346.2
1967-68	2,534.3	2,725.2
1968-69	2,884.0	2,995.3
1969-70	3,209.3	3,442.4
1970-71	3,807.0	3,928.9
1971-72	4,226.9	4,575.8
1972-73	4,732.5	5,055.1
1973-74	5,440.4	5,698.1
1974-75	6,921.5	7,028.6
1975-76	7,917.7	8,791.1
1976-77	9,217.3	10,208.4
1977-78	11,168.3	12,052.4
1978-79	11,923.5	13,398.0
1979-80	13,306.7	15,123.2
1980-81	14,681.4	17,558.7
1981-82	17,471.6	20,359.8
1982-83	19,210.3	22,259.3
1983-84	21,411.0	24,523.5

Sources: *Annuaires du Québec* and *Public Accounts of the Province of Quebec.*

Throughout the period, technocratic centralization has given rise to tension that efforts at decentralization, regionalization and participation have not succeeded in resolving.

Public Finance

The growth of the state's administrative machine has been reflected in the rapid growth of public spending, which has increased by a factor of forty in less than a quarter of a century (table 1). The psychological barrier of $1 billion was quickly broken in the early 1960s, and inflation contributed to an even faster increase in spending in the 1970s. In the latter part of the 1970s, the machine seemed to have got out of control and the government tried to slow it down through budget restraint. While revenues also increased at a rapid rate, it was not fast enough to keep up with the spending increases. The government consistently ran a small deficit until 1975-76, when much larger deficits began to appear. The deficit quickly passed the $1-billion mark and headed for $3 billion before being stabilized there in the 1980s.

There was a substantial change in the sources of revenue as developments that had begun in the previous period continued. James Iain Gow has identified three major trends: "the relative decline of non tax revenues, the predominance of tax revenues, and the growth of revenue coming from the federal government." Income from royalties on natural resources, licences of all kinds and liquor sales, which for many years had represented a significant portion of the Quebec government's budget, still accounted for nearly 20 per cent of revenues in 1960-61 but had fallen to 8 per cent by 1983-84. Consumption taxes continued to make a substantial contribution to revenues, although the share they represented fell from 29 to 19 per cent. The lion's share has been attributable to income taxes and succession duties, which increased from 34 to almost 43 per cent of revenues. The most dramatic growth has been in the share accounted for by the personal income tax: from 10 to 32 per cent. This has occurred as the federal government has gradually yielded a portion of this tax field (13 per cent in 1960, 50 per cent in 1970) to the government of Quebec. In addition, direct transfers from the federal government, which represented 12 per cent of the Quebec government's revenues in 1960-61, accounted for almost 30 per cent in 1983-84. Equalization payments, which amounted to more than $3 billion at the end of the period, represented a little more than half of these transfers.

To finance its deficits and capital investments, the Quebec government borrows on a large scale from the public and financial institutions. Its debt, which stood at only $300 million in 1960, was more that $18 billion in 1984. In addition to its own debt, the government had guaranteed loans — notably those of Hydro-Quebec — amounting to more than $20 billion.

* * * * * *

The growth of government intervention in Quebec started well before the Quiet Revolution. However, in the quarter-century beginning in 1960 it took place at such a pace that the position of the state in society and in the daily lives of Quebecers changed completely. The most decisive changes occurred in the way government intervention was managed and in the administrative apparatus that underlay it. Reform of the state in Quebec was not carried out in a vacuum. Quebec followed the example of other governments, notably those of France and Sweden, to which it paid close attention, and that of Canada, which had the advantage of having started much earlier to adapt to the administrative needs of the welfare state. The Canadian government also modernized its own management methods during the period, following the recommendations of the Glassco Commission. It faced many of the same difficulties as the Quebec government: problems of planning, tensions between centralization and decentralization, and a steep growth in public spending and the deficit. Administrative reform was also undertaken at the local level, especially by municipal governments.

At the beginning of the Quiet Revolution, unanimous agreement was quickly reached on the need to turn Quebec into a welfare state. As the consequences of this decision became clear, however, people began to reexamine it, and there was a reaction to the reform of the state. The government's emergence as the leading dispenser of jobs led to concern in the private sector and aggravated relations with the trade unions. The development of a technocratic, bureaucratic government apparatus made more rational management possible but also led to a degree of inefficiency, which came under increasing criticism. Businesses and individuals deeply resented the regulations this apparatus imposed, while a renewed civil service benefited from its growth. The civil service provided attractive, well-paid careers for the Francophone middle class, but it was seen as a privileged group. Tension between the public and private sectors increased. In the 1980s, government intervention was seen less and less as a solution and more and more as a problem. For many social actors, the situation had become ripe for a fundamental reexamination of the role of the state.

CHAPTER 49

THE RENEWAL OF PARTY POLITICS

Political life in the period since 1960 has been intense and effervescent. While until the death of Duplessis the political contest retained many of its traditional aspects, some of them dating back to the nineteenth century, since 1960 there has been a thorough renewal of party politics. The parties and the electoral system have been transformed. Several new parties have emerged while the structures of existing ones have undergone major changes.

Transformation of the Party System

Before 1960, political parties had little formal structure and were controlled by the leader, the treasurer and a few organizers. They have become much more highly structured organizations, with permanent employees and democratic institutions that meet regularly, and are more broadly based at the local level.

That parties have tried to become more democratic is beyond question. The goal has been to create mass parties with thousands of individual members who choose delegates, participate in defining the party's overall orientation, contribute to its financing, and serve as an army of election workers during campaigns. Party platforms are adopted at policy conventions after consultation with the membership. Party leaders, formerly chosen by a small group of MLAs and organizers, are now elected at leadership conventions by delegates representing all of Quebec's ridings. In 1985, the Parti Québécois went even further, choosing its new leader by a vote of its entire membership.

At the base of the major parties' new structures is the riding association, which groups party members at the local level, elects representatives to higher levels of the party hierarchy, and chooses the party's official candidate at election time. Other major party institutions are the "general" or "national" council and the convention. Each party also has committees or commissions with special functions, whose concerns include such matters as the party platform, financing and youth. The wide dissemination of written party platforms has been another new development of the period.

While parties previously had only tacit recognition, since 1963 they have been officially recognized by the government, which contributes to the financing of major parties and, more clearly than before, establishes the rules of the political game. In an effort to make the financing of election campaigns more open, the PQ government banned contributions from companies and organizations and established a legal limit on contributions by individuals in 1977. Parties have become much more complex organizations, with full-time employees serving as technocrats of election campaigns and party politics.

A large number of new parties were established in the 1960s and 1970s, but most of them had only a limited constituency. Despite this flowering of new parties, Quebec has still had what is essentially a two-party system — the Liberals and the Union Nationale at the beginning of the period and the Liberals and the Parti Québécois later on. Between 1970 and 1980, a fundamental realignment took place that led to a brief period

Parti Québécois convention, 1981. (*Le Journal de Montréal*)

of multiparty politics. The 1981, 1985 and 1989 elections, however, showed that the two-party system had firmly reestablished itself, although it was somewhat shaken in 1989 by the upsurge of the Equality Party.

Elections

Elections are the high points of political life. There has been a marked change in the way elections are run: some inequities have been corrected, election practices have been cleaned up, and the style of campaigning has changed from previous periods.

The system never provides for perfectly adequate representation of the will of the voters and some inequities always creep in. However, efforts have been made to correct some of these inequities and make the political contest more democratic. New legislation has broadened the electorate by lowering the minimum voting age from twenty-one to eighteen (1964) and removing restrictions on specific groups: natives (1969), judges (1978) and prisoners (1979). The gradual reform of the electoral map has been even more significant. In the early 1960s, the electoral map was still seriously distorted: rural regions were overrepresented and there were widely divergent numbers of voters in different constituencies. Initially, the number of urban constituencies was increased. Then in 1970, a clause in the BNA Act that made it difficult to change the boundaries of a few protected ridings was repealed. During the 1970s, precise rules regarding the number of voters per constituency were spelled out and an independent permanent commission was established to submit proposals for revising the electoral map at regular intervals. The number of constituencies increased steadily, from ninety-five in the 1960 and 1962 elections to 108 in 1966 and 1970, 110 in 1973 and 1976, 122 in 1981 and 1985, and 125 in 1989.

However, the reform of the electoral map did not eliminate another distortion. As a result of the first-past-the-post system, the percentage of seats a party obtains does not correspond to its percentage of the popular vote. During the 1970s, there were lengthy discussions of ways of reforming this system and especially of introducing elements of proportional representation, but no government could make up its mind to implement any such proposal.

The way elections are run has also been cleaned up significantly. After the 1956 election, two priests, Gérard Dion and Louis O'Neill, criticized electoral corruption, and starting in 1960 governments gradually strengthened controls on election practices. Many forms of fraud that marred the electoral process were eliminated. Candidates were identified by party on the ballot, limits were placed on authorized election expenses, and the government even began to reimburse officially recognized parties for a portion of those expenses. The way the voters' list is drawn up was improved, and the list was made permanent in 1972.

Election campaigns have increasingly been run by specialists in advertising and communications, so that image has become an important factor in politics. The electronic media — radio and television — are now central to election strategy. Efforts have also been made to revitalize personal contact between candidates and voters through new practices such as informal gatherings in people's homes. More characteristic of the period, however, are large rallies in sports arenas, with considerable use of audiovisual techniques.

Politicians

In an era of major changes, one aspect of political life has remained the same: representatives have continued to come from an elite. As in most parliamentary democracies, the composition of the Quebec legislature is completely unrepresentative of the population at large. It contains hardly any farmers, workers or lower level clerical employees, and women are underrepresented. But while politicians are recruited from an elite, the characteristics of this elite have been changing, reflecting changes in society as a whole.

The political scientist Robert Boily has studied the members elected to the Quebec Legislative Assembly between 1956 and 1966. He found that while a majority came from the countryside and small towns, as a group they were highly educated, with 58 per cent being university-trained. The liberal professions supplied the largest number (53 per cent), with law and medicine especially well represented. Merchants accounted for 17 per cent of MLAs and industrialists 13 per cent. MLAs had deep roots in their local communities: 40 per cent had sat on a city or town council or a school board before being elected to the Legislative Assembly. Starting with the 1966 election, these characteristics began to change. The proportion of highly educated members increased, while a smaller number came from rural areas. Workers and farmers almost completely disappeared from the legislature and industrialists and merchants occupied a less prominent position, while an increasing number came from the teaching profession and related occupations.

These new features became even more pronounced as the period progressed, especially after the Parti Québécois came to power in 1976: 80 per cent of PQ members were university-trained and half worked in intellectual professions, with education accounting for 40 per cent and culture for 10 per cent. Only 18 per cent came from the liberal professions and fewer than 6 per cent were business people. The political scientist Jean-Pierre Beaud has shown that the PQ caucus was a reflection of the party's membership more than of people who entered politics in Quebec as a whole. A larger proportion of Liberals elected to the legislature were still business people, senior executives and members of the liberal professions. Réjean Pelletier's study of members elected in 1981 confirms these tendencies: PQ members came primarily from the cultural and social spheres while Liberal members were mostly from the economic and social spheres. Overall, the composition of the Quebec legislature reflects the wider variety of career choices within the Quebec elite and is characterized by a higher level of education and, overwhelmingly, by urban origins.

Although women are still seriously underrepresented, they have succeeded in gaining a foothold in this male world. It has not been an easy task. It was not until 1961 that the first woman, Claire Kirkland-Casgrain, was elected to the Legislative Assembly; Kirkland-Casgrain became the first female cabinet minister in 1964. And it was another decade before women began to be elected in significant numbers: five in 1976, eight in 1981, eighteen in 1985, twenty-three in 1989. The number of women in the cabinet has also increased, but there is still a long way to go: as of 1989, only six cabinet ministers were women.

The Liberal Party

In the 1950s the Quebec Liberal Party undertook a major change of direction, turning itself from an organization of *notables* into a mass party. This significant development was begun under Georges-Émile Lapalme and continued under Jean Lesage, who succeeded Lapalme as leader in 1958. It involved setting up new structures with specialized functions and broadening the membership, and became a model for similar changes in other parties. In another noteworthy change, the federal and provincial wings of the party, which had hitherto been a single organization, became clearly distinct. The Quebec Liberal Party asserted its autonomy by establishing its own institutions, forcing its federal counterpart to follow suit.

In the early 1960s, the Liberal Party was the embodiment of the reform forces it had brought together. However, tension soon developed among the party's various elements: reform and conservative wings, different nationalist tendencies. When René Lévesque left the party in 1967, tensions eased for a time. The Liberals defined themselves as a clearly federalist party and the reform wing lost some of its strength.

A number of changes occurred with the election of Robert Bourassa as leader in 1970. The party became more centrally focused on its leading figures. Its staunchly federalist orientation was tempered by its concern with defending Quebec's autonomy against the federal Liberals — although this didn't make the party any less vigorous in its battle against the Parti Québécois. The party's thinking tended to be managerial, although there was room within that framework for pursuing goals that its leaders considered social democratic. It was a demoralized and somewhat hidebound Liberal Party that chose Claude Ryan as its new leader after its defeat in the 1976 election. Ryan tried to breathe new life into the party's thinking and democratize its structures, and turned it into a significant force in byelections and the referendum campaign. However, he could not resolve the tensions between the ideals he pursued and the realities of day-to-day political life.

When Bourassa returned as leader in 1983, the party went back to some of its older ways. It sought to strengthen its managerial image and emphasized efficiency in economic development. This time, however, it had little room for ideas that did not come from the business community.

The Union Nationale

The Union Nationale in 1960 was a classic case of a traditional party of *notables*, worn out by too many years in power. The deaths of Maurice Duplessis (1959) and Paul Sauvé (1960) in quick succession followed by factional rivalry under Antonio Barrette's leadership (1960-61) gave an impression of drift. In addition, the party was discredited by the revelations of the Salvas Commission, which was appointed by the Lesage government and brought to light the wrongdoing of the previous regime. The party's first leadership campaign in 1961 was a divisive one, but the election of Daniel Johnson as leader marked the beginning of a period of rebuilding. The party tried to revitalize itself by modernizing its structures, but it ran into substantial difficulties, especially since Johnson's victory represented a triumph for the old guard. However, when the Union Nationale held its first policy convention in 1965, it became clear that significant changes had taken place, notably the accession of younger people to leading positions in the party.

After its 1966 election victory, the Union Nationale was divided by tension between federalists and supporters of more radical nationalist options. The ambiguous position of Premier Johnson, with his slogan *"Égalité ou indépendance"* (Equality or independence) did not help clarify the issue. Johnson's death in 1968 was followed by a struggle for succession between Jean-Guy Cardinal and Jean-Jacques Bertrand that sapped the party's strength. Bertrand won, but he proved both a weak leader within the party and incapable of dealing with the political issues of the day, giving the impression that the Union Nationale was something of a spent force. Events — notably the student protests of 1968 and the language crisis — seemed to have moved too fast for the party. It was a discredited government that faced the electorate in 1970, and it did not inspire much confidence in the voters.

Bertrand resigned as leader a few months after the party lost the election, but his successor, Gabriel Loubier, was no more successful in dealing with the Union Nationale's problems. He tried to give the party a new image, but neither changing its name to Unité-Québec between 1971 and 1973 nor surrounding himself with a new team was enough to reverse its steep decline. After failing to elect a single member in 1973, the party conducted a fruitless search for a new leader. Squeezed between the Liberals and the Parti Québécois, the Union Nationale no longer had any clear reason for existence and lost supporters to both its rivals. Although it rebounded in 1976 with Rodrigue Biron as leader, it was again wiped off the political map in 1981 and has since been moribund.

Jean-Jacques Bertrand, premier of Quebec (1968-70), surrounded by his senior ministers. (*Le Soleil*)

The Créditistes

Although Social Credit had been part of Quebec political life since the 1930s, it did not enter provincial politics until 1970. It was initially a political protest movement based on the theories of a British engineer, Maj. C.H. Douglas, and traditionalist ideology. Social Credit succeeded in gaining a foothold in some of Quebec's rural and semiurban regions: Abitibi, Saguenay-Lake St. John and the Eastern Townships. It contested several election campaigns with little success, and then in the 1950s it increasingly turned into a religious movement that became known as the *"bérets blancs."* In 1957, a dissident group led by Réal Caouette established a political party, the Ralliement des Créditistes, concentrating on federal politics. They burst onto the federal scene in the 1962 election, gaining 26 per cent of the vote in Quebec and winning twenty-six seats. Despite splits in 1963 and 1966, the Créditistes won seats in every federal election through 1979.

There was a strong temptation to enter provincial politics, but Caouette resisted it for a long time. Some dissident Créditistes ran in the 1966 Quebec election under the banner of the Ralliement National, but none were elected. In 1970 the Ralliement Créditiste du Québec was set up with Camil Samson as leader, and it won twelve seats in the National Assembly with 11 per cent of the vote. From 1972 on, the provincial

Créditistes were divided by a series of splits. After winning only two seats in the 1973 election, they quickly disappeared from the political scene.

The Rassemblement pour l'Indépendance Nationale

The Rassemblement pour l'Indépendance Nationale (RIN) is a good example of a party that grew out of an ideological movement. When it was founded in Montreal in 1960, its goal was to promote the cause of Quebec independence through popular education. After considerable hesitation, the RIN decided to turn itself into a party in 1963. Some of the features it retained from its original incarnation were quite new in the Quebec political context: it organized street demonstrations, it was financed by its membership, its members were very militant, and it held meetings in private homes. In its short life it moved rapidly towards the left, to the point where its right wing split off in 1964. In the 1966 election the RIN showed its vitality by winning 6 per cent of the popular vote. However, the establishment of the Mouvement Souveraineté-Association the following year brought about a crisis in the party. After the Parti Québécois was founded in 1968, the party dissolved itself and most of its 14,000 members joined the PQ.

The Parti Québécois

It did not take long for the Parti Québécois to bring Quebec's pro-independence forces together and get them working towards a common goal. Founded in 1968, the PQ was the product of a merger between the Mouvement Souveraineté-Association (sovereignty-association movement), established the previous year by René Lévesque, and the more marginal Ralliement National. Its ranks were soon swelled by the militants of the disbanded RIN, as well as by a large number of nationalists unhappy with the federal regime. The PQ was able to have such a diverse membership because the concept of sovereignty-association was an ambiguous one that allowed different and even opposing tendencies, ranging from uncompromising supporters of independence to advocates of decentralized federalism, to coexist and work together. This broad ideological base became one of the PQ's major sources of strength.

Another source of strength was the role and personality of the PQ's founder and leader, René Lévesque. For seventeen years, the leader and the party were inseparable, as Lévesque lent his good name and much of his popularity to the PQ. With his unrivalled communication skills, he succeeded in mobilizing the PQ membership towards the goal of taking power. Because Lévesque appeared to be the only leader who could give the party the cohesion it needed to make gains at election time, his leadership was firmly established. The strategy the PQ adopted after the 1973 election proved to be a prudent one. In an effort to avoid frightening the voters, most of whom did not want independence, the PQ emphasized the issue of good government and promised not to begin the process leading to independence without first holding a referendum. This strategy led to the election victory of 1976.

In some respects, the PQ appeared to be a new kind of party, with its high proportion of intellectuals and people working in the cultural sphere. It also had an aura of youth as a result of its appeal to the postwar baby boom generation. The way people worked within the PQ was also highly unusual. As the successor to ideological movements such as the RIN, it inherited some of their characteristics: enthusiasm, egalitarianism, meetings in private homes, public demonstrations.

However, once the PQ achieved power, a wide gap opened up between the parliamentary caucus and the party. Except during election campaigns, the party played second fiddle to the caucus, and the enthusiasm of many party activists dimmed as a result. The shock of the 1980 referendum defeat and Ottawa's successful manoeuvring of a repatriated constitution in 1982 accentuated the decline in party activism. Many Quebecers sympathetic to the PQ were hard hit by the government's decision to cut civil servants' pay in 1982 and by the recession of the early 1980s, and the party lost support as a result. Finally, the party's decision to shelve the idea of independence in 1984 brought about a split, as those who were most firmly committed to independence, including several high-profile ministers, quit the party. The PQ was left in disarray. Lévesque resigned as leader and was succeeded by Pierre Marc Johnson, but the leadership change was not enough to heal the party's wounds in time for the 1985 election. Buffeted by internal tensions, Johnson was forced to resign in 1987. The choice of Jacques Parizeau to succeed him as leader represented a return to the primacy of the idea of independence.

Other Parties

The proliferation of third parties became a significant feature of the Quebec political scene after 1960. Their number and variety increased as the years went on, reflecting Quebec's ideological pluralism and its greater politicization as a society.

Although activists in working-class organizations have regularly expressed the view that Quebec needed a party that would represent workers' interests, no left-wing party has ever succeeded in establishing deep roots. Although many attempts have been made to create a working-class party, the goal has never been achieved — witness the vicissitudes of the Quebec Communist Party, the weakness of the Quebec NDP both federally and provincially, and the marginal nature of the socialist parties that have existed at various times. In the 1970s, small groups of Marxist activists tried to establish a party aimed at the working class, but without success.

New parties, as ephemeral or weak as the ones on the left, also sprang up on the right. Usually organized around a leader, they lasted only a few months or through one election. Examples are Yvon Dupuis's Parti

Présidentiel in 1974 and Jérôme Choquette's Parti National Populaire in 1975-76.

This proliferation of parties is evidence that Quebec was open to a variety of forms of political expression, but their influence did not extend very far and none of them ever obtained a substantial share of the popular vote.

The 1989 election was characterized by a new phenomenon: the creation of new parties to channel Anglophone voters' discontent with the policies of the Liberal Party. These parties succeeded in gaining the support of a significant proportion of Anglophone voters and one of them, the Equality Party, won four seats in the National Assembly.

Terrorism and the October Crisis

Outside the framework of legal political action, a new phenomenon appeared: terrorism. Generally operating under the banner of the Front de Libération du Québec (FLQ), small groups chose political violence as a means of speeding up the process of achieving Quebec independence. The political scientist Marc Laurendeau has identified eleven terrorist networks that came on the scene in succession between 1963 and 1970. Police action and arrests of their members brought all of these networks to a quick end. The earliest groups attacked federal institutions such as

Terrorist bombing at the Montreal Stock Exchange, 1969. (*La Presse*)

the army or the post office, which they saw as symbols of colonialism. Starting in the mid-1960s, however, the FLQ developed an increased awareness of social conflicts and intervened in labour struggles.

Terrorism in Quebec reached its climax with the October Crisis of 1970. An FLQ cell abducted a British diplomat posted to Montreal, James Richard Cross. Its demands included the freeing of political prisoners and the dissemination of a manifesto outlining the FLQ's position. The authorities refused to negotiate, and another cell kidnapped Quebec Labour Minister Pierre Laporte, who was found dead a few days later. Quebec was plunged into a crisis of unprecedented seriousness. The Quebec and Canadian governments decided to stand firm against the FLQ. Troop reinforcements were called into Quebec, and then Ottawa proclaimed the War Measures Act, substantially restricting democratic rights. Thousands of searches were undertaken and hundreds of people were arrested. Two months after Cross was abducted, his kidnappers were located by the police and obtained safe conduct to Cuba in exchange for freeing the diplomat.

While many Quebecers had some sympathy for the FLQ at the beginning of the crisis, the atmosphere changed after Laporte's death. The FLQ's initiative proved to be a failure, and it brought about the end of terrorism in Quebec for all practical purposes. However, the way the police handled the crisis left a lasting impression on the hundreds of people who were unjustly arrested.

The impact of the terrorist activity that took place in Quebec between 1963 and 1970 is difficult to evaluate. The first FLQ bombs no doubt contributed towards making Francophones more aware of their situation and speeding up the pace of change. Throughout its eventful history, however, the FLQ never succeeded in gaining broad support among the population. The October Crisis appears to have had a variety of effects. It probably led some activists to favour the democratic route to independence through support for the Parti Québécois. It may also have contributed to the radicalization of other activists who were concerned with social change and to the development of the Marxist-Leninist groups on the far left that appeared during the 1970s.

Quebec and Federal Politics

In the federal arena, the most notable characteristic of the period was the dominance of the Liberal Party in Quebec. After their crushing defeat in 1958, the Liberals regained their old stronghold. In every election between 1962 and 1980 they were the leading party in Quebec, in terms of both number of seats and popular vote. Liberal support in Quebec was further enhanced by the accession of Pierre Elliott Trudeau to the party leadership in 1968.

The seats they won in Quebec made it possible for the Liberals to stay in power from 1963 to 1979 and 1980 to 1984. This situation gave Quebec representatives a stronger voice in running Canada's affairs than they had ever had before. On an organizational level, circumstances led the Quebec section of the Liberal Party of Canada to set up structures distinct from those of the Liberal Party of Quebec.

The Conservative Party was discredited by the poor performance of the Diefenbaker government and its leading Quebec figures. Although the two leaders who followed Diefenbaker, Robert Stanfield and Joe Clark, made genuine efforts to be open to Quebec and the French reality in Canada, the party never managed to rebuild a solid base in Quebec and consistently won fewer than ten seats with about a fifth of the popular vote from 1963 on. However, in 1983, a bilingual Quebecer of Anglophone origin, Brian Mulroney, was elected Conservative leader, and Trudeau retired from politics the following year. As a result of these developments the Tories were able to turn the situation around and win a majority of seats in Quebec — and the country as a whole — in the 1984 and 1988 elections.

Until the last years of the period, the real opposition to the federal Liberals in Quebec came from the Créditistes, who won more seats than the Conservatives in every election between 1962 and 1979. They clearly had a measure of popular support, winning between 16 and 27 per cent of the Quebec vote during the period, and their strength was magnified by the geographical concentration of Créditiste voters.

The NDP did not succeed in winning any seats in Quebec in any general election during the period. It turned in its best performance in the 1965 election, when it won 12 per cent of the popular vote. Its first and only Quebec seat was won in a byelection in 1989.

* * * * * *

The period has been characterized by a proliferation of parties and intense political activity. The most significant developments, however, have been the cleanup of election practices and the enhanced democracy that has been conspicuous at all levels of political life.

CHAPTER 50
GOVERNMENT IN A TIME OF CHANGE

Quebec went to the polls twenty times between 1960 and 1989: ten times for federal elections, nine times for provincial ones and once for the 1980 referendum. There was also a more rapid turnover of Quebec governments than during the previous period: there were five different governments, none of them winning more than two consecutive elections. A major realignment of political forces took place around 1970, the most significant aspect of which was the virtual disappearance of the Union Nationale and the rise of the Parti Québécois. In Ottawa, the period opened and closed with the Conservative Party in power, but the leading phenomenon of the years in between was the dominance of Pierre Elliott Trudeau's Liberals and their "French Power." On the whole, Quebec politics in the 1960s — both provincial and federal — was characterized by reform and the theme of modernization. In the 1970s, however, these issues were increasingly overshadowed by the national question, which culminated in the 1980 referendum on sovereignty-association.

1960-66: The Lesage Liberal Government

As the 1960s opened, the Union Nationale had been in power in Quebec City for sixteen uninterrupted years. This very conservative government, dominated by Maurice Duplessis, increasingly appeared to be a throwback to an earlier time. A number of groups seeking to modernize Quebec banded together to oppose the regime, and these opposition forces rallied to the Liberal Party, led by Jean Lesage. The Liberals presented a bold reform program and attracted prestigious candidates such as the journalist René Lévesque and the legal scholar Paul Gérin-Lajoie. These high-profile Liberals became known as the *"équipe du tonnerre"* and their slogan "It's time for a change" symbolized the theme of renewal on which the election of June 22, 1960 focused.

Table 1
Results of Quebec Elections, 1960-1989

Election	Party	% of pop. vote	No. of seats
1960	Liberals	51.3	51
	Union Nationale	46.6	43
	Other	2.1	1
1962	Liberals	56.5	63
	Union Nationale	42.2	31
	Other	1.3	1
1966	Union Nationale	40.9	56
	Liberals	47.2	50
	RIN	5.6	-
	RN	3.2	-
	Other	3.1	2
1970	Liberals	45.4	72
	PQ	23.1	7
	Union Nationale	19.6	17
	Créditistes	11.1	12
	Other	0.8	-
1973	Liberals	54.7	102
	PQ	30.2	6
	Créditistes	10.0	2
	Union Nationale	4.9	-
	Other	0.2	-
1976	PQ	41.4	71
	Liberals	33.8	26
	Union Nationale	18.2	11
	Créditistes	4.6	1
	Parti National Populaire	0.9	1
	Other	1.1	-
1981	PQ	49.2	80
	Liberals	46.1	42
	Union Nationale	4.0	-
	Other	0.7	-
1985	Liberals	56.0	99
	PQ	38.7	23
	Other	5.3	-
1989	Liberals	49.9	92
	PQ	40.2	29
	Equality Party	3.7	4
	Other	6.2	-

Reports of the Quebec Director General of Elections

The Liberal victory in that election, which ushered in what became known as the Quiet Revolution, was anything but a landslide (table 1). Although the Union Nationale was divided and had a weak leader, Antonio Barrette, it held onto a substantial portion of its support. But the Liberals, while retaining their support in urban constituencies, made gains in rural areas, where they won almost half the seats. The result was very close, but the gains made by the Liberals were enough to give them a narrow victory. In sixty-one of Quebec's ninety-five ridings, the successful candidate won with a margin of less than 10 per cent of the votes cast.

In 1962, the Lesage government decided to call a snap election, maintaining that it had to consult the voters directly on its proposal to nationalize Quebec's private electricity companies. It also hoped to take advantage of the disorganized state of the Union Nationale to consolidate its position. The Liberal campaign was based on the slogan *"Maîtres chez nous"* (Masters in our own house) and the strong personality of Natural Resources Minister René Lévesque. The Liberals sang the praises of economic nationalism and the reform movement they had begun in 1960, while the opposition appealed to caution and conservative "good sense." The results fulfilled the hopes of the Liberals, who substantially increased the number of seats they held and their share of the popular vote (table 1).

During its six years in power, the Lesage government was notable for the number of reforms it undertook and their often dramatic nature. Its policies were aimed at modernizing and democratizing the structures of Quebec society and putting Quebec on the map. Its favoured instrument to accomplish these goals was the state, whose administrative structures it reformed from top to bottom.

Jean Lesage flanked by René Lévesque and Paul Gérin-Lajoie, 1962. (*La Presse*)

Government intervention radically transformed a number of areas of Quebec society. The government set up the Parent Commission to rethink Quebec's whole education system, and it established a Department of Education in 1964. It agreed to cooperate with the federal government to put a hospital insurance program into effect, redefined all of Quebec's social security policies and inaugurated the Quebec Pension Plan. Other important measures included the adoption of a new labour code, the recognition of the legal equality of married women and the establishment of a Department of Cultural Affairs. In the economic sphere, the government got involved in planning and development and was much more interventionist than its predecessors: it established the Société Générale de Financement and the Caisse de Dépôt et Placement, strengthened Hydro-Quebec and worked towards setting up a Quebec steel mill. These measures were also viewed as a means of increasing Francophone control over Quebec's economic development.

In addition to these internal policies, the Lesage government took a much more aggressive stance in its relations with the federal government and increased Quebec's presence on the international scene, notably by establishing a number of delegations outside Canada and by signing cooperation agreements with France.

1966-70: The Union Nationale Governments of Daniel Johnson and Jean-Jacques Bertrand

The paradoxical result of the 1966 election was a dramatic manifestation of the irregularities of the electoral map and the effects of the first-past-the-post system. Receiving a lower percentage of the popular vote than the Liberals (and a lower percentage than it had in the 1960 and 1962 elections, which the Liberals had won), the Union Nationale nevertheless succeeded in forming a majority government under Daniel Johnson.

The election did demonstrate a significant loss of support for the Liberals, who in the campaign showed signs of being a tired, divided government. The reforms of the previous years had led to internal fractiousness, and their cost and less than complete success were a source of discontent in some sectors of the population. The Union Nationale skilfully exploited this dissatisfaction. In addition, with two pro-independence parties (the Rassemblement pour l'Indépendance Nationale and the Ralliement National) in the race, the clear lines of the two-party contest became somewhat blurred. The two new parties took support away from the Liberals and allowed the Union Nationale to gain seats.

Once in power, the Union Nationale was forced to take into account the state of public opinion revealed by the election result. The new government, initially under Johnson and later under Jean-Jacques Bertrand, pursued the major goals of the Quiet Revolution. In education, it established the cegeps and the University of Quebec. In the economic sphere, it followed through with the creation of the Quebec government's steel company, SIDBEC, and set up a forest products enterprise, REXFOR.

Daniel Johnson, premier of Quebec (1966-68).

It continued the reform of the state by establishing the Department of the Public Service, abolishing the Legislative Council, and changing the name of the remaining house of the legislature from the Legislative Assembly to the National Assembly. Among the government's new reform initiatives were crop insurance, Quebec's own family allowance program, a Department of Immigration and Radio-Québec.

The Union Nationale government was also sensitive to the rise of nationalism, especially during Johnson's premiership. It demanded a thorough reform of the constitution and the distribution of powers. It also increased Quebec's international presence, notably at the time of Expo 67 and the visit of French President Charles de Gaulle.

After Johnson's death, however, the Bertrand government was increasingly overwhelmed by the post-Expo economic slowdown and the rise of student and labour protest. Furthermore, in response to the Union Nationale's inability to deal adequately with the language problem (and especially the adoption in 1969 of Bill 63, allowing parents free choice in language of education), a massive opposition movement grew up that weakened the government considerably.

1970-76: The Bourassa Liberal Government

In the 1970 election, for the first time in Quebec history, four major parties entered the fray. Robert Bourassa's Liberals, campaigning on promises of creating new jobs and defending "profitable federalism," saw that their

Robert Bourassa, premmier of Quebec (1970-76 and 1985-   ), during the
1970 October Crisis. (*La Presse*)

most serious rival was not the ruling Union Nationale, which had failed
to redefine what it stood for, but the newly formed Parti Québécois. The
PQ, led by René Lévesque, tried to rally Quebec's nationalist forces
around its proposal of sovereignty-association and its appeal to national
pride and the achievements of the Quiet Revolution. Finally, Camil Samson's Ralliement Créditiste based its campaign strategy on the federal
Social Credit Party's regional strength and ran on a very conservative
platform.

The election results showed that Quebec's political forces were now
divided into a number of currents of significant size, enough to disturb
the smooth functioning of the traditional two-party system, at least for a
time (table 1). With the votes divided among four parties, the Liberals
were able to win a comfortable majority even though their percentage of

the popular vote was lower than it had been in the three previous elections. The Union Nationale's support dissolved, but it still managed to form the official opposition. The Créditistes, with their regionally concentrated vote, won a relatively large number of seats. But the most striking development was the success of the Parti Québécois, which received more votes than either the Union Nationale or the Créditistes and emerged as the leading rival to the Liberals even though it won only a handful of seats.

The 1973 election confirmed this trend. The Union Nationale, which under Gabriel Loubier's leadership had changed its name to Unité-Québec, was shut out of the National Assembly, while the Créditistes won only two seats. The PQ thus became the official opposition. The Liberals campaigned against the "separatist threat," and the resulting polarization allowed them to win an overwhelming victory. At the same time, however, the PQ continued to broaden its support and became a force in all areas of Quebec, even though it again won only a few seats.

In its two terms, the Bourassa government placed much of its emphasis on economic issues. Seeking to stimulate growth through large-scale public works, it built superhighways and government buildings, inaugurated the James Bay project, and participated in the construction of the facilities for the 1976 Olympics in Montreal. At the same time, it reorganized Quebec's publicly owned corporations and rationalized the management of forest resources. In the area of health and social security, it established Quebec's health insurance plan, modernized the hospital system and established the Centres Locaux de Services Communautaires (CLSCs). In the legal sector, its innovations included the establishment of small claims courts and legal aid, the adoption of a bill of rights, and consumer protection measures.

Refusing to abandon the nationalist field to the PQ, the Liberals also posed as the defenders of Quebec's constitutional powers and what they called its cultural sovereignty within Canada. Thus, the Bourassa government rejected the proposed Victoria Charter for the repatriation of the constitution, asserted Quebec's jurisdiction in communications and culture, made French the official language of Quebec by adopting Bill 22, and consolidated Quebec's presence on the international scene.

But despite these achievements, the Bourassa government ran into serious problems. The October Crisis in the fall of 1970 was a baptism of fire. The government subsequently became embroiled in repeated and intense struggles with the trade unions: the Common Front strike of 1972 ended with the union leaders in jail; the James Bay construction site was destroyed; and there were strikes at utilities and the Olympic site. The government also appeared increasingly cut off from the population, its relations with the media deteriorated, and there were constant rumours of corruption and mismanagement that the government could not convincingly deny. Even the Liberals' allies took to criticizing the government. The federal Liberals saw the Bourassa government's positions as leaning too far towards autonomy, while many Anglophones and immigrants were outraged by Bill 22. There was a growing impression of political and social chaos, and the government, even with 102 seats in the National Assembly, seemed powerless to stop it.

1976-85: The Parti Québécois Government of René Lévesque and the 1980 Referendum

The 1976 election, which Bourassa called well before the end of his mandate, was a clear expression of the dissatisfaction with the Liberal government. The Liberals again tried to raise the spectre of the "separatist threat," but this time they were unsuccessful. The PQ defused the Liberals' strategy through its own strategy of *"étapisme"*: instead of beginning to implement sovereignty-association as soon as it attained power, the party now promised that it would first hold a referendum on the issue.

René Lévesque, premier of Quebec (1976-85), and his successor, Pierre Marc Johnson (1985).

It campaigned on its ability to provide "good government" and bring social peace and progress back to Quebec.

On November 15, 1976, for the first time ever, a party advocating sovereignty was elected to form the government of Quebec. The election result sent shock waves throughout Quebec and beyond. The PQ's victory was attributable to the effectiveness of its campaign, the discredit into which the Bourassa government had fallen, and the opportunism of the Union Nationale, which under its new leader, Rodrigue Biron, staged an unexpected recovery by reaping the support of Anglophone and Francophone federalists who were dissatisfied with the Liberal government.

Although the PQ won a solid majority of seats and its victory was of major symbolic significance, it was by no means based on majority popular support. Counting on the dynamism of its programs and the means of persuasion available to it as a government, the party hoped to build its support over the next four years so that it could win the referendum it kept putting off but eventually had to call. At the same time, it laid the groundwork for the referendum by establishing a legislative framework for popular consultations, publishing white papers divulging the details of its proposal, and then bringing out a question that it formulated as cleverly as it could:

> The Government of Quebec has made public its proposal to negotiate a new agreement with the rest of Canada, based on the equality of nations.

This agreement would enable Quebec to acquire the exclusive power to make its laws, administer its taxes and establish relations abroad — in other words, sovereignty — and at the same time, to maintain with Canada an economic association including a common currency.

Any change in political status resulting from these negotiations will be submitted to the people through a referendum.

On these terms, do you agree to give the Government of Quebec the mandate to negotiate the proposed agreement between Quebec and Canada?

The referendum was called for May 20, 1980, and the two sides plunged into an intense battle that polarized public opinion as never before. The Yes side, led by René Lévesque, ran a rather defensive campaign. The No campaign, whose standardbearer was the new Liberal leader, Claude Ryan, received strong political and financial support from Prime Minister Trudeau and the federal Liberal government. The No side appealed to Canadian solidarity, pointed out the risks of sovereignty and promised a renewed federalism. More than 85 per cent of Quebecers voted in the referendum, with 40.4 per cent voting Yes and 59.6 per cent voting No. On an overall basis, this may have been a decisive victory for the No side, but breaking down the vote by ethnic group shows the result in a different light. If, as would be expected, Anglophones and other ethnic minorities voted overwhelmingly against sovereignty-association, Francophones were divided into two camps of virtually equal size. According to some analysts, the No side won only a very narrow majority of the Francophone vote.

Even though voters rejected the PQ's sovereignty-association proposal, there was still a high level of satisfaction with the government. At the same time, Premier Lévesque continued to enjoy considerable prestige — much more than Opposition Leader Ryan. The 1981 election reflected these developments. The Liberals, confident after their referendum victory, again campaigned on an antiseparatist platform. But the PQ countered by promising not to resubmit its sovereignty-association proposal during its second term and portraying the provincial Liberals as subordinate to their federal counterparts. On the basis of this strategy, the PQ was reelected with a popular vote of close to 50 per cent (table 1). Its support extended to all regions of Quebec and almost all sectors of the population. The Liberals also increased their share of the vote, while third parties, including the Union Nationale, were eliminated from the National Assembly. Thus, this election marked the completion of the realignment of forces that had begun around 1970.

In its nine years in power, and especially during its first term, the Lévesque government represented a continuation of the Quiet Revolution. It carried through with reforms that had been underway for a number of years and placed great emphasis on the role of the state. The characteristics that distinguished the PQ government from its predecessors were its management style, which made heavier use of consultation and the mass media, and the more firmly nationalist and "social democratic" orientation of its policies.

In the economic sphere, the government nationalized a substantial part of the asbestos industry and kept Quebecair under Quebec control. Even more important, it sought to ensure that its own corporations were subject to government priorities. It also supported the rise of Francophone business through its advocacy of entrepreneurship and through a variety of programs aimed at aiding the development of small business and the cooperative movement, notably export promotion and assistance for capital formation and financing. In agriculture, it sought to increase Quebec's self-sufficiency in food production and adopted an agricultural land preservation policy.

In the social sphere, the government's responsibilities became broader and more diverse under the PQ. New initiatives included partial nationalization of automobile insurance, consumer protection legislation, and greater concern for youth and senior citizens. The government also emphasized promoting equality for women, notably by instituting maternity leave, reforming family law and extending Quebec's system of daycare centres. Starting off by declaring that it was "prejudiced in favour" of workers, the government raised the minimum wage substantially, established minimum labour standards, adopted antiscab legislation and improved job health and safety regulations.

In the cultural sphere, the PQ considered the language problem an urgent one and energetically pursued a solution. In 1977, it brought in Bill 101, which gave priority to French in all sectors, including immigrant absorption, the workplace and public signs. At the same time, it established new programs relating to minority ethnic communities, emphasized the economic and industrial dimensions of culture, and took an interest in the development of science and technology. The Lévesque government also introduced several innovations into Quebec's political life, including election financing legislation, reorganization of the parliamentary process and revitalization of municipal institutions. Quebec's cultural and economic presence on the international scene was also a major concern of the government.

Despite its convincing victory in the 1981 election, the Lévesque government quickly ran into trouble on all fronts and its popularity dropped. In 1981-82 it had to face the world recession, which in Quebec took the form of very high unemployment and a serious crisis in public finance. This situation forced the PQ to make drastic cuts in some areas and led to a brutal confrontation between the government and unionized workers in the public and parapublic sectors. Also as a result of the recession, many Quebecers become more keenly aware of the heavy weight and high cost of the bureaucratic machinery with which the PQ was closely identified. When the economy recovered, the government tried to recapture its earlier dynamism and regain its lost support, but it could not. The PQ was also suffering from the effects of having been beaten in the referendum and outmanoeuvred by the federal government in the negotiations leading to the adoption of a new constitution in 1982. The party took positions that were increasingly out of touch with most Quebecers, and severe internal dissension followed. The crumbling of the government led to a major crisis within the PQ, the departure of several prestigious figures, and finally the resignation of Lévesque himself.

Heading into the 1985 election, the new premier, Pierre Marc Johnson, inherited a disoriented and seriously weakened party. Meanwhile, the Liberals had carried out a successful reorganization under the renewed leadership of Robert Bourassa. They counted on voters' weariness with the PQ and a widespread desire for a less interventionist government. Although the PQ struck a similar note, proposing a reduced role for the government and emphasizing economic issues, voters saw the Liberals as being best able to carry out a program of this sort (table 1). With both parties campaigning against big government, the 1985 election appeared to represent a break with the spirit of the Quiet Revolution and perhaps the beginning of a new phase in Quebec's political life.

Table 2
Federal Election Results in Quebec and Canada as a Whole, 1962-1988

Election	Party	Quebec % of popular vote	Quebec No. of seats	Other provinces % of popular vote	Other provinces No. of seats	Canada % of popular vote	Canada No. of seats
1962	Cons.	29.6	14	40.1	102	37.3	116
	Liberals	39.2	35	36.5	65	37.4	100
	Soc. Cred.	25.9	26	6.3	4	11.6	30
	NDP	4.4	-	16.9	19	13.5	19
1963	Liberals	45.6	47	40.3	82	41.7	129
	Cons.	19.5	8	37.7	87	32.8	95
	Soc. Cred.	27.3	20	6.3	4	11.9	24
	NDP	7.1	-	15.4	17	13.1	17
1965	Liberals	45.6	56	38.2	76	40.2	132
	Cons.	21.2	9	36.4	88	32.4	97
	NDP	12.0	-	20.0	21	17.9	21
	Soc. Cred.	17.5	10	5.0	3	8.3	13
1968	Liberals	53.6	56	42.5	99	45.5	155
	Cons.	21.4	4	35.1	68	31.4	72
	NDP	7.5	-	20.4	22	16.7	22
	Soc. Cred.	16.4	14	0.0	-	4.4	14
1972	Liberals	49.1	56	34.5	53	38.5	109
	Cons.	17.4	2	41.5	105	35.0	107
	NDP	6.4	-	21.9	31	17.7	31
	Soc. Cred.	24.4	15	1.4	-	7.6	15
1974	Liberals	54.1	60	39.3	81	43.2	141
	Cons.	21.2	3	40.4	92	35.4	95
	NDP	6.6	-	18.5	16	15.4	16
	Soc. Cred.	17.1	11	0.9	-	5.1	11
1979	Cons.	13.5	2	44.6	134	35.6	136
	Liberals	61.7	67	31.7	47	39.8	114
	NDP	5.1	-	22.8	26	17.8	26
	Soc. Cred.	16.0	6	0.2	-	4.5	6
1980	Liberals	68.2	74	35.5	73	44.1	147
	Cons.	12.6	1	39.8	102	32.3	103
	NDP	9.1	-	23.7	32	19.7	32
	Soc. Cred.	5.9	-	0.1	-	1.7	-
1984	Cons.	50.2	58	49.7	153	50.0	211
	Liberals	35.4	17	25.1	23	28.0	40
	NDP	8.8	-	22.5	30	18.8	30
1988	Cons.	51.8	63	39.3	106	42.7	169
	Liberals	29.7	12	32.4	71	31.7	83
	NDP	13.7	-	22.6	43	20.2	43

Cons. = Conservatives; NDP = New Democratic Party; Soc. Cred. = Social Credit

Note: Votes and seats obtained by other parties and independent candidates are not included in this table.

Source: *Historical Statistics of Canada* and Director, Elections Canada, *Report of the Chief Electoral Officer.*

Federal Politics

Throughout the period, Quebec's political development and assertion as a society had direct repercussions on the federal scene, and Quebec came to play a leading role in federal politics as a result. In this perspective, the period can be divided into two major phases.

During the first phase, between 1960 and 1968, Ottawa was seen as having little sensitivity to Quebec's development and aspirations. A noteworthy indication of this perception was the substantial support Quebec voters gave Réal Caouette's Créditistes in the 1962, 1963 and 1965 elections (table 2). By reducing the Liberals' traditional majority in Quebec, the Créditiste vote contributed to the election of three straight minority governments.

At the beginning of the period, the Conservative government of John Diefenbaker, in power since 1957, had to struggle with a recession that had a severe impact in Quebec. In addition, the Conservatives had a hard time appreciating the significance of the Quiet Revolution or the issues involved in it. They gave the appearance of being an Anglophone government in which Francophone representatives had little influence. This situation changed with the election of the Liberals under Lester B. Pearson in 1963, who were more responsive to Quebec's concerns and sought to enhance the position of its representatives in Ottawa. Towards this end, the government established the Royal Commission on Bilingualism

Lester B. Pearson, prime minister of Canada (1962-68). (Duncan Cameron, National Archives of Canada, PA-57932)

Pierre Elliott Trudeau, prime minister of Canada (1968-79 and 1980-84).

Joe Clark, prime minister of Canada
(1979-80). (National Archives of
Canada, PA-116450)

Brian Mulroney, prime minister of
Canada (1984-)

and Biculturalism (the Laurendeau-Dunton Commission) in 1963. In addition, in keeping with its policy of "cooperative federalism," it accepted a number of Quebec's demands in the areas of taxation and social affairs. In an effort to strengthen the Francophone wing of his party, Pearson also recruited three prestigious Quebecers (soon nicknamed the "three wise men") in 1965: the intellectuals Gérard Pelletier and Pierre Elliott Trudeau, who had been cofounders of the journal *Cité Libre*, and the labour leader Jean Marchand. On the basis of this policy of increased openness to Quebec, the Liberals were able to gain a substantial number of seats and win the 1963 and 1965 elections.

After Pearson resigned, Pierre Elliott Trudeau became Liberal leader and prime minister. The 1968 election was marked by an outbreak of "Trudeaumania" in all regions of Canada and resulted in a solid Liberal victory. Trudeau's accession represented the beginning of the second phase, which lasted until 1984. The Liberals were in power throughout this phase except for a nine-month interruption in 1979-80. Their support in Quebec steadily increased and was largely responsible for their ability to remain in office (table 2).

Trudeau and his associates considered Quebec nationalism excessive and provincialist and had entered federal politics to act as a counterweight to it. Hence, they believed that Francophone Quebecers should define themselves first and foremost as Canadians and should be able to regard the federal government as serving their interests as well as those of English Canadians. While upholding a multicultural version of

Canadian nationalism and progressive social policies, the Trudeau Liberals also brought in the Official Languages Act in 1969 and tried to make federal institutions bilingual and increase Francophone influence in the federal administration. The expression "French Power" became a catchword for these developments. At the same time, they fought fiercely against any attack on federalism or erosion of the federal government's power, notably by imposing the War Measures Act in October 1970 and participating vigorously in the referendum campaign in 1980.

Seeing his party's popularity drop all over Canada and feeling that he had achieved his major political goals after the constitution was repatriated in 1982, Trudeau retired from politics in 1984. A few months later, the Conservatives came to power, winning majority support in Quebec for the first time since 1958 (table 2). The new government was headed by Brian Mulroney, who advocated an end to confrontation in federal-provincial relations and a reduction in the role of government in favour of a new emphasis on private enterprise. Social and constitutional issues, which had been the dominant ones under the Liberals, were placed on the back burner as economic concerns and the question of free trade with the United States came to the fore.

CHAPTER 51
THE CONFRONTATION BETWEEN QUEBEC AND CANADA

In intergovernmental relations, both continuity and discontinuity with previous decades can be seen in the period under study. In line with Quebec's traditional position, all Quebec governments continued to demand respect for provincial autonomy as provided for in the BNA Act. But unlike Duplessis's defence of autonomy, their stance no longer took the form only of reacting against federal policies in the name of a legalist interpretation of the constitution. Instead, the Quebec government now took a much more pragmatic and positive attitude. This led, on one front, to demands for a revised constitution that would grant more powers to Quebec. On another, it meant that the government took an increasing number of initiatives that challenged the traditional functioning of the federal system. From 1976 on, the PQ government took this strategy a step further, questioning the existence of the federal structure itself. These changes were in large part the result of the new conception of the role of the state that took hold in Quebec, as well as the rise of the new nationalism and the independence movement.

Of course, the new attitude has had substantial effects on Quebec's relations with the federal government. But it has also taken the form of a new desire to establish relations with the other Canadian provinces and with foreign governments. Thus, what might be called Quebec's external affairs took on new scope and significance during the period.

A New Dynamic in Federal-Provincial Relations

As of the late 1950s, the results of the new national policy the federal government had been implementing since the Second World War had not fully met Ottawa's expectations. Instead of reducing inequalities among the different regions of Canada, large-scale economic intervention inspired by Keynesian theory had often had the effect of exacerbating them. Nor had these policies succeeding in preventing unemployment and inflation from rising, as the government realized during the recession that began in 1957. At the same time, the provinces had to deal with increased responsibilities in the areas of education and social affairs, which were under their jurisdiction, but their share of the tax pie did not give them enough resources to do an adequate job. Even Ottawa recognized that no coherent economic policy could be put into effect without the active cooperation of the provinces.

As a result, the climate of federal-provincial relations changed noticeably. Dissatisfied with Ottawa's management and convinced that they knew more about the needs of their residents, the provincial governments believed that they had a right to more power and autonomy. They became vocal in defence of their less centralist vision of federalism. These tensions came to a head during the world energy crisis, in which the problem of managing natural resources came to the fore and substantial economic interests were at stake. The movement became especially strong in some provinces, notably Alberta and Newfoundland, and also took the form of a virtual interprovincial common front standing against Ottawa. While the new national policy of the 1940s and 1950s ignored regionalism and demands for autonomy, their resurgence has become a major factor in contemporary federalism.

The Quebec government has been an active participant in this challenge to a centralized federal system. Going beyond the demands it holds in common with the other provinces, it has defined itself as the government of a distinct society or even a distinct nation within Canada. As a result, it has demanded broad powers and corresponding resources, especially in the areas of culture, communications, social services, regional development and immigration. In some cases — hospital insurance, health insurance, aid to higher education — it has participated in shared-cost programs conceived by Ottawa, making sure that it has as much control as possible. In other cases it has refused to participate in programs of this sort and has preferred to establish its own. In 1964 it succeeded in getting Ottawa to institutionalize the principle of opting out, according to which a province has the right to decide not to participate in a federal program. Such a province can receive fiscal compensation making it possible to implement its own policies instead. Quebec has been the only province to make use of this right. Since 1964 it has withdrawn from twenty-eight programs, including bursaries, loans and allowances for students and aid to municipalities. Quebec also decided to establish its own pension plan instead of participating in the Canada Pension Plan, which operates in the other provinces. This gave Quebec the autonomy to manage the large amounts of money that accumulate in its pension fund and are entrusted to the Caisse de Dépôt et Placement. In addition, Quebec has obtained special powers in areas such as immigration and broadcasting. Although the constitution has never been amended to that effect, all these extensions of Quebec's powers have effectively given it a kind of special status within Canada.

In response to these autonomist tendencies in Quebec and other provinces, the federal government's attitude has changed over time. Initially, it agreed to let the provinces have a larger share of the tax pie and even made major concessions to Quebec. But this did not mean that the spirit of the new national policy had disappeared: Ottawa sought to maintain an active presence among citizens by inaugurating a number of new programs of "national" scope. It also tried to assert itself as the government of all Canadians through such measures as the adoption of the maple leaf flag. Nevertheless, there was unease in some quarters about the risk of "balkanizing" the country, and after a while Ottawa responded to these concerns by taking more hard-line positions and fiercely defending its powers, resources and leadership against encroachment by the provinces. The "cooperative federalism" of the early 1960s gave way to a period of unrestrained competition, repeated confrontation and endless quarrelling between the two levels of government. Although this policy pitted Ottawa against all the provinces to some degree, it created a state of permanent conflict with the government of Quebec in particular. The tension reached a paroxysm as the 1980 referendum approached.

Despite these often stormy political confrontations and constitutional debates between the two levels of government, they were forced by the very nature of the federal system to cooperate with each other in running the country, especially since the state was more active than ever before in all sectors of society. The proliferation and intensification of intergovernmental exchanges of all sorts has been one of the major characteristics of the period. Thus, Quebec took the initiative in reviving interprovincial conferences, where the provincial premiers meet to coordinate their policies. There are also regional meetings where specific provinces, such as the western provinces or the Atlantic provinces, get together. Other provinces, following Quebec's lead, have established departments or agencies dealing with intergovernmental affairs. There have also been federal-provincial exchanges of unprecedented scope. They are reflected not only in numerous official federal-provincial conferences but also in hundreds of meetings between ministers or officials from the two levels of government in the course of managing all the programs where federal and provincial responsibilities meet and often overlap. Canadian federalism has thus taken on the appearance of a huge mechanism of permanent cooperation and confrontation, in which Quebec's role is especially important.

This new dynamic in federal-provincial relations has made it possible for the provinces to increase their financial resources substantially. In particular, they now receive a larger share of the taxes paid by Canadians. This is especially true of Quebec, whose government has decided to withdraw from a number of federal programs in exchange for fiscal compensation. But this increase in Quebec's share of the pie should not lead to illusions about its financial autonomy, for Quebec is still heavily dependent on Ottawa. In 1983-84, almost 30 per cent of Quebec's revenues were transfers from the federal government, in the form of equalization payments and shared-cost programs, carried out under rules that in the final analysis were determined by Ottawa. The federal government also retains substantial fiscal powers and controls such major instruments of economic intervention as the Bank of Canada, monetary policy and control of international trade. Finally, Ottawa still has the right to resort to any mode or system of taxation and has what is referred to as an "unlimited" spending power: in other words, it can spend money for whatever purpose it wants. In short, Ottawa still has a preponderant role in managing the Canadian economy.

The Constitutional Debate

The great debate on the constitution that had begun during the Depression and the Second World War continued and indeed intensified after 1960. The early 1980s represented a turning point, with the Quebec referendum in 1980 and the new constitution promulgated in Ottawa in 1982. In this debate, the federal and Quebec governments were the major adversaries, with each side trying to win the support of the other provinces. In the end, the other provinces rallied to Ottawa's side and Quebec was left to do battle on its own.

Quebec's position, as put forward by governments of all political parties, was that Quebec should have special status within the Canadian federation. The constitution already stipulated that Quebec had a bilingual government and a distinct civil code and that three of the nine Supreme Court justices should come from Quebec. Quebec's traditional defence of its autonomy was based on this special status. After 1960, however, the idea of special status was taken much further. Governments not only continued to defend Quebec's autonomy but also demanded a new constitution that would give Quebec increased powers and resources. This would make it possible for Quebec to take its proper place as a distinct society with a state that could fulfil its role as the national government of French Canadians. If these changes were not made, it was argued, decisions made by Canada's Anglophone majority would affect the essential characteristics of the French-language minority concentrated in Quebec. In this perspective, the new constitution would turn Canada into a decentralized country based on the principle of equality of the two major ethnic groups. Quebecers attached a variety of formulations and labels to this idea: "two nations," "associate states," "special status," "cultural sovereignty," "sovereignty-association." Each of these formulations may have had its own particular content, but they were all primarily inspired by the idea of asserting Quebec's specific character.

The federal government had a completely different vision of Canada. In its view there was only one Canadian nation, and the ethnic and cultural differences within that nation should not be translated into constitutional terms beyond the provisions made in the BNA Act. The "national" government was the one in Ottawa, and for it to play its internal and external role in full measure it had to maintain a preponderant position relative to the provinces, including Quebec. During the 1960s, circumstances may have forced Ottawa to make some accommodations, so that Quebec was allowed to enjoy a measure of autonomy reflecting its ethnic and cultural difference. But Ottawa refused to recognize any formal special constitutional status for Quebec, and the other provinces and English Canadian public opinion supported it in this posi-

The arrival of the "three wise men" (Pierre Elliott Trudeau, Jean Marchand and Gérard Pelletier) in Ottawa marked the beginnings of "French Power."

tion. Starting in the late 1960s, notably with the arrival of "French Power," this position was combined with a desire to respond to Quebec's demands by strengthening the position of Francophones in federal institutions and extending bilingualism to all of Canada, so that Ottawa would be seen as the government of French as well as English Canadians. Ottawa's preeminence would thus be legitimized, and Quebec would remain, in constitutional terms, a province like the others.

The constitutional debate had wide ramifications, but it crystallized around a number of specific issues. As already noted, Quebec's primary objective was to obtain major revisions to the constitution. Ottawa saw no need for such revisions, but it wanted to repatriate the constitution to Canada and bring in a formula that would make it possible to amend the constitution without going to the British Parliament. Quebec was not fundamentally opposed to repatriation or to an amending formula so long as it had a veto. But it refused to agree to repatriation if it didn't obtain satisfaction on the distribution of powers. In the 1970s, Ottawa also sought to add to the constitution a charter of rights that would apply to all citizens. The charter would take precedence over the usual legislative powers of governments and its application would ultimately be the responsibility of the Supreme Court. Quebec — which already had its own charter of rights — objected to this proposal as well, regarding it as a threat to some of its traditional powers, especially since all the Supreme Court justices were appointed by Ottawa.

While Quebec and Ottawa were embroiled in the constitutional debate continuously throughout the period, there were three major flareups: 1964, 1971 and 1980-82. At a federal-provincial conference in 1964, Ottawa proposed that the constitution be repatriated and that what was known as the Fulton-Favreau amending formula be adopted. Under this formula, the agreement of the provinces — unanimous in some cases, majority in others — would be required for any constitutional amendment that concerned them, but Quebec would not have a formal veto. The Lesage government, which had just got Ottawa to agree to opting out, initially joined the other provinces in accepting the federal proposal. But nationalist groups and the official opposition in Quebec City vigorously attacked the agreement, which gave Quebec neither a new distribution of powers nor adequate protection of its rights. The government finally had to retreat in the face of this reaction and block the adoption of Ottawa's formula.

A similar scenario was played out at the time of the Victoria Conference in 1971. The federal government again proposed repatriation. This time it agreed to a veto for Quebec, but Quebec was still demanding that the distribution of powers be revised in its favour and Ottawa refused to budge on that question. Once again, Quebec was tempted to accept Ottawa's proposal, but the government had to yield to pressure from the PQ opposition and a large segment of public opinion. While opponents of the Victoria Charter acknowledged the significance of the veto, they

A meeting of the Yes forces, 1980. (*Le Journal de Montréal*)

saw it as a purely negative weapon that could leave Quebec a prisoner of the constitutional status quo. For the second time, Quebec was the sole opponent of a federal proposal and brought about its failure.

After the Victoria Conference there were no constitutional discussions for a time. Then with the provinces making increasing demands to which Ottawa did not want to give in, the federal government declared that it was prepared to repatriate the constitution — unilaterally if necessary. Intense negotiations were resumed, in which the Lévesque government, setting aside its sovereignty-association proposal, joined in a common front with the other provinces, which demanded a decentralized federal system. Faced with this situation and the rise of the sovereignty movement in Quebec, the Trudeau government established the Pépin-Robarts Commission on Canadian unity. However, it ignored the commission's conclusions, which it regarded as too favourable to the provinces' demands and the concept of Canadian duality. Meanwhile, a variety of solutions and formulas were put forward in Quebec, notably by the Liberal Party in an effort to offer an alternative to the government's sovereignty proposal. Just before the referendum, Prime Minister Trudeau solemnly promised that if the No side won there would be a new constitution, but he said nothing about what it would be. In November 1981 he called a federal-provincial conference for this purpose, and it ended with a dramatic reversal: all the English-speaking provinces,

A supporter of the No side. (*Le Journal de Montréal*)

even those that had joined with Quebec in rejecting the federal position, agreed to Ottawa's proposal, leaving Quebec completely isolated. This time, however, Quebec's refusal didn't prevent Ottawa from acting. After obtaining the agreement of the Supreme Court of Canada, the federal government went to London to get its proposal assented to there. The new Constitution Act was formally promulgated in April 1982; no representatives of the government of Quebec were present at the ceremony.

In essence, the provisions of the BNA Act (now officially renamed the Constitution Act, 1867) remain intact under the new constitution. However, the constitution can now be amended by the federal Parliament with the consent of at least seven provinces representing 50 per cent of Canada's population. If an amendment transfers provincial legislative powers relating to education or culture to the federal government, a province can opt out of the transfer and receive reasonable financial compensation. The 1982 constitution also makes a number of other additions to the BNA Act: official recognition of native rights, entrenchment of the principle of equalization and, most notably, a charter of rights based on the principles of a free and democratic society, similar to those recognized by other major western countries. The Canadian charter departed from precedent, however, in dealing explicitly with language and educational rights. It makes English and French the official languages of Canada, with equal status and privileges in all federal institutions. It also stipulates that citizens who received their primary education in Canada in English or French have the right to have their children educated in the same language, even if it is a minority language in the province where they live.

The Lévesque government objected to the new constitution for a number of reasons. First, it didn't accept the abandonment of what it regarded as the principle of the unanimous consent of the provinces for any fundamental change to the constitution. Second, the government considered it risky to entrust the Supreme Court, an exclusively federal and majority Anglophone institution, with the task of interpreting the Charter of Rights, a number of whose provisions could eventually affect its own powers. Third, in the educational sphere, it objected to the imposition of rules that contradicted its own policies as defined in Bill 101. And finally, it regarded limiting the principle of financial compensation to the educational and cultural sectors as unacceptable.

Despite the Lévesque government's protests and its refusal to ratify the 1982 constitution, the constitution went into effect in Quebec as it did in the rest of the country, except as provided for within the act itself. Subsequently, the Mulroney and Bourassa governments resumed negotiations in an effort to create conditions under which Quebec could officially recognize the new constitution. This was the aim of the Meech Lake Accord of 1987, which became the subject of considerable controversy when it was submitted for ratification by the provinces.

Quebec and the World

Until the 1960s, the Quebec government had little interest in international relations and engaged in them only occasionally and in limited fashion. However, from the beginning of the Quiet Revolution and throughout the next two decades, it mounted a steadily increasing effort in this area. As its international economic, cultural and political ties grew, the Quebec government developed the position that it was its responsibility to represent Quebecers internationally in areas within its jurisdiction. In this perspective, Quebec gradually established a network of foreign delegations and offices, first in western Europe, then in major cities in the United States, and finally in other parts of the world. In 1985, there were twenty-five of these missions in fourteen countries on four continents. Their role is to represent Quebec's interest by encouraging commercial and cultural exchanges, participating at the source in the selection of immigrants who come to Quebec and, in some cases, overseeing a variety of projects in which Quebec cooperates with other jurisdictions.

The most significant of the missions is the Quebec Delegation-General in Paris, which was opened in 1961 and is recognized diplomatically by the French government. In the early years of the Quiet Revolution, the Lesage government sought to develop Quebec's position as a French-language culture and society, and all of its successor governments followed it in this respect. As a result, the government saw relations with France as a high priority and went about establishing close links with Paris, especially in the educational and cultural spheres. This policy got a very favourable reception in Paris and resulted in the signing of a variety of cooperation agreements, the establishment of the Office Franco-Québécois pour la Jeunesse, many exchanges of civil servants, teachers and experts, commercial and industrial agreements, state visits and, in general, steadily intensifying relations of all kinds between the people of France and those of Quebec.

These agreements between Quebec and France led to a major constitutional problem within Canada. Quebec saw these initiatives as simply the projection of its internal powers onto the international stage. In Ottawa's view, however, Canada had to speak with only one voice in international affairs, and only the federal government was qualified to reach agreements with other countries. Thus, the first international agreement reached by Quebec, the France-Quebec agreement of 1965, was signed in the context of a general agreement between Paris and Ottawa. Subsequently, the federal government kept a very vigilant eye on Quebec's international initiatives, even trying on some occasions to prevent them or limit their extent. A series of squabbles over flags and protocol conflicts ensued.

The issue took a new turn when President de Gaulle, visiting Expo 67, made his celebrated "Vive le Québec libre" speech from the balcony of Montreal City Hall. De Gaulle followed this gesture with a policy of systematic support for Quebec's international initiatives, which resulted in open conflict between Paris and Ottawa for several years. Subsequent French presidents continued to support Quebec and did not disavow de Gaulle, but they avoided direct confrontations with Ottawa. In the description of Valéry Giscard d'Estaing, president from 1974 to 1981, Paris's stance was "a policy of noninterference and nonindifference."

While it has pursued relations with France, Quebec has also endeavoured to establish links with other Francophone countries, notably by encouraging a proliferation of cultural, technical and economic exchanges with French-language communities in Europe and Africa. It has also seen itself as the home of French culture in America and established a variety of ties with Francophones of Louisiana, New England, Haiti and the other provinces of Canada. On a more official level, it has obtained the status of a participating government in the Agence de Coopération Culturelle et Technique, the organization of Francophone countries established in 1970, and at the first Francophone Summit in 1986. As a result of Quebec's international activities, the Francophone element has played a larger part in Canada's foreign policy and international cooperation programs than in the past.

The Quebec government's growing presence on the international stage is only one aspect of a much deeper phenomenon, which began to affect Quebec society at least as early as the Second World War. Through travel, radio and television, and cultural, commercial and religious exchanges, Quebecers have become much more open to the world. Since 1960, this tendency has become steadily more intense, spread to new fields of endeavour, and had an impact on increasing numbers of Quebecers. Government activity has further strengthened this tendency and given it more direct political significance, making it possible for Quebecers as a national collectivity to maintain a presence in the world.

*   *   *   *   *   *

By using its powers under the BNA Act and by negotiating with Ottawa and the other provinces, Quebec succeeded in obtaining changes in the functioning of the federal system, leading to a degree of decentralization and increased cooperation between the federal and provincial levels of government. It even managed to establish a significant international presence. As a result of these changes, Ottawa has become more sensitive to Francophones' expectations. However, Ottawa is still clearly preeminent, both within Canada and internationally. At the end of the constitutional debate, Quebec had not succeeded in obtaining the fundamental reorganization it had been seeking for twenty years. Quite the reverse: the 1982 constitution represented a victory for the federal position.

CHAPTER 52

THE FLOWERING OF CONSUMER CULTURE

Consumer culture began to develop in Quebec in the period between the wars. By 1960, a set of conditions — a heavily urbanized society, prosperity, increased leisure time, widespread availability of radio and television, the rise of youth — had come together to speed up this development in unprecedented fashion. Under the influence of the Quiet Revolution, the climate in Quebec was more favourable than ever before to the rejection of traditional models and the adoption of new modes of cultural consumption, especially those inspired by the United States. By the 1970s, this rise in consumption had led to the virtual industrialization of the cultural sphere, in which mass production was dominant but there was little domestic control.

Radio and Television

During the period, Quebec became a full participant in the age of electronic media, which were now the chief instruments for disseminating mass culture. Far from being rivals or competitors, radio and television meshed neatly with each other to form a huge electronic fabric that covered all of Quebec and turned it into what the prophet of the media age, Marshall McLuhan of the University of Toronto, called a "global village."

As table 1 shows, even though virtually every Quebec household had a radio and a television set by 1961, Quebecers continued to acquire electronic equipment at an increasing rate. The purchase of a number of radios or TVs reflected a change in listening and viewing habits. In the 1960s, listening to the radio switched from being a family activity to a more individual one; the same thing happened to television viewing starting in the 1970s. In addition, as a result of technological innovation, when one market was saturated another could be opened up. This hap-

Table 1
Audiovisual Equipment in Quebec Households, 1961-1983

% of Quebec households with:	1961	1965	1970	1975	1980	1983
at least one radio	97.6	96.4	97.5	98.4	98.9	99.2
two or more radios	29.3	34.6	53.8	64.6	64.4	69.7
at least one FM radio	7.4	24.1	56.9	81.7	90.4	96.0
at least one car radio	34.5	47.2	62.3	70.1	75.1	n.a.
at least one car FM radio	n.a.	n.a.	n.a.	22.1	42.4	n.a.
at least one TV (of any kind)	90.8	95.5	97.7	97.8	98.6	99.1
two or more TVs (of any kind)	3.7	12.1	26.0	37.2	44.7	50.6
at least one colour TV	n.a.	n.a.	9.7	49.7	80.3	90.9
a cable subscription	n.a.	n.a.	17.1	28.7	40.4	51.3
at least one VCR	n.a.	n.a.	n.a.	n.a.	n.a.	22.8
at least one record player	43.9	57.9	68.1	75.5	77.7	n.a.
at least one tape recorder	n.a.	n.a.	n.a.	26.9	38.3	n.a.

n.a.: data not available

Source: Annual Statistics Canada estimates (64-202).

pened with frequency modulation (FM) radio in the 1960s and with colour television (introduced in 1966) and cable in the 1970s. There were other factors as well: miniaturization and computerization, which improved productivity and reduced costs, and the entry into the market of audio and video cassette recorders, which made it possible for individuals to record their favourite programs.

While Quebec's capacity for receiving electronic signals was expanding in this way, the production and distribution system was also growing substantially. The Fowler Report in the 1950s gave rise to the federal Broadcasting Act of 1958, which took regulatory powers away from the CBC and transferred them to a new body, the Board of Broadcast Governors. (In 1968, this body gave way to the CRTC — initially Canadian Radio-Television Commission, renamed Canadian Radio-television and Telecommunications Commission in 1976.) The 1958 act also provided for a much larger role for private enterprise, which took advantage of the new situation to increase its already substantial position in radio broadcasting. In the wake of the Fowler Report's recommendation that FM radio be developed, most private AM stations now acquired FM transmitters, while stations broadcasting only in FM also began operation. At the same time, two existing Montreal radio stations, CKAC and CJMS, became the flagship stations for two new major private networks, Télémédia and Radio-Mutuel respectively. The programming on many regional radio stations changed as a result. In 1982, there were more than 160 AM and FM stations in Quebec, three quarters of them Francophone.

Radio was overwhelmingly commercial, except for CBC radio, which eliminated advertising in 1975, and a few community and university stations with low-power transmitters and limited audiences.

The effects of privatization and easier access to the airwaves were even more dramatic in television. In 1960, two local movie entrepreneurs, Paul L'Anglais and J.-A. de Sève, established Télémétropole, channel 10 in Montreal, which soon became the flagship station of a network, TVA, that reached 94 per cent of Quebecers in 1977. An English-language private station, CFCF-TV, also began broadcasting in 1961. Thus, after having been a captive audience for a single network, the CBC (which continued to expand until it reached all of Quebec), Quebecers began to discover multichannel television. The pace of diversification speeded up considerably in the 1970s. The UHF band came into use, allowing viewers to receive Radio-Québec (1975); even more important, distribution by cable became common, making available the major American networks. As well, technical innovations ranging from the converter to the VCR have improved TV reception and allowed new forms of use.

Radio and television complement each other in a number of ways. While radio is directed primarily to a morning and afternoon audience — especially housewives and rush-hour commuters — television occupies people's evenings, which have come to extend further and further into the night. There is a similar division in programming. In the 1960s, radio completely abandoned dramatic entertainment and concentrated even more heavily on two areas where it was already strong: information and music, especially recorded popular music. A new development was the widespread use of the telephone for "open line" programs. Radio's ability to communicate quickly and with simple technology has made it a leading vehicle for information. And while music had been a staple of AM radio since the 1950s, the growth of FM provided a new set of opportunities, offering higher-quality sound and making possible the emergence of specialized stations.

There has been little change in the content of television programming during the period. Television has tended to concentrate on pure entertainment. Information is still an element of television programming, and its presentation has become more dramatic, with satellites transmitting images live from all over the world and even the moon. However, the percentage of air time devoted to information was the same in 1976 as in the early 1960s: 15 per cent. The bulk of air time went to entertainment programming: variety, serials, drama, movies and sports. While sports occupied only 6.7 per cent of air time in 1967, that proportion had risen to 15.2 per cent in 1976, not counting weekend afternoon sports reports. The biggest change has been in the quantity of entertainment programming, which increased as channels proliferated. Entertainment has also been the area where American television has come to occupy an increasingly prominent place on Quebec screens. This has occurred in a number of ways: through American channels received directly, through American programs and movies broadcast on Quebec channels in English or in translation, and through Quebec-made programs that imitate American models and standards.

Television has remained primarily commercial and as a result has become somewhat more uniform. To stay profitable, each station seeks to get the highest ratings and therefore aggressively goes after its competitors' viewers by broadcasting the same kind of programs they do. There were experiments with alternative, parallel, educational and community television in the 1970s, but their success has been limited. Among such stations, only Radio-Québec has been able to carve out a modest place for itself.

By the end of the period, radio and television were ubiquitous in Quebecers' lives and played a central role in mass culture. The position of television is supreme. A 1978 survey showed that Quebecers spent an average of twenty-five hours a week in front of their television sets. As a consequence, any cultural product — whatever it is — had to go through television if it wanted to reach the masses.

Publishing

With the domain of the audiovisual media growing rapidly, the traditional media had little room to expand. This was especially true of the daily press, which went through a period of stagnation and even decline. Having lost its monopoly on information and advertising, it had a hard time keeping its readers. Well-established newspapers such as *Montréal-Matin*, the Montreal *Star*, *L'Action* and *L'Événement-Journal* ceased publication. New ones, born out of the enthusiasm of the Quiet Revolution (*Le Nouveau Journal*) or the independence movement (*Le Jour*), lasted only a few years. None of the newspapers that survived increased its circulation significantly, despite the growth of the population and the overall rise of its educational level. The only newspapers that really did well were morning tabloids such as *Le Journal de Montréal* (1964) and *Le Journal de Québec* (1967), which systematically followed the definitions of reality established by television.

With the possible exception of *Le Devoir*, almost half of whose small circulation is outside Montreal, no daily could really be called a national newspaper. Even if daily newspapers are read in other regions, they remain closely tied to Quebec's major centres. In Quebec as a whole, weekend newspapers — whose number and total circulation went up by about 50 per cent between 1957 and 1972 — are the most widely read. Most of these newspapers are published in Montreal. They are heavily illustrated and concentrate on news from the worlds of sports, radio and television. Meanwhile, regional weeklies and the neighbourhood press changed significantly during the period. Before 1960, some of these newspapers offered a wealth of high-quality local news. Since then, while their numbers have grown and there has been a tendency towards concentration, their content has become more mediocre and they are now primarily

Le Journal de Montréal, a daily newspaper success story.

advertising vehicles. At the same time, the circulation of the ethnic press, concentrated in Montreal, increased from 80,000 in 1957 to more than 250,000 in 1972.

The 1960s and 1970s were difficult years for magazine publishing in Quebec. Religious journals, which continued to flourish as late as the 1950s, disappeared or stagnated, as did agricultural publications, and there was a substantial drop in the number of general-interest magazines. Some, such as *Châtelaine* and *L'Actualité*, managed to survive through mergers and takeovers by English Canadian corporations, but they were subject to intense competition from French and American periodicals. Meanwhile, specialized magazines, devoted to very specific subjects such as sports, popular science, interior decorating, music, business, comic strips, computers and others, grew rapidly during the 1970s. Some magazines of this sort have been started in Quebec, but many more come from foreign countries, especially France and the United States, and these have tended to be the most popular ones.

Another aspect of publishing consists of mass-circulation books, and this sector has grown rapidly during the period. This growth has been due both to the expansion of the reading public as a result of mass education and to more modern methods of producing and selling books. Publishers outside Quebec have largely dominated the market for mass-circulation books and they reaped most of the benefit from the growth of popular literature — fiction, adventure, crime novels, true stories, romance, the occult. Their products have reached large sectors of the population and taken a variety of forms: paperback series such as Marabout, J'ai Lu and Harlequin, comic-strip collections and, during the 1970s, blockbuster novels, often translations of American bestsellers. Sales figures for these books were far ahead of those for the few popular successes published in Quebec towards the end of the period, such as Antonine Maillet's *Pélagie*, Yves Beauchemin's *The Alley Cat* and Michel Tremblay's Montreal novels. Meanwhile, a few Montreal publishers — Éditions de l'Homme (1957), Éditions du Jour (1961), Héritage (1968), Stanké (1975) — succeeded in establishing a place for themselves in other areas: current events, biographies of popular artists and how-to books (cooking, sex, sports, gardening, personal growth and the like). In general, the growth of mass-circulation books brought vast changes to Quebec publishing. Cultural concerns have tended to give way to economic and marketing considerations.

Movies

It took movies some time to recover from the crisis that began in 1952 with the coming of television. Attendance at movie theatres continued to decline. Total attendance stood at twenty million in 1975, and dropped to fourteen million by 1984. As a result, movies had to redefine their role and their place in the spectrum of cultural consumption. Until the 1960s, movies were mass entertainment, with large theatres, relatively low admission prices, and form and content designed to appeal to as large an audience as possible. The decline of this kind of movie production and distribution was inevitable, as television was bound to have a negative impact. Radio had begun to adjust to the new conditions created by television as early as the 1950s; to survive, movies had to do the same thing.

This adjustment began to take place in the late 1960s. Admission prices went up, double features gradually disappeared and there were a variety of changes in film distribution. The opening of the first drive-in theatres in 1969 was one such change. More significant, however, was the closing of many traditional neighbourhood theatres during the 1970s and the appearance in downtown areas and suburban shopping centres of multiscreen theatres, showing a number of movies at the same time to smaller audiences. As a result of this development, the number of theatres in the Montreal area increased from fifty-eight in 1965 to eighty-one in 1975. At the same time, content changed as well. The trend was towards offering something clearly different from what was available on television, and was reflected in the rise of "adult" films, made possible by the easing of censorship in 1967. In 1975-76, 42 per cent of the movies reviewed by the Cinema Supervisory Board were for viewers eighteen and over, as compared with only 22 per cent in 1969-70.

Another aspect of specialization was the growing place occupied by repertory films, which appealed to an ever larger and more knowledgeable audience of cinephiles. These people, many of whom developed their taste in school film societies, are inveterate moviegoers, and their influence has encouraged the showing of a wider variety of films: the French "new wave," art films, experimental films, films of social and political protest, retrospectives of the classics of world cinema. All these kinds of films get very little play on television and as a result are distributed through repertory cinemas, film festivals and the Cinémathèque Québécoise, established in 1971.

Despite its difficulties, moviegoing is still a major element in Quebec's cultural life. According to surveys carried out in 1977 and 1983, moviegoing is the leading form of entertainment outside the home for Quebec adults. Movie theatres may be empty for long periods, but they are still full whenever there is a major hit, often an American blockbuster. And no assessment of the movies' true impact can ignore the fact that they increasingly reach their audience through means other than theatre showings: television, pay television and especially videocassette. Videocassettes spread so rapidly in the early 1980s that they have become a major means of film distribution and have made movies another cultural product that, to an increasing extent, is consumed individually.

International productions continue to dominate the Quebec film market. Almost all new feature films shown commercially have come from outside Quebec: more than a third from the United States, about 20 per cent from France and 12 per cent from Italy. In 1975, 71 per cent of the movies shown were French-language films and 28 per cent were English-language; in 1983, however, only 57 per cent were French and more than 40 per cent were English. More than half the movies shown on television are of American origin; on the video rental shelves, the proportion is even higher.

Quebec film production, all but nonexistent since 1953, did not begin to come together again until the late 1960s, primarily as a result of growing support from the state — the only institution that can serve in some measure as a counterweight to the power of foreign producers in an industry where financial constraints are a determining factor. The renewal of Quebec film production began at the National Film Board. Francophone directors, who formed an autonomous section from 1964 on, revived the documentary through the use of "direct cinema," a technique with considerable social and political impact. Short subjects such as Gilles Groulx's *Golden Gloves* (1961) and Arthur Lamothe's *Les bûcherons de la Manouane* (1962) were models for this form of filmmaking, but the film that stood out was Pierre Perrault and Michel Brault's *Pour la suite du monde* (1963), which astounded audiences and film professionals both for its technique and for its content. Throughout the period, the NFB has been the chief locus of documentary film production in Quebec, and films such as *On est au coton* (Denys Arcand, 1970), *L'Acadie, l'Acadie* (Perrault and Brault, 1971), *Action* (Robin Spry, 1974) *Derrière l'image* (Jacques Godbout, 1978) and many others presented a critical view of

Quebec society and culture. Meanwhile, a number of NFB directors began making fiction movies and opened the way to a new era in Quebec film.

This era was at its height around 1970. Between 1968, the year of *Valérie* (Denis Héroux), and 1973, the year of *Kamouraska* (Claude Jutra), *Réjeanne Padovani* (Denys Arcand) and *La mort d'un bûcheron* (Gilles Carle), nearly 120 feature films were made. A number of these, such as *Deux femmes en or* (Claude Fournier, 1970), *Mon oncle Antoine* (Claude Jutra, 1971), *Les Colombes* (Jean-Claude Lord, 1972) and *La vraie nature de Bernadette* (Gilles Carle, 1972), gained considerable popular success. The NFB played an important role in this output, but the private sector — itself heavily dependent on government assistance — was becoming an increasingly significant factor. In 1968, Ottawa established a financing agency, the Canadian Film Development Corporation (CFDC; later Telefilm Canada), and introduced tax breaks for private film investors. The CBC was also a major source of funds for the private film industry. In 1977, the Quebec government also began to support film production through its new Institut du Cinéma, later the Société Générale du Cinéma. These various forms of government intervention made possible the creation of a domestic film industry, but its existence was slightly artificial. Films produced in this way were rarely profitable enough to compete seriously with those made by foreign producers, who also controlled film distribution and most of the theatres.

These problems started to become glaring in the mid-1970s. The making of serious films proceeded only with difficulty (Michel Brault's *Les ordres*, 1974; Francis Mankiewicz's *Les bons débarras, 1979)* or again retreated to the haven of the NFB (Jean Beaudin's *J.A. Martin photographe*, 1977). Meanwhile, most of the Quebec film industry turned its attention to making purely commercial movies. Many of these were international coproductions, often in English, or series made with television in mind (Gilles Carle's *Les Plouffe*, 1981). While Denys Arcand achieved considerable success with his *Decline of the American Empire* (1986), this was an isolated phenomenon.

Changing public tastes were also a factor in this development. In the strong atmosphere of cultural nationalism that prevailed around 1970, people favoured the establishment of an indigenous Quebec cinema and liked seeing themselves in the stories, characters and language presented in Quebec films — so much so that in many cases they were willing to forgive technical or artistic flaws. But both the enthusiasm and the indulgence waned in subsequent years, perhaps because the Quebec film industry was slow to explore new themes and perhaps because people's tastes and judgements were increasingly influenced by international standards.

Popular Music and Live Shows

Ever since radio, records, movies and concerts had begun to make popular music a form of mass entertainment, young people had always been its most enthusiastic audience. In the 1960s, when the baby boom generation grew into adolescence, the scope of this phenomenon changed completely. Popular music became the most significant manifestation of "youth culture" — young people's favourite means of expressing and identifying themselves.

Three major forms of popular music have gained public favour in Quebec during the period. The most significant one in quantitative terms is rock. Originating in the United States and Britain, rock in its various manifestations has been the dominant sound of the period. Its leading interpreters have been international superstars such as the Beatles, and it has been associated with rapidly changing fashions, dances and ideological currents. Powerful and sophisticated equipment is used to create the rhythm and "sound" that are basic to rock. Ubiquitous on the radio and disseminated on 33 RPM records, cassettes and more recently "video clips," rock represents a huge industry, in which Quebec producers and artists have only a tiny share.

The second form consists of sentimental ballads, and the emphasis here is on melody and interpretation. Originating in nightclubs, this music is popular with older audiences as well as the young. In the 1960s it was disseminated on 45 RPM records, while in the 1970s it received considerable play on AM radio and some FM stations. Although the sentimental ballad is largely Anglophone in origin, Quebec audiences hear it primarily as performed by local and French singers.

The third form of popular music is the Quebec *chanson*, produced by local writer-composers who generally perform their own music. There were two stages in the development of the *chanson*. In the early 1960s, a group of singer-songwriters called *chansonniers* appeared, influenced by the postwar French chanson of Léo Ferré, Georges Brassens, Jacques Brel and Quebec's own Félix Leclerc. A Montreal group, les Bozos, first brought this form of music to Quebec in 1960, and with the opening of clubs called *boîtes à chansons* in various parts of Quebec the *chansonniers* had access to a young and enthusiastic audience. *Chansonniers* such as Claude Léveillée, Jean-Pierre Ferland, Gilles Vigneault and Claude Gauthier sang with only an acoustic guitar or piano as accompaniment. Poetic, echoing folk tradition, and often socially committed, their songs dealt with women, the grandeur of nature, solidarity, their homeland of Quebec. These songs captured the new spirit of national and cultural self-assertion that characterized the Quiet Revolution.

The *chansonnier* movement lasted until the late 1960s. Those who continued to perform after that time were forced to become more commercial, worked as professionals rather than craftspeople and tended to be less political. Times had changed, and in 1968 a new kind of Quebec

Gilles Vigneault, *chansonnier.*

music and song began to appear. First introduced by Robert Charlebois, this new form came as a revelation, and Charlebois's influence spread quickly among the young generation of Quebec singer-songwriters, performers and musical groups. Less interested in producing poetic lyrics than a new sound, they bore the stamp of rock and the California counterculture. The themes they dealt with were much closer to city life than those of their predecessors, and their sensibility was in greater harmony with the violence of the times, the spirit of protest and the realities of the consumer society. The acoustic guitar gave way to an electric guitar or a synthesizer, the rivers of the North Shore to the streets of Rosemount, and the checked shirt to the wild costumes of "punk" stars.

Quebec popular music around 1980 consisted of a wide variety of styles and tendencies. In the wake of the *chansonnier* movement, however, it has steadily moved closer to international trends. As it lost some of its specificity, it was increasingly subject to competition from France and especially the United States, the dominant players in the market. Sales of recorded music in Quebec stood at $60 million in 1973, but the share of Quebec-produced records was barely 25 per cent. That proportion has decreased steadily in subsequent years.

Live shows in Quebec changed considerably over the period. Initially, in the early 1960s, forms of urban entertainment such as nightclubs and dance halls quickly disappeared; discotheques came along to replace them a little later. Popular theatre, virtually nonexistent since the early 1950s, made a partial comeback with the opening of Montreal's Théâtre des Variétés in 1967 and with the establishment of summer theatres in many vacation areas. While the new popular theatre took some of its inspiration from the burlesque and *boulevard* tradition, it was to a greater degree an extension of television, whose stars and dramatic techniques it borrowed. The only real innovators in popular theatre were monologists,

Diane Dufresne, a Quebec star of the 1980s. (*Le Journal de Montréal*)

mimics and comedians who, with the help of records and television, became steadily more popular during the 1970s.

The most common form of live performance throughout the period was the popular music concert, featuring the latest Quebec and foreign stars. Initially, these concerts were relatively small. They took place at the Comédie Canadienne in Montreal or in *boîtes à chansons*, college auditoriums and movie theatres elsewhere in Quebec. Later on, new theatres such as the Place des Arts in Montreal, the Grand Théâtre in Quebec City and the many arts centres built for Canada's centennial in 1967 offered better locations for popular concerts. Another kind of show was introduced in the 1970s: popular music festivals inspired by Woodstock that took the form of giant popular gatherings. These included the Manseau festival, St. Jean Baptiste Day festivals in Montreal's Mount Royal Park, Chant'âout and Superfrancofête on the Plains of Abraham in Quebec City, and later huge shows in the Montreal Forum and the Olympic Stadium. The main form of entertainment presented in these latter locations, however, was professional sports, which had become a major media phenomenon. During the period Quebec acquired a new major-league hockey team, the Quebec Nordiques, in addition to the existing Montreal Canadiens, as well as a major-league baseball team, the Montreal Expos.

Industrialization and Americanization

The consumption of all aspects of mass culture — radio and television, records, movies, popular literature, live shows — has grown extremely rapidly in recent years, in Quebec as in other advanced societies. On the production and distribution side, the most significant development has been what might be called industrialization: the introduction in the cultural sphere of the same rules, ways of doing things and methods of competing that prevail in other sectors of the economy. In this way, cultural production was reorganized, the pace and quantity of its output increased and its distribution methods became more refined. More and more, individual producers and small companies organized along craft lines were squeezed out. Instead, huge organizations with powerful financial and technical means at their disposal monopolized cultural production. In book publishing, for example, Sogides owns several publishing houses, a printing firm and a distribution company. Most of the major newspapers and magazines belong to press empires such as Power Corporation, Unimédia and Québecor. All but a few private radio and television stations are part of the major Quebec and Canadian networks. And in all cultural enterprises, including government-owned ones, industrial methods of producing and marketing culture have been adopted.

An even more striking aspect of this development has been the opening up of the Quebec cultural market and the steadily growing market share occupied by foreign and especially American products. Supported by all-powerful marketing and advertising structures, these products are sought after all over the world. In this context, Quebec cultural industries do not have an easy time of it, despite government efforts to help them. Their position is precarious, even in the local market, and it tends to get worse as demand grows for more, better and more varied movies, records, videocassettes and television programs. At the same time, Quebec producers have had little success with foreign sales. They have made a few dramatic breakthroughs in France, especially in popular music, but these have tended to be one-time successes. On the whole, exchanges are very one-sided, even with France.

In addition to these economic difficulties, the gradual Americanization of mass culture exerts pressure on the specificity of Quebec culture itself. Some people see this as a process of acculturation that can only become more intense as French gives way to English, the dominant language of mass culture. A growing proportion of Francophones, especially young ones, not only prefer American and British music but also increasingly consume English-language television, movies and magazines. Other people see this phenomenon as a new challenge for Quebec to meet. In either case, it represents the result of a long process of cultural modernization and catching up with other western societies. This process began in the years between the wars, became more intense in the 1940s and 1950s, and since 1960 has taken place at a faster pace and spread to more sectors of society than ever before.

CHAPTER 53
A TIME OF CULTURAL FERMENT

In literature and the arts, there were dramatic and extremely rapid changes after 1960 that affected the whole situation of culture in Quebec society. Esthetic and ideological modernization, which had taken place in fairly limited circles in the 1940s and 1950s, continued, became stronger and extended its reach considerably after 1960. Modernization of Quebec's cultural institutions, largely a function of increasing government involvement in the cultural field, was a major contributing factor to this trend. Institutional modernization could be seen in at least four developments: a growing audience for culture and a rapid increase in consumption; the establishment of new facilities; an improvement in artists' status; and an increase in the scope and variety of cultural production.

While modernization was a feature of the whole period, it can be divided into two distinct phases, corresponding roughly to the 1960s and the period after 1970. During the first, intense phase, Quebec culture caught up, laid foundations and was transformed. A new audience emerged, the government made its entry onto the cultural stage, and improvements in Quebec's cultural facilities were initiated. After 1970, this climate of reform and innovation gave way to a new phase whose main feature was consolidation and expansion of the developments that had taken place in the previous decade.

The Audience

The number of people interested in literature, classical music, theatre and the visual arts grew substantially. First of all, wider access to education meant a much larger number of students, who always represent a pool of particularly active cultural consumers. The rise in the general educational level also meant a wider circle of culturally knowledgeable people. Meanwhile, with higher incomes and more leisure time, the constraints that had made access to books, works of art, concerts and plays difficult if not impossible were now eased for many Quebecers. What took place, in a word, was democratization: forms of culture hitherto reserved for a very small number of connoisseurs, concentrated in the most privileged sectors of urban society, were now available to wider groups, more varied in their social origin.

But the change was not only quantitative: ideas, attitudes and tastes changed as well. This was largely the doing of the new postwar generation that was becoming the largest and most influential part of the population. Numbers represented only one aspect of this generation's power. It devoted more time to reading, listening to music and going to shows and exhibitions than its elders had and consumption of cultural products was a more central element in its way of life. This was true not only in Montreal and Quebec City but also in smaller cities and towns. At the same time, this generation was less submissive to clerical authority, less attached to traditional values and more aware of new trends and styles originating in other countries. It not only accepted modern ideas and works that challenged accepted notions and represented a break with the past — it preferred them.

This was especially true during the 1960s. The new audience supported esthetic innovation, political involvement, affirmation of a distinctly Quebec culture and, a little later, the emergence of the counterculture. As this generation aged, however, the cultural climate settled down somewhat after 1970. Consumption continued at a high level, and even grew. But cultural audiences were less interested in formal or ideological audacity than in quality, originality and variety. In the 1960s, feelings inspired by Quebec nationalism had led people to hold "authentically Quebec" products in high regard. This preference and the fervour that went with it waned after 1970. At the same time, while youth during the Quiet Revolution had been more or less unanimous in its tastes and interests, there was now an increasing tendency towards segmentation in which groups of more specialized connoisseurs developed within the culturally knowledgeable public. These connoisseurs were often more demanding and had more intense likes and dislikes than in the past.

Cultural Facilities

As a result of these changes, demand for and consumption of cultural goods and services, whether produced in Quebec or elsewhere, rose steadily as the period progressed. Quebec's facilities for cultural dissemination and promotion were seriously outdated, and the Quebec government took measures to satisfy and stimulate these growing demands.

The public library system was one of the areas where these efforts were most conspicuous. In 1967, the old Saint-Sulpice Library in Montreal became the Bibliothèque Nationale du Québec, with a mandate to collect and make available works published in Quebec. At the same time, Quebec's network of municipal libraries improved significantly. The number of municipal libraries increased from seventy-one in 1960 to 114 in 1967 and 138 in 1983. In addition, twelve central lending libraries were established in the late 1970s to serve nearly 750 rural municipalities in the various regions of Quebec. In the large cities, municipal libraries opened new branches: in 1982, Montreal's municipal library had twenty-one branches while Quebec City's had six. In this way, the proportion of the population served by public libraries grew from 45 per cent in 1960 to 63 per cent in 1970 and reached 83 per cent in 1984. It also became easier for Quebecers to buy books. Following the recommendations of the Bouchard Report (1963), Quebec established an accreditation system for bookstores that broke the virtual monopoly held by religious communities and educational institutions. The new system established favourable conditions for independent bookstores so long as they were Quebec-owned and their stock was of high quality. In 1985, there were 172 such accredited bookstores in Quebec, ninety-one of them in Montreal and twenty-six in Quebec City.

There was a similar improvement in Quebec's concert halls and theatres. The years 1965-75 were a particularly intense period of building and establishing new facilities, and some of the most serious inadequacies were corrected during this time. Here too, improvement was most notable in Montreal and Quebec City. A complex offering music, opera, dance, theatre and variety shows was built in each city: Montreal's Place

The Grand Théâtre in Quebec City.

des Arts (1961-67) and Quebec City's Grand Théâtre (1967-71). At the same time, older, smaller halls, movie theatres and other public buildings were renovated or redeveloped, usually with government help. In a number of middle-sized cities, arts centres were built as part of the celebration of Canada's centennial. The result was the establishment of a circuit that touring Quebec or foreign theatre companies, orchestras or soloists could travel.

In the visual arts, several new museums and exhibition centres were opened. These new facilities — notably the Musée d'Art Contemporain (1965) and the Saidye Bronfman Centre (1967) tended to specialize in modern art. At the same time, a whole system of alternative galleries developed. In 1972, the Quebec government changed the Montreal Museum of Fine Arts from a private institution into a joint public-private one, making it possible for the museum to grow and to stage major international exhibitions. Most of the arts centres in middle-sized cities also had art galleries, which presented frequent exhibitions of works by local artists. The number of commercial galleries also increased rapidly during the 1960s, as did the variety of styles they promoted.

Another significant development was the large number of artistic/commercial events that attracted large numbers of people in Montreal and other cities starting in the 1970s. These include book fairs and festivals of all kinds: film, video, classical music, jazz, theatre and others. Here too, government financial and technical assistance has played a determining role.

Finally, no picture of the development of Quebec's cultural facilities would be complete without taking into account the contribution of educational institutions all over Quebec. Polyvalent schools, cegeps and universities maintain libraries, auditoriums and exhibition halls that are used by the public as well as by students.

In general, Quebec's cultural infrastructure made considerable progress in twenty years. Of course, many deficiencies persist. But the contrast with the situation before 1960 is such that it has truly been a time of new beginnings. In Quebec as a whole and especially in Montreal, a commercial and institutional network has developed that makes cultural activities and goods hitherto reserved for a minority available to almost everyone. Never in the past have books, records, shows, concerts and exhibitions been accessible in such quantity and variety.

But this wider access doesn't necessarily mean that all citizens take advantage of the cultural services available to them. Even though consumption has greatly increased, it remains limited by economic and especially educational factors. Thus, despite the wider availability of books, a 1979 survey showed that 77 per cent of Quebecers never go to public libraries, 50 per cent have never been in a bookstore, and 44 per cent virtually never read — in 1983, this last figure had gone up to 49 per cent. A similar situation prevails with respect to art museums, which attract less than 25 per cent of adult Quebecers. While these percentages may seem discouraging, they do represent progress in comparison with earlier eras. Since the 1970s, however, they appear to have stabilized, so that the overall proportion of Quebecers interested in so-called "elite" culture can be estimated as at best about 20 per cent. This is comparable with the figure in other western societies.

Artists

Another manifestation of Quebec's cultural ferment has been a change in the place of artists in society: their position has become less marginal and their status and living conditions have improved, especially since the late 1960s. There has been a significant rise in the number of artists as a result of increased demand, greater availability of means of production and wider dissemination of artistic knowledge through the educational system. Thus, the number of professional actors in Quebec increased from fewer than 400 in 1971 to more than 1,000 in 1981. In 1975, there were 2,770 artists working in the visual arts, of whom 1,800 lived in Montreal and 560 lived in Quebec City. At the same time, artists have tended to come from a wider variety of social origins and the proportion of women in the arts has increased significantly.

With the modernization, extension and reorganization of specialized training schools, self-taught artists became rarer. Previously, these schools had been autonomous and rather marginal institutions, but now they were integrated into the college and university systems. As a result, it became possible to establish such schools all over Quebec and to make better resources accessible to them. At the same time, the number of artists who study outside Quebec has increased, as has the number who participate in major international competitions.

More numerous and better trained than ever before, artists and other people working in the cultural field have increasingly tended to regard themselves as professionals and have become more aware of their socioeconomic interests. In theatre, music, radio and television, they were already represented by well established unions, and these unions' influence has increased as the market has broadened. A new development since 1970 has been the emergence of groups of painters, engravers, writers and other independent artists making a collective effort to promote their works and lobby the government on questions that concern them.

It is still rare for artists to be able to make a living from their art alone. A few well-known writers, painters and actors were able to achieve this position, especially in the 1970s. For the vast majority, the income derived from their art (royalties, fees and sales of works as well as government bursaries, grants, prizes and orders), while tending to increase over the period, remained small, and almost all of them had to depend on a second source of income. This other work tended to be closer to the artist's field of expression than in the past: in addition to radio, television and journalism, work was now available in the educational field — community cultural work and especially college and university teaching. Jobs of this sort allowed artists to pursue their creative activities with considerable freedom. On the whole, however, according to a study done for the Canada Council in 1979, the material conditions in which artists lived were still far below those enjoyed by other groups with a comparable level of education.

Finally, there were significant changes in the political and ideological role of intellectuals and artists and the positions they tended to take. Until roughly 1970, they saw themselves and were seen most frequently as people challenging the system. They were active in opposition movements, trade unions, and pro-independence and Marxist groups. They openly criticized Quebec's institutions and deliberately sought to subvert the system through their works. Among such artists were the writers of the *Parti Pris* group, painters and sculptors who supported the democratization of art, and actors in neighbourhood and factory troupes. Some of them made the authorities sufficiently nervous that they were arrested during the October Crisis in 1970. After 1970, however, this notion of the artist's role waned, gradually giving way to a more apolitical attitude and a return to specialization. Artists increasingly ignored social and political struggles and concerned themselves strictly with esthetic and professional questions.

The 1960s

Each of the period's two major phases had its own practices, ideas and climate. If we examine each phase in turn, a more accurate picture of the abundance and variety of cultural output in contemporary Quebec emerges than if we look at each cultural sector for the period as a whole.

During the 1960s, the means of cultural production in Quebec were still on a fairly modest scale. Cultural output, while clearly greater than in previous decades, was still relatively small. However, it had a resonance that extended to more Quebecers and was more intense than before. There was a degree of thematic and formal unity to the works of the decade. They represented a continuation of the esthetic modernization of the 1940s and 1950s, but they differed from the works of that period in that their creators saw them as much more directly related to social and political struggles. Fired by the climate of the Quiet Revolution, artists sought through their works to develop a specifically Quebec culture and encourage national awareness. While they identified with international and especially French currents and favoured modern forms, they also endeavoured to produce works rooted in the traditions, language and realities of the Quebec homeland. Journals such as *Liberté* (established in 1959), *Situations* (1959-62) and *Parti Pris* (1963-68) were notable expressions of this spirit, which also provided the energy for the *chansonnier* movement and Quebec film in the 1960s.

Literature: Literature was clearly the most active cultural sector. Quebec publishing finally came out of the slump in which it had been mired since the end of the Second World War and entered a new period of

Table 1
Average Number of French-Language Literary Works Published Each Year in Quebec, 1962-1982

Genre	1962-65	1966-69	1970-73	1974-77	1978-82
Novels and stories	40	57	74	83	155
Poetry	40	42	81	87	110
Theatre	7	15	19	26	33
Juvenile literature	21	10	29	43	86
Essays					
a)Literature	21	33	45	47	66
b)Arts	5	13	25	24	33
c)History/geography	18	36	59	47	91
d)Social sciences	20	37	70	58	91

Source: Annual bibliographies in the journal *Livres et Auteurs Canadiens/ Québécois* (includes some reprints).

growth. The annual number of books published increased substantially (table 1), and several new publishing houses were founded, including Leméac (1957), HMH (1960), Boréal Express (1963), Parti Pris (1964) and Éditions du Jour (1961). Éditions du Jour combined literary publishing with mass-circulation popular books and was a major force in the renewal of the novel that was one of the significant developments of the decade.

Before 1960, the wave of modernization that had transformed other areas of expression such as poetry and painting had largely passed the novel by. In the 1960s, however, novelists began to break the traditional rules of their art. They violated chronological order, brought together a number of different points of view, ignored verisimilitude, used *joual*, wrote erotic passages, and created characters who were in open revolt against the established order, religion and morality. They wrote what the critic Gilles Marcotte has called *"le roman à l'imparfait."* For readers, these daring works came as a surprise and were often diametrically opposed to what they had been accustomed to, but they were willing to be won over. The extent of their conversion can be seen in the larger press runs for Quebec novels and the prestige accorded to the new novelists, a number of whom remained in the limelight in the 1980s. Among the more noteworthy novelists of this school were Gérard Bessette (*Le libraire*, 1960), Jacques Ferron (*Contes du pays incertain* [*Tales from the Uncertain Country*], 1962), Jean Basile (*La jument des Mongols*, 1964), Réal Benoît (*Quelqu'un pour m'écouter*, 1964), André Major (*Le cabochon*, 1964), Andrée Maillet (*Les remparts de Québec*, 1964), Jacques Renaud (*Le cassé* [*Broke City*], 1964), Hubert Aquin (*Prochain épisode* [in English under the same title], 1965), Marie-Claire Blais (*Une saison dans la vie d'Emmanuel* [*A Season in the Life of Emmanuel*], 1965), Claude Jasmin (*Pleure pas, Germaine*, 1965), Claire Martin (*Dans un gant de fer* [*In an Iron Glove*], 1965), Réjean Du-

Writers from *Parti Pris*, 1964: André Major, Gérald Godin, Claude Jasmin, Jacques Renaud, Laurent Girouard and Paul Chamberland. (Jean-Pierre Beaudin)

charme (*L'avalée des avalés* [*The Swallower Swallowed*], 1966), Jacques Godbout (*Salut Galarneau!* [*Hail Galarneau!*], 1967) and Roch Carrier (*La guerre, yes sir!* [in English under the same title], 1968).

The works of these novelists — and especially Aquin and Godbout — were marked by the ideological and political ferment of the period, but not as much as Quebec poetry, in which the dominant themes were the homeland and the "*fondation du territoire.*" The first to express these themes were the poets of the l'Hexagone generation, whose works had great impact in the 1960s: Paul-Marie Lapointe (*Arbres*, 1960), Jean-Guy Pilon (*Recours au pays*, 1962), Gaston Miron (*La vie agonique*, 1963), Roland Giguère (*L'âge de la parole*, 1965). They were also found in collections by newcomers such as Gratien Lapointe, whose *Ode au Saint-Laurent* was published in 1963, and Paul Chamberland, who sang the praises of *Terre-Québec* in 1964. This school of consciously militant poetry also gave rise to collective readings such as the "*Poèmes et chants de la résistance*" in 1968, memorable for Michèle Lalonde's passionate recital of her poem "Speak white." The works of other poets of the period, such as Jacques Brault (*Mémoire*, 1965), Fernand Ouellette (*Le soleil sous la mort*, 1965) and Gilbert Langevin (*Pour une aube*, 1967), were marked by a more personal and less politically involved form of lyricism. In the latter part of the decade, younger poets — such as Michel Beaulieu and Nicole Brossard, who were among the founders of the magazine *La Barre du Jour*, and others who were involved with the counterculture — began to challenge the dominant theme of the homeland in poetry. This led to the explosion of forms and themes that would mark the next decade, dramatically presaged by the "poetry night" organized by the National Film Board in 1970.

The passion for change and new climate of freedom that characterized the Quiet Revolution gave rise to all kinds of reexaminations, discussions and reflections and hence made the 1960s a rich time for essays in Quebec. Some essays were book-length, such as those of Gilles Leclerc (*Journal d'un inquisiteur*, 1960), Pierre Vadeboncoeur (*L'autorité du peuple*, 1965), Fernand Dumont (*Le lieu de l'homme*, 1968) and Pierre Vallières (*Nègres blancs d'Amérique* [*White Niggers of America*], 1968). But most essays were shorter, written ad hoc and polemical in nature, appearing in newspapers or magazines in response to circumstances and the concerns of intellectual circles. Some of these essays were the work of writers, such as Fernand Ouellette, Pierre Maheu, Jacques Ferron and Hubert Aquin. Others were written by journalists such as Jean-Louis Gagnon, André Laurendeau and André Langevin. Still others were interventions in the controversies of the moment by social scientists such as Pierre Elliott Trudeau, Marcel Rioux, Michel Brunet and Léon Dion. The number and variety of essays and the often passionate interest they aroused among readers show how intensely ideas were expressed and circulated in the 1960s and how thoroughly the ideological and intellectual barriers of the past were overcome.

Perhaps in no other era in Quebec's history did writers and writing enjoy such influence or play such a central role in their society's cultural life. Literature was a crucial forum for the debates, new perceptions, worries and expectations that made up the mindset of the new culturally knowledgeable elites. Increasingly, this "literature in ferment," as Gérard Bessette has called it, asserted its autonomy and specific character. Quebec literature was now taught in schools, academic journals were devoted to it, older works were reissued and reinterpreted, and new syntheses were developed. The latest contributions to Quebec literature were closely followed by critics such as Gilles Marcotte, Pierre de Grandpré and Jean Éthier-Blais.

Theatre: The theatre of the 1960s was a more or less direct extension of that of the 1950s, except that it continued to grow and Quebec plays occupied an increasingly important place. In addition to well-established professional companies such as the Rideau-Vert and the Théâtre du Nouveau Monde, there were new troupes such as the Nouvelle Compagnie Théâtrale (1964) and the Théâtre Populaire du Québec (1966), which sought to broaden the theatregoing public by staging tours and performances for student audiences. These companies presented high-quality traditional theatre, devoting much of their attention to the classical repertoire. At the same time, other groups such as l'Egrégore (1959) and the Saltimbanques (1962) were more interested in experimentation and in new forms of avant-garde and political theatre. And in many Quebec cities and towns, amateur troupes were organized, often in a college setting.

In general, theatre presented in Quebec remained centred on the playwright, and the text was still the most important element. The most novel feature of the theatre of the 1960s was the prominent place occupied by Quebec plays, which explored themes of questioning and revolt. Recognized Quebec writers were major participants in this movement: Gratien Gélinas (*Bousille et les justes*, 1960), Jacques Ferron (*La tête du roi*, 1963), Jacques Languirand (*Klondyke*, 1965), Anne Hébert (*Le temps sauvage*, 1967), and especially Marcel Dubé, who enjoyed his most fruitful years in the 1960s, with plays such as *Les beaux dimanches* (1965) and *Au retour des oies blanches* (1966). But younger writers also made a significant contribution, including several who participated in the activities of the Centre d'Essai des Auteurs Dramatiques, established in 1965. The most notable of these younger writers were Françoise Loranger (*Une maison ... un jour*, 1965), Robert Gurik (*Hamlet, prince du Québec*, 1968), Jean Sauvageau (*Wouf-wouf*, 1969), and especially Michel Tremblay, whose *Les belles-soeurs*, staged in 1968 by André Brassard, opened the way to a new form of theatre distinguished by use of *joual* and popular culture.

Visual arts: Painting in the 1960s was also largely dominated by artists who had emerged in the postwar years and whose works were now considered classics. The Montreal Museum of Fine Arts devoted major retrospectives to Alfred Pellan, Paul-Émile Borduas, Jean-Paul Riopelle and Jean-Paul Lemieux, while the new Musée d'Art Contemporain did the same for Jean-Paul Mousseau and the sculptor Robert Roussil. At the same time, the advent of new and younger art aficionados who favoured modern forms led to a widening of the market for art. According to Guy Robert, some 300 exhibitions were held annually in Montreal between 1960 and 1967 and 90 per cent of them featured nonfigurative art. There continued to be two major tendencies within nonfigurative art, lyrical and geometric. Geometric painting, strongly represented by neo-*plasticiens* such as Guido Molinari, Claude Tousignant and Yves Gaucher and buttressed by the influence of American op art and hard edge, was clearly the dominant trend. Many women artists — notably Marcelle Ferron, Lise Gervais, Rita Letendre and Marcella Maltais — painted lyrical works and gave new life to that tendency, but they soon moved off in other directions.

After having emerged with great difficulty in Quebec since the 1930s, nonfigurative art was now so widely accepted and disseminated that it was perceived almost as a new form of academic art, and reactions to it began to appear in the 1960s. Thus, both Edmund Alleyn and Marcella Maltais had painted *automatiste* works, but Alleyn became more interested in schematic figurative painting while Maltais turned to landscapes and portraits. But it was primarily younger artists who criticized abstract art, which they considered bourgeois and decadent. Starting in 1964, artists such as Serge Lemoyne and Jean Sauvageau organized "happenings" and other artistic events based on the idea of a synthesis of the arts and the desire to create a participatory art. This movement would continue into the 1970s and a variety of developments emerged from it, ranging from the occupation of the École des Beaux-Arts in Montreal in 1968 and the formation of groups of artists seeking more committed forms of art to the more radical tendencies of the counterculture. The movement provided material for the alternate galleries and was expressed in the same kinds of challenges to established institutions that were occurring in other fields at the time.

The 1960s were also a decisive period in the development of engraving and printmaking. Unlike a canvas, an engraving or a print is a work of art with multiple copies. Susceptible to wide public distribution and lending itself naturally to experimentation, such art was very compatible with the spirit of democratization that infused the 1960s. An abundance of works emerged from the workshops of young engravers such as Richard Lacroix, Pierre Ayot, Marc Dugas, René Derouin and Janine Leroux-Guillaume, trained by Albert Dumouchel at the École des Beaux-Arts in Montreal. The Guilde Graphique and the GRAFF studio, both founded in 1966, played a significant role in stimulating and distributing this work.

There were also a variety of experiments aimed at integrating art more fully into the social environment, again related to the desire to make art more democratic. Thus, the first outdoor sculpture symposium was held in Mount Royal Park in Montreal in 1964. In this vein as well, artists were called on to contribute to the environment of public places. Notable examples were Mousseau's neon-lit fibreglass mural in the Hydro-Quebec building in Montreal (1962) and the stained-glass windows, murals, reliefs and sculptures that decorate Montreal's metro stations. This integration of the arts into the environment, encouraged by government policies, would come into full flower in the 1970s.

Music: In music, modern tendencies continued to occupy a prominent place. Under the leadership of the composer Pierre Mercure, the *Semaine Internationale de Musique Actuelle* (International contemporary music week) took place in Montreal in 1961 and provided music lovers with a glimpse of the newest and most surprising experiments in modern music. Another step forward in the promotion and development of modern music was the establishment of the Société de Musique Contemporaine du Québec in 1966. The new tendencies in music — electroacoustic music, the twelve-tone scale, aleatoric music, multimedia music — were represented in Quebec by composers such as Gilles Tremblay, Jacques Hétu, François Morel, Clermont Pépin, Micheline Coulombe-Saint-Marcoux, Claude Vivier and especially Serge Garant. The audience for music, a considerable part of which still preferred the classical and romantic repertoire, was larger than before and also better served, thanks to records, FM radio, visiting orchestras, conductors and soloists, and concerts by local ensembles. Chorales, chamber orchestras and ballet companies were founded, and in 1965 the Montreal International Competition for piano, violin and voice began. At the same time, the Montreal Symphony Orchestra moved into its new home in Place des Arts and entered a very fruitful period under its young conductor Zubin Mehta (1961-67).

After 1970

The transition from the 1960s and the years after 1970 was far from being a complete break. In many ways, the 1970s represented simply an extension and intensification of the movement that began in the 1960s. But the general climate and the conditions under which culture was produced were sufficiently different that the 1970s can be considered the beginning of a new phase of cultural creation. A number of developments in the late 1960s foreshadowed this new phase: the establishment of the cegeps, the opening of the University of Quebec, student protest, the hippie movement, and the great festival of youth and cultural consumption that took place at Expo 67 in Montreal.

At least two elements distinguished the new phase from its predecessor. The first was the dramatic growth in the number of works produced and the inception of new ways of marketing culture. The Bibliothèque Nationale's legal delivery service received a total of 653 books published in Quebec in 1968. By 1976 the figure had risen to 2,446, and in 1982 it was 4,336. Similarly, while there were three professional dance companies in Quebec in 1970, there were ten in 1982. In the visual arts, exhibitions proliferated to the point where Guy Robert described the market as being saturated. Along with this quantitative explosion came a new approach to the market, as more unabashedly commercial methods were introduced, including greater use of advertising, publicity and sales agents, specialized magazines, television programs, and festivals and other major local and international events. Even "alternate" institutions, which proliferated in the early 1970s, were by no means completely outside the market; in fact, most of them ended up being part of the market in one way or another. Increasingly taking on the character of a commodity within the economic mainstream, "elite" culture was subject to the cyclical fluctuations of the economy. Thus, during the 1981-82 recession there was a drop in the consumption of books and works of art, from which cultural industries took several years to recover.

If the first major change was the increased quantity of works of art, the second was their unprecedented variety. The relative unity that still held in the 1960s has given way to an ever greater profusion of styles and expressions as artists explore different tendencies, themes and inspirations. It is very difficult to detect any central or dominant current in the assortment of old and new experiments, ideas, forms and themes that Quebec culture has become. Artists are not influenced by French and other European models as exclusively as they once were, as styles and ideas coming from the United States have played a more important role. One of the results of this diversification has been the decline of national-

Some major women writers, including Madeleine Ouellette-Michalska, Madeleine Gagnon, Yolande Villemaire, Nicole Brossard, Suzanne Paradis and Madeleine Ferron. (Kèro)

ism, which has lost its central position while other tendencies such as mysticism, the ecology movement, Marxism and feminism have made corresponding gains. Feminism in particular has been a major concern and source of inspiration for many artists since 1975, in literature, the visual arts and theatre as well as history and the social sciences.

A look at Quebec's cultural magazines gives an idea of the profusion and eclecticism that characterize recent cultural output. In the 1960s a few journals occupied a more or less predominant position: *Parti Pris*, *Libertéç* and *La Barre du Jour*. Since then, there has been an explosion of magazines, many of them ephemeral and each with its own area of specialization: psychedelic drugs and the counterculture (*Mainmise*, 1970-78; *Hobo-Québec*, 1972-81), socialism and nationalism (*Presqu'Amérique*, 1971-73; *Possibles*, 1976-), Marxist theory and criticism (*Stratégie*, 1972-77; *Chroniques*, 1975-78), the Third World (*Dérives*, 1978-), feminism and new values (*Le Temps Fou*, 1974-83; *La Vie en Rose*, 1980-87).

Literature: All cultural sectors have been marked by this growth and diversification, and literature is no exception. As table 1 shows, the number of books of all sorts published increased rapidly in the early 1970s. The rate of growth slowed in the middle of the decade, but gathered strength again around 1980. On the other hand, the number of sales per title tended to decline. According to the Bibliothèque Nationale, the average sale for all books published in Quebec in 1968 was 5,406, while in 1982 the figure was only 2,733.

Taking into account numbers of titles published, circulation and reception by the critics and the public, the novel emerged as the most important form of literature in Quebec in the 1970s, displacing poetry which had held that position in the 1950s and early 1960s. This development was related to the process of commercialization mentioned above. A wide variety of novels have been written in Quebec, but it is primarily the works of previously published writers that have received the most attention: Gabrielle Roy, Anne Hébert, Jacques Godbout, Réjean Ducharme, Gérard Bessette, Roch Carrier, Antonine Maillet, André Major, Marie-Claire Blais, Gilles Archambault. Notable among the newcomers have been Jacques Poulin, Victor-Lévy Beaulieu, Jacques Benoît, Louis Caron, Michel Tremblay, Yolande Villemaire and Yves Beauchemin. Novelists have continued to experiment with form, but not as much as in the sixties. Instead, novels in which plot, character and setting are the major elements have made a comeback. There has even been talk of a return to realism.

Even if poetry has been pushed off centre stage, more of it has been published than ever before. There has been an extremely varied array of poetry collections, published in small editions and read almost entirely in specialized circles. One tendency has been formalism, which rejects personal expression in favour of highly experimental "texts" reflecting a passion for theory. Meanwhile, supporters of socially involved literature write poetry that is committed and critical. Others take their inspiration from mass culture and rock music, while still other poets give voice to a new spirituality drawing from the mysticism of the East and California. Within these diverse and often overlapping tendencies, what has come to be known as "women's writing" has occupied a large place. And despite the prominence of the daring and vocal avant-garde, a simpler, stricter lyricism not only has survived but even began to make a comeback among a number of younger poets around 1980.

Two literary genres have made especially rapid strides since 1970. The first has been children's and young people's literature. In this area, high production costs had prevented Quebec publishers from competing with European imports, but the modernization of the production and distribution system along with support from educational institutions has corrected the situation somewhat and many more Quebec titles have been published since 1975. The other rapidly expanding area has been essays and works about literature, the arts, history and the social sciences; the growth of scholarly journals has been a related development. This has happened partly because of the expansion of Quebec's universities and other research institutions, which produce and consume a large number of theses, studies and reference works. In addition, these disciplines have been in methodological and conceptual ferment since the 1960s. Literary and esthetic studies have been renewed by structuralism, psychoanalysis and sociological criticism, historical studies have seen the rise of the new economic and social history, and new analytical models have also made their appearance in sociology, political science, demography and economics. Most works published in these fields — some of which reach the general public as well as scholarly readers — have dealt with subjects of Quebec interest. This was especially true in the period leading up to the referendum.

Theatre: Theatre was one of the areas in which particularly significant changes occurred during the 1970s. Especially before 1975, theatre underwent what some people consider an identity crisis, manifested primarily in a rejection of traditional methods, which were considered poorly adapted to modern sensibilities. The large institutional companies continued their activities, but they felt the effects of this challenge directly. Their prestige waned, and they were shunned by younger audiences, who preferred what Laurent Mailhot has called the "new Quebec theatre." As this new theatre emerged in the early 1970s, there was a flowering of companies of young actors whose approach to theatre was deliberately experimental and daring and whose attitude towards language, inspiration and interpretation was free of traditional constraints. The Grand Cirque Ordinaire and the Théâtre du Même Nom, both founded in 1969, were leaders in this regard. The themes favoured by these new companies tended towards protest, social and political criticism, commitment, sometimes outright propaganda. They tried to be close to people's immediate concerns and to reach new audiences by performing — with varying degrees of success — in factories, working-class neighbourhoods and schools. But their most striking innovations were in the areas of form and staging. They rejected the script and the primacy of the playwright and instead gave pride of place to the actor and the audience, emphasizing collective creation, improvisation and audience participation. Theatre became less a branch of literature and more pure performance.

This period of effervescence lasted only a short time. By the late 1970s, the ideas introduced by the new theatre were accepted and regarded as routine, and hence they lost their bite. But the ferment had a beneficial effect, making it possible for Quebec theatre to become more varied and distinctive. It also brought a new generation of actors, directors and "writers for the stage" to the fore: Michel Tremblay, Jean Barbeau, Jean-Claude Germain, Michel Garneau. In the early 1980s, theatre that sought only to entertain was still quite popular, while a number of companies continued — sometimes with difficulty — to stage experimental and innovative theatre.

Visual arts: No sector provides a better example of the wide diversification of Quebec's cultural output after 1970 than the visual arts. As artists, works of art, and places where art could be exhibited proliferated, it became a sector where literally everything could be expressed. There

Michel Tremblay's play *L'Impromptu d'Outremont*. (André Le Coz)

were no longer any dominant schools or styles. Thus, in painting, the avant-garde returned to figurative art by way of pop art and later super realism. This trend did not mean that abstraction was no longer practised, but only that it did not have the theoretical and commercial supremacy that it enjoyed as late as the 1960s. In fact, the dichotomy between figurative and nonfigurative art has seemed increasingly irrelevant. Some painters have stuck to abstract and others to representational art, but many have gone blithely back and forth from one to the other or tried to combine the two.

At the same time, other disciplines such as sculpture, photography and tapestry have used a variety of new forms and materials. Two developments in particular have contributed to their growth: the more frequent staging of collective events (symposiums, biennial exhibitions, retrospectives) and the movement to integrate art into the environment, in which both government and an increasing number of private companies have been involved. Murals, frescos, mobiles, sculptures and, more recently, "installations" have been used to decorate buildings (both inside and outside), public places and parks. In some cases, these works have offended conservative groups, as happened with Jordi Bonet's mural for the Grand Théâtre in Quebec City in 1971 and the works produced for the Corridart project in Montreal in 1976.

Some artists have still sought to be provocative — by ridiculing art and its institutions, for example. In general, however, art's subversive edge has been blunted somewhat, as more emphasis has been placed on personal expression and purely formal experiments. Finally, there has been a proliferation of new media that break with traditional categories: laser and computer design, kinetic and conceptual environments, use of the body and voice for "performance" or "installations." Some of these forms are part of a new tendency that first appeared in Europe and New York and gradually gained favour in the early 1980s — postmodernism. Postmodern art represents a critique of modernism using methods in which purely subjective expression by the artist is the dominant element.

The explosion of disciplines and styles and the proliferation of exhibitions and signatures have resulted in a crowded market for art. Competition among artists has become very intense. It has been essential for an artist's works to bear his or her particular stamp, through unusual themes, an easily identifiable style or a newly invented technique. At the same time, the confusion in the art market has made the public very cautious. Some connoisseurs have been interested only in a very specific portion of Quebec's artistic output, while others have fallen back on tried and tested criteria. As a result of the latter trend, the reputations of such artists as Marc-Aurèle Fortin, Léo Ayotte and Jean Dallaire have made a comeback.

Music: In music, the 1970s were marked by two major phenomena. First, musical life in Quebec and especially in Montreal became livelier, as the number of performances increased, their quality improved and their variety broadened. It was a period of consolidation for Quebec's major musical institutions, which won new acclaim both inside and outside Quebec. This was especially true of the Montreal Symphony Orchestra. After undergoing a financial crisis in 1973-74, it had to reorganize and develop a wider — and mostly Francophone — audience. It burst into prominence after Charles Dutoit became its conductor in 1978: it has given more concerts, enjoyed growing popularity, gone on international tours and made many recordings. The major ballet companies, the Opéra de Montréal (founded in 1980) and the Quebec Symphony Orchestra have all developed in a similar if less dramatic way. At the same time, many other local professional and semiprofessional groups — chamber orchestras, vocal ensembles, youth orchestras — have also presented regular programs. The increased number of institutions, concerts and performances has been beneficial both to music lovers and to musicians, singers, dancers and composers, who have been able to find more work.

The second noteworthy development has been a tendency towards specialization. In addition to performances seeking to attract the general public, there has been an increasing number of activities directed towards more limited groups of music lovers: organ recitals; baroque music, often played on period instuments; various kinds of contemporary music, notably jazz; folk music and dance. Networks of enthusiasts, institutions and artists devoted to these musical forms have taken shape and maintain close contact with similar networks outside Quebec.

*   *   *   *   *   *

The ferment of the years since 1960 presents a striking contrast to the rarefied atmosphere of Quebec's literary, artistic, theatrical and musical life in the 1930s or even just before the Quiet Revolution. Of the many factors that have contributed to Quebec's cultural effervescence, three are especially worth noting. The first is government support, discussed in detail in the next chapter. The second is Quebec's lively ideological and political scene, which until roughly the late 1970s not only served as a constant backdrop for cultural developments but also directly sparked artistic creation and innovation. A third factor is the improvement in means of communication, which has made possible both better circulation of artistic works within the domestic market and more intense and sustained communication with developments outside Quebec. Through books, films, records, exhibitions and touring performers and companies from Europe and the United States along with more frequent exchanges and other opportunities for travel, Quebec artists and audiences have become direct participants in major international cultural trends to a greater extent than before. At the same time, Quebec's artistic output has gained better distribution and recognition elsewhere, especially in France. Internationalization, however, also represents a challenge. Now that the public has increased access to the best cultural products from outside Quebec, local works no longer have quite the privileged status they once did. These works face increased competition, and it is their competitors that largely set the standard for quality and content.

CHAPTER 54

CULTURE AND THE STATE

One of the major elements in Quebec's recent cultural history has been the increasing role of government in supporting and directing cultural output and distribution. This new reality, which emerged after the Second World War, has steadily broadened in scope since 1960, while its orientation has gradually changed. As noted from time to time in the preceding chapters, the governments in Ottawa and Quebec City have become active and essential players in all sectors of cultural life.

Initial Awareness

Even before the 1950s, government was not completely absent from the cultural sector. Quebec City and Ottawa provided modest financial support for a few art schools and institutions aimed at conserving cultural goods. From time to time they would commission or buy works from particular artists or give them grants or prizes, such as the Prix Littéraires et Scientifiques de la Province, first awarded in 1922, and the federal Governor General's Awards, instituted in 1937. But these activities were carried out on a small scale, were not part of any overall plan, and were designed to meet only limited needs. There was no government department with specific responsibility for coordinating or directing these initiatives, so that they depended on the good will of a few enlightened members of the government.

This situation was a result of two factors. The first was the overall idea that political elites and the ruling class as a whole had of culture. Providing no obvious economic return, culture was viewed either as a luxury product reserved for limited circles of connoisseurs or else as a suspect activity that involved criticizing morality and the established order. In either case, it was strictly a private matter. The only areas to which government paid a little more attention were radio and, to a lesser extent, movies; because these media reached much wider audiences, they were seen as utilities, means of conveying information and, where necessary, propaganda instruments. There was also another argument for hesitancy about government intervention in the cultural sphere that appealed strongly not only to the country's leaders but also to many intellectuals. This was that the only examples of interventionist governments at the time were the totalitarian regimes in Nazi Germany and the Soviet Union where, as politicans were fond of repeating, freedom of expression had been replaced by censorship and government control of culture.

During and after the Second World War, however, the idea of government responsibility in the cultural sphere began to emerge. Groups of artists, writers and representatives of local institutions criticized the pathetic state of Canada's cultural infrastructure and demanded government action. At the same time, in many parts of the western world, ideas about both culture and the role of government were changing. Instead of being seen as strictly decorative or as the monopoly of a privileged few, culture began to be viewed as an essential part of the life of a society, reflecting solidarity among people, visions of the world, and values of concern to the society as a whole. The establishment in 1945 of the British Council, chaired by the economist John Maynard Keynes, and the founding the next year of the United Nations Educational, Scientific and Cultural Organization (UNESCO) were notable manifestations of these new ideas.

An additional — and crucial — circumstance in the Canadian context was a strong resurgence of cultural nationalism, fuelled both by the international recognition that participation in the war had brought to Canada and by an increasingly widespread desire in federal political circles and among educated Canadians to see Canada assert its own identity. The establishment of the Massey Royal Commission on National Development in the Arts, Letters and Sciences in 1949 was a response to this concern.

Its report, published in 1951, suggested that it would be desirable for Canadian writers, painters and musicians of recognized stature to be able to express Canada's sensibility, history and landscape — its very soul — to Canadians from coast to coast and to the world. But in the commission's view, there were two obstacles to the flowering of Canadian culture. The first was Canada's small and scattered population, which made it impossible for Canadian cultural activities to be profitable or even financially self-sufficient. The second was the overwhelming presence of foreign and especially American influence: Canadian writers had to have their books published in London, Paris or New York; painters lived and exhibited their works abroad; musicians went into exile. Research in the social sciences was largely funded by private American foundations, as were scholarships for students, grants for artists, and assistance to museums, libraries and universities. Moreover, Canadian cultural products were in no position to compete with foreign imports in their own market. For the future, it would be necessary for the government to do for Canadian culture as a whole what it had done for radio since the 1930s: protect it and provide it with funds. The government had to overcome considerable resistance to implement the Massey Report's recommendations, but it finally did so in 1957 by establishing the Canada Council.

Elites in Quebec had always been concerned with maintaining cultural identity, but two factors delayed government involvement in this sector. First, the Duplessis government, faithful to its anti-interventionist ideology, not only attacked Ottawa's initiative but also saw culture as outside its own area of concern. Second, the threat of becoming culturally assimilated into the United States has always been less strongly felt in Quebec than in the rest of Canada. In the 1950s, however, the reform-minded opposition to Duplessis began to demand government intervention. The intellectuals who surrounded *Cité Libre* saw it as natural, even preferable, that government action in the cultural sphere should come from Ottawa. They cited the prevailing conservatism and authoritarianism in Quebec institutions on the one hand and, on the other, the pluralist and even culturally progressive nature of federal agencies such as the CBC and NFB at the time. Meanwhile, neonationalists were suspicious of the concept of Canadian culture that formed the basis of the Massey Report and feared that policies coming from Ottawa would be harmful to Quebec's identity. They wanted to see the Quebec government get involved in cultural activity rather than leave the whole field to Ottawa.

Taking its lead from the French model as conceived by Charles de Gaulle's minister of culture, the writer André Malraux, the Quebec Liberal Party made the establishment of a department of cultural affairs part of its platform. The department was finally established in 1961. Here too, nationalism was a determining influence. According to Premier Jean Lesage, the new department would be "a department of French Canadian civilization, [which will be] the most effective servant of the French fact in America — that is, of the soul of our people."

The Instruments of Government Intervention

By the early sixties, culture had become a public matter, and governments felt justified in acting in this area. Over the next twenty years, government intervention in culture became steadily more extensive and varied, as culture played an increasing role in economic and social life and cultural professionals presented their case for government assistance more strongly, arguing that they advanced the interest of society as a whole. Thus, government became much more than just a partner in the cultural field: it became a central, indispensable actor. In contemporary Quebec, the material base for cultural development is almost entirely a government responsibility.

The two senior levels of government — and, to a marginal degree, some of the larger municipalities — have assumed this role. Both Quebec City and Ottawa have departments responsible for culture: the Quebec government has the Department of Cultural Affairs, while the federal government placed the Canada Council and other cultural agencies under the umbrella of the Department of the Secretary of State in 1963; after 1980, this responsibility was switched to the Department of Communications. On the whole, until the mid-1970s, Ottawa was the more dynamic of the two governments in this area. Its programs were better orchestrated and more visible, used greater human and financial resources, and sought to be more attentive to the demands of the artistic community. Artists, for their part, appeared largely satisfied with Ottawa's performance, even if they always asked for more.

By comparison, Quebec's Department of Cultural Affairs looked like a poor relation. It had neither resources nor initiative, and despite repeated declarations of intent, few concrete actions were undertaken. In absolute terms, the department's expenditures increased substantially, from $2.7 million in the 1960-61 fiscal year to $38.9 million in 1975-76. However, this represented no increase in its share of overall government expenditures but rather a slight decline: from 0.46 per cent in 1960-61 to 0.43 per cent in 1975-76. The cultural community grew steadily more dissatisfied, and in 1975 a group of artists and intellectuals drew up a blistering *Rapport du Tribunal de la culture* (Report of the tribunal on culture). The next year, Liberal Cultural Affairs Minister Jean-Paul L'Allier issued a green paper entitled *Pour l'évolution de la politique culturelle* (For the development of cultural policy) in which improvements were announced. This desire for change was taken up by the new Parti Québécois government. Cultural development became one of the four major areas into which government activity was divided; funds allocated to the Department of Cultural Affairs were increased by a third in a single year and in 1980-81 stood at almost $100 million or 0.56 per cent of overall government expenditures; and a voluminous white paper on cultural development, *La politique québécoise du développement culturel*, was solemnly issued in 1978. The department gradually improved its programs and administrative methods, and its activities became more numerous and relevant. By 1980, something of a balance between Quebec City and Ottawa had been achieved, although there were still a number of areas of overlap.

But the activities of departments and agencies that are formally responsible for culture are far from being the only ways in which government intervenes in cultural affairs. A number of other government institutions are directly or indirectly involved in culture and their influence is sometimes greater than that of strictly cultural agencies. The clearest example of this phenomenon in Quebec throughout the period has been the Department of Education, which plays an essential role in distributing works, educating artists and the public, putting infrastructure in place and even providing direct assistance for artistic creation. In the 1970s, the same was true for departments such as Immigration, Leisure, Intergovernmental Affairs and even Public Works. In Ottawa, agencies such as the Centennial Commission and the office of the Commissioner of Official Languages intervened in the cultural sphere, as did the departments of External Affairs, Indian Affairs and Regional Economic Expansion. Finally, public bodies such as the organizing committee for Expo 67 or for the celebration of the 450th anniversary of Jacques Cartier's voyage devoted large sums of money to cultural activities.

This fragmentation makes it difficult to plan an overall policy — something Ottawa has never attempted and Quebec has only sketched. Even at the end of the period, there was considerable confusion in government cultural policy. There is no general agreement on just what the cultural sector includes nor on what methods should be used for research or intervention. As a result, it is virtually impossible to obtain a reliable measure of the extent of the government presence in the cultural field. Thus, the historian Bernard Ostry has estimated that Quebec's expenditures on culture and recreation increased from $5.9 million in 1957-58 to $24.6 million in 1967-68 and then to $197.4 million in 1977-78. By contrast, statisticians at the Institut Québécois de Recherche sur la Culture estimate the same expenditures at about $238.4 million in 1976-77 and at more than $428.2 million in 1980-81. There are similar discrepancies in calculations of federal expenditures in Quebec, which are generally regarded as being comparable to those of the Quebec government. The only safe statement is that allocations to cultural activities have grown rapidly during the period, and especially during the 1970s. Around 1980, combined expenditures of the two governments affecting the cultural sector in Quebec were estimated at about $1 billion.

The Major Directions of Cultural Policy

Despite what Ostry has referred to as the lack of a coherent cultural policy, it is possible to identify a clear line of development in the major directions that government intervention has followed. In the 1960s, it was almost exclusively directed towards professional cultural activity and was aimed at creating conditions that favoured the local production of high-quality works, to which as many citizens as possible would have access. While the expression of a "national" culture was a goal pursued by both Quebec City and Ottawa (with each defining "national" in its own way), both governments had considerable confidence in the ability of the cultural community to achieve this goal on its own. Because the cultural community was so small, and because governments' limited resources had to meet a variety of pressing needs, culture was not seen as a major political issue. This explains why there were so few confrontations and jurisdictional conflicts between Quebec City and Ottawa in this field, at a time when there were so many in other areas.

In the 1970s, some significant changes of direction occurred as a result of the impact of the ideological and political climate and the extension of the concept of culture. The first change was a substantial broadening of the field of government intervention, which now tended to include not only arts and letters but also a whole variety of other activities involving a larger number of people: crafts, amateur theatre and music, local history, community movements and the whole area of sociocultural recreation. While government continued to encourage professional artists, it also devoted more attention and resources to these other activities, and changed its vocabulary and methods of action to accommodate them. Ideas and concerns such as animation, participation and democratization made their appearance. Ottawa initiated its Canadian Horizons Program in 1971, followed by Explorations in 1973. Meanwhile, many of the grants it gave out under Opportunities for Youth and the Local Initiatives Program went to cultural organizers and groups operating in working-class neighbourhoods, rural areas and isolated regions. The same concerns led to more intensive efforts to decentralize cultural services. In Quebec, this led to the establishment of Conseils Régionaux de la Culture (Regional cultural councils) in 1977.

Another major change was the emergence of the new idea of cultural development, which found its most significant expression in the Quebec white paper of 1978. This change was both a logical extension and a broadening of the preceding one and involved three points. First, every citizen or group of citizens was viewed as a cultural actor with full rights, as consumer, producer and participant. Second, culture became a central element in all the activities that together make up the life of a society. Culture is reflected and created not only in the arts and literature but also in education, language, communications and recreation and in the way people work, eat, have fun and the like. Third and most important, it was not enough for government to take on the role of patron and protector of culture. It had to be the initiator and planner of cultural development, which meant that it had to take cultural impact and concerns into account in all its activities, whatever they might be.

In the late 1970s, government cultural activities also became increasingly political. While it would be going too far to talk of government control of culture, there was a tendency towards disputes over powers and responsibilities between Ottawa and Quebec City, as in the struggle for control of cable television, and towards greater ideological and political content in both governments' cultural activities. This tendency was at its height on the eve of the referendum, when the federal government tightened its control over the CBC and other cultural agencies and reminded them that their mandate was to promote the expression and strengthening of Canadian unity. The competing national celebrations of June 24 and July 1 became battlegrounds in which "cultural" grants served as ammunition. Each government aimed to maximize its visibility and influence, especially in mass culture: television, large shows, and fairs and exhibitions of all kinds.

The Sectors of Government Activity

Few studies have been devoted to government activity in the cultural sphere, and there are large gaps in the data. Nevertheless, it is possible to provide a quick overall view, at least in the area of the arts and professional culture. Four major sectors can be identified.

The first consists of activities undertaken directly by government either as a conserver or as a producer of cultural goods. Although government has been involved in this sector for a long time, it has more recently allocated new resources to it and updated its initiatives. In the area of conservation, Quebec City and Ottawa have restructured institutions such as national libraries, archives and museums, widening their mandates, increasing their staffs and encouraging their expansion. At the same time, they have improved government services aimed at cataloguing and managing Quebec's and Canada's historical and natural heritage. In the area of production, the two large federal agencies, the CBC and the NFB, both of which grew rapidly until the late 1970s, have made Ottawa unquestionably the dominant player. More recently, however, there has been a tendency for the federal government to seek to withdraw from direct production and finance private-sector activities instead. Quebec has established its own television outlet, Radio-Québec (1969), hesitantly set up a film board (1961), and reactivated its official publisher, but on the whole it has not been very active as a direct cultural producer.

Another sector is legislative action. Throughout the period, governments have adopted a variety of legislative measures concerning the arts, culture and communications. Some of these measures have been aimed at stimulating the production and sale of local works. Thus, the so-called 1 per cent law, adopted by Quebec in 1961 and by Ottawa in 1966, made it obligatory for governments to set aside a portion of the cost of public buildings for the purchase of works of art. Other legislation has endeavoured to regulate particular cultural markets, such as bookselling, movie theatres or cable television. The most significant measures, however, have been those aimed at limiting the influence of foreign cultural producers in publishing, movies, radio and television. Both governments have enacted a number of such protectionist measures.

The other two sectors — investment in cultural infrastructure and aid to artistic creation — have involved higher levels of expenditures. Government has played a leading role in establishing the major instruments for distributing and consuming cultural goods: public libraries, concert halls, theatres, museums, cultural centres. While Ottawa's contribution in this area has been far from negligible, the major effort has come from Quebec City, which has financed the construction of buildings and the establishment of institutions and then assumed responsibility for the bulk of their operating costs.

Finally, government is virtually alone in playing the role of patron through its direct assistance to artistic creation and scientific research. Some of this assistance goes to individuals in the form of bursaries, grants, prizes and direct purchases. Another segment goes to such institutions as orchestras, theatre, opera and dance companies, and private film, recording and publishing companies, as well as to universities and research groups. Until the mid-1970s, Ottawa was the most active player in this sector. The Canada Council, which at its inception was a small agency with something of a philanthropic flavour, soon became a major dispenser of bursaries and grants through its various direct assistance programs and initiatives such as the Art Bank (1972) and the Touring Office (1973). Expenditures on these programs rose from $1.4 million in 1960-61 to $10.3 million in 1970-71 and then to more than $43 million in 1980-81. The council also financed research in the social sciences and higher education for many young Canadians both inside and outside Canada, thus contributing, especially in the 1960s, to the training of a whole new generation of university professors and researchers. In 1978, these programs were transferred to another federal agency, the Social Sciences and Humanities Research Council.

Starting in the mid-1970s, there were two significant changes in this area. The first was the growing involvement of the Quebec government, which substantially increased its bursaries and grants for artistic creation, notably through the Fonds pour la Formation des Chercheurs et l'Aide à la Recherche (Fund for the training of researchers and assistance to research, known initially as FCAC and later as FCAR). Quebec also established a special agency, the Institut Québécois de Recherche sur la Culture (Quebec institute for research on culture). The second change was the new emphasis placed by both governments on the concept of cultural industries. Governments increasingly encouraged the emergence and consolidation of private companies — sometimes to the detriment of individual initiatives — and the criteria applied to these companies were more clearly economic: profitability, financial self-sufficiency, and effective management and marketing. This new approach led to the establishment of the Société de Développement des Industries Culturelles du Québec (Quebec cultural industries development corporation) in 1979 and was reflected in Ottawa's Applebaum-Hébert Report in 1982.

Overall, over the course of the period Quebec's programs encouraging the arts and cultural production have made it one of the leading western societies in this area — as is Canada as a whole. While this situation is justified by the weakness of the domestic private sector in the face of international competition, it has not been without its problems.

First, to the extent that government acts as a patron, this patronage constantly creates new needs, and these increased needs rapidly outstrip the capacity of the available resources to deal with them. The function that government patronage performs also changes over time. Until roughly the early 1970s, government primarily encouraged works of art that were emerging, innovative, in many cases even daring and challenging. Subsequently, however, what had emerged in this way needed its support on a continuing basis. As a result, there were fewer and fewer resources available to encourage new developments, and the stimulating effect once produced by government assistance gave way to caution and even, in the area of research, constraint.

But the most serious problem has been the dependence of artists and cultural institutions on the state. There is hardly a theatre, publishing house or film producer that doesn't need public funds to survive. A company's viability or even an artist's career is often decided by bursaries and grants. And a cutback in government expenditures is enough to create a crisis atmosphere in the cultural community, as happened in the early 1980s.

* * * * * *

It is difficult to come to any overall conclusions about government cultural intervention in Quebec since 1960. It has clearly been a success in the area of arts and letters: the cultural ferment that Quebec has seen since the Quiet Revolution would undoubtedly not have had the same scope without it. In literature, the visual arts, theatre, art film, classical music and dance, government support has made possible the emergence of a Quebec culture that has produced an abundance of works and become increasingly confident of its originality and quality. However, success has been much less evident in the area of communications and mass culture: television and popular movies, music and publishing. In this area, government action has been necessarily defensive, and far from preventing the overwhelming penetration of foreign — essentially American — cultural products, the most it has been able to do has been to keep afloat a few fragile vessels of what could be called national culture.

GENERAL
CONCLUSION

What conclusions about the development of Quebec society arise out of the history outlined in these two volumes? Quebec society has been shaped by a number of fundamental processes, which have slowly and steadily done their work of redefining the relationships both among individuals and between individuals and nature. A few processes in particular stand out: industrialization and the growth of the service sector; urbanization and the rural exodus; technological innovation; the demographic transition and immigration; the development of capitalism and the working class; the rise of literacy, education and cultural development; nationalism and federalism; government intervention; women's assertion of their rights. These processes have operated concurrently, interacting with one another and each proceeding at its own pace, contributing to the shape of Quebec society today.

Our study has shown that any analysis that traces the origins of present-day Quebec to the Quiet Revolution or even the Second World War is shortsighted. The roots of today's Quebec extend far back in time. Some phenomena — the French presence, the concentration of the population in the St. Lawrence Valley, the development of the two urban poles of Montreal and Quebec City — can be traced to the early years of New France. Other developments became significant in the second half of the nineteenth century — the era when modern Quebec truly begins.

The Stages of Development

We have divided the history of modern Quebec into five major periods. In the first, from 1867 to 1896, Quebec society adjusted slowly and painfully to a set of economic, social and political transformations that had first become significant in the 1840s. The most important was clearly industrialization, which not only radically changed the structure of production but also transformed social relationships, leading to the rise of the new capitalist bourgeoisie and the formation of the working class along with its instrument, the trade union movement. Industrialization was supported by the revolution in transportation arising out of the gradual disappearance of the wooden sailing ship and especially the growth of railways, which became the leading sector for long-term investment. In turn, industrialization stimulated urbanization, which had been going on for a long time but increased greatly in scope after 1850.

At the same time, the gradual specialization of Quebec agriculture represented the beginning of a response to the severe crisis that had afflicted the agricultural sector for several decades. However, the economic growth brought about by these changes was not enough to sustain Quebec's rapid increase in population, and even though there was very little immigration in the years following 1867 and thus little competition in the urban labour market, many of the people who left the Quebec countryside had to go to the towns of New England.

Quebec also had to adapt to the new context created by Confederation in 1867. Confederation directed the axis of economic development towards the west and established an integrated domestic market structured around the National Policy. While it established a Quebec state with limited autonomy and a Francophone majority, it also enshrined French Canadians' minority status in Canada as a whole. It was a struggle for the new Quebec state to organize its institutions and define its priorities. Finally, the Catholic Church consolidated its power over Quebec's institutions and culture between 1867 and 1896.

The next period, from 1896 to 1929, was one of expansion. The long phase of adaptation was completed, and while there were a few discordant voices, Quebecers in general entered enthusiastically into an era of rapid growth, which was seen as synonymous with economic and social progress. The development of natural resources became the lynchpin of the Quebec government's economic strategy, and it brought industrialization, urbanization and proletarianization to what had previously been colonization regions. At the same time, Quebec's traditional industries benefited from the quantitative and qualitative expansion of the Canadian domestic market, especially the settlement of the prairies. The increased number of jobs attracted a new wave of immigrants and reduced the impact of the exodus to the United States. The merger movement radically changed the corporate structure, set in motion the growth of the service sector, and led to increasingly centralized economic power. The new prosperity was very unequally distributed and the working class was still subject to difficult living and working conditions, although there were some improvements in Quebec's infrastructure and public health.

This period was an era of great political stability in which the major features were the dominance of the Liberal Party, an increase in the resources at the government's disposal, and a "golden age" of provincial autonomy. Quebec's political serenity was, however, disturbed by lively debates on the national question and the emergence of a nationalist movement that made unsuccessful attempts to win acceptance for its conservatively oriented political program. It was also in this period that the first attempts to adapt Quebec's institutions to the new economic realities were made: the first social programs were hesitantly introduced, as were partial reforms in the field of education. Quebec's educational system, however, was still mired in a jumble of structures and programs and Quebec clearly lagged behind Ontario in this area. The Catholic Church maintained a powerful position in Quebec society and tried as best it could to adapt to the cultural changes that were taking place. The pace of these changes was speeded up by American influence, which affected urban society and the workplace.

After the optimism of the early decades of the twentieth century came a troubled period, lasting from 1930 to 1945 and marked by the successive shocks of the Depression and the Second World War. The Depression seemed to indicate that the mode of development that had prevailed until then had failed, and it led to a fundamental reexamination of capitalism. The turbulent decade of the 1930s, in which conditions were ripe for an unprecedented flowering of ideologies, saw a political realignment in Quebec whose effects would be felt for a long time. Production was in chaos; unemployment was massive; insecurity and misery were widespread. Public works programs, the dole and colonization represented only a partial, ineffective response to the Depression. Also as a result of the Depression, the way Canadian federalism functioned was called into question and a realignment of forces began in which the federal government would come out on top. The Quebec nationalist movement showed new vigour but did not succeed in translating it into long-term political gains.

The war put the economy back on the rails and set Quebec on a path towards renewed economic growth. It meant a new period of prosperity and full employment for Quebecers and an improvement in living and working conditions. However, the war upset the political balance of Canadian federalism by making it possible for Ottawa to concentrate resources and decision-making power in its hands. Ottawa took advantage of the situation to fully embrace Keynesian economic policy and to introduce the first programs of what would become the welfare state. A Liberal Quebec government also undertook some fundamental social reforms, but it was defeated in 1944 when the conscription crisis led to a nationalist upsurge.

During the period between 1945 and 1960, Quebecers basked in prosperity and enjoyed a significant improvement in their living standards. Industrialization and urbanization, which had faltered during the Depression, once again proceeded at a steady clip. The price of prosperity, however, was increased economic and cultural integration into the American orbit. The baby boom and renewed immigration brought about rapid population growth, which in conjunction with higher living standards led to a substantial increase in the demand for social, health and educational services. Existing institutions were poorly equipped to deal with these new demands and the Quebec government's conservatism delayed the necessary reforms. The social and economic climate that prevailed under clerical ascendancy and in the long shadow of Maurice Duplessis seemed stifling and led to the emergence of a reform movement demanding the modernization of government institutions. While official nationalism, identified with conservatism, rallied to the defence of provincial autonomy in the face of Ottawa's centralizing thrust, a new nationalism seeking to make the Quebec state an instrument of development in the interest of French Canadians began to be expressed. This contradiction dramatically came to the fore in 1960.

The impact of the Quiet Revolution has been felt throughout the period that began in 1960. Quebec's new political leaders were supporters of reform liberalism and the welfare state, and they undertook a thorough reform of Quebec's state apparatus and institutions providing educational, health and social services. With the Quiet Revolution, a new ruling class arising out of the postwar middle class and the Francophone bourgeoisie came to power, with the support of broad sectors of the population. Its actions were based on an aggressive nationalism that sought to change existing power relationships. Within Quebec, it aimed to ensure that Francophones had a preponderant voice in determining the direction of the economy and society, while in Canada, it not only resisted Ottawa's centralization but demanded increased powers for Quebec, both domestically and on the international scene. The role of government in the development of Quebec society was seen as that of a master builder, and government intervention was extended into every area as the state took advantage of Quebec's rapid declericalization. The new leaders were also avowed democrats, and they sought to improve access to services, increase participation and open up the political system.

It wasn't long before tensions and contradictions began to appear. On the national question, the new elite was divided by the question of just how much autonomy Quebec should seek as the independence movement gained strength. In the social sphere, the opposition between the major trade union centrals and the government led to confrontation while the burden of unemployment and social assistance became increasingly heavy. Moreover, the drop in Quebec's birth rate meant that its population was aging. Displacement of the economic centre of gravity towards Toronto and Quebec's declining position in Canada as a whole represented a drag on its economic growth. By the late 1960s, the long-term processes of industrialization and urbanization had been completed; service activities dominated the economy more than ever and mass culture was ubiquitous. It was a very fertile cultural period for Quebec as new artists and interpreters made their presence felt. The Francization of the economy took place at a rapid pace and led to the rise of the Francophone bourgeoisie. But this too was not an entirely smooth process, and its effects could be seen in the language crisis and the Anglophone exodus. Another major development of the period was the growth of the women's movement, which led to a redefinition of relationships between the sexes.

Some of the reforms of the period represented a reversal of long-term trends, such as clerical ascendancy over Quebec's social and ideological life. However, the ground had been prepared in the decades preceding the Quiet Revolution, and most of the reforms represented the completion or acceleration of processes that had been in motion for a long time. Government intervention and the rise of the Francophone bourgeoisie are examples of such processes. There were also persistent trends that the Quiet Revolution did not succeed in changing, such as Quebec's economic and technological dependency and the dominant position of Montreal with respect to the other regions of Quebec. Quebec's long-term development is punctuated by periods of rapid change alternating with periods of slower change, adaptation and even retreat. Ultimately, the Quiet Revolution was one such period of rapid change. The fact that it has given way, in the 1980s, to a time of reexamination makes that easier to see.

The Direction of Quebec's Development

In the 1960s, it would have been virtually impossible to write a synthesis of modern Quebec history such as this one. Since then, great strides have been made in historical research and whole strata of Quebec's recent past have been laid bare. The limited scope of our work makes it impossible to do justice to the full richness of this research or to all its nuances. Nevertheless, the thousands of published studies by historians and social scientists, which have served as the basis for our synthesis, allow us to ask the question: what has been the direction of Quebec's development?

The first conclusion that arises out of our overview of more than a century of history is that the image of Quebec as a monolithic, unanimous society does not stand up to serious examination. Like other societies, Quebec society is complex. The first sign of its diversity is the coexistence on Quebec soil of different ethnic and cultural groups that interact with and influence one another. The varying and sometimes divergent efforts by Francophones to define themselves in relation to other groups mark the entire history of Quebec.

But even if we look at French Canadians alone, we see complex situations and a lack of unanimity. Research in recent decades has highlighted some of the factors leading to these divisions and distinctions. There has been a sharper perception of differences and conflicts between classes, regions, sexes, economic sectors and generations, and of the ramifications of these differences in the form of relations of domination and dependence and efforts to obtain enfranchisement or autonomy.

A second myth, which arose out of looking at Quebec in isolation, was the uniqueness and originality of Quebec society. This myth has also been shot down. The processes Quebec society has undergone, such as industrialization and urbanization, have taken place throughout the West, perhaps even throughout the world. Quebec has borrowed widely: technology from Britain and the United States, debates about liberalism and ultramontanism from Europe, contemporary artistic trends from all over. Of course, this transposition has been accompanied by varying degrees of adaptation to the Quebec context, as occurs in all other societies. How adaptation occurs can vary from one part of Quebec to another, between city and country, or among different social and cultural groups. All of Quebec's development has been marked by the constant flux of transposition and adaptation, of borrowing and creation, of universality and specificity.

A third myth has proved inadequate as an explanation of the recent history of Quebec: the myth of a traditional society propelled brutally into the modern era. On the contrary, modernization can be seen as an evolutionary process, and furthermore one that is constantly being redefined. It is not a linear process; rather, it is punctuated by advances and retreats, by times of rapid change and periods of stagnation. Different aspects of modernization reach people at different rates, while such factors as region, social group, sex and generation also affect the pace at which the impact of modernization is felt.

A fourth conclusion has to do with nationalism, which shows up at all stages of Quebec history. While at various times groups have adopted the nationalist label and formulated political programs based on the nation, no group has ever had a monopoly of nationalism. It is important to distinguish the deep, almost visceral nationalism present in all segments of the Francophone population from specific nationalist programs formulated and argued by clearly identified groups. Beyond these specific programs, modern Quebec history is unquestionably marked by Francophones' assertion of their identity and desire to regain a dominant position in Quebec. This social process is a product of demographic, economic, political, ideological and cultural developments, and like all processes it has no definitive end.

Thus, in the space of a few years, we have gone from seeing Quebec as fixed and monolithic to seeing it as evolving and complex. Instead of perceiving Quebec as a relic of the past, we now analyse it as a society, with all the hierarchies, struggles, differences and transformations that such a status entails.

GENERAL BIBLIOGRAPHY

Specialized works covering particular topics are listed at the end of each chapter. However, there are also some basic general works, a few of which are listed below.

Research tools

Both the Quebec and federal governments publish annual compilations of statistics on a very wide range of subjects. These are useful research tools. The *Quebec Yearbook* was published annually until 1976; it was published irregularly thereafter and its title was changed to *Le Québec statistique* with the 1985-86 edition. The *Canada Year Book* was published annually until 1980-81, and then skipped to 1985-86. The *Census of Canada*, published every ten years until 1951, and then every five years after that, is another major source of information on Canada's population, economy and society. As well, both Statistics Canada and the Bureau de la statistique du Québec put out many specialized publications containing a wide variety of statistical series. There is also a collection in which significant statistical series are presented in historical perspective:

Leacy, F.H. and M.C. Urquhart, eds. *Historical Statistics of Canada*. Second edition. Ottawa: Statistics Canada, 1983.

A number of guides to the literature are useful supplements for the period under consideration:

Aubin, Paul and Louis-Marie Côté. *Bibliography of the History of Quebec and Canada, 1945-1965*. 2 vols. Quebec City: Institut québécois de recherche sur la culture, 1987.

Aubin, Paul and Paul-André Linteau. *Bibliographie de l'histoire du Québec et du Canada, 1966-1975*. 2 vols. Quebec City: Institut québécois de recherche sur la culture, 1981.

Aubin, Paul and Louis-Marie Côté. *Bibliography of the History of Quebec and Canada, 1976-1980*. 2 vols. Quebec City: Institut québécois de recherche sur la culture, 1985.

The most useful encyclopedia is:

The Canadian Encyclopedia. Second edition. 4 vols. Edmonton: Hurtig, 1988.

General Works

The first work that must be mentioned here is Robert Rumilly's monumental *Histoire de la province de Québec* in forty-one volumes. (Montreal: different publishers, 1940-1969). This sprawling narrative deals primarily with Quebec politics, but touches on many other topics as well. Volumes 31 to 41 cover the period from 1930 to 1945.

The following works are particularly useful for situating Quebec history in its Canadian context:

Thompson, John Herd and Allen Seager. *Canada 1922-1939, Decades of Discord.* Toronto: McClelland and Stewart, 1985. 438 pp.

Bothwell, Robert, Ian Drummond and John English. *Canada Since 1945: Power, Politics and Provincialism.* Toronto: University of Toronto Press, 1981. 489 pp.

Granatstein, J.L. et al. *Twentieth Century Canada.* Toronto: McGraw-Hill Ryerson, 1983. 440 pp.

An annual public affairs review is:

Canadian Annual Review of Public Affairs. Toronto: University of Toronto Press, since 1960.

Finally, there are a number of major syntheses of Canadian and Quebec history in French. Three of them are:

Brown, Craig. *The Illustrated History of Canada.* Toronto: Lester & Orpen Dennys, 1987. 574 pp.

Charpentier, Louise, René Durocher, Christian Laville and Paul-André Linteau. *Nouvelle histoire du Québec et du Canada.* Montréal: Boréal Express/CEC, 1985. 448 pp.

Robert, Jean-Claude. *Du Canada français au Québec libre: Histoire d'un mouvement indépendantiste.* Paris and Montreal: Flammarion, 1975. 323 pp.

Hamelin, Jean, ed. *Histoire du Québec.* Toulouse: Privat, 1976. 538 pp.

CHAPTER BIBLIOGRAPHIES

Chapter 1

Angers, François-Albert and Roland Parenteau. *Statistiques manufacturières du Québec.* Montreal: École des hautes études commerciales, 1966. 166 pp.

Bolduc, André, Clarence Hogue and Daniel Larouche. *Québec: Un siècle d'électricité.* Second edition. Montreal: Libre Expression, 1984. 431 pp.

Minville, Esdras, ed. *Notre milieu. Aperçu général sur la province de Québec.* Montreal: Fides and École des hautes études commerciales, 1946. 443 pp.

Safarian, A.E. *The Canadian Economy in the Great Depression.* Toronto: McClelland and Stewart, 1970. 258 pp.

Vallières, Marc. "Les industries manufacturières du Québec 1900-1959." MA thesis (history), Laval University, 1973. 243 pp.

Chapter 2

Blanchard, Raoul. *L'Est du Canada français; Le Centre du Canada français; L'Ouest du Canada français.* 5 vols. Montreal: Beauchemin, 1936-54.

Drummond, W.M., and W. Mackenzie. *Progress and Prospects of Canadian Agriculture.* A study published by the Royal Commission on Canada's Economic Prospects. Ottawa: Queen's Printer, 1957.

Gendreau, Louis. "La politique agricole du Québec sous trois gouvernements (1920-1966)." MA thesis (political science). University of Montreal, 1971. Chapters 1 and 2.

Haythorne, G.V. and L.C. Marsh. *Land and Labour: A Social Survey of Agriculture and the Farm Labour Market in Central Canada.* Toronto: Oxford University Press, 1941. 568 pp.

Kesteman, Jean-Pierre, with Guy Boisclair and Jean-Marc Kirouac. *Histoire du syndicalisme agricole au Québec UCC-UPA, 1924-1984.* Montreal: Boréal Express, 1984. Part 2. Pp. 97-175.

Lemelin, Charles. "Transformations économiques et problèmes agricoles." *Culture,* vol. 19, no. 2 (June 1958), pp. 129-152.

Létourneau, Firmin. *Histoire de l'agriculture (Canada français).* N.p., 1968. pp. 253-317.

Minville, Esdras, ed. *L'agriculture.* Montreal: Fides, 1943. 555 pp.

Rioux, Albert. *Le problème rural.* Appendix 7 of the report of the Royal Commission of Inquiry on Constitutional Problems. N.p., 1955. 166 pp.

Chapter 3

Bolduc, André, Clarence Hogue and Daniel Larouche. *Québec: Un siècle d'électricité.* Second edition. Montreal: Libre Expression, 1984. Chapter 7.

Canada. Dominion Bureau of Statistics. *System of National Accounts: National Income and Expenditure Accounts, the Annual Estimate 1926-56.* 203 pp.

Canada. Royal Commission on Dominion-Provincial Relations (Rowell-Sirois Commission). *Report.* Vol. 1: Canada: 1867-1939. Ottawa: King's Printer, 1940. 259 pp.

Finkel, Alvin. *Business and Social Reform in the Thirties.* Toronto: Lorimer, 1979. 224 pp.

McInnis, Edgar. *Canada: A Political and Social History.* New York: Holt, Rinehart and Winston, 1984. Chapters 18 to 20.

Pelletier, Michel and Yves Vaillancourt. *Les politiques sociales et les travailleurs.* Book II: *Les années 30.* Montreal, 1975. Chapter 3.

Quebec. Royal Commission of Inquiry on Constitutional Problems (Tremblay Commission). *Report.* 4 vols. Quebec City, 1956.
Safarian, A.E. *The Canadian Economy in the Great Depression.* Toronto: McClelland and Stewart, 1970. 258 pp.
Struthers, James. *No Fault of Their Own: Unemployment and the Canadian Welfare State 1914-1941.* Toronto: University of Toronto Press, 1983. 268 pp.

Chapter 4

Blanchard, Raoul. *L'Ouest du Canada français: Montréal et sa région.* Montreal: Beauchemin, 1954. Pp. 297-382.
—*L'Est du Canada français.* Montreal: Beauchemin, 1935. 2 vols.
Copp, Terry. "Montreal's municipal government and the crisis of the 1930s." In *The Usable Urban Past: Planning and Politics in the Modern Canadian City*, edited by A.F.J. Artibise and G.A. Stelter, pp. 112-29. Toronto: Macmillan, 1979.
Minville, Edras, ed. *Montréal économique.* Montreal: Fides and École des hautes études commerciales, 1943. 430 pp.
Nader, George A. *Cities of Canada.* Volume 1: *Theoretical, Historical and Planning Perspectives.* N.p.: Macmillan, 1975. Chapter 7.
Stone, Leroy O. *Urban Development in Canada.* Ottawa: Dominion Bureau of Statistics, 1967. 293 pp.

Chapter 5

Abella, Irving M. *Nationalism, Communism and Canadian Labour.* University of Toronto Press, 1973. Pp. 1-65.
Auger, Geneviève and Raymonde Lamothe. *De la poêle à frire à la ligne de feu.* Montreal: Boréal Express, 1981. 232 pp.
Canada. Royal Commission on Price Spreads. *Report.* Ottawa: Printer to the King, 1935. 506 pp.
CNTU-CEQ. *History of the Labour Movement in Quebec.* Montreal: Black Rose Books, 1986. 299 pp.
Dionne, Bernard. "Les 'unions internationales' et le Conseil des métiers et du travail de Montréal, de 1938 è 1958." Ph.D. thesis (history), University of Quebec at Montreal, 1988.
Dumas, Evelyn. *The Bitter Thirties in Quebec.* Montreal: Black Rose Books, 1975. 151 pp.
Gérin-Lajoie, Jean. *Les métallos 1936-1981.* Montreal: Boréal Express, 1982. Pp. 15-62.
Harvey, Fernand. *Le mouvement ouvrier au Québec.* Montreal: Boréal Express, 1980. Pp. 288-89.
Lévesque, Andrée. *Virage à gauche interdit: Les communistes, les socialistes et leurs ennemis au Québec 1929-1939.* Montreal: Boréal Express, 1984. 186 pp.
Morton, Desmond. *Canada and War.* Toronto: Butterworths, 1981. Pp. 104-49.
Morton, Desmond and Terry Copp. *Working People.* Ottawa: Deneau and Greenberg, 1980. Pp. 139-86.
Pierson, Ruth Roach. *Canadian Women and the Second World War.* Ottawa: Canadian Historical Association, 1983. 31 pp.
Rouillard, Jacques. *Histoire de la CSN, 1921-1981.* Montreal: Boréal Express/CSN, 1981. Pp. 61-164.
—*Histoire du syndicalisme québécois.* Montreal: Boréal Express, 1989. Pp. 153-97.
—"Le militantisme des travailleurs au Québec et en Ontario, niveau de syndicalisation et mouvement de grève." *Revue d'histoire de l'Amérique française*, vol. 37, no. 2 (September 1983), pp. 201-25.
Stacey, C.P. *Arms, Men and Governments: The War Policies of Canada, 1939-1945.* Ottawa: Queen's Printer, 1970. 681 pp.
Thompson, John H. and Allen Seager. *Canada 1922-1939.* Toronto: McClelland and Stewart, 1985. Pp. 350-51.
Webber, Jeremy. "The Malaise of Compulsory Conciliation: Strike Prevention in Canada during World War II." *Labour/Le travail*, no. 15 (1985), pp. 57-88.
Weisbord, Merrily. *The Strangest Dream.* Toronto: Lester & Orpen Dennys, 1983. Pp. 10-121.

Chapter 6

Auger, Geneviève and Raymonde Lamothe. *De la poêle à frire à la ligne de feu*. Montreal: Boréal Express, 1981. 232 pp.

Clavette, Suzanne. "Des bons aux chèques: aide aux chômeurs et crise des années 1930 à Verdun." Master's thesis, University of Quebec at Montreal, 1986. Chapters 3-5.

CNTU-CEQ. *History of the Labour Movement in Quebec*. Montreal: Black Rose Books, 1986. 299pp.

Copp, Terry. "Montreal's Municipal Government and the Crisis of the 1930s." In *The Usable Urban Past: Planning and Politics in the Modern Canadian City*, edited by A.F.J. Artibise and G.A. Stelter, pp. 112-29. Toronto: Macmillan, 1979.

Gagnon, Jean-Louis. *Les apostasies*. Vol. 1. Montreal: La Presse, 1985. Pp. 261-79.

Gravel, Jean-Yves. "Le Québec militaire, 1939-1945". In *Le Québec et la guerre*, edited by Jean-Yves Gravel, pp. 77-108. Montreal: Boréal Express, 1974.

Johnston, Wendy. "Keeping Children in School: The Response of the Montreal Roman Catholic School Commission to the Depression in the 1930s." Canadian Historical Association/Société Historique du Canada, *Historical Papers/Communications Historiques*. (Montreal), 1985, pp. 193-217.

Larivière, Claude. *Crise économique et contrôle social: le cas de Montréal (1929-1937)*. Montreal: Albert Saint-Martin, 1977. Pp. 121-238.

League for Social Reconstruction. *Social Planning for Canada*. Reprint ed. Toronto: University of Toronto Press, 1975. 528 pp.

Marsh, Leonard. *Canadians In and Out of Work*. Toronto: Oxford University Press, 1940. Chapters 13-15.

—*Report on Social Security for Canada*. Reprint ed. Toronto: University of Toronto Press, 1975. 333 pp.

Minville, Esdras. *Labour Legislation and Social Services in the Province of Quebec: A Study Prepared for the Royal Commission on Dominion-Provincial Relations*. Ottawa: King's Printer, 1939. 97 pp.

Vaillancourt, Pelletier, Michel, and Yves *Les politiques sociales et le travailleur*. Book 2: *Les années 1930*. Montreal, 1975. Chapter 3.

Rumilly, Robert. *Histoire de Montréal*. Vol. 4. Montreal: Fides, 1974. Chapters 11-20.

—*La plus riche aumône*. Montreal: Éditions de l'Arbre, 1946. Chapters 7-8.

Sautter, Udo. "Government and Unemployment: The Use of Public Works before the New Deal." *The Journal of American History*, vol. 73, no. 1 (June 1986), pp. 59-86.

Thompson, John H. and Allen Seager. *Canada 1922-1939*. Toronto: McClelland and Stewart, 1985. Pp. 193-302, 350-51.

Vaillancourt, Yves. *L'évolution des politiques sociales au Québec 1940 — 1960*. Montreal: Presses de l'Université de Montréal, 1988. 513 pp.

Chapter 7

Anctil, Pierre and Gary Caldwell, eds. *Juifs et réalités juives au Quéec*. Quebec City: Institut québécois de recherche sur la culture, 1984. Chapters 2 and 5.

Audet, Louis-Philippe. *Histoire de l'enseignement au Québec, 1608-1971*. Vol 2. Montreal: Holt, Rinehart and Winston, 1971. 496 pp.

Charland, Jean-Pierre. *Histoire de l'enseignement technique et professionnel*. Quebec: City: Institut québécois de recherche sur la culture, 1982. 482 pp.

Denault, Bernard and Benoît Lévesque. *Éléments pour une sociologie des communautés religieuses au Québec*. Montreal and Sherbrooke: Presses de l'Université de Montréal, 1975. Pp. 34-108.

Duchesne, Raymond. *La science et le pouvoir au Québec (1920-1965)*. Quebec City: Éditeur officiel, 1978. 126 pp.

Frandrich, René. *L'école primaire supérieure*. Montreal: Éditions Albert Lévesque, 1934. 181 pp.

Frost, Stanley. *McGill University*. Vol. 2. Montreal: McGill-Queen's University Press, 1984. 493 pp.

Galarneau, Claude. *Les collèges classiques au Canada français 1620-1970*. Montreal: Fides, 1987. 287 pp.

Hamelin, Jean and Nicole Gagnon. *Histoire du catholicisme québécois*. Part 3: *Le XXe siècle*. 2 vols. Montreal: Boréal Express, 1984. Vol. 1, p. 504; vol. 2, pp. 11-102.

Johnston, Wendy. "Keeping Children in School: The Response of the Montreal Roman Catholic School Commission to the Depression in the 1930s." Canadian Historical Association/Société Historique du Canada, *Historical Papers/Communications Historiques*. (Montreal), *1985*, pp. 193-217.

Rousseau, Louis. "L'évolution des association volontaires dans les paroisses montréalaises, 1940-1970." Paper given at the Symposium sur le renouveau communautaire. Montreal, 1973. 8 pp.

Thivierge, Nicole. *Écoles ménagères et instituts familiaux*. Quebec City:, Institut québécois de recherche sur la culture, 1982. 475 pp.

Voisine, Nive, André Beaulieu and Jean Hamelin. *Histoire de l'Église catholique au Québec (1608-1970)*. Montreal: Fides, 1971. Pp. 55-79.

Chapter 8

Archibald, Clinton. *Un Québec corporatiste?* Hull: Asticou, 1973. Part 1: "L'Avant-Révolution tranquille," pp. 53-144.

Bélanger, André J. *L'apolitisme des idéologies québécoises: Le grand tournant de 1934-1936*. Quebec City: Presses de l'Université Laval, 1974. 392 pp.

—*Ruptures et constantes—Quatre idéologies au Québec en éclatement*. Montreal: Hurtubise HMH, 197. Chapter 1: "Les idéologies pionnières: la Relève et la JEC." Pp. 13-61.

"Cinquante années de nationalisme positif." Special issue of *L'Action Nationale*, vol. 52, nos. 7-8 (March-April 1963), pp. 641-903.

Comeau, Robert and Bernard Dionne. *Les communistes au Québec 1936-1956*. Montreal: Presses de l'Unité, 1980. Chapter 1. Pp. 1-31.

Dumont, Fernand, Jean Hamelin and Jean-Paul Montminy, eds. *Idéologies au Canada français 1930-1939*. Quebec City: Presses de l'Université Laval, 1978. 361 pp.

—*Idéologies au Canada français 1940-1976*. 3 vols. Quebec City: Presses de l'Université Laval, 1981.

Fournier, Marcel. *Communisme et anticommunisme au Québec (1920-1950)*. Montreal: Albert Saint-Martin, 1979. 165 pp.

Gauvin, Bernard. *Les communistes et la question nationale au Québec*. Montreal: Presses de l'Unité, 1981. Chapters 3 and 4. Pp. 77-128.

Hamelin, Jean and Nicole Gagnon. *Histoire du catholicisme québécois*. Part 3: *Le XXe siècle*. 2 vols. Montreal: Boréal Express, 1984. Vol. 1, pp. 357-451;. vol. 2, pp. 11-108.

League for Social Reconstruction. *Social Planning for Canada*. 1935. Reprint ed. Toronto: University of Toronto Press, 1975. 528 pp.

Lévesque, Andrée. *Virage à gauche interdit: Les communistes, les socialistes et leurs ennemis au Québec 1929-1939*. Montreal: Boréal Express, 1984. 186 pp.

Neatby, Blair. *The Politics of Chaos: Canada in the Thirties*. Toronto: Macmillan, 1972. 196 pp.

Pelletier, Michel and Yves Vaillancourt. *Les politiques sociales et les travailleurs*. Book 2: "Les années 30." Montreal, 1975. Chapter 2: "Le contexte politique et idéologique." Pp. 51-174.

Saint-Germain, Yves. "La société québécoise et la vie économique: quelques échos de la décennie de la grande ambivalence 1920-1929". In *Économie québécoise*, pp. 433-64. Montreal: Presses de l'Université du Québec, 1969.

Chapter 9

Beck, J.M. *Pendulum of Power: Canada's Federal Elections*. Scarborough, Ont.: Prentice-Hall, 1968. 442 pp.

Black, Conrad. *Duplessis*. Toronto: McClelland and Stewart, 1977. 743 pp.

Canada. Royal Commission on Dominion-Provincial Relations (Rowell-Sirois Commission). *Report*. Vol. 1. Ottawa: King's Printer, 1940. 261 pp.

Dupont, Antonin. *Les relations entre l'Église et l'État sous Louis-Alexandre Taschereau, 1920-1936*. Montreal: Guérin, 1972. 366 pp.

Durocher, René. "Le Fasciste canadien, 1935-1938." In *Idéologies au Canada français 1930-1939*, edited by Fernand Dumont, Jean Hamelin and J.-P. Montminy, pp. 257-71. Quebec City: Presses de l'Université Laval, 1978.

Hamelin, Jean, Jean Letarte and Marcel Hamelin. "Les élections provinciales dans le Québec 1867-1956." Special issue of *Cahiers de géographie de Québec*, vol. 4, no. 7 (October 1959-March 1960).

Lamontagne, Maurice. *Le fédéralisme canadien*. Quebec City: Presses de l'Université Laval, 1954. 298 pp.

LaTerreur, Marc. *Les tribulations des conservateurs au Québec, de Bennett à Diefenbaker*. Quebec City: Presses de l'Université Laval, 1973. 265 pp.

Lévesque, Andrée. *Virage à gauche interdit: Les communistes, les socialistes et leurs ennemis au Québec 1929-1939*. Montreal: Boréal Express, 1984. 186 pp.

Neatby, H. Blair. *William Lyon Mackenzie King*. 2 vols. Toronto: University of Toronto Press, 1963.

Quebec. Royal Commission of Inquiry on Constitutional Problems (Tremblay Commission). *Report*. 4 vols. Quebec City, 1956.

Quinn, Herbert F. *The Union Nationale*. 1963. Second edition. Toronto: University of Toronto Press, 1977. 342 pp.

Rumilly, Robert. *Maurice Duplessis et son temps*. Vol 1: *1890-1944* Montreal: Fides, 1973. Vol. 1.

Vigod, Bernard L. *Quebec before Duplessis: The Political Career of Louis-Alexandre Taschereau*. Montreal: McGill-Queen's University Press, 1986. 312 pp.

Young, Walter D. *The Anatomy of a Party: The National CCF, 1932-1961*. Toronto: University of Toronto Press, 1969. 328 pp.

Chapter 10

Auger, Geneviève and Raymonde Lamothe. *De la poêle à frire à la ligne de feu*. Montreal: Boréal Express, 1981. 232 pp.

Beck, J.M. *Pendulum of Power: Canada's Federal Elections*. Scarborough, Ont.: Prentice-Hall, 1968. 442 pp.

Black, Conrad. *Duplessis*. Toronto: McClelland and Stewart, 1977. 743 pp.

Comeau, Paul-André. *Le Bloc populaire 1942-1948*. Montreal: Québec/Amerique, 1982. 478 pp.

Genest, Jean-Guy. "La vie et l'oeuvre d'Adélard Godbout, 1892-1956." Ph.D. thesis (history), Laval University, Quebec City, 1971.

Hamelin, Jean, Jean Letarte and Marcel Hamelin. "Les élections provinciales dans le Québec 1867-1956." Special issue of *Cahiers de géographie de Québec*, vol. 4, no. 7 (October 1959-March 1960).

Laurendeau, André. *La crise de la conscription, 1942*. Montreal: Éditions du Jour, 1962. 157 pp.

Morton, Desmond. *A Military History of Canada*. Edmonton: Hurtig, 1985. 305 pp.

Pierson, Ruth Roach. *"They're Still Women After All!": The Second World War and Canadian Womanhood*. Toronto:, McClelland and Stewart, 1986. 301 pp.

Quinn, Herbert F. *The Union Nationale*. 1963. Second edition. Toronto: University of Toronto Press, 1977. 342 pp.

Rumilly, Robert. *Maurice Duplessis et son temps*. Vol. 1. *1890-1944*. Montreal: Fides, 1973.

Stacey, C.P. *Arms, Men and Governments: The War Policies of Canada, 1939-45*. Ottawa: Queen's Printer, 1970. 681 pp.

Chapter 11

Canada. Royal Commission on Dominion-Provincial Relations (Rowell-Sirois Commission). *Report*. Vol. 1. Ottawa: King's Printer, 1940. 261 pp.

"Cinquante années de nationalisme positif." Special issue of *L'Action nationale*, vol. 52, nos. 7-8 (March-April 1963), pp. 641-903.

Durocher, René. "Maurice Duplessis et sa conception de l'autonomie provinciale au debut de sa carrière politique." *Revue d'histoire de l'Amèrique française*, vol. 23, no. 1 (June 1969), pp. 13-34.

Genest, Jean-Guy. "La vie et l'oeuvre d'Adèlard Godbout, 1892-1956." Ph.D. thesis (history), Laval University, Quebec City, 1971.

Lamontagne, Maurice. *Le fédéralisme canadien*. Quebec City: Presses de l'Université Laval, 1954. 298 pp.

Quebec. Royal Commission of Inquiry on Constitutional Problems (Tremblay Commission). *Report*. 4 vols. Quebec City, 1956.

Rémillard, Gil. *Le federalisme canadien.* Montreal: Québec/Amerique, 1980. 553 pp.

Sabourin, Louis. *Le système politique au Canada: Institutions fédérales et québècoises.* Ottawa: Éditions de l'Université d'Ottawa, 1970. 507 pp.

Trudeau, Pierre Elliott. *Federalism and the French Canadians.* Toronto: Macmillan, 1968. 212 pp.

Chapter 12

Beaulieu, André and Jean Hamelin. "Aperçu du journalisme québécois d'expression française." *Recherches sociographiques,* vol. 7, no. 3 (September-December 1966), pp. 305-48.

Canada. Royal Commission on Broadcasting (Fowler Commission). *Report.* Ottawa: Queen's Printer, 1957.

Dumont, Fernand. *Le lieu de l'homme: la culture comme distance et mémoire.* Montreal: HMH, 1969. 233 pp.

Dupont, Jean-Claude. *Contes de bûcherons.* Montreal: Quinze, 1976. 215 pp.

Hébert, Chantal. *Le burlesque au Québec: un divertissement populaire.* Montreal: Hurtubise HMH, 1981. 302 pp.

Houle, Michel and Alain Julien. *Dictionnaire du cinéma québécois.* Montreal: Fides, 1978. 366 pp.

Lamonde, Yvan and Pierre-François Hébert. *Le cinéma au Québec: essai de statistique historique (1896 à nos jours).* Quebec City: Institut québécois de recherche sur la culture, 1981. 478 pp.

Laurence, Gérard. "Dans un Québec réticent, la radio d'un pays directement impliqué." In *La guerre des ondes: histoire des radios de langue française pendant la Deuxième Guerre mondiale,* edited by Hélène Eck, pp. 283-366. Montreal: Hurtubise HMH, 1985.

Lavoie, Elzéar. "L'évolution de la radio au Canada français avant 1940." *Recherches sociographiques,* vol. 12, no. 1 (January-April 1971), pp. 17-49.

—"La constitution d'une modernité culturelle populaire dans les médias au Québec (1895-1950)." In *L'avènement de la modernité culturelle au Québec,* edited by Yvan Lamonde and Esther Trépanier, pp. 253-98. Quebec City: Institut québécois de recherche sur la culture, 1986.

Pagé, Pierre. *Répertoire des oeuvres de la littérature radiophonique québécoise 1930-1970.* Montreal: Fides, 1975. 826 pp.

Kallmann, Helmut, Gilles Potvin and Kenneth Winters. *Encyclopedia of Music in Canada.* Toronto: University of Toronto Press, 1981. 1076 pp.

Proulx, Gilles. *L'aventure de la radio au Québec.* Montreal: Éditions La Presse, 1979. 143 pp.

Veronneau, Pierre. *Histoire du cinéma au Québec.* Vol. 1: *Le succès est au film parlant francais.* Montreal: Cinémathèque québécoise, 1979. 164 pp.

Chapter 13

Archives des lettres canadiennes. Vol. 5: *Le Théâtre canadien-français.* Montreal: Fides, 1976. Pp. 169-318.

Blais, Jacques. *De l'ordre et de l'aventure: la poésie au Québec de 1934 à 1944.* Quebec City: Presses de l'Université Laval, 1975. 410 pp.

Gagnon, François–Marc. "La peinture des années trente au Québec." *Annales d'histoire de l'art canadien/The Journal of Canadian Art History,* vol. 3, nos. 1-2 (Fall 1976), pp. 2-20.

Giguère, Richard. *Exil, révolte et dissidence: étude comparée des poésies québécoise et canadienne, 1925-1955.* Quebec City: Presses de l'Université Laval, 1984. 283 pp.

Hill, Charles C. *Canadian Painting in the Thirties.* Ottawa: National Gallery of Canada, 1975. 223 pp.

Kallman, Helmut, Gilles Potvin and Kenneth Winters. *Encyclopedia of Music in Canada.* Toronto: University of Toronto Press, 1981. 1076 pp.

Klinck, Carl Frederick, ed. *Literary History in Canada: Canadian Literature in English.* Toronto: University of Toronto Press, 1965. 945 pp.

Lamonde, Yvan, ed., *Imprimé au Québec: aspects historiques (18e-20e siècles).* Quebec City: Institut québécois de recherche sur la culture, 1981.

— and Esther Trépanier, eds. *L'avènement de la modernité culturelle au Québec* . Quebec City: Institut québécois de recherche sur la culture, 1986. 313 pp.

Lemire, Maurice, ed. *Dictionnaire des oeuvres littéraires au Québec.* Vols. 2 (1900 to 1939) and 3 (1940 to 1959). Montreal: Fides, 1980-82.

Marcotte, Gilles. "Les années trente: de Monsigneur Camille à *La Relève." Voix et images*, vol. 5, no. 3 (Spring 1980), pp. 515-24.

Ostiguy, Jean-René. *Modernism in Quebec Art, 1916-1946.* Ottawa: National Gallery of Canada, 1982. 167 pp.

Robert, Guy. *La peinture au Québec depuis ses origines.* Sainte-Adèle, Quebec: Iconia, 1978. Chapters 2 and 3.

Trépanier, Esther. "Crise économique/crise artistique: parallèle ou convergence?" Association for Canadian Studies/Association des études canadiennes, *Canadian Issues/Thèmes canadiens*, no. 8 (1987), pp. 177-92.

—*Peintres juifs et modernité/Jewish Painters and Modernity, Montreal 1930-1945.* Montreal: Saidye Bronfman Centre, 1987. 181 pp.

Chapter 14

Abella, Irving and Harold Troper. *None Is Too Many: Canada and the Jews of Europe, 1943-1948.* Toronto: Lester & Orpen Dennys, 1982. 336 pp.

Boily, Robert et al. *Données sur le Québec.* Montreal: Presses de l'Université de Montréal, 1974. 270 pp.

Charbonneau, Hubert. *La population du Québec: études rétrospectives.* Montreal: Boréal Express, 1973. 110 pp.

Desrosiers, Denise et al. *La migration au Québec: synthèse et bilan bibliographique.* Quebec City: Government of Quebec (Department of Immigration), 1978. 106 pp.

Dufour, Desmond and Yves Péron. *Vingt ans de mortalité au Québec: les causes de décès, 1951-1971.* Montreal: Presses de l'Université de Montréal, 1979. 204 pp.

Gauthier, Hervé. *Évolution démographique du Québec.* Quebec City Office de planification et développement du Québec, 1977. 168 pp.

Henripin, Jacques. *Trends and Factors of Fertility in Canada.* Ottawa: Statistics Canada, 1972. 421 pp.

Kalbach, Warren E. *The Effect of Immigration on Population.* Ottawa: Manpower and Immigration, 1974. 93 pp.

— and Wayne McVey. *The Demographic Basis of Canadian Society.* Second edition. Toronto: McGraw-Hill Ryerson, 1979. 402 pp.

Québec. Bureau de la statistique. *Démographie québécoise: passé, présent, perspectives.* Quebec City: Éditeur officiel, 1983. 457 pp.

Chapter 15

Aitken, Hugh G.J. et al. *The American Economic Impact on Canada.* Durham, N.C.: Duke University Press, 1959. 176 pp.

Bonin, Bernard. *L'investissment étranger à long terme au Canada: Ses caractères et ses effets sur l'économie canadienne.* Montreal: École des hautes études commerciales, 1967. 462 pp.

Clement, Wallace. *The Canadian Corporate Elite. An Analysis of Economic Power.* Toronto: McClelland and Stewart, 1975. 478 pp.

— *Continental Corporate Power. Economic Linkages Between Canada and the United States.* Toronto: McClelland and Stewart, 1977. 408 pp.

Cuff, R.D. and J.L. Granatstein. *American Dollars—Canadian Prosperity: Canadian-American Economic Relations 1945-1950.* Toronto: Samuel-Stevens, 1978. 286 pp.

Levitt, Kari. *Silent Surrender: The Multinational Corporation in Canada.* Toronto: Macmillan, 1970. 185 pp.

Porter, John. "Concentration of Economic Power and the Economic Elite in Canada." *Canadian Journal of Economics and Political Science*, vol. 22, no. 2 (May 1956), pp. 199-220.

— *The Vertical Mosaic — An Analysis of Social Class and Power in Canada.* Toronto: University of Toronto Press, 1965. Chapter 8.

Raynauld, André. *La propriété des entreprises au Québec: Les années 60.* Montreal: Presses de l'Université de Montréal, 1974. 160 pp.

Chapter 16

Boismenu, Gérard. *Le duplessisme: Politique économique et rapports de force, 1944-1960.* Montreal: Presses de l'Université de Montréal, 1981. 432 pp.

Bolduc, André, Clarence Hogue and Daniel Larouche. *Québec: Un siècle d'électricité.* Montreal: Libre Expression, 1964. Chapter 16.

Lebel, Gilles. *Horizon 1980: Une étude sur l'évolution de l'économie du Québec de 1946 à 1968 et sur ses perspectives d'avenir.* Quebec City: Department of Industry and Commerce, 1970. 263 pp.

Le Bourdais, D.M. *Metals and Men. The Story of Canadian Mining.* Toronto: McClelland and Stewart, 1957. Chapter 18.

Raynauld, André. *Croissance et structure économiques de la province de Québec.* Quebec: Department of Industry and Commerce, 1961. 657 pp.

Chapter 17

Lebel, Gilles. *Horizon 1980. Une étude sur l'évolution de l'économie du Québec de 1946 à 1968 et sur ses perspectives d'avenir.* Quebec City: Government of Quebec, 1970. 263 pp.

Main, J.R.K. "An Outline of the Development of Civil Air Transport in Canada." *Canada Year Book,* 1967, pp. 838-43.

La radiodiffusion au Canada depuis ses origines jusqu'à nos jours. Montreal: Canadian Institute for Adult Education, 1964. 262 pp.

Neufeld, E.P. *The Financial System of Canada.* Toronto: Macmillan, 1972. 645 pp.

Chapter 18

Blais, André. "La politique agricole du gouvernement québécois, 1952-1973." *Recherches sociographiques,* vol. 20, no. 2 (1979), pp. 173-203.

Dagenais, Pierre. "Le mythe de la vocation agricole du Québec." *Cahiers de géographie du Québec,* no. 6 (April-September 1959), pp. 193-201.

Fortin, Gérald. *La fin d'un règne.* Montreal: Hurtubise HMH, 1971. Pp. 17-55.

Gendreau, Louis. "La politique agricole du Québec sous trois gouvernements (1920-1966)." MA thesis (political science), University of Montreal, 1971. 210 pp.

Kesteman, Jean-Pierre, with Guy Boisclair and Jean-Marc Kirouac. *Histoire du syndicalisme agricole au Québec UCC-UPA, 1924-1984.* Montreal: Boréal Express, 1984. Pp. 97-208.

Keyfitz, Nathan. "L'exode rural dans la province de Québec, 1951-1961." *Recherches sociographiques,* vol. 3, no. 3 (1962), pp. 303-16.

Lavigne, Benoît. "Changements récents dans la structure de notre industrie agricole." *Agriculture,* vol. 15, no. 2 (March-April 1938), pp. 53-60, 64.

Lebel, Gilles. *Horizon 1980: Une étude sur l'évolution de l'économie de Québec de 1946 à 1968 et sur ses perspectived d'avenir.* Québec, Department of Industry and Commerce, *1970. 263 pp.*

Lemelin, Charles. "Social Impact of Industrialization on Agriculture in the Province of Quebec." *Culture,* vol. 14, no. 1 (March 1953), pp. 34-46.

— "Transformations économiques et problèmes agricoles." *Culture,* vol. 19, no. 2 (June 1958), pp. 129-52.

Perron, Normand. "Genèse des activités laitières au Québec, 1850-1960." In *Agriculture et colonisation au Québec,* edited by Normand Séguin, pp. 113-40. Montreal: Boréal Express, 1980.

Quebec. Commission royale d'enquête sur l'agriculture au Québec. *L'évolution de l'agriculture et le développement économique du Québec, 1946-1976.* Quebec City: Government of Quebec, 1967. 159 pp.

Quebec. Comité d'enquête pour la protection des agriculteurs est des consommateurs. *Rapport* (Héon Report). Quebec City, 1955. 455 pp.

Roy, Jean-Louis. *La marche des Québécois: Le temps des ruptures (1945-1960).* Montreal: Leméac, 1976. Chapter 4.

Séguin, Normand. "L'histoire de l'agriculture et de la colonisation au Québec depuis 1850." In *Agriculture et colonisation au Québec, 1850-1960,* edited by Normand Séguin, pp. 9-37. Montreal: Boréal Express, 1980.

Trépanier, René. "Modern Trends in Agriculture, a Glance at Rural Quebec/Coup d'oeil sur le Québec agricole et son orientation." *Canadian Geographic Journal*, vol. 15, no. 1 (1967), pp. 119-30.

Wampach, Jean-Pierre. "Les tendances de la productivité totale dans l'agriculture: Canada, Ontario, Québec, 1926-1964." *Canadian Journal of Agricultural Economics*, vol. 15, no. 1 (1967), pp. 119-30.

Chapter 19

Blais, André. "La politique agricole du gouvernement québécois, 1952-1973." *Recherches sociographiques*, vol. 20, no. 2 (May-August 1979), pp. 173-203.

Boismenu, Gérard. *Le duplessisme: Politique économique et rapports de force, 1944-1960*. Montreal: Presses de l'Université de Montréal, 1981. 432 pp.

Bothwell, Robert, Ian Drummond and John English. *Canada Since 1945: Power, Politics and Provincialism*. Toronto: University of Toronto Press, 1981. 489 pp.

Bourque, Gilles and Jules Duchastel. *Restons traditionnels et progressifs: Pour une nouvelle analyse du discours politique: Le cas du régime Duplessis au Québec*. Montreal: Boréal Express, 1988. 399 pp.

Brewis, T.N. et al. *Canadian Economic Policy*. Revised edition. Toronto: Macmillan, 1965. 463 pp.

Cuff, R.D. and J.L. Granatstein. *American Dollars—Canadian Prosperity: Canadian-American Economic Relations 1945-1950*. Toronto: Samuel-Stevens, 1978. 286 pp.

Chapter 20

Beauregard, Ludger, ed. *Montréal, guide d'excursions/Field Guide*. Montreal: Presses de l'Université de Montréal, 1972. 197 pp.

Choko, Marc H., Jean-Pierre Collin and Annick Germain. "Le logement et les enjeux de la transformation de l'espace urbain: Montréal, 1940-1960." *Urban History Review/Revue d'histoire urbaine*, vol. 15, no. 2 (October 1986).

Collin, Jean-Pierre. *La cité coopérative canadienne-française: Saint-Léonard-de-Port-Maurice, 1955-1963*. Montreal and Quebec City: INRS-Urbanisation and Presses de l'Université du Québec, 1986. 184 pp.

Couillard, Robert. *Marché immobilier et création d'un centre-ville: le cas de Québec*. "EZOP-Québec," Book 2. Quebec City, 1972. 251 pp.

Divay, Gérard and Jean-Pierre Collin. *La communauté urbaine de Montréal: de la ville centrale à l'île centrale*. Montreal: INRS-Urbanisation, 1977. Pp. 38-47.

Divay, Gérard and Louise Richard. *L'aide gouvernementale au logement et sa distribution sociale*. Montreal: INRS-Urbanisation, 1981. 95 pp.

Kaplan, Harold. *Reform, Planning and City Politics: Montreal, Winnipeg, Toronto*. Toronto: University of Toronto Press, 1982. Chapter 7.

Mathews, Georges. *Évolution générale du marché du logement de la région de Montréal de 1951 à 1976: données synthétiques sur une réussite méconnue*. Montreal: INRS-Urbanisation, 1980. 69 pp.

Trotier, Louis. "Les sites industriels dans l'agglomération québécoise." *Cahiers de géographie de Québec*, no. 10 (April-September 1961), pp. 245-55.

Chapter 21

Bédard, Roger, ed. *L'essor économique du Québec*. Montreal: Beauchemin, 1969. 524 pp.

Behiels, Michael D. *Prelude to Quebec's Quiet Revolution: Liberalism versus Neo-Nationalism, 1945-1960*. Montreal: McGill-Queen's University Press, 1985. Chapter 1.

Bellavance, Claude. "Patronat et entreprise au XXe siècle: l'exemple mauricien." *Revue d'histoire de l'Amérique française*, vol. 38, no. 2 (Fall 1984), pp. 181-201.

Boismenu, Gérard. *Le duplessisme: Politique économique et rapports de force, 1944-1960*. Montreal: Presses de l'Université de Montréal, 1981. 432 pp.

Bouchard, Gérard, Yves Otis and France Markovski. "Les notables du Saguenay au 20e siècle à travers deux corpus biographiques." *Revue d'histoire de l'Amérique française*, vol. 39, no. 1 (Summer 1985), pp. 3-23.

Durocher, René and Paul-André Linteau, eds. *Le retard du Québec et l'infériorité économique des Canadiens français*. Montreal: Boréal Express, 1971. 127 pp.

Falardeau, Jean-Charles. "Des élites traditionnels aux élites nouvelles." *Recherches sociographiques*, vol. 7, no. 2 (January-August 1966), pp. 131-45.

Galarneau, Claude. *Les collèges classiques au Canada français.* Montreal: Fides, 1978. 287 pp.

"Les classes sociales au Canada français." Special issue of *Recherches sociographiques,* vol. 6, no. 1 (January-April 1965).

Ouellet, Fernand. *Histoire de la Chambre de commerce de Québec.* Quebec City: Faculty of Commerce of Laval University, n.d. 105 pp.

Porter, John. "Concentration of Economic Power and the Economic Elite in Canada." *Canadian Journal of Economics and Political Science,* vol. 22, no. 2 (May 1956), pp. 199-220.

— *The Vertical Mosaic: An Analysis of Social Class and Power in Canada.* Toronto: University of Toronto Press, 1965. 626 pp.

Raynauld, André. *La propriété des entreprises au Québec: Les années 60.* Montreal: Presses de l'Université de Montréal, 1974. 160 pp.

Rioux, Marcel and Yves Martin, eds. *La société canadienne-française.* Montreal: Hurtubise HMH, 1971. 404 pp.

Rocher, Guy. "Multiplication des élites et changement social au Canada français." *Revue de l'Institut de sociologie,* 1968-1, pp. 79-94.

Roy, Jean-Louis. *La marche des Québécois: Le temps des ruptures (1945-1960).* Montreal: Léméac, 1976. 383 pp.

Chapter 22

Abella, Irving M. *Nationalism, Communism and Canadian Labour.* Toronto: University of Toronto Press, 1973. Chapters 5 and 10.

Barry, Francine. *Le travail de la femme au Québec: L'évolution de 1940 à 1970.* Montreal: Presses de l'Université du Québec, 1977. 80 pp.

Boismenu, Gérard. *Le duplessisme: Politique économique et rapports de force, 1944-1960.* Montreal: Presses de l'Université de Montréal, 1981. 432 pp.

CNTU-CEQ. *History of the Labour Movement in Quebec.* Montreal: Black Rose Books, 1986. 299 pp.

Cousineau, Jacques. *L'Église d'ici et le social, 1940-1960.* Montreal: Bellarmin, 1982. Chapter 3.

Gagnon, Mona-Josée. "Les femmes dans le mouvement syndical québécois." In *Travailleuses et féministes: Les femmes dans la société québécoise,* edited by Marie Lavigne and Yolande Pinard, pp. 139-60. Montreal: Boréal Express, 1983.

Gérin-Lajoie, Jean. *Les Métallos, 1936-1981.* Montreal: Boréal Express, 1982. Chapter 3.

Harvey, Fernand, ed. *Le mouvement ouvrier au Québec.* Montreal: Boréal Express, 1980. Chapters 6 and 9 and appendices.

Lebel, Gilles. *Horizon 1980: Une étude sur l'évolution de l'économie du Quéébec de 1946 à 1968 et sur ses perspectives d'avenir.* Quebec City: Department of Industry and Commerce, 1970. Chapters 3 and 5 and appendices.

Morton, Desmond and Terry Copp. *Working People.* Ottawa: Deneau and Greenberg, 1980. Pp. 187-238.

Palmer, Bryan D. *Working-Class Experience.* Toronto: Butterworths, 1983. Chapter 6.

Rouillard, Jacques. *Histoire de la CSN, 1921-1981.* Montreal: Boréal Express, 1981. Pp. 166-213.

— *Histoire du syndicalisme québécois.* Montreal: Boréal Express, 1989. Pp. 199-286.

— "Le militantisme des travailleurs au Québec et en Ontario, niveau de syndicalisation et mouvement de grève (1900-1980)." *Revue d'histoire de l'Amérique française,* vol. 37, no. 2 (September 1983), pp. 201-25.

— "Mutations de la Confédération des travailleurs catholiques du Canada (1940-1960)." *Revue d'histoire de l'Amérique française,* vol. 34, no. 3 (December 1980), pp. 377-405.

Roy, Jean-Louis. *La marche des Québécois: Le temps des ruptures (1945-1960).* Montreal: Leméac, 1976. Pp. 87-161.

Rumilly, Robert. *Quinze années de réalisations.* Montreal, 1956. Pp. 41-72.

Trudeau, Pierre Elliott, ed. *The Asbestos Strike.* Toronto: James Lewis and Samuel, 1974. 382 pp.

Chapter 23

Choko, Marc, Jean-Pierre Collin and Anick Germain. "Le logement et les enjeux de l'espace urbaine: Montréal, 1940-1960." *Urban History Review/Revue d'histoire urbaine*, vol. 15, no. 2 (October 1986), pp. 127-36; no. 3 (February 1987), pp. 243-53.

Guest, Dennis. *The Emergence of Social Security in Canada*. Vancouver: University of British Columbia Press, 1980. 257 pp.

Lebel, Gilles. *Horizon 1980: Une étude sur l'évolution de l'économie du Québec de 1946 à 1968 et sur ses perspectives d'avenir.* Quebec, Department of Industry and Commerce, 1970. 263 pp.

Levasseur, Roger. *Loisir et culture au Québec.* Montreal: Boréal Express, 1982. Chapter 3.

Quebec. Study Committee on Public Assistance. *Report* (Boucher Report). Quebec City Government of Quebec, 1963. 230 pp.

Roy, Jean-Louis. *La marche des Québécois: Le temps des ruptures (1945-1960).* Montreal: Leméac, 1976. 383 pp.

Saint-Germain, Maurice. *Une économie à libérer: Le Québec analysé dans ses structures économiques.* Montreal: Presses de l'Université de Montréal, 1973. 471 pp.

Tremblay, Marc-Adélard and Gérald Fortin. *Les comportements économiques de la famille salariée du Québec: Une étude des conditions de vie, des besoins et des aspirations de la famille canadienne-française d'aujourd'hui.* Quebec City: Presses de l'Université Laval, 1964. 405 pp.

Vaillancourt, Yves. *L'évolution des politiques sociales au Québec, 1940-1960.* Montreal: Presses de l'Université de Montréal, 1988. 513 pp.

Chapter 24

Anctil, Pierre and Gary Caldwell, eds. *Juifs et réalités juives au Québec.* Quebec City: Institut québécois de recherche sur la culture, 1984. Chapters 2 and 5.

Audet, Louis-Philippe. *Histoire de l'enseignement au Québec.* Vol. 2. Montreal: Holt, Rinehart and Winston, 1971. 496 pp.

— "Les cadres scolaires." In *Structures sociales du Canada français*, edited by Guy Sylvestre, pp. 29-66. Quebec City and Toronto: Presses de l'Université Laval and University of Toronto Press, 1966.

Canada. Royal Commission on National Development in the Arts, Letters and Sciences (Massey Commission). *Report, 1949-1951.* Ottawa: Printer to the King, 1951. 517 pp.

Charland, Jean-Pierre. *Histoire de l'enseignement technique et professionnel, 1867-1982.* Quebec City: Institut québécois de recherche sur la culture, 1982. Pp. 223-338.

Conférence provinciale sur l'éducation. *L'éducation au Québec face aux problèmes contemporains.* Saint-Hyacinthe: Éditions Alerte, 1958. 180 pp.

Cousineau, Jacques. *L'église d'ici et le social, 1940-1960.* Montréal: Bellarmin, 1982. Pp. 19-128.

Dandurand, Pierre and Marcel Fournier. "Développement de l'enseignement supérieur, classes sociales et luttes nationales au Québec." *Sociologies et sociétés*, vol. 12, no. 1 (April 1980), pp. 101-32.

Denault, Bernard and Benoît Lévesque. *Éléments pour une sociologie des communautés religieuses au Québec.* Montreal: Presses de l'Université de Montréal, 1975. Pp. 18-117.

Desbiens, Jean-Paul. *The Impertinences of Brother Anonymous.* Montreal: Harvest House, 1962. 126 pp.

Dion, Gérard and Louis O'Neill. *Le chrétien et les élections.* Montreal: Éditions de l'Homme, 1960. 123 pp.

Dionne, Pierre. "Une analyse historique de la Corporation des enseignants du Québec (1936-1968)." Master's thesis (industrial relations), Laval Univesrsity, Québec City: 1969. 260 pp.

Duchesne, Raymond. *La science et le pouvoir au Québec (1920-1965).* Quebec City:, Éditeur officiel, 1978. 126 pp.

Galarneau, Claude. *Les collèges classiques au Canada français.* Montreal: Fides, 1978. 287 pp.

Gow, James Iain. *Histoire de l'administration publique québécoise 1867-1970*. Montreal and Toronto: Presses de l'Université de Montréal and Institute of Public Administration of Canada, 1986. Pp. 248-57.

Gutwirth, Jacques. "Hassidim et judaïcité à Montréal." *Recherches sociographiques*, vol. 14, no. 3 (1973), pp. 291-325.

Hamelin, Jean. *Histoire du catholicisme québécois: Le XXe siècle*. Vol. 2: *De 1940 à nos jours*. Montreal: Boréal Express, 1984. Pp. 11-207.

Hamelin, Louis-Edmond. "Évolution numérique séculaire du clergé catholique dans le Québec." *Recherches sociographiques*, vol. 2, no. 2 (April-June 1961), pp. 189-241.

Lasry, Jean-Claude M. "Une diaspora francophone au Québec: Les juifs sépharades." *Questions de culture*, no. 2 (1982), pp. 113-35.

Mair, Nathan H. "The Protestant Churches." In *The English of Quebec: From Majority to Minority Status*, edited by Gary Caldwell and Eric Waddell, pp. 219-32. Quebec City: Institut québécois de recherche sur la culture, 1982.

Quebec. Royal Commission of Inquiry on Constitutional Problems (Tremblay Commission). *Report*. 4 Vols. Quebec City, 1956.

Rousseau, Louis. "L'évolution des associations volontaires dans les paroisses montréalaises, 1940-1970." Paper given at the Symposium sur le renouveau communautaire. Montreal, 1973. 8 pp.

Roy, Jean-Louis. *La marche des Québécois: Le temps des ruptures (1945-1960)*. Montreal: Leméac, 1976. pp. 245-358.

Tremblay, Arthur. *Contributions à l'étude des problèmes et des besoins de l'enseignement dans le province de Québec*. Appendix 4 to the Tremblay Report, 1955. 406 pp.

Vigeant-Galley, Paulette. *Les enseignants et le pouvoir: Histoire de l'Alliance des professeurs de Montréal: les luttes syndicales et le développement social (1952-1958)*. N.p.: CEQ and APM, 1981. 128 pp.

Voisine, Nive, André Beaulieu and Jean Hamelin. *Histoire de l'Église catholique au Québec (1608-1970)*. Montreal: Fides, 1971. Pp. 73-85.

Chapter 25

Behiels, Michael. *Prelude to Quebec's Quiet Revolution: Liberalism versus Neo-Nationalism, 1945-1960*. Montreal: McGill-Queen's University Press, 1985. 366 pp.

Bélanger, André-J. *Ruptures et constantes: Quatre idéologies du Québec en éclatement*. Montreal: Hurtubise HMH, 1977. Chapter 2.

Bourque, Gilles and Jules Duchastel. *Restons traditionnels et progressifs: Pour une analyse du discours politique: Le cas du régime Duplessis au Québec*. Montreal: Boréal Express, 1988. 399 pp.

Brunet, Michel. "Trois dominantes de la pensée canadienne-française, l'agriculture, l'anti-étatisme et le messianisme." In *La présence anglaise et les Canadiens*, pp.112-66 Montreal: Beauchemin, 1958.

Comeau, Robert et Bernard Dionne. *Les communistes au Québec 1936-1956*. Montreal: Presses de l'unité, 1980. Chapter 2.

Dumont, Fernand, Jean Hamelin and Jean-Paul Montminy, eds. *Idéologies au Canada français 1940-1976*. 3 vols. Quebec City: Presses de l'Université Laval, 1981.

Durand, Gilles. "La pensée socio-économique d'André Laurendeau." In *Économie québécoise*, pp.485-95. Montreal: Cahiers de l'Université du Québec, 1969.

Léonard, Jean-François, ed. *Georges-Émile Lapalme*. Sillery: Presses de l'Université du Québec, 1988. 297 pp.

McRoberts, Kenneth and Dale Posgate. *Quebec: Social Change and Political Crisis*. Toronto: McClelland and Stewart, 1976. 216 pp. Chapter 5.

Rioux, Marcel. "Sur l'évolution des idéologies au Québec." *Revue de l'Institut de sociologie*, no. 1 (1968), pp. 95-124.

Roy, Jean-Louis. *La marche des Québécois: Le temps des ruptures (1945-1960)*. Montreal: Leméac, 1976. 383 pp.

Trudeau, Pierre Elliott. "The Province of Quebec at the Time of the Strike." In *The Asbestos Strike.*, Toronto: James Lewis & Samuel, 1974, pp.1-81.

Chapter 26

Beck, J.M. *Pendulum of Power: Canada's Federal Elections*. Scarborough, Ont.: Prentice-Hall, 1968. 442 pp.

Bernard, André and Denis Laforte. *La législation électorale au Québec 1790-1967*. Montreal: Éditions Sainte-Marie, 1969. 197 pp.

Bibeau, Gilles. *Les bérets blancs*. Montreal: Parti pris, 1976. 187 pp.

Black, Conrad. *Duplessis*. Toronto: McClelland and Stewart, 1977. 743 pp.

Canada. Royal Commission on Government Organization (Glassco Commission). *Reports*. Vol. 1. Ottawa: Queen's Printer, 1962.

Cardinal, Mario, Vincent Lemieux and Florian Sauvageau. *Si l'Union nationale m'était contée*. Montreal: Boréal Express, 1978. 348 pp.

Comeau, Paul-André. *Le Bloc populaire canadien 1942-1948*. Montreal: Québec/Amérique, 1982. 478 pp.

Gow, James Iain. *Histoire de l'administration publique québécoise 1867-1970*. Montreal and Toronto: Presse de l'Université de Montréal and Institute of Public Administration of Canada, 1986. Chapters 6 and 7.

Hamelin, Jean, Jean Letarte and Marcel Hamelin. "Les élections provinciales dans le Québec, 1867-1956." Special issue of *Cahiers de géographie du Québec*, vol. 4, no. 7 (October 1959-March 1960).

Lapalme, Georges-Émile. *Mémoires*. 3 vols. Montreal: Leméac, 1969-73.

Lemieux, Vincent. *Le quotient politique vrai: Le vote provincial et fédéral au Québec*. Quebec City: Presses de l'Université Laval, 1973. 274 pp.

— *Personnel et partis politiques au Québec*. Montreal: Boréal Express, 1982. 347 pp.

Léonard, Jean-François, ed. *Georges-Émile Lapalme*. Sillery: Presses de l'Université du Québec, 1988. 297 pp.

Pelletier, Réjean, ed. *Partis politiques au Quéec*. Montreal: Hurtubise HMH, 1976. 299 pp.

— *Partis politiques et société québécoise. De Duplessis à Bourassa, 1944-1970*. Montreal: Québec/Amérique, 1989. 397 pp.

Quinn, H.F. *The Union Nationale*. Toronto: University of Toronto Press, 1963. 247 pp. Second edition, 1982. 347 pp.

Regenstreif, Peter. *The Diefenbaker Interlude*. Don Mills, Ont.: Longmans, 1965. 194 pp.

Rumilly, Robert. *Maurice Duplessis et son temps*. Montreal: Fides, 1973. Vol. 1.

Thomson, Dale C. *Louis St. Laurent, Canadian*. Toronto: Macmillan, 1967. 564 pp.

Whitaker, Reginald. *The Government Party: Organizing and Financing the Liberal Party of Canada 1930-1957*. Toronto: University of Toronto Press, 1977. 507 pp.

Chapter 27

Brunet, Michel. "Le fédéralisme, l'Acte de l'Amérique du Nord britannique et les Canadiens français." *Québec/Canada anglais: deux itinéraires, un affrontement*. Montreal: Hurtubise HMH, 1968, pp. 233-86.

Canada. Royal Commission on National Development in the Arts, Letters and Sciences (Massey Commission). *Report, 1949-1951*. Ottawa: Printer to the King, 1951. 517 pp.

"Cinquante années de nationalisme positif." Special issue of *L'Action nationale*, vol. 52, nos. 7-8 (March-April 1963), pp. 641-903.

Durocher, René and Michèle Jean. "Duplessis et la Commission royale d'enquête sur les problèmes constitutionnels, 1953-1956." *Revue d'histoire de l'Amérique française*, vol. 25, no. 3 (December 1971), pp. 337-64.

Lamontagne, Maurice. *Le fédéralisme canadien*. Quebec City: Presses de l'Université Laval, 1954. 298 pp.

Lapalme, Georges-Émile. *Mémoires*. 3 vols. Montreal: Leméac, 1969-73.

Quebec. Royal Commission of Inquiry on Constitutional Problems (Tremblay Commission). *Report*. 4 Vols. Quebec City, 1956.

Rémillard, Gil. *Le fédéralisme canadien: Éléments constitutionnels de formation et d'évolution*. Montreal: Québec/Amérique, 1980. 553 pp.

Sabourin, Louis. *Le système politique au Canada. Institutions fédérales et québécoises*. Ottawa: Éditions de l'Université d'Ottawa, 1970. 507 pp.

Trudeau, Pierre Elliott. *Federalism and the French Canadians*. Toronto: Macmillan, 1968. 212 pp.

Chapter 28

Barrett, Caroline and Michel René. "Littérature de masse au Québec." *The French Review*, vol. 53, no. 6 (May 1980), pp. 872-79.

Beaulieu, André and Jean Hamelin. *Les journaux du Québec de 1764 à 1964.* Quebec City: Presses de l'Université Laval, 1965. 329 pp.

Beaulieu, André and Jean Hamelin. "Aperçu du journalisme québécois d'expression française." *Rechereches sociographiques,* vol. 7, no. 3 (September-December 1966), pp. 305-48.

Beaulieu, Pierre. "La belle époque des nuits de Montréal." *La Presse,* January 19, 1980, pp. B1 and B9.

Houle, Michel and Alain Julien. *Dictionnaire du cinéma québécois.* Montreal: Fides, 1978. 366 pp.

Lamonde, Yvan and Pierre-François Hébert. *Le cinéma au Québec: essai de statistique historique (1896 à nos jours).* Quebec City,: Institut québécois de recherche sur la culture, 1981. 478 pp.

Laurence, Gérard. "La naissance de la télévision au Québec 1949-1953." *Communication et information,* vol. 2, no. 3 (Autumn 1978), pp. 25-64.

— "La rencontre du théâtre et de la télévision au Québec (1952-1957)." *Études littéraires,* vol. 14, no. 2 (August 1981), pp. 215-49.

— "Le début des affaires publiques à la télévision québécoise 1952-1957." *Revue d'histoire de l'Amérique française,* vol. 36, no. 2 (September 1982), pp. 213-39.

Lavoie, Elzéar. "La constitution d'une modernité culturelle populaire dans les médias au Québec (1895-1950)." In *L'avènement de la modernité culturelle au Québec,* edited by Yvan Lamonde and Esther Trépanier, pp. 253-98. Quebec City: Institut québécois de recherche sur la culture, 1986.

Legris, Renée and Pierre Pagé. "Le théâtre à la radio et à la télévision au Québec." *Archives des lettres canadiennes.* Vol. 5: *Le théâtre canadien-français,* pp291-318 Montreal: Fides, 1976, pp. 291-318.

Lever, Yves. *Histoire générale du cinéma au Québec.* Montreal: Boréal Express, 1988. 551 pp.

Pagé, Pierre. *Répertoire des oeuvres de la littérature radiophonique québécoise 1930-1970.* Montreal: Fides, 1975. 826 pp.

— and Jacques Belleau. "Jalons pour une histoire de la radio au Québec 1940-1965." *Communication et information,* vol. 4, no. 2 (Winter 1982), pp. 116-22.

Proulx, Gilles. *L'aventure de la radio au Québec.* Montreal: Éditions La Presse, 1979. 143 pp.

Canada. Royal Commission on Broadcasting (Fowler Commission). *Report.* Ottawa: Queen's Printer, 1957.

Véronneau, Pierre. *Histoire du cinéma au Québec I: Le succès est au film parlant français; II: Cinéma de l'époque duplessiste.* Montreal: Cinémathèque québéoise, 1979.

— *L'Office national du film, l'enfant martyr.* Montreal: Cinémathèque québécoise, 1979, pp. 3-60.

Chapter 29

Archives des lettres canadiennes. Vol. 3: *Le roman canadien-français.* Second edition. Montreal: Fides, 1971. 514 pp.

Archives des lettres canadiennes. Vol. 4: *La poésie canadienne-française.* Montreal: Fides, 1976. Pp. 143-204.

Archives des lettres canadiennes. Vol. 5: *Le théâtre canadien-français.* Montreal: Fides, 1976. Pp. 249-340.

Dionne, René, ed. *Le Québécois et sa littérature.* Sherbrooke: Naaman, 1984. 426 pp.

Godin, Jean-Cléo and Laurent Mailhot. *Le théâtre québécois.* Montreal: HMH, 1970. 254 pp.

Harper, J. Russell. *Painting in Canada: A History.* Toronto: University of Toronto Press, 1966. 443 pp.

Lajeunesse, Marcel. "La lecture publique au Québec au 20e siècle: l'ambivalence de ses solutions." In *L'imprimé au Québec, aspects historiques (18e-20e siècle),* edited by Yvan Lamonde, pp. 189-205. Quebec City: Institut québécois de recherche sur la culture, 1983.

Lefebvre, Marie-Thérèse. "La modernité dans la vie musicale." In *L'avènement de la modernité culturelle au Québec,* edited by Yvan Lamonde, pp. 173-88. Quebec City: Institut québécois de recherche sur la culture, 1986.

Lemire, Maurice, ed. *Dictionnaire des oeuvres littéraires du Québec.* Vol. 3: *1940-1959.* Montreal: Fides, 1982. 1252 pp.

Mailhot, Laurent and Pierre Nepveu. *La poésie québécoise des origines à nos jours.* Anthology. Montreal: Presses de l'Université du Québec/Hexagone, 1981. 714 pp.

— *Le Temps des poètes.* Montreal: HMH, 1969. 251 pp.Marcotte, Gilles. *Une littérature qui se fait.* Montreal: HMH, 1962. 295 pp.

Mullins, Stanley G. "A Review of Creative Writing in English Canada, 1946-1959." *Quebec Yearbook,* 1962, pp. 196-222.

Ostiguy, Jean-René. *Un siècle de peinture canadienne 1870-1970.* Quebec City: Presses de l'Université Laval, 1971. 206 pp.

Potvin, Kallman, Helmus, Gilles and Kenneth Winters, eds. *Encyclopedia of Music in Canada.* Toronto: University of Toronto Press, 1981. 1076 pp.

Quebec. Commission d'enquête sur le commerce du livre (Bouchard Commission). *Rapport.* Quebec City: Department of Cultural Affairs, 1963.

Robert, Guy. *L'art au Québec depuis 1940.* Montreal: La Presse, 1973. 501 pp.

Chapter 30

Desjardins, Bertrand and Jacques Légaré. "Le vieillessement de la population du Québec: faits, causes et conséquences." *Critères,* no. 16 (Winter 1977), pp. 143-69.

Dufour, Desmond and Yves Péron. *Vingt ans de mortalité au Québec: Les causes de décès, 1951-1971.* Montreal: Presses de l'Université de Montréal, 1979. 204 pp.

Dumas, Jean. *Current Demographic Analysis: Report on the Demographic Situation in Canada.* Ottawa: Statistics Canada, 1983. 138 pp.

Gauthier, Heré. *Évolution démographique du Québec.* Quebec City: Office de planification et de développement du Québec, 1977. 168 pp.

Mathews, Georges. *Le choc démographique. Le déclin du Québec est-il inévitable?* Montreal: Boréal Express, 1984. 204 pp.

Quebec. *Démographie québécoise: passé, présent, perspectives.* Québec City: Éditen officiel, 1983. 457 pp.

La situation démographique au Québec. Édition 1985. Quebec City: Les publications du Québec, 1986. 242 pp.

Chapter 31

Canadian Forum. *A Citizen's Guide to the Gray Report.* Toronto: New Press, 1971. 189 pp.

Clement. Wallace. *The Canadian Corporate Elite. An Analysis of Economic Power.* Toronto: McClelland and Stewart, 1975. 479 pp.

— *Continental Corporate Power. Economic Linkages Between Canada and the United States.* Toronto: McClelland and Stewart, 1977. 408 pp.

Fournier, Pierre, ed. *Le capitalisme au Québec.* Montreal: Albert Saint-Martin, 1978. 436 pp.

Levitt, Kari. *Silent Surrender: The Multinational Corporation in Canada.* Toronto: Macmillan, 1970. 185 pp.

Litvak, I.A. and C.J. Maule. *The Canadian Multinationals.* Toronto: Butterworths, 1981. 184 pp.

Niosi, Jorge. *The Economy of Canada: A Study of Ownership and Control.* Montreal: Black Rose Books, 1978. 179 pp.

— *Canadian Capitalism: A Study of Power in the Canadian Business Establishment.* Toronto: Lorimer, 1981. 224 pp.

— *Canadian Multinationals.* Toronto: Between The Lines, 1985. 200 pp.

Quebec. *Bâtir le Québec—Énoncé de politique économique.* Quebec City: Éditeur officiel, 1979.

Quebec. Interdepartmental Task Force on Foreign Investment. *A Quebec Policy of Foreign Investment:/ report of the Interdepartmental Task Force on Foreign Investment* (Tetley Report). Quebec City: Government of Quebec, Executive Council, 1974.

Raynauld, André. *La propriété des entreprises au Québec: Les années 60.* Montreal: Presses de l'Université de Montréal, 1974. 160 pp.
Sales, Arnaud. *La bourgeoisie industrielle au Québec.* Montreal: Presses de l'Université de Montréal, 1979. 322 pp.

Chapter 32

Bélanger, Yves and Pierre Fournier. *L'entreprise québécoise: Développement historique et dynamique contemporaine.* Montreal: Hurtubise HMH, 1987. 187 pp.
Bolduc, André, Clarence Hogue and Daniel Larouche. *Québec: un siècle d'électricité.* Second edition. Montreal: Libre Expression, 1984. Chapters 17 to 23.
Chanlat, Alain with André Bolduc and Daniel Larouche. *Gestion et culture d'entreprise: Le cheminement d'Hydro-Québec.* Montreal: Québec/Amérique, 1984. 250 pp.
Faucher, Philippe and Johanne Bergeron. *Hydro-Québec: La société de l'heure de pointe.* Montreal: Presses de l'Université de Montréal, 1986. 221 pp.
Fournier, Pierre, ed. *Le capitalisme au Québec.* Montreal: Albert Saint-Martin, 1978. 436 pp.
— *Les sociétés d'État et les objectifs du Québec: une évaluation préliminaire.* Quebec City: Éditeur officiel, 1979. 135 pp.
— ed. *Capitalisme et politique au Québec.* Montreal: Albert St-Martin, 1981. 290 pp.
Jobin, Carol. *Les enjeux économiques de la nationalisation de l'électricité.* Montreal: Albert Saint-Martin, 1978. 206 pp.
McRoberts, Kenneth and Dale Posgate. *Quebec: Social Change and Political Crisis.* Toronto: McClelland and Stewart, 1976. 216 pp.
Niosi, Jorge. *Canadian Capitalism: A Study of Power in the Canadian Business Establishment.* Toronto: Lorimer, 1981. 224 pp.
Paquette, Pierre. "Industries et politiques minières au Québec: une analyse économique, 1896-1975." *Revue d'histoire de l'Amérique française,* vol. 37, no. 4 (March 1984), pp. 573-602.
Quebec. *Bâtir le Québec—Énoncé de politique économique.* Quebec City: Éditeur officiel, 1979.
Quebec. *L'épargne: Rapport du groupe de travail sur l'épargne au Québec.* Quebec City: Éditeur officiel, 1980. 687 pp.

Chapter 33

Bolduc, André, Clarence Hogue and Daniel Larouche. *Québec: un siècle d'électricité.* Second edition. Montreal: Libre Expression, 1984. Chapters 17 to 23.
Carré, Ronald et al. *Analyse structurelle à moyen terme de l'économie du Québec.* Quebec City: Office de planification et de développement du Québec, 1977. 262 pp.
Girard, Jacques. *Géographie de l'industrie manufacturière du Québec.* 2 vols. Quebec City: Éditeur officiel, 1979.
Quebec. *Bâtir le Québec—Énoncé de politique économique.* Quebec City: Éditeur officiel, 1979.
Quebec. *L'économie: Document de référence.* N.p.:Le sommet économique du Québec, 1977. 130 pp.

Chapter 34

Blais, André. "La politique agricole du gouvernement québécois, 1952-1973." *Recherches sociographiques,* vol. 20, no. 2 (1979), pp. 173-203.
Canada. Federal Task Force on Agriculture. *Canadian Agriculture in the Seventies: A Report of the Federal Task Force on Agriculture.* Ottawa: Queen's Printer, 1969. 475 pp.
Charbonneau, André and Vincent Harvey. "Ottawa sacrifie l'agriculture québécoise à celle de l'Ouest." *Maintenant,* no. 119 (October 1972), pp. 18-25.
Chartier, Jean. "L'agriculture peut-elle être rentable au Québec?" *Forces,* no. 40 (1977), pp. 4-19.
Dagenais, François. "The Development of a Food and Agriculture Policy in Quebec." *American Journal of Agricultural Economics,* vol. 60, no. 5 (December 1978), pp. 1045-50.
— "Les progrès de l'agriculture au Québec." *Le Devoir,* January 6, 1981, p. 13.

Kesteman, Jean-Pierre, with Guy Boisclair and Jean-Marc Kirouac. *Histoire du syndicalisme agricole au Québec UCC-UPA 1924-1984*. Montreal: Boréal Express, 1984. Pp.
181-309.
Lafrenière, Danielle. "Les composantes prix et productivité du revenu agricole moyen
au Québec de 1961 à 1976." MA thesis (agricultural economics), Laval University,
Quebec City, 1978.
Quebec. *L'agro-alimentaire. Pour une stratégie de développement*. Quebec City, 1978. 85 pp.
— *L'économie. Point de vue sur notre réalité: Le développement économique du Québec
1961-1980. Une synthèse*. Quebec City, 1977. 65 pp.
Quebec. Bureau de la statistique du Québec. *Statistiques agricoles du Québec, 1977 et
1978*. Quebec City: Éditeur officiel, 1980. 191 pp.
Quebec. Commission Royale d'enquête sur l'agriculture au Quebec. *Rapport*. 14 parts.
Quebec City, 1967–69.
Roy, Jean-Baptiste. *L'agriculture au Québec*. Quebec City: Department of Agriculture,
1975. 93 pp.
Union des producteurs agricoles: Évolution historique. Montreal: UPA, 1974. 23 pp.
Veeman, Terrence S. and Michèle M. Veeman. "The Changing Organization, Structure
and Control of Canadian Agriculture." *American Journal of Agricultural Economics*,
vol. 60, no. 5 (December 1978), pp. 759-68.

Chapter 35

Bélanger, Gérard. "Le transport urbain." *Annuaire du Québec 1977/1978*, pp. 1090-96.
"Les institutions financières canadiennes et québécoises à l'heure du changement."
Special issue of *Forces*, no. 72 (Autumn 1985). 115 pp.
Quebec. *Comptes économiques du Québec: Revenus et dépenses: Estimations annuelles 1961-
1975*. Quebec City: Éditeur officiel, 1977. 22 pp.
— *Comptes économiques des revenus et dépenses. Québec 1971-1983*. Quebec City:
Bureau de la statistique du Québec, 1985. 126 pp.
— *L'épargne: Rapport du groupe de travail sur l'épargne au Québec*. Quebec City:
Éditeur officiel, 1980. 625 pp.
Ryba, André. *Le rôle du secteur financier dans le développement du Québec: un essai de
finance régionale*. Montreal: Centre de recherches en développement économique,
Université de Montréal, 1974. 347 pp.
— "Le secteur financier et le développement économique du Québec." *Actualité
économique*, vol. 50, no. 3 (July-September 1974), pp. 379-400.
Virthe, Gérard. "Commerce de détail et services: des secteurs en constante évolution
au Québec." *Annuaire du Québec 1977/1978*, pp. 1197-1204.

Chapter 36

Banville, Charles. *Les opérations dignité*. Quebec City: Fonds de recherches forestières
de l'Université Laval, 1977. 128 pp.
Canada. Economic Council of Canada. *Living Together: A Study of Regional Disparities*.
Ottawa, 1977. 247 pp.
Dugas, Clermont. *Les régions périphériques*. Quebec City: Presses de l'Université du
Québec, 1983. 253 pp.
Gagnon, Alain-G. *Développement régional, État et groupes populaires*. Hull: Asticou, 1985.
Gagnon, Gabriel et Luc Martin, eds. *Québec 1960-1980: La crise du développement*. Mon-
treal: Hurtubise HMH, 1973. 500 pp.
Lévesque, Gérard-D. "Les politiques de développement régional au Québec." In *Re-
gional Economic Development*, edited by O.J. Firestone, pp. 7-15. Ottawa: University
of Ottawa Press, 1974.
Parenteau, Roland. "L'expérience de la planification au Québec (1960-1969)." *Actualité
économique*, vol. 45, no. 4 (January-March 1970), pp. 679-96.
Quebec. *Perspectives démographiques régionales, 1981-2006*. Quebec City: Bureau de la
statistique du Québec, 1984. 436 pp.
Simard, Jean-Jacques. *La Longue marche des technocrates*. Montreal: Almbert Saint-Martin, 1979. pp.75-113.

Chapter 37

Andrew, Caroline, Serge Bordeleau and Alain Guimont. *L'urbanisation: une affaire: L'appropriation du sol et l'État local dans l'Outaouais québécois*. Ottawa: Éditions de l'Université d'Ottawa, 1981. 248 pp.

Aubin, Henry. *City for Sale*. Montreal and Toronto: L'Étincelle and Lorimer, 1977. 389 pp.

Beauregard, Ludger, ed. *Montréal. Guide d'excursions/Field Guide*. Montreal: Presses de l'Université de Montréal, 1972. 197 pp.

Benjamin, Jacques. *La communauté urbaine de Montréal: Une réforme ratée*. Montreal: L'Aurore, 1975. 157 pp.

Bouchard, Louis-Marie. *Les villes du Saguenay: Étude géographique*. Montreal: Leméac, 1973. 212 pp.

Collin, Jean-Pierre. *Le développement résidentiel suburbain et l'exploitation de la ville centrale*. "Études et documents," no. 23. Montreal: INRS-Urbanisation, 1981. 141 pp.

— *La cité coopérative canadienne-française: Saint-Léonard-de-Port-Maurice (1955-1963)*. Montreal and Quebec City: INRS-Urbanisation and Presses de l'Université du Québec, 1986.

Divay, Gérard and Jean-Pierre Collin. *La Communauté urbaine de Montréal de Montréal: de la ville centrale à l'île centrale*. Montreal: INRS-Urbanisation, 1977. 250 pp.

Divay, Gérard and Marcel Gaudreau. *La formation des espaces résidentiels: Le système de production de l'habitat urbain dans les années soixante-dix au Québec*. Montreal and Quebec City: INRS-Urbanisation and Presses de l'Université du Québec, 1984. 262 pp.

Godbout, Jacques and Jean-Pierre Collin. *Les organismes populaires en milieu urbain: contre-pouvoir ou nouvelle pratique professionnelle?* Montreal: INRS-Urbanisation, 1977. 311 pp.

"La ville de Québec." Special issue of *Recherches sociographiques*, vol. 22, no. 2 (May-August 1981).

Léveillé, Jacques. *Développement urbain et politiques gouvernementales urbaines dans l'agglomération montréalaise, 1945-1975*. N.p.: Société canadienne de science politique, 1978. 608 pp.

Mathews, Georges. *Évolution générale du marché du logement de la région de Montréal de 1951 à 1976: données synthétiques sur une réussite méconnue*. "Études et documents," no. 17. Montreal: INRS-Urbanisation, 1980. 69 pp.

Quesnel-Ouellet, Louise. "Aménagement urbain et autonomie locale." In *L'État du Québec en devenir*, edited by Gérard Bergeron and Réjean Pelletier, pp. 211-38. Montreal: Boréal Express, 1980.

Chapter 38

Bélanger, Yves and Pierre Fournier. *L'entreprise québécoise: Développement historique et dynamique contemporaine*. Montreal: Hurtubise HMH, 1987. 187 pp.

Clement, Wallace. *The Canadian Corporate Elite: An Analysis of Economic Power*. Toronto: McClelland and Stewart, 175. 479 pp.

Dubuc, Alain and Laurier Cloutier. *Le club des milliardaires et l'épargne des Québécois*. Montreal: La Presse, n.d. 42 pp.

Fournier, Pierre, ed. *Le capitalisme au Québec*. Montreal: Albert Saint-Martin, 1978. 436 pp.

— *Le patronat québécois au pouvoir: 1970-1976*. Montreal: Hurtubise HMH, 1979. 308 pp.

— *Les sociétés d'État et les objectifs économiques du Québec: une évaluation préliminaire*. Quebec City: Éditeur officiel, 1979. 135 pp.

— ed. *Capitalisme et politique au Québec*. Montreal: Albert Saint-Martin, 1981. 292 pp.

Grand'Maison, Jacques. *La nouvelle classe et l'avenir du Québec*. Montreal: Stanké, 1979. 272 pp.

Laurin-Frenette, Nicole. *Production de l'État et formes de la nation*. Montreal: Nouvelle Optique, 1978. 176 pp.

Légaré, Anne. *Les classes sociales au Québec*. Montreal: Presses de l'Université du Québec, 1977. 197 pp.

"L'entreprise canadienne-française." Special issue of *Recherches sociographiques*, vol. 24, no. 1 (January-April 1983).

Newman, Peter C. *The Canadian Establishment*. Vol. 1. Toronto: McClelland and Stewart/Bantam, 1977. 551 pp.

— *The Canadian Establisment*. Vol. 2: *The Acquisitors*. Toronto: McClelland and Stewart/Bantam, 1982. 566 pp.

Niosi, Jorge. *Canadian Capitalism: A Study of Power in the Canadian Business Establishment*. Toronto: Lorimer, 1981. 224 pp.

Raynauld, André. *La propriété des entreprises au Québec: Les années 60*. Montreal: Presses de l'Université de Montréal, 1974. 160 pp.

— and François Vaillancourt. *L'appartenance des entreprises: le cas du Québec en 1978*. Quebec City: Éditeur officiel, 1984. 143 pp.

Sales, Arnaud. *La bourgeoisie industrielle au Québec*. Montreal: Presses de l'Université de Montréal, 1979. 322 pp.

Simard, Jean-Jacques. *La longue marche des technocrates*. Montreal: Albert Saint-Martin, 1979. 198 pp.

Vaillancourt, François. "Les cadres francophones au Québec." *Recherches sociographiques*, vol. 21, no. 3 (September-December 1980), pp. 329-37.

Chapter 39

Barry, Francine. *Le travail de la femme au Québec: L'évolution de 1940 à 1970*. Montreal: Presses de l'Université du Québec, 1977. 80 pp.

Clio Collective. *Quebec Women: A History*. Toronto: Women's Press, 1987. 396 pp.

CNTU-CEQ. *History of the Labour Movement in Quebec*. Montreal: Black Rose Books, 1986. 299 pp.

David, Hélène. *Femmes et emploi: Le défi de l'égalité*. Quebec: Presses de l'Université du Québec, 1986. 477 pp.

Demers, François. *Chroniques impertinentes du 3ème Front commun syndical, 1979-1980*. Montreal: Nouvelle Optique, 1982. 170 pp.

Dupont, Pierre and Gisèle Tremblay. *Les syndicats en crise*. Montreal: Quinze, 1976. 152 pp.

Gagnon, Mona-Josée. "Les femmes dans le mouvement syndical québécois." In *Travailleuse et féministes: La femme dans la société québécoise*, edited by Marie Lavigne and Yolande Pinard, pp. 139-60. Montreal: Boréal Express, 1983.

Gérin-Lajoie, Jean. *Les métallos, 1936-1981*. Montreal: Boréal Express, 1982. Chapters 4 and 5.

Harvey, Fernand. *Le mouvement ouvrier au Québec*. Montreal: Boréal Express, 1980.

Lamonde, Pierre and Jean-Pierre Bélanger. *L'utopie du plein emploi: Croissance économique et aspirations au travail, Québec 1971-2001*. Montreal: Boréal Express, 1986. 175 pp.

Lesage, Marc. *Les vagabonds du rêve: Vers une société des marginaux?* Montreal: Boréal Express, 1986. 141 pp.

Morton, Desmond and Terry Copp. *Working People*. Ottawa: Deneau and Greenberg, 1980. Pp. 239-317.

Palmer, Bryan D. *Working-Class Experience*. Toronto: Butterworths, 1983. Chapter 6.

Pontaut, Alain. *Santé et sécurité: Un bilan du régime québécois de santé et sécurité au travail, 1885-1985*. Montreal: Boréal Express, 1985. Chapters 4 to 6.

Rouillard, Jacques. *Histoire de la CSN, 1921-1982*. Montreal: Boréal Express. Chapter 5.

— "Le militantisme des travailleurs au Québec et en Ontario, niveau de syndicalisation et mouvement de grève (1900-1980)." *Revue d'histoire de l'Amérique française*, vol. 37, no. 2 (September 1983), pp. 201-25.

Chapter 40

Anctil, Pierre and Gary Caldwell, eds. *Juifs et réalités juives au Québec*. Quebec City: Institut québécois de recherche sur la culture, 1984. 371 pp.

Benjamin, Claire. "Les entrées internationales au Québec." *Démographie québécoise: passé, présent, perspectives pp. 314-44*. Quebec City: Bureau de la statistique du Québec, 1985.

Boissevain, Jeremy. *The Italians of Montreal: Social Adjustment in a Plural Society*. Ottawa: Queen's Printer, 1970. 87 pp.

— *La population du Québec: études rétrospectives*. Montreal: Boréal Express, 1973. 110 pp.

Charbonneau, Hubert and Robert Maheu. *Les aspects démographiques de la question linguistique*. Quebec City: Éditeur officiel, 1973. 438 pp.

Desrosiers, Denise, Joël W. Gregory and Victor Piché. *La migration au Québec: synthèse et bilan bibliographique*. Quebec City: Ministère de l'Immigration, 1980. 106 pp.

"Enjeux ethniques: Production de nouveaux rapports sociaux." Special issue of *Sociologie et sociétés*, vol. 15, no. 2 (October 1983).

"Hommage aux communautés culturelles du Québec." Special issue of *Forces*, no. 73 (March 1986).

Ioannou, Tina. *La communauté grecque du Québec*. Quebec City: Institut qué bécois de recherche sur la culture, 1983. 154 pp.

Malservisi, Mauro F. *La contribution des groupes ethniques autres que français et britannique au développement du Québec*. Quebec City: Éditeur officiel, 1973. 336 pp.

"Migrations et communautés culturelles." Special issue of *Questions de culture*, no. 2 (1982).

Rudin, Ronald. *The Forgotten Quebecers: A History of English-Speaking Quebec, 1759-1980*. Quebec City: Institut québécois de recherche sur la culture, 1985. 315 pp.

Chapter 41

Breton, Raymond and Gail Grant. *La langue de travail au Québec*. Montreal: Institut de recherches politiques, 1981. 107 pp.

Canada. Royal Commission on Bilingualism and Biculturalism (Laurendeau-Dunton Commission). *Final Report*. Ottawa: Queen's Printer, 1968-70.

The Canadian Annual Review of Politics and Public Affairs. Toronto: University of Toronto Press, 1960-84.

Cappon, Paul. *Conflit entre les Néo-Canadiens et les francophones de Montréal*. Quebec City: Presses de l'Université Laval, 1974. 288 pp.

Charbonneau, Hubert and Robert Maheu. *Les aspects démographiques de la questions linguistique*. Quebec City: Éditeur officiel, 1973. 438 pp.

Daoust, Denise. "La planification linguistique au Québec: un aperçu des lois sur la langue," *Revue québécoise de linguistique*, vol. 12, no. 1 (1982), pp. 9-75.

Gémar, Jean-Claude. *Les trois états de la politique linguistique du Québec: D'une société traduite à une société d'expression*. Quebec City: Éditeur officiel, 1983. 201 pp.

McWhinney, Edward. *Quebec and the Constitution 1960-1978*. Toronto: University of Toronto Press, 1979. 170 pp.

Quebec. Commission of Inquiry on the Position of the French Language and on Language Rights in Quebec (Gendron Commission). *The Position of the French Language in Quebec*. 3 vols. Quebec City: Éditeur officiel, 1972.

Rudin, Ronald. *The Forgotten Quebecers: A History of English-Speaking Quebec, 1759-1980*. Quebec City: Institut québécois de recherche sur la culture, 1985. 315 pp.

Taddeo, Donat J. and Raymond C. Taras. *Le débat linguistique au Québec: La communauté italienne et la langue d'enseignement*. Montreal: Presses de l'Université de Montréal, 1987. 246 pp.

Chapter 42

Brodeur, Violette et al. *Le mouvement des femmes au Québec: étude des groupes montréalais et nationaux*. Montreal: Centre de formation populaire, 1982. 77 pp.

Canada. Royal Commission on the Status of Women (Bird Commission). *Report*. Ottawa: Information Canada, 1970. 488 pp.

Clio Collective. *Quebec Women: A History*. Toronto: Women's Press, 1987. Chapters 12 to 15.

Johnson, Micheline. "La parole des femmes: les revues féminines, 1938-1968." In *Idéologies au Canada français 1940-1976*, edited by Fernand Dumont, Jean Hamelin and Jean-Paul Montminy, vol. 2, pp. 5-45. Quebec City: Presses de l'Université Laval, 1981.

"La nouvelle famille et la loi 89." Dossier in *La vie en rose* (December 1981-January 1982).

Lamoureux, Diane. *Fragments et collages: Essai sur le féminisme québécois des années 70.* Montreal: Remue-ménage, 1986. 169 pp.

Lanctôt, Martine. *La genèse et l'évolution du mouvement de libération des femmes à Montréal, 1969-1979.* MA thesis, University of Quebec at Montreal, 1980. 207 pp.

Lavigne, Marie and Yolande Pinard. *Travailleuses et féministes: les femmes dans la société québécoise.* Montreal: Boréal Express, 1983. 430 pp.

Lemieux, Denise and Lucie Mercier. *La recherche sur les femmes au Québec: bilan et bibliographie.* Quebec City: Institut québécois de recherche sur la culture, 1982. 336 pp.

Quebec. Conseil du statut de la femme. *Pour les Québécoises: égalité et indépendance.* Quebec City: Éditeur officiel, 1978. 335 pp.

Therrien, Rita and Louise Coulombe-Roy. *Rapport de l'AFÉAS sur la situation des femmes au foyer.* Montreal: Boréal Express, 1984. 214 pp.

Chapter 43

Dostaler, Gilles, ed. *La crise économique et sa gestion.* Montreal: Boréal Express, 1982. 256 pp.

Dubuc, Alain. "Sommes-nous plus riches qu'en 1950?" *La Presse*, March 15, 1986.

Jurdant, Michel. *Le défi écologiste.* Montreal: Boréal Express, 1984. 432 pp.

Lamonde, Pierre and Jean-Pierre Bélanger. *L'utopie du plein emploi: Croissance économique et aspirations au travail, Québec, 1971-2001.* Montreal: Boréal Express, 1982. 187 pp.

Lesage, Marc. *Les vagabonds du rêve: Vers une société de marginaux?* Montreal: Boréal Express, 1986. 141 pp.

Levasseur, Roger. *Loisir et culture au Québec.* Montreal: Boréal Express, 1982. 187 pp.

Quebec. *Comptes économiques des revenus et dépenses: Québec, 1961-1982.* Quebec City: Bureau de la statistique du Québec, 1982. 123 pp.

Saint-Germain, Maurice. *Une économie à libérer: Le Québec analysé dans ses structures économiques.* Montreal: Presses de l'Université de Montréal, 1973. 469 pp.

Chapter 44

Fréchette, Pierre, Roland Jouandet-Bernadat and Jean P. Vézina. *L'économie du Québec.* Montreal: HRW, 1975. Chapters 9 and 10.

Gaucher, Dominique. "L'organisation des services de santé mentale au Québec: tendances actuelles." *Sociologie et sociétés*, vol. 17, no. 1 (April 1985), pp. 41-49.

Guest, Dennis. *The Emergence of Social Security in Canada.* Vancouver: University of British Columbia Press, 1980. Chapters 10 to 12.

Lesemann, Frederic. *Services and Circuses: Community and the Welfare State.* Montreal: Black Rose Books, 1984. 276 pp.

Latouche, Daniel. "Questionner l'État-providence." *Forces*, no. 49 (1979), pp. 4-14.

McGraw, Donald. *Le développement des groupes populaires à Montréal (1963-1973).* Montreal: Albert Saint-Martin, 1978. 184 pp.

Pelletier, Michel, and Yves Vaillancourt. *Les politiques sociales et les travailleurs.* Book 4: *Les années 60.* Montreal, 1974. 304 pp.

Quebec. Comité d'étude sur l'assistance publique. *Report of the Study Committee on Public Assistance (Boucher Report).* Quebec City, 1963. 230 pp.

Quebec. Commission of Inquiry on Health and Social Welfare (Castonguay-Nepveu Commission). *Report.* 7 vols. Quebec City: Éditeur officiel, 1967-72.

Renaud, Marc. "Réforme ou illusion? Une analyse des interventions de l'État québécois dans le domaine de la santé." *Sociologie et sociétés*, vol. 11, no. 1 (April 1977), pp. 127-52.

Sénéchal, Marcel. "Les C.L.S.C. et la santé mentale." *Santé mentale au Québec*, vol. 11, no. 1 (1986), pp. 117-23.

Vaillancourt, François and Julie Grignon. "L'aide sociale au Canada et au Québec, 1970-1985: évolution et analyse." Paper delivered at the ninth meeting of the Comité-Québec of the C.D. Howe Institute, Montreal, November 1985.

Vaillancourt, Yves. *Le P.Q. et le social: éléments de bilan des politiques sociales du gouvernement du Parti québécois, 1976-1982.* Montreal: Socialisme et indépendance, 1983. 92 pp.

Chapter 45

Anctil, Pierre and Gary Caldwell, eds. *Juifs et réalités juives au Québec.* Quebec City: Institut québécois de recherche sur la culture, 1984. Chapters 2 and 5.

Chagnon, Roland. *Les charismatiques au Québec.* Montreal: Québec/Amérique, 1979. 211 pp.

Denault, Bernard and Benoît Lévesque. *Éléments pour une sociologie des communautés religieuses au Québec.* Montreal: Presses de l'Université de Montréal, 1975. Pp. 18-117.

Gosselin, Jean-Pierre and Denis Monière. *Le trust de la foi.* Montreal: Québec/Amérique, 1978. 166 pp.

Gutwith, Jacques, "Haddidim et judaïcité au Québec." *Recherches sociographiques* Vol. 14, no. 3 (1973), pp. 291-325

Hamelin, Jean. *Histoire du catholicisme québécois.* Part 3. *Le XXe siècle.* Vol. 2. *De 1940 à nos jours.* Montreal: Boréal Express, 1984. Pp. 209-376.

Lasry, Jean-Claude M. "Une diaspora francophone au Québec: Les Juifs sépharades." *Questions de culture,* no. 2 (1982), pp. 113-35.

Mair, Nathan H. "The Protestant Churches." In *The English of Quebec: From Majority to Minority Status,* edited by Gary Caldwell and Eric Waddell, pp. 211-23. Quebec City: Institut québécois de recherche sur la culture, 1982.

Rousseau, Louis. "L'évolution des associations volontaires dans les paroisses montréalaises, 1940-1970." Paper delivered at the Symposium sur le renouveau communautaire, Montreal, 1973. 8 pp.

Voisine, Nive, André Beaulieu and Jean Hamelin. *Histoire de l'Église catholique au Québec (1608-1970).* Montreal: Fides, 1971. Pp. 73-85.

Chapter 46

Audet, Louis Philippe. *Histoire de l'enseignement au Québec* Vol.2. Montreal: HRW, 1971.Pp. 385-474.

Bélanger, Pierre. *Le mouvement étudiant quécois: son passé, ses revendications et ses luttes, 1960-1983.* Montreal: Association nationale des étudiants du Québec, 1984. 208 pp.

CNTU-CEQ. *History of the Labour Movement in Quebec.* Montreal: Black Rose Books, 1986. 299 pp.

Conseil de la science et de la technologie. *Science et technologie: Conjoncture 1985.* 2 vols. Quebec City, 1986.

Dion, Léon. *Le bill 60 et la société québécoise.* Montreal: HMH, 1967. 197 pp.

Duchesne, Raymond. *La science et le pouvoir au Québec (1920-1965).* Quebec City: Éditeur officiel, 1978. 126 pp.

Galarneau, Claude. *Les collèges classiques au Canada français.* Montreal: Fides, 1978. 287 pp.

Hamelin, Jean. *Histoire du catholicisme québécois.* Part 3. *Le XXe siècle.* Vol. 2. *De 1940 à nos jours.* Montreal: Boréal Express, 1984. 415 pp.

Milner, Henry. *The Long Road to Reform: Restructuring Public Education in Quebec.* Montreal: McGill-Queen's University Press, 1986. 170 pp.

Quebec. Royal Commission of Inquiry on Education (Parent Commission). *Report.* 5 vols. Quebec City, 1963-66.

Chapter 47

Arnopoulos, Sheila McLeod and Dominique Clift. *The English Fact in Quebec.* Montreal: McGill-Queen's University Press, 1980. Chapters 8 and 11.

Balthazar, Louis. "La dynamique du nationalisme québécois." In *L'État du Québec en devenir,* edited by Gérard Bergeron and Réjean Pelletier. Montreal: Boréal Express, 1980, pp. 37-58.

Bélanger, André-J. *Ruptures et constantes: Quatre idéologies du Québec en éclatement.* Montreal: Hurtubise HMH, 1977 Chapter 3.

Brunelle, Dorval. *Les trois colombes.* Montreal: VLB éditeur, 1985. 308 pp.

Caldwell, Gary and Eric Waddell. *The English of Quebec: From Majority to Minority Status.* Quebec City: Institut québécois de recherche sur la culture, 1982, 479 pp.

CNTU-CEQ. *History of the Labour Movement in Quebec.* Montreal: Black Rose Books, 1986. Chapters 5 and 6.

D'Allemagne, André. *Le RIN et les débuts du mouvement indépendantiste québécois.* Montreal: L'Étincelle, 1974. Pp. 13-25 and 31-44.

Désy, Marielle, Marc Ferland, Benoît Lévesque and Yves Vaillancourt. *La conjoncture au Québec au début des années 80: les enjeux pour le mouvement ouvrier et populaire.* Rimouski: Librairie socialiste de l'Est du Québec, 1980. 200 pp.

Dumont, Fernand, Jean Hamelin et Jean-Paul Montminy, eds. *Idéologies au Canada français 1940-1976.* 3 vols. Quebec City: Presses de l'Université Laval, 1981.

Gagnon, Alain, ed. *Quebec State and Society.* Toronto: Methuen, 1984. Part 1.

Latouche, Daniel and Diane Poliquin-Bourassa. *Le manuel de la parole: Manifestes québécois.* Vol. 3: *1960-1976.* Montreal: Boréal Express, 1979. 289 pp.

Laurin-Frenette, Nicole. *Production de l'État et formes de la nation.* Montreal: Nouvelle Optique, 1978. 176 pp.

"Manifeste 1964-1965." *Parti pris,* vol. 2, no. 1 (September 1964), pp. 2-17.

"Manifeste 1965-1966." *Parti pris,* vol. 3, no. 1 (August-September 1965), pp. 2-41. Reprinted in *Les Québécois,* pp. 249-80. Montreal and Paris: Parti pris and Maspero, 1967.

McRoberts, Kenneth and Dale Posgate. *Quebec: Social Change and Political Crisis.* Toronto: McClelland and Stewart, 1976. Chapters 6 to 8.

Trudeau, Pierre Elliott. "New Treason of the Intellectuals." In *Federalism and the French Canadians,* pp. 151-81. Toronto: Macmillan, 1968.

Chapter 48

Bergeron, Gérard and Réjean Pelletier, eds. *L'État du Québec en devenir.* Montreal: Boréal Express, 1980. Chapters 3 and 4.

Gagnon, Gabriel and Luc Martin, eds. *Québec 1960-1980: La crise du développement: Matériaux pour une sociologie de la planification et de la participation.* Montreal: Hurtubise HMH, 1973. 500 pp.

Gow, James Iain. *Histoire de l'administration publique québécoise, 1867-1970.* Montreal and Toronto: Presses de l'Université de Montréal and Institute of Public Administration of Canada, 1986. Chapters 6 and 8.

McRoberts, Kenneth and Dale Posgate. *Quebec: Social Change and Political Crisis.* Toronto: McClelland and Stewart, 1976. 350 pp.

Orban, Edmond, ed. *La modernisation politique au Québec.* Montreal: Boréal Express, 1976. Chapters 6 and 7.

Simard, Jean-Jacques. *La longue marche des technocrates.* Montreal: Albert Saint-Martin, 1979. 198 pp.

Chapter 49

Bellavance, Lionel. *Les partis indépendantistes québécois de 1960-1973.* Montreal: Les anciens canadiens, 1983. 98 pp.

Bernard, André. *Québec: élections 1976.* Montreal: Hurtubise HMH, 1976. 173 pp.

Cardinal, Mario, Vincent Lemieux and Florian Sauvageau. *Si l'Union nationale m'était contée...* Montreal: Boréal Express, 1978. 348 pp.

D'Allemagne, André. *Le RIN et les débuts du mouvement indépendantiste québécois.* Montreal: L'Étincelle, 1974.

Latouche, Daniel, Guy Lord and Jean-Guy Vaillancourt, eds. *Le processus électoral au Québec: les élections provinciales de 1970 et 1973.* Montreal: Hurtubise HMH, 1976. 288 pp.

Laurendeau, Marc. *Les Québécois violents.* Montreal: Boréal Express, 1974. 240 pp.

"Le gouvernement du Parti Québécois." Special issue of *Recherches sociographiques,* vol. 25, no. 1 (January-April 1984).

Lemieux, Vincent. *La fête continue: La vie politique au Québec depuis la Révolution tranquille jusqu'au référendum.* Montreal: Boréal Express, 1979. 201 pp.

— ed. *Quatre élections provinciales au Québec, 1956-1966.* Quebec City: Presses de l'Université Laval, 1969. 246 pp.

— Marcel Gilbert and André Blais. *Une élection de réalignement: L'élection générale du 29 avril 1970 au Québec.* Montreal: Éditions du Jour, 1970. 182 pp.

McRoberts, Kenneth and Dale Posgate. *Quebec: Social Change and Political Crisis.* Toronto: McClelland and Stewart, 1976. 350 pp.

Murray, Vera. *Le Parti Québécois: de la fondation à la prise du pouvoir.* Montreal: Hurtubise HMH, 1976.

Pelletier, Réjean, ed. *Partis politiques au Québec.* Montreal: Hurtubise HMH, 1976. 299 pp.

— *Partis politiques et société québécoise: De Duplessis à Bourassa, 1944-1970.* Montreal: Québec/Amérique, 1989. 397 pp.

Trait, Jean-Claude. *FLQ 70: offensive d'octobre.* Montreal: Éditions de l'Homme, 1970. 230 pp.

Chapter 50

Barberis, Robert and Pierre Drouilly. *Les illusions du pouvoir: les erreurs stratégiques du gouvernment Lévesque.* Montreal: Sélect, 1980. 238 pp.

Beck, J.M. *Pendulum of Power: Canada's Federal Elections.* Scarborough, Ont.: Prentice-Hall, 1968. 442 pp.

Bernard, André. *Québec: élections 1976.* Montreal: Hurtubise HMH, 1976. 173 pp.

Bernard, André and Bernard Descoteaux. *Québec: élections 1981* Montreal: Hurtubise HMH, 1981. 229 pp.

Drouilly, Pierre. *Le paradoxe canadien: Le Québec et les élections fédérales (1963-1974).* Montreal: Parti pris, 1978. 235 pp.

— *Statistiques électorales du Québec, 1867-1981.* Quebec City: Bibliothèque de l'Assemblée nationale, 1982. 687 pp.

— *Statistiques électorales fédérales du Québec, 1867-1980.* Montreal: Université du Québec à Montréal, 1983. 937 pp.

Dupont, Pierre. *How Lévesque Won.* Toronto: Lorimer, 1977. 136 pp.

Laurin-Frenette, Nicole and Jean-François Léonard. *L'impasse: enjeux et perspectives de l'après-référendum.* Montreal: Nouvelle Optique, 1980. 162 pp.

Lemieux, Vincent. *Le quotient politique vrai: Le vote provincial et fédéral au Québec.* Quebec City: Presses de l'Université Laval, 1973. 274 pp.

ed. *Quatre élections provinciales au Québec, 1956-1966.* Quebec City: Presses de l'Université Laval, 1969. 246 pp.

Marcel Gilbert and André Blais. *Une élection de réalignement: L'élection générale du 29 avril 1970 au Québec.* Montreal: Éditions du Jour, 1970. 182 pp.

Monière, Denis. *Pour la suite de l'histoire.* Montreal: Québec/Amérique, 1982. 182 pp.

Murray, Don and Vera Murray. *De Bourassa à Lévesque.* Montreal: Quinze, 1978. 264 pp.

Québec, un pays incertain: réflexions sur le Québec post-référendaire. Montreal: Québec/Amérique, 1980. 312 pp.

Chapter 51

Beaudoin, Gérald. *Essais sur la constitution.* Ottawa: Éditions de l'Université d'Ottawa, 1979. 422 pp.

Canada. Task Force on Canadian Unity (Pépin-Robarts Commission). *Report.* 3 vols. Ottawa: Department of Supply and Services, 1979.

Hamelin, Jean. "Quebec and the Outside World, 1867-1967." *Quebec Yearbook,* 1968-69, pp. 37-60.

McWhinney, Edward. *Quebec and the Constitution 1960-1978.* Toronto: University of Toronto Press, 1979. 170 pp.

— *Canada and the Constitution, 1979-1982: Patriation and the Charter of Rights.* Toronto: University of Toronto Press, 1982. 227 pp.

Patry, André. *Le Québec dans le monde.* Montreal: Leméac, 1980. 167 pp.

Rémillard, Gil. *Le fédéralisme canadien: Éléments constitutionnels de formation et d'évolution.* Montreal: Québec/Amérique, 1980. 553 pp.

— *Le fédéralisme canadien.* Vol. 2.: *Le rapatriement de la constitution.* Montreal: Québec/Amérique, 1985. 721 pp.

Roy, Jean-Louis. *Le choix d'un pays: le débat constitutionnel Québec-Canada, 1960-1976.* Montreal: Leméac, 1978. 366 pp.

Sabourin. Louis, ed. *Le système politique du Canada: Institutions fédérales et québécoises.* Ottawa: Éditions de l'Université d'Ottawa, 1970. 517 pp.